I0817389

"Richard Melick has written an exegetically wise, theologically faithful, practically fruitful exposition of Philippians. Philippians is full of wisdom and instruction for the Christian life and the Christian community. Pastors, students, and anyone interested in learning about Philippians will find Melick's exposition to be an edifying and instructive."

– Thomas R. Schreiner, James Buchanan Harrison Professor of New Testament Interpretation, The Southern Baptist Theological Seminary

"It is great to see this revised edition of Richard Melick's commentary on Philippians! This is a significant update with particularly helpful attention given to the literary structure and flow of thought of the letter. Deeply exegetical, richly theological, and warmly pastoral, this commentary will be a wonderful resource for pastors, students, and anyone wanting to understand and live out the book of Philippians."

– Ray Van Neste, Dean of the School of Theology & Missions and Professor of Biblical Studies, Union University

"More than thirty years ago, Richard Melick published the first volume in the New American Commentary. Building on his previous research, Melick's expanded work continues to feature solid and faithful theological exposition. The work, however, is not merely a reprint for a new series. This volume has been strengthened by careful research, fresh exegesis, and the rethinking of matters of interpretation brought about by years of thoughtful reflection on the writings of the apostle Paul. Pastors, teachers, and students will be blessed by the seriousness and reverence with which Melick approaches the biblical text. It is a joy to recommend this fine volume on Paul's Letter to the Philippians."

– David S. Dockery, President and Distinguished Professor of Theology, Southwestern Baptist Theological Seminary

"Richard Melick is one of the most trusted New Testament scholars in Baptist life. His exceptional commentary on Philippians is exegetically precise, theologically faithful, pastorally wise, and consistently insightful. I'll personally be turning to it each week as I preach through Philippians."

– Christopher W. Morgan, Dean and Professor of Theology, School of Christian Ministries, California Baptist University

"Richard Melick's original NAC commentary was a model of faithful and reverent exegesis from the pen of a scholar that has sat at the feet of the great Apostle to the Gentiles for decades. Pastors learned to trust that commentary for careful attention to the structure and syntax of the original text, sound theology, and love for the Lord and his church. This new updated and expanded commentary on Philippians is an even greater gift to those seeking guidance in expounding this epistle. It will be a rich resource for all who seek to correctly handle the word of truth."

– Charles L. Quarles, Research Professor of New Testament and Biblical Theology, Southeastern Baptist Theological Seminary

I am grateful that the next generation of pastors, scholars, and Bible students will have access to Dr. Richard Melick's clear and insightful Commentary on Philippians, especially in this updated and refined edition. Always a model of evangelical scholarship and statesmanship, he perfectly blends rigorous exegesis with theological fidelity and pastoral sensitivity. Whether scaling the doctrinal heights of Christology or exploring the practical terrain of church unity, Melick helps every reader apprehend the beauty and impact of Paul's epistle of joy.

– Herschel W. York
Southeastern Baptist Theological Seminary

PHILIPPIANS

PHILIPPIANS

Richard R. Melick, Jr

Christian Standard Commentary: Philippians

ISBN: 978-1-5359-3586-9

Dewey Decimal Classification: 227.6

Subject Heading: BIBLE. NT. PHILIPPIANS-COMMENTARIES

1 2 3 4 5 6 • 28 27 26 25

Printed in China

RRD

Dedication

To Shera,
who shares my life in every way and more than anyone I know displays "the mind of Christ."

To Our Children
Rick and Joy Melick, Kristi and Michael Ent, Karen and Darren Draeger

And to
our ten grandchildren and two great grandchildren
(see author's preface)

TABLE OF CONTENTS

Series Introduction	xi
Author's Introduction	xv
Abbreviations	xxv
Introduction Outline	1
Introduction	3
Commentary	67
Bibliography	411
Name Index	419
Scripture Index	423

SERIES INTRODUCTION

The Christian Standard Commentary (CSC) aims to embody an "ancient-modern" approach to each volume in the series. The following explanation will help us unpack this seemingly paradoxical practice that brings together old and new.

The *modern commentary* tradition arose and proliferated during and after the Protestant Reformation. The growth of the biblical commentary tradition largely is a result of three factors: (1) *The recovery of classical learning* in the fifteenth-sixteenth centuries. This retrieval led to a revival of interest in biblical languages (Greek and Hebrew). Biblical interpreters, preachers, and teachers interpreted Scripture based on original languages rather than the Latin Vulgate. The commentaries of Martin Luther and John Calvin are exemplary in this regard because they return to the sources themselves. (2) *The rise of reformation movements* and the splintering of the Catholic Church. The German Reformation (Martin Luther), Swiss Reformation (John Calvin), and English Reformation (Anglican), among others (e.g., Anabaptist), generated commentaries that helped these new churches and their leaders interpret and preach Scripture with clarity and relevance, often with the theological tenets of the movements present in the commentaries. (3) *The historical turn in biblical interpretation* in the seventeenth and eighteenth centuries, with an emphasis on the historical situation from which biblical books arise and in which they are contextualized.

In light of these factors, the CSC affirms traditional features of a *modern commentary*, evident even in recent commentaries:

- Authors analyze Old and New Testament books in their original languages.
- Authors present and explain significant text-critical problems as appropriate.
- Authors address and define the historical situations that gave rise to the biblical text (including date of composition, authorship, audience, social location, geographical and historical context, etc.) as appropriate to each biblical book.
- Authors identify possible growth and development of a biblical text so as to understand the book as it stands (e.g., how the book of Psalms came into its final form or how the Minor Prophets might be understood as a "book").

The CSC also exhibits recent shifts in biblical interpretation in the past fifty years. The first is the literary turn in biblical interpretation. Literary analysis arose in biblical interpretation during the 1970s and 1980s, and this movement significantly influenced modern biblical commentaries. Literary analysis attends to the structure and style of each section in a biblical book as well as the shape of the book as a whole. Because of this influence, modern commentaries assess a biblical book's style and structure, major themes and motifs, and how style impacts meaning. Literary interpretation recognizes that biblical books are works of art, arranged and crafted with rhetorical structure and purpose. Literary interpretation discovers the unique stylistic and rhetorical strategies of each book. Similarly, the CSC explores the literary dimensions of Scripture:

- Authors explore each book as a work of art that is a combination of style and structure, form and meaning.
- Authors assess the structure of the whole book and its communicative intent.
- Authors identify and explain the literary styles, poetics, and rhetorical devices of the biblical books as appropriate.
- Authors expound the literary themes and motifs that advance the communicative strategies in the book.

As an *ancient commentary,* the CSC is marked by the theological bent with respect to biblical interpretation. The bent is a tacit recognition that the Bible is not only a historical or literary document, but is fundamentally the Word of God. That is, it recognizes Scripture as fundamentally both historical *and* theological. God is the primary speaker in Scripture, and it is with him readers must deal. Theological interpretation affirms that although God enabled many authors to write the books of the Bible (Heb 1:1), he is the divine author, the subject matter of Scripture, and the One who gives the Old and New Testaments to the people of God to facilitate her growth for her good (2 Tim 3:16–17). Theological interpretation reads Scripture as God's address to his church because he gives it to his people to be heard and lived. Any other approach (whether historical, literary, or otherwise) that diminishes emphasis on the theological stands deficient before the demands of the text.

Common to Christian (patristic, medieval, reformation, or modern) biblical interpretation in the past two millennia is a sanctified vision of Scripture in which it is read with attention to divine agency, truth, and relevance to the people of God. The *ancient commentary* tradition interprets Scripture as a product of complex and rich divine action. God has given his Word to his people so that they may know and love him, glorify him, and proclaim his praises to all creation. Scripture provides information that leads to spiritual and practical transformation.

The transformative potential of Scripture emerges in the *ancient commentary* tradition as it attends to the centrality of Jesus Christ. Jesus is the One whom God sent to the world in the fullness of time, whom the OT anticipates, about whom the OT testifies. Further, he is the One whom the NT presents as the fulfillment of the OT promise, in whom the church lives and moves and has her being, and who the Old and New Testaments testify will return to judge the living and the dead and who will make all things new.

With Christ as the center of Scripture, the *ancient commentary* tradition reveals an implicit biblical theology. Old and New Testaments work together as they reveal Christ in a promise-fulfillment schema, among other patterns. Thus, the tradition works within a whole-Bible theology in which each Testament is read in dialectic relationship, one with the other.

Finally, the *ancient commentary* tradition is committed to spiritual transformation. The Spirit of God illumines the hearts of readers so that they might hear God's voice, see Christ in his glory, and live in and through the power of the Spirit. The transformational dimensions of Scripture emerge in *ancient commentary* so that God's voice might be heard anew in every generation and God's Word might be embodied among his people for the sake of the world.

The CSC embodies the *ancient commentary* tradition in the following ways:

- Authors expound the proper subject of Scripture in each biblical book, who is God; further, they explore how he relates to his world in the biblical books.
- Authors explain the centrality of Jesus appropriate to each biblical book and in the light of a whole-Bible theology.
- Authors interpret the biblical text spiritually so that the transformative potential of God's Word might be released for the church.

In this endeavor, the CSC is ruled by a Trinitarian reading of Scripture. God the Father has given his Word to his people at various times and in various ways (Heb 1:1), which necessitates a sustained attention to historical, philological, social geographical, linguistic, and grammatical aspects of the biblical books which derive from different authors in the history of Israel and of the early church. Despite its diversity, the totality of Scripture reveals Christ, who has been revealed in the Old and New Testaments as the Word of God (Heb 1:1; John 1:1) and the One in whom all things hold together (Col 1:15–20) and through whom all things will be made new (1 Cor 15; Rev 21:5). God has deposited his Spirit in his church so that they might read spiritually, being addressed by the voice of God and receiving the life-giving Word that comes by Scripture (2 Tim 3:15–17; Heb 4:12). In this way, the CSC contributes to the building up of Christ's church and the Great Commission to which all believers are called.

AUTHOR'S INTRODUCTION

People love Philippians! Whenever groups of Christians are asked to share their favorite verses, Paul's letter to the Philippians shines among the replies. For example: "I am able to do all things through him who strengthens me" (4:13). "And my God will supply all your needs according to his riches in glory in Christ Jesus" (4:19). "I am sure of this, that he who started a good work in you will carry it on to completion until the day of Christ Jesus" (1:6). "For me, to live is Christ and to die is gain" (1:21). "And the peace of God, which surpasses all understanding, will guard your hearts and minds in Christ Jesus" (4:7). "Our citizenship is in heaven, and we eagerly wait for a Savior from there, the Lord Jesus Christ" (3:20).

My pilgrimage reflects much the same. When I was in college, it was popular to select a life verse that would guide your life and reflect your values. I oscillated between Phil 1:20 and 3:10–11: "My eager expectation and hope is that I will not be ashamed about anything, but that now as always, with all courage, Christ will be highly honored in my body, whether by life or by death" (1:20). "My goal is to know him and the power of his resurrection and the fellowship of his sufferings, being conformed to his death, assuming that I will somehow reach the resurrection from among the dead" (3:10–11). The verses served me well, whichever one I selected at a given time. Both were true! They were appropriate for one looking ahead to a life of ministry. Now, looking back some fifty plus years, the focus has changed. There is still the longing to be faithful and to know Christ; but looking ahead, another ambition takes prominence: "not having a righteousness of my own . . . but one that is through faith in Christ—the righteousness from God based on faith" (3:9).

When Paul penned Philippians, he was likely between sixty and seventy years of age. He was held under house arrest, awaiting one of the most significant events of his ministry: he would speak personally with the leader of his world, the Roman emperor. The issues that challenged Paul's life and ministry persisted. Preachers at Rome divided over him. Some Jewish teachers opposed him viciously. He was forced to entertain the possibility of martyrdom. What did he have to offer God? Despite an exemplary life first as a Jewish leader and then as a Christian hero, Paul saw his significance elsewhere. Indeed, what a privilege to be able to trust Jesus—to have his righteousness—rather than our own!

Aligning one's personal life with the teaching of Philippians comes naturally. It was Paul's intent in writing, though the contexts between then and now are radically different. Philippians is autobiographical. Paul writes candidly and with a sometimes-shocking transparency that enables the reader to examine personal sensitivities and life-patterns. The style is intentional. Philippians has the warmth that comes from personal relationships; it is distinctively different from Ephesians and Colossians, written at approximately the same time according to traditional dating. The literary pattern through most of it is *syncrisis* (comparison). Ultimately, the life of Christ stands as the model for all to follow. Secondarily, Paul's exemplary life reflected Christ's in thought and deed. The Philippians faced internal discord and theological threats on the horizon. Paul had faced both! His experience reveals an underlying theology foundational for us all.

No wonder Philippians has been dear to Christians throughout the two millennia since its writing. There are many valuable and necessary ways to argue for the inspiration of Scripture, but to see the ongoing dynamic and spiritual power of an ancient narrative surely gives testimony to the fact that God spoke through human language. Indeed, the very words themselves taken in context stand as testament to the revelation that is Scripture.

This commentary represents a unique privilege. Almost thirty-five years ago I wrote *Philippians, Colossians, and Philemon* in the NAC series. The prefaces of the NAC and CSC provide the distinctive characteristics for each set and the approach taken with each commentary. I am grateful for the thousands of people who purchased, read, and found my prior work on Philippians for the NAC series helpful in their understanding and in teaching/preaching the letter to the church at Philippi. The intervening years have brought time for reflection and more mature appreciation. Time has deepened my understanding in at least two major ways.

First, I am grateful for the continued interest in the letter to the Philippians. The literature since my first volume is expansive. Select periodicals brought better understanding of specific portions of the letter. Comments from those who read my first volume and those from the many students who studied it with me broadened my understanding. At the same time, new commentators effectively addressed the letter with nuanced approaches and insights. I am particularly indebted to Kown, Fee, Holloway, Fowl, Reed, Reumann, Witherington, and Guthrie for their insights. Many other writers stimulated my thought in various ways. Doubtless there are more in process that will rightly demand consideration in the future.

Second, I am grateful for the opportunity to rethink my conclusions about the letter. There are minor places where I have changed my position. For one, multiple literary discussions have enabled me to see the letter in a different light. Most scholars now classify the letter to the Philippians as either a friendship letter or a family letter. Both had still-available templates in the Greco-Roman world. The differences between the two are minor, but important. I have organized the letter (outlined it) differently from before. Even with some changes in approach and text, however, my understanding of the message of Philippians has remained the same.

It is a joy to publish again with Holman Reference, one of the publishing arms of my denomination. Ray Clendenen and Brandon Smith, general editors of the series at its beginning, gave me the opportunity to write. I thank them. Brandon has made valuable comments in reading the first draft, particularly with his keen theological eye. Sheri Klouda Sharp helped me in many ways as Project Manager for the series. Gateway Seminary (formerly Golden Gate Theological Seminary) has been my academic home for almost thirty years. I have appreciated the support of the administration and my faculty colleagues. In particular, Dr. Jonathan McCormick, Director of Library Services, has been extremely helpful and supportive.

As always with regard to my writing, my family has been the greatest encouragement. Dr. Shera Melick served as Associate Professor of Educational Leadership and Chair of the Educational Leadership department at Gateway Seminary (then Golden Gate Theological Seminary) until retirement. Our professional interaction has been of inestimable value. We jointly wrote an integrative textbook, drawing on the resources of our various disciplines. More importantly, she is my wife of over five decades and has brought continual support and exercised patience with the long hours of research and writing. Her love is constant and consistent. She personalizes having "the mind of Christ" (1 Cor 2:16). Living with her has stimulated my own quest to be like Jesus. Others in my family provide constant encouragement. My three children and their spouses, all professionals, continue to serve our Lord effectively in full-time Christian ministry. At the same time, I continually benefit from children, grandchildren, and great-grandchildren who love me and our Lord. Rick Melick, III pastors in Des Moines, Iowa, and his wife Joy is children's director at the church. Kristi, a piano teacher and writer/editor, serves with her husband, Michael Ent, a pastor in Homewood, Alabama. Karen, a homeschool supervisor for the public school system, is married to Darren Draeger, a full-time hospital chaplain. Our ten grandchildren (though one passed away at age fifteen) and two great grandchildren are growing up in Christian homes. Their eagerness in things Christian continually stimulates. Their love for our Lord is exemplary. They are Richard and Eden Melick, with daughter Emory; Nathan Melick; Anna (Ent) and Jeff Poon with son Anzo; Michael David, Abbie (deceased), and Sam Ent; Rachael and Maddie Draeger. We could not be more grateful for them all.

Commentaries impact the writers more than the readers. The hours spent grappling with the technical aspects of the text force precision and clarity not otherwise found. Integrating specific biblical texts and books with others of the same author, or with the entire canon, reinforces the wonder of Scripture. The various books display different writers' personalities, vastly different politico-cultural and language settings, and multi-layered challenges. Yet Scripture has an amazing Christo-centric unity within diversity. Moving from text to theology requires a grasp of broader meaning and its application to life. Each of these calls for its own discipline, but the commentator rightly endeavors to integrate them all. The purpose of biblical study is to see the text and through it to see more clearly the Lord whom it reveals. Philippians points us to Christ: who he is, what he did, and how he empowers his followers in multiple ways. It calls us to be as well as to do. May we, like Paul, adopt "the mind of Christ." My work has been worship, and it is offered to the Lord for his glory.

Soli Deo Gloria

Richard R. Melick, Jr
Senior Distinguished Professor of New Testament
Gateway Seminary
May 2024

ABBREVIATIONS

Bible Books

Gen
Exod
Lev
Num
Deut
Josh
Judg
Ruth
1, 2 Sam
  1, 2 Kgdms (LXX)
1, 2 Kgs
  3, 4 Kgdms (LXX)
1, 2 Chr
Ezra
Neh
Esth
Job
Ps (pl. Pss)
Prov
Eccl
Song
Isa
Jer
Lam
Ezek
Dan
Hos
Joel
Amos
Obad
Jonah
Mic
Nah
Hab
Zeph
Hag
Zech
Mal
Matt
Mark
Luke
John
Acts
Rom
1, 2 Cor
Gal
Eph
Phil
Col
1, 2 Thess
1, 2 Tim
Titus
Phlm
Heb
Jas
1, 2 Pet
1, 2, 3 John
Jude
Rev

Commonly Used Sources for New Testament Volumes

AB	Anchor Bible
ACCS	Ancient Christian Commentary on Scripture

AnBib	Analecta Biblica
Ant.	Josephus, *Jewish Antiquities*
ANE	Ancient Near East
ANF	Ante-Nicene Fathers
BA	*Biblical Archaeologist*
BBR	*Bulletin for Biblical Research*
BAGD	Bauer, Walter, William F. Arndt, F. Wilbur Gingrich, and Frederick W. Danker, Greek-English Lexicon for the New Testament and Other Early Christian Literature
BECNT	Baker Exegetical Commentary on the New Testament
Bell.civ.	*Appion Belle Civilia*
BHGNT	Baylor Handbook on the Greek New Testament
Bib	Biblica
Biblnt	Biblical Interpretation Series
BibR	*Biblique Revue*
BNTC	Black's New Testament Commentary
BSac	*Bibliotheca Sacra*
BZNW	Beihefte zur ZAW
CBQ	*Catholic Biblical Quarterly*
CSB	Christian Standard Bible
CTR	*Criswell Theological Review*
EBC	Everyman's Bible Commentary
ExpTim	*Expository Times*
EQ	*Evangelical Quarterly*
HBD	HarperCollins Bible Dictionary
HNTC	Harper's New Testament Commentaries
HTR	Harvard Theological Review
ICC	*International Critical Commentary*
Int	*Interpretation*
JBL	*Journal of Biblical Literature*
JETS	*Journal of the Evangelical Theological Society*
JSNT	*Journal for the Study of the New Testament*
JSNTSup	Journal for the Study of the New Testament Supplement Series
JSOT	*Journal for the Study of the Old Testament*
JSOTSup	Journal for the Study of the Old Testament Supplement Series
JTI	*Journal of Theological Interpretation*
JTS	*Journal of Theological Studies*
LCL	Loeb Classical Library
LNTS	The Library of New Testament Studies
LXX	Septuagint
NAC	New American Commentary
NBBC	New Beacon Bible Commentary
NCB	New Century Bible
Neot	*Neotestamentica*
NBBC	New Beacon Bible Commentary
NIBCNT	New International Bible Commentary of the New Testament
NICNT	New International Commentary on the New Testament

NIDNTT	*New International Dictionary of New Testament Theology*
NIV	New International Version
NIVAC	NIV Application Commentary
NLT	New Living Translation
NovT	*Novum Testamentum*
NovTSup	*Novum Testamentum,* Supplements
NTC	New Testament Commentary
NTS	*New Testament Studies*
NTTS	New Testament Theological Studies
PNTC	Pelican New Testament Commentaries
PRS	*Perspectives in Religious Studies*
R&T	*Religion and Theology*
RB	*Revue biblique*
RTR	*Reformed Theological Review*
SBJT	*Southern Baptist Journal of Theology*
SBLDS	Society of Biblical Literature Dissertation Series
SBLMS	SBL Monograph Series
SGBC	The Story of God Bible Commentary
SHBC	Smyth and Helwys Bible Commentary Series
SNTS	*Society for New Testament Series*
SNTSMS	*Society for New Testament Studies Monograph Series*
TDNT	G. Kittel and G. Friedrich, eds., *Theological Dictionary of the New Testament*
THNTC	Two Horizons New Testament Commentary
TynBul	*Tyndale Bulletin*
WGRWSup	Writings from the Greco-Roman World Supplements
WUNT	Wissenschaftliche Untersuchungen zum Neuen Testament
ZECNT	Zondervan Exegetical Commentary on the New Testament

INTRODUCTION OUTLINE

- 1 The City and Its People
  - 1.1 Location
  - 1.2 History
  - 1.3 People and Language
  - 1.4 Religion
- 2 The Origin of the Church
  - 2.1 Gentile
  - 2.2 Women
  - 2.3 Generosity
  - 2.4 Loyalty
  - 2.5 Disunity
  - 2.6 Spiritual Strength in Persecution
- 3 The Occasion
- 4 Authorship
  - 4.1 Timothy
  - 4.2 Paul
- 5 The Integrity of the Epistle
- 6 Origin and Date
  - 6.1 Origin
  - 6.2 Date
- 7 Paul's Opponents at Philippi
- 8 Theological Themes
- 9 Genre and Style
- 10 Interpreting the Letter

INTRODUCTION

Paul stood at the summit of the mountain pass that rose up from Neapolis. Having first sailed across the Aegean Sea to Samothrace, he had joined the Via Ignatia, the famous road built in the previous century to facilitate east-west travel to and from Rome. From the place where he stood, Paul could see below the city of Philippi. As he rested from his climb, he knew he had entered Europe for the first time. He and his companions traveled on an eighteen-foot wide paved expressway leading 600 miles across what would one day be northern Greece. Thousands of soldiers, merchants, wagons, horsemen, and pedestrians used the road. It facilitated travel like few other Roman roads could.

His mind raced. So, this was the place! The surrounding mountains once filled with gold. The tall acropolis nearby, with its many temples for the various gods of history, stood prominently off to the right. The city he aimed to reach soon was the home of Philip of Macedon's dream to conquer the world. Philip had renamed the ancient city Philippi and unified the Greek city-states, forming one powerful nation: Greece. It had become the capital of the Greek Empire under Alexander the Great, Philip's son. Its topography provided the location for historic military battles in one of the few plains in Greece sufficient for major combat. The city was known around the world for its allegiance to Rome; indeed, it was a Roman outpost surrounded by Greek culture and language. Perhaps Paul had hoped his entire life to stand in this spot.

Other thoughts would crowd his mind. What was so important about Europe? His plans to evangelize Asia (modern Western Turkey) had been interrupted by the restlessness of his spirit. God had moved him in a different direction. Rather than west to Ephesus, he would go north and west to Troas on the sea. The strange but clear guidance had climaxed in a vision, the only one Paul's friend Luke had felt significant enough to record among the meticulous travel notes he always made. The physician, believed to be from Troas, had joined Paul's missionary team before they had sailed toward Neapolis. In the vision, a European called to Paul. He implored him to cross the sea and help him. Paul had immediately understood it was a message from God. Silas was with him, his companion from Syrian Antioch; young Timothy had joined them in Lystra. Before sailing to Neapolis he met a remarkable man most likely from Troas: Luke. The physician Luke joined Paul's team which would prove to be a providential relationship. Standing above Philippi, Paul no doubt wondered. Why was he here? What did God intend? It was more than a road trip. God wanted him there!

No one knows the intricacies of God's plans. In some ways this one was ironic. God wanted a primarily Jewish team to enter such a solidly Roman city. Jews, Paul knew, were not welcome in Philippi. In fact, he intended to quietly hire himself out to a tent maker and practice the family trade there in relative anonymity until God's purposes became clearer. Silas and Timothy, meanwhile, could find work as scribes, an always in-demand occupation. Luke, Paul was certain, could put out his shingle and practice medicine anywhere they went. It would work out. He knew in time he would move to other cities to tell the story of the Messiah.

Hardly could he have imagined how history would unfold. But in time, he would leave that city and work his way down the coast to Corinth, and from there to Ephesus. It was a circuitous route to complete his original plan of preaching again in Asia. Even so, his travels would bring him back through Philippi several times so he could visit and encourage the church he founded there. A strong bond would develop. Deep friendships would form. And though Paul sought no financial support from churches he founded, the Philippians would insist on providing him help. It was, in fact, the only church identified as a financial and material partner in Paul's work.

A decade later, Paul would find himself under arrest in Rome, awaiting trial before Caesar Nero; the Philippians again came to his aid. It is unsurprising he remembered the church with a unique fondness in his writings, having a special place in his heart as he said, "from the first day until now." The letter he wrote to them indicated as much.

More than any other Pauline letter, Philippians reveals insights into Paul's situation, commitments, and background. In it Paul spoke candidly to his strongest supporters. He explained his current situation at Rome and how his imprisonment caused mixed reactions among the Christians there. He thanked his dear friends for their financial and prayer support and urged them to continue in the faith in spite of opposition. By sharing his thoughts and actions, Paul hoped to provide a model of the truth. This incarnational principle permeates his writing in this missive. He found that he could even counter false teachers by appealing to his past experiences. As a rabbi, after all, he had lived what they taught and found it lacking.

In addition to revealing much about the life of Paul, the letter contains a fresh presentation of Jesus. In a lofty poem about Jesus Christ, Paul called his readers to an examination and interpretation of the mind of Christ. Hearing it perhaps repeatedly, they were reminded to live like Jesus did. Paul clearly believed his life had been transformed radically because of following Christ, and so every portion of the letter reveals the Lord through his servant.

The epistle reads easily. Paul's thoughts flow logically and personally, and apart from a few notable questions of syntax/structure, there are few places where interpreters question the nature of the language or what it discloses. Other than Philemon, Philippians is the most personal of all the Pauline corpus. Contemporary readers naturally and properly honor the apostle Paul. He, however, sought to honor his Lord, Jesus Christ. Any focus on Paul, then, can only be acceptable if it brings a clearer picture of the grace of God in Christ. This commentary intends to honor that aspect of Paul's life. One goal of the commentary is to help readers see the apostle Paul in a new light, with real and vital, life-changing commitments. Another goal is to help readers to feel the depth of his understanding and practical insights. This volume's overriding aim, however, is to help readers see the Lord through the pages of the biblical text. Millions of Christians have found encouragement through the words penned here. Pastors may struggle to preach and teach some of the biblical books, but all love the letter to the Philippians. It draws the reader into living practical Christianity that strengthens both individuals and churches.

1 THE CITY AND ITS PEOPLE

Philippi is one of the better-known NT cities. Scholars have done extensive historical and archaeological investigation at the site of Philippi, and information is readily available. The French Archaeological School of Athens excavated the site from 1914 until 1937.[1] The Greek Archaeological Service continued the excavations after that time. Philippi's main street was the Via Ignatia, the main east-west Roman road of Macedonia. This ancient expressway was eighteen-feet wide and followed the coast south through Thessalonica, then east. The present ruins of Philippi include the forum, agora, streets, gymnasium, baths, library, and acropolis. In addition to what may be a 400 BC temple of Apollo and Artemis,[2] the site has produced numerous inscriptions and coins.

1.1 Location

Philippi was located in the northeast section of the Roman province of Macedonia, between the Strymon and Nestos Rivers. The city's location made it strategic in ancient times; it was situated about eight hundred miles from Rome and approximately ten miles from the seaport of Neapolis. Originally the city lay on a steep hillside on the edge of an inland plain. Abundant natural resources, such as water supplies, timber, and metals, made the city important.[3] Significantly, the area contained extensive gold mines. Mount Pangaion, a mountain of almost 6,500 feet, contained extensive gold and metal mines in its lower slopes. At the peak was the Hill of Dionysus, not far from

---

[1] See P. Collart, *Philippes, ville de Macedoine depuis ses origines jusqu'a la fin de l'époque romaine* (Paris: E. de Boccard, 1937).

[2] See P. Ducrey, "The Rock Reliefs of Philippi," Arch 30 (1977): 102–7; and P. Davies, "The Macedonian Scene of Paul's Journeys," BA 26 (1963): 95ff. An excellent master's thesis on Philippi records significant information about the city and its people: J. G. Armistead, "The Social Setting of the Early Christian Community at Philippi" (M.A. thesis, University of Mississippi, 1987).

[3] See S. Casson, *Macedonia, Thrace, and Illyria* (Oxford: University Press, 1926), 3ff.

town.[4] Indeed, these mines attracted the early settlers and suited the city to become the capitol of the Greek armies.

The most imposing geographical feature was a high rock cliff which overlooked Philippi, a part of Acropolis Hill. Many reliefs depicting the religious cults popular at Philippi were sculpted on and in it. By looking toward it, everyone who entered the city was immediately confronted with the religious symbolism of the area. Approximately eighty percent of the inscriptions were written in Latin, obviously another major language spoken in Greek-speaking Macedonia.[5]

Neapolis was the major seaport of the north Aegean Sea but at the time of Paul, Philippi eclipsed it in importance. At the time of Alexander the Great (333 BC) some spoke of Neapolis as Philippi's seaport and later the Via Ignatia passed through it. Yet by the first century, all citizens looked to Philippi, ten miles inland across the mountain pass.

1.2 History

Philippi had a long, varied history. The occurrence of several name changes may indicate its importance. Many scholars suggest the earliest name was Tasibasta, "the place of the Thasians,"[6] and some believe the city was also called Datus.[7] All agree that an ancient name was Crenides, "fountains" or "springs," a name given because of the abundant water supply there.

The city rose to prominence when it became the capital of the Greek Empire. In 359/358 BC, Philip II of Macedon gained control of the city after the residents appealed to him for help against the neighboring warring Thracians. He renamed the city Philippi, which was the first time a city had been named for its benefactor.[8] With the resources there, especially gold and timber, Philip believed he could accomplish his dream of uniting Greece and conquering the world. Given that 80 percent of Greece is mountainous, his was an ambitious dream. The

---

[4] Appion, Bella Civilia, 4:106. Quoted in Armistead, 16.

[5] Sculptures and inscriptions are sometimes difficult to date and at least some of these may be second century, later than Paul's visit. Certainly, however, given the varied religions background of the city, some dated back much earlier.

[6] Casson, *Macedonia*, 49.

[7] Casson, 49. Others think that Datus was another place close by.

[8] N. G. L. Hammond and G. T. Griffith, *A History of Macedonia* (Oxford: Clarendon, 1972), 2:360. The plural name of the city is interesting. Perhaps it indicates that several settlements existed in the area. Further, this was the first Macedonian colony. The practice was later repeated in the advance of the Greek armies.

population lived primarily in city-states, each with its own government and dialect. The dialects differed so that often one city-state could not communicate with another even though they both spoke what we now call Classical Greek.[9] Philip's untimely death ended his plans, but his son, Alexander, inherited his vision and united the Greek city-states. In 336 BC, at the age of nineteen, Alexander and his armies ventured from Philippi, and in twelve years three decisive battles established one of the greatest empires the world has known, with dominion for the Greeks stretching as far east as India. Philippi became the showpiece of Greek culture, and Alexander devoted significant energies to its development. Throughout the conquered empire, the Greeks built cities modeled after Philippi. He created the Greek *polis*, the cities (*poloi*) becoming centers of Greek culture and politics. Aristotle, Alexander's boyhood tutor until the age of sixteen, spread his philosophy everywhere with government encouragement. Alexander unified the Greek dialects by simplifying grammatical forms and establishing a universal pronunciation. His language, Koine Greek, prevailed in the Greco-Roman Empire for 700 years, and it served as the common language of the Roman Empire during the first century AD.

About two hundred years after Alexander, Roman soldiers conquered Macedonia (168 BC). They divided the territory into four districts, each having its own legislature, and discontinued the mining operations.[10] The city's significance diminished until about 40 BC, with the battle of Philippi.

Civil war broke out following Julius Caesar's death in 44 BC. Antony and Octavian aligned their armies and fought the armies of Brutus and Cassius on the plains near Philippi. Two battles ensued. Antony's army defeated Cassius first, and two weeks later Octavian defeated Brutus. Antony and Octavian disbanded the defeated armies and established a colony at Philippi in 42 BC and in 30 BC, respectively. Consequently, the city was repopulated and revived by Roman army veterans, giving the city a predominant Italian flavor. In addition, when Octavian became emperor (taking the name "Augustus") he conferred upon Philippi the *ius Italicum,* giving the colonists the same privileges and rights as those who lived in Italy.[11]

---

[9] The phrase Classical Greek represents several different dialects represented in the city-states. Strictly speaking, there was no unified "classical Greek."

[10] Armistead, "The Social Setting," 19.

[11] Armistead, 20–22.

Although Roman colonies emulated Rome, each enjoyed considerable self-government. Colonies elected their officials in pairs: two *duumviri* (judicial and political figures), two *aediles* (public works officials), and two *quaestores* (financial officers).[12] Each Roman colony also had a territorium composed of land surrounding the city. Philippi's territorium consisted of 730 square miles which encompassed many small villages.[13] This made the city significant to the area, but Macedonia also had five other colonies. By the first century AD Philippi lost its grandeur and never again enjoyed the status of Thessalonica, the principal city of the province, located 100 miles away.

1.3 People and Language

In the first century, Philippi contained a diverse population. Three primary ethnic groups lived there, but many others came for various reasons, including commerce. The native Thracians remained from the days when they were the primary ones who occupied Tasibasta, by the first-century called Philippi. Many extant Latin inscriptions found there contain Thracian elements. This witnesses to the strength of the Thracian community even after Greek and Roman dominance.

The second major population group was Greek. Originally the Greeks were fourth-century BC colonists who shared Philip's dream of a world empire. Later, others moved to Philippi because of the commercial opportunities. Greek culture and language quickly eclipsed the Thracian culture, and by Paul's time any traveler with a knowledge of Greek could easily move about Philippi.

Finally, the Romans occupied the territory. From appearances, the Roman element was the strongest. Although it is impossible to know the precise population of the various groups, clearly the Romans ruled every aspect of life in the city. Perhaps the double colonization of veterans after the Roman civil war gave them this prominence.

The strong Roman element suggests that Latin was the primary language of the city. The inscriptions bear this out as do the tombstones.[14] It continued to be the primary language into the second

[12] G. H. Stevenson, *Roman Provincial Administration* (New York: Strechert, 1939), 172ff.

[13] Collart, *Philippies*, 185ff, 276ff.

[14] B. Levick, *Roman Colonies in Southern Asia Minor* (Oxford: Clarendon, 1967), 161, reported that of 421 inscriptions found in Philippi, 361 were in Latin and sixty were in *Greek* (some of them were pre-colonial). Collart(Philippians, 301) said the number of tombstones in Latin is double the number in *Greek*.

century and survived until after the time of Constantine.[15] Greek was always spoken as well. Although anyone could navigate the city with a knowledge of Greek, Latin was necessary to be fully conversant with the affairs of the city. Other than Rome itself, Philippi was no doubt the most Roman of all the cities Paul visited.

Other cultures mixed at Philippi, but there is little evidence of a Jewish population. Paul did not go to the synagogue as was his custom, presumably because there was not one in the city. Instead, he went to a river where he expected Jews and Jewish proselytes worshiped (Acts 16:13). Even there, those he met were Gentile women. Since Jewish law commanded that a synagogue be established where ten male heads of household lived (a *minyan*), apparently few Jewish males lived in Philippi. Possibly the military nature of the city did not attract the Jews. More likely, the pro-Roman flavor of the colony had caused the Jews to be expelled as they were from Rome in AD 49 under Emperor Claudius. Paul entered the city in approximately AD 50–51. Jews would likely have been allowed to return when Claudius lifted his ban in AD 54. Certainly such a devoted Roman colony shared the same political sentiments as the mother city. This would include anti-Semitism.

Although emperors banned Jewish people from Rome at least three times, Claudius's edict has significance for Christian history. The Roman historians claim that the Jews argued over *Crestus*. Most think this was the Latin translation of *Christos*, "Messiah." It could be that the evangelistic efforts of Christian Jews living in Rome were a major disruptive force in the city. According to Acts 2:10, at Pentecost in Jerusalem there were "visitors from Rome (both Jews and converts)." A decade after founding the church at Philippi, Paul wrote Philippians and explained there were divisions among those who proclaimed Christ in Rome. Some thought if "Christ" became the topic that caused division, the Roman government would silence Paul. Others preached Christ to encourage the efforts of advancing Christianity through Paul. For those who opposed Paul, perhaps the moniker "Christ" was a lightning rod to alert the government to the activities of those they opposed (Phil 1:12). At any rate, the Roman government tolerated the Jews but with a watchful eye to avoid popular disruption. Philippi's leaders surely took the same approach. At that time, it appears the Roman government considered Christianity a subset of

[15] Collart, *Philippies*, 313.

Judaism. That would change later when the church became predominantly Gentile and Christianity would be listed as *illicita*, "illegal." At Philippi, one of the charges brought against the Pauline group was that they promoted an illegal religion.

As with most ancient cities, it is difficult to estimate the population. A reliable construction suggests that the city proper contained about 10,000 inhabitants. Thriving ancient cities also had suburbs immediate to them. Philippi was no exception. Population estimates basically come from the size of the large amphitheater (8,000 seats) and the population density of Pompeii, Italy, as a model. The surrounding territory, economically and politically dependent on Philippi, contained possibly 46,000 people. Peter Oakes suggests the following:[16]

—elite	3%
—colonist farmers	20% (half owning, half renting)
—service groups	37% (a mix of Greek and Roman)
—slaves	20%
—poor	20% (mostly Greeks)

1.4 Religion

Most large cities of the Roman Empire had complex religious environments. Philippi was no exception. Native Thracian religions were "somewhat crude and barbaric, oftentimes involving animal-worship, human sacrifice and orgiastic rites."[17] Three prominent Thracian gods were Liber Pater, Thracian Rider, and Bendis. Liber Pater was identified with the grape harvests and, therefore, with wine. He frequently was equated to the Greek Bacchus or Dionysus and was the great local god of Philippi. Thracian Rider was associated with hunting and represented the native hunter cult. He was always depicted on a horse. Bendis was a Thracian goddess often erroneously identified with the

[16] Peter Oakes, *From People to Letter*, *SNTSMS* 110 (Cambridge: Cambridge University Press, 2001), 40–54. Also quoted, among others, in George H. Guthrie, *Romans: Zondervan Exegetical Commentary*, ed. Clinton E. Arnold (Grand Rapids: Zondervan Academic, 2023), 8; and Mark J. Keown, *Philippians: Evangelical Exegetical Commentary*, ed. H. Wayne House (Bellingham: Lexham Press, 2017), 1:38. It is likely that by AD 60 the Romans were a minority in population but enjoyed prominence in influence.

[17] Armistead, "The Social Setting," 47.

Greek Diana and Artemis. She always dressed in boots and short skirt, carried a spear or knife, and appeared extremely athletic. Worship directed to her involved orgiastic practices.[18]

In addition to the Thracian religions, many Greek and Roman cults entered the city. The inscriptions, rock reliefs, and scriptural testimony reveal the worship of a number of these deities.[19] Paul encountered a follower of Apollo in Acts 16:16.[20] Apollo was particularly known for divination, but he was also associated with music, archery, medicine, and shepherding. A favorite Italian god was Silvanus, god of the woodland. A temple dedicated to him was completed in about AD 20–30.[21] One of Paul's companions had the name of this god. Paul consistently called him Silvanus; Luke always called him a shorter version of the name, Silas (cf. Acts 16:19).

Archaeological finds reveal the strength of the Eastern cults in Philippi as well. The Egyptian cult of Isis was most popular, but many others appeared.[22] The religious climate produced more than two dozen cults at the time of Paul. Some, however, estimate there were more than forty varieties of these cults actively carrying on their religious practices in the area.[23]

Finally, the emperor cult was a favorite religion. In fact, the specific charge brought against Paul and his company was that he advocated customs "not legal for . . . Romans to adopt or practice" (Acts 16:21). The acknowledgment and worship of the emperor served Rome's political interests and distinguished Roman loyalists. Inscriptions mention Julius, Augustus, and Claudia. Rome had a relatively tolerant attitude toward religion at that time, and one could easily practice both a national religion and the imperial cult. Of the two, the imperial cult was the more important to Rome since it unified the people of the empire and confessed obedience to the emperor.

---

[18] She was not the Diana or Artemis of Ephesus who is depicted with rows of breasts. That Diana was a local goddess. Much of the information in the text comes from Armistead.

[19] They include Zeus-Jupiter, Hera-Juno, Apollo, Athena-Minerva, Aphrodite-Venus, Cupid, Ares-Mars, Hermes-Mercury, Heracles-Hercules, Dionysus-Bacchus, and Artemis-Diana (Armistead, "The Social Setting," 50).

[20] This is evidenced by the *Greek* text which states the slave girl had the spirit of the "python" ("who had a spirit"), a tradition associated with the worship of Apollo.

[21] Davies, "The Macedonian Scene," 101.

[22] These included Harpocrates and Serapis (Egyptian), and Cybele (Anatolia).

[23] Armistead, "The Social Setting," 45–46.

In that light, the Roman attitude toward religion emerges. Rome determined two classifications of religion: legal and illegal. Legal religions were affirmed by the senate or the emperor, who generally accepted the ethnic, national religions of its conquered people. Some religions were unsanctioned (illegal). In general, however, if the people of the religion did not promote public discord, anti-Roman sentiments, or excessive debauchery, Rome gave significant freedom to them. At the time of Paul, Christianity had not been accepted or rejected by the Roman officials. In fact, after the Roman trials of Jesus, the first Christian encounter with the Roman government occurred at Philippi. Since the first missionary leaders were Jews, it seems likely that Rome considered Christianity a sect of Judaism and its practice was protected under the umbrella of Judaism as a national religion. The growing Gentile nature of Christian churches, especially after the destruction of the Jewish temple in AD 70, made it increasingly clear that Christianity did not have the necessary tie to Judaism to qualify as a national religion. The potential for persecution from the Roman government was exacerbated. Roman persecution of Christians continued until the fourth century when Constantine became emperor (and reportedly a Christian). During that pre-Constantine time, Christianity was never declared legal. The continued practice of an unsanctioned religion put Christians into the category of criminals deserving punishment.[24]

2 THE ORIGIN OF THE CHURCH

The church at Philippi was founded by the apostle Paul on his second missionary journey from Antioch, Syria, recorded in Acts 16. The precise time of Paul's arrival is unknown, but most likely it was around AD 51.[25] When Paul determined to return to the churches he founded on the first missionary journey, he and Barnabas differed on taking their previous associate John Mark. They parted company, and Silas

---

[24] Of course, there were many underlying issues that fueled the fires of persecution. One was the absolute refusal of Christians to declare the creed "Caesar is Lord." Officially, however, the illegal nature of Christianity brought the persecution. Ironically, the major struggle to separate Christianity from Judaism, though both had a common origin in the OT, also brought severe persecution of Christians as they lost their protected status with Rome.

[25] Although estimates vary as to the exact date, the best chronology places the second missionary journey at about AD 50, shortly after the Jerusalem Council. Paul was in Corinth in about AD 52 because he appeared before Gallio during his pro-consulship there. Paul probably entered Europe in the middle of this second journey.

accompanied Paul to the churches of Lystra and Derbe. At that time Timothy joined them, and they traveled west. Forbidden by the Holy Spirit to speak in Asia (Acts 16:6–7), they journeyed northwest to Troas, a major seaport on the west coast of Asia. The journey was approximately 300 miles long and likely took several weeks. Paul's intent to go to Ephesus was redirected by the Holy Spirit for unknown reasons. But at Troas Luke joined the party of three, indicated by the change to the "we" accounts in Acts rather than third person narrative. Luke's origins, especially his coming to faith in Jesus, are unknown. Typically Luke seems reluctant to put himself in prominence. In Troas Paul had a vision of a Macedonian calling for help. Subsequently, he and his team sailed across the Hellespont waterway to Neapolis and walked to Philippi. As was his habit, Paul looked for a synagogue where he could initiate conversations about Christ. Apparently, there were none in the city, so on the Sabbath Paul went to the riverside outside the city gates to meet with those few who practiced the Jewish faith. Presumably these consisted primarily of women, some proselytes, since the Jewish law required an official synagogue if there were ten male heads of households locally. With the paucity of the Jewish community, the people may have recognized Paul as a Jew, exacerbating his problems there.

In Acts 16:11–40, Luke recorded three significant events associated with the beginning of the Philippian church. The first European convert was Lydia. This significant believer in Christ came from the Asian city of Thyatira.[26] She probably moved to Philippi to further her import business, which consisted of selling the purple cloth so famous in Thyatira. No doubt she had considerable resources since the purple dye was quite expensive. At the time, pure purple dye was found only in the region of Thyatira and it became a favorite of kings and royalty. The best dye was available in shellfish alone, which made it quite expensive, but a less expensive process was developed in Thyatira to make purple dye from the root of the madder plant. After her conversion, Lydia invited Paul and Silas into her home. Since there were at least four in Paul's travel group, she must have had a large home and possibly servants to care for them all. Unlike Philippi,Thyatira contained a large Jewish population and it is likely that Lydia was already

[26] F. W. Beare suggests Lydia "was probably not her personal name but a nickname: 'the Lydian.'" *The Epistle to the Philippians*, HNTC (San Francisco: Harper & Row, 1959), 11.

a proselyte to Jewish religion. Her conversion to Christ was a natural outworking of her desire to know God. Her household followed in her decision to accept Paul's message, and all were baptized.

A feature of the period, as Beare notes, was the proliferation of "private brotherhoods. These were cult-associations devoted to the worship of a chosen god; and there were many such groups at Philippi."[27] The groups needed some influential person(s) to provide resources, including the locations for the meetings, and the new church was no exception. Lydia may have become the local patroness of the church. She also may have provided a link to the Gentile population of the city and, perhaps, to the more influential business community.

Lydia helped Paul introduce Christianity to Europe. In identifying with him and his message she may well have also had her own witness. Regardless of whether she shared her testimony, she is the first of women who are significant in Philippi's young church. In the Acts account of the ministry in Europe, Luke mentions women often. He includes Lydia, a slave girl set free of a demonic spirit, and Euodia and Synteche in Philippi (Acts 16:11–21; Phil 4:2); "a number of the leading women" in Thessalonica (Acts 17:4); "a number of prominent Greek women" in Berea (Acts 17:12); "a woman named Damaris" in Athens (Acts 17:34); and Priscilla in Corinth (Acts 18:2). Luke emphasizes women in his Gospel as well. This reflects the importance of women in the contemporary Greek and Roman society. In the first century AD, Gentile women were given a number of new legal privileges such as "initiating divorce, signing legal documents, even holding honorary public titles."[28] Significantly, women had a major role in the spread of the gospel from the start, as was evidenced when Paul and his group entered Greece.

The second significant event at Philippi was the exorcism of demons from a slave girl. Although the Scriptures do not state that she became a convert to Christianity, there is every reason to assume she did. The masters of the demon-possessed girl made considerable money from her ability to predict future events.[29] She had the spirit

---

27 Beare, Philippians, 9.

28 J. B. Polhill, *Acts*, NAC 26 (Nashville: Broadman & Holman, 1992), 349.

29 Some suggest her ability was actually ventriloquism, such as R. Martin, *Philippians*, NCB (London: Oliphants, 1976), 8–9. That hardly explains her ability to foretell events, which brought the owners great gain.

of "the python," a phrase reflecting the worship of Apollo, who surrounded himself with the snake. The prophecies connected with Apollo worship caused the snake to be the symbol of the phenomenon. Future telling was valued in the Roman Empire. Even generals wanted some word of assurance from one with the gift before they led into battle. This girl followed Paul and cried out, "These men, who are proclaiming to you a way of salvation, are servants of the Most High God." Luke does not record how she understood who they were. Perhaps she heard Paul's and Silas's messages as she followed them and decided to validate them herself. Alternatively, she may have received the information by revelation. The Gospels record that spirit-possessed people often had correct information about Jesus's identity.[30] Though neither she nor her hearers understood her message, it was an irritant to have her following them. Interestingly, her description of the missionaries, "servants" (*douloi*), is exactly the way Paul introduced himself and Timothy in his letter to the church (Phil 1:1). Paul encountered her, and through the gospel the demon was exorcised.

The masters, realizing they would lose their living if their slave girl converted, dragged the missionaries to court to have them silenced. This was Paul's first Roman trial. The charges included being "Jews," causing a disturbance, and introducing a foreign religion. The accusers said they were "promoting customs that are not legal for . . . Romans to adopt or practice" (Acts 16:21). Perhaps that referred to the illegal status of Christianity, but that seems unlikely since Christians were assumed to be a sect of Judaism at that time. Whatever the specific accusations, clearly the new church faced a formidable challenge: the populous and government considered it illegal. Paul and Silas were stripped of their clothing, beaten with rods, and thrown into a dungeon with common criminals. It is unclear why Scripture does not record that Timothy and Luke endured the same punishment. Perhaps because Timothy was younger he was not considered a promoter of the faith. Luke was a Gentile, possibly known in the area since Paul probably met Luke in Troas. Perhaps the Roman officials assumed if they could deal effectively with the leaders, Paul and Silas, they could silence the others. Wright comments,

---

[30] See, for example, Mark 1:24. The witness of the demonic spirits to the truth is one of Mark's important evidences of who Jesus is.

> . . . the motive for the charge was clear, even though the underlying sequence of thought was bewildering. Paul's exorcism of the girl (an initially "religious" problem) quickly translated into loss of income (an economic problem), and this was turned, vengefully, into the accusation that Paul and Silas were Jews (an ethnic problem) who were teaching customs that it would be illegal for Romans to practice (a political problem).[31]

The third event Luke recorded in Acts 16 occurred while Paul and Silas were in jail, secured by stocks attached to the walls. In spite of the adverse circumstances, the missionaries sang praises to God at midnight. At that late hour, an earthquake shook the prison; the cells opened so that all could escape. The jailer, assuming the prisoners had fled, feared for his own life at the hands of the Roman officials. He drew his sword to kill himself, but Paul assured him that all the prisoners were in their cells. The frightened jailer fell at the feet of the missionaries, and that night he and his family were converted to Christianity. They welcomed Paul and Silas into their home, bathed and cared for them, and gladly received the gospel message.

Luke records the clear gospel message that Paul preached. He also indicated who heard the message. Paul gave the simple form of the message to the jailor: "Believe in the Lord Jesus, and you will be saved" (Acts 16:31). Interestingly, he did not include the title "Christ." Certainly Christ is an essential part of Jesus's identity; it was also the distinctively Jewish part of the gospel. Could it be that Paul avoided the sometimes-inflammatory word "*Chrestos*" that Emperor Claudius claimed was the source of controversy and dissension in Rome? The topic caused the relocation of many Jews from Rome and, presumably, Philippi as well. If so, by the time of the letter to Philippi, "Christ" was a topic of conversation in the Roman world, but the word "Lord" is strangely absent from the first half of Philippians (see Phil 1-2 where Paul consistently identifies Jesus as "Jesus Christ," with Christ before Jesus! Apart from the letter salutation, 1:2, and the poem to Christ, 2:11, it is not until chap. 3 that "Lord" is introduced). It was part of Jesus's name and title that offended Rome since for them "Caesar is Lord."

---

[31] N. T. Wright, *Paul: A Biography* (San Francisco: Harper One, 2018), 181. He further notes there is no evidence that the law forbade Romans to practice Jewish customs.

Twice in the founding account, Luke indicates the primary house member became a Christian, but so did the related household. Lydia brought her "household" to hear and be baptized (Acts 16:15). The jailor took Paul to his house where Paul explained the gospel in greater detail, and all believed and were baptized (Acts 16:32-33). There is no evidence in Scripture the decisions of the householder were efficacious to others in the household. Everywhere faith in Christ Jesus is a personal matter. Without doubt, however, the response of these two sensitized their households to listen carefully.[32] The first two believers at Philippi populated the church plant with multiple people eager to worship Jesus.[33]

Paul sent word to the city magistrates that it was unlawful for Roman citizens to be subject to such treatment. The next morning the city officials asked Paul and Silas to leave the city. The officials fearfully apologized to them and sent them on their way.

This was the first time Paul appealed to his Roman citizenship. Naturally, the magistrates would assume Jews were not citizens, for few were or wanted to be. Rome protected its citizens, making sure of a proper trial and limiting the punishments that could be inflicted. The Philippian officials had disregarded both. Apparently, Silas had citizenship as well (Acts 16:37). This situation gave Paul the upper hand. One other time Paul would claim Roman citizenship: when other officials threatened scourging in Jerusalem. He appealed to Caesar for safety and a trial (Acts 22:25). One wonders why in Philippi the missionaries waited until after the imprisonment and scourging before they pulled this trump card. All that could have been avoided.[34]

---

[32] Furthermore, the statement is made of a woman, Lydia, and a man, the jailor. Each had influence over their households. Presumably Lydia was married, but her business acumen may have made her the *de facto* person of influence.

[33] Roman households included the parents and children, but also servants and, perhaps, other domestics. Scripture includes them in the commands to the domestic code in Eph 5:22–6:9 and Col 3:18–4:1. Given that, the households' presence in the first meetings of the church could have included multiple people: parents, children, servants and their spouses and children if they had them.

[34] Roman citizenship was the right of every Italian, but relatively few outside of Italy or Roman heritage actually had that status. Given the tumultuous relationship between Rome and the Jews, even fewer Jews enjoyed the privilege. Paul inherited citizenship, a highly valued way of achieving it (Acts 22:28). Most likely Paul's father or grandfather served a Roman emperor in a special way. Perhaps he used the family business of tent making to create tents or sails for the military. No certain evidence exists, however.

Two important points emerge that have significance for Philippians. First, Paul used political (primarily citizenship) terms in explaining the outworkings of the gospel. After explaining the conflicted situation among the churches of Rome, Paul urged the Philippians to "live . . . worthy of the gospel of Christ" (Phil 1:27). Paul normally used the words "walk" or "conversation"(KJV) for Christian conduct. Here he used a word rooted in politics: *politeuoμai*. As a result, they were to live as worthy citizens of the gospel. Second, in explaining the ultimate hope of Christians, Paul claimed their citizenship is in heaven. While imprisoned at Rome awaiting trial, perhaps Paul's mind embraced afresh the implications of Roman citizenship and used that to help illustrate the Christian community. It was an ideal the Philippians prized.

At a deeper level for Acts and the early church, Luke affirmed repeatedly the good conduct of Christians and that they were never convicted of Jewish or Roman lawbreaking. Creating a sub-theme of Luke and Acts, the writing forms a defense of the history and growth of the early church for Roman officials, though the books are addressed to Theophilos, unknown to us. Luke hoped Rome would grant legal status to Christianity. Rome finally did when Constantine became both a Christian and emperor in the fourth century.

Paul could well have expected mistreatment. On the first missionary journey he was stoned and left for dead (Acts 14:19). This occurred in the first advance of the gospel into what is now Turkey (Lystra/Derbe). Now, in the first advance of the gospel into Europe, once again Paul was beaten. In both cases, he took his suffering as a privilege to be so identified with Jesus.

Paul maintained contact with the Philippian church. The missionaries visited the city again on the third missionary journey (Acts 20:1). The church also took advantage of several occasions to send financial support to Paul (cf. Phil 4:15; 2 Cor 11:9) and to the believers at Jerusalem (2 Cor 8:1–5). When Paul was sentenced to prison at Rome, the church sent Epaphroditus, a leader among the brethren, to minister to Paul. The apostle responded by sending Timothy to them and planned to visit in person after his impending trial. It appears Luke joined Paul at Troas since the Acts account changes from "they" to "we" during this time. This was the first of three "we" sections in Acts, and the "they" terminology resumes after Luke recorded the events in Philippi (Acts 16:17). Luke joined Paul on three occasions, each related narrative longer than the previous. The "we" sections denote personal involvement in the spread of the gospel. It may be that as Paul aged, or faced increasingly intense physical difficulties, Luke joined him to provide much needed medical treatment.

The Philippian church became a model. From its beginning it was healthy, even though at the time of Paul's writing it was experiencing a minor problem of disunity in the congregation (Phil 4:2–7). The NT evidence suggests several characteristics of this congregation.

2.1 Gentile

Philippi's first converts were Gentiles, and Gentiles predominated in the fellowship. The Gentile character of the church may be questioned from Phil 3:1–4:1, which has a Jewish flavor to it; nevertheless, the historical data supports a primarily non-Jewish congregation. More specifically, the Roman influence dominated in the first century AD. As previously noted, other ethnic groups either remained from former days or migrated to the city for commercial reasons. Assuming the Jews were expelled in AD 49 but allowed to return in AD 54, there may have been serious anti-Semitic attitudes prevalent.

2.2 Women

Women played an important role in the life of the church at Philippi.[35] The NT mentions four women there: Lydia and the slave girl, the first converts, and Euodia and Syntyche, who were identified as co-laborers with Paul. Lydia doubtless provided the church's first meeting place in her home, since early clubs and groups needed a benefactor who could provide for plenary sessions. Though Lydia remains unknown after the events recorded in Acts, she had critical significance in the founding of the church. The slave girl likely became a Christian, although that is not certain. She was the unintended cause of the turmoil against Paul and Silas. Euodia and Syntyche were noted for their involvement in the spiritual battles of the area (Phil 4:2–7). They uniquely assisted Paul, obviously effective in their evangelistic activity. Although they occupied a prominent place, when the disturbance between them occurred,

[35] Luke also recorded the prominence of women at Thessalonica, another prominent church of Macedonia (Acts 17:1–9).

Paul urged his "true partner" to care for it (4:3). The women did not have the chief place of leadership in the congregation.

2.3 Generosity

The congregation was an example of generosity to the other churches of Macedonia and Achaia (2 Cor 8:1), contributing to Paul and to the Jerusalem saints who were in need. The church apparently was not wealthy, although it seems some persons of means were members. At one point Paul said the members gave beyond themselves and out of their "extreme" poverty (2 Cor 8:2–4). The Philippian congregation was the only one specifically mentioned as sending a financial gift to Paul. Their giving remains an example of genuine Christian concern manifesting itself in tangible ways.

2.4 Loyalty

The Philippian church stood by Paul throughout his life, as evidenced in the gifts it gave for his support and in its desire to know Paul's state in Rome. It thoughtfully and lovingly maintained contact with its founder. Caird suggests this church "was the one which gave [Paul] the most satisfaction and the least trouble."[36]

The church remained strong into the second century. Its location on the Via Ignatia made it ideally suited for hospitality to travelers. Fifty years after Paul's letter to the church, Ignatius was escorted to Rome by Roman soldiers to be tried for his faith in Christ and was comforted by the church at Philippi on the way.

2.5 Disunity

The Philippian church was one of the friendliest and most supportive of the Pauline churches. Despite that, the congregation suffered serious disunity (4:2). Euodia and Syntyche, well-known and influential people, were unable to resolve their difficulties by themselves. Paul urged another to help them. Their discord may not have been the only disruption of harmony. Regardless, Paul urged the church toward unity in at least two ways. First, he subtly implied unity had the potential of damaging the progress of the gospel. The Christ-followers were to

---

[36] G. B. Caird, *Paul's Letters from Prison* (Oxford: University Press, 1976), 98.

shine like lights among a distorted generation around them (2:14–16). Second, he implied their disunity disrupted their movement toward completeness at the day of the Lord (2:16). Paul encouraged the entire church toward unity (2:1–4) illustrated by the life of Jesus (2:6–11).[37]

2.6 Spiritual Strength in Persecution

The Philippian church faced persecution. Paul urged the believers to stand firm "in one spirit, in one accord, contending together for the faith of the gospel, not being frightened in any way by . . . opponents" (1:27–28). Whether this was a general exhortation or Paul had specific persons in mind, clearly the terms suggest conflict. Persecution could have come from the Roman elite of Philippi because of the church's refusal to acknowledge Nero's ultimate power. Certainly later in the first century refusal to bow to the emperor was a capital offense. Additionally, opposition may have come from the encroaching Judaizers who sought to "correct" Pauline doctrine in its assumed disregard of Torah law. If that opposition did not exist in Philippi at the time, there is no doubt it was coming (3:2) and the church needed spiritual strength to stand against it.

3 THE OCCASION

Why did Paul write the epistle when he did? Several suggestions come from the epistle itself. Perhaps Paul wanted to inform the believers of Timothy's approaching visit and prepare them for it (2:19). Likewise, Paul intended to visit the church in the near future, and the letter could have prepared for his arrival (2:24). Others suggest Paul felt the need to address the problem of disunity which had surfaced in the congregation (4:2–4). None of these, however, have significant enough material devoted to them to offer a plausible answer to the matter of the reason for and timing of the letter.

More likely, Paul wanted to thank the Philippians for a gift received for his support. In 1:3, 7 and 4:10–20, he expressed his thanks for their gift and took advantage of the opportunity to instruct them in a theology of material resources. Clearly the church's support had significant impact on Paul for two reasons. First, no other church gave to

---

[37] Frank Thielman, *Theology of the New Testament* (Grand Rapids: Zondervan, 2005), 314–15, identifies these two problems.

support his missions work like it did (4:15). Second, Paul's situation in Rome probably caused him to reflect on his ministry to churches of other cities. It no doubt lifted his spirits to receive a tangible expression of confidence. Even so, there could have been other occasions for expressing his appreciation. This suggestion may have contributed to the timing, but another possibility fits the data better.

Paul's companion Epaphroditus wanted to return to his friends at Philippi. The church had sent Epaphroditus to Paul as a personal embodiment of its concern. In the meantime, Epaphroditus almost died from a prolonged sickness. The church heard of his situation, and he, in turn, heard of its concern for him. He recovered and Paul was eager to send him back to the church (2:28). Since he almost gave his life in service to Paul as a proxy for fellow believers, Paul anxiously desired they honor him appropriately. He would be better off at home. The apostle took advantage of Epaphroditus's desire to return to the church. He wrote the letter expressing two concerns: thanks for the gift and a plea for unity.[38]

Paul's exhortations to unity permeate the epistle. The most obvious case of disunity involves the dispute between Euodia and Syntyche (4:2). Subtly, however, many texts reveal an underlying concern that the church stand strong together. The most powerful incentive occurs in the example of Christ, whose attitude of humility was to characterize all believers (2:5–11). Furthermore, the epistle is a letter of biographical contrasts. On the one hand, Jesus (2:6–11), Paul (4:9), Timothy (2:20–22), and Epaphroditus (2:29–30) stand as positive examples of the proper attitudes. They are the only male persons identified by name in the body of the letter. On the other hand, Euodia and Syntyche (4:2), the opposing preachers at Rome (1:15–17), and the approaching false teachers (3:2) all exemplify discordant and improper behavior.

If this analysis is correct, it clarifies the nature of the letter. Paul wrote a warm, friendly letter to his loyal children in the faith. A problem of Jewish false apostles who attempted to bring the church under

[38] M. Silva, *Philippians*, WEC (Chicago: Moody, 1988), 5, suggests Paul had to explain why he sent Epaphroditus without their beloved Timothy. He states, "Aware that the Philippians would be deeply disappointed to see Epaphroditus rather than Timothy return, Paul was faced with a serious challenge. How would he cushion this inevitable disappointment? Might Epaphroditus become the object of undeserved criticism?" This reconstruction may capture the tone of 2:19–30, and it deserves consideration. Nothing in the text explicitly states that such disappointment would occur, however.

the law loomed on the horizon. The problem did not require an urgent reply like the situation which prompted Galatians. Thus, it accentuated the positive relationships between the congregants and Paul.

The problems identified in Philippians should not be over simplified. In two places Paul evidenced at least two different challenges. In 1:14–17, Paul explained a tension regarding himself and some preachers in Rome. The churches in Rome were divided over Paul's distinctive position related to Jewish law. Some preachers loved him and sought to encourage him by proclaiming the same message as he. Others rejected him, hoping that by preaching they would bring a negative judgment from Caesar when Paul stood before him. Paul had concerns about their motivations, but he accepted their message as promoting Christ. Consequently, the opposition in chapter 1 is within the accepted parameters of Paul's message. He mentioned it briefly simply to inform his readers that he was well in spite of some ill-willed preachers.

In 3:1–21 Paul addressed a different problem. He knew there was a coming challenge from false teachers, apparently regarding keeping the law, challenging the doctrine of justification by faith. Paul addressed this straightforwardly (see commentary on chapter 3). Indeed, some of the harshest language Paul ever penned in Scripture comes in this section. The heresy does not seem to arise within the church at that time, however. Judaizers followed Paul, seeking to "recapture" Jewish followers of Jesus to their own cause. Finally, many believe the challenge of chapter 3 also reveals the flip side of legalism: perfectionism. More will be said of that later. These two issues seem to assume the letter in its present form does not have the flavor of urgency. Often Paul changed tone when he turned his attention to a theological problem. Here, however, he handled it appropriately as an apostle.

This discussion of the occasion of the letter assumes Paul wrote the missive from Rome during his first Roman imprisonment. Many, however, opt for an origin in Ephesus, assuming that Paul was in prison there. Overall, the Roman origin is better. This will be discussed in detail later.

4 AUTHORSHIP

No one seriously questioned Pauline authorship of Philippians until the eighteenth century when F. C. Baur expressed his extreme view that it was spurious.[39] Few followed him since his arguments rested "on grounds which even his disciples of the Tübingen School found unconvincing."[40] At least one author selected the letter as the standard by which to measure Pauline thought.[41] Contemporary questions relate to the integrity of the letter, but even most of those who see two or three letters collated into one accept the Pauline authorship of the fragments—apart from those who posit that 2:6–11 was pre-Pauline. It is agreed, therefore, that the letter is Paul's. Polycarp (ca. AD 135) commented on the letter of Paul to the Philippians, and the letter appears in all the lists of canonical writings. The letter claims to have been written by Paul and the external evidence for Pauline authorship is overwhelming, so no serious objection to Pauline authorship exists today. Timothy is also identified as an author in 1:1. Several reasons support why Paul might have included Timothy, but clearly the letter is Pauline (see exposition). The normal first-person style found in the epistle confirms its Pauline origin.

4.1 Timothy

Timothy occupied a prominent place in Paul's ministry. Paul met him on the first missionary journey in Lystra/Derbe. Timothy had a strong Jewish heritage through his mother and grandmother. Paul names them in 2 Tim 1:5: grandmother Lois and mother Eunice. They raised Timothy in a strong faith background that Paul commends. It was a Jewish background that Paul traced back three generations. When he embarked on his second journey, returning first through Lystra/Derbe, Paul asked Timothy to accompany him, and Timothy became a prominent member of the ministering team. It is likely Timothy impressed Paul on Paul's first missionary journey, but because Timothy was so young at that time, and Paul and Barnabas intended to return to Antioch from Lystra, he did not join the group. On the second missionary journey, Timothy would have been at least two years older and Paul intended to move westward from Lystra toward Ephesus.

[39] F. C. Baur, *Paul: The Apostle of Jesus Christ*, 2 vols. (London: Williams & Norgate, 1875), 2:45–79.

[40] Caird, *Paul's Letters*, 98–99.

[41] C. L. Mitton attempts to prove that Ephesians was not written by Paul. He compares it with Philippians to prove his point. Cited in Caird, Letters, 99.

Approximately fifteen to seventeen years later, Paul wrote to Timothy, urging him not to allow any of his parishioners to "despise [his] youth" (1 Tim 4:12). This evidence suggests when Timothy first joined Paul and Silas (AD 50) he was likely in his early twenties at most. At the time of writing the letter to Philippi, Timothy was in Rome with Paul approximately ten years after Paul invited him to join him in Lystra. After Paul's release in AD 64, Timothy became a pastor in Ephesus and received two letters from Paul (1–2 Timothy). The second letter was written when Paul was in a Roman prison for the second time, awaiting his death under Nero (AD 67/68).

Timothy was no stranger to the church at Philippi. He was with Paul when Paul experienced the vision of going into Macedonia. Although he is not explicitly mentioned in the Philippi narrative, he was with Paul for the events of founding the church there. The scene in Acts 16 focuses on Paul and Silas, no doubt the leaders of the missionary band. They were beaten and imprisoned for preaching the gospel. They were the ones who appealed to their Roman citizenship. Timothy and Luke both accompanied them. No one knows what happened to them during the persecution of their leaders. It may be they were not identified as Jewish and the anger of the Roman officials was against Jews. Luke was certainly Gentile, and Luke makes explicit mention of Timothy having a Greek father. Paul, in fact, circumcised him since his mother was a Jewess.[42] Circumcising Timothy avoided the unfair accusation that Paul's message was to draw Jews away from their culture when he intended the opposite. Paul's team consisted of both Jews and Gentiles, embodying the now clear kingdom culture brought by Christ.[43] Timothy was known and beloved by the Philippian church. Later, when Paul was in Ephesus, he sent Timothy and Erastus to Macedonia, expecting to join them soon (Acts 19:22). A short time later he sent Timothy to Corinth in his stead (1 Cor 4:17). Many in the divided and troubled church of Corinth questioned Paul's leadership, and Timothy was sent as an envoy on Paul's behalf to calm the turbulent waters there.

---

[42] Acts 16:1–3. Though Jewish heritage was noted through the father from tribe to tribe, Jewish identity was affirmed through the mother.

[43] Even when Paul was imprisoned at Rome he had a mixed team with him. Colossians 4:10–14 mentions Aristarchus, Mark, and Jesus (Justus) "of the circumcised," and Epaphras, Luke, and Demas who are Gentiles. This commentary assumes Colossians was written by Paul during the same imprisonment he endured while writing Philippians.

Paul mentioned him in the salutations of six letters (2 Cor; Col; Phil; 1, 2 Thess; Phlm) and wrote two letters that bear his name as addressee. He and Titus had a special relationship to Paul, and Paul likely saw them as the inheritors of the mission after his death.

4.2 Paul

The apostle Paul is familiar even to those with little knowledge of the Bible. The biblical accounts focus on Paul as a primary shaper of the early church and Christian theology. He wrote thirteen extant letters, leaving us with more books than any other person connected with the early church. Luke chronicled Paul's travels and church planting activity in sixteen of Acts's twenty-eight chapters. Through Paul, Christianity spread north-westward into modern Turkey (ancient Asia Minor), Europe (Greece and Italy), and Spain.[44] As the church matured and produced multiple writings, Paul's theology became a major criterion as to whether any of the writings should be received as canonical.[45]

Paul was well prepared for the ministry God had for him. Before his conversion to Christianity, he zealously pursued the righteousness that comes from the OT law. He chose to be a Pharisee (Phil 3:5; Acts 26:5) after studying with one of the leading Pharisees, Gamaliel, in Jerusalem itself (Acts 22:3). Doubtless, Paul's family had both adequate resources and political/religious connections to provide an envied education in Jerusalem with one of the two leading rabbis of the time. Paul found favor with the Judean Jewish leadership, being able to secure soldiers (apparently) and financial support to search out, find, and imprison Jewish converts to Christianity even outside of Judea (Acts 19:1–9). He witnessed the martyrdom of Steven, the church's first martyr, giving his approval (Acts 8:1). Some suggest he was a member of the highest Jewish court, the Sanhedrin.[46] Whether or not he was, his Jewish credentials were impeccable.

[44] Because of Acts and the letters, it is often thought Christianity only spread northwest through Paul. Other early church missionaries took the gospel into different geographical directions: Thomas went to India, Mark to North Africa, and Peter to Cappadocia (eastern Turkey). Early Bible translations reveal mature congregations in other parts of the Mediterranean, and by AD 800 there is evidence of the gospel in southern China (Nestorianism). God chose to preserve only Paul's activities in the canon.

[45] The *Regula Fida*, "rule of faith," primarily based on Paul's theological emphases, was one of the tests as the church recognized the emerging canon.

[46] This is based at least in part on Paul's testimony before King Agrippa that "When they were put to death, [he] was in agreement against them" (Acts 26:10). This suggests Paul had an

Paul's background also gave him awareness of Gentile culture. He was born in Tarsus of Cilicia (Acts 21:39). Most likely his birth was around the turn of the century, about AD 01. He was roughly a contemporary of Jesus, though he possibly claimed he did know him "according to the flesh" (2 Cor 5:16)[47] Apparently Paul's family had lived in Tarsus for generations as Diaspora Jews. Paul learned a trade, leather/canvas-working, from his father, which he used to support himself in his missionary travels. At least one of his ancestors must have found favor with the Roman government, and the family was awarded Roman citizenship, an extreme rarity for Jews. One likely suggestion is that his father or grandfather made tents for the army or sails for the navy, and the family was given citizenship in gratitude. Regardless, Paul used his status as a Roman citizen at least twice in his missionary service: at Philippi after being beaten and jailed for a night (Acts 16:37), and when enduring trials and imprisonment in Judea (Acts 25:10–11; 25:25; 26:32). In the strongly pro-Roman city of Philippi, Paul's citizenship probably brought him some measure of additional respect. His birthplace, Tarsus, was on the main road to the Cilician Gates, the primary (only southern) east-west route through the Cilician mountain range. He would have learned Greek, the trade language (Acts 21:37), Roman culture, and gained some knowledge of other countries because of the constant caravans, ships in port, and travelers through Tarsus. He was no stranger to the privileges of the Roman Empire even though his family probably lived in the Jewish quadrant of Tarsus.

Paul's imprisonment in Rome and the writing of Philippians occurred in the last decade of his life. His Damascus Road conversion was likely in the mid to late AD 30s (perhaps 36), the time Paul recognized the lordship of Jesus. Luke provided three accounts of Paul's conversion, each adding information to the others because of different audiences. The narrative is first provided in Acts 9:1–9. Paul also gave his testimony to a riotous crowd in Jerusalem (Acts 22:1–21) and to King Agrippa, with Festus, as a trial defense (Acts 26:12–23). Quickly

---

official vote regarding the fate of the early Christians. That would have meant he was a Sanhedrin member. If so, that honor was bestowed on Paul at a young professional age.

[47] The phrase "according to the flesh" (κατὰ σάρκα) indicates a standard of knowing, in a "fleshly" way. The phrase does not indicate of itself that Paul knew Jesus physically. In 2 Corinthians Paul argues that his old way of viewing things has passed as he is the new creature. The "standard" of measurement is confirmed by his statement that he knew no one "according to the flesh."

after his conversion, Paul became an able apologist and evangelist in Damascus (Acts 9:19–25) and journeyed possibly twice to Jerusalem to align himself with the Jewish Christian leadership there (Acts 9:26–30; Gal 1:18–20). Paul became one of five prophets and teachers of the church at Antioch, Syria (early AD 40s), and took a relief offering from the church to the famine-struck believers in Jerusalem (ca. AD 45). The Holy Spirit led the Antioch church to "Set apart . . . Saul and Barnabas" as missionaries from the church to the northwest, eventually as far as Italy (Acts 13:2–3). Subsequently, Paul led three missionary journeys from Antioch, introducing the gospel to Jews (first) and Gentiles who had not heard of Jesus (AD 47–49, Acts 13:1–14:28; AD 50–52, 15:36–18:22; and AD 53–58, 18:23–21:3). After each of the journeys, Paul went to Jerusalem. He was warned not to go after his third journey, but he chose to follow his normal pattern. While he was there, some Jews recognized him and accused him of defiling the temple by bringing Gentiles into it. It was a false charge, but Paul spent two years defending himself and waiting for a positive outcome of his trials (AD 58–60, Acts 21:15–26:23). During this time, he was led to exercise his Roman citizenship and appeal his case to Caesar Nero. In AD 60 he set sail for Rome on a prison transport.

Little is known about Paul regarding this time.[48] Luke records that when he arrived, the "brothers and sisters" from Rome came to meet them and encouraged him. Paul was allowed to live by himself in a rented place guarded by soldiers (Acts 28:15) since he was a Roman citizen and not accused of a capital crime or insurrection. Consistent with his theological and practical convictions, Paul called together the leaders of the Jewish community first (Rom 1:16) and explained his message of Jesus from the Law and Prophets (Acts 28:23). It was a message they rejected, so Paul invited Gentiles to visit and hear about the kingdom of God and the Lord Jesus Christ (Acts 28:30–31). While imprisoned under house-arrest and waiting trial before Nero, Paul wrote four known letters, often called Prison Letters (AD 60–62, Philemon, Colossians, Ephesians, and Philippians).[49] At Rome the Jewish

[48] Some scholars do not see a correlation between Acts 28 and Paul's imprisonment when he wrote the Prison Letters. See the following discussion of the origin of the letter.

[49] Those familiar with the history of Pauline studies will know that the dates, authorship, and origins of each of these has been debated. In particular, the dates of Ephesians, Colossians, and Philippians are debated and the authorship of Ephesians and Colossians generates much discussion. In the account above, the traditional approach to these seems best and no

community rejected Paul's message, but even the Christian congregations were divided over supporting him (Phil 1:12–15). Several of Paul's friends and co-laborers were with Paul in Rome, perhaps intermittently. These included Tychicus (Eph 6:21), Aristarchus, (John) Mark, (Jesus) Justus, Epaphras, Luke, and Demas (Col 4:10–14; Phlm 23–24). Only Timothy and Epaphroditus are mentioned in Philippians.

Why Paul was in prison in Rome naturally arises. Luke alone provides the history of the early church movement ending with Paul there. Luke's purpose in writing was to demonstrate the power of the gospel and chronicle its spread into Europe. It certainly was not to provide Paul's biography. Nevertheless, early church growth into Europe and Paul's ministry intertwine. There is a trail of evidence as to why Paul stood in the shadow of his trial before Nero.

Both the receptions of Paul's sermons and the accusations brought against him provide the answer. Paul's sermons may be divided into those to Jews and those to Gentiles. The longest recorded in a Jewish setting occurs in the synagogue at Antioch of Pisidia (Acts 13:13–52). He rehearsed the history of Israel and the coming of Jesus prophesied throughout the OT. He warned them to believe to be "justified through [Christ] from everything that [they] could not be justified from through the law of Moses" (13:39). Cryptically, he spoke to the limitations of justification by law and that complete justification could only occur through Jesus. This statement is truly and typically Pauline. The other sermons in Acts focus on Jesus as the anticipated Messiah for Jews (17:3; 18:5) and Jesus as God's appointed Judge and inaugurator of the kingdom of God for both Jews and Gentiles (19:8; 28:23). A major component of his message was the resurrection from the dead, with Jesus serving as the evidence of that reality (17:32; 24:15; 26:8, 23). Of particular note is Luke's silence about much of the theology found in Paul's writings. For example, Luke hardly mentions the Christians' relationship to the Law of Moses; yet in Paul's epistles it is a major component (see Galatians; Rom 6–8; Col 2 for example).

Luke also records the history of Paul's relationship to political officials and the courts. Since Paul was under arrest in Rome awaiting trial, Luke provides a clear picture of how that trial might end. In short, none of the political officials find Paul guilty of breaking

---

compelling reasons exist for forsaking it. The chronology of Paul's life, above, has also followed traditional dating. Discussions of these issues lie outside the parameters of this commentary.

a law. If there were a case against Paul and Christianity, it would have been tried at Philippi. Instead, the political officials apologized to Paul and asked him to leave (Acts 16:38–40). Approximately two years later, Jews in Corinth brought Paul to the tribunal when Gallio was proconsul of Achaia. They accused Paul of "persuading people to worship God in ways contrary to the law" (18:13). Gallio refused to take the case and "drove them from the tribunal" (18:16). After a riot in Ephesus, the people demanded legal action against Paul. The matter was silenced when the city clerk stated "there is no justification that we can give as a reason for this disturbance" (19:40). On Paul's last recorded trip to Jerusalem, the Jewish crowd rioted against him, claiming he "taught against [their] people, [their] law, and[that] place" and defiled the temple with a Gentile guest (21:28–29). Paul subsequently appeared before the Sanhedrin and Governor Felix, who postponed any verdict against Paul. Felix was replaced by Festus, who was anxious to hear the notorious Paul. In his hearing, Paul made his appeal to Caesar (25:11–12). Out of curiosity, King Agrippa asked to hear Paul, which Festus arranged. Paul provided an extended defense, including his testimony of God's call on the Damascus Road. At the end, Agrippa and his wife Bernice, and Governor Festus agreed: "This man is not doing anything to deserve death or imprisonment . . . [He] could have been released if he had not appealed to Caesar" (26:31–32). The point of Luke's detail is that no official of any government ever indicted Paul. The courts did not exonerate him—they did not consider his cases trial-worthy.

This somewhat lengthy and well-known account still requires an answer to the question: Why was Paul in a Roman incarceration awaiting trial before Nero? In spite of sometimes popular uprisings because of religious differences, every political official minimized the issues. Beyond cultic reasons, Paul was accused regularly of advocating a religion (or philosophy) contrary to Roman law. Specifically, it was opposed to "Caesar is Lord" and therefore treasonous. Yet no official court saw it that way. The Nero trial was unnecessary except for Paul's insistence that his case be heard by the emperor. Perhaps it was Paul's impatience after two years in Judea awaiting an outcome. According to Phil 1:12–15, some Christian preachers in Rome hoped the trial would go against Paul. Were they advocates of Christianity in addition to law for salvation? That would make them align more with the Judaizers of Phil 3. Paul leaves the issue with multiple questions unanswered, stating they hoped to "cause me trouble in my imprisonment" (Phil 1:17). History records that Nero released Paul in this instance, not finding Paul's message contrary to the interests of the Roman government.[50]

5 THE INTEGRITY OF THE EPISTLE

The question of authorship quickly passes to the integrity of the written letter. Generally, the question of integrity involves multiple authors of or multiple documents within a given letter. Regarding Philippians, most scholars agree Paul wrote the entire thing. They disagree, however, on how many fragments of letters Paul composed and whether Philippians reflects one letter or more. Today there are advocates of one letter, two letters, and three letters now contained in the canonical book of Philippians. Holloway generalizes the current state of the study: "A generation ago most critical scholars were agreed that Philippians as it appears in the manuscript tradition is a composite document pasted together from two or three originally separate Pauline letters. Today that view has largely been abandoned, but there are complications."[51] He also attributes the different positions, in many cases at least, to the advocates following theological or methodological assumptions which color the conclusions reached.[52]

Some support for the view that there are multiple letters in Philippians comes from Polycarp, who mentioned that Paul "wrote letters, by which, if you study them carefully, you will be able to edify yourselves in the faith imparted to you."[53] Some have taken the plural words ("letters . . . them . . .") to mean there were actually *multiple* letters from Paul to the Philippians. A. Harnack thought the Thessalonian letters were included in Polycarp's plural since the two cities were in Macedonia. E. Schweizer regarded 2 Thessalonians as a letter sent by

---

[50] It should be noted Christians were sometimes considered a nuisance to the empire. In AD 64, Nero blamed the burning of Rome on Christians who disturbed the city with their discussions about "*Crestus*" (Latin: Christ). Later, the Roman attitude changed significantly toward the defiant Christians who refused to confess "Caesar is Lord." Christianity remained illegal until AD 317. Apparently, thousands of Christians were martyred up to that point.

[51] Paul A. Holloway, *Philippians: A Commentary,* Hermeneia: A Critical and Historical Commentary on the Bible (Minneapolis: Fortress Press, 2019), 10.

[52] Holloway, 10.

[53] (Polycarp to Philippians, 3:2) Quoted in Martin, *Philippians*, 11.

Paul to the church at Philippi. A. Wikenhauser suggested Polycarp was making a guess because of the abruptness of the canonical epistle at Phil 3:2.[54] Perhaps J. B. Lightfoot correctly assessed the situation when he interpreted the plural "letters" as referring to a letter of importance which had a plural designation because of its significance.[55]

Those who challenge the integrity of Philippians identify various fragments in the letter. The chronologically first assumed fragment is 4:10–20, where Paul thanked the church for its financial support. Proponents say it would have been written shortly after Epaphroditus arrived in Rome with the Philippians's gift. Certainly, Paul would be eager to thank the church for their generosity. The support for this takes several lines of argument. (1) Advocates say that Paul would not have waited for months to write a note of thanks for their support, especially by that point of his life. They assume it would have taken months for news to travel back and forth from Rome to Philippi, and that Paul would have sent thanks immediately after receiving the gift. Some assume 2:25–30 presupposes a communication from Paul to Philippi outside this letter. There Paul stated "But I considered it necessary to send you Epaphroditus." The aorist form of the verb "consider" suggests, to them, a past event. The remainder of that section, however, counters that assumption. Paul stated, "I am very eager to send him so that you may rejoice again when you see him (2:28)." The best understanding is that Paul sent Epaphroditus along with the letter. It is typical in the letters to use the aorist tense for present writing. In so doing, the author puts himself in the place of the reader for whom the narrative would be past. (2) In addition, why would Paul put the word of appreciation at the end of the letter rather than the beginning? Normally Paul thanked his readers at the beginning of his letters, and that would have been appropriate here as well. It should be noted Paul did include his normal pattern of thanksgiving at the beginning of the letter. He noted their "partnership in the gospel" (1:5, 7). These early statements in the letter follow Paul's pattern. He usually reserved more extended mention of personal concerns for

---

[54] Martin, 11–12.

[55] J. B. Lightfoot, *St. Paul's Epistle to the Philippians*, reprinted (Grand Rapids: Zondervan, 1953), 142. He stated, "Whenever it occurs in prose of a single epistle, [it] seems to denote a missive of importance, such as a king's mandate or a bishop's pastoral." See also his section "Lost Epistles to the Philippians?," 138–42.

the end. That is the case here. Holloway notes that the claim that 2:25–30 is late

> assumes that the primary purpose of Paul's letter was to express thanks. This assumption is by no means obvious . . . Indeed, a major rhetorical hurdle facing Paul in corresponding with the Philippians was how to thank them for their gift while at the same time maintaining that such externals do not really matter.[56]

(3) Philippians 4:10–20 appears to have the shape of a letter by itself. Some, noting the major repetition of words between chapter 1 and 4:10–20, conclude that Paul actually introduced another letter in 4:10 in his typical way. Somehow it was included into the canonical Philippians.

The second assumed fragment begins at 3:2. At this point, the tone of the letter changes radically. No one doubts Paul employed different writing styles in his correspondence, but they question whether he did so in one letter. Scholars who hold this view differ on where the fragment ends: at 4:1, 3, 9, or 20. The arguments supporting this break fall into three general categories: (1) the situation addressed differs from the previous writing; (2) the previous section ends like a travel itinerary (2:19–3:1); and (3) the section is a radically different style from the remainder of the letter. Some assume the change of tone (style) is unusual because Paul addressed the same opponents in 3:2 as he did in 1:17. If true, the change is remarkable. It is highly unlikely, however, that the two opponents are the same. The differences are because Paul addressed different subjects.

The suggestion of a previous letter segment starting at 3:2 is based in part on the identity of the person/issues addressed. Bockmuehl explains, "The confrontational material about Judaizing (3.2 or 3:1b–11) and libertine (3.18–19) adversaries is introduced very abruptly and without a clear transition from the warm and irenic flavour of chapters 1–2, in which the only opposition seemed to be pagan."[57] The opponents in 1:28 seek to make Paul's life more difficult before the Roman government, while those in 3:2 challenge the church. Could

[56] Holloway, *Philippians*, 16–17: "Paul has been exhorting the Philippians not to place too much value in things that do not matter, and now he must not be seen to be doing so himself."

[57] Markus Bockmuehl, *A Commentary on The Epistle to the Philippians*, BNTC (London: A & C Black, 1997), 21.

this abrupt change indicate a different set of circumstances in Paul's life? It is better to understand that the shift is simply to change subject rather than reflecting a changed life situation. The Judaizers were ever-present in the background of Paul's letters. It was natural for the apostle to warn of these opponents since they were a constant nemesis.

The third assumed fragment is 1:1–3:1. Here the question is why the letter seems to come to a Pauline end in 2:19–3:1. They say this represents the original letter, with one or two other fragments added.

Today most scholars accept the canonical form of Philippians. Those who reject the idea it started as one letter divide into those who accept two (3:2 as inserted into the original letter) and those who accept three (3:2 and 4:10–20 inserted into the original one). Nevertheless, there is little agreement on the number of letter fragments, and there is even less on the precise verses which comprise each.[58]

Fragment theories have difficulties. There must have been some reason for preserving and joining the fragments into the form in which they are preserved, and there must be clear evidence they do not fit into the original document. It is impossible to prove either of these in the case of Philippians. The most that can be said is that it is possible the book incorporates more than one source document, but the evidence suggests otherwise. From the methodological perspective, several points argue for the integrity of the letter. No external evidence exists for any other form of the letter than the canonical one.[59]

There is no apparent motive for joining letter fragments into one and concealing the parts. Paul's letters vary in length from the short letter of Philemon to the longest letters. There was no reason to put several together because of their length. Some suggest the three proposed source letters were Paul's way of addressing separate problems, but in letters like 1, 2 Corinthians multiple problems were addressed in the same letter. The theories of interpolation raise the question of the thinking of the interpolator. Why would anyone insert a document in such an awkward place as 3:2, and why would someone place the note of thanks at the end if everyone knew it should come

---

[58] An encyclopedic but cryptic overview of the issue of integrity is in Mark J. Keown, *Philippians 1*, 15–23.

[59] The earliest extant form of the letter is the Chester Beatty Papyrus (P-46) dated about AD 200. If the letter existed in fragments, it did so well before that time, and there is no textual evidence to suggest such a history.

first? Finally, why would the church be so sloppy as to lose the introductions and conclusions of the letters from one so dear to them as Paul?[60]

The two main "fragments" reveal more in common with the letter than is often thought. The thank-you note of 4:10–20 is placed well if two matters are considered. If Epaphroditus's sickness occurred on his way to Paul, so that the journey was completed only after Epaphroditus's recovery, Paul's note may have been written immediately after receiving the money. Perhaps word of Epaphroditus's sickness (and perhaps restored health) returned to Philippi before Paul knew of the illness, likely from a traveler going west to east instead of east to west. It is conceivable that after Epaphroditus arrived at Rome with the gift, a messenger from Philippi also arrived to inquire about Epaphroditus. Thus, a delay of some months before sending the thanks letter is not the only possibility. C. J. Bahr suggested Paul put the thanks at the end purposely so as to sign it with his own hand.[61] In that case, the thanks would have more personal significance since it came from Paul's own hand, which was customarily at the end.[62] Furthermore, there are "preparatory allusions to [the gift] in 1:5 and 2:30."[63] Additionally, the verbal parallels and cohesive elements shared between 1:1–3:1 and 4:10–20 reveal closely connected themes.[64] These consid-

---

[60] Jeffery T. Reed, *A Discourse Analysis of Philippians: Method and Rhetoric in the Debate over Literary Integrity*, ed. Stanley E. Porter (Sheffield, England: Sheffield Academic Press, 1995), 145, lists six possible reasons the supposed fragments were joined: (1) the compilation of fragments could have been accidental; (2) the redactors may have been motivated by prestige, wanting to create a more theologically profound letter than Paul wrote; (3) combining letters to save writing materials; (4) beginning and ending Philippians with "positive" letters leaves the impression of Paul's successful ministry at Philippi and his cordial relationships; (5) to update Paul's letter because it was no longer relevant; and (6) Paul's thanksgiving in supposed letters A and C cannot be assumed, so the redactor excised portions from other letters. Each of these is speculative and without clear basis. Reed rejects them all.

[61] C. J. Bahr, "The Subscriptions in the Pauline Letters," *JBL* 87 (1968): 27–41.

[62] Judging from Gal 6:11, two factors may be seen regarding the Pauline signatures. First, they authenticated the letters. Second, sometimes they had a personal message associated with them (Gal 6 ends some seven verses after Paul stated he signed in his own hand). Both of these factors would have relevance to the Philippian situation.

[63] Caird, *Paul's Letters*, 100.

[64] See, for example, Holloway, *Philippians*, 17, n. 133, who repeats the list of W. J. Dalton, "The Integrity of Philippians" Bib 60 (1979): 97–102. Also, several chapters in Reed, *Discourse Analysis of Philippians*; George H. Guthrie, "Cohesion Shifts and Stitches in Philippians," in *Discourse Analysis and Other Topics in Biblical Greek*, ed. Stanley Porter and D. A. Carson, JSNTSup 113 (Sheffield: Sheffield Academic Press, 1995), 36–59.

erations reveal that the "fragment" is not necessarily as disconnected as some have thought.

The second so-called fragment (starting at 3:2) has also been explained reasonably. Paul often wrote with abrupt shifts in style, and it would not be surprising that he would do so in a warm, personal letter such as Philippians (see Rom 16:16–19; 1 Thess 2:13–16). The change in tone from warmth to harshness is difficult only if the opponents were the same ones as in Phil 1:15–17. If he had addressed his Judaizing enemies earlier, the new invective would be startling. If he had not, a change in tone might be expected. Paul clearly was more soft-spoken with the opponents of 1:15–17, treating them as misguided Christians. In 3:2, the opponents were represented as being motivated by the things of the world and hardly could have been Christians. The harsh tones do not continue throughout the entire section (3:2–21). At 3:7, the language of faith and commitment predominates. The section is not radically different from the previous portions of the letter. Similar words and themes were used in this section.[65] The ethical admonitions of 2:12 resume in 3:2. Similarly, the issues raised in 1:28, 29, and 2:14–16 also continue in 3:2; and the types of dangers were hardly compatible with each other.[66]

Many point to the repetition of "finally"[67] in 3:1 and 4:8 as indicating the end of a letter. The Greek phrase is usually translated "finally" as in 4:8 of CSB. Strictly speaking, the definition of *to loipon* ("finally") in the accusative case means something like "toward the rest." It frequently marks transitions rather than endings.[68] More will be said in the commentary. At this point, it should be noted this use does not indicate the concluding of a letter. The evidence for this segment as a fragment is unconvincing.

---

[65] This and the previous three arguments are well stated in G. Hawthorne, *Philippians*, WBC (Waco, TX: Word, 1983), xxxi. This discussion is an excellent overview of the subject. See also Holloway, *Philippians*, 18–29, who provides lexical and thematic parallels between 2:6–11 and 3:20–21 and the critical analysis of the unity of chapters 2 and 3.

[66] These last three points come from Martin, *Philippians*, 15.

[67] τὸ λοιπόν in 3:1 and 4:8.

[68] In CSB, 3:1 opens with the words "In addition." See also J. Harold Greenlee, *An Exegetical Summary of Philippians*, 2nd ed. (SIL International, 2008), 150. He includes various translations: "a. λοιπόν . . . "for the rest" (Mou, NTC, PI; NAB;), "as for the rest" (ICC), "finally" (HNTC, LN, WEC; KJV,NASB, NIV, NJB, NRSV], "in conclusion" (*TEV*), "from now on" (LN), "and now" (REB, TNT), "furthermore" (LNS), "well then" (WBC). See also Andreas J. Kostenberger and Robert W. Yarbrough, *Philippians: Exegetical Guide to the Greek New Testament* (Nashville: B & H Academics, 2015), 168.

Recently several scholars have approached the integrity of the letter from a literary perspective. Without any manuscript evidence, the contrary arguments to unity are also literary. An early helpful approach is by D. Garland.[69] Others contributed significant literary analyses since Garland. In 1995 Stanley Porter and D. A. Carson edited a volume entitled *Discourse Analysis and Other Topics in Biblical Greek*, which contained contributions related to discourse analysis. About half the essays used Philippians as the exemplar for the method.[70] Soon thereafter, Jeffrey Reed wrote an extensive study of discourse analysis in his doctoral dissertation converted to a monograph.[71] Surveys of contributions and approaches to structural and rhetorical issues can be found in most modern commentaries.[72]

Garland argues the epistle has a solid literary unity intended to build to the point of addressing Euodia and Syntyche. The so-called harsh elements must be reevaluated in light of linguistic and semantic evidence. When this is done, the hard language is considerably softened. One obstacle to unity, the change of tone, is removed. The text shares greater affinity with other passages in Philippians, and the assumed need for a fragment hypothesis no longer exists. The details of this exegesis surface in the specific sections of the commentary as they are appropriate. The work of these scholars offers a new way of analysis which complements traditional exegesis and provides a way beyond the seeming impasse of contrary literary analysis.[73]

It is helpful to present an example of the structure of the letter from a literary perspective because discourse methodologies denominate some circles of biblical exegesis. One of the most recent commentaries

---

[69] D. Garland, "The Composition and Literary Unity of Philippians: Some Neglected Factors," *NovT* 27 (1985): 141–73. This article is very significant in the analysis of Philippians. Among the strengths in it are a good survey of the history and current state of the problem, extensive bibliography for further reading, proper application of literary criteria in exegesis, and a new and effective way to solve the problem of the fragment theories. The direction of scholarly argument changed as a result of this article.

[70] Stanley Porter and D. A. Carson, *Discourse Analysis and Other Topics in Biblical Greek*, JSNTSup 113 (Sheffield: Sheffield Academic Press, 1995).

[71] Reed, *A Discourse Analysis*.

[72] For example, see Markus Bockmuehl, *A Commentary*, 20–25, 34–40; Stephen F. Fowl, *Philippians*, THNTC, ed. Joel B. Green and Max Turner (Grand Rapids: Eerdmans, 2005), 8–9; Holloway, *Philippians*, 10–19; Keown, *Philippians 1:15–23*.

[73] The literature on this subject is extensive. An excellent summary is provided in Garland's article, and Hawthorne's commentary also provides good bibliographic data.

on Philippians was written by George Guthrie.[74] He affirms the unity of the letter in both stylistic examination and literary features.

Guthrie notes verbal parallels throughout the epistle that suggest cohesion. Gerald Peterman demonstrated extensive verbal and conceptual parallels between 1:3–11 and 4:10–20. These parallels frame the book between opening and closing.[75] Guthrie lists thirteen parallels, particularly with Greek words.[76] Building further on the work of David Garland, Guthrie notes seventeen linguistic and conceptual parallels between 1:27–2:4 and 3:15–4:4. Consequently, the two sets of parallels argue for unity of authorship both at the "ends" and in the main body of the letter.[77] Finally, Guthrie argues the words "joy" and "rejoice" form a tight structural pattern throughout the letter with several inclusions forming a seam for the book.[78] Together these present a tightly structured and linguistic argument for the book's integrity. In addition, Guthrie argues the brief volume has three primary sections, each with subsections: The Letter Opening, 1:3–11; The Letter Body, 1:12–4:9; and The Letter Closing, 4:10–23.

In addition to discourse analysis, which focuses on the written patterns of an ancient letter, many recent scholars conclude Paul's letters have an oral base; therefore, they approach them rhetorically. While there are some similarities between rhetoric and discourse analysis, there are also core differences. Ben Witherington, III makes a case for a rhetorical interpretation: "The dominant communication ethos was oral and rhetorical, not epistolary, not least because only about ten to fifteen percent of the population could read."[79] He notes that

> no epistolary conventions include thanksgiving prayers in ancient letters . . . Nor do ancient letters normally include the sort of lengthy arguments and discourse material we regularly find in Paul's epistles. But rhetorical speeches do include such arguments, and we would be much better served to realize that it is rhetorical

---

[74] George H. Guthrie, *Philippians*, ZECNT (Grand Rapids: Zondervan, 2023).

[75] Gerald Peterman, *Paul's Gift from Philippi: Conventions of Gift Exchange and Christian Giving*, SNTSMS 92 (Cambridge: Cambridge University Press, 1997), 91–93.

[76] Guthrie, *Philippians*, 31.

[77] Guthrie, 32–33.

[78] Guthrie, 34.

[79] Ben Witherington, III, *Paul's Letter to the Philippians, A Socio-Rhetorical Commentary*, (Grand Rapids: Eerdmans, 2011), 12.

> conventions not epistolary conventions that Paul is mainly following in Philippians.[80]

Further, the epistolary handbooks used as models of ancient letters "were too late to have influenced Paul."[81] Witherington's outline of the letter contains seven parts:

1) epistolary prescript, 1:1–2;
2) exordium, 1:3–11;
3) narratio, 1:12–26;
4) propositio, 1:27–30;
5) probatio, 2:1–4:3;
6) peroratio, 4:4–9;
7) concluding arguments, 4:10–20; and
8) epistolary greetings and closing, 4:21–23.

This reflects that Paul follows accepted rhetorical devices which knit the letter together as a unity.[82]

Some have offered cautions about applying the principles of discourse too rigidly. Bockmuehl states:

> They frequently require one to conform Philippians to rigid rhetorical schemes and conventions—or to interpret it solely through the myopically "synchronic" spectacles of a strictly internal linguistic analysis, analysing [sic] the text in splendid isolation from the historical flesh-and-blood complexities affecting the author and his readers.[83]

Stephen Fowl concludes, "Christians have no real option but to treat the canonical form of Philippians as the basis for theological reflection.

---

[80] Witherington, III, 13. He further states, "Paul knew perfectly well that proclaiming a monotheistic Jewish message in a polytheistic culture where anti-Semitism was rife required more than just words spoken in earnest and with passion. It required persuasion."

[81] Witherington. III, *Paul's Letter*, 13. These include Libanius (4th century) and pseudo-Demetrius (late 1st or 2nd century).

[82] Witherington, III, 29–30.

[83] Bockmuehl, *A Commentary*, 23. He emphasizes his argument further: "Rhetorical, epistolographic and text-linguistic arguments for unity . . . too often remain methodologically arbitrary, inappropriately prescriptive in their use of ancient parallels and patterns, or indeed mutually contradictory."

It is, ultimately, Philippians's status in the canon that demands this, not arguments for or against the literary integrity of the epistle."[84]

After analyzing all the arguments, a conclusion may be reached. Significant evidence suggests the unity of the letter although some notable scholars disagree. The following reasons argue for the unity of Philippians. Definitive evidence of any kind supporting the fragment theories is absent. Those who accept a fragment theory have been unable to agree on the exact length of the fragments. Knowledge of a specific situation which called for the loss of portions of the two or three letters is lacking, as is the lack of knowledge of any time when the supposed fragments were put together. A clear motivation for joining the fragments is also lacking. The redactor, if there were one, did sloppy work when he chose to leave the letter with such changes of tone and abrupt breaks after attempting to collatc thcm. Good explanations exist as to how the proposed fragments actually fit into the plan and purpose of Philippians. More recent literary analysis demonstrates a valid way of explaining the unity of the epistle. In short, the fragment theories do not contain compelling evidence, and there are at least two different methods of approaching Philippians which support the unity and integrity of the letter.[85]

6 ORIGIN AND DATE

Opinions about the date of the letter depend in large measure on conclusions about the provenance of the letter. The questions regarding these issues basically fall into two divisions: the circumstances of Paul and the theology of the letter These must be considered both separately and together since the theology has compelled some to look to a date that differs from the traditional.

---

[84] Fowl, *Philippians*, 8.

[85] Bockmuehl, *A Commentary*, 25, summarizes well in accepting the unity of the letter: "On balance . . . it seems fair to conclude that partition theories have turned out to raise more questions than they answer. The best course of action will be to acknowledge the structural problems of Philippians as it stands, and to try as far as possible to account for each in turn as we come to it . . . That, at any rate, is the conclusion drawn by all the major recent commentaries in English."

6.1 Origin

Numerous criteria need consideration before determining the origin of the letter.[86] The most important of these are discussed below. Luke records four Pauline imprisonments: Philippi (Acts 16:23–31, in about AD 50); Jerusalem (Acts 22:24–23:22, in about AD 58); Caesarea (Acts 23:33–26:32, in about AD 58–60); and Rome (Acts 28:17–31, in about AD 60–62). Paul makes clear, however, in writing to the Corinthians (2 Cor 11:23) that before his third missionary journey had been completed, he was imprisoned "many" times. Prior to 2 Corinthians, written from Ephesus, Philippi was the only known imprisonment. Obviously, Luke does not give a full account of Paul's experiences. Although Luke does not record an imprisonment at Ephesus, there are good reasons to suggest it. The current discussion centers on one of two locations, Ephesus or Rome.

ROME. The traditional view (i.e., the view that stems from the earliest centuries of Christianity) is that Paul wrote the letter from Rome during his first Roman imprisonment. No other tradition survived from the second century until the eighteenth. The only external evidence available comes from the Marcionite prologue to the letter. The writer, speaking about the Philippians, stated, "The Apostle praises them, writing to them from Rome, from prison, carried by Epaphroditus."[87] Although it is the only history available, no one knows the origins of this prologue or what basis lay behind it.

The traditional view fits most of the details required by the text. Many factors enter into discussions regarding the origin of the letter that support it. Some of the more important are that Paul was in prison at the time of writing (better, house-arrest rather than prison); Paul had the freedom to entertain friends, write letters, and lead a movement which was possibly suspect in the eyes of the government; Paul faced a trial, the outcome of which was uncertain; the church engaged in extensive evangelistic work apart from Paul; and Paul planned to visit Philippi, assuming he received a favorable verdict. The interpreter

---

[86] For example, Hawthorne list seven factors. Keown, *Philippians*, I:24–45, gives perhaps the most extensive list of eleven. Scholars differ on how they weigh the importance of some of these.

[87] The Latin Marcionite prologue dated from the second century. Quoted by Beare, *The Epistle*, 24.

must also account for the number of times Paul's companions traveled to and from Philippi.[88]

Each of these easily fits into the Roman hypothesis, except the travel itinerary. The strongest objection to a Roman hypothesis is the distance between Philippi and Rome. Objectors to the Roman hypothesis point out that the evidence calls for a minimum of four trips between Philippi and Rome, and perhaps as many as six would be necessary. The trips would have been (1) news of Paul's imprisonment was sent to Philippi; (2) Epaphroditus was sent from Philippi to Rome with a gift and an offer of help (Phil 2:25); (3) news of Epaphroditus's sickness (after some time?) reached Philippi (2:26); (4) word reached Paul and Epaphroditus that the Philippians were concerned about Epaphroditus (2:26); (5) Paul hoped to send Timothy before he could go himself (2:23–24); and (6) Paul possibly expected that Timothy would return and journey with him to Philippi.[89]

The trip to Rome from Philippi was approximately 800 miles. From Rome the traveler would follow the Ignatian Way to Brundisium (360 miles), take a ship across the Adriatic to Dyrrachium (two days with favorable weather), and follow the Ignatian Way to Philippi (370 miles).[90] Sir William Ramsay estimated a foot-traveler covered fifteen to twenty miles per day on the Roman roads.[91] This would suggest travel took fifty-two days by the slower rate and thirty-nine days by the faster pace. Imperial couriers traveled at a rate of fifty miles per day, perhaps with the help of chariots or horses,[92] making the travel time only fifteen land travel days, two sea travel days, and whatever intervals were needed for rest or inclement weather. Some estimate that the travel requirements of five months traveling round trip, and thus ten months total for four one-way trips, easily fit into one year of time.[93] It is difficult to see how earlier commentators, such as A. Deissmann, concluded the travel was impossible in less than two years.[94]

---

[88] Many sources provide extensive details regarding these matters. Helpful recent surveys from commentaries, with good bibliographies, include Martin, *Philippians*, 36–57; Hawthorne, *The Epistle*, xxxvi-xliv; and Beare, *The Epistle*, 15–24.

[89] This list includes the most important criteria developed from within the letter.

[90] Beare, *The Epistle*, 18.

[91] W. Ramsay, "Roads and Travel (NT)," *HDB* 5:375–402.

[92] See Silva, *Philippians*, 6, n. 4.

[93] Beare, *The Epistle*, 19; Silva, *Philippians*, 7.

[94] Quoted in Martin, *Philippians*, 41.

Many scholars also question the necessity of four to six trips from Rome to Philippi. Some have suggested fewer trips were necessary. The travel could be reduced to a minimum with the following reconstruction. The Philippians heard Paul was going to be sent (or possibly had been sent) to Rome to await trial; immediately they sent Epaphroditus with a gift for Paul's support, perhaps having heard he would have to rent housing. On the way, Epaphroditus took sick and news of his sickness reached Philippi.[95] The church dispatched the news of their concern for him, knowing the courier would reach him on the way to or in Rome. And Epaphroditus continued his journey upon his recovery and presented the money to Paul. This would have required two trips to Rome, which may have been undertaken simultaneously in part, although there would obviously be delays for the illness and recovery.

While this reconstruction is possible, it is hardly likely. The travel scenario is overdone. Too much may be built on unnecessary assumptions. The normal way to read the text allows for some time for Epaphroditus's sickness, and surely enough time elapsed for more than two trips from Rome to Philippi. Even if four seem likely, they could easily have been done in ten months and Paul was imprisoned for two years. This removes the greatest obstacle to the Roman origin of the letter.[96]

Other problems with the Roman origin have surfaced. Primarily, they are Paul's expected visit to Philippi upon his release and the nature of the content of the letter. Paul could have changed his earlier plans to visit Rome after the relief offering was deposited in Jerusalem. Although in Rom 15:23–29 Paul spoke as though he had finished his ministry in the eastern Mediterranean, things changed. Time passed and five years in prison could easily redirect thoughts and intentions. F. W. Beare's sentiments regarding this should be heard:

---

[95] This was suggested by C. O. Buchanan, "Epaphroditus' Sickness and the Letter to the Philippians," *EQ* 36 (1964): 157–66. Martin, *Philippians*, 42, objects to Buchanan's thesis because it contains "all manner of speculation," but nothing in Philippians states when Epaphroditus became sick. The primary speculative element is how the illness occurred, not that it may have occurred earlier than his arrival to Rome.

[96] The problem of the distance from Rome to Philippi seems to have been the issue that called for another reconstruction. Shorter travel distances and time would seem, to some, to be plausible.

> This argument is singularly weak. When Paul wrote Romans, he was a free man, and at the height of his powers. It would not be strange if after five years in custody he would no longer have the impulse to start new work in strange territory, but would long to return to the Aegean cities to see his old friends once again.[97]

Some also point to the fact that Timothy is not mentioned in Acts as being with Paul in Rome. He is mentioned as one of the writers of Philippians, indicating Timothy's strong relationship to the church there. Further, it is likely Timothy accompanied Paul to Rome. He was with him in the final journey to Jerusalem (Acts 20:4) and, presumably, remained with Paul through Paul's legal difficulties. He is included in the salutation of three of the traditional four Prison Letters (Col 1:1; Phil 1:1).[98]

The letter's content is another matter. The argument is that the content of the letter resembles Romans, Corinthians, and Thessalonians, written four to eight years earlier. Both the content and the apparent opponents resemble these other books. After scrutiny, however, no compelling theological parallels demand an earlier date.[99] The letter may have been written earlier, but nothing demands such a conclusion. The argument from the content of Paul's letters assumes Paul would only write certain themes at certain times in his life so his argument against the Judaizers, for example, could only take place during the mid 50s.[100] The very nature of the mission of the Judaizers, however, reveals their desire to travel to Pauline churches to undermine Paul's message of grace. Their itinerant work suggests

---

[97] Beare, *The Epistle*, 19. This makes good sense. It should be noted, however, that history records Paul did make a later trip to Spain as he hoped earlier.

[98] It should be noted (1) the mention of Timothy in Philippians is for some beside the point, since that does not substantiate a Roman origin, and (2) many scholars question both the Pauline authorship of Colossians and its origin from Rome. Traditionally, until the 1700s, all thought Paul wrote Colossians from Rome.

[99] Beare, *The Epistle*, 21, quotes Mitton's study on the subject, concluding that "there is little evidence of passages from other letters exerting a sustained or a recurring influence in Philippians. . . . The parallels appear to be unrelated to each other." He continues, "Thus it appears that no light can be thrown on the date of Philippians by any conspicuous degree of similarity to one group of the other epistles. There is nothing in the style or language to deter us from affirming that it is the latest of them all."

[100] This would also compel an argument for the date of Galatians being mid-50s and a North Galatia destination. Most scholars today reject that in favor of the South Galatian destination and a date in the late 40s.

movement from place to place. Certainly, it would be easy for them to move from Asia Minor (Ephesus) or Southern Europe (Corinth) to Macedonia (Philippi) in a matter of five to seven years. Most often it is assumed by earlier date advocates that Philippians most resembles Thessalonians, Corinthians, and Romans. Dating the letters according to their content often fails to account for the circumstances in the receiving churches and places the emphasis on Paul's developing theology. In considering internal evidence, both "the imperial guard"(Phil 1:13) and "Caesar's household" (4:22) demand interpretation. The best understanding of these point to a Roman origin, but see below.

The arguments against the traditional date do not compel the reader to forsake it. Conversely, nothing in the letter requires a late date, and the traditional date rests on slim evidence. The question that must be answered is this: Does the evidence seem to fit better in another setting and time? If it does not fit better elsewhere, the traditional dating of Rome in AD 60–62 should be accepted.[101] Nevertheless, three other suggestions demand consideration.

EPHESUS. The Ephesian hypothesis goes back to 1900 when H. Lisco suggested Paul may have written from there about AD 54–57.[102] He has been followed by several scholars, including G. S. Duncan, who popularized the theory.[103] The theory basically assumes the distance between Ephesus and Philippi makes the logistics more likely than from Philippi to Rome.[104]

Other considerations arise from those who favor the Ephesian hypothesis. Most of them are prompted by the distance from Rome to Philippi, but other data is produced in a supplemental way to make

---

[101] This is the conclusion of many modern scholars, including Beare, *The Epistle*, 24; Silva, 8; C. H. Dodd, *New Testament Studies* (Manchester: University Press, 1953); P. N. Harrison, "The Pastoral Epistles and Duncan's Ephesian Theory," *NTS* 2 (1955–56): 250–61.

[102] See Hawthorne, *Philippians*, xxxviii. His discussion of all these theories is well worth reading for specific data.

[103] G. S. Duncan has written several works espousing this position. They include *St. Paul's Ephesian Ministry* (London: Hodder & Stoughton, 1929); "A New Setting for Paul's Epistle to the Philippians," *ExpTim* 43 (1931–32): 7–11; "Paul's Ministry in Asia:—The Last Phase," *NTS* 3 (1956): 211–18. Others have agreed with Duncan, but generally the hypothesis is associated with him.

[104] Other arguments supporting the theory are these: Timothy was with Paul in Ephesus and where Philippians was written; there was a praetorium at Ephesus if it can refer to any provincial governor's residence; extensive evangelistic activity occurred at that point in Paul's ministry; and Acts records great difficulty and public riot in Ephesus (19:23–41). See also 2 Cor 1:8–10 and 11:23ff.; moreover, the language and style of the letters of that time parallel Philippians.

the Ephesian hypothesis more likely. In arguing for Ephesus, proponents realized it became necessary to argue against Rome. Discrediting the Roman hypothesis paves the way for accepting another, most likely the Ephesian hypothesis.

The focus of argumentation has been twofold, revolving around the praetorium (1:13, often translated "imperial guard," as in CSB), and "Caesar's household" (4:22, often assumed to be Caesar's family). The two go together in the arguments. If the praetorium is not a reference to a Roman official building, as some argue, then Caesar's household is unlikely to be located in Rome. A few pivotal points seem to argue against a Roman origin.

First, some question whether Philippians should be correlated with Luke's account in Acts. As Flexsenhar states, "[T]he deeper problem with many historical reconstructions of Paul's situation is the tendency to read Philippians alongside the canonical Acts as if they form one harmonious historical account."[105] At the core of the issue is whether Acts 28:16 should read "[w]hen we entered Rome, Paul was allowed to live by himself with the soldier who guarded him"[106] or "when we came to Rome, *the centurion delivered the prisoners to the captain of the guard*, but Paul . . . "[107] The preferred reading makes no mention of the "captain of the guard," supposedly the head of the imperial guard. According to Flexsenhar, "[T]he Praetorian/Imperial Guard interpretation of Phil 1.13 has not only conflated Acts 28:16 and Phil 1:13 but, from its inception, has conflated the two using an inferior textual witness."[108] His conclusion is that it is incorrect to read Philippians through the history recorded in Acts. The suggestion of "imperial guard," and the Roman origin, he believes, are presupposed from Acts.[109] Is it necessary, however, that Paul include Luke's history in a friendly letter like Philippians to make sure everyone knows the two

105 Michael Flexsenhar, III, "The Provenance of Philippians and Why it Matters: Old Questions, New Approaches," *JSNT* 42:1 (2019): 27.

106 See the CSB, HCSB, NIV, RSV, ESV, and most modern translations.

107 So KJV, NKJV, and many of the majority text witnesses. The emphasis is added.

108 Flexsenhar, III, "The Provenance," 23–25, traces the connection of the two to Bishop J. B. Lightfoot.

109 Further, "Acts never states that when Paul was in Rome he was imprisoned, chained, or in a *praetorium* . . . Acts never states that Paul was under the watch of the Praetorian Guard . . . Acts uses the same word as Paul does (πραιτώριον) . . . for a provincial, administrative building (Acts 23:35) . . . Acts envisions that Paul was not in prison at all but in 'a rented lodging," Flexsenhar, III, "The Provenance," 28.

are the same? In spite of the detailed argument presented, it remains an argument from the silence of Philippians on details the church might well know already.

Second, for Ephesus advocates, the mention of the praetorium or imperial guard does not necessitate a Roman provenance. Flexsanhar well establishes the fact that there were multiple provincial buildings throughout the Roman Empire called "praetorium," which had a variety of uses.[110] His basic argument is that it is not necessary to confine a praetorium to Rome alone. Combined with other "evidences," he discounts a Roman origin. One Achilles heel in his argument, however, is there is absolutely no evidence of a praetorium in Ephesus. In fact, "Ephesus was in a senatorial, not imperial, province; and there is no known evidence that refers to a senatorial governor's palace as a praetorium."[111]

That Paul references more than an official palace building seems clear from the phrase "and from everyone else (1:13)." It makes little sense to assume it means "all the praetoriums in the empire" or "all the other buildings in the area." It strongly suggests the persons who occupy the building and others beyond it are on Paul's mind. The remainder of the people certainly knew of Paul's situation. This likely happened because Paul was surrounded by individuals connected to the praetorium as they talked about their new prisoner. Thus, the interpretation of the soldiers as Praetorium officers fits well into the narrative. As a Roman citizen, Paul had appealed to Caesar. He had that right. The entire scenario, described in Acts, fits well into the practices of ancient Rome. Paul's plight was heard and evaluated by soldiers of the highest order, the imperial Praetorium Guard (Caesar's own), and he became a topic of conversation throughout their home base.

The bulk of attention goes to the discussion of the praetorium. As mentioned above, however, the identification of believers in "Caesar's household" deserves comment. Unlike Paul's use of praetorium in a technical sense, household is generic.[112] It is conceivable, like many of non-Roman origin suggest, that "Caesar's household" refers to

---

[110] Flexsenhar, III, 31–37. He further provides a possible location of a praetorium in Ephesus if there were one.

[111] Gordon D. Fee, *Paul's Letter to the Philippians*, NICNT (Grand Rapids: Eerdmans, 1995), 35, n.87.

[112] Praetorium is a Latin word which Paul left untranslated into *Greek*. Obviously it occurred in common parlance. Even so, it is specific to referencing a government facility. Household (οἰκία) occurs with broader connotations.

people beyond blood relations or immediate and vital house servants/employees. Sometimes it is enlarged by suggestion to any of Caesar's employees around the empire. Fee offers a caution about this assumption: "Nowhere outside of Rome is there a known concentration of them [sic. Caesar's household] of such size that some of its 'members' are noteworthy for having become believers in Christ, nor is there any evidence for the use of this terminology outside of Rome."[113] Further, the question arises as to why Paul identifies them in Philippians and not in other letters where, presumably, some government officers would have become Christians. The best answer is that Paul wanted to reinforce connections between the Roman government and the Philippian church. He chose several political words and metaphors throughout the book. They must have been chosen to communicate clearly to Roman citizens, such as at Philippi. The best understanding is that these are related to Caesar in Rome. Their inclusion is striking.

Not all who support an Ephesian origin for Philippians argue along these lines. Many accept the accuracy of the Acts history, but they do not find the data in Philippians compelling to a Roman situation. They find the suggestions of (1) Paul imprisoned in Ephesus; (2) the problem of the distance between Philippi and Rome; and (3) internal matters, likely point against it.[114] The Ephesus origin notion seems to be gaining popularity among many, so that for some "[t]he Ephesian provenance theory of the letter appears destined to become the consensus view of NT scholars in the near future."[115]

Four considerations argue against the Ephesian hypothesis. First, it is based on conjecture. No evidence confirms Paul's imprisonment there, though such an imprisonment was possible. Second, the letter does not mention the "collection for the saints" which so occupied Paul's thoughts during this period. Further, it is unlikely that Paul would have received a gift for himself when he was so involved in fund-raising for this project.[116] Third, Paul spoke in Philippians as though he had no friends with him at the time except Timothy (2:19–21), yet Aquila and Priscilla were in Ephesus when he was (Acts

---

[113] Fee, *Philippians*, 36.

[114] Hawthorne, *Philippians*, 1, exemplifies these. He notes in his first edition he opted for a Caesarean origin. In the second edition, he changed his mind and "espoused the proposal of an Ephesian provenance (which is in keeping with the trends of recent scholarship)."

[115] Andreas J. Kostenberger, L. Scott Kellum, and Charles L. Quarles, *The Cradle, The Cross, and the Crown* (Nashville: B&H Academic, 2009), 566.

[116] Hawthorne, *Philippians*, xxxix. See 1 Cor 16:1-3.

18:18–26).[117] Fourth, it does not appear he faced death at Ephesus, especially since he had not yet appealed to Caesar. To these may be added the fact that Paul probably would not have had the freedoms described in Philippians at Ephesus since he would have been imprisoned because of a riot.[118] To these should be further added, by way of review, that no external evidence exists for anything but a Roman origin; moreover, the descriptions in Phil 1 suggest a capital crime against the state.

The idea of the Ephesian hypothesis is attractive, but it does not fit the details as well as the Roman theory. If concrete evidence existed that Paul was in prison in Ephesus, that there were a Praetorium in Ephesus, and that he had the freedoms and friendships demanded by the letter to the Philippians, the hypothesis could be accepted. The theory gained prominence in reaction to the Roman view and because of the matter of the distance. It offers a solution which contains more problems than what it intends to solve.[119]

CAESAREA. As early as 1779, H. E. G. Paulus proposed Caesarea as the place of origin for Philippians.[120] Unlike the Ephesus hypothesis, the distance between Rome and Philippi did not prompt the development of the Caesarean hypothesis. Caesarea is further from Philippi than Rome, approximately 1,200 miles over land, so other issues need to be considered besides accessibility to Philippi when deciding between Caesarea and Rome.[121] The primary reason for suggesting Caesarea is that it reconciles with Paul's travel plans after his release.[122]

---

[117] Hawthorne, xxxix.

[118] Beare, *The Epistle*, 23, says, "It was not every prisoner who would be free to turn his cell into an executing office for the propagation of a religion of doubtful legality." The same fact holds for Caesarea, where Paul was imprisoned because of a riot, and he had a change of venue because of the threat on his life. There he did appeal to Caesar.

[119] Martin, *Philippians*, 56–57, gives three reasons why continental scholars hold to the Ephesian origin: the theory of Philippians being a composite document made up of several letters, the letter's affinities with 2 Corinthians, and the identity of the rival preachers in Phil 1:12–18. Those who argue these points seem to want to hold on to other theories which are best served by this one as well.

[120] Cited in Hawthorne, *Philippians*, xli. Hawthorne is the most recent commentator to accept the Caesarean origin of the letter. His arguments should be consulted for a good defense of the hypothesis.

[121] Hawthorne, vlii, states, "If distance from Philippi is the major objection for considering Rome as the site for the origin of Philippians (so Collange), then there exists no possibility for suggesting Caesarea in its place."

[122] Other factors do accord with the facts as well: Luke stated that the Caesarean imprisonment was in the palace of Herod (Acts 23:35); the imprisonment was for two years, which

Paul easily could have expected to visit the church at Philippi because the overland route to Rome would take him through Philippi. It also reconciles with his earlier intention to go to Spain.

Apart from the resolution of the supposed conflict in mission plans, little commends the Caesarean hypothesis. The primary reason for the Ephesian theory was to avoid the distance in travel. That problem is more difficult with a Caesarean origin. Unlike the Ephesian hypothesis, it can claim the support of Acts, which records a lengthy imprisonment in Caesarea. In reality, however, nothing commends the hypothesis positively to such a degree that it should replace the traditional view, and certain problems persist.

CORINTH. The final suggestion is that Paul wrote Philippians from Corinth. It too claims early support since the first suggestion occurred in 1731 by G. L. Oeder. S. Dockx revived the theory in 1973.[123] The suggestion suffers some of the same problems as the Ephesus hypothesis, but it also solves some of the same problems.[124] The hypothesis dates Philippians early, about AD 50–51.

Against the proposal, some major obstacles remain. First, Acts does not record an imprisonment in Corinth. The account reveals Paul had less trouble at Corinth than other places, such as Caesarea or Ephesus. Second, at Corinth Paul had several good friends surrounding him, but in Phil 2:19–21 it seems only Timothy remained with him. Few today hold to this option. It creates more problems than the Ephesus hypothesis and has even less to commend it.

The most likely suggestions as to origin, then, are Rome and Ephesus. Ephesus is, in many ways, an attractive alternative. On the whole, however, the Roman origin seems less problematic and enjoys a longer history of acceptance. It is assumed here.

Given such attention to the matter of provenance, the question arises as to its importance. Is this just the interest of scholars who

---

allowed plenty of time for the travel; Paul had some liberty (Acts 24:23); Paul apparently already had made some defense, such as was the case at Caesarea (Acts 24:20–21); Paul's opponents in Phil 3:2 seem to have been Jews, and that would fit this scenario; Paul delivered the collection for the saints and thus felt no restraint in accepting gifts. See Hawthorne, xli-xlii.

[123] See Martin, *Philippians*, 44; S. Dockx, *"Lieu et Date de l'epitre aux Philippiens," RB* 80 (1973): 230–46.

[124] Martin, *Philippians*, 44, gives the following support: Corinth had a proconsul, by inference, a praetorium (Acts 18:12); the geographical problem is solved; the anti-Judaizing polemic occurs in other writings of the time as well; Paul's statement in Phil 4:10–20 that there was no opportunity for a gift fits well in the time frame.

inevitably and consistently debate such matters? Opinions on that vary. Fowl states, "I would also add . . . that it is not clear that one's decisions on these matters make much interpretive difference."[125] Flexsenhar represents the opposite, rewriting the commonly assumed Christian history. He says,

> The 'Praetorian' or 'Imperial Guard' interpretation of Phil 1.13 elevates Christianity's social and political position in history and, by extension, Christianity's authority in the world today. To think that Paul's message of Christ permeated the elite personal bodyguard of the most powerful person in the Roman world . . . insinuates an excessive exultation of the 'gospel' and indeed the superiority of Christianity. Such an interpretation is always susceptible to triumphalism.[126]

More to the importance of this discussion, Keown speaks to the impact of the political terminology in the Roman sensitive church.[127] Fee adds, "The gospel, with its proclamation of a heavenly Lord who had become the incarnate Savior, had penetrated the household of the (merely earthy) Roman "lord and savior."[128]

6.2 The Date

The date of the letter depends on its origin. Scholars who locate the writing at Corinth suggest an early date, about AD 50–51, shortly after the founding of the church at Philippi. Those who locate the writing at Ephesus date Philippians in the mid-50s, when Paul ministered at Ephesus on the third missionary journey. Those who locate the writing at Caesarea date the epistle later, about AD 58–60. Finally, those who affirm the traditional view, from Rome, generally date the letter at about AD 60–62, during Paul's first Roman imprisonment. This is the preferred view in this commentary.

Some interpreters attempt to date the epistle even more precisely. Was it at the beginning, middle, or end of the imprisonment? There is

---

125 Fowl, *Philippians*, 9.

126 Flexsenhar, III, "The Provenance," 38–39.

127 Keown, *Philippians*, 1:33, n.22. He states, "A Roman provenance in particular does affect interpretation, heightening the contrast between the Roman world and empire and the *politeuma* of heaven."

128 Fee, *Philippians*, 32.

no way of knowing this. The letter seems to imply that when it was written Epaphroditus had been in Rome for a short time. Additionally, the letter reveals that repercussions of Paul's imprisonment were widespread, suggesting some time of development after his arrival. Moreover, it may be Paul expected a quick trial in the near future. These factors suggest Paul had been in Rome for some time. Conversely, he *hoped* for a quick verdict and a visit to Philippi soon (2:24). The best suggestion, therefore, is the letter was written from the middle to near the end of his stay in Rome, around AD 61–62.

The relationship of Philippians to the other Prison Epistles also causes some interest. Apparently, Colossians, Ephesians, and Philemon belong together in time. The same person served as courier for Colossians and Ephesians (Tychicus, Eph 6:21–22; Col 4:7–8). Also, Tychicus traveled with a runaway slave, Onesimus, who returned to his master, Philemon (Col 4:9; Phlm 12). Further, Archippus occurs in both Colossians (4:17) and Philemon (2). The connections among these three of the Prison Epistles suggests they were sent at the same time. Most likely, the occasion was the return of Onesimus to Philemon after Onesimus's conversion. Since the courier would have to pass through Ephesus, it is natural to include the letter to that church. It is possible the couriers could have taken the Via Ignatia through Philippi as well, but it was not a necessary route. In content, Ephesians and Colossians share both a common outline of contents and significant similarity of instruction.[129] Thus, multiple reasons suggest the purpose and timing of these three of the Prison Epistles. It is likely Paul would have delayed these letters carried by Onesimus/Tychicus and Epaphras if he had expected a quick release. The three of them could have traveled together.[130] It seems, therefore, that Ephesians, Colossians, and Philemon may have been sent separately and, perhaps, earlier. Philippians has a different style of writing, different content, and a different purpose.

[129] Numerous studies have demonstrated the parallels between Ephesians and Colossians. William Hendriksen, *Exposition of Ephesians*, NTC (Grand Rapids: Baker, 1967), 5–26, gives a good presentation of the parallels.

[130] He obviously did expect to be free soon. He asked them to "prepare" for his coming (Phlm 22).

7 PAUL'S OPPONENTS AT PHILIPPI

Who were Paul's opponents at Philippi? The question is not easily answered, though the Philippian letter provides ample information regarding them in four basic passages: 1:15–17; 1:27–28; 3:2; 3:18–19. Scholars question whether these passages refer to the same group, two groups, or three groups.

Several observations guide the investigation. In 1:15–17 Paul referred to the opponents as preachers of Christ. He exposed them by describing their unfortunate motivations, but his ultimate evaluation was joy that they preached Christ. Clearly, he considered them Christian brethren, and their differences were relatively minor. Given the fact there were likely multiple congregations in Rome scattered throughout Rome's urban sections, it is easy to understand how preachers would have different ideas about how to promote the gospel. In addition, the fact that most, if not all, had never met Paul personally renders the division explainable. As will be noted in the commentary, however, the surface issue seemed to be what to do with Paul. At a deeper level, perhaps giving them the benefit of the doubt, the issue was how best to protect the gospel and churches from political interference. Regardless, the situation changed in chapter 3. There the apostle addressed those opponents sharply and condemned both their message and activities. Could the opponents of chapter 1 have been the same as the opponents of chapter 3? It seems not.

In chapter 3 Paul first addressed the opponents as "dogs, evil workers, those who mutilate the flesh" (3:2). Later the problem was libertinism, and Paul described the opponents as "enemies of the cross" (3:18–19). The difficulty appears to have been a mixture of legalism related to law and liberty related to foods. Were all the opponents the same people with the same message? It seems not.

Another difference is worth noting. The opponents in 1:15–17 were within the Christian community at Rome; the opponents in 3:2. appear to have been outside the Christian community at Philippi. Did something tie together people from two different places who had different attitudes toward Christianity? Paul seems to have identified them differently. In 1:15–17 he knew well those who opposed him. Perhaps he could have called at least some of them by name. In chapter 3, however, another group with whom he was not personally acquainted opposed his message. They loomed on the horizon, ready to invade the church from outside. Paul's attacks were general, relating to the group and its characteristics rather than to specific individuals.

Finally, the interpreter must determine what Paul's opponents opposed in Paul. The apostle identified his opponents' message in 1:15 as "Christ," and he handled it as though that content of their message was no problem to him. Presumably he could have preached the same message! The point of division was probably the same as Paul encountered everywhere he went. He proclaimed implications of the gospel that some could not accept. His distinctive insight was that Gentiles were included in the gospel and they did not need to accept the Jewish social and religious obligations as a part of their salvation. The Roman church had discussed the same matters earlier (Rom 14:1–15:6), and divisions occurred as convictions formed.

The opponents in chapter 3 definitely opposed Paul's teaching that Gentiles were saved as Gentiles and that the law was fulfilled in them by the Spirit. The opponents taught salvation required keeping the law, usually by becoming proselytes if interested parties were not Jews already. It is likely, therefore, the issue was one of degree rather than kind. The law was the issue. The early part of the letter reflects a long-term situation in Rome and the tension between differing motivations in preaching. The third chapter reflects an alarming situation like the ones at Galatia and Corinth. The opponents attacked the heart of the message; they preached another gospel. Thus, it appears two different groups were addressed in the epistle. The first were those who opposed Paul in Rome (chap. 1); the other posed the threat to the church at Philippi (chap. 3).

The history of identifying the opponents reveals several different options for chapter 3. Some suggest they were entirely Jewish, either Judaizers (from within the church community at large) or Hellenistic Jews (from outside). Their preoccupation with law formed the basis of Paul's attacks. First, they displayed legalism regarding circumcision (3:2). In some ways that reflects Acts 15:1, the issue of the Jerusalem Council (AD 50): "Unless you are circumcised according to the custom prescribed by Moses, you cannot be saved." Although Paul's letter to Philippi came approximately ten years after the Council, the issue of the relationship to the law was still alive. Since for Jews circumcision was the entrance point into keeping the commandments, the focus on it symbolized the need to be under the entire law. The issue had been settled at the Jerusalem Council, but many Jewish persons, including Jewish Christians, did not have clarity about it. The issue struck at the heart of the freedom of the gospel presented by Jesus and explained well by Paul. Indeed, his entire ministry emanated from the freedom from the law because of Jesus's death. Paul defended his position by claiming genuine circumcision is spiritual. He was not the first to understand the spiritual reality behind circumcision. Deuteronomy presented the truth that there is a circumcision of the heart (30:6). Paul wrote of it almost four years earlier to the Roman Christians (2:29), and even earlier had called the heresy of legalism to circumcision "another gospel" (Gal 1:6–9, which he quickly explained as no gospel at all).

Second, they had fascination with OT food laws as a part of the ceremonial law. In Phil 3:19 Paul said their "god is their stomach," referring to the scrupulous manner of choosing foods carefully. Speaking partially in irony, he suggested their entire lives were lived under the consciousness of food restrictions. It was worship for them. In both cases, then, the opponents were Jewish zealots who opposed Paul's mission to the Gentiles. Later in chapter 3 he identifies other characteristics of these opponents.[131]

Others have seen a Gnostic influence in the chapter. Perhaps the opponents were teachers who claimed to have membership in the Jewish-Christian-Gnostic community by virtue of their circumcision. They boasted of their own circumcision but added to it a perfectionist element. In their minds, they already had been raised to a heavenly, spiritual life on earth and moral and nutritional restraints made no difference to them.[132] For that reason, Paul countered these opponents with revelation of his personal attitudes regarding Christian perfectionism (3:12–16). He directly dealt with their claims of freedom from any restraints on diet or morality (3:18–19). This more fits the discussion in the middle of the chapter than the first part. It suggests there may be at least two opponents identified in chapter 3. Most scholars today reject the Gnosticism position since Gnosticism was not an issue until later in the first century. The commitments Paul opposes so strongly can be found in various streams of those who claim to remain within Judaism.

---

[131] Those who hold to this view of one Jewish opponent are, among others, J. Gnilka, M. Dibelius, K. Barth, O. Michaelis, Beare, Hawthorne, and Silva. See Martin, *Philippians*, 23–24; Hawthorne, *Philippians*, xlvx; Silva, *Philippians*, 9–11.

[132] See the discussion in Martin, *Philippians* 28–29.

Finally, the data has led some commentators to see two or more kinds of opponents in the chapter. These opponents generally are considered to be Judaizers who attacked the church from outside (3:2) and libertine heretics who may have come from within (3:19).

In summary, the opponents of chapter 3 appear to have preached the Jewish law (perhaps in addition to Christ). While Gnostic influence is possible although improbable, the data may be well understood and satisfied by the position that these false teachers were Jews. Some of Paul's Jewish opponents practiced esoteric and experiential religious principles that resembled those practiced by some later Christian Gnostics. They are most precisely described in Col 2:8–3:4. Nothing, however, in the Pauline writings seems to reflect Gnosticism.[133] It appears the opponents came from outside the church since Paul's words hardly referred to Christian brothers and a Jewish context is likely. The opponents of chapter 3, then, called the church to accept the laws of the OT, boasting in their own self-effort. The opponents of chapter 1 preached with a view to hindering Paul's universal application of Christianity. These taught that as Christians it was necessary to keep the law.

The Jewish flavor of the argument predominates. One question remains. Why would Paul have to engage in such a Jewish dialogue with a church in a city with few Jews? If there were too few of them in Philippi to have a synagogue and the first converts were Gentile, by what avenue did the Jewish teachers come in? The answer must be that they had a concern to oppose Paul's preaching wherever they encountered it. That is likely the tie between the opponents of 1:15 and 3:2. They both had an interest in "the Christ" and his relationship to Gentiles, one more affirming than the other. See also the extensive introduction to chapter 3.

[133] Some scholars in the past two-hundred years viewed the Letter to the Colossians as written "against" Gnosticism. This found support from their higher critical assumptions that 1) Colossians was not Pauline, and 2) Colossians was written later, perhaps in the second century AD. With the discovery of the Qumran scrolls, however, it is now known that some sects in Jewish life were perfectionistic (e.g., the Qumran community). They also practiced ascetic rituals that produced visions (hallucinations) and glossolalia ("worship of [like] angels"). Paul's references to Jews in Phil 3, however, do not have the same descriptions and detail found in his polemic against his opponents at Colossae. Even so, there is no reason to postulate a Gnostic background to any portion of Philippians. See Richard R. Melick, Jr, *Philippians, Colossians, Philemon,* The New American Commentary: An Exegetical and Theological Exposition of Holy Scripture, ed. David S. Dockery et al (Nashville: B&H, 1991), 171–83.

8 THEOLOGICAL THEMES OF THE EPISTLE

After the greeting and prayer for the church, Paul had definite concerns which he wanted to express, and he also wrote to warn of false teachers who threatened the church. Unlike many of Paul's letters, Philippians cannot be divided into theological and practical sections. Every section is incarnational. Paul's theological interests are expressed in biographical, first-person form. Within this motif, however, certain movements occur.

Paul explained his situation at Rome (1:12–26). Although he was concerned about the divided Christian community there, his outlook was strengthened by the knowledge that Christ was magnified. Paul's theology of life formed the basis of his optimism. Whether he lived or died, whether he continued his service to others or went to his own rewards, or whether he was appreciated or not, he wanted Christ to be glorified. Philippians describes this commitment better than any other of Paul's letters.

Paul exhorted the church to unity (1:27–2:18). Two factors influenced him. The church at Rome was divided, and he lived with a daily reminder of the effects of disunity. Further, similar disunity threatened the Philippian church as two prominent women differed with each other: Euodia and Synteche (4:2). Selfishness lay at the heart of the problems at Rome and Philippi. The answer came in an incarnational vehicle. Paul reminded the believers of Jesus's humility. If they would allow the outlook of Christ to guide their lives, harmony would be restored. The poem about Christ dominates the letter (2:5–11). Although the poem is presented as an illustration of proper attitudes, many see it as foundational for the entire letter It is possible to extend the statements of the hymn to provide a basis for Paul's exhortations throughout. While this is true, and the poem contains the most explicit Christology of the letter, Paul includes it as a well-known illustration.

Paul warned the church to beware Jewish legalists (3:2–21). Legalistic Jewish teachers threatened to destroy the vitality of the congregation by calling it to preoccupation with external religious matters. Paul countered the legalists with a forceful teaching about justification by faith. He chose to express his theology through his personal experience. He had lived their message and found it lacking.

Paul thanked Philippi's believers for their financial support. The church had sent money and a trusted leader, Epaphroditus, to care for Paul. Its generosity encouraged Paul at a time of personal need.

Even here he took advantage of the situation to express the rewards of giving and to teach Christian living. Again, theological instruction was occasional.

The letter abounds with Christian models for imitation. Most obviously, the church was to imitate Jesus, but other genuine Christians also merit appreciation. Paul, Timothy, and Epaphroditus embodied the selflessness God desires in his people.

Philippians also instructs in the meaning of salvation. Salvation was provided by Christ who became "obedient to the point of death" (2:6–8). Salvation was proclaimed by a host of preachers who were anxious to advance the gospel, and it was promoted through varying circumstances of life—both good and bad—so that the lives of believers became powerful witnesses. Finally, salvation would transform Christians and churches into models of spiritual life.

This little letter provides insight into church relationships. Paul expressed his concern for unity. Christian unity was achieved when individuals developed the mind of Christ. In more difficult situations, the church collectively solved problems through the involvement of its leadership (4:2–3). Harmony, joy, and peace characterize the church which functions as it should.

Paul taught about Christian stewardship. The Philippian church had reached a level of maturity regarding material possession, and it knew how to give out of poverty. It recognized the value of supporting the gospel and those who proclaim it, and it felt confident that God could provide for its needs as well. Paul also demonstrated his attitude toward material things. He could live with spiritual equilibrium in the midst of fluctuating financial circumstances. Christ was his life, and Christ's provisions were all he needed. In everything, Paul's joy was that Christ was glorified in his life.

Providing a theme that surfaces in significant places, Paul wrote of suffering. He did so by reflecting on several positive elements that redeem the natural negative perspective about Christian suffering. It is important to distinguish in the text the differences between tribulation and suffering, yet both have common causes on the surface and in a deeper appraisal. On the surface, suffering is caused by the popular reaction to Christians and their message. The uniqueness of Jesus's person and work always causes opposition. There is no evidence such opposition is deserved. That is, that Christians live in such a way as to arouse the antagonism of their neighbors. Their suffering is related to the message they proclaim and the lifestyle it requires. Often, therefore, the rationale for persecution has to do with the prevailing religions and, especially powerful, the claim that Christianity is anti-Roman. Growing emperor worship coupled with the Roman practice of approving or rejecting which religions could be practiced contributed to the fear of persecution.

At the deeper level, however, Paul lived with an eschatological awareness. Jesus suffered. It was a fulfillment of expected reactions to the Messiah's appearance. Therefore, Jesus's followers should expect to participate in suffering as they identified with him. Living through Christ was more than identification, however. The sufferings it brought enabled believers to know Christ better, experiencing something of what he did and for the same reasons. Christians could never suffer redemptively, since that would imply a weakness in the provision of salvation through the cross. The suffering Paul described he endured with resolution, understanding it was part of his new life. If he were to gain Christ and all that comes with it, he must suffer. It paralleled Jesus humbling and emptying self to gain God's vindication.

Philippians contributes to knowledge of genuine Christianity. Most of its themes occur elsewhere in Scripture, but the lessons impact life most powerfully in this letter. It is filled with theology, Christian commitment, and Christlikeness. Every Christian should learn these lessons well.

9 GENRE AND STYLE

Ancient letter writing took defined forms. Letters penned in ancient times followed developed patterns, much like we see in modern templates for business or cover letters, depending on the purpose of a missive. The form of a letter, therefore, often reveals the intent of the author. There is, of course, a reciprocal nature to the study. First, ancient letters are analyzed according to purpose and typical patterns emerge which are applied to specific writings. Second, the content of the letters is studied to determine if a given letter conforms to a known literary style. When the two correspond, the purpose of the letter is more clearly known. The study has helped to clarify ancient authorship and, at times, the situations it addresses.

Many have studied Philippians, comparing it to known ancient styles.[134] Recent scholarship "has tended to describe Philippians either (1) as a 'letter of friendship' or (2) as a type of 'family letter' (a genre not discussed in handbook traditions but in evidence in the papyri)."[135] Friendship letters include "mention of being 'absent' from those addressed (Phil 1:27; 2:12), the current situation of the writer and the recipients (1:12, 27; 2:19, 23), and acknowledgment that the recipients in some way have participated in meeting the needs of the letter's sender (4:14)."[136] Philippians fits this description. It includes more, however, speaking of a more intimate relationship secured by commitment to Christ and partnership in his mission, expanding beyond the desired information shared between writer and recipients. Indeed, Paul's letter includes strong elements of moral exhortation that has given rise to the designation "family letters."[137] This designation is preferred. Beyond simply finding the purpose of the letter, "the hortatory nature of the writing also suggests that we should give attention to the common rhetorical conventions the apostle used in the course of the letter's production."[138] As a very personal letter, Philippians also has the freedom to depart from the templates at times, producing at best a "mixed form" or even a very non-traditional form.

The Greek text of Philippians contains challenges. For the most part the language and vocabulary are simple and straightforward. There are few places where the text is lexically challenging. Seldom is there a text-critical issue that significantly alters interpretation. The letter contains frequent metaphors that demand attention, however, especially in theological and vitriolic passages (e.g., 2:6–11; 3:11–21). Also, the syntax and structure of Philippians presents challenges. Some texts are the most puzzling of any in the Pauline corpus. On a larger scale, these include the proper divisions in 1:12, the number of verses and arrangement of the poem in 2:6–11, chapter 3 as a parenthesis or continuation of Paul's argument, the ending of chapter 3 and/or the literary unit of which it is a part, and the organization of chapter 4:1–10 (do parts go with chapter 3 or on what basis are the verses subdivided?). The

[134] Holloway, *Philippians*, 24–36, provides an excellent overview and bibliography. He contends Philippians is a letter of consolation, given the grief evidenced in the letter at many points. See also 1–10.

[135] Holloway, 32. The ἐπιστολὴ φιλυκή, "letter of friendship," is a growing option for many.

[136] Guthrie, *Philippians*, 27, and Fee, *Philippians*, 3.

[137] Fee, *Philippians*, 2–7, 12–14.

[138] Guthrie, *Philippians*, 27.

organization of every chapter is vague enough for interpreters to vary on these points and others. On a smaller scale, sections like 1:9–11 bring various structural analyses. The small, warm, and friendly letter (of only four chapters) contains many challenges due, likely in part, to the free flow of the ideas from one to another. These matters are discussed in the appropriate places of the commentary.

10 INTERPRETING THE LETTER

The commentary to follow incorporates basic elements of biblical interpretation. Looking at the larger picture, biblical exegesis involves principles of CONTEXT, CONTENT, and CONCERN. The CONTEXT includes historical backgrounds and larger literary features (such as genre and canonical "locations"). CONTENT involves textual, lexical, structural, and literary approaches (such as rhetoric, discourse, conventions of speech, textual patterns). CONCERN looks back to the author's purpose and forward to contemporary theology and applications. In trying to be sensitive to these matters, this current commentary includes locating the text in the lives of Paul and the Philippian church(es). In addition, it uses a foundational visual presentation of structure. For practical reasons the structure has followed the Bible translation for this series, the Christian Standard Bible, with comments about Greek structure and other features being included where they are helpful. Since communication is hierarchical, all communicators oral or written have various ways of presenting their messages. There are main points and developing points. These are embedded in structural clues and highlighted by lexical and linguistic patterns. The interpretation section of the commentary interacts with Pauline thought in Philippians and in the traditional Pauline corpus. At the end of units of text, there are theological and practical sections that highlight some of the major themes.

The Greek text of Philippians is typical Koine Greek as may be found in communication among friends. There are, however, significant syntactical and literary challenges more numerous than in most Pauline letters of this size. Frequently these give rise to optional ways of outlining the letter, with scholars differing on how to connect them. Optional positions are presented in these places.[139]

---

[139] For example, Philippians is probably the most used letter for beginning Gk. students to translate. At the other extreme in Paul's writing, Colossians contains many unusual or unclear

OUTLINE OF THE LETTER

1 Salutation (1:1–2)
  1.1 The Writers (1:1a)
  1.2 The Readers (1:1b)
  1.3 The Greeting (1:2)
      Theological and Practical Points
2 Introductory Matters: Paul's Prayer for the Church and His Circumstances in Rome (1:3–26)
  2.1 Thanksgiving and Prayer for the Philippians (1:3–11)
    2.1.1 Paul's Thanksgiving (1:3–8)
    2.1.2 Paul's Prayer for the Philippians (1:9–11)
      Theological and Practical Points
  2.2 Paul's Joy in the Progress of the Gospel in Rome (1:12–26)
    2.2.1 Paul's Circumstances (1:12–18a)
      Theological and Practical Points
    2.2.2 Paul's Attitude (1:18b–26)
      Theological and Practical Points
3 Body of the Letter: Paul's Concerns for the Church (1:27–4:9)
  3.1 Exhortation to Christlike Character (1:27–2:18)
    3.1.1 A Unified Stand (1:27–30)
      3.1.1.1 The Nature of Their Stand
      3.1.1.2 Christian Suffering
      Theological and Practical Points
    3.1.2 A Unified Mind (2:1–4)
    3.1.3 A Unified Focus: The Example of Christ (2:5–11)
      Theological and Practical Points
    3.1.4 The Command to Obedience (2:12–18)
      Theological and Practical Points
  3.2 Paul's Future Plans Related to Philippi (2:19–30)
    3.2.1 Concerning Timothy (2:19–24)
    3.2.2 Concerning Epaphroditus (2:25–30)
      Theological and Practical Points
  3.3 Exhortation to Avoid False Teachers (3:1–21)
    3.3.1 Paul's Experience Explained (3:1–16)
      3.3.1.1 True Circumcision
      3.3.1.2 True Values
      3.3.1.3 True Zeal

words, even though most of the structure is clear. Examples of syntactical questions are Phil 1:9–11, 18; 3:1–2; 4:1.

3.3.2 The False Teachers' Character Exposed (3:17–21)
Theological and Practical Points
3.4 Exhortations to the Philippians: (4:1–9)
3.4.1 Exhortation to Steadfastness (4:1)
3.4.1.1 The Address to the Readers
3.4.2 Exhortation to Unity (4:2–3)
3.4.3 Exhortation to Joy and Peace (4:4–9)
Theological and Practical Points
4 Concluding Matters: Expression of Thanks for the Philippians' Support (4:10–20)
4.1 Paul's Situation (4:10–14)
4.1.1 Appreciation (4:10)
4.1.2 Contentment (4:11)
4.1.3 Adaptability (4:12)
4.1.4 Dependency (4:13)
4.1.5 Blessing (4:14)
4.2 Paul's Attitude Toward Those Who Gave (4:15–20)
4.2.1 Commendation (4:15–17)
4.2.2 Blessings (4:18–19)
4.2.3 Doxology (4:20)
Theological and Practical Points
5 Conclusion: Greetings from Rome (4:21–23)
5.1 From Paul (4:21a)
5.2 From the Brothers (and Sisters) with Paul (4:21b)
5.3 From All the Saints at Rome (4:22a)
5.4 From Believers in Caesar's Household (4:22b)

Philippians is one of Paul's shorter letters. Even so, there are various ways it is outlined. Some connected movements seem obvious to all. Others not so much. The following considerations guide the outline for this commentary.

1. Like all Paul's letters Philippians begins and ends with a greeting (1:1–2; 4:21–23).

2. Like ancient letters of friendship, the opening section includes a wish for the readers' well-being and a description of the author's life situation (1:3–26).

3. The body of the letter follows, with the message(s) the author desired to communicate. Alternate outlines often follow the type of letter Philippians is supposed to be (see above).

4. Beginning in 1:27 there are three basic imperatives Paul gives to the church. These form the pattern for 1:27–2:18 ("live your life worthy of the gospel" 1:27; "make my joy complete" 2:2; and "work out your own salvation" 2:12). Philippians 2:5–11 is an illustrative parenthesis, though its elements are interwoven throughout the letter.

5. After the commands, Paul reveals his plans for future contact with the church(es), involving Timothy, Epaphroditus, and himself 2:19–30.

6. Paul then warns about approaching false teachers. Philippians 3:1 is variously interpreted as either introductory to 3:2 and following, or 3:2 is an interruption to Paul's train of thought. Two keys for this text are 1) the phrase "in the Lord" occurs here as the first of four occurrences. The phrase seems to be dividing points in the narrative, revealing a pattern that holds the next section together. 2) Paul states he is addressing a problem again. It seems likely he is addressing the false teachers of 3:2. With that, the next section is 3:1–4:9. It includes various matters of concern.

7. Paul then addresses the financial support the church had provided for him (4:10–20).

COMMENTARY

1 SALUTATION (1:1–2)

SECTION OUTLINE

1 Salutation (1:1–2)
   Structure
   1.1 The Writers (1:1a)
   1.2 The Readers (1:1b)
   1.3 The Greeting (1:2)
         Theological and Practical Points

[1] Paul and Timothy, servants of Christ Jesus: To all the saints in Christ Jesus who are in Philippi, including the overseers and deacons. [2] Grace to you and peace from God our Father and the Lord Jesus Christ.

Structure

Paul and Timothy, [writing] to all the servants of Christ Jesus
                                              who are in Philippi,
                                              including the overseers and deacons:

Interpretation

The greeting Paul sent the church resembled the greetings of other first-century letters. Commonly, they contained three elements:

identification of the writer(s), identification of the readers, and actual greeting. Some differences occur compared to secular letters, however, which reinforce the Christian nature of the letters. Paul changed from the typical greeting *charein* to *charis* ("grace"); he added "peace" and explained that "grace and peace" come from both God the Father and Christ.[1]

The greeting reveals Paul chose to write this in a letter format. Ancient letters may be formal or informal.[2] Formal letters tend to reflect forethought in subject matter, stylized writing, and an organized presentation. Informal letters generally contain a tone of warmth and spontaneity and, at times, reflect intimacy regarding specific contexts that leave the modern interpreter puzzled.[3] Philippians has been considered informal. This does not assume Paul had no plan in mind. As noted, recent developments in both epistolary and rhetorical studies suggest Paul follows an established pattern in his communication.

Currently, two primary formats apply to this brief book: friendly letter and family letter.[4] Gordon Fee makes the case for a friendly letter with extensive supporting data.[5] He concludes:

> Philippians is a "hortatory letter of friendship: . . . But above all, Philippians is an especially Pauline, and therefore intensely Christian, expression of that letter form, so that in his hands form does not come first, Christ and the gospel do, first and always. Thus, the letter reflects known first-century conventions; but the conventions themselves are mere scaffolding for Paul.[6]

Witherington, among others, points out the language of friendship—*philos* and *philia*—are missing in Philippians. Further, the style of Philippians also does not fit friendship, he says, since "friendship

---

[1] Many point out the similarity between Paul's letters and other first-century correspondence. Hawthorne, however, suggests in the differences between Paul and his surroundings, Paul contributed to the history of letter writing. Hawthorne, *Philippians*, 2.

[2] These categories need revision because of the many ways letters are being classified, but they serve adequately the point made here.

[3] E.g., when Paul wrote in 1 Thessalonians, "You don't need me to write you" (stated in various ways, but see 4:9; 5:1). At other times the references are not so explicit.

[4] Keown, *Philippians 1:1–2:18*, 69–78, provides an excellent survey and summary of current scholarship. See also Witherington, III, *Paul's Letter*, 17–37, for an overview of genre, literary, rhetorical, and social approaches.

[5] Fee, *Philippians*, 1–14. His support includes the nature of friendship in the Greco-Roman world.

[6] Fee, 14.

language did not connote a parity relationship but rather ironically masked the opposite in polite language." Friendship was between the lower status person whose responsibility was to honor the higher as their friend. The relationships indicated in Philippians more fit the family.[7] Many point out that family letters were considered a subset of friendly letters.[8] Finally, a word of caution may be appropriate. Some approaches to the letter seem to be too neat, leaving the interpreter too tied to the system to appreciate the dynamics of the letter. As Keown aptly observes, "Philippians should be read for what it is: a letter from a Jewish apostle, in prison in Rome, whose life is now shaped by the crucified and risen Christ, to his converts in Philippi, seeking to persuade, dissuade, warn, and encourage them."[9]

In any event, there is no doubt that Paul's content could have altered a perfect letter form. This conversation between friends, using today's terminology and not that of Greco-Roman social conventions, suggests two important truths. First, the letter is not systematic. This means much of the writing simply flowed from Paul's mind. At no place in the letter did Paul sustain a fully developed, systematic presentation. The closest to it is in 2:5–11, which has the marks of more formal writing, but it illustrates another point and may well have not been Pauline (see exposition). This does not invalidate the letter as epistle or rhetoric since the form may be intuitive for Paul. Second, the letter is occasional. Some specific situation(s) prompted Paul to write. The letter is theology in street clothes. Paul answered the Philippians' specific concerns in ways they could understand. That is the beauty of such portions of Scripture: they are applied theology. At the same time, that approach brings some frustration to modern readers because the interpreter must always ask what lay behind the writing. A critical question to answer is, What is the reason for writing this letter?

---

[7] Witherington, III, *Paul's Letter*, 18. He notes the use of *agapetos* (beloved) twice (4:1). He notes the importance of the family letter since it reveals Paul's understanding of the church as a Christian family, rather than a friendship or social club.

[8] Guthrie, *Philippians*, 27.

[9] Keown, *Philippians*, 1:78.

1.1 The Writers (1:1a)

[1] *Paul and Timothy, servants of Christ Jesus:*

1:1a The letter identifies two writers: Paul and Timothy. Other NT books reveal significant information about both men, and the church at Philippi knew them very well.[10]

Specifically, why was Timothy mentioned? Various suggestions have been made. The most obvious answer lies in the close relationship Timothy had with the Philippians. He was part of the team that founded the church (Acts 16–18), Paul intended to send Timothy to the church not long after writing the letter (Phil 2:19), and Paul had no one who better shared his outlook and burden for his ministry (2:20). M. Silva suggests that, given the prominence of Timothy in Macedonian evangelism, the surprise would have been if he were not included in Paul's letter.[11]

Paul referred to himself and Timothy as "servants of Christ Jesus." He generally reserved the title *doulos* ("servant" or "slave") as a description of himself, and even then it occurs sparingly. This is the only place he referred to Timothy as a "servant/slave" of Christ, and he rarely called persons other than himself by the title. In Col 4:12, Paul called Epaphras a "servant of Christ" (*doulos Christo*), and others are called "fellow-servants" (*sundoulos*: Epaphras, Col 1:7; Tychicus, Col 4:7).[12] In this way Paul identified Timothy by a title which revealed high esteem for Timothy's commitment to Jesus and his effective and humble service (see Phil 2:20–24).[13] Even so, Paul reserved the title for a select few. Other Christian ministers are called "ministers" or "servants" (*diakonos*, Rom 16:1, for example). It is

---

[10] See the Introduction, "Authorship."

[11] Silva, *Philippians*, 39.

[12] Hawthorne, *Philippians*, 3–4, states regarding Paul's calling Timothy a slave, that it is unique. "In describing only himself as a 'slave,' or 'apostle,' or 'prisoner' of Christ Jesus—never anyone else. . . . The fact that it is shared only this once demands explanation." He later asked: "Why then did the apostle dare to share, for this one time only, his otherwise carefully and jealously guarded uniqueness?" Other commentators share Hawthorne's observation and sentiments. In fact, the point he makes is a proper one, but others are called "slaves."

[13] Hawthorne, 3–4, lists the following in his discussion of why Timothy was called a servant (though he uses the word slave). He was with Paul in his imprisonment; he was co-author of the letter; he was Paul's amanuensis; he was a co-founder of the church at Philippi; Paul wanted to be courteous to a loved associate; Paul wanted to show his humility in describing Timothy as a co-laborer (3–4). To these might be added the following reasons: Paul wanted to substantiate his testimony, and Paul intended to send him to Philippi in his place.

not apparent why Paul was so selective, but it remains an interesting feature of his writing.

Translations do not always distinguish between the two Greek words often translated "servant." *Doulos*, used here in the opening of Philippians, included the idea of a "slave-servant," often used in the OT of the bond-slave. In some ways it is the more restrictive of the two terms because of the implicit ownership idea associated with it. The second term, *diakonos*, is almost always translated "servant." It implies the idea of volitional, intentional giving in benefitting others. This word root occurs in the word for the office of "deacon," used sparingly then but frequently now. In 1 Tim 3:8–13 Paul used the term of an office in the church. In the same letter, however, he told Timothy to be faithful in his "service" (*diakonos*). It seems Paul used the word "servant" as a symbol of his (and Timothy's) authority in the mission God gave them. Too much may be made of that, however, since in a companion letter Paul identifies Timothy in the salutation as simply "Timothy our brother" (Col 1:1). Its use necessarily also brings to mind humility.

The word *doulos* occurs in only three salutations (Romans, Philippians, and Titus). Elsewhere Paul used the term "apostle" to describe himself. Before considering the meaning of "servant," it is necessary to ask why Paul used *doulos* here and elsewhere. He had not met the Roman church personally, but neither had he met the Colossian congregation, so lack of previous acquaintance does not seem to be the rationale for use.[14] In Romans Paul used both "servant" and "apostle" (1:1). There "servant" designates his humility, and he stated even his apostleship came by divine call. Perhaps more to the point, he did not have to assert his authority at Rome or Philippi. In Romans, Paul hoped to solve the problem of division between the Jewish and Gentile factions, but ultimately he had no personal responsibility for the church. When writing to Titus, Paul did not need to assert his apostleship. Titus knew him well and accepted his authority. Further, the problems addressed in Titus related to sub-Christian practice, not specifically false teachers entering the Christian community.[15] It may

[14] There was a difference in the two, however, in that the church at Colossae was Pauline in many ways.

[15] This latter distinguishes the letters to Timothy from the Letter to Titus. The heresy at Ephesus (addressed in Paul's note to Timothy) demanded an authoritative voice, even in a personal letter. Perhaps Paul assumed Timothy would read the letter to the congregation.

be, therefore, Paul used *doulos* when he could address the congregants without concern for major controversy in their midst.[16]

The word "servant" or "slave" has been defined in various ways. Its basic meaning is clear, but it may have implied one of two different ideas. The first comes from Greco-Roman culture. Slaves were common because of war, and Christian slaves probably worshiped in the churches alongside their masters.[17] Slavery was a common and familiar practice. In the Roman world, including Philippi, "slavery was an integral part of every aspect of life."[18] Possibly 85–90 percent of the people in Rome served as, or were related to, slaves. Additionally, up to a third of the population of urban areas were slaves.[19] Slaves were considered chattel. Sociologically, many were victims of war, dominated by the more powerful Roman military machine. Slaves often had professions which were disrupted by their captivity, but sometimes used by their Roman owners. Slaves occupied a distinct social class, the opposite of the political and economic leaders. No one sought to be a slave. A slave had no rights or privileges, and all personal interests and ambitions had to be repressed. Everything related to the master.[20] This title did not refer to a position of honor in the first-century, Gentile world. Given the strong Roman heritage of Philippi, the Philippians no doubt thought it strange, if not shocking. Was Paul, the son of privilege, intentionally identifying with the lowest class of persons in Rome? Paul chose his words carefully and "servant" truly characterized his life.[21]

The second possibility comes from the OT. Frequently the Septuagint used the word "servant" for one who served Yahweh (e.g., Num 12:7). Moses was the "servant" of the Lord, and from his day onward, the title became one of honor (Josh 14:7). It was also used of David (Ps 89:3; 2 Sam 7:5–8) and Elijah (2 Kgs 10:10). At least once it described Israel (Isa 43:10). The designation stood for one

---

[16] If that is correct, that will temper the dispute between Syntyche and Euodia in 4:2. It may not have been as serious as some surmise.

[17] See Phlm 15–16; the instructions in Eph 6:5–9, especially Col 3:22–4:1; and the greetings from "Caesar's household" in Phil 4:22.

[18] Keown, *Philippians 1:1–2:18*, 98.

[19] Keown, 98–99.

[20] Some slaves had considerable privileges and some autonomy, but only if the master allowed it.

[21] There were, of course, honorable slaves. Many had positions of responsibility, and some gained great personal wealth. It is doubtful Paul communicated that to his Roman audience.

who was commissioned by God for a special task. From a historical vantage point, the Jewish readers could have associated it with honor and privilege. God's chosen and called servants spoke in the name of God and occupied the place of God for the populous. But even with that high calling, the word itself implied one whose life was committed to the master and whose gifts and activities promoted the purposes of the master. The OT background may have influenced Paul, but he employed the word because it spoke of humility. This is reinforced by the strong, explicit commands to humility, the example of Christ (Phil 2:5–11), and the implicit responsibilities Christians had to view all of life with humility. Paul used it of himself in letters written largely to Gentile audiences (though the Roman church was full of Gentiles and Jews), where they would not necessarily perceive the OT tradition.

Christian churches included slaves. According to Roman culture, they were considered part of the household and became the responsibility of the head of the house. Paul's letter to Philemon concerned a runaway slave, and he gave other explicit directions as to how to treat slaves as members of the household (Eph 6:5–9; Col 3:22–4:1, for example). Presumably Christian slaves and their families worshipped with non-slave families.

It seems harsh to modern sensitivities that Paul did not advocate abolition. The Roman system, including slavery, was strong and when slaves rebelled there was mass killing and maiming of revolting slaves. What Paul did do was lay the groundwork for emancipation. In both Ephesians and Colossians Paul taught that slaves had a master, but even masters were slaves to Christ. He called for mutual respect and humane treatment. Even more pointedly, Paul expressed to Philemon that Onesimus, the slave, was his brother. The shock value of Paul's self-description "servant" intentionally reminded the readers of a deep and pervasive commitment to Christ.

The term represented the Christian era. Whether it was heard with Hellenistic or Hebraistic ears, it became a Christian ideal. Paul certainly knew of its centrality to the poem found in 2:6–11. If the term characterized the Lord, it was equally appropriate as a model for his servants.

1.2 The Readers (1:1b)

To all the saints in Christ Jesus who are in Philippi, including the overseers and deacons.

1:1b Paul identified two groups of readers. They were the church at large and special persons, leaders, within the congregation. The church was called "the saints." Biblically, the term has no other meaning than Christian people, and Paul used it in place of "the church," a phrase which he had used earlier in his ministry. According to the traditional dating of the Pauline letters, in the earlier ones he addressed the congregations simply as "churches" (1, 2 Thessalonians; 1, 2 Corinthians; Galatians). Later, he consistently used the term "saints" or "holy ones" (Romans, Philippians, Colossians, Ephesians). There is consistency in the pattern, but too much could be made of this. For example, the change in nomenclature could be the result of the messages Paul wanted to convey, rather than a developing theology. The saints were those who were set apart by God at conversion, they were in process of becoming like Christ, and their eternal destiny was secure. The term reminded the church of its special status in God's redemptive plan.

The word "saints" should hold special meaning for Christians. The word means "to be set apart." Consistent with its OT precedent, this "set apartness" became known as "holy," a word always used in a spiritual sense. "Holy" refers to God himself, to the places where God chooses to meet people (tabernacle and temple), to supernatural beings associated with God and his purposes (angels), and of the people whom he considers his own. The use of the word for Christians identifies Christ-followers with a special group of "the holy." In Pauline parlance, the word included the righteousness already imputed by God to believers because of the work of Christ on their behalf. There is no place in the NT where the word "saints" refers to those who have reached a higher level of spirituality, nor does it describe only the deceased. All true Christians are saints.

Paul identifies the dual location of the saints. They are "in Christ Jesus" and "in Philippi." The order reveals his thought. Being in Christ Jesus was the higher and better location. "In Christ" is a common designation, so much so that some have considered it the theme of Paul's theology. The phrase "in Christ Jesus" occurs multiple times in Philippians and over thirty times in other Pauline letters.[22] In its most basic meaning, it locates Christians in their spiritual environment once they submit to the lordship of Jesus at conversion. To be saved is to be "in Christ," and, in turn, once saved Christ is "in you" (Col 1:27).[23] Paul generally uses the phrase to express a more comprehensive and total relationship of the believer and Christ. It speaks of intimate connection, the believer and Christ joined in an eternal spiritual relationship. It identifies the spiritual power available to the believer: that of Christ (see Phil 4:13 "him who strengthens me"). It brings responsibility to represent to the world the Christ within (he is "the head"; we are "the body," Col 1:18). It speaks of the believer's primary identity as separate from the world. To be "in Christ" is to be connected to God. It is the place of ultimate victory over sin and death. It is the believer's spiritual location.

At the same time, believers on earth have a physical location. The rather natural and mundane expression "in Philippi" may be simply perceived as necessary to identify a specific location of part of Christ's body, those who receive this letter. It should not be overlooked, however, that the believer has obligations, concerns, and sometimes fears from this world. Paul warns the Philippians of some of their responsibilities and impending dangers from their location "in Philippi." Consequently, believers are located "in Christ" and "on earth." The state of being in Christ should affect their attitudes and behaviors here.

The other group consisted of bishops and deacons. This is the only time Paul used the word "bishop" outside of the Pastoral Epistles.[24] The word means "overseer," (so CSB), and the question here is whether "overseer" refers to an office or simply a function. The most basic understanding of the word is that bishops had some supervision over church functions: worship, fellowship, and ministry. At that time in church history, the title "bishop" did not refer to one person who

---

[22] For Philippians: 1:1, 26; 3:3, 14; 4:7,21.

[23] Paul's primary point in Col 1:27 is Christ is "among the Gentiles" and not only Jews. Nevertheless, Paul's statement is "Christ in you, the hope of glory."

[24] It only occurs twice there, 1 Tim 3:2 and Titus 1:7. A related form, ἐπισκοπῆς (feminine rather than the masculine ἐπισκοπος), occurs in 1 Tim 3:1. Peter used each word (1 Pet 2:12; 2:25). Ἐπίσκοπος also occurs in Acts 20:28. It is not clear why 1 Tim 3:1 uses the -ης ending rather than the one in 1 Tim 3:2, -ον. George Knight is likely correct: "It is coined on the basis of the title ἐπίσκοπος, which had a meaning established in the early church. This is the more easily possible, of course, because ἐπίσκοπή is clearly used for 'office' in the language of the LXX." George W. Knight, III *The Pastoral Epistles: A Commentary on the Greek Text*, The New International Greek Testament Commentary (Grand Rapids: William B. Eerdmans, 1992), 54.

had the charge of a number of churches in a geographical area; the use of this meaning of the term (sometimes translated "bishop") evolved in the second century as a later development.

Was there some type of office in the church this early? The text reveals several factors. Overseers were singled out in a special way, not as simply "saints" and not as "deacons." They also were placed second in Paul's opening remarks. But perhaps this revealed his concern that they had a secondary importance. Third, the term is plural, eliminating the possibility of a "one man" rule over several churches. Conceivably, the plural could refer to several churches located at Philippi, each with its own leader. Since the church was founded less than a decade previously, it may be considered highly unlikely the Christian community numbered enough to have multiple congregations. Conversely, the plural suggests several had this function or office. Since it is quite possible the population of Philippi, including the surrounding area which depended on Philippi's economy, could have been as much as 46,000 people, multiple congregations are likely.[25] In the only Lukan use of the term, overseers were called to service by the Holy Spirit (Acts 20:28).

There was precedent for offices in the church. The early church probably adopted the worship patterns of the synagogue, which had two chief officers. Likewise, some scholars point to a parallel in Essene communities, which had an administrative supervisor who was responsible for community leadership.[26] Finally, some suggest the titles "overseers" and "deacons" simply reveal "the Roman penchant for organization" which "gave the Philippian church a regular system of office-bearers."[27] How much any congregation was influenced by these organizational precedents is impossible to know.

The lists of leadership positions reveal at least an informal structure (Eph 4:11–13), which probably grew out of the natural ability and spiritual giftedness of some congregants, reinforcing the evidence of God's call on some to a special oversight responsibility. Clearly the early church was organized. The word and office of "overseer,"

---

[25] See Peter Oakes, *From People to Letter*, 40–54, quoted in Guthrie, Philippians, 21. He suggests ten thousand in Philippi and five thousand people in suburbs—plus those of the surrounding territory.

[26] See J. Jeremias, *Jerusalem in the Time of Jesus* (Philadelphia: Fortress, 1969), 260–61. Jeremias states the "overseer" was the same as the office in Essene communities.

[27] Beare, *The Epistle*, 48. Beare does not suggest this as the most likely possibility. He prefaces the comment by saying, "if it is not simply an indication."

however, does not appear in any list of gifts in the church apart from the qualifications lists of 1 Timothy and Titus. Similarly, in Acts 20:28, Luke recorded the presence of "overseers." In just a few years after the Letter to the Philippians was written, the church had defined offices with qualifications clearly identified (e.g., 1 Tim 3:1). Since 1 Timothy may have been written only two to five years after Philippians, it seems there was an emerging or developing structure.

Conversely, the precise function of "bishops and deacons" is not clear. In writing to the Ephesians at about the same time as Philippians, Paul did not mention "bishops and deacons," even though he listed several offices which helped the church develop (4:11–13). Ephesians has perhaps the most profound theological presentation of the church in the Pauline letters, and the fact that bishops and deacons were not mentioned there is significant even though Paul acknowledged overseers in his last visit with Ephesian church leadership. In that visit (Acts 20:17–38) three terms for church leadership are used. It is one of the few places where they occur together. First, he summoned the "elders of the church" (20:17). Then, summarizing his final message, he challenged them to "be on guard for themselves and for all the flock of which the Holy Spirit had appointed them as overseers, to shepherd the church of God" (Acts 20:28). Since he summoned "elders" and challenged them with overseeing and shepherding, obviously there is overlap; it seems the terms refer to the same persons. Apparently the "elders" do not include "deacons," but the term includes "overseers" (bishops) and shepherds.[28]

In Phil 4:3, Paul alluded to another church leader, asking for his help in solving the misunderstanding between Euodia and Syntyche.[29] He addresses him as "true partner" (*suzuge*) and not bishop or deacon. It is quite possible that he was the pastor of the church, though so little is known about the whole situation that no clear conclusions can be drawn.

Two other factors deserve mention. First, many commentators identify the overseers with the gift sent to Paul; perhaps they generated

---

[28] By occurring here synonymously, the three titles seem to refer to the same person's responsibility or office: elder, overseer, shepherd.

[29] This person is surrounded with obscurity, and not everyone agrees as to who or what he is. What is clear is Paul could appeal to someone in a position *of authority* to address these women, apparently because he had the responsibility to do so. His function was also known well enough that all would understand Paul's cryptic reference there.

the gift. Since the letter is, in part at least, a thank you, their "oversight" role was acknowledged.[30] The title "bishop" was common in Greek society and had a variety of uses in the LXX.[31] Perhaps it was a natural term to identify leaders within the church community. It is perhaps strange that some translators translate the Greek word *episcopos* ("overseer") as "bishop," reflecting later church polity.

Second, if this were a description of formalized church officers, it is surprising that "elder" is omitted. That title drew more on Jewish/Christian background than overseer/bishop,[32] although there is sufficient evidence that "bishop" and "elder" referred to the same persons.[33] The title probably related to a function rather than an office. Providing oversight in the areas of teaching and administration were the primary functions of a bishop or elder. As a result, bishops had some overseer function. It is doubtful, however, that addressing them in this fashion recognized a hierarchy of pastors culminating in one overseer over many others. Later, writing to Timothy and Titus, Paul described the qualifications for an "overseer" (often translated bishop) and for deacons. There, he does not include other offices in the church (1 Tim 3:1–7; Titus 1:5–9).

The word "deacons" described the other group. It was used in a technical sense (1 Tim 3:8) to refer to an office in the church. This use probably draws its origin from Acts 6:1–6, though the word "deacon" is not used of the seven who were elected to oversee the administration of community funds.[34] There the allotment to the widows was called a "distribution" (*diakonia*), a variation of the same word as "deacon." That word certainly refers to function and not office. Furthermore, the word root occurs again in Acts 6:2: "to wait on tables" (*diakonein*). It provides a rationale for electing the seven. The apostles's task and the theology of the church would be hindered without the seven. Given

---

[30] Lightfoot, *Saint Paul's Epistle*, 82, seems to have been one of the first of modern times to make this suggestion. He said further, "It seems hardly probable that this mention was intended, as some have thought, to strengthen the hands of the presbyters and deacons, their authority being endangered."

[31] Lightfoot, 95–99, gives an excellent discussion of this data.

[32] Lightfoot, *Saint Paul's Epistle*, 96.

[33] See the following references where overseer and elder are used either interchangeably, or explain each other: Acts 20:17 with 20:28; 1 Pet 5:1–2; 1 Tim 3:1–7 with 5:17–19; Titus 1:5–7.

[34] It is perhaps significant that the word root occurs twice in these verses, but not as a title for the seven. The Hellenistic women were neglected in the διακονία (6:1), and the twelve had to give themselves to the διακονεῖν of the word.

the neglected persons recorded in Acts 6, it is likely the task is to oversee the distribution which may have involved multiple locations and gathering places. Neither of these occurrences is necessarily used as a technical term for an office. The word servant (*diakonos*) also occurs non-technically in many passages (1 Cor 3:6; Eph 3:7 of Paul; Col 1:7 of Epaphras; 1 Tim 4:6). It may be difficult to suggest the word "overseers" here could be functional in nature and the word "deacons" official. Since neither "bishops" nor "deacons" occurs elsewhere in this letter or the other Prison Epistles written at approximately the same time, obviously the letter was written to the church at large, the saints. "Saints" included all Christians at Philippi, including the overseers and deacons. Their prominence in Paul's mind is evidenced by his addressing them first. If there is a major issue with unity in the churches at Philippi, mentioning the plenary group of believers first honors their importance and, perhaps, stresses unity.

1.3 The Greeting (1:2)

[2] *Grace to you and peace from God our Father and the Lord Jesus Christ.*

Structure

Grace . . . and peace [be]
  to you. from God our Father and the Lord Jesus Christ

Typically in such cryptic greetings, verbs are omitted. The point is clear without them. The verb is supplied above in brackets to complete the logic of the sentence.

Interpretation

1:2 The specific greeting, "[g]race . . . and peace," adds to the normal epistolary introductions.[35] Since grace always reminded Paul of God's grace in Christ, no doubt this word conveys full Christian meaning. This means "may God's grace be with you." The word "grace" occurs only twice in the letter, in the first verse and in the last (4:23).[36] Both occurrences have the same meaning and import. Paul saw all of life

[35] The word "grace" (χάρις) also differs from the typical Gk. letter which begins with χαρεῖν or χαρά.

[36] Interestingly, there are multiple instances of the same words at the beginning (1:2) and

in Christ as built on God's grace. It is where a believer lives (stands) as the recipient of God's grace (Rom 5:2). The word appropriately describes the basis of salvation by grace (Eph 2:8). Here, however, he writes to believers who have already received the grace of salvation. Requesting God to supply his grace to them in their situations reveals Paul's understanding that one's entire life is based on, energized with, and guarded by grace. The first word to the church, therefore, is to acknowledge what they already have and receive. They receive rather than achieve what makes life meaningful. Although mentioned sparingly in this letter, it reminded the Philippians of the central fact of a relationship with God: everything is by grace. In asking for God's grace to be applied to them, Paul tacitly requests God take care of their every need. If God chose to do so, it would evidence the fulfillment of Paul's prayer: the application of grace in their lives.

Paul's placement of grace before "peace" may indicate further his theological orientation that grace provided for and secured peace. "Peace" no doubt conveyed Paul's Hebrew background and the typical greeting "shalom." It had the full sense of "may all things be well with you." Paul used the word peace in ways similar to grace. Peace describes the relationship of believers to God. It is the peace of proper standing before him, sometimes referred to as legal peace. When used this way, it is a further description of salvation indicating the "war" between persons and God has come to a proper truce (Rom 5:1). When this meaning is meant, the stress is on relationships, not emotions. Like the recipients of grace, the Philippians were also already recipients of peace with God. The relationship was already established, never to be undone, as Paul notes in Phil 1:6. Here Paul invokes the peace of God. It is a prayer for the presence of God to overshadow the Philippians in their circumstances, resulting in spiritual equilibrium regardless of the situation. Paul speaks further about God's peace in 4:7–9. The use in Phil 1:2 most closely parallels with 4:7: "the peace of God . . . will guard your hearts and minds in Christ Jesus." Consequently, the believers' new life comes out of peace (with God) and is characterized by peace within (of God). Paul separated grace and peace by the insertion of "to you" after grace. This reinforces the idea that peace may be the result of grace. Theologically, that conforms to

---

the end (4:21–23) of the letter. These include "saint(s)," "grace," and the phrase "Lord Jesus Christ" which only occurs three times.

Paul's understanding. Both words as used by Paul imply a petition as well as a greeting. Paul implores God and Christ to provide peace.[37]

Grace and peace come jointly "from God our Father and the Lord Jesus Christ." The provision of grace and peace to believers by God was no surprise. Many Gentile religionists prayed to their gods for the same qualities, usually more for peace than grace. The addition of "Lord Jesus Christ" adds a profound Christological dimension to the blessing. The church knew well that grace was embodied in Jesus (Titus 2:11–14), and peace was his gift to the believer (John 14:27; 16:33). In so combining the work of God and Jesus, Paul reflected his deep conviction about the deity of Jesus. He does what God the Father does.[38] The individual activities of each member of the Trinity occur in several NT passages (Eph 1:3–14 may be the most explicit). The Father (God) is most often described as the planner or initiator of the eternal plan of creation and redemption (sometimes called the *pactum salutis*). Jesus, the Son, most often acts as the accomplisher because of and through his death on the cross. The Holy Spirit applies the plan of God and the work of Jesus. He actively works in the world, effecting the work of Jesus in specific persons and events. While there is not complete separation of activities—sometimes these sources of tasks overlap—the general revelation of the work of the Godhead follows this pattern.

As a result, Paul's salutation bears its own emphasis. First, a reference to the Holy Spirit does not occur here. Paul is not providing a complete picture of the working of the Godhead.[39] Second, Paul does combine God and Jesus as corporately providing both grace and peace. Linking them demonstrates that both can engage in the same way in the life of the believer. It may be God accomplishes sending peace through the work of Jesus. Still, each member maintains his own distinct identity. God is qualified as "our Father." Clearly, "our Father" modifies God by position and logic. Paul avoids saying God is the Father of Jesus Christ. Jesus is qualified by the word "Lord." The result is that Paul emphasizes God as the Father of believers (showing

---

[37] Significantly, here Paul employs the preposition "from" in its normal sense "peace from God" (ἀπό θεοῦ) rather than "peace toward God" (πρός θεόν).

[38] The use of the title "Lord" with Jesus Christ also identified him in that way.

[39] "Spirit" occurs only three times in Philippians. In 1:19 it is deliverance by "the Spirit of Jesus Christ"; in 3:3 Paul serves "by the Spirit of God"; and in 2:1 there is "fellowship with the Spirit." Each will be discussed later. It should be noted many do not take 2:1 to refer to the Holy Spirit; moreover, many who do, do not interpret it as "with" the Holy Spirit. The paucity of references to the Spirit is noteworthy.

again the origin of the Christian faith) and Jesus as the Sovereign One who demands our allegiance.

This is one of the few times in the letter the words "Lord Jesus Christ" are put together in this complete fashion.[40] The combination of the three may well have been an early Christian confession. Technically, each word of this identifier conveys meaning. Jesus is the human name given by prophecy and at his birth (Matt 1:21, 25). It unites him with Israel both in history and in theology since it was connected to "God is with us" (Matt 1:23). "Lord" is a title given to Jesus. The disciples, particularly Thomas, recognized Jesus's lordship (John 20:25, 28). It is first articulated publicly at Pentecost when Peter declared God made "this Jesus, whom [the Jews] crucified, both Lord and Messiah" (Acts 2:36). The title was bestowed by God and recognized by the apostles (Phil 2:9–11). It refers to his sovereignty. It may be particularly applicable to devout Jews who called God "Lord."[41] Taken in this context, Paul acknowledged the sovereignty of Jesus who is over all, and who is to be understood in specific places as the person the OT text identified as God (Ps 110, and following Jesus himself, Matt 22:43–45). The word also has application to Gentiles. The Roman emperors referred to themselves as "Lord." They did so to remind their subjects they had control over the affairs of their kingdoms. They were "sovereign." In either case, and for either Jewish or Gentile readers, the point is made: Jesus is the Sovereign One over all. At Philippi there was a decidedly pro-Roman flavor. Paul subtly reminded them whether in Philippi, where they were, or in Rome, where he was, Jesus was in charge.

"Christ" had particularly Jewish associations. It referred to the anticipated "Messiah" expected as predicted from Israel's Scriptures. The early Christians recognized Jesus was the Messiah, and the title applied to him became a household moniker then and throughout history.[42]

---

[40] This occurs three times in Philippians: 1:2; 2:11; 4:23. In CSB, 2:11 says, "Jesus Christ is Lord." He writes "Jesus Christ" (15 times) in 1:6, 8, 11, 19, 26: 2:5 (reversed order): 3:4 (reversed order), 8, 12, 14, 20: 4:7, 19, 21, . He writes simply Christ (17 times) in 1:10, 13, 15, 16, 18, 20, 21, 27, 29: 2:1, 16, 21, 30: 3:7, 8, 9, 18.

[41] Both "Jehovah" and "Adonai" are translated in the LXX by the Gk. word *kurios* (κύριος) and the English follows this pattern as well (see Ps 110:1). Devout Jews refused to pronounce the Hb. words for God.

[42] The following chart provides the places where Paul uses the various name and titles associated with Jesus.

Theological and Practical Points

1. *Paul and Timothy.* As noted, Paul graciously included Timothy with him as co-writer. Everyone agrees that Paul was the primary author, however. Including Timothy was both gracious and revealed that Paul was no *prima dona,* thinking only of his prominence. Especially since he was in prison (under house arrest) and was awaiting trial, the church would be naturally concerned about Paul and his well-being. The mention of Timothy underscores Paul was a team player! Additionally, the fact that he included Timothy may be because . . .

1) Timothy was with Paul at the founding of the church, and the congregation had known him from the beginning. Timothy had other occasions to visit the Christians at Philippi. Interestingly, Paul includes Timothy in three of the four Prison Letters (omitting Ephesians). At the least, Paul wanted to identify with Timothy.

2) Paul was uncertain of his future and already had plans to make Timothy prominent as an heir of his own ministry. This is perhaps particularly remarkable in that none of Paul's other companions at that time were mentioned.

3) Paul intended to send Timothy to the church as his own personal representative (2:19ff). The letter provided a proper authority for this loved, though younger, companion of Paul in ministry.

2. *Saints including Bishops and Deacons.* Paul's commitment to the church is congregational, not hierarchical. The designation "saints," which includes the entire Christian community, is Paul's focus. Leadership is presented as a subset of the congregation. Perhaps this is to strengthen the unity of the church, a major theme in Philippians. Perhaps it was the way Paul naturally envisioned the church: all equal in

TITLE	CHAPTER 1	CHAPTER 2	CHAPTER 3	CHAPTER 4	TOTAL
Lord Jesus Christ	1:2	2:11		4:23	3
Christ Jesus/ Jesus Christ	1:1, 6, 8, 11, 19, 26	2:5	3:8, 12 ,14, 20	4:7, 19, 21, 23	15
Christ	1:10, 13, 15, 18, 21, 27, 29	2:1, 30	3:7, 8, 9, 18		13
Lord Jesus		2:19			1
Lord		2:29		4:4, 5, 10	4
	14	**6**	**8**	**8**	**36**

the body of Christ. The salutation certainly diminishes heavy-handed authoritarianism so characteristic of many leaders. "The saints" are equipped differently for service in the church and the world (Rom 12:3–8; Eph 4:11–14; 1 Cor 12:4–11). The properly functioning church recognizes the value of each saint and provides an environment in which each one contributes to the others.

3. *Bishops and Deacons*. Already there was a need for organization. It is best to understand there were likely multiple Philippian congregations who would receive this letter. Each would have a pastor (bishop) and ministry helpers (deacons). Chronologically, this is the first hint of church organization in the Gentile mission. Three or four years later, Paul would provide more detailed requirements for those who held these offices (1–2 Timothy; Titus). No doubt the pattern was primarily derived from the Jerusalem church, with its apostles and helpers (Acts 6).

4. *Grace and Peace*. As described above, these two qualities are naturally linked together in Christian thought. While they occur commonly in general greetings in the first century, doubtless they are filled with Christian theology. Consequently, for Paul and the early church the mundane greeting called the believers to remember their position before God and the benefits provided to Christians alone.

5. *God our Father and the Lord Jesus Christ*. [Much of this relates to 2:6–11 as well]. Significantly, both names, God and Jesus, are linked in the text as they are introduced with one preposition. Both are included in Paul's "from." That both are jointly sending grace and peace indicates Paul's conviction that Jesus operates on the same level as God the Father. Jesus does what God does. The use of the words "God our Father" in no way diminish Christ's deity. "God" can be considered as the one true deity, or in some texts the word may indicate "God the Father" as one personality (more traditionally understood as "person") of the Triune God. This reflects Paul's understanding of plurality within the one God because God is here known by his activity ("from God") and jointly with Jesus. These two, along with the Holy Spirit, complete the Godhead. Though subtle, this counters the Jewish idea of monotheism which was usually understood as that God existed as one person and one personality. Yet, consistent with Jesus's argument with some of the Pharisees, the Christian understanding broadens the idea of the one God into three persons and reflects Paul's detailed exegesis of OT passages—such as the plural word for deity in Genesis and the

conversation God had at creation:"Let *us* make man in our image" (Gen 1:26; emphasis added). As mentioned in the commentary, other places in the OT speak of beings higher than humanity.

Paul easily and naturally identifies the persons of the Godhead by their distinct works in the world. For example, he calls God "Father," a title reserved only for that person. Neither Jesus nor the Spirit is called "Father." These relations make sense of the economic subordination with the Son and Spirit taking and fulfilling specific roles (sometimes called "operations" or "missions") in the economic work of God, initiated by the Father. "Economic" is used here in a purist sense of how tasks are allocated to accomplish the whole within the work of God in the world. "Economic subordination of divine persons" describes the division of divine tasks among each of the three persons. These roles are seen in both creation and redemption, the two focal points of Scripture and, indeed, all of life. In creation, God creates (Gen 1:1). Yet, for Paul and other biblical writers, Jesus is the actual agent of creation as the Creator himself (John 1:1–2; Col 1:16; Heb 1:1–3). In redemption, God the Father elects people to salvation (Eph 1:4–6). Yet it is in Jesus that election is actuated in time and history (Eph 1:7–12). Ephesians follows the work of these two persons with that of the Spirit, who seals the salvation of believers and assures those who are redeemed that God will keep his word (Eph 1:13–14). He guarantees the believer's eternity with God. Although Scripture consistently follows this pattern relating to the Godhead, the persons are equal in power and will, and each one can also be described as sharing in the work of the others.[43]

Care should be taken not to understand the distinctive work of each person of the Trinity in too isolated a way. Reading the canon as a whole reveals that while there is emphasis on distinct personhood, these are also inseparable operations in which each person of the Trinity both delights in and shares in the work of the others. Taking too extreme a view on each having specific and isolated functions approaches thinking in terms of *tri-theism*, a belief in three separate

[43] "Economic Subordination" applies to the Father, Son, and Spirit in describing their functions (their work). This is balanced by "Essential Equality," often referred to as "ontological equality." "Essential equality" describes the fact that there is only one God, and each person is, in essence, the same as the others. There is no "essential (ontological) subordination." Furthermore, the economic relationships do not seem to be eternal. Based on 1 Cor 15:27–28, for example, changes in the functions may occur eschatologically.

gods acting independently though harmoniously. Yet Scripture consistently affirms the one God cooperatively shares in the mission and work of each of the three persons. Inseparable operations among the three reinforce the reality that each person of the Godhead is co-equal in every way, so there is essential equality even if there is economic subordination in creation and redemption.

Much of Paul's understanding grows immediately out of his conversion experience on the Damascus Road. When conquered by Jesus, Paul asked, "Who are you, Lord?" He was told, "I am Jesus, the one you are persecuting" (Acts 9:5–6). Paul knew previously of Jesus's death in Jerusalem and had heard people of The Way proclaiming Jesus's resurrection. Here, however, Paul encountered the risen Lord. His thoughts about Jesus changed. He spoke with the risen Lord, and from that time on the resurrection convinced Paul that Jesus was the Lord—God himself. In that moment, his Jewish theology expanded. "Listen, Israel: The Lord our God; the Lord is one" (Deut 6:4) came more clearly into focus and Paul realized "one" in this case is more complex than simply a unique singular reference. His monotheism expanded. Jesus is Lord and God!

Paul, therefore, extends common Jewish thought based on both his particular reading of the OT and his personal experience of Jesus's resurrection (Acts 9:5). Paul shared in the mission of the apostles, to search the OT for its anticipation of Jesus as Lord which was confirmed by Jesus's resurrection. Their task became fitting the OT into their new understanding of Jesus's lordship (Acts 2:36).

2 INTRODUCTORY MATTERS: PAUL'S PRAYER FOR THE CHURCH AND HIS CIRCUMSTANCES IN ROME (1:3–26)

SECTION OUTLINE

2 Introductory Matters: Paul's Prayer for the Church and His Circumstances in Rome (1:3–26)
- 2.1 Thanksgiving and Prayer for the Philippians (1:3–26)
  - 2.1.1 Paul's Thanksgiving for the Philippians (1:3–8)
  - 2.1.2 Paul's Prayer for the Philippians (1:9–11)
    - Theological and Practical Points
- 2.2 Paul's Joy in the Progress of the Gospel in Rome (1:12–26)
  - 2.2.1 Paul's Circumstances (1:12–18a)
    - Theological and Practical Points

2.2.2 Paul's Attitude (1:18b–26)
Theological and Practical Points

2.1 Thanksgiving and Prayer for the Philippians (1:3–11)

The letter proper begins like many of Paul's epistles—with thanks to God for the church. Here Paul also includes a specific petition on behalf of the believers at Philippi. The pattern of thanksgiving occurs regularly enough that it no doubt reflects Paul's natural inclination in prayer. He begins each letter, except Galatians, with some form of thanksgiving.[44] In the letters, four times he expresses his appreciation for their response to the gospel. In Rom 1:8 it is because their faith "is being reported in all the world." In 1 Cor 1:5 he appreciates that the gospel came to them not just in word but in power that fully assured them of its truth. First Thessalonians 1:3 says, "We recall, in the presence of our God and Father, your work produced by faith, your labor motivated by love, and your endurance inspired by hope in our Lord Jesus Christ." In Phil 1:5 Paul said he prayed with joy "because of [their] partnership in the gospel from the first day." In each situation Paul disclosed his joy that his converts continued in the faith. The thanksgiving was not nebulous, something left purposely vague. Rather, Paul revealed his knowledge of their situations and their growth within or in spite of them. Paul frequently disclosed his prayer life of thanksgiving for them.

Together the thanksgiving and prayer form the opening of the letter. They are a unit of thought in two movements. Several factors reveal the unity: the synonyms "I give thanks to my God" (1:3) and "I pray this" (1:9), the general content of praise and petition, and Paul's epistolary pattern in introductions. The section divides naturally into two subsections, however. First, vv. 3–8 express thanksgiving for the Philippians. The verb translated "I give thanks" literally means "to grace well,"[45] but both Greek and English contain the idea of thanksgiving. Furthermore, all of vv. 3–8 modify that one main verb: "I give thanks." Second, vv. 9–11 express Paul's more specific petition.

---

[44] See Rom 1:8; 1 Cor 1:4; 1 Thess 1:2; Phil 1:3; Col 1:3; and Phlm 4; all have "give thanks" (εὐχαριστοῦμεν). Second Thess 1:3 "ought to give thanks (εὐχαριστεῖν ὀφείλομεν). Second Cor 1:3; Eph 1:3 have an alternative, "blessed be . . . " (εὐλογητὸς); Gal has no expression of appreciation.

[45] The verb contains the root word *charis* (χαριστέω), to "give grace," "I grace." With the prefix *eu* (εὐ) it is heightened so that it means "to give thanks (well)," forming the verb εὐχαριστέω.

He introduced his prayer with a consecutive conjunction ("and," *kai*) which both continues the previous idea and introduces another. Technically, these verses contain one long sentence in Greek, but it is natural and correct to see the conjunction "and" as a consecutive connection. Most translations, therefore, divide the text into two or more sentences. The CSB renders it with five sentences, the longest of which is vv. 9–11.[46] Most readers, like average American English readers, find more ease of understanding in shorter sentences. Consequently, the translator must find ways to show dependency in sentence to sentence relationships, which is often difficult to do. Unfortunately, the CSB fails to communicate the nuances of sentence connections here.

2.1.1 Paul's Thanksgiving (1:3–8)

3 I give thanks to my God for every remembrance of you, 4 always praying with joy for all of you in my every prayer, 5 because of your partnership in the gospel from the first day until now. 6 I am sure of this, that he who started a good work in you will carry it on to completion until the day of Christ Jesus. 7 Indeed, it is right for me to think this way about all of you, because I have you in my heart, and you are all partners with me in grace, both in my imprisonment and in the defense and confirmation of the gospel. 8 For God is my witness, how deeply I miss all of you with the affection of Christ Jesus.

Structure

As noted above, vv. 3–8 consist of one long sentence. Proper analysis requires noting the grammatical and syntactical hierarchy of clauses within the sentence. Careful analysis, therefore, requires some discussion of the grammar of the Greek text. The grammatical relationships may be pictured with the most important elements on the left and the descriptive elements indented. For further clarification, the primary thoughts of each sentence (independent grammatically) are placed first with explanatory (modifying) elements under them. Thus the structure

---

[46] Translators must be sensitive to the language and thought patterns of the receptor language reader. In this case, the sentence with its subordinate clauses indicated by conjunctions and dependent participles has been divided by clause without any indication of structural hierarchy.

rearranges the English text to conform more explicitly to the grammatical and syntactical patterns of the Greek text.

3 I give thanks to my God for every remembrance of you,
4 always **praying** with joy for all of you in my every prayer
5 because of your partnership in the gospel from the first day until now.
6 **I am sure** of this, that he who started a good work in you will carry it on to completion until the day of Christ Jesus.
7 Indeed, **it is right** for me to think this way about all of you,
because I have you in my heart,
and you are all partakers with me in grace,
both in my imprisonment
and in the defense and confirmation of the gospel.
8 For God is my witness, how deeply I miss all of you with the affection of Christ Jesus.

This graphic presentation of structure intends to highlight several aspects of the Greek text. First, the primary element is Paul's statement that he gives thanks to God. Second, three main ideas modify that statement, or, more precisely, modify the verb "I give thanks." Two different but common ways of subordination support this and they are indicated by the bold, underlined type. The first two are participles ("praying" and "I am sure").[47] The third is introduced by a conjunction of comparison ("indeed"). The relationship is untranslated in the CSB which simply states "it is right." Subordinating conjunctions, like Greek participles which function similarly to subordinate clauses, normally modify a verb,[48] and so the statement "it is right . . . ." parallels the two participial clauses that precede it (as above). Finally, v. 8 reinforces Paul's emotion by appealing to God as a witness. It summarizes vv. 3–7. This pattern provides the structure for the comments on this section later.

Highlighting the unity of this section, Gordon Fee proposed "a kind of (conceptual) chiastic arrangement."[49] Though it is conceptual

[47] The actual words are "making my prayer," δέησιν ποιούμενος (*deasin poioumenos*), "having confidence," πεποιθὼς (*pepoithos*), and "even as" untranslated in CSB but followed by "it is right," καθώς (*kathos*).

[48] Almost all subordinating conjunctions in Gk. are adverbial, thus modifying a verb or verbal idea. The most notable exception is when a relative pronoun introduces a clause in which case the relative pronoun functions as an adjectival conjunction and normally modifies a noun. Attributive participles, those with an article associated with them, function adjectivally and may function as a noun clause in a sentence.

[49] Fee, *Philippians*, 76. The chart that follows is based on his translation.

and not grammatical, the flow of ideas supports the meaning of the passage:

A I thank God at all my remembrance of you (personally)
  B I pray with joy because of your fellowship in the gospel
    C I am convinced God will keep this going until the end
  B′ I have every right to this confidence because I have you in my heart and because of your fellowship in the gospel
A′ God is my witness as to my deep longing for you all

Looking at the text this way emphasizes Paul's confidence in the Philippians' continuing in the faith.[50] Although he looks back at their mutually good relationships, he has heightened appreciation that their past promises a good future as well. The comments below in the commentary follow the grammatical/syntactical structure of the text rather than the "conceptual" literary pattern observed by Fee.

The format for this thanksgiving resembles others but the content is unique. Paul remembered God's working in the believers' lives as well as their participation in his ministry. He did not simply recite a pre-conceived thanksgiving that could be true of any group of Christians. These verses are warm and personal. The best analysis is thematic building on the structure. Three ideas support Paul's main statement in the opening verb: "always praying with joy" (1:4), "[being] sure of this" (1:6), and "it is right for me to feel this way" (1:7).[51] Following these structural components, the text reveals that Paul's thanksgiving was joyful (1:4–5); it was confident (1:6); and it was proper (1:7–8).[52]

---

[50] In Gk. chiastic constructions the primary emphasis is on the A/A′ members (outside members) unless there is a "C" element. In these cases, the "C" takes priority and the A/A′ become second emphases.

[51] In this sense, then, this is simply an alternate form of petition so typical for Paul. He used participles in these introductory sections and sometimes followed them with clauses of one type or another. For the former, see 1 Thess 1:1–5; for this type, see Col 1:3–8, an almost identical structure. In Col 1:6 the καθώς clause introduces a new direction but ties this new direction to the previous statement as well.

[52] The first two of these are predicate participles which modify the main verb. Their structure is parallel. Third is a comparative clause (καθώς) which continues the sentence. As noted above, the CSB stresses this with a new sentence. The NIV makes a new paragraph with it, indicating the strength of this usually relatively minor construction. The UBS Greek text separates it with a colon. It is a strong comparison, however, equal in structural weight to the two participles, and the outline of the passage reflects that analysis. There is no need to separate this statement from the rest.

Interpretation

1:3 Paul expressed his pleasure over the church. He let the believers in on his thoughts. Two significant aspects of Paul's thanksgiving emerge in v. 3. These aspects reveal information about Paul's prayer life and his fondness for the Philippians. First, Paul was thankful for them even though a problem of disunity threatened the fellowship of the congregation. He lived his life in response to the love of Christ (2 Cor 5:14–15), hoping to reach people everywhere and that they would do the same. The validation of his ministry was that people actually responded to the gospel he preached and that they remained true to their faith in such ways. He stated as much in 1 Thess 2:19; 3:8. Any positive response to the gospel brought Paul joy. When a place embraced the Lord and the gospel message as enthusiastically as the Philippians did, it was cause for great thanksgiving. It is noteworthy that Paul directs his thanksgiving to God, though obviously he intends the church to hear his appreciation. In this, Paul subtly affirms his conviction that God accomplishes his work through people.

Second, Paul's thankfulness never wavered. It was "for every remembrance of you." The reasons for that are detailed in v. 5. Here he stressed the consistency of his memories. Paul turned each thought of them into praise for them.[53] The CSB correctly translates "for every remembrance of you." What kind of church produced such memories? They had shared hard times which served to deepen their friendship.

Two grammatical questions arise in this first statement. The first is how to understand "for every remembrance." The CSB correctly translates this as a clause which could be rendered "because of every remembrance." The Greek preposition *epi* with the dative case, as here, properly provides a basis for the statement it modifies. This is typical of Greek syntax and is supported by the use of the same preposition in v. 5 ("because of your partnership"). The force of the construction is not temporal "when I remember you," but rather "because I remember you."

Most often, those who understand the statement as indicating time rather than cause point to opening thanksgivings in other letters which contain a temporal element, "when I remember you." They also

[53] The Gk. construction of ἐπί with the dative/locative actually provides a basis for the thanksgiving. It therefore is conducive to temporal ideas, such as "when I remember you." The most basic idea, however, is that the remembrance provided a basis for thanksgiving.

assume the resolution of the somewhat ambiguous "of you" which follows determines the interpretation. This results in Paul's saying "because of your remembering me," instead of "because I remember you." This, however, is a second issue and need not be connected to the meaning of the preposition *epi*. It is best to keep the meaning of "because."

Second, ambiguity exists in Paul's statement "remembrance of you." "Of you" takes the Greek construction in an objective sense, that Paul remembers them. Some take the words "of you" in Greek to be a subjective idea. Understood in this way, Paul speaks of their remembrance of him, and normally is assumed to recall specifically, though not exclusively, perhaps, their financial support. In that case, it anticipates Paul's thanksgiving for the gift they sent which occurs in 1:5 with their "partnership" and later in chapter 4. This interpretation reads too much into Paul's introductory prayer. Are we to assume in the other places where Paul expresses his thanksgiving for the churches that they, too, have done something for Paul akin to what the Philippians did? Rather, he states no church has done so (at least in the early days, 4:15), yet he gives thanks to God for them. Further, the word translated remembrance typically takes an object or modifier in the genitive case in an objective sense, as here.[54] Thus, Paul remembers *them*, not *they* remember him. The thrust of the discussion in 1:4–8 supports this as well, unless one understands their "partnership" to be exclusively the financial gift. It seems, then, that Paul thanks God for them because he remembers them.[55] The CSB translation "for every remembrance of you" suggests this.[56]

1:4 The first characteristic of Paul's thanksgiving for them was that it was joyful. The Greek text stresses this by placing the words

---

[54] This is so consistently the pattern because of the root meaning of "remembrance" that Fee, Philippians, states, "There is no known instance of the combination of this noun with a personal pronoun in the genitive where it is not an objective genitive," 78, n.28.

[55] Most commentators connect the preposition and pronoun together in arriving at an interpretation: 1) "when I remember you," or 2) "because you remember me." As noted, there is no need for the two to influence each other. I interpret "because I remember you" contrary to most interpreters. Halloway, Philippians, supports this stance: "We are left, then, with the natural sense of the Gk.: 'I give thanks to my God *for* every remembrance *of you*," 72.

[56] For a comprehensive view of the options, see Keown, *Philippians 1:1–2:18*, 122–24, and Fee, *Philippians*,75–80. Both make the statement temporal: "when I remember . . . " Fee, *Philippians*, 78, calls this the traditional understanding and "it is the better of it by far." But ἐπι literally provides a "foundation" for the associated noun and is literally translated "upon." The temporal is a derived syntactical meaning.

"with joy" before the words "I always pray." To highlight this attitude, the CSB brings the Greek construction "with joy making my request" from the end of the clause to the beginning. It is difficult, however, to know whether Paul stressed the consistency of his thanksgiving and therefore put it first, or the joyful nature of his thanksgiving by putting it last.[57] The CSB opts, correctly, for emphasizing it first. This is the first reference to joy, a major theme in the epistle.

The grammatical and syntactical relationships in this section are quite complicated. Several questions must be answered that pertain to vv. 4–5 and their function in the sentence. Is the NIV text correct in starting a new thought at the beginning of v. 4? Does the phrase "because of your partnership in the gospel" connect with the main verb "I give thanks," or does it go with something else? Where does the phrase "from the first day until now" go?

Regarding the first question, how should the thoughts of v. 4 be arranged?[58] The CSB correctly interprets the sense of the passage. This observation is based on some literary patterns which prevail. Twice the same root word for "prayer" occurs, though in different parts of speech ("in my every prayer" and "always praying"). These two occurrences, which go together logically, also somewhat repeat and specify the phrase "I give thanks." Paul informed his readers his thanksgiving was actually made in prayers.[59] Therefore, the sense of the thanksgiving was resumed in the two words for "prayer."

1:5 The resolution of the second question begins at this point. Does the phrase "because of your partnership" (*koinonia*) go with v. 3 or v. 4? The parallelism of the text suggests it goes with v. 4. The two terms for prayer belong together in sense, and the two clauses which provide a reason for the prayers conform to each other as well. The first clause, "for all of you in my every prayer," provided a reason for Paul's thankfulness.[60] The second, "because of your partnership," provided a corollary reason for his specific joyful prayers. His remembrance was stirred by the gift they gave him. Their partnership

[57] Emphasis in Gk. is often demonstrated either by bringing something to the front of the sentence, or by moving something to the end.

[58] There are three good possibilities. The entire verse begins a new thought, a new thought begins in the middle of the verse, and the entire verse is a thought unto itself.

[59] As pointed out earlier, the participles are typical structural indicators, and this one seems to carry the other form of the word for prayer with it.

[60] It should be noted again that the preposition translated "for" is *epi* (ἐπί), the same as in 1:3: "for every remembrance of you."

cannot be limited to the specific financial gift, though that may have occasioned the letter. As Paul states in the following, they were partners from the beginning of his relationship with them, not only in their recent gift. Their partnership was also the non-financial support they rendered to the apostle.[61] Here it is emphatic, not careless.[62] Paul adds the statement of joy, which emphasizes the importance of the phrase "with joy."

The third question is the location of "from the first day until now." Some scholars want to place it with "I give thanks to my God"; others, with "I am sure of this"; still others, with "always praying." Taking it with "I give thanks to my God" makes the sentence extremely awkward and surely should be rejected. Understanding it with "I am sure of this" causes an abrupt change of direction from the emphasis on the gifts of the church to the attitudes of Paul. That interpretation, too, should be rejected. The church participated with Paul in the gospel from the first day until the time he penned the letter. That considers the normal flow of the text and satisfies the need for consistency of subject matter. Though it properly goes with partnership, clearly the entire context supports Paul's reason for thanksgiving. Distinctions should not be pressed to the extreme.

Since the primary contribution of v. 4 is the identification of Paul's joy, the basis of Paul's joy is revealed in v. 5. The CSB correctly captures the relationships by stating "because of your partnership in the gospel."[63] The relationship between Paul and the church went deeper than human friendships. They had a tie that came from joining in the work of God in the world. Such cooperation in the spread of the gospel was something Paul appreciated very much. That fellowship with Paul was only in an intermediate sense; the ultimate contribution they made was to the spread of the gospel itself.

"Fellowship"(CSB "partnership") is a major theme of the brief book though the word is rarely used. It occurs primarily in the Pauline Letters (thirteen of nineteen times in the NT) and three times in

---

[61] This reconstruction makes good sense of the structural arrangements but is somewhat awkward by its repetition of ideas. No matter what structural arrangement, there is repetition.

[62] The repetition is seen in the four Gk. words for prayer (essentially meaning "I thank," "I remember you," "my prayers," and "I always pray") and in the four times words for "all" are used. This analysis makes the opening clauses basically parallel as well.

[63] The Gk. construction is the preposition ἐπί followed by the dative/locative case. Two such constructions are in these first two verses, and for reasons suggested in the text, they are complementary and somewhat repetitive.

Philippians.[64] In 2:1 Paul urged, "[I]f any fellowship with the Spirit," and in 3:10 he expressed his desire to share in the "fellowship of [Christ's] sufferings." Additionally, the verbal form of the word occurs in 4:15, which the CSB translates as "shared with me." This last occurrence presents a context for understanding Paul's use of the word in Philippians. It referred to the believers' involvement with Paul by sending a gift to support his work. The grammar of 1:5 confirms this primary meaning. The English word "fellowship" does not capture the meaning of the Greek term *koinonia*. The word implies far more mutual engagement than enjoying a common meal. It implies a commonness of purpose born out of mutual values and sustained by mutual commitment. Partnership implies an ongoing mutuality in the relationships. That is appropriate within the church and between the church and Paul. The noun "partnership" may be followed by various cases or parts of speech. For example, in the other two occurrences of "fellowship" in Philippians, the word "of" occurs. Here the word "unto" follows.[65] In other places where the preposition "unto" follows, the people experience "fellowship" by contributing to a gift (Rom 15:26; 2 Cor 9:13). Consequently, when Paul thanked God for their partnership "in [*eis*] the gospel," he meant they were contributing to the spread of the gospel in tangible ways, that is, primarily through their support. This may well have been in Paul's mind in 1:5, but the span of their relationship, identified as from the first day, indicates Paul has much more in mind, too. The financial gift was accompanied by Epaphroditus. Was he part of the gift from the church? Further, the first day must mean from the day the apostolic band entered Philippi. Their partnership referenced the entirety of their relationship. Paul could thank God for them all the time since they were his partners in the faith the entire time!

---

[64] With other forms built on this root, appearing forty-four times in the NT; twenty-seven are Pauline and six are in Philippians: 1:5, 7; 2:1; 3:10; 4:14, 15.

[65] The difference is that in 1:5 the preposition εἰς follows the word κοινωνία, whereas in 2:1 and 3:10 it is followed by a genitive case noun (2:1, "fellowship of the spirit" πνεύματο; 3:10, "of his sufferings" παθημάτων). A Pauline pattern emerges: κοινωνία is either followed by the genitive case (1 Cor 1:9; 10:16; 2 Cor 8:4; 13:13; Phil 2:1; 3:10; Phlm 6) or the preposition εἰς (Rom 15:26; Phil 1:5; 2 Cor 9:13). Two times it has no modifiers. When the genitive occurs, Paul identified the tie which produced the fellowship or the entity within which fellowship occurs. When the preposition εἰς occurs, Paul described something larger than the two to which they contribute. That pattern holds in this reference. My reading contrasts with the CSB.

The gospel was not only the environment of their fellowship but also its goal. Had it not been for the gospel, they would not have met. Paul generally stated that the tie that bound Christians together was trust in the gospel message. Here, however, the construction suggests that the advancement of the gospel united them. In their support of Paul, they contributed to the work of God in the world through the gospel. When the Philippians were converted, they were given the privilege of promoting the gospel. In part through their relationship with Paul, they were true to that aspect of their faith.

Paul mentioned the gospel nine times in Philippians.[66] His other letters reveal he conceived of the gospel as a message of salvation for a world under the curse of death based on historical, theological, and experiential evidence.[67] Yet Paul can go deeper than the personal benefits of the gospel. In 1 Thess 2:4 Paul explained he was "approved by God to be entrusted with the gospel." The gospel message was God's message. It did not belong to Paul or the churches. It was bigger than any individual possessed or proclaimed.

In this letter, the gospel was proclaimed (1:15–17), defended (1:16), and was said to have advanced by the lives of those who knew it (1:12; 2:22). In this text, Paul used the term to suggest the gospel was the movement of God through history and that it was perpetuated by God's human spokespersons. Both he and the church had the privilege of promoting God's gospel in the world.

Paul's joy came as he remembered the history of the church, as well as the relationship it had with him. Immediately upon Paul's preaching, some had responded to the gospel, and the church remained firmly committed to Paul, who had delivered God's message to them. Paul, therefore, looked back to the beginning and appreciated its general support from the first day. Acts 16 records the early history of the Philippian church. The beginning was difficult for both believers and the apostolic band. In addition to the common difficulties faced in spreading the gospel, Paul faced imprisonment for his faith. His joy as he remembered the Philippians, therefore, was not because of his good circumstances when they believed; rather, it was because of the

[66] These are 1:5, 7, 12, 16, 27 (2x); 2:22; 4:3, 15. The word occurs seventy-six times in the NT.

[67] The historical evidence is twofold: the life of Jesus and the resurrection (1 Cor 15; see Acts 2). The theological evidence is the continuity between the OT and the NT (see Galatians). The gospel actually fulfilled OT expectations. The experiential evidence came in the testimony of Paul and other believers who responded to the gospel message (Phil 3).

firm faith of the believers in spite of their difficulties. As they grew in their Christian maturity, they also grew in their appreciation of Paul. He remembered them with joy.

It is remarkable Paul could mention joy so early in this letter. On the one hand, it anticipated his assurance of his well-being that surely caused them anxiety. It relieved their minds to hear of Paul's joy. On the other hand, it revealed an important character trait of Paul. Many circumstances in his recent past and his present could prohibit his joy, and no one would blame him for that. He had been imprisoned for three to four years, though in Rome it was house-arrest. He had been shipwrecked on the sea voyage to Rome. Perhaps, most difficult of all, his arrival in Rome signaled an intra-church conflict over his character and message (1:14–28). All of this happened as he prepared to present his case and defend Christianity before Emperor Nero. Focus on any of these could be derailing; together they could seem almost insurmountable. Neverthelesss, Paul had learned joy is an attitude born of a choice. It is a decision to see the big picture and acknowledge God ultimately controls everything, and he can be trusted to do what is best. At times in the letter, clearly Paul reflects the kind of joy brought only by resolve! Circumstances do not produce it. In the broad spectrum, however, thoughts of the church at Philippi lifted his spirits. They provided an alternate set of circumstances, reminding Paul of ultimate joys found in Christ. They brought him joy.

1:6 The second characteristic of Paul's thanksgiving for the Philippian believers was that he prayed with confidence based on the working of God in their midst, not on his own ability or persuasiveness. Two matters emerge as significant emphases: the nature of the work in the Philippians and the time orientation involved.

God began the work in the church. Obviously if he starts something he will also complete it. Paul easily moved between the tensions of human agency and divine initiative, accepting both in a natural way. The Philippians established a partnership with Paul through the work of God. The contrasts between these two realities and Paul's comfort with each deserve attention. What work had God begun? Referring to the immediate context only, some interpreters prefer to explain it as the support the church gave to Paul. They say Paul meant the "sharing in the gospel."[68] The rule of context always guides the interpreter, but it

[68] So Hawthorne, *Philippians*, 21.

is conceivable Paul may have drawn on the wider context of Christian experience as well. The experience of God's grace always lay under the surface of Paul's words. Most likely that is true here since a reference to the gift-support seems awkward. First, this would be better suited to an articular expression in Greek, like "the good work," that is, the previously mentioned participation in the gospel. The text, however, says simply "good work," leaving the precise nature of that work to the reader's understanding. Second, it is difficult to see how the work of the gift to Paul could have been unfinished, and it is equally difficult to know what would have completed it. Paul never approached his congregations with the expectation of continued support; instead, he did just the opposite. He seemed surprised when they sent a gift for him. If each gift were a complete act, which seems likely, what was left undone? Further, how does the reference to the "day of Christ" relate to their completion of the gift? Did Paul expect them to continue supporting him until the Second Coming?

Paul had a general Christian characteristic in mind when he made this statement. Even those who interpret the passage as referring to the specific financial gift normally generalize it by referring to the Spirit who produced the gift or the opportunity and responsibility of supporting the gospel.[69] It is more likely, however, that Paul saw the Philippians' generosity as evidence of the grace of God in their lives, and in this text he spoke to that grace. In 2 Cor 8:7, a passage that urged the Corinthians to be like the Philippians (Macedonians) in generosity, Paul encouraged the development of the grace of giving. Giving evidenced the maturity of their thoughts and understanding. The "good work" in Phil 1:6 refers to what lay behind their generosity: the calling and Christian maturity of the church. If the specific gift occupied Paul's thoughts here, it was only because the gift represented the genuineness of the Philippian church's faith.

Since Paul spoke of the work beginning and ending it remains unlikely he had only their initial salvation experience in mind, but also an ongoing process of growth in the Christian's life (Phil 2:12). The whole salvation process, particularly the progressive element, is what Paul meant here. Since God began a work of Christian growth,

---

[69] Hawthorne, *Philippians*, 21–22, says, "Paul was certain that the Philippians would never waiver in their generosity, would never cease sharing their good gifts to help spread the gospel, until the Parousia". He does say other interpretations can "be right by extension."

evidenced in part by their giving, he would complete that growth.[70] "Carry it on to completion" means more than just seeing something to its finish. The idea means "to bring to a proper conclusion, the pieces in place."[71] Paul's confidence stemmed from the realization that his initial expectations from the first day would be fulfilled in time. Judging from Paul's preaching in general, these expectations would include the visible lordship of Jesus and full development of Christian character (1:11).

Paul expressed the confidence that the growth would take place "until the day of Christ Jesus." He glanced backward to their salvation and forward to the completion of their character when the Lord returns. The reference to the "day of Christ Jesus" is synonymous with the "day of the LORD" so common in the OT (Joel 2:1; Amos 5:20). Some question why the end times were included at this point. Although Paul could have thought in terms of the imminent coming of the Lord, he also was more aware of a delay than earlier in his ministry.[72] Paul's use of the phrase "until the day" called to mind the consummation of the present age. It was Paul's way of making two points: sanctification was an ongoing process and the process would continue to the end of the age. At that time the believers would be complete in character. They needed to relinquish fear of the judgment which characterized that day.[73]

---

[70] This suits the need of some progressive element in this passage, as well as the fact that for Paul giving is one aspect of the Christian life which measures growth (2 Cor 8:1–7). Commentators sometimes draw attention to the fact that these words recall the LXX translation of creation. There are some parallels in Gen 1, 2. They point out the allusion to God's work in the beginning and Paul's commitment to the truth that God will consummate it. The allusion may be significant (see Martin, *Philippians*, 66, and Hawthorne, *Philippians*, 21), but the linguistic correspondence is not as significant as the conceptual correspondence (the work was finished in creation), the correspondence with Genesis is incomplete, and Paul used the expression of "beginning and completion" elsewhere (2 Cor 7:1; Gal 3:3). See Silva, *Philippians*, 51–52. The parallel to Genesis is vague and hardly provides the basis for understanding. It may, at best, recall the fact that God begins and ends the process.

[71] The verb here is *epitelesei* (ἐπιτελέσει), a future tense. τελέω suggests a logical finish of what was begun. It is that all things fit together properly (as they should) when completed.

[72] He wrote of a delay in the Lord's return as early as 2 Thess 2:1–12, so by the time of the writing of Philippians this delay had been reinforced in his mind.

[73] A similar time orientation occurs in Phil 1:10–11 where Paul prayed they would be filled with the fruit of righteousness at the day of Christ. Paul's use of the preposition ἄχρι parallels the use of εἰς in 1:10.

Some scholars understand Paul's confidence to be directed to the church at large, rather than to individuals within the church.[74] The plural "you" makes the text uncertain, suggesting it may have been addressed to the church collectively. On the other hand, the distributive plural commonly occurs in the letters so that nuance seems better here. Paul's thankfulness came with the confidence that God would work in the individual Christians until the day of Christ. This confidence occurred for two reasons. First, Paul was confident that what God began God would complete, and his words came from a deep conviction that God worked in them. Second, Paul saw the manifestations of their right relationship with God. Their gift evidenced their Christian maturity. Since God worked in them and they responded, Paul's confidence was justified.

Paul's thoughts span the entirety of the Philippians' Christian experience. He looks back to the first day, bringing their awareness to the present. He follows with a return to the beginning of a good work, the same as "the first day," and projects it to the end of the church age. His observation of their character and ministry was intermediate. From his perspective on the continuum of their Christian experience, what he observed enabled him to look back with pleasure and look ahead with confidence.

1:7 The third characteristic of Paul's thankful attitude was its appropriateness: it was right! The Greek text has the word "right, just" (*dikaion*), a descriptive term expressing the sense of propriety. Paul most commonly uses the "right" word group (*dik–*) in its proper legal sense; consequently, an activity can be "declared right," legally appropriate rather than illegal. In common parlance, not judicial, the term means appropriate, given the circumstances which call for it. Paul appeals to his strong relational tie with the church as the obvious foundation for the properness, and truthfulness, of his statement. One other time in Philippians Paul used the word "just, right." In his list of virtues to embrace, he includes "whatever is just" (4:8), applying this common word describing God's work in Christ in justifying believers or defending God's character. In Philippians the term describes right conduct.

A structural question should be asked here: What does this clause modify? It could explain why Paul felt such confidence in God's

[74] Martin, *Philippians*, 65, says, "The Philippian church will be preserved to the end time."

working in the Philippians. Alternatively, it could add a reason Paul was thankful for them, expressing a thought parallel to his great joy for them.[75] The latter is better. The "even as" clause (CSB "Indeed, it is right") parallels the two verbal ideas found here ("always praying" and "sure of this"). Further, Paul's confidence that God would complete his work hardly rested on emotional ties with them, but his thankfulness for them could.

Here is the first of many occurrences of "to be minded."[76] The CSB translates it "to think" this way. It is distinctively Pauline, occurring twenty-six times in the NT, but only twice outside of the Pauline corpus. It occurs frequently in Philippians.[77] Based on the attitude of Christ (2:5), the church was to develop a distinctively Christian mindset. Fee points out the word occurs seven times in Rom 12–15, a section introduced by renewing of the mind.[78] It is a way of thinking, a "mindset," a disposition to develop. As Paul used it here, it speaks of his attitude toward the Philippians. He is justly "minded" to entertain positive thoughts of them, which produced continual thankfulness for them.

Paul provided three reasons explaining his attitude toward them. First, he had them in his heart. Commentators differ over the precise meaning of this structure. On one hand, the Greek could read, "You have me in your heart," and the context could be interpreted to support it,[79] suggesting Paul could be explaining his appreciation for their gift on his behalf. Perhaps here he continued his appreciation for their financial support. On the other hand, the construction more naturally reads, "I have you in my heart."[80] Understood this way,

---

[75] The former takes καθώς ("even as") to modify the participle πεποιθώς ("having this confidence"). The latter takes the καθώς to modify the verb εὐχαρίστω ("I give thanks").

[76] This Gk. form is the infinitive of φρονέω (*phroneo*), to have understanding or to think. It is a characteristic of Philippians, likely frequently used because it characterizes Jesus in the hymn to Christ (2:5–11). BAGD translates it "hold an opinion, judge, set one's mind on"; Louw-Nida says, "to hold a view, to have an opinion, to consider, to regard." It is more comprehensive than our idea of "to think."

[77] Phil 1:7; 2:2, 5; 3:15, 19; 4:2, 10.

[78] Fee, *Philippians*, 89, n. 80.

[79] The infinitive construction in Gk. has two accusatives with it. The first is με ("I"); the second is ὑμᾶς ("you").

[80] This follows a rule of thumb in such constructions, that the accusative nearest the verb is the subject. Further, if the existing subject works in a statement, it is best to retain it. Both of these rules fit well with taking "I" as the subject, in spite of the early commentary of Chrysostom to the contrary. The evidence for "I" being the object is well presented by Hawthorne, *Philippians*,

Paul's thanksgiving was more than a response to the gift they sent and to the knowledge of God's working in their behalf. It came from a true blending of hearts. Emotional ties bound them together, evidencing the deeper relationship commitment between them.

The second reason for this attitude was their fellow-service in the apostolic ministry. Paul's circumstances did not hinder their relationship but strengthened it. His being a prisoner could have presented an obstacle to their wholehearted support because of the pro-Roman commitments of many in Philippi. But the Philippians adopted the attitude they shared in Paul's imprisonment. No doubt this meant more to Paul because the church at Rome divided into two groups concerning him—to some, his imprisonment was part of the problem. Some preachers in Rome supported his presentation of the gospel while others opposed, preaching primarily to anger the authorities in hopes they would punish Paul further. Either way, Paul was a prisoner of Rome. Could they support one whom the Roman government considered [at least] a potential criminal? No church was in a more patriotic setting than the Philippian church, but Paul's chains proved to be no obstacle.

Paul mentioned his "defense" and "confirmation of" the gospel. The words are legal terms, denoting official language for a formal defense, and some interpret them as evidence that Paul had presented his case in court. In fact, he had presented himself and the gospel to various political officials in Judea.[81] His presence in Rome was also an opportunity to defend the gospel. Based on the previous imprisonments, Paul considered it that. He stated later the topic of conversation in Rome was "Christ" (1:13). The ordeal of his incarceration may be correctly called a defense and confirmation, since it was the ultimate opportunity for Christians to present their claims to the emperor. The words "defense" and "confirmation" may refer to specific activity while he was in prison, or they may refer in a general sense to the fact that they stood with him whether he was free or bound. The latter seems more historically true. They supported him in the relief offering, and now they supported him directly in his own trials.

22–24. The evidence to the contrary is well presented by Silva, Philippians, 56–57, especially see n. 21 with its instructive data surveys.

[81] These defenses were before the rioting crowd (Acts 22:1–22); before the Sanhedrin (Acts 23:1–10); before Felix (Acts 24:1–21); before Drusilla (Acts 24:24–27); before Festus (Acts 25:4–12); and before Agrippa and Bernice (Acts 26:1–32). Since the Caesarean imprisonment was two years in duration, it is likely the church heard of these opportunities to defend the gospel.

Paul was committed to the gospel message by life or death. The church stood by him in it. Whether good or bad times came, Paul relied on the Philippian church. Their support evidenced they were true "partners. They joined with him in his apostolic calling to reach Gentiles for Christ. The partnership between them formed the strong tie which Paul addressed in the next verse.

Paul referred to his apostleship with the word "grace." The term may identify general Christian attitudes, a state of grace in which a Christian stands, or Paul's specific calling of grace. The last correctly describes this reference. To understand it as depicting a general state of grace does not consider the immediate context seriously. The defense and confirmation of the gospel directly relate to the grace since they are the arena in which the grace operates. Here is another reference to his apostolic function. The Philippians recognized Paul's unique place in God's economy as apostle of God's grace, and they demonstrated their support for it by participating with him as they could.

1:8 The third reason for Paul's attitude in prayer was the deep Christian tie between them. The force of this statement is demonstrated in two ways. First, the new sentence is in the form of an oath, as Paul called God to the witness stand ("God is my witness"). They could not see Paul's heart for them, but God did. Second, this intense desire was distinctly Christian. Paul used two terms: "long for" (CSB "deeply miss"), (*epipothō*), which expresses a strong desire, and "affection" (*splanchnois*), which identifies the entrails as all being involved in the emotion. Such affection was actually that of Christ Jesus, an obviously anthropomorphic statement which attributes to God the strongest of human emotion. Paul thereby expressed the fact that his feelings came from the Lord. His was deep Christian emotion that resulted from their shared faith and participation in what God was doing in Christ.

2.1.2 Paul's Prayer for the Philippians (1:9–11)

[9] *And I pray this: that your love will keep on growing in knowledge and every kind of discernment,* [10] *so that you may approve the things that are superior and may be pure and blameless in the day of Christ,* [11] *filled with the fruit of righteousness that comes through Jesus Christ to the glory and praise of God.*

Structure

Before addressing the structure of this sentence, some explanations are required. Though the basic idea is clear, the actual structure, and therefore the flow of Paul's thought, is questioned. It is one of the most challenging syntactical constructions in the letter. Regardless, there is progression in thought: love seems to be the intermediate concern and being pure and blameless at the Lord's return is ultimate.

1. What is the antecedent of "I pray this?" Typically, pronouns refer back to some previously clear reference point, the antecedent. "This," however, is not always so clear. It may point backward or forward. The basic guidelines are (1) is there some clear reference point in the immediately preceding verses? More importantly, (2) is the content of "this" provided anywhere in the text? The key to understanding it in 1:9 fits both of these criteria. As for (1), there is nothing previous to which this could refer. There is no prayer content, though Paul indicates he brings his thanksgiving to God for them. While it is possible that it incorporates all of vv. 3–8, that is unlikely and unwieldy since that translation would better be understood with a plural pronoun of "these things" identifying the various elements of verses vv. 3–8. Regarding (2) there is/are content indicators found in vv. 9–11 that provide Paul's prayer-concern.

2. How does "I pray" influence interpretation? It should be observed earlier when Paul was giving "thanks," he described it using a word for prayer twice (*deasis*, 1:4). In the characteristic pattern of Paul's prayer language, that term refers to a specific request. There it refers specifically to "give thanks." In contrast, "I pray" (1:9) is *proseuchomai,* which typically refers to the activity of praying in general, though here there is some specific content. More to the point, Paul has not expressed a prayer until 1:9. Earlier he described his thankfulness and called it a request, but it is not technically a prayer or a prayer report.

3. The function of "that" (*hina,* twice: 1:9, 10b). Here is where there is a critical divide. In Greek, "that" is *hina* which can introduce a noun clause, such as an object of a verb, or it can be adverbial, providing a purpose (or result rarely) of the primary verbal statement. Context decides. Most interpreters correctly understand the first *hina* (1:9) to be in apposition to the pronoun "this" as the noun equivalent. The relative clause "that" functions as an object clause and the "antecedent" of the pronoun "this," and is used to explain it further.

The result is "I pray this: that your love will keep on growing." The CSB correctly translates the verse this way.

There is a second *hina* clause ("that," 1:10b). The same questions pertain. Is it used as a noun clause or an adverb expressing purpose? If it functions as introducing purpose, as many do, the statement reads "that your love will keep on growing . . . so that you may approve the things that are superior . . . *in order that* you may be pure and blameless . . . " The problem is that approach requires taking the two *hina* clauses in different ways when they are only a few words apart and in the same sentence. The alternative, and the one adopted here, is both are noun clauses in apposition to the demonstrative "this" that opens the sentence. In that scenario, the "this" has two components, two petitions as part of the prayer rather than one; [82] that is "and this I pray (1) that your love will keep on growing . . . . (2) that you may be pure and blameless."

The options for the second "that" are

1. as parallel to the first "that," *hina* clause.
2. as modifying (i.e., subordinate to) that previous "that," *hina*, clause.
3. as modifying "so that you may approve the things that are superior."

This commentary opts for the first as the simplest and most straightforward explanation.

[82] The Gk. constructions are quite complicated. The factors to consider regarding the clauses are: 1) Paul rarely uses two ἵνα clauses in close proximity unless they relate to different thoughts (different "verses," for example). 2) ἵνα functions as a "strong" conjunction. Other conjunctions occur within ἵνα clauses as a norm. 3) Rarely, if ever, does a ἵνα clause occur within another subordinating clause. 4) It is very awkward for the two ἵνα clauses to be taken in two different ways when used in proximity. This all argues for two parallel statements.

The structure, then, may be viewed three different ways. Each is presented here with the best presented last.

As the CSB [1st *hina* as object; 2nd *hina* as object parallel so "so that" or a parallel purpose]

And I pray this: that [*hina* #1] your love will keep on growing
in knowledge and every kind of discernment,
so that you may approve the things that are superior
and [*hina* #2] may be pure and blameless in the day of Christ,
filled with the fruit of righteousness
that comes through Jesus Christ,
to the glory and praise of God.

As Hellerman[83] ***and others*** [1st "that" (*hina*) as object; 2nd "that—in order that" (*hina*) a purpose]

And this I pray: that [*hina* #1] your love will abound more and more
in knowledge and discernment
so that you can determine what really matters
in order that [*hina* #2] you may be pure and blameless in the day of Christ
filled with the fruit of righteousness
that comes through Jesus Christ
to the glory and praise of God.

---

[83] Joseph H. Hellerman, *Philippians: Exegetical Guide to the Greek New Testament*, ed. Andreas J. Kostenberger and Robert W. Yarbrough (Nashville: Broadman & Holman, 2015), 33. Lidija Novakovic, *Philippians: A Handbook on the Greek Text* (Waco: Baylor University Press, 2020), 14, gives three options for the second "that" (*hina*) but all three are purpose clauses (adverbial): "(1) gives the purpose of Paul's overall prayer, modifying the main verb προσεύχομαι in verse 9, (2) offers another purpose . . . of Paul's prayer for increased love described in the previous ἵνα clause, or (3) provides the purpose of the preceding infinitival phrase (εἰς τὸ δοκιμάζειν ὑμας . . .)." He does not consider the possibility the ἵνα could be a noun clause with a second petition.

Best rendering:[84] [1st *hina* as object; 2nd *hina* as parallel object]

And this I pray: that [*hina* #1] your love will abound yet more and more
in knowledge and discernment
so that you can determine what really matters
that [*hina* #2] you may be pure and blameless in the Day of Christ
having been filled with the fruit of righteousness
through Jesus Christ
to the glory and praise of God.

The third approach provides a grammatical balance with the text. The two requests are each modified by a subordinate clause: the first with "so that" and the second with "having been filled." Furthermore, it is unusual for Paul to place a *hina* clause within a previous *hina* clause. He usually writes with a hierarchy of grammatically subordinate ideas. It is extremely unnatural to make the second *hina* clause come within (and modifying) another "so that" or purpose clause.

Interpretation

Paul's thoughts easily moved from thanksgiving to a petitioning prayer report. The two were part of the same spiritual activity, but more than that, Paul acknowledged that the good done in the Philippians' lives came from God. As a corollary to his thanksgiving, he prayed God would continue his work in them through the development of Christian virtues and character.

This prayer resembles the prayer in Col 1:9–11. The similarity goes beyond the fact that the prayer follows quickly after thanksgiving. Similarities of words reveal a similarity of content. There Paul pondered the same thoughts on Christian growth, perhaps because of his own situation in life.[85] The lexical and conceptual parallels reflect the natural tone and consistency of Paul's prayers for his converts. They include . . .

[84] See also John Reumann, *Philippians: A New Translation with Introduction and Commentary*, AB: 33B (New Haven: Yale University Press, 2008), 127.

[85] This fact is often overlooked in Colossians, where most accept the fact the prayer was suited to the specific problem faced there. While it is true the problem colors specific expressions, it is equally true the concepts are shared with other letters, such as Philippians. That fact diminishes the urgency of the impact of the false teachers at Colossae and emphasizes the thought naturally flowed from Paul's mind.

Phil 1:9–11	***Col 1:9–11***
I pray	praying
(*proseuchomai*)	(*proseuchomenoi*)
growing in knowledge	growing in knowledge of God
(*epignoμsei*)	(*epignoμsin*)
every kind of discernment	in wisdom and understanding
(*aisthesei*)	(*sophia kai synesei*)
filled	you may be filled
(*pepleμroμmenoi*)	(*pleμroμtheμte*)
fruit of righteousness	bearing fruit
(*karpon dikaiosyneμs*)	(*karpophorountes*)
	power of his glory
	(*kratos teμs doxeμs*)
	every good work
(*ergon agathon*)	(*ergoμagathoμ*)

These parallels reveal Paul thought consistently on the matter of Christian growth, and since they are parallel, emphasize the basic themes found in his somewhat normal requests.[86]

The prayer report contains two basic petitions. These are known by two "that" (*hina*) clauses in the Greek text. The CSB fails to pick up this distinction and even makes the second petition part of a parallel statement ("and may be pure and blameless").[87] The two petitions are "that your love will keep on growing . . . so that you may approve the things that are superior" (1:9–10a); and that you "may be pure and blameless . . . filled with the fruit of righteousness" (1:10b–11). The first looks to the time interval between the present situation and the return of the Lord. The second adopts the perspective of the Second Coming and looks back to the preparation of the church for that event. Paul prayed for growing love (1:9–10b) and for complete character (1:10b–11a).[88] The first is an immediate concern, their process of

[86] The list of parallels is adapted from Silva, *Philippians*, 57–58.

[87] It is most awkward to fail to acknowledge a major conjunction like ἵνα ("that"). CSB has taken a purpose infinitive (εἰς τό plus infinitive) as the beginning of a new clause rather than the end of the first ἵνα clause. Of the ways to understand the relationships, this is the least likely.

[88] It is possible the two primary clauses are consecutive so that the translation is "that your love will keep on growing . . . in order that you may be sincere and void of offense." This takes the two ἵνα clauses in different relationships, however. The first one would be an object clause the second a purpose clause. This construction would be awkward in the same sentence. In addition, another purpose element is in the verse: εἰς τό with the infinitive. The sentence is actually quite balanced structurally, which is not uncommon in Paul's prayers. The first has a

Christian growth. The second is an ultimate concern, their readiness for the day of Christ.

1:9–10a Love occupied Paul's thoughts first. Perhaps that was because of the Philippians' love demonstrated in supporting him at such a crucial time in his life. Perhaps it was because love summarized the Ten Commandments, as presented in Deut 6:5 and Luke 10:27. Love also epitomized Christian responsibility to other Christians (John 13:35; 1 John 2:7–11).

To these rather obvious commands regarding love, Paul added his own insights. If the Philippians' love abounded, they would be well on the way to Christian maturity. Here Paul described the nature of a growing love, the environment for a growing love, and the result of a growing love.

1:9a Some confusion always exists in discussing love. It is at the same time the universal ideal to which all should aspire and the most personal and existential of all expressions.

The definition of love is addressed in this part of v. 9. Paul used the word *agape*. The term predominates in Scripture as the expression of love.[89] It is sometimes difficult to distinguish *agape* from *philos* because the two occur frequently in Scripture with seemingly interchangeable meaning. Nevertheless, *philos* often includes an element of mutuality not found in *agape*. *Philos* is a satisfying interaction with others. What is clear is that for Paul *agape* emphasized the self-sacrificial love of Christ (Rom 5:6–8), since it is a selfless action to benefit someone else. The model for this love is Jesus, who gave himself for the sins of the world (John 3:16). Noting that, in Scripture love is rooted in God himself who may be partially defined in terms of love.

As Paul prayed for the readers' love to grow, he prayed for their Christlike attitude of self-sacrifice to continue as it had been demonstrated earlier in their giving.[90] The sacrificial nature of the love is further stressed in that there is no object for the love; it is a characteristic

---

non-final conjunction (ἵνα) modified by a purpose infinitive; the second has a non-final ἵνα modified by a predicate participle.

[89] Though Fee points out it is used "only sparsely among Greek writers." Fee, *Philippians*, 98, n.11. He continues that it became "the ultimate theological word to describe God's character and to articulate the essence of Christian behavior."

[90] See 2 Cor 8:1–6 where Paul spoke of their "extreme poverty" (v. 2), of their gift exceeding their ability (v. 3), of their begging Paul to accept the gift (v. 4), and of their gift as an expression of commitment to the Lord (v. 5).

of the "lover" regardless of the object.[91] It is tempting to limit love's object by stating the obvious: the Philippians are to love God. This attitude corresponds in Scripture with the obligation to love one's neighbor as oneself (the "Greatest Commandment"). Paul used the word three other times in Philippians. In 1:16 the term is used of Roman ministers preaching "out of love, knowing that [Paul is] appointed for the defense of the gospel." In 2:1 he appeals to what the church has in common, "if any consolation of love." In 2:2 they should express "the same love" for each other. All three of these place *agape* in a context of relating to other persons correctly. As a result of the disunity that existed in the church, Paul prayed for love that would unite the church in mutual commitment. Even though these were doubtless in Paul's mind at some level, the lack of specific object for love points one even beyond loving everyone, unspecified. His point places emphasis on the subject who loves more than the objects who are loved. The modifying pronoun, "your love," calls the entire church to be the initiators of love rather than its recipients.

Jesus taught that aspect in the parable of the Good Samaritan (Luke 10:25–37). The lawyer asked, "[W]ho is my neighbor?," seeking to come to a clear understanding of his neighborhood and of his responsibility (10:29). Jesus responded, "Which [man] ... proved to be a neighbor?," informing the man he had framed the question incorrectly (10:36). There are no boundaries to a Christian's neighborhood. Love was to follow in the wake of their living.[92] It is to be indiscriminate as to object and fostered by the maturing of the subjects.

The dynamic growth of love is presented in this first clause. The verb translated "will keep on growing" (*perisseueo*), which means to "be present in abundance,"[93] occurs in the most dynamic of expressions possible, emphasizing continuation.[94] Their love was to keep on

---

[91] It is always easier to measure love if there is a specific object who should be loved. The absence of such parameters makes love all the more the responsibility of the initiator, not the receiver.

[92] Beare, *The Epistle*, 54, correctly sees this aspect of syntax. He states it is not only love for God or others, but "love in the most comprehensive sense as the central element of the Christian life."

[93] BAGD, 650–51. Hawthorne, *Philippians*, 26, points out that the word is typically Pauline (twenty-six of thirty-nine times in the NT) and that it typifies the new age brought by Christ. This assessment is correct and insightful.

[94] It is a present subjunctive. The progressive idea is a product of the verb root, the tense, and the context which demands it. Together they stress the dynamic nature of the love.

abounding. Second, the adverbial expression "more and more" stresses the dynamic of love. The Greek text has the expression "still more and more," the first part of which is omitted in the CSB. The translation "keep on growing" (CSB) is emphatic. The expression builds layer upon layer to make the point. "More" would have sufficed, "more and more" was better, but "still more and more" accentuated the point being made. With this expression, Paul does not command initiating love. He assumes the church displays love and cares for each other. Although exemplary in their love, the Philippians had not yet reached perfection. There was still room for growth.

1:9b The prayerful exhortation to love came with instructions about how to implement it. The words "knowledge and every kind of discernment" provide the twofold environment in which love may grow.[95] They are, in fact, the most basic elements which foster love.[96] The first aspect of the environment for growing love is knowledge. The Greek word for "knowledge" (*epignosis*) is difficult to translate into acceptable English. The root word is *gnosis*, and the preposition *epi* ("upon") is prefixed to it. Both parts of the compound need explanation.

The basic word used here (*gnosis*) contains a slight contrast with its synonyms. Most often it is compared or contrasted with the common Greek term for "knowledge" (*oida*). This latter term generally signifies intellectual knowledge (the product of the mind). It may convey the idea of complete knowledge because the other terms are not well suited to the idea of completion. In contrast, *gnosis* generally conveys the idea of an experiential knowledge (the product of experiencing by living). It easily lends itself to expressing relationships since they come from experiences. Further, since experiences provide the process of learning, *gnosis* often stresses the process of knowing rather

---

[95] Hawthorne, *Philippians*, 26, seems to provide an alternate option. He states love is to be "accompanied by knowledge and understanding," and, later, "One of the things that directs love is knowledge." In actuality, he is not far from the position of this commentary, but the principle followed here is if the locative idea with ἐν ("in") will work, it should be employed. That is its most common and natural force, and to understand these as locatives of sphere works well in this passage.

[96] Martin, *Philippians*, 68, suggests these terms are common among Hellenistic philosophers "in the twofold sense of an intellectual apprehension of the good in life and a moral choice which determines a man's course of action." Paul probably had the philosophers in mind in this statement, but certainly the intellectual and moral combine here. The outline captions for this section reflect that understanding.

than the outcome. Here Paul used the term in its full sense of real, personal knowledge. It is not the product of deductive reasoning and intellectual (*oida*). Nevertheless, it is not fully relational, indicating only relationships with persons. Paul wanted them to have personal knowledge which, as he stated later in this prayer, would surface in practical ways as well. The compound form heightens the definition. In Greek, prefixed prepositions may be either directive, pointing to a specific knowledge, or perfective, emphasizing an accurate knowledge. Since this context does not provide a direction, clearly Paul used the word in the perfective sense.[97] This first aspect of love aims for an accurate knowledge. Part of that knowledge is its ability to apply what is known to the practical aspects of life, much like wisdom in the OT.[98]

Paul added judgment, the moral environment, to knowledge. The term "discernment" occurs only here in the NT, although a form of the root word occurs in Heb 5:14 "solid food is for he mature—for those whose *senses* have been trained to distinguish between good and evil." It conveys the sense of moral discretion.[99] Thus morality affects the growth of love.

Although the terms knowledge and discernment have no specific modifiers, two matters are clear. First, Paul wrote in Christian terms. The love and judgment he espoused were those seen in Christ and consistent with Scripture. While the words sometimes occur in secular contexts discussing general morality, Paul certainly rooted his prayers in Christ and the resources which come from the Holy Spirit. The Philippians would realize, therefore, that in disclosing his prayer for them, Paul called them to the highest and best of Christian qualities and growth. Second, these two terms provide a collective environment which fosters growth. If either is lacking, love will not grow. In this, Paul's expression is consistent with his Jewish-Christian ethical background. Knowing and living go hand in hand. Failure to grow in the knowledge God expects of Christians hinders love. Similarly, failure to discipline the moral life hinders love. Attention to both of these realms promotes a healthy and positive Christian life.

---

[97] Lightfoot, *St. Paul's*, 86, called it an intensive preposition.

[98] Silva, *Philippians*, 63, points out Paul preferred the compound term in the chronologically later letters and there may be no significance to the form. Silva's observation may be partially correct. That is, Paul may well have developed such a preference, but that preference no doubt came from his insistence on real knowledge. The word became his favorite later because of its suitability to his theological outlook.

[99] Emphasis added. BAGD, 25.

Like "love," the terms "knowledge" and "discernment" have no expressed objects. They speak to broad, general concerns. The comprehensive knowledge includes an accurate understanding of God and the world, as well as of the "lover" himself.[100] Similarly, the moral insight comes from various sources and is comprehensive in nature. It exposes the rightness and wrongness of all thoughts and actions.

Although growing love is the subject of this sentence, some have suggested Paul's real prayer is for knowledge, not love.[101] Since the statement moves toward approving "the things that are superior," they say the goal of the prayer is the knowledge necessary to arrive at that ability. As knowledge and discernment increase, so does the ability to discern. Presumably, discernment relates to knowledge so it qualifies what kind of knowledge actually helps.[102] Thus, for them, the key to this part of Paul's prayer is his focus on knowledge as essential to successful Christian living. In that scenario, discernment relates to the nature of the knowledge. It is discerning knowledge, not random facts. Care must be exercised in this, however. Knowledge is parallel with discernment, not a modifier of it. If Paul had meant knowledge was the foundation of love, he might well have used the preposition *epi* (upon) rather than *en* (in).

The emphasis on the importance of accurate knowledge should be noted well. The question remains, however, whether that is the point of Paul's prayer. It must be observed that love is the theme of this sentence, evidenced by Paul's making it the subject. Dynamic love receives the stress and is the key to understanding. The difference is significant. If the point is to gain knowledge, then knowledge refined by discernment enables sorting out what really matters. There are multiple times Paul commends knowledge as necessary.[103] Conversely, if

[100] Thus love is fostered by seeing a model (God), knowing the object (the world), and being an intimately personal expression (myself).

[101] So Holloway, *Philippians*, 78–79: "A prayer not for love but for *knowledge* and what Paul wants for the Philippians is the 'knowledge and discernment' required to ascertain 'the things that really matter.'"

[102] It is noteworthy that "knowledge" and "discernment" are two nouns joined by "and," introduced by one preposition: "in." The two are thus joined in some fashion as two of some similarity.

[103] One passage illustrates this, which is so common in Paul's writing. The Thessalonian Christians were to walk and please God "[f]or you know what commands we gave you through the Lord Jesus" (1 Thess 4:2). First Thessalonians 4:13 is also helpful on this point: "We do not want you to be uninformed, brothers and sisters, concerning those who are asleep, so that you will not grieve like the rest." Paul's writing in general was to supply knowledge for growth.

love is the point, then the ability to sort things that differ comes from love informed by knowledge and discernment. Paul also affirms this relationship. First Corinthians consistently discusses the relationship between love and knowledge. Paul states, "Love never ends" though "knowledge . . . will come to an end" (1 Cor 13:8). Similarly, he prayed that the Thessalonians would "overflow with love for one another and for everyone"(1 Thess 3:12). Why did Paul make love the subject of this sentence rather than knowledge? Surely it was that growing love occupied the primary focus in his prayers for them.[104]

That leads to another critical question. How does love grow through discernment? Christian love as here is not a sentimentalizing of emotion that follows wherever excitement leads. It is a determined, attitudinal commitment to what is best, sourced in the (biblical) heart and mind. As such, love is both a motivator and a guide. Love motivates one to believe and embrace the best in others and in life. Similarly, love serves as a thermometer. It reveals both what is best and indicates when there is less than the best. Knowledge and discernment combined help to focus love in a proper direction. In the difficulties and dilemmas of life, where knowledge is unclear or uncertain, love pulls one through. Christian love, rooted in and devoted to Christ, finds a way to live as God intends.

The reciprocal relationships between these, however, should be emphasized. That is the thrust of Paul's prayer. Love can and will grow given the proper environment of knowledge and discernment. While love can surpass knowledge and guide to proper discernment (Eph 3:17–19), love is also the product of reflection. In Ephesians Paul uses the same word, *gnosis* (and its verbal form). Accurate knowledge and reflective discernment enable flourishing love. In the mental and moral contexts of life, love receives the impetus to flourish. No one should diminish the importance of knowledge and discernment. Paul intimates as much in Rom 12:1–2, where growth is attributed to the renewed mind. It should be noted, however, that in Romans Paul actually speaks of the mind (*noia*) rather than knowledge. The point of

[104] George Hunsinger, *Philippians*, Brazos Theological Commentary on the Bible. ed. R. R. Reno et al. (Grand Rapids: Brazos Press, 2020), 15, notes "Ultimately, therefore, there can be no such thing as a neutral knowledge of God detached from love (as in some philosophical theologies), nor a true love of God apart from knowledge (as in some 'Spiritualities'). A God not worshiped with love in true knowledge is no God at all."

Paul's prayer here is love. Perhaps love receives the emphasis because of the Philippian problem of church disunity.

In reading the Letter to the Philippians, this is a somewhat strange prayer, utilizing unusual words. This question may be asked: What prompted this prayer? The similarity to Colossians, written at the same time, has been noted. Perhaps, therefore, it is a general prayer for the apostle to voice. If, however, he has in mind the context of Philippians, is there some specific issue on his heart? The most obvious reference would be the Christ hymn. The commands preceding encourage love, sometimes explicitly. *Agape* is a rare word for Paul in Philippians; it occurs only three times. It appears in relational contexts of Christians to which, when followed, accomplishes proper relationships in the church. As noted, the word translated "discernment" in CSB is a *hapax legomena*, occurring only once in the NT. Most agree it has moral overtones, and therefore "discernment" is the best translation. It is unlikely Paul is advocating discernment in knowledge, a theme unfound in the Pauline corpus directly. The combination is moral (discernment) and mental (knowledge). The more one knows, and the more care one has for proper conduct, the more love will grow.

1:10a Paul envisioned mature Christians who had the ability to distinguish right from wrong. He directed his prayer toward that end.[105] The CSB translates what may be understood in several ways: "so that you may approve." It is a purpose clause rather than result, although either could be implied with the Greek construction. Result, however, would be understood as looking at the accomplishment of the main idea. It would be "with the result that you approved," a translation which does not fit the flow and the syntax of the sentence. The word "approve" has the meaning of "test by trial." The concept occurs frequently in the NT and in Paul's writings in particular. It was used of purifying metals through the fire of a furnace and of testing coins for their authenticity.[106] The nuance of the word implies coming through testing with purified character. The term best emphasizes the result of that testing. The phrase need not stress the fact that some things are harmful and, therefore, should be avoided. It has equal application to affirming and embracing the best of good choices, and that reading fits this text better. Although it cannot be confined to

---

[105] The construction εἰς τό plus the infinitive shows purpose in this case as it often does when the "governing" ἵνα clauses are non-final.

[106] Hawthorne, *Philippians*, 67.

issues in the Philippian church, it certainly may commend the best way of living, implementing the mind of Christ in local disputes such as between Euodia and Syntyche. Since this context calls for wisdom related to life, the words suggest the ability to discern moral conduct and values so that life and energy are not misdirected. The picture of having been refined by fire supports the power of knowledgeable and discerning love. Refinement comes in experience, rather than by a textbook or ethical list of optional choices. A growing love, fed by proper knowledge and moral insight, enables one to see the best way to live in light of the day of Christ. When behavior options confront and leave one somewhat bewildered, growing love will guide.

1:10b–11 The second petition takes the ultimate perspective. If the first, growing love, enables one to navigate the murky waters of life, the second points to the glory of Christ's return. At that time, Christian character commends us to God and glorifies him. In a sense, then, Paul's first prayer guides us from now until then; his second prayer affirms the intended goal and takes a backward glance to the processes that produce character.

The two are logically related. Discerning what is best (that is, "superior") develops character. Growing love provides for character development and completion. As Paul prayed, his thoughts moved to the day of accountability. He prayed the Philippians would live in such a way they would be without blame at that time. In this second petition, therefore, Paul foresaw the end of life on earth. As always, the return of the Lord and Christians' preparation for it occupied his thoughts. Paul identified through prayer the nature of complete character, the means to it, and the purpose of it.

1:10b Three words describe Paul's concern for the Philippians: he wanted them to be "pure and blameless." Strictly defined, these words convey two slightly different ideas. "Pure" (*eilikrineos*) occurs only one other time in the NT (2 Pet 3:1), although other words with the same root occur (i.e., 1 Cor 5:8). The most common etymology of pure suggests that it derives from the two words "sun" (*helios*) and "to judge" (*krinoo*) and the word originally involved being held "up to sunlight for inspection."[107] The point of inspection was to reveal flaws in the finished product. In the sunlight a jar may be seen to have a crack, a blemish, or impurity in its workmanship. No one expects

[107] Hawthorne, *Philippians*, 28

total perfection but that should be the goal. Purity, therefore, points to the person. It calls for turning from sin and the character following sinful desires produces. It compels embracing Christlikeness. As will be noted below, it embodies the righteousness given by God through Christ and embraced by consistent Christian living informed by love.

"Blameless" (*aproskopoi*) also occurs rarely in the NT.[108] The term may have an active meaning ("not to blame") or a passive one ("to be free from blame").[109] The decision is a difficult one since both have a precedent (cf. Acts 24:16; 1 Cor 10:32). The active sense is understood as a person *who does not blame*. Understood that way, the text must read something like arriving at the day of Christ accepting full personal responsibility for the path taken, rather than making excuses so easily transferred to others. In modern life, one common approach to achieving self-respect is to place blame on others. Arriving at the end of life without a victim mentality is certainly a good thing and a Christian ambition. It is not found by casting blame, however.[110] Coupled with "pure," and the general direction of this text, this takes us to the passive meaning of "blame." No one can successfully accuse the believer of thinking or acting improperly. Rather than an outlook toward others, it is a personal quality of self-examination. Paul referenced the believers' blamelessness in potential accusation in Rom 8:33–34. There he affirms the legal standing of a follower of Christ before God. Through Christ, God accepts us no matter what anyone may say. Used here, however, "blameless" speaks to the life lived out of purpose and love. It is standing before God having cared for imperfect actions and their damage to others, so that a pattern of right decisions and correct living characterizes one's life. The text follows with a reference to the "fruit of righteousness," a phrase which implies character and favors the passive sense. Paul hoped they would live blamelessly. Innocence of character (purity) and harmless living (blamelessness) encapsulate Paul's hope for his readers.

Mention of "the day of Christ" raises some questions as to the specific meaning. What is clear is the day of Christ, the same as the

[108] Phil 1:10; Acts 24:16; and 1 Cor 10:32. BAGD, 102.

[109] Lightfoot, *Saint Paul's*, 87. He argues in this context any reference to conduct toward others is out of place. Paul spoke only of their relationship to God here.

[110] Thus, practically, one is often told to blame parents, environments, lack of opportunities, and the like for complexes to overcome. But Adam and Eve were certainly guilty of such by Adam blaming Eve and Eve blaming Satan for their fall.

"day of Christ Jesus" (1:6), references the day of the climax of history. It is the time when Jesus comes again to receive his own, to judge the world, to establish a new heavens and earth, and to usher in eternity. It is the believer's ultimate and blessed hope fulfilled. What is unclear is the meaning of the preposition *eis*, "unto, into, for." Paul only uses the exact expression here and in 2:16. The preposition is not to be confused with "*en*" (in), which contains a static idea of location.[111] The preposition *eis* implies movement, motion toward and into the noun with which it is associated. Therefore, some want to translate the text as "unto the day of Christ." The most blatant problem with this rendering is that Paul knows some will not live "unto" the day of Christ (see 1 Thess 4:13–18, for example). In Phil 1:6 Paul states "until" using the preposition *achri*. (Here, too, CSB uses "in" but allows for "until" as an alternate). It is doubtful he intends the two different prepositions in the same way. Most likely the meaning is "for." This means they have "the day of Christ in view as their ultimate goal,"[112] and preparation for it as a primary concern.

1:11a Creating similar structure to the first petition, Paul provided a context out of which such character could come. In the first, the environment of knowledge and morality will produce a discerning love. In this petition the fruit of righteousness produces complete character.

The phrase "fruit of righteousness" also demands interpretation. The primary concern is the use of the term "righteousness."[113] Some interpret it to mean the fruit produced by their imputed righteousness.[114] Most, however, understand the phrase to mean the result of righteous activity as Christians, referring to ethical righteousness. The OT supports this conclusion (Hos 10:12), and it fits Paul's attitude expressed in Philippians. Paul does not say "fruit of *the* righteousness," which favors imputed righteousness. The article goes with "*the*

---

[111] The CSB translates this "in the day of Christ" with an optional "until." "In" may be understood as "at the day of Christ," which would satisfy the translation.

[112] Fee, *Philippians*, 102, n.23. Also Keown, *Philippians 1:1–2:18*, 164 (referring also to Lightfoot, 87).

[113] The construction is actually capable of three possible translations of the genitive "righteousness": fruit which is righteousness (appositional genitive); the fruit which righteousness produces (subjective genitive); the fruit which is righteous fruit (descriptive genitive). Regarding the definition of righteousness, there are two options: forensic (imputed righteousness) or ethical (moral conduct).

[114] So Beare, *The Epistle*, 55.

fruit of righteousness," which supports the righteous character and activity that comes from being righteous.

Here Paul used an agricultural metaphor which included the word "fruit." Some translate the word as "harvest," a translation which no doubt captures Paul's thought well. The fruit was that which Jesus Christ produced in them and parallels Gal 5:22. For that reason, the participle is best understood as a passive idea, "having been filled" (e.g., by Christ or more specifically, the work of the Holy Spirit).[115] The prayer was for them to live in such a way that Christ could work in them the harvest of morality and righteousness which would be acceptable at the day of Christ. The ultimate goal is the glory and praise of God. Rather than boasting about personal achievements of righteousness (cf 3:2ff), true believers boast of Christ's power to produce and reward righteous living. Since it is "through Jesus Christ" it brings glory to God.

Righteous living would protect the church; it would be blameless. As Paul would clarify later (see 3:4–6), his concern was that blamelessness be the result of Christ and his righteousness, not one's own. The passage assumes if those who are righteous by God's grace through faith (imputed righteousness) live as they should, the fruit of their lives will be true blamelessness. No one will condemn them, and they will stand the test of judgment day.

1:11b Paul concluded this prayer with a reference to God's glory. The day of Christ characterized Paul's thoughts; the glory of God motivated Paul's actions. He saw the entire scope of salvation as an outworking of God's grace and as a contribution to God's glory.[116] The chief end of persons is the glory of God. He reminded the Philippians of their ultimate calling to reflect God's character in their lives. He explained the reason for their careful living: "the glory . . . of God."

With this prayer for God's glory, Paul ended the first section of the letter. The epistle began with appreciation for the church's relationship to Paul from the beginning. Paul called them to realize God began a work in them and it must continue, and it reminded them of the need

[115] In contrast to Beare, *The Epistle*, 55, who takes it as middle (produce a harvest). It is equally difficult to see how Hawthorne, *Philippians*, 28–29, takes the participle as an adjective (attributive function) when it fits the normal structural patterns of adverbial participles (predicate forms), and the context makes good sense with this reading.

[116] This is specifically clear in Eph 1:3–14 where three sections of doxology are marked by some form of the phrase "to the praise of his glorious grace" (1:6, 12, 14).

to prepare for the day of Christ's appearing. Paul masterfully revealed his concerns for them, introducing each of the major themes of the letter. In a manner appropriate to friends, Paul spoke first in appreciation for who they were, then urged them to continue in Christian growth. Even his prayer provided a positive approach to them. His was no disinterested concern. He prayed they would achieve the character prized so highly for them and himself (3:8–11). The concern for spiritual completion, however, did not bypass the present life. Love was to characterize all Christians. It uniquely expressed their relationship to Christ and prepared them for meeting him at the end of this life.

Theological and Practical Points

This is an introduction to Paul's letter and supremely warm, as it ought to be. Nevertheless, there are solid theological and practical principles that undergird this section and, therefore, the entire letter

1. *Paul's prayer life.* Like most of Paul's letters (Galatians excluded), Paul begins with a prayer or at least a disclosure of how he prays. Here he does both. Twice the specific word for prayer, *deesis*, occurs in the first eleven verses of chapter one (1:4, 2x). This word suggests a specific request and the hearers need explanation of what that request is. Other words also occur: "I give thanks" (*euxaristeo*, 1:3); "always praying" (*mneia*,1:4); and "I pray" (*proseuxomai*, 1:9). This section is saturated by prayer, and Paul's vocabulary of prayer is natural and unforced. It is far from a nicety or religious obligation. Several observations come from this: Paul naturally thanked God as he remembered them. He disclosed that he lived in a God-ordered world and his coming to Philippi was God-led. The warm relationship that developed in spite of serious opposition was God-ordained and thus, appropriately, Paul genuinely, and first, thanked God for them.

Additionally, Paul prayed consistently as he remembered them. Few people can say honestly that God is to be thanked every time they remember someone else. Paul's claim might be easier to understand if it were based on their generosity alone, but Paul carefully notes it began from the first day. That was a day at the riverside where he met some devout women who promptly trusted in Jesus, but it soon included a beating and imprisonment. Paul does not thank God for the imprisonment, but he is able to think beyond it to the overriding good that came out of it: the salvation of the jailer and his family. Given that, he found himself easily thankful and joyful for the divine appointments at Philippi. It was natural to appreciate God for these personal intersections in life. One wonders about the scope of his prayer list if he felt this way about all the churches he planted!

2. *Paul's Commitment to the Metanarrative of History.* The metanarrative is the historical movement as God accomplished his plans. In Philippians, this took two dimensions, one related to Paul and the other to the church at Philippi. First, Paul saw himself as privileged to be a steward of God's movement in the world and through history. This is most clearly stated in the salutation where Paul identifies himself as a servant of Christ Jesus. Consequently, his activities are ordered by and dedicated to his master, Jesus. Elsewhere, however, Paul clearly states his specific stewardship. In 1 Thess 2:4 Paul recounts his visit to Thessalonica and references his previous time at Philippi. He states, "[W]e have been approved by God to be entrusted with the gospel." The gospel is God's primary way of revealing himself to the world. Sometimes Paul spoke of it as the effective power that enabled God's plans. Paul understood he was selected by God to carry God's message of redemption to the world. He noted the gospel "truly is the word of God, which also works effectively in [all] who believe" (1 Thess 2:13). The gospel was not Paul's idea, and it was not Paul's choice to commit himself to it. Rather, God selected him and privileged him with the stewardship of the message. He saw himself in a train of people from earliest history recorded in the OT all the way up to the witness of the early church. The gospel did not belong to him.

Second, Paul understood the unique position of the Philippian church in carrying out God's purposes. From the beginning they partnered with him in promoting the gospel, the same gospel Paul was selected to proclaim. It was God who worked in them on day one, through the instrumentality of Paul, and God would take them to the end: the day of Christ. The church responded as they could by sending their support to Paul. It was a partnership of love (Paul wrote, "I have you in my heart") as they both understood and promoted the gospel—the grace of God (Phil 1:7). Paul expressed strong confidence that the church existed as a result of God's working in Philippi and, given that, they would remain the object of God's care until the end of time.

The metanarrative found in Scripture is that God has a plan for his creation and is carrying it forward generation to generation. He chooses some individuals and gifts them for involvement in this plan. The OT testifies to that. In many ways it is a history of the people

God used. The biographical nature of Scripture encourages each individual of each generation to take his or her turn in promoting God's purposes. One of the strengths of Scripture is the biographies included describe both successes and failures. Yet God still worked through those chosen. In Paul's longest recorded sermon, given at Antioch of Pisidia, he said of King David, "[A]fter serving God's purpose in his own generation, fell asleep, was buried with his fathers, and decayed" (Acts 13:36). As David had served his generation well, Paul, and the early Philippian church, took their place in God's economy to serve their generation well. Such was their lap in the race!

3. Paul's concern for the church's spiritual growth. Throughout this first section, Paul has a specific prayer in mind. The use of *deesis* as his word for prayer evidences this. It refers to a specific entreaty rather than a general attitude of prayer. It is likely that Paul prayed a general and all-encompassing prayer for them,[117] but in this context his plea is more specific. It revealed his understanding of the church's situation and the remedy for its disunity. The prayer has two petitions: for a growing love and completeness of character.

Though love is prominent in this prayer as an introduction to the epistle, *agape* occurs only four times in Philippians (see the commentary). It may well be the apostle's mind is on the present discord in Rome where the leaders of the churches were divided over the validity of Paul's mission. He then transferred that easily to the lesser discord in the church at Philippi whose disunity could be resolved in part by their encouraging each other.

Paul's prayer for their love is at the heart of his concern. When he addressed the problem at Philippi he did not speak of love. He urged them to be of the same mind. Perhaps Paul intended the same mind to be the result of knowledge and discernment. Discernment occurs twice in the simple prayer to describe growing love. It occurs with the word itself (discretion or discernment) and it occurs in the goal of increasing love. In the various issues of life, it is often difficult to determine the bad from the good and the good from the best. Love navigates these treacherous waters successfully, but only in the crucible of life itself. Knowledge and discernment enable the church to arrive at more congeniality through the growth of love they promote. Paul's prayer for

[117] This would be similar to modern prayers like "God bless the missionaries."

growing love is connected to character (the "fruit of righteousness") As noted in the commentary above, growing love motivates.

The second petition, wholeness of character, is founded on righteousness. Paul notes purity and blamelessness come as the fruit of righteousness (1:11). The concept of righteousness occurs four times in Philippians. Apart from this reference, it occurs in 3:6 and twice in 3:9. Chapter three is Paul's polemic against his non-Christian opponents, much of which concerns righteousness. First, it is a category of measurement (3:6). He compares himself to the Judaizers in zeal and righteousness. These same categories appear in Rom 10:2–3 as the standard of measurement for Israel's failure. They had "zeal for God, but not according to knowledge" and "they are ignorant of the righteousness of God and attempted to establish their own righteousness." These appear to be the common fall back characteristics the Jewish people used to justify their claim to be God's people. Philippians 3 replicates that. These texts inform us of the particular nuance of Paul's prayer here. Paul sometimes stated believers stand in a state of righteousness by God's grace through the believer's faith. One clear occasion of this is Rom 5:1: "we have been justified by faith." The verbal form of the word stem for righteousness is usually translated as justified, thus it refers to a state of justness. It is described as a declaration from God that he has provided righteousness for us through Christ. For example, Paul states, "[I]n [Christ]we might become the righteousness of God" (2 Cor 5:21). In Phil 3, the contrast is between "righteousness . . . [from] the law" and that provided by God. Yet though given by God to the believer, righteousness is not passive. It motivates the believer to good deeds, actually accomplishing God's plan of changed character. As will be noted, it is character unavailable through law and human effort.

Paul prayed the Philippi Christians would evidence the result of God's righteousness in their lives. Rather than considering it a work, which implies human effort, Paul calls it fruit. It is something that naturally happens out of the seedbed of righteousness. The fruit coming from righteousness is itself righteous and bears its own offspring, character. In this passage, the fruit refers specifically to purity and blamelessness. The Philippians are to live in such a way that their lives have the character of righteousness. Since he references the day of Christ, clearly he envisions a lifetime of righteousness producing its own product in the lives of the believers. Though this is described as a future characteristic, as the expected result of being righteous, the church was to understand that they were to strive to be pure and blameless. They were to have transparent and genuine sincerity of life, living without giving any occasion for them to be justly blamed for ill. Love and righteousness should characterize the church in its relationships to each other as well as for the glory of God. The Judaizers of 3:2 might well have said "keep the Torah" to develop the character God expects. Paul replaces Torah with love: keep love as your guiding principle.

2.2 Paul's Joy in the Progress of the Gospel in Rome (1:12–26)

After opening the letter with a preliminary thanksgiving and a prayer for the church, Paul turned his thoughts to matters at hand. The church desired to know Paul's situation, and Paul wanted to relieve them of anxiety regarding it. Philippians 1:12 introduces a chiastic structure that guides the reader through the letter with major changes in tone and style. The change of tone is noted most dramatically in grammar. These patterns reveal the letter proper begins with 1:12 and ends with 4:19. The text changes from indicative first person verbs to imperative second person commands intermittently. The change in verbal moods between indicative and imperative indicates a major stylistic feature of the letter. This is further emphasized by the interchange of subjects expressed primarily by personal pronouns. The indicative sections have Paul as the subject, and therefore the pronoun "I" predominates. The imperative sections have the church as the subject, and therefore the pronoun "you" does. This may be seen graphically:

A 1:12–26 Indicative ["I" predominant]
  B 1:27–2:18 Imperative ["you" predominate]
    [2:5–11 illustrate the core values Paul encourages]
    C 2:19–3:14 Indicative ["I" predominate, though two different subjects]
  B′ 3:15–4:9 Imperative ["you" predominate but interchanges with "I"]
A′ 4:10–19 Indicative ["I" predominate]

At least three observations emerge from this. 1) The graphic presentation above is a chiastic pattern. The pattern may not hold true regarding every technical aspect of a chiasm. In particular, in chiasms when there is a "C" member (the middle and "unbalanced" member), it receives the primary emphasis. It is difficult to see how sending Timothy and Epaphroditus would constitute the primary message of the letter. The most that can be observed is this is a grammatical chiasm with the "C" member unclear, but it should be noticed the C is in two thematic sections: sending Timothy and Epaphroditus, and warning about Judaizers. 2) In both the "A" components (A and A′), Paul reveals his own personal circumstances. This is a major concern of the Philippian church. A and A′ each have a different emphasis, however. In 1:12–26 Paul reveals his confidence in the midst of both intra-church divisions and the uncertainty of the Roman government trial. In either and both, Paul had confidence in the sovereignty of God and thus maintained his spiritual equilibrium. In 4:10–19, Paul revealed his genuine thankfulness for the gifts sent by the church, but in that context he also revealed his sense of sufficiency. He knew he could "do all things through [Christ]" who strengthened him. Thus, from an internal perspective rather than external, he is content. 3) The "B" members also complement. The first, 1:27–2:18, urges the church to guard its own unity by standing together and implementing the attitude of Christ in their midst. The second, B′ 3:15–4:9, encourages the church to remember to imitate both Paul and Christ in living appropriately as citizens of heaven.

In this analysis, a major section has been purposely omitted: 2:5–11. This primarily records the poem about appropriating the "mind" of Christ. Paul expects in the readers' minds, this strikingly emotive and powerful section should be highlighted rather than diminished. The major question, however, is the structural importance of this section to the message of the book. It appears as illustrative, yet beautifully exemplifies the Christian's ideal. Is it more than illustrative? Some have analyzed the entire letter around the centrality of this section. As in many cases, the illustration often eclipses the point it illustrates.

With 1:12, Paul began a discussion of his situation in Rome. He rarely wrote about his own situation so early in an letter.[118] Perhaps several reasons prompted this approach. First, the church anxiously awaited this news; it had sent Epaphroditus to Paul's side, anticipating his needs. Perhaps it had heard of the potential difficulties Paul

[118] He does in 2 Cor 1:8–11, but there he summarized what happened to him in order to address their attacks against him. In Philippians Paul wrote a "free standing" disclosure of his situation and placed it at the beginning. That calls for some explanation. Galatians has two chapters of autobiographical information, but that actually is part of his argument. Fee, *Philippians*, 106, n. 4, states, "Nowhere else is there anything like this—reflection on his own present and future circumstances."

might have with the Roman government. Although at this time being a Christian was not a capital crime, no one knew how the emperor would rule regarding Christians. This was the test case.

The second reason Paul discussed his circumstances so soon was that the Philippians would hear a firsthand report from Epaphroditus and Paul needed to address their concerns quickly. Their anxiety regarding Epaphroditus would turn to continued anxiety about Paul. Although the former's report would be accurate, it could easily be filled with only his impressions. Little could be done constructively to address the needs of the church if readers were waiting to hear how Paul responded to his circumstances.

Third, Paul saw firsthand how divisions affected the work of the gospel. The divided church at Rome surely grieved Paul. Although he did not complain in his letter, and he pointed out the positive aspects of the situation, the disunity concerned him. An explanation of his circumstances provided a natural and easy way to encourage the Philippians in the qualities he saw lacking at Rome. Thus, the description of his situation served to anticipate his point to the readers. Surely they would conduct themselves differently from the Roman churches.

Finally, this section responded to the gift they had sent. They wanted to know Paul's circumstances because they were friends; because of their stewardship, they needed to know how the work progressed. At specific intervals Paul wrote autobiographically, informing the readers of his own thoughts. Three times this occurs in major sections: 1:12–26, regarding his circumstances; 3:1–14, regarding his experience of salvation; and 4:10–20, regarding the gift from the church. In each case, Paul's experiences became an effective vehicle for communicating his concerns.

This section of the letter also reveals circumstances can and do change intended activities. Paul wrote earlier to the churches at Rome that he hoped they would help him take the gospel to Spain (Rom 15:28). He desired to go to Rome, but not by the circumstances that took him there. He also expected the churches of Rome would support his work in the gospel. Yet in Philippians and the other Prison Letters, there is no indication of Paul's desire to go to Spain. Rather, every evidence suggests he wished to go east and visit the churches he wrote from Rome, including Philippi.

In Romans he also acknowledged there were problems within the churches in Rome. They were theological/historical in nature (who had Abraham as father, 4:9–12); they included God's plans for the redemption of the world (how were Gentiles included and did Jews lose their identity after Christ?, 4:9–11); and what amoral practices were appropriate for Christian people (14:1–15:6)? It is doubtful these issues were settled by the time Paul entered Rome, some five to six years after writing the letter to the Romans. Though none of the divisive issues lie in the background of Philippians, at least directly, the nature of the Roman churches circulated to other churches. Indeed, Paul complemented the Roman Christians that "news of [their] faith [was] being reported in all the world" (Rom 1:8). Still, there was enough to cause concern in the Philippian churches who so partnered with Paul. He faced difficulties of travel (by modern standards); the Roman political system to which he had entrusted his future and, indeed, his own life; and the inability of the Roman churches to agree on secondary matters of the faith, including the nuances of Paul's message and matters of personal conduct.

A major structural question concerns the ending of this first major section of Philippians. It is difficult to know whether 1:27–30 concludes the first section by applying Paul's concerns regarding Rome to the church at Philippi, or whether it begins the first set of exhortations. There are thematic and conceptual ties to both sections.

The problem is to determine what criteria actually indicate a new section has begun. Philippians has the marks of a personal letter, and informal allusions to the tie between writer and reader occur throughout. In 1:27–30 Paul made reference to his desire to hear of the Philippians' firm stand. Such a stand confirmed his apostolic ministry. In 2:1–11 Paul appealed to the common bond between himself and the church. The humility he advocated was a fulfillment of his joy. In 2:12–18 he urged them to obey and work out their salvation even if he were sacrificed. Their obedience vindicated his sufferings for them. The criterion for structural divisions may be personal allusion, but such allusions are frequent in the section. In each portion Paul appealed to their friendship. On the other hand, the criterion may be that the form changes to exhortation rather than information. In support of that, it is noteworthy that Paul uses a predominance of first-person communication in 1:12–26 (twenty-three times). Later the basic pattern shifts to second-person communication, the normal person for commands. Three primary commands occur in 1:27–2:18.

This change of tone appears most significant, and the three no doubt form a major section to themselves. The first section ends at 1:26.[119] It divides naturally into two secondary sections: Paul's circumstances (1:12–18a) and Paul's attitudes (1:18b–26). Even so, these two fit naturally into one primary theme. This is apparent in part by an inclusio consisting of the two times the word "advanced" (1:12) and "progress" (1:25) occur. They are the same Greek word though translated differently by CSB. Repeating them reveals Paul's commitment to understanding that life's circumstances move the gospel forward.

The section is emotion packed. Paul was moved by what surrounded him at Rome, and yet his joy was found elsewhere: in Christ and his purposes. The Philippians may have assumed the difficulties at Rome would discourage Paul. Paul's opening section assured them the opposite happened. Negative circumstances have, in separate ways, promoted the gospel. Paul saw beyond himself as the center of the events around him to the mission that organized his life.

Furthermore, this section is Christ-filled, contributing to Paul's joy. He was allowed the privilege of being Christ's follower in every kind of life situation. "Christ" occurs nine times in 1:12–26 and two times more in 1:27–30. Paul's "imprisonment is because [he is] in Christ"(1:13). He was pleased that "Christ" is preached, whether as a pretext or sincerely (1:15–18, three times). Paul expected deliverance from the "Spirit of Jesus Christ" (1:19). In the meantime, "Christ [would] be highly honored in [his] body" (1:20). The reason given is "to live is Christ" (1:21). He longed to "be with Christ" (1:23). He hoped through coming to see them again their "boasting in Christ Jesus [would] abound" (1:26). Paul's life cannot be understood apart from Christ, and his joy was obviously rooted in Jesus being prominent in every situation.

This first section of Philippians does not directly address Paul's concerns in writing. It is preliminary to the body of his message to them, beginning in 1:27. Yet the information brings more than casual interest. One would expect a friendly letter to begin in this way.[120]

[119] The difficulty in determining structure points should be considered in discussions of the unity of the letter. The fabric has few clear seams since firsthand references and bases of appeal occur throughout. There are also few section indicators: 1:12, "now I want you to know, brothers"; 1:27, "In addition"; 3:1, "finally"; 4:8. Twice "so that" (ὥστε) occurs as well as a minor sectional marker (2:12 and 4:1).

[120] See, for example, the excellent discussion in Witherington, III, *Paul's Letter*,71–78.

2.2.1 Paul's Circumstances (1:12–18a)

[12] Now I want you to know, brothers and sisters, that what has happened to me has actually advanced the gospel,[13] so that it has become known throughout the whole imperial guard, and to everyone else, that my imprisonment is because I am in Christ. [14] Most of the brothers have gained confidence in the Lord from my imprisonment and dare even more to speak the word fearlessly. [15] To be sure, some preach Christ out of envy and rivalry, but others out of good will. [16] These preach Christ out of love, knowing that I am appointed for the defense of the gospel; [17] the others proclaim Christ out of selfish ambition, not sincerely, thinking that they will cause me trouble in my imprisonment. [18] What does it matter? Only that in every way, whether from false motives or true, Christ is proclaimed, and in this I rejoice . . .

Structure

[12] Now I want you to know, brothers and sisters,
that what has happened to me has actually advanced the gospel
so that it has become known throughout the whole imperial guard,
and to everyone else,
that my imprisonment is because I am in Christ
[14] Most of the brothers have gained confidence in the Lord from my imprisonment
and dare even more to speak the word fearlessly.
[15] To be sure, some preach Christ out of envy and rivalry,
but others out of good will.
[16] These preach Christ out of love,
knowing that I am appointed for the defense of the gospel:
[17] the others proclaim Christ out of selfish ambition, not sincerely,
thinking they will cause me trouble in my imprisonment.
[18] What does it matter?
Only that . . . Christ is proclaimed
in every way
whether from false motives or true,
and in this I rejoice.

Note that 1:15–17 are in a chiastic arrangement. The corresponding parts are indicated by indention. The first statement of 1:15 corresponds to 1:17. The second statement of 1:15 corresponds to 1:16.

Interpretation

Verses 12–14 are one sentence in the Greek text. There is a statement of events (1:12) followed by two results (1:13–14), highlighting the progress of the gospel (1:12). The resulting witness about Christ to Roman guards (1:13) and preachers being encouraged (1:14–17) provide the actual manner in which the gospel went forth. This is followed by Paul's conclusion of the matter (1:18a).

The church desired to know Paul's circumstances, and he wanted to inform them. While his description is in some ways quite explicit, in other ways many questions remain unanswered. For one thing, Paul assumed that the church knew the details. If it did not, Epaphroditus would surely report more than Paul could write. Writing all that he felt could have jeopardized his legal situation. For another, what he wrote was one-sided, and the readers had to piece things together as best they could.

1:12 Rather than detail the hardships he faced, Paul took a divine perspective. He recognized that all events could be redeemed for the Lord's sake, and he took what advantage he could to continue his mission. The primary concern was that the gospel move forward. This happened through adverse circumstances, but as long as it happened, Paul could be joyful.

Paul did not specifically mention his imprisonment. The Greek text says simply "the things to me" (*ta kat' eme*). Most likely he included all the events from his imprisonment at Jerusalem through his imprisonment at Rome. These were the riot in Jerusalem at Passover, the two-year imprisonment at Caesarea, the appeal to Caesar, the threat on his life, the trip to Rome with its shipwreck, his house-arrest and restricted freedom, and the impending trial. However, the focus is on the events in Rome.[121] As Paul described them, he spoke in terms of their effect on the soldiers and the Roman church. In a purely descriptive way, he spoke of his "chains" (CSB "imprisonment," 1:13, 14, 17), which indicates his concern was primarily what happened in Rome.

The Philippian church might have expected the worst, but Paul countered that quickly. The gospel was advancing in Rome! The term "advanced" (*prokopen*) was used in the Greek-speaking world

[121] A. T. Robertson, *Paul's Joy in Jesus: Studies in Philippians* (Nashville: Broadman, n.d.), 41, adds all these events to the statement. It seems unlikely Paul stressed them all.

to describe blazing a trail before an army, the philosophical progress toward wisdom, and the progress of a young minister.[122] Paul, therefore, saw the events as forging new territory for the gospel. They took Paul into contact with a select group of people, soldiers and Roman officials, who otherwise would have had no relationship to him, and they also prompted a renewed evangelistic effort in the city. While others may have seen the events as marking the end of missionary activity, Paul saw the new ways the gospel could advance. The events which seemed to inhibit the freedom of the gospel became its catalyst. Paul did not say "in spite of" these events, but rather through them. There is a note of sacrifice here. Paul's private concerns did not matter; the gospel did.

2.2.1.1 Prisoner of Christ (1:13)

In explaining the situation at Rome, Paul disclosed two important results of the events that happened to him. Neither of these was expected, and thus Paul's word was news to them. At the same time, both reactions advanced the gospel; Paul made specific what he had claimed to be the case in 1:12. His statement there did not come without evidence. Even here, however, one of the reactions continued to be a mixed blessing, and it proved to be a continuing issue of the gospel's advance through difficulties.

1:13 In this undesirable situation at Rome, the gospel spread through the ranks of the soldiers. In essence Paul said they knew he was a prisoner of Christ, not just of Rome. The clarification of that fact was an encouragement since Paul would later state "to live is Christ" (1:21). Two matters deserve comment: the meaning of the phrase "in Christ" (derived from *phanerous en Christo*), and the meaning of "the imperial guard" (*praitoriom*).

Paul's basic reason for encouragement was that his real imprisonment became clear. Commentators differ on the meaning of the words "in Christ." Some think they imply something like "it became evident that I was a Christian," or "that I was a prisoner of Christ." Since Paul lived for the gospel, perhaps he stated he was not guilty of any charge brought against him and that the soldiers knew he could be released

---

[122] Robertson, 40–41. Interestingly he says, "The opposition to Paul in Rome had kicked the gospel upstairs" in this instance. Paul alone uses this verb and that only three times: 1:12, 25; and 1 Tim 4:15. In the latter instances, CSB translates the term "progress" instead.

except for his commitment to Christ. In the truest sense, he was a prisoner of Christ.[123] That prior relationship had led to him becoming a literal prisoner of Rome. Others interpret the phrase to mean that the chains of his imprisonment were "for Christ." Pointing out the awkward construction in Greek if any other interpretation holds, they state Paul was really a prisoner for the sake of Christ.[124] His predicament was because of the Christian message he proclaimed.[125]

Paul took advantage of the situation to call to mind a deeper slavery (1:1). In Eph 3:1, he referred to himself as "the prisoner of Christ." Surely, he intended a similar meaning here. Paul used words in such a way that they conveyed deeper meanings (not in violation of simpler meanings, however). The first interpretation above fits the context better than the second. Paul's joy came because what he lived for, the manifestation of Christ, was actually occurring. Further, the principle he held so dear was clarified to those around. They understood his slavery to Christ, which had made him an innocent prisoner of Rome.

Second, Paul said this knowledge spread in the praetorium. Considerable debate focuses on whether the *praetorium* (or palace guard) was a place (i.e., a barracks, or government administrative building) or a people (i.e., an elite imperial guard). On one hand, the *praetorium* was a place.[126] Those who interpret it as a place assume the place

---

[123] Caird, *Paul's Letters*, 110, provides a list of charges brought against Paul as found in Acts. They were sacrilege (21:28) and political agitation (24:5). He continues, "[Paul] had therefore been at pains to prove to all he met that loyalty to Christ was his sole offence."

[124] The Gk. construction puts "in Christ" after "my chains manifest." That is awkward if "chains in Christ" belong together. However, the verb "became" is also dislocated from the rest; the entire construction is unusual. The literal Gk. order is "so that my imprisonment manifest in Christ became." The CSB translates it, "my imprisonment is because I am in Christ."

[125] K. Barth, *The Epistle to the Philippians* (Richmond: John Knox, 1962), 26–27, n. 1, assumes such interpretations were commonly accepted but fail to satisfy the text. They assume Paul was expecting release because it became apparent his "crime" was being a Christian. At that time, that was no crime. Barth argues: (1) the positive outcome was an assumption of the interpreters and would not have been prominent in Paul's opening words; (2) the Roman Christians would have taken courage because there was nothing to fear for being a Christian is a wrong assumption; and (3) the Gk. order argues against it. His arguments lose their weight because this is not an essential assumption to the position. In fact, regardless of the outcome of the trial, Paul lived for Christ being honored in his body (1:20), and so would have joy regardless. Barth offers the rather strange interpretation that the bonds were "publicized in Christ," that the fact of Paul's imprisonment became a problem to all concerned, and many were reached through this word. His interpretation has little to commend it.

[126] Lightfoot, *Saint Paul's*, 99–104, indicates the word could mean the general's tent, the residence of a governor or prince, any spacious palace, the imperial residence on the Palatine, the barracks attached to the imperial palace itself, the great camp of the praetorian soldiers, or

was either the barracks of the imperial guard or a general government administration building.[127] The evidence from Acts reveals Paul had his own leased dwelling, so he could not have been incarcerated at the praetorium (Acts 28:30). If the matter is seen this way, Paul stated the topic of conversation in the barracks, or in the head Roman administration building, was Paul and Christ. On the other hand, the praetorium was also a group of men. The term stood for the emperor's bodyguard of nine cohorts. They were the only troops stationed in Italy after Augustus.[128] Although Paul did not claim people of the guard were converted, he did claim they heard his message.[129]

That Paul referred to the Praetorian Guard is further supported by the statement "and to everyone else." In Greek, one preposition introduces the two, which are also joined by "and." This reads, then, "in the whole praetorium and all the rest." "All the rest" cannot mean all the other buildings.[130] The rest must be people elsewhere who also knew the significance of Paul's imprisonment. Since they are associated with the Praetorian Guard, perhaps they were other government officials who knew first-hand of Paul's situation.

This reveals an amazing aspect of God's working in and through Paul. How would the young and relatively obscure (Christian) faith gain a hearing among the empire's elite? Such people had little interest in a novel idea that sprang from so ideologically insignificant a place as Judea. Jews were notoriously anti-Rome. Judea was an imperial province because of its strategic importance to the Roman Empire,

---

a body of men, the imperial guard. His discussion provides the basic evidence of the varieties of usage.

[127] As noted earlier, Flexsenhar, III, "The Provenance," 27, clearly demonstrates there were praetorium(s) [English] in many Greco-Roman cities, particularly those of strategic importance to the empire. His work intends to demonstrate a different provenance for Philippians than Rome. See Introduction. He argues against the word being used of people, more particularly a "palace guard."

[128] Caird, *Paul's Letters*, 110.

[129] This conclusion assumes Paul wrote from Rome. If Ephesus or Caesarea were the location of writing, the term possibly could have referred to a building. The arguments for and against a building rest on some assumptions. Certainly Paul would not call the emperor's residence on Palatine Hill a "praetorium," yet some say a visitor from the east could easily call a building something it was not. The text is best satisfied if Paul had the guard in mind. Naturally, the guard needed barracks, but the stress appears to be on the people who heard and transmitted the word.

[130] Fee, *Philippians*, 114, n. 36 well states, "Some earlier interpreters (Chrysostom, Calvin) suggest 'in all other places' (KJV; cf. Moffatt). But that is against all analogy, and in this case is nearly impossible."

largely due to its geographical location as the gateway from Europe/Asia to Africa. Few Romans ruled the Jews well. There was constant discord and threat of rebellion.[131] The gospel advanced to otherwise inaccessible new people in new places because of the things that "happened to" Paul. Keown references Gromacki's observation that if soldiers rotated in six-hour shifts with no soldier repeating shifts for the period of Paul's two-year imprisonment, Paul would have had access to 3,000 different soldiers (assuming one soldier per shift). If four-hour shifts, the number would be 4,380 shifts.[132] Whether or not that is a close estimation, Paul had a significant impact.

2.2.1.2 Christians Encouraged to Speak (1:14–18a)

1:14 The first result of the events Paul mentions refer to Rome's military and political organizations. The second result of Paul's circumstances involved the church(es) at Rome. A new evangelistic effort sprang up, affecting the entire Christian community. Paul saw his situation was the catalyst for renewed interest in outreach, and he knew that would be encouraging news to the church at Philippi. Living with the vestiges of strongly Roman influence, they, perhaps more than other churches, exercised their faith against the ever-present backdrop of Rome. If the gospel could find some acceptance in Rome and preachers were encouraged to speak, perhaps the same dynamic could operate with full power in Philippi.

In actuality, the churches at Rome had two different reactions. Some preachers were encouraged by Paul and preached out of sympathy; others hoped to get Paul into more trouble with the Roman officials. Paul focused first on the brethren who supported him. It was a positive statement in what could have appeared as discouraging news. After the strong statement about the advance of the gospel, Paul spoke of the divided state in the churches at Rome. He was able to see beyond the differences in motivation and realized Christ was proclaimed. He was comforted by this reality.

---

[131] Numerous facts bear this out. Among them are these: (1) Rome had Senatorial Provinces and Imperial Provinces. Usually, Imperial Provinces were more strategic to Rome's economy. (2) Procurators generally had short careers in Judea. Pontius Pilate was the most successful, serving from AD 26–36. He was, however, banished to Spain for mishandling the Jews. (3) Herod built a Roman fortress on one corner of the temple complex to assure Roman access to potential uprisings associated with the temple.

[132] Keown, *Philippians 1:1–2:18*, 191, n. 69.

Most of the Christians took heart from Paul's situation.[133] They preached more courageously and fearlessly. Some commentators have suggested that the increase in believers' preaching occurred because they knew that Paul's only crime was Christianity, and that was no crime at all. Before they had feared their own imprisonment; now that fear no longer existed. There is no evidence for that interpretation, however. While Paul's general tone was optimistic, he never indicated he knew the trial would exonerate him. Paul stated, "Most of the brothers have gained confidence in the Lord from my imprisonment." He emphasized their spiritual motivation, not the evidence they might have derived from Paul's circumstances.

A major concern occurs in the placement of the phrase "in the Lord." Some see the phrase as "brothers in the Lord," i.e., Christians, who were encouraged. The primary arguments in favor of this understanding include the notion the natural reading of the text makes a prepositional phrase follow what it modifies, and normally "gained confidence" (*pepoitha*) comes first in its clause. Other views take the phrase as "gained confidence in the Lord." They say the phrase "brothers in the Lord" involves a redundancy (where else would brothers be?); "in the Lord" comes first for emphasis, and other times the verb *pepoitha* is followed by the preposition "in." The arguments do not clearly favor one over the other. Nevertheless, similar constructions with the verb occur in 2:24; 3:3–4, and the prepositional phrase follows (see also, for example, Rom 14:14; 2 Thess 3:4). The better understanding is that these are brothers who have "gained confidence in the Lord," as CSB indicates.

Further, the context assumes their preaching came from Paul's imprisonment, not the expected release. As the next verses indicate, their support for Paul had given them courage to preach God's word.[134]

---

[133] Some statements reveal Paul expected to be freed. He knew how law operated because he was a Jewish lawyer and knew where he stood with the Roman government officially. Nevertheless, Christianity was an unknown factor in the empire, and Paul was the first serious test case of the official Roman attitude toward it. Paul's optimism resulted from his reading of the situation coupled with his spiritual insights. There is no evidence he had an inside track on the outcome of the trial. But see 1:19.

[134] The UBS Greek text simply says "to be speaking the word." Some translations follow, including the KJV, as does the CSB. The NIV, however, has "to proclaim the gospel." This interpretation is no doubt correct, as the variant readings affirm. The stronger external evidence supports it, and the internal evidence is indeterminate. The words "of God" may have been part of the original, but if not, the earliest interpretations worked their way into the text. Given the principle of the shorter reading preferred, "of God" probably should not be included.

1:15–17 After disclosing the positive fact of supporting preachers, Paul turned his thoughts to the more complex situation. Not all agreed with Paul. It seems he expected his audience to know that by his introducing words "[t]o be sure, some preach . . . " Paul acknowledged they preached Christ, but not everyone preached about Christ with proper motivations. Paul described two groups of preachers who reacted to him. His descriptions fall into a literary pattern of a chiasm, a common literary device for indicating contrasting elements and relative importance between them:[135]

A To be sure, some preach Christ out of envy and rivalry,
  B but others out of good will [proclaim Christ.]
  B′ These preach out of love,
    knowing that I am appointed for the defense of the gospel;
A′ the others proclaim Christ out of selfish ambition, not sincerely,
    thinking that they will cause me trouble in my imprisonment.

Several observations may be made. First, there are two contrasting classes of preachers: those opposed to and those supporting Paul. In addition, because of the emphases found in chiasms, the "A, A′" members receive the emphasis. Therefore, Paul's mind turned to his opposition. Furthermore, Paul stated the message is "Christ." It occurs in this chiasm in two places, summarizing each set of preachers. Preaching Christ is synonymous to "speak[ing] the word fearlessly" (1:14). Moreover, two different constructions are used consistently of the preachers. "[O]ut of envy and rivalry" and "out of good will" occur with an accusative construction in Greek, typically revealing the standard by which they are measured. Preaching "out of love; out of selfish ambition" occur in the genitive (ablative) case, indicating a source of their preaching. The two sets of contrasts are, therefore, different in their constructions and interpretive nuances (grammatically, A, B are the same; A′, B′ are too). These characteristics, then, are not simply lined up to reinforce Paul's point. They are presented in different ways, indicating different explanations for each. Finally, the last two contrasts of each (A′ and B′) have more extensive modifying clauses explaining them (B′: "knowing that I am appointed for the defense of the gospel"; A′: "thinking that they will cause me trouble in my

[135] A chiasm is a literary device containing two or more sets of members arranged in an ABBA pattern. In chiasms, the outside members (A, A′) receive the emphasis.

imprisonment"). The primary points are clear; the secondary points add color and precise understanding.

The ones preaching to harm Paul are discussed in 1:15a, 17. The content reveals a close connection between vv. 14–15, but the translators show a separation. The only complaint against the preachers of 1:15 is they had wrong motives. They were nevertheless brothers. The first portion of the chiastic unit mildly changes to describing an activity unexpected of brothers. The translation "[t]o be sure" captures the thought. Some opposed Paul, but that was a minor obstacle.

1:15a Paul exposed their method and motivations. The motive was "(through) envy and rivalry."[136] The words always suggest relationships which have spoiled, and the terms normally occur in Paul's lists of sins to avoid. In fact, in Rom 1:29 such language is used of those who should know God through creation but have rejected him. More specifically, in Gal 5:21, those who practice such things identified there "will not inherit the kingdom of God." Since Paul referred to them in 1:14 as "brothers," he does not consider them unsaved. They are acting in ways characteristic of non-Christians, however. One other time Paul used the words instructively. In 1 Tim 6:3–4 they are used of "anyone [who] teaches false doctrine"; that person is "conceited." This comes closer to Paul's use here. In 1 Timothy, however, Paul used the term to refer to those who also have doctrinal and practical deviations from the faith, thus promoting ungodliness. It is surprising Paul chose such strong, negative words to describe some of Rome's preachers: words often associated with unbelievers.

Of what were these Christians jealous and contentious? The two clues presented together describe one activity. They are joined by one preposition (CSB says "out of"). "Envy" implies jealousy or activity directed toward someone who has something desired by the actor. It seems quite inappropriate directed toward a Roman prisoner! Paul's imprisonment is beside the point, though they hope to make use of it to further their cause. Rather, they must have had some issue with Paul's popularity among Roman Christians. Perhaps his previous letter to

[136] The Gk. construction has the preposition διά with the accusative case for these. Strictly speaking, it should show the standard by which something is measured. Modern linguistics, however, has warned about pressing classical semantic and grammatical distinctions without warrant from the context. These warnings should be heeded, and the distinction made here may press the construction and the difference between it and the description of v. 17 (ἐξ ἐριθείας). Nevertheless, the shades of variation do occur, and at least a slight difference exists between the two.

them (the book of Romans) may have displayed his wisdom and courage in addressing both theological and practical areas of contention in that Christian community (see Rom 14–15, for example). Along with his generally perceived stature in the emerging Christian world, Paul was a popular and persuasive preacher.

Their envy expressed itself in activity, as it usually does. "Rivalry" describes taking sides for or against the envious. The men's activity involves not only preaching, but some form of political interests within the Christian community. Who will be first among them? Paul, or someone else? To make their case, they combine their jealousy with preaching Christ. Jealousy and preaching Christ do not go together, as argued by the Philippian correspondence. Yet even Christian leaders can act in ungodly ways, often in the name of the Christ they proclaim. The first description of Paul's opponents is their polarizing activity in the Christian community. It is, of course, the first obvious characteristic since motives are often subliminal.[137]

1:15b–17 Paul used the same construction in stating others preached "out of (through) good will." Certainly, their good will was not directed toward the Roman authorities. Roman emperors had a record of opposing Jews in Rome and that could easily include Christians, as happened shortly after this with Emperor Nero's change of heart toward Christians in AD 64. It was unlikely it was good will toward the church. In fact, some would no doubt think the best course of action for the church would have been to remain silent and allow unity and harmony to prevail. The good will must be directed to Paul. The apostle describes here how the events in Rome focus on him, which is the interest of the Philippian church, and his statements are couched in personal terms. "Good will" refers to favor toward him. It is highly unlikely Christian preaching could or would influence a high-level Roman trial. They were not seeking to lobby for Paul's release; instead, they were hoping their renewed ambition to preach Christ would somehow lift Paul's burden and fulfill the joy of his mission. They would cooperate with Paul.

In 1:16, Paul continued his description of supporting preachers who "preach out of love." As noted above, the construction used here indicates source. It is used of Paul's supporters first, and the same

[137] Fee, *Philippians*, 120, suggests they have a "kind of unsavory delight that enjoys kicking an opponent who is down; they now view Paul's imprisonment (evidence of God's judgment?) as their chance to preach Christ 'correctly.'"

construction, with different wording, occurs with his opposition. The work of supporting Paul through their preaching emanated from their love. Paul does not directly indicate an object for love, though the subject is obviously the preachers. It is similar to 1:9, and the reader is left to understand the broadest application of love. It encompasses love for God (and Christ), but in a more pointed sense it includes love for Paul. Identifying this motivation comforts the anxious Philippians who wonder if anyone is supporting their friend. There are preachers in Rome who care, though their care may be confined to what they can do—preach the gospel.

Their love-motivated preaching is encouraged by what they know. "Knowing" is factual, rather than experiential.[138] They are aware of God's plan for Paul and the deeper reason he is in prison. Paul makes the reason explicit by stating he is "appointed for the defense of the gospel." Two words elucidate this: appointed and defense. The first reveals a theological understanding of Paul's unique place in God's missionary program. The words "I am appointed" translate the Greek word *keimai* ("I have been set").[139] Paul used the word (*keimai*) to express the divine purpose of his imprisonment, which was "the defense of the gospel."

Paul revealed a similar self-understanding in Gal 1:15–16. In a statement that parallels Jeremiah's experience (cf. Jer 1:5), Paul explained God set him apart even while he was in his mother's womb, called him by grace, and prepared him to preach the gospel to the Gentiles (Gal 1:15).[140] He could not foresee all the situations he would encounter in responding daily to God's call on his life. He knew his appointment involved suffering as a regular part of his ministry,[141] however, and he knew God called him to defend and present the truth of the gospel to both Jews and Gentiles. His defense before Jews

---

[138] This is a perfect participle from οἶδα, to know by perception or intellect rather than γινώσκω, to know by experience or knowledge in process. The understanding of Paul's calling was clearly known, not something to "grow into" (1:9 uses ἐπιγινώσκω, by contrast).

[139] The word κεῖμαι is "lie or recline" literally. It is built on a perfect tense paradigm and, thus, came to express an appointment. It could well be translated "I have been set" toward the end its context describes.

[140] The parallel with Jeremiah goes beyond the words and the concept of election in the womb. Perhaps Paul began to identify with Jeremiah early in his ministry (at the time of writing Galatians, ca. AD 49). Jeremiah suffered during his lifetime as a fulfillment of the divine plan. In a similar way, Paul would suffer, too.

[141] See Acts 9:16; Col 1:24; Phil 3:10.

reached a theological climax at the Jerusalem Council when it was decided Gentiles did not need to adopt Jewish patterns of life, worship, and service. Throughout his ministry, however, he had to live out that agreement, many times among those who did not accept it as well as the Jerusalem apostles did. Paul's presence in Rome occasioned this segment of the ongoing debate. His defense before Rome also had a long developing history. In several cities where he founded churches, Paul defended himself against Gentile attacks which often involved the accusation that he preached something unlawful for them (cf. Acts 17:6–9; 18:12–14; 19:24–41; 26:19–20).

Paul recognized from these experiences that he not only encountered Jewish opposition but also had to answer to Rome. No doubt as he traveled the many miles of Roman roads, he planned how to defend the gospel should such an occasion arise. Paul's defense involved the gospel. Others may have thought about the repercussions of their preaching in relation to their own lives, but Paul lived for the gospel. For him, the opportunity to appear before Caesar provided a test case for the gospel. Would it be accepted? Perhaps there is a note of anticipation as well as resolution. He was the apostle to the Gentiles. He struggled to deliver the gospel to them, yet soon he would have opportunity to present the "new ideology" to the emperor. Paul knew in a real way the task of Gentile evangelism was his, and he had opportunity for a major step forward. The emperor of the whole empire would actually hear the gospel.

Paul would naturally present the claims of Christ to the emperor. He also recognized his privilege of possibly changing the world's official attitude toward Christianity. In the early years, the church thrived in part because the Roman government mistook it for a sect of Judaism. Judaism was a sanctioned religion (*religio licita*). With the spread of Christianity beyond Jewish geography and the increasingly Gentile character of the church, the central Roman question was, "Is it legal?" In addition to proclaiming Christ is Lord, even over Caesar, Paul hoped to convince the Roman government that Christians were harmless to it and that Christianity should be legalized. Only God could orchestrate such an encounter, and Paul was prepared to take full advantage of it. He would "defend" the gospel, and his supporters joined with him as they could.

Following the two statements describing friendly preaching, Paul returned to his opponents. As the "outside" members of the chiasm, they receive the emphasis since the source of their activity is "selfish ambition." The origins of the word designating "selfish ambition" are obscure. If the term derives from *eritheia*, the word occurs only in Aristotle's writings prior to the NT. There it denotes seeking political office for personal ambition.[142] Others trace it to the root *erithos* which denotes hired labor, or day labor.[143] Either word conveys something done for personal gain or advantage. These preachers somehow hope to improve their reputation or status by their preaching. On the surface, it is difficult to see how bringing more trouble to Paul would improve their status.

Paul stated his supporters knew he was "appointed for the defense of the gospel" (1:16), while his antagonists hoped to "cause [him] trouble in [his] imprisonment" (1:17). Opponents saw this as the time to silence Paul. They hoped—or perhaps imagined[144]—to bring affliction to him and, perhaps, to sway the sympathies of the emperor against him. Paul described their intent to raise up trouble, for which he used a word normally translated tribulation (*thlipsis*). It is unlikely they sought bodily harm, which would be difficult to accomplish given Paul's circumstances. Perhaps their zeal was to influence Rome against him at his impending trial, hoping to add to his distress. Doubtless they rejoiced that Paul's fate lay in the hands of Rome and they added to that the emotional pressures that came when what Paul believed and promoted was effectively used against him.

Whether for or against Paul, the proclamation subject was Christ. Three times in 1:15–18 Paul used the expression Christ is being proclaimed (vv. 15, 17, 18). These amplify his words in 1:14 in his general statement introducing the situation. The majority of the brothers dared "to speak the word fearlessly." The word is explained as Christ. His readers would understand proclaiming Christ involved more than the uniqueness of Jesus. The title symbolized the entirety of the gospel message. It was of Jesus Christ: his virgin birth, his sinless life, his vicarious death, his powerful resurrection, and his reign as Lord. If they had deviated from any portion of this, Paul would certainly have identified their points of heresy. He seemed content to accept their message apparently as the same as his.

---

142 Fowl, *Philippians*, 41, n. 16. The word is ἐπιθεία (*epitheia*).

143 Fee, *Philippians*, 121, n. 21; Keown, *Philippians 1:1–2:18*, 109.

144 This may better capture the feeling of this word οἰόμενοι.

1:18a This attitude is reinforced in Paul's summary. "What does it matter?" is a good translation of the literal "for what?" What is the ultimate significance of this? Paul moved to the critical point which serves to summarize up to v. 18, then is reinforced by what follows (1:18b–25). Once again he presents the alternate positions: "false motives or true." "False motives" comes from the Greek word usually translated "pretense." A pretense is a cover for something else. The opponents' preaching was a cover intended to hide their motives, and while the pretense was insufficient to cover their blatant attitudes, they did preach Christ. Contrasting with pretense, Paul's supporters preached truthfully. Truth indicates their motives were consistent with their message: there was no hypocrisy.

Paul derived joy from their preaching Christ by looking at the positive side of all their preaching. Summarizing this section, Paul ends with "in this I rejoice." "This" could refer to the entire previous section, 1:12–17. It is unlikely Paul rejoiced that some were opponents and their strategy was to defeat him by more energetic preaching. "This" refers to the immediately preceding statement, which has been repeated verbatim in this section. When Christ was the topic of conversation, Paul rejoiced. It mattered little about his circumstances; what mattered greatly was Christ.

Such a disclosure of the situation at Rome prompts the question of who the rival group was. Some have suggested they were Judaizers like those who troubled Paul at Galatia and, perhaps, in Phil 3. Paul had little sympathy for Judaizers, however. His harshest words were against their theology and methodology.[145] They hardly fit the accepting attitude of Paul in this text. He would have noted their heresy as he did on virtually every other occasion where they appear. Others suggest they were preachers who believed martyrdom was a high ideal. They preached with an intent of bringing Paul to martyrdom, while realizing that whatever consequences he received, they would likely bear as well.[146]

---

[145] See Galatians, Paul's most abrupt letter. In Galatians, Paul did not even thank God for the believers or their Christian experience. His concern for them brought him straight to the point at hand. Even Corinth with its party spirit did not receive such harsh treatment.

[146] This suggestion fits the second century better than the first. When persecution became widespread and martyrdom became quite probable, a theology of martyrdom developed and Christians prayed for it. A form of this, however, is argued in Hawthorne, *Philippians*, 35, and in his earlier article "Phil 1:12–19 with special reference to vv. 15, 16, 17," *ExpTim* 62 (1950–51): 316ff.

These preachers, however, preached against Paul out of jealousy. They could hardly have hoped to bring Paul to a higher spiritual stature if they were envious of what he already had. This suggestion has little to commend it. A third possibility is that they preached against the Jews for what they did to Paul.[147] The Jewish flavor of the situation is quite likely, but preaching against the people who opposed Paul does not fit the context. Furthermore, the Jewish Christian population of Rome seemed large. Nothing would be gained by denigrating them. Paul stated they preached with reference to him.

Finally, some scholars note the opponents preached against Paul. Perhaps they did so because of his weaknesses. The fact that he was a prisoner demonstrated for them he was not who he claimed to be. Surely, he would triumph in Christ if God were with him. Instead, they said that God had manifested his presence through them. Paul responded by saying what was manifest about him: Christ.[148]

More than likely, the problem arose from the dynamics of the Roman church and Paul's relationship to it. Possibly the situation resembled that of Corinth, where the various factions rallied around one great leader or another.[149] The situation at Rome was pluralistic. No great Christian leaders were there before Paul arrived, so there was no primary apostle. Perhaps many vied for the position or, at the least, they did not want someone from the outside claiming that status.

Rome welcomed various ethnic groups and cultural practices. Normally immigrants lived in common tenement houses arranged by ethnic and language neighborhoods. Sometimes various groups subdivided by ideologies or places of origin. For example, the city had at least thirteen Jewish synagogues, which probably served Jews from different places in the empire.[150] How the church fit into that social and ethnic structure is difficult to discern. The issues that separated the Gentile and Jewish Christians had become more pronounced with

---

[147] F. C. Synge, *Philippians and Colossians* (London: Torch Bible Commentaries, 1951), 24–25.

[148] This suggestion has much to commend it based on the situation at Corinth, where Paul's opponents did attack his weaknesses with a "theology of triumphalism." There is little in the epistolary context to support it except the reference to "manifest," a word which does not appear in CSB. Greater evidence may come from the historical context since Philippi was at the north end of the peninsula from Corinth. See R. Jewett, "Conflicting Movements in the Early Church as Reflected in Philippians," *NovT* 12 (1970): 362–90.

[149] Beare, *The Epistle*, 59.

[150] Caird, *Paul's Letters*, 111.

the expulsion of all Jews from Rome in AD 49 and their return in AD 54. No doubt Gentiles dominated at least during the period of expulsion, and they probably vied for power and leadership when the Jews returned. Earlier, Paul had written to the Roman church with a major concern about unity between Jews and Gentiles. Although the letter to Rome was written five years before Philippians, the complexities of the situation surely continued until Paul arrived in Rome.[151]

The situation regarding Paul is difficult to untangle. Tensions arose between and among the various groupings: Jews against themselves, Gentiles against Jews, Jews against Gentiles, and various Gentile factions against each other. Further, Paul entered this difficult situation with the authority of the apostle to the Gentiles but limited by the Roman government. All of the groups within the church knew him, but not all welcomed him.

Perhaps a theological tension underlay the social and economic situation. Paul championed Gentile freedom from the law. In his Roman letter, he had sided with the Gentiles in affirming they did not need to keep the practices of Jewish culture.[152] Although the Jewish Christians would have expected support from Paul, no doubt it forced an intense debate on the matter. The debate followed Paul wherever he went, and his arrival at Rome perhaps triggered it again. Most likely it involved the law. Paul's writings and the historical data reveal Paul had intense conflicts over the relevance of the Ten Commandments and the ceremonial aspects of Jewish law. Additionally, the argument in Phil 3 concerned these matters. There the debate intensified and broadened beyond the concerns of the preachers of Phil 1.

Paul evaluated these preachers carefully and objectively. Three areas of concern emerge in his evaluation of others: their methods, their motives, and their message. They clearly had a correct message. Christ was proclaimed (1:14–18). Likewise, their methods caused no

---

[151] On the situation at Rome, see the excellent though dated article by W. Wiefel, "The Jewish Community in Ancient Rome and the Origins of Roman Christianity," reprinted in *The Romans Debate*, ed. Karl Donfried (Minneapolis: Augsburg, 1977), 100–19.

[152] The debate between Jews and Gentiles permeates the letter, but the focal passage is Rom 14:1–15:6. There the specific matters included days and diet. On the surface they sound like Jewish versus Gentile distinctions. On deeper reflection, however, they clearly were in some measure Gentile Christian issues as well. The meat issue was neither clean versus unclean nor meat offered to idols. It was over vegetarianism. These make the specific identity of the problem difficult. On the other hand, they do point out the complexities of the varieties of Christian experiences at Rome.

problem. The text reveals only one way of ministry: they preached. The point of difference was their motives. Motivations generally remain inside and quiet, but these preachers quite openly explained their motives.[153] Paul had a great concern for motives in the ministry,[154] yet he did not attack these preachers the way he did others. Apparently, this was because they acted against him personally, not toward the gospel or the general Christian community. He chose to look on the bright side since the message and the method furthered the truth. God alone can deal with motives!

Theological and Practical Points

Though Paul's description of his circumstances will continue below, it is helpful to note some overriding themes.

1) Paul experienced joy. The section culminates with that idea twice (1:18). His discussion of his circumstances served to anticipate what he expected might come their way in Philippi. Their suffering amounted to little compared with Paul's (1:29). Disclosing his genuine joy in spite of hard things served both to inform the church of his well-being and to model Christ's attitude even in the shadow of the cross (Heb 12:2). Later Paul would reinforce joy by challenging them to live their Christian faith. They were to "Rejoice in the Lord" (Phil 4:4). Here, however, Paul's joy was in the proclamation of the gospel. At conversion, he was called by Christ to "take [his] name to Gentiles, kings, and Israelites" (Acts 9:15). As his thought developed, Paul saw that commission was directly foretold in the OT but largely misunderstood by Jewish Christians (Eph 3:1–7). He approached this commission like he had approached all of life: he gave everything to it. His ultimate satisfaction was in the conversion of Gentiles, and he saw that conversion as the fulfillment of his life work (Phil 2:16). In Rome, even in house arrest, he anticipated presenting the gospel to the emperor. In odd ways and circumstances, his commission to "take [Jesus'] name to . . . kings" would be fulfilled. Joy emerges as people live in accord with God's call on their lives. The closer their

---

[153] Otherwise Paul could not have known them for sure, and it is doubtful that he would have discussed them so openly had their motives not been common knowledge. This in itself points out the arrogance of the situation—they openly and energetically opposed Paul.

[154] This is evidenced by the way he defended his own motives when he was attacked (1 Thess 1–2; 1 Cor 1–4; 2 Corinthians and his warnings regarding other preachers' motives (2 Tim 3:1–9; Titus 1:10–11).

lives align with that call, the more eagerly they anticipate what God can do. There is joy. Regardless of motives, Christ became the topic of conversation throughout Rome, validating Paul's life and his calling.

The conflicting circumstances force an understanding of genuine Christian joy. Joy comes from the choices made to live as God intends. Suffering and inconvenience may accompany that. Even in the difficulties of life, the privileges of being "in Christ" outweigh them. Knowing God who "started a good work" and "will carry it on to completion until the day of Christ" brings a foundation and reference point for life. We "eagerly wait for a Savior" (1:5–7; 3:20–21) and the fulfillment of what lies ahead in Christ. Confidence that God is bringing us to that point enables right choices and inner joy. Paul chose to look at the positive benefits of God's working rather than the inconveniences it brought to him. Joy was not based on external circumstances. He lived with joy.

2) Paul lived above the turmoil of personal or party interests in ministry. The preachers could—and did—have their own reasons for preaching. They apparently rallied believers to their perspectives as they could. Paul did not side with either openly. He let them preach; they were not accountable to him. He lived his life true to his calling and expected others to do the same. As long as the message was correct, preaching Christ, Paul was vindicated. Without doubt he preferred proper motives in the preachers and alliance with him in proclaiming the gospel. Nevertheless, Paul was satisfied that people were hearing the gospel. He had his own calling to fulfill.

3) The gospel unifies. The gospel is the critical point of church unity. Better stated, correct understanding and proclamation of Jesus Christ is the rallying point for the church. While in Rome, Paul did not identify the multiple issues we find addressed in the Letter to the Romans, written four or five years earlier, which they would have read since that letter or vestiges of it were circulated. Rather than obscure the gospel by making secondary issues primary, Paul knew that if all would focus on the lordship of Jesus Christ, the churches could move ahead in unity. That was his previous message when addressing amoral issues so prevalent at Rome. "Before his own Lord he stands or falls. . . . [W]e live for the Lord . . . we die for the Lord . . . we belong to the Lord" (Rom 14:4, 8). The letter to his supportive friends at Philippi could have represented a time to vocalize discontent about those who differed with him and divided the church. He refrained. The secondary issues were secondary. The gospel united, and in that Paul was joyful.

4) Evaluating preachers. This passage contains a helpful way to evaluate the various preachers of Christ. Three concerns arise potentially causing division: motive, methods, and message. Here Paul reveals his satisfaction in both the message and the method. In other places he expressed concern about them both (Gal 1:6–9; 1 Tim 6:3–10). He knew and understood the motives found in the divided Roman Christian community. He exposed the various motives for preaching, using both strongly affirming and harshly condemning language. Beyond that, he was content to allow God to search hearts and render judgment where and if appropriate.

5) Confidence in God's sovereignty. Underlying all was Paul's confidence in God's sovereignty. God will accomplish his plan, and he is able to take the events of life and incorporate them into his purposes. Perhaps this, more than anything, gave Paul joy.

2.2.2 Paul's Attitude (1:18b–26)

18b *Yes, and I will continue to rejoice* 19 *because I know this will*
lead to my salvation through your prayers and help from the Spirit
of Jesus Christ. 20 *My eager expectation and hope is that I will not be*
ashamed about anything, but that now as always, with all courage,
Christ will be highly honored in my body, whether by life or by death.
21 *For me, to live is Christ and to die is gain.* 22 *Now if I live on in the*
flesh, this means fruitful work for me; and I don't know which one I
should choose. 23 *I am torn between the two. I long to depart and be*
*with Christ—which is far better—*24*but to remain in the flesh is more*
necessary for your sake. Since I am persuaded of this, I know that I
will remain and continue with all of you for your progress and joy in
the faith, 26 *so that, because of my coming to you again, your boasting*
in Christ Jesus may abound.

Structure

Yes, and I will continue to rejoice
  19 because I know this will lead to my salvation
    through your prayers
    and help from the Spirit of Jesus Christ.
20 My eager expectation and hope is that I will not be ashamed about anything,
  but that now as always, with all courage, Christ will be highly honored in
    my body,
      whether by life or by death.
21 For me, to live is Christ and to die is gain.

22 Now if I live on in the flesh, this means fruitful work for me;
  and I don't know which one I should choose.

23 I am torn between the two.
  I long to depart and be with Christ—which is far better—
  24 but to remain in the flesh is more necessary for your sake.

    Since I am persuaded of this, I know that I will remain and
      continue with all of you for your progress and joy in the faith,
        26 so that, because of my coming to you again, your
          boasting in Christ Jesus may abound.

Interpretation

Paul's situation caused deep reflection. His concerns were twofold: the outcome of his imprisonment and trial and the possibility of death. These verses reveal the tensions in Paul's life. The tribulations he endured reached their zenith as he awaited his trial. In many ways, that was his finest hour for the gospel. The commitments which drove him in his life now kept him as he contemplated his death. Even in the midst of such deep reflection, Paul was optimistic. He would be saved, Christ would be glorified one way or another, and the gospel would go forth.

Structurally, two questions arise in these verses. The first is, Where does the section begin? The second relates to the progress of thought through 1:18–26: Are there one, two, or three movements? Regardless of the number of movements, Paul's argument progresses with one discussion flowing from a previous idea. The thought of joy (1:18a) brought to mind the expectation of continued joy in the future (1:18b). In v. 20 Paul introduced the concept of death, and in 1:21–24 the themes of life and death are further developed. Finally, 1:24 ends with a desire to do what was best for the Philippians, and 1:25–26 continues the themes of remaining on earth and sacrificing for them.

It is a carefully composed section that expressed Paul's commitments and his emotions.

2.2.2.1 Paul's Joy In Salvation (1:18–24)

1:18 The section begins in v. 18. The CSB translators (and HCSB) assumed 1:18b continues 1:12 and makes the paragraph break at 1:20. Alternatively, the NIV breaks the text at 1:18a, with 1:18b beginning a new paragraph that continues through 1:26. Most contemporary commentators make a break after 1:18a.[155] The theme of the preachers continues until that point, and Paul ended the previous section on a note of joy. The repetition of the word "rejoice" serves as a transition, providing another reason for Paul's joy: his own anticipation of success in the trial that lay before him, or in a greater sense, the salvation he expects.[156]

The second structural question relates to the movements within the section. The question is whether they should be seen as three different ideas or two. Those who see three separate units argue the grammar suggests them. The first unit is 1:18b–20, which is one sentence in the Greek text. It is noted by "for" (*gar*) as Paul states "because ["for"] I know this will lead to my salvation . . ." The second unit is 1:21–24. This contains the section about life and death and is introduced by "for" (*gar*), as is the first section ("For me, to live is Christ"). The third unit is 1:25–26, which is one sentence in Greek introduced by the expression "and having this confidence."[157]

This arrangement is quite possible, but so is a two-unit arrangement. Two basic parallels confirm the flow of thought. The main verb of 1:18b–19 is "I know,"[158] and that same verb is repeated in 1:25. The other parallel is a conceptual tie between "I will . . . rejoice,"

---

155 For good argumentation for the break here, see Fee, *Philippians*, 128–129; Hellerman, *Philippians*, 56; Keown, *Philippians 1:1–2:13*, 221; Thomas Moore, *Philippians: An Exegetical Guide for Preaching and Teaching*, Big Greek Idea Series, ed. Herbert W. Bateman, IV (Grand Rapids: Kregel Academic, 2019), 76–77.

156 Hawthorne, *Philippians*, 39, refers to the work of M. E. Thrall, *Greek Particles in the New Testament*, NTTS 3 (Grand Rapids: Eerdmans, 1962), 11–16, to demonstrate the construction "but and" (ἀλλὰ καί) begins a new section. He translates it well: "And in addition I will be glad for still another reason."

157 The CSB translates it, "Since I am persuaded of this." This three-unit arrangement acknowledges the two times the conjunction is γάρ and the sentence units. Further, the thematic analysis reveals the cogency of these units as "self-contained" in thought.

158 This is not the main verb of the sentence; technically, that is "rejoice." That, however, is introductory and not as tightly tied grammatically to the γάρ clause that follows.

which introduces the phrase "I know," and "persuaded of this," which introduces the second. Paul's joy and confidence were two expressions of the same attitude: He would be able to achieve his deepest desires of glorifying Christ. The same ideas and root words occur in 1:4–6, where Paul's prayer for the Philippians was both joyful and confident. Here Paul's desire was that Christ would be magnified in his life, and his confidence was that he would remain for their edification.[159]

Paul's optimism was obvious. But why was he optimistic? Was it because he expected to be released from prison soon? Was it that he knew whatever happened, he was surely to be delivered from this evil world? Was it a joy that came from a backward glance to his conversion experience that sustained him through the difficulties of the present? These three suggestions call for careful analysis, and they are not necessarily mutually exclusive. The first section contains two parts: a description of Paul's salvation and hope (1:18b–20) and an expression of his commitment to them (1:21–24).

1:18b–20 Paul fully expected deliverance, and these verses express that hope clearly. He wrote with a joyful tone as he contemplated what that meant for him and for the Philippians. The first question to answer in this text is about the nature and means of Paul's salvation.

Paul spoke of his salvation with a note of certainty. The verb "know" (*oida*) used here reflects an air of confidence. The term may be used of complete knowledge identified with the mind rather than the process of knowledge which comes from the experience.[160] How

---

[159] This suggests the "this" (τοῦτο) of v. 25 looks ahead to the "that" (ὅτι) clause that follows, though it could look backward. A forward look is somewhat unusual, but it does occur in 1:6 and 1:9, the only other two occurrences of the pronoun to this point in the letter. After 1:25 the pronoun looks ahead for its antecedent in 2:5. It does not in 2:23. The difficulty of determining the antecedent of "this" in 1:25 is that the same themes occur before and after it. In 1:21–24 Paul spoke of the necessity of remaining for their betterment, and in 1:25–26 he made that explicit. Could the antecedent be ambiguous, referring to the general concept which brought confidence? Further, the confidence is derived, not from his expected release from prison, but from his knowledge of their need of his ministry. This point will be developed later.

[160] The differences between οἶδα and γινώσκω have been studied often with diverse conclusions. The verb was translated "knowing well" by M. R. Vincent, A *Critical and Exegetical Commentary on the Epistles to the Philippians and to Philemon*, ICC (Edinburgh: T & T Clark, 1897), 23. Others disagree with a fast distinction between the two (Hawthorne, *Philippians*, 39). Whether the certainty of knowledge comes from the fact that Paul used the word οἶδα or whether it comes from the context, the term does imply a certainty and confidence. It appears that Paul chose this word because of its suitability to that meaning. Hawthorne's Pauline examples do not support the point because there is not an equivalent of the terms in the passages. Οἶδα is used in 1 Cor

Paul knew salvation in this way is unknown, and the many suggestions depend on the meaning of the word "salvation." The term has been interpreted in two primary ways. First, a common interpretation today is that Paul knew he would be delivered (saved) from death and/or imprisonment. Since Rome had nothing against Christians at this early date, Paul had no reason to suspect anything but a positive decision at his trial. In previous trials there was no verdict and at least one, before Agrippa, stated he could have been released if he had not appealed to Rome (Acts 26:32). Two main lines of argumentation support this conclusion. The word "salvation" may have the sense of "deliverance from death."[161] Those who accept this interpretation invoke that meaning in this passage. Additionally, 1:25 expresses Paul's certainty that he would remain on earth. The last argument is the most significant.

Against this interpretation, several factors in the context must be considered.[162] First, Paul stated that his adversity would result in his deliverance. His words indicate the difficulty would itself have the positive results he anticipated; this view hardly fits deliverance from prison. Second, Paul entertained the possibility of death but that did not affect his optimism. His deliverance would come in spite of imprisonment or even death. Third, Paul anticipated gaining his hope of "not be[ing] ashamed." Finally, Paul's statement in this section is similar to Job 13:13–18. As a result, while many equate the passage with an expectation of release, that interpretation does not fit all the details well.

The second interpretation of salvation takes the word in its full, eschatological sense. The completion of the salvation begun with commitment to Christ would be the final vindication of the believer when he meets Christ. Paul knew he would arrive at that great day and see the complete salvation he so desired. This longing did not come from an unsettledness or unassured attitude toward salvation. Paul knew

8:1–3 to introduce a principle which is explained by the consistent use of γνω- root words. In 2 Thess 1:8 Paul quoted the LXX and then applied it with the word "obedience" (ὑπακούω), a moral term synonymous with πιστεύω more so than γινώσκω. CSB uses the word "obey."

[161] The definition of the term influences interpretations significantly. BAGD indicates the word means "deliverance, preservation." It is "generally of preservation in danger, deliverance fr. impending death." Further, "quite predom. salvation, which the true religion bestows . . . In our lit. this sense is found only in connection w. Jesus Christ as Savior. This salvation makes itself known and felt in the present, but it will be completely disclosed in the future" (801).

[162] The best presentation of these comes from Silva, *Philippians*, 76–80.

perseverance through this life was one of the identifying characteristics of a Christian. Knowing he had been saved, he also anticipated the full joy of finished salvation. Several factors support this interpretation.

Paul's wording in this section clearly reflects Job 13:13–18 in the LXX text. Both the Greek wording and the circumstances parallel each other. If Paul quoted Job in context, as he normally did when he referred to the OT, he must have consciously derived comfort from Job's course of life. Paul's life had, in fact, often taken much the same course. When nothing made sense to Job and everyone opposed him, his "salvation" (his "deliverance" in CSB) was that he knew he was justified and that when he stood before God he would be vindicated.

A significant question to answer in Phil 1:19 is the reference to the demonstrative "this" ("this will lead to my salvation"). The pronoun must look to the mixed preaching of the Christians at Rome. It makes little sense to insert "this imprisonment" since the discussion concerned the preachers. In that way, many brought their accusations against Paul and his righteousness. Like Job, he would stand vindicated at last.

A second reason for this interpretation is that it deals seriously with the question of life and death (1:21–24). Paul would be saved regardless of his physical condition. The element of uncertainty regarding the trial did not affect his confidence inside.

Third, Paul's real joy was that Christ was proclaimed. The factor of his life call enters this context. Paul wanted to hear "well done" when he stood before God (see Matt 25:21). His task was to reach the Gentiles for Christ, and how that was accomplished was of secondary consequence. The mixed preaching at Rome furthered his deepest Christian desire, which was to make Christ known.

Finally, the passage contains terms that relate to spiritual deliverance: salvation and hope. The better interpretation is to see Paul's salvation in an eschatological sense—he looked forward to his entrance into heaven and vindication by the Lord himself. Although in 1:21 he turned to the present situation, that does not warrant reading it back into these statements. Confidence in his ultimate, eschatological salvation was the bedrock of his life and ministry. It is not superfluous to provide it first in his response. Given that, he easily turned to the earthly situation he faced. The confidence of his salvation gave him confidence and hope in the present.

In spite of Paul's confidence in his destiny, he sought the Philippians' help. His deliverance would come "through [their] prayers and help from the Spirit of Jesus Christ" (1:19). Paul considered these two ideas to be closely related because they both provided the means through which his goal was achieved.[163] He sought their prayers on his behalf, realizing God answers prayer and works through it to accomplish his purposes. There was no resignation to the inevitable here. Paul combined his foundational trust in Christ with the need for prayers on his behalf.

The help given by the Spirit goes along with the prayers. The related Greek phrase has been handled in different ways. Some scholars take it to be "the supply that the Spirit gives," or the "help from the Spirit of Jesus Christ" (CSB). In this case, the noun "supply" (Greek: *epichoregias*) is understood to be assistance given by the Spirit. It should be noted that "help" is never a meaning suggested for the Greek word "supply" in the lexicons. It has worked its way into the commentary traditions, however. It is also accepted by the CSB. It is a logical translation often made in English but is not technically the meaning of the word. Others understand it to mean "the help which consists of the Spirit."[164] A parallel idea occurs in Gal 3:5 of HCSB ("[D]oes God supply you with the Spirit,")[165] where Paul asked how they had received God's Spirit, obviously meaning the gift of the Spirit himself. Most likely this translation is correct. Paul expected the Holy Spirit to provide whatever he needed to meet life's demands. He already had the indwelling Spirit. It is unlikely he thought in terms of a greater or lesser manifestation of the Spirit depending on various circumstances. This help would occur along with their prayers as well.

The grammatical construction leads to understanding. "Prayers" and the Holy Spirit's assistance go together, although some are prone to separate the two. The two make a natural and normal expression of how God works in the world. They work in tandem, not in

---

[163] The grammar reinforces that. The two nouns "prayers" and "help" are joined in a phrase introduced by the one preposition, introduced further by one article which goes with both (when in prepositional phrases no articles are actually needed and yet they occur, they are emphatic), and joined by the word "and" (καί). Gk.

[164] In Greek, the former is a subjective genitive and the latter is a descriptive or even appositional genitive. Fee, Philippians, 133–135, emphatically calls for the subjective genitive, "Jesus Christ's Spirit."

[165] In Gal 3:5 Paul uses the verbal form (participle) of the root: ἐπιχορηγέω rather than the noun ἐπιχορηγίας as found here.

sequence. Here Paul used the word for a specific entreaty (*deesis*) that he used twice earlier in 1:4. There he brought specific requests coming out of his memory of them and accompanied with joy.[166] Praying is the responsibility of Christian people. Though understanding the complexity of prayer defies understanding, everywhere Scripture encourages prayer for both our desires and God's will, and specifically that the two will mirror each other. There are places where it seems God does not accomplish his intent because his people did not pray. Through prayer Christians identify with God's plans rather than their own, and they actively participate in bringing them about.

On the other hand, the "help from the Spirit of Jesus" takes a different perspective. Jesus partially (along with the Father) controls what the Holy Spirit does (John 14:16, 26; with 15:26; 16:7). Keown notes, "The Spirit's character is consistent and in continuity with Christ . . . Christ [is] imparter of the Spirit."[167] The parallel statements do not show sequence. Paul did not say "pray in order to get help from the Spirit . . ." That would put the responsibility on Christian people. The two are parallel in time as well as grammar. Even while people are praying, God is supplying.

1:20 The second portion of this section focuses on a new topic. "My eager expectation and hope" introduces the content of Paul's hope.[168] The anticipation of his deliverance accorded perfectly with his lifelong hope that Christ would be glorified in him.

Paul stated his desire in two ways.[169] First, he hoped he would "not be ashamed"; second, that Christ would be "highly honored" in his body. What did he mean by "not be ashamed?" The word

---

[166] It is not the word used in 1:9, which says, "I pray this: that your love will keep on growing . . . ." προσεύχομαι normally suggests the practice of praying, rather than a specific request. At times, however, the difference is blurred.

[167] Keown, *Philippians 1:1–2:13*, 233.

[168] Hawthorne, *Philippians*, 39, makes a good case for taking the two ὅτι clauses as parallel, as providing two reasons for Paul's joy. His interpretation depends on taking "salvation" as deliverance from Rome, and with the second ὅτι Paul looked to his spiritual triumph. The suggestion fits well with the Gk. of the text, although the parallels are a little contrived. However, the flow of thought seems to fit better with understanding this portion as a modifier of the previous. That is, Paul's expected spiritual deliverance is completely in accord with his anticipated success in standing true to the Lord. I have taken these verses to have one primary statement with the second ὅτι clause as a modifier in apposition of it.

[169] This interpretation understands the second ὅτι clause to be a restatement of hope. It is appositional rather than parallel, as the previous footnote explains. It is unusual for Paul to have a clause express the nature of the hope since he normally did it with a genitive. The natural way to read this, however, suggests an exception.

translated "ashamed" does not express the feeling of guilt which the English word often conveys. There is an objective aspect to it. Paul uses the objective aspect of "hope" or "trust" as it was used in Isa 28:16, NRSVA. He referenced this verse both in offering the gospel and as one of its foundations (Rom 9:33; 10:11). The verses from Romans help interpret Paul's understanding of the passage. In Rom 9:33, he contrasted stumbling over a rock (Christ) with those who do not trip (i.e., are not put to shame). In Rom 10:10–11, Paul stated the one who confesses Christ "with his mouth" after believing "with the heart" will not stumble (i.e., be put to shame). Confession seals the commitments, and those commitments do not lead to embarrassment. This suits the context of Isa 28:16, where the Lord spoke through the prophet that Israel should remain true to the Lord. If it did, it would not be shaken. These texts have little to do with being ashamed to confess Christ. They do not speak to the point of timidity. Rather, they speak to the security of believers and the certainty they are on a solid foundation when they believe on the "cornerstone." Believers will not be disgraced.

Paul expected not to be put to shame about anything. He confidently confessed Jesus as Lord. It was not a thoughtless or quick confession, but represented the direction of his life. He had OT Scripture to support his contention that the Lord aids those who confess him. Perhaps his thoughts turned to the day of judgment. That is the greatest test, and Paul hoped to be bold (not to "be ashamed") on that day. The context points to the present life as the contrasting clause to this one makes clear ("Christ will be highly honored in my body"). He expected God would give him grace so he would not be put to shame in his confession there and then. The Roman trial was another opportunity for him to triumph in Christ. In no way would he fail. Christ would give him the strength.

The positive side of Paul's hope was that Christ would be exalted in his body. This clearly identifies the hope with an earthly situation rather than the final judgment. "I will not be ashamed" presents the hope Paul would stand strong through the various situations of life. This clause makes that hope concrete: "in my body." They both refer to the same aspects of existence. The use of the term "body," which Paul used for the physical body, and the discussion of life or death as the means of accomplishing this hope demonstrate Paul's expectation.

Two matters help interpret Paul's statements here: "with all courage" and "in my body."

The phrase "with all courage" translates a strong Greek expression (lit., "have all presence"). Usually, Paul employed it referring to the proclamation of the gospel (2 Cor 3:12; Eph 6:19) so it described boldness in witness. If the Philippians passage is understood that way, Paul is expecting boldness in affirming the gospel through these circumstances, more probably in his trial before Caesar. It describes, however, courage of life. He hoped he would have the courage to live or die as a true Christian should. The phrase "in my body" is rather odd if used of speech. How else could speech occur but in the body? The redundancy suggests a broader use of courage. Paul's ministry encompassed both living and speaking, and he needed courage for both. He had enjoyed success before, but now he faced greater tests. He expected to end as he began: courageous in his witness.[170]

The location of this witness was "in [his] body." Paul consistently used the term for the physical body, and there is no need to suggest some metaphorical use of the term here.[171] In Rom 6:6 Paul spoke of crucifixion with Christ to "paralyze the physical body of sin" (my translation). Later, in vv. 12–14, he made it clear the body was the mortal body, and sin had to be overcome there. Further, in a positive command, in Rom 12:1–2 Paul employed the metaphor of sacrifice to exhort the believers to consecration. He still used the terms of the physical body. It is not surprising, therefore, he thought here in terms of the body's responsibility in Christian commitment.

Paul knew Christian commitment cannot happen apart from the body. In fact, Christian growth requires focusing on the body as the vehicle of expression of the true person, and as the instrument for receiving the communications of others. Each person is intimately connected to his or her body, and Paul easily localized Christian commitment in the physical parts of his. Since, therefore, he had committed his body to God and served him in it, he had to continue to glorify

---

[170] Some object to another interpretation besides a speaking ministry because of a pattern of Pauline usage of the phrase. It is not impossible for him to have used the phrase in other contexts, however (2 Cor 7:4), and this was an unusual situation to address. To confine Paul's use of the term in such a way unnecessarily encumbers his expression.

[171] See R. H. Gundry, *SOMA in Biblical Theology: With Emphasis on Pauline Anthropology*, SNTSMS 29 (Cambridge: University Press, 1976), 37.

him there as well. The immediate context confirms this conclusion where, in Phil 1:24, he again referred to life in the body ("flesh").

No matter what the cost, Christ would be honored by everything about this apostle. Glorifying God in the body involved both living and when the time came, dying in a Christ-honoring way. Paul's commitment to Christ, his confession of him, and his understanding of the power of God to sustain the believer demanded no less.

There may be an even deeper understanding of the body glorifying Christ at death. This question should be raised: What does it mean to glorify God in the body "by death?" The literal construction is "through death," the preposition conveying a vehicle or means through which something can be accomplished.[172] It is short-sighted to understand the phrase to mean "at death" since the term is not temporal. Aquinas commented on this text: "Christ is honored in our body in two ways: in one way, inasmuch as we dedicate our body to his service by employing our bodies in his ministry . . . ; in another way by risking our body for Christ . . . the first is accomplished by life, the second by death."[173] The body displays character, as it is employed in the service of who we are at our cores. If Paul disgraced himself "by recanting under torture—Paul's body would display something crucial about his character."[174] The Roman Empire exerted pressure seeking to control its subjects through their bodies, often through fear associated with physical punishment. Paul expected he would remain true while living, but also in the way he died, through death. Fowl comments,"Whether he lives or dies, Paul's body will be, as he has always been, Christ's text rather than the empire's."[175] This, in fact, became both the power of the gospel's hope and the downfall of the Roman government. Rome could never conquer Christians. Following Paul's and others' examples, the martyrs glorified Christ not only at their deaths but through their deaths. Government fails miserably when it finds itself powerless to persuade even with the threat of death.

In 1:21–24, Paul revealed a deep inner struggle. The contrasts between life and death indicate that Paul seriously contemplated the

---

[172] The preposition in both parts of the statement is δία (*dia*). It literally implies that the noun associated with it is a "conveyor." We understand this better as "through life" and "through death."

[173] Aquinas, *Philippians*, 69. Quoted in Fowl, *Philippians*, 47.

[174] Fowl, 47.

[175] Fowl, 48.

possibilities of both. Of course, he did not have power over his destiny; it was in the hands of God (perhaps as he might work through Rome). Nevertheless, Paul faced the alternative situations with forethought. In his own mind, he resolved the tension by the same principle that guided his life to that point. He would serve Jesus to the end.

1:21 The themes of life and death explain how Paul would glorify God in his body—even death would not keep him from it. These themes also prompted him to evaluate the purpose of living. With this introduction to 1:21–24, it seems the section explains the commitment of the previous verses (vv. 18b–20). As far as Paul was concerned, "to live is Christ and to die is gain."[176]

This differs from what others thought and what might have been expected. Normally, one would say to live is gain and to die is Christ, but Paul reversed these. At death a Christian gains a more intimate relationship with the Lord and receives the full blessings promised at conversion. Ironically, death opens the door to the ultimate fulfillment of everything promised in the gospel. The statement "to live is Christ" is magnified by the statement "to die is gain."[177]

Often Paul spoke of Christ as his life. In Gal 2:20 he said, "I live by faith in the Son of God." In Col 3:4 he stated of other believers that Christ "is [their] life." These two passages differ in context and concern. The emphasis in Gal 2:20 is soteriological; in Col 3:4, Paul speaks to the mysterious union between Christ and the believer. Paul did not mean precisely either here, however. In this context he spoke of glorifying Christ through whatever means he had, providing the interpretive environment. The statement is completed by envisioning death as a better state than life. Thus, "to live is Christ" must mean that Paul so completely wanted to glorify Christ that as long as he lived, everything about him was to point people to Jesus. This was accomplished in part by his imprisonment, which was "manifested in Christ" (1:13); but even if he were called to die, it would be an occasion for Christ to become prominent. Death was a gain because he would see the Lord, enjoy him, and no longer endure the difficulties he was called to bear on this fallen earth.

1:22–24 These verses describe both Paul's dilemma and his resolution of it. The literary pattern emphasizes his conviction that he

---

[176] This is a dative of reference.

[177] Some commentators want to break the equation and make it say something like "to live or die is Christ." That is unnecessary and confuses the passage.

would remain, that the result of his trial would be life not death. The pattern is chiastic:

A. "Now if I live on in the flesh, this means fruitful work for me;
  B. I don't know which one I should choose.
  B′ I am torn between the two. I long to depart and be with Christ
A′. but to remain in the flesh is more necessary for your sake.

In 1:22 he expressed the conviction that fruit would result from his continued physical life. The way the letter precedes reveals the interpretation of "fruitful work for [Paul]" (1:22). This statement corresponds to the conviction that he would remain for the sake of the Philippians (1:24). While it may appear the fruit was some spiritual development in Paul's life, the context clearly relates it to the service Paul performed.

In between these two statements, he posed the troublesome question of his choice, essentially, "What shall I choose? . . . I am torn between the two."[178] It was helpful to them for Paul to remain; the fruit was what resulted from his work for others. The phrase Paul used, literally "the fruit of work" is to be understood as either a subjective genitive construction ("the fruit work produces") or a genitive of description expressing the kind of work he expected ("fruitful work"). The CSB adopts the latter. Either way, fruit is the expected outcome of his ministry. He knew from past experiences that God used his efforts to further the kingdom, and nothing less would be expected in the future.

The longer Paul lived, the more people would be touched by his life.[179] Many understand Paul to say he would reap the harvest of his

---

[178] This chiastic arrangement emphasizes the expectation that he would continue to serve them. The "outside" members of the chiasm (first and last) receive the greater emphasis. The question of which is better is there, but it remains a question. The answer is clear: they needed him, and he expected to remain rather than die.

[179] Verse 22 has had many diverse interpretations. The syntax is ambiguous. Paul introduced the statement with a first-class condition format, εἰ ("if"), but where the apodosis begins is not clear. Is it with "this means fruitful work" or with "what shall I ask?" The NIV takes the former and makes the rest of the one sentence in Gk. introduce a new idea. There are three ways of rendering it: 1) If my living on in the body means that I could reap the fruit of my past toil, then I do not know which to prefer. 2) If I am to live on in the body, that will mean that I can reap the fruit of my toil. Yet I do not know which to prefer. 3) What if my living on in the body means that I could reap the fruit of my toil? I do not know which to prefer. The second appears to be the best even though it means introducing an apodosis with καί ("and"), and the τοῦτο ("this") seems unnecessary. There are fewer problems with it.

past work. Therefore, it would benefit him to remain in the flesh.[180] These interpretations seem to neglect the fact that Paul's rewards, and therefore his benefits, awaited him after death. That is why dying was gain. Further, this passage reveals Paul's concern for others, not himself (1:24, 26). He must have been thinking of the future and the harvests that would come from his life should God allow him to continue on this earth. The statement should be understood, therefore, like this: "If I am to live on in the body, that will mean that I can reap the additional fruit of my toil. Yet I do not know which to prefer."

The statement "I don't know which one I should choose" (1:22) is problematic. Normally the verb used for "know" means, for Paul, a disclosure. He most often preferred this verb for a disclosure of something he assumed his readers did not know.[181] If it is to be understood in this normal way, Paul expressed his reticence to reveal his future: "I am not ready to disclose this to you," implying Paul had a choice relating to his future activities, or his restraint in action. He could foresee—if not control—the circumstances of his own death.[182] This could possibly be supported by his strong affirmation that he will glorify Christ through death. Fee prefers the clause to mean something like "I can't tell."[183] The context fits this latter understanding better.

Further, "I should choose" contains a difficulty. First, there is a textual variant concerning whether it should be read as a subjunctive ("I should choose") or a future form ("I will choose"). The former implies a moral aspect to the decision. What *should* be done? "I will choose" suggests uncertainty rather than obligation. Second, understood on the surface, Paul stated his choice was unclear to him. He may choose death over life. However, v. 25 states he knows his choice is following the will of God. God's plan for his life as much as he can see it is to remain with them. Many, however, approach this as though Paul were saying "I do not know what I prefer (and therefore choose)." Choices reflect preferences. He expressed his preference: to depart and be with Christ which is far better. In this case, then, Paul's choice may not reflect his preferences, for to remain alive is far more

---

[180] It may be that every Christian wants to see the work he has done and to enjoy it. Paul, however, wanted to see Christ more than all.

[181] The verb is *gnorizo* (γνωρίζω). See, for example, its use in Rom 16:26; 2 Cor 8:1; Gal 1:11.

[182] Holloway, *Philippians*, 97–98, interestingly and insightfully suggests 1) Paul could commit suicide in prison, or, alternatively, 2) a courtroom display of boldness that would be fatal.

[183] Fee, *Philippians*, 145.

"useful, better."[184] His life glorified Christ in large part by his choices to fulfill God's call on his life. He lived the choice of service. Here he reflects his life-long characteristic of others-orientation. He will remain for their benefit. The phrase "I should/will choose" is based on the call of God on his life, not on his own wishes.

Beyond the mention of rewards, however, Paul expressed the strong desire to "be with Christ" (1:23) since it was better. Paul used a very strong emotional term for desire (*epithumia*), normally translated "lust," suggesting more than a whimsical or flippant comment. He allows the Philippians to see his passion to depart and be with Jesus. The word translated "depart" historically denoted the movement of a ship from harbor, or the embarking of an army for a battle. It serves for Paul as another metaphor for death, and by using it, Paul reveals his certainty that death is not an end, but a beginning of a new phase of living. Thinking of the two stages of life put Paul in a dilemma. The passive verb translated "I am torn" (*sunexomai*) subtly indicates a dilemma not of his own making, perhaps deriving from his personal relationship with Christ, or from his intentional theological study of being in Christ. Either way, the tension between continued life and fruitfulness or ultimate satisfaction being with Christ captivated his thoughts and consumed his energy. The discussion of rewards clouds the basic issue. Paul's longing for death was a longing for a more intimate, open, and total relationship with Christ himself. Such a relationship could only occur after he left this life behind. The practical dilemma consisted of whether Paul would choose his own preference or remain to benefit others. His conviction was he would remain. While the statement obviously takes an optimistic perspective on the trial Paul faced, it spoke more to his conviction regarding his life service. His work remained unfinished. He thought, therefore, God would have him remain and accomplish it.

One final concern emerges from these verses. Some commentators introduce the problem of the topic of soul sleep here.[185] Generally

---

[184] *kreisson* (κρεῖσσον).

[185] Caird, *Paul's Letters*, 113–4, says Paul taught consistently "Christians who die remain in a state of sleep until the Advent of Christ, who will then raise them to eternal life." This conclusion is not so clear, however, even from the passages he draws upon for support (1 Thess 4:13–5:11; 1 Cor 15:35–55; 2 Cor 5:1–10; Rom 8:18–25). For example, there is a two-part experience in 1 Thess 4:13–18, as Paul said those who are asleep (a euphemism for death) in Jesus will be raised with him. They are alive and conscious; they come to be reunited with their bodies. It is the resurrection that awaits the Advent, not presence with Christ (see Luke 23:39-43).

those who do must address the fact that these verses do not teach the doctrine. They must harmonize the passage with what they have deduced from others. For example, 1 Thess 4:13–18 uses the word "sleep" of the believing dead, and Paul further indicates the "dead in Christ will rise first" at the rapture. Neither of these make the case. Sleep was a common euphemism for death, used by Paul and others (John 11:11 for example). The metaphor must be interpreted in light of clearer passages that teach at death Paul expects to be immediately with Christ (2 Cor 5:8). Regarding Paul's eschatology, 1 Thess 4:14 states, "God will bring with him those who have fallen asleep." Deceased believers are with Christ awaiting the resurrection to gain their bodies made new. The intermediate state is not one of sleep, but one of activity in Christ's presence.[186] Paul directly stated in death he would be "with Christ," and the language speaks of being immediately in Christ's presence (cp. David's language in Ps 16:11b). Further, Paul would hardly have been comforted by being away from Christ after death. He was already with him and looked forward to a more open relationship with him at death. Why would Paul want to sleep (away from the conscious presence of Christ which he enjoyed on earth) when his tension resulted from the desire to enjoy Christ more fully? Finally, making this passage conform to an already assumed position such as soul sleep is difficult.[187] The natural way to read the passage speaks against it, as do the other Pauline discussions of life after death.[188] The fact is, Paul did not discuss the doctrine of soul sleep in this text at all. He simply expressed his conviction that if he died, he would gain because death was a departure through which he would be in the presence of the Lord (*syn Christo* 1:23).

---

[186] Holloway, *Philippians*, 99, affirms the interpretation that Paul expected to be with Christ upon his death. He states, however, this represents development in Paul's eschatological understanding, maturing from his previous idea of "soul sleep."

[187] Caird, *Paul's Letters*, 113, an advocate of soul sleep, states, "This verse seems to present the contrary view that those who 'die in the Lord' go directly into his presence." He then attempts to explain why the obvious cannot be so to his mind.

[188] Bockmuehl, *A Commentary*, 92–93, helpfully observes, "At the end of the day, . . . the questions persist—perhaps because they demand the impossible: a description of transcendence and eternity in immanent temporal terms. As poets and children know well, transcendent reality can be known only through metaphor."

2.2.2.2 Paul's Confidence of Future Ministry (1:25–26)

1:25 The second section of this passage begins here. It continues Paul's attitude in light of his circumstances of house arrest. It not only looks back to the discussion of 1:18–20 but also expresses Paul's hope in new ways. Specifically, Paul shared his confidence he would remain with the Philippians to advance the gospel and to further their progress and joy in the faith as they saw him again.

Looking back, Paul based his statement on the confidence expressed in 1:18–20. The glory of Christ would be achieved best by Paul's remaining on earth to continue his ministry. Paul did not explain to the readers why he felt this conviction. Perhaps he knew Rome had no reason to punish him, and his optimism lay in the confidence that Rome would act justly. At a deeper level, his confidence grew out of his understanding of the ministry God had given him. Paul lived for others; he knew their needs well, and he knew they would grow spiritually through his presence with them. This statement applied the hope that Christ would be honored (1:20) to the realities of daily life. He might have chosen to go on to heaven and enjoy fully the Lord whom he loved, but the task was unfinished, and he must remain.[189]

Paul would remain because of their needs, which he first stated in an overview and then in specific terms. The overview is "for [their] progress and joy in the faith." The word "progress" (*prokopen*) was used earlier of the advancement of the gospel message (1:12; there CSB translates it as "advanced"). There Paul's circumstances propelled the message forward into new territory. In a similar way, his return to the church would push its faith forward. As the events became opportunities for preaching the gospel, his presence with the church could only help it. This advancement of its faith was also called a joy. Both "progress" and "joy" are modified by "of the faith."[190] As the Philippians matured in their understanding of Christ, their joy in the faith would deepen and would be encouraged. This thought is repeated in v. 26.

---

[189] Paul's confidence of remaining receives emphasis two ways. First, twice he stated he expects to remain (μένω and παραμένω). Second, the word παραμένω is a perfective form, stressing his expectation to remain beside them.

[190] CSB says, "in the faith." The Granville Sharp rule applies here: Two nouns joined by καί and introduced by one article refer to the same person or thing. Progress and joy are two sides of the same idea. The construction "in the faith" is an objective genitive, that is, "Progress and joy directed toward their faith."

Significantly, Paul associates "progress" and "joy." The grammar puts them together as part of the same ideological package. Does lack of progress remove joy? Does joy enable progress? Without doubt, discouragement often hinders people from achieving the goals for which they strive. Paul's case differed, however. In 1:12 he affirmed the gospel had "advanced." In spite of his undesirable and somewhat difficult circumstances in house-arrest, he was able to "rejoice" that Christ was preached (1:18). Paul always found a reason for joy and, we are to assume, he was a joyful person. Coupling the two nouns is intentional. The best understanding is that they accompany each other. Since "progress" comes first, perhaps it bears the subtle stress. Regardless, progress relates to Christ proclaimed. The next verse, 1:26, interprets it for us: "your boasting in Christ Jesus may abound." Progress relates to the vocal—and public—exaltation of Christ. Before it was through preaching (1:12), now it is through "spoken pride" in Christ.[191] Why, then, did he hope to promote their "progress and joy?"

1:26 The specific statement is that Paul's presence would bring great joy.[192] It was joy in Christ through Paul's release. A similar statement occurs in 4:10, where Paul said, "I rejoiced in the Lord greatly because once again you renewed your care for me." Their financial support caused Paul to worship and praise the Lord who sent it through them. Naturally, the gift brought joy, but the greater joy was what it meant in the work of the Lord. Applying that understanding here, Paul realized his presence provided an occasion for worship and praise. In spite of the similarity of 1:26 and 4:10, two different words describe "joy." In 4:10, Paul used *chairo* "to rejoice" or "be glad."[193] Here, the word is *kauchepma* "to boast or be proud."[194] The word often suggests an occasion or object of the joy and has the sense of "taking pride in" something specific.[195]

---

[191] The word *kauchomai* (καύχομαι) implies taking pride in something and therefore speaking about it. While the spoken element is a derivative idea not a core meaning, in this context it applies.

[192] In Gk., this verse is a purpose clause that shows the goal of his statement. Dividing the commentary into "overview" and "specific" seems to satisfy the demands of that construction. The overview is expressed with "εἰς," which also speaks to a goal of living; the specific is expressed with ἵνα showing purpose.

[193] BAGD, 873.

[194] BAGD, 426.

[195] Vincent, *Critical and Exegetical Commentary*, 30, said it "is the matter or ground of glorying, not the act of glorying."

Three complementary phrases explain the ground of their glorying. First, it would "abound" in Christ Jesus. For Paul, Jesus was always the basis of joy. Second, it would be through Paul representing Christ. Paul, as apostle, brought Christ to them, and they longed to see him again. He was their best example of Jesus. Third, they would boast because of Paul's presence with them again. Additionally, there may be an overtone of joy that the trial would be over and that the work of the Lord could go forth.

Paul's words express his optimism. Without a doubt, he expected to continue his ministry after the trial. Even so, he contemplated the realities of what could happen and how he would respond to the worst of situations. He would triumph. If he went to be with his Lord, that was triumph. If he stayed with them, they would be helped. But as he understood the work of the Lord, he would remain to further their faith.

This passage reveals Paul anticipated a visit to Philippi upon his release. The same expectation occurred in Colossians and Philemon. Paul's plans to go to Spain had been postponed. Perhaps he sought the strength of fellowship his converts provided. Perhaps he knew they needed him. At any rate, they would prosper if God allowed him to remain on earth.

We are at the end of Paul's disclosure of his circumstances. A structural note is in order. As mentioned earlier, vv. 12 and 25 include an inclusio by the repetition of the rather unusual word *prokopen.* Verses 25 and 26 belong together in completing the thought of Paul's remaining on earth. In fact, v. 26 completes the sentence begun in v. 25 with a purpose clause giving the purpose of Paul's expectation to remain on earth. The grammar, sentence structure, and inclusio with "advanced/progressed" indicate vv. 12–26 are one main unit of thought. They inform the church of Paul's circumstances and his attitude toward them.

Theological and Practical Points

Although autobiographical, Paul's discussion was rooted in his foundational theology. Like much of the letter, his life was lived anchored to confidence in God's control and supervision of his life. It is helpful to see both the theology and how the principles work out in the difficulties of a life of service.

1. *The progress of the gospel.* This passage revolves around Paul's commitment to the progress of the gospel. It is similar to Paul's joy described earlier and somewhat repetitive to it, but appropriate here. The statement of 1:12 revealed past events have furthered the gospel. Paul's call was to spread the gospel to the Gentiles. He saw that as unique among the apostles, even calling it a "mystery" (*musterion*, Eph 3:3–7). In explaining his life calling, he stated he was "made a servant of this gospel" (Eph 3:7), the gospel that understands Gentiles are "coheirs, members of the same body, and partners in the promise in Christ Jesus through the gospel" (Eph 3:6). All events of his life, whether positive or negative, enabled the gospel to find fertile soil in new places. While some would consider Paul's experience a failure, Paul took advantage of every opportunity to spread the gospel. For years Paul had hoped to take the gospel to Rome, the capitol of the empire. Although there were churches in Rome, Paul wanted first-hand knowledge of them and desired to contribute his unique gifts to their success (Rom 1:10–12). He considered that a part of the divine will for his life. God worked in strange ways, inconvenient and in many ways limiting. Yet Paul saw through personal difficulties that God was accomplishing his purposes. He was in Rome and he would not only speak to the churches at Rome, he would appear before the emperor, the highest representative of the Gentiles. In strange ways his hopes, and God's plans, came to fruition. The gospel moved forward.

2. *Strengthening the Church.* Paul was a churchman. He devoted his energy to planting new churches as his priority. He also maintained contact with the churches he started and with some he considered Pauline in origin even though another founded them (Colossae; Rome). Communication was difficult by modern standards, but he had regular communication with them. He knew their situations, their successes, and their tendencies toward unforeseen difficulties theologically or in relationships. The letter to Philippi reveals he knew their partnership with him and the division caused by Euodia and Syntyche. In this passage he reveals his strong commitment to the churches' success. Facing an unknown future with an unprecedented appearance before the emperor, he contemplated death or life. He expected to be exonerated of any wrongdoing. His concern for after the trial was the Philippians' "progress and joy in the faith" (1:25). Before his imprisonment in Judea, he hoped to evangelize westward, taking the gospel as far as Spain (Rom 15:23–24). Plans change as God orchestrates events. Paul

did not expect to be in Rome in the current circumstances. Nevertheless, he expected release from imprisonment and freedom to engage in more active ministry again. Contemplating whether he wished to live or die, he came to the conclusion that, contrary to his own inclinations to die and be with the Lord, he would live and serve. His was a life of service rather than personal gain on earth or in promptly passing into eternity to receive his eternal rewards.

3. *Deliverance from opposition.* After speaking to the issue of divided preachers, and doubtless divided sermons for or against him, Paul turned his thoughts to his own situation. Preachers may preach what they will, but what about Paul? How was Paul doing? Given the church's concern for their founding apostle, Paul now spoke from the depths of his own commitment. The Philippians were to see what is inside triumphs over surroundings on the outside. Inside, Paul had the deepest commitment to Christ. He could look beyond the circumstances of life to the spiritual relationships that prevail after earthly circumstances fade. He expected salvation. As discussed in the commentary, it is most likely the salvation he saw coming would be based on his own ability to stand strong and true in the midst of human opposition. As in Job's case, the criticisms raised against him had no merit. Tempted to quit, Paul recognized his own resolve and persistence would see him through. His salvation was that he did not fail, did not lash out against his opponents, and did not lose the focus of his commitment. Even so, Paul realized the precarious nature of self-sufficiency. As always in the patterns of his life, he sought others' help. Support need not come financially, though they gave to him out of love. What he saw as essential was their prayers, prayers for his endurance (salvation). He implored them to join with his own prayers for the specific need of the hour. Prayer support encouraged, but he also called for the present power of the Holy Spirit. The Spirit alone could supply what Paul needed to stand unashamed before God.

4. *Christ magnified the "body."* Paul wrote about the body more than any other NT writer. Apart from the thirteen Pauline letters, the physical body is seldom mentioned. Jesus spoke of it occasionally in the Gospels (Matt 5:29–30 relate to this idea). Beyond that, there are few places where the body is of concern. In one of the most focused of statements about Christian commitment, Paul declared his commitment would involve his physical body. It is easy to confine spiritual principles to the realm of the spirit. Feelings, thoughts, and values are

often intangible. Yet they are an essential reflection of genuine spirituality. Christian commitment, however, goes beyond that. It takes place "in the body." Paul's prayer that "Christ . . . be highly honored in [his] body" reveals his deep understanding about the totality of life. The physical body enables the intangible aspects of a person to become tangible. Thoughts often work their way out by physical activities. Feelings prompt laughter or tears. Abused values express themselves in and through the body. The body is the person in action. If God is to be glorified, it will be in large part in the body.

God cares about the physical body. He created it as part of humanity being in his own image. Though God cannot be reduced to a physical image, in creating humans he chose to package his image in specific human forms. When God created people "he created him in the image of God; he created them male and female" (Gen 1:27). Yet the image of God goes beyond the body being a vehicle of the soul, which was a pagan idea. The image of God required the creation of a physical body to complement, express, and personalize the soul. The body's origins are in God's creative acts. Furthermore, the created body is destined for eternity. As Paul noted with regard to our fallen bodies, "flesh and blood cannot inherit the kingdom of God, nor can corruption inherit incorruption" (1 Cor 15:50). Thus, the body "must be clothed with incorruptibility, and this moral body must be clothed with immortality" (1 Cor 15:54). Such is the final stage when "death has been swallowed up in victory" (1 Cor 15:54). The divine act of transformation enables a fleshly body to be equipped and suited for an eternal dimension of existence.[196]

The eternal nature of the body brought, for Paul, temporal implications. He warned the Corinthians not to engage in extramarital sexual activities because "the body is not for sexual immorality but for the Lord, and the Lord for the body" (1 Cor 6:13). This is explained as "your bodies are part of Christ's body," and it is not proper to

[196] Paul wrote about the body more than any other NT writer. The OT assumes the resurrection of the physical body and provides some brief theology about it. David "knew" he would see his son again after his infant's death; Enoch was taken from earth in bodily form; they never found Elijah's body. These bear witness to life after death in the body. In the apocryphal literature they knew of Michael the Archangel wrestling with the Devil over Moses's body, available to them after death. One highlight of Jesus's life was his transfiguration when his body was changed, and he met and talked with the deceased Moses and Elijah. These scant references leave many questions. Paul wrote more, and more clearly, about the importance of and implications of the body.

"take a part of Christ's body and make it part of a prostitute" (v. 15). In a broader context, Paul explained his conservative lifestyle: "I discipline my body and bring it under strict control, so that after preaching to others, I myself will not be disqualified" (1 Cor 9:27). More positively, genuine Christian growth into Christlikeness involves the body: "I urge you to present your bodies as a living sacrifice, holy and pleasing to God; this is your true worship" (Rom 12:1). God speaks to the mind through increasing knowledge, but that knowledge reaches maturity when it affects both the immaterial and the material aspects of Christians.

What does this brief overview have to do with Paul's statement in Phil 1:20: "Christ will be highly honored in my body, whether by life or by death?" Genuine spiritual life works its way to and through the physical body. Conversely, issues related to the physical body often influence the spiritual life. Paul speaks to that in 4:12 where his understanding of contentment includes "whether well fed or hungry." In the difficulties and frustrations of Roman imprisonment, even though it was house arrest, physical sufferings had the potential to dampen the spirit. Depression and failure often arise from physical roots. Paul had endured suffering for Christ. He identified such with "Christ's afflictions" (Col 1:24) and triumphed over them, even with joy (at Philippi, Acts 16:25). Matters related to the body would not deter his mission. Christ would be honored in his body as well as in his spirit. He fully expected to triumph in the future, even if it came to martyrdom ("by life or by death," 1:20), so that his commitment to Christ was complete. He honored Christ in his body.

5. *"To live is Christ."* This statement has been variously interpreted. As noted above, it is best to understand it as something like "living is for Christ,"[197] which fits the flow of this passage and encapsulates Paul's attitude in brief, slogan-like form. For one thing, this explained Paul's attitude toward the divided preaching in Rome. His perspective was that "Christ is proclaimed," and he rejoiced in this. For another thing, his restatement of joy in 1:18b reveals the

[197] Grammar must be observed. First, this is a present infinitive, bringing it into the foreground as a present, ongoing experience. Second, with the article, the infinitive serves as the subject of the sentence, rather than "Christ" or a supplied subject. Third, the infinitive is less specific than if a noun were used, thereby making a general observation about Paul's existence. All this is set against the background of the aorist infinitive "to die," presented as more remote, though possible.

more Christ was proclaimed, becoming the topic of conversation and faith, the more he continued to rejoice. Additionally, Paul's future joy related to how Christ could become the most obvious part of his life as expressed by the devotion of his energies to promoting Christ's reputation, his sacrifice, and most importantly his lordship. Paul's deeper ambition was that the more people came in contact with Paul's life and ministry, the more they would understand the beauty of Christ himself. In sum, "to live is Christ" explains how he could endure negative circumstances and could affirm the divided motives and purposes of the Christian preachers at Rome in positive light.

6. *"To die is gain."* On the surface, thinking of death as a positive experience for believers brings nothing new. It stems from Jesus himself and is embedded solidly in Christian thought from the time of the early church. Everyone looks for a better afterlife. For many people that is at the heart of their evangelistic efforts; they ask, "Do you want to go to heaven when you die?" Comparing life and death in such a manner does capture one aspect of Christian hope, but it is inadequate to express the fullness of hope promised in the gospel. For believers, in earth's time orientation, eternal life begins at the moment of conversion. It is a life of fullness, blessing, and confident hope.

What, then, does Paul mean by death as gain? Using the word "gain" (*kerdos*) indicates Paul expected a reward at death, like an investment with expected positive results. Since he identified it with death, some in the church may immediately think of martyrdom and the special crown reserved for those who make the ultimate sacrifice. In that sense, it would be a special reward for Paul and the others who die in service. Paul, however, did not speak of any desire for martyrdom, nor did he hold out the promise of special blessings for those who are martyred.

Paul used the word "gain" one other time in Philippians. In 3:7, Paul compared his present life with his past life under the law. Then he considered his achievements and activities as gain. That is, that what he achieved was a benefit to him compared with the time before he achieved them. Perhaps his former "gain" was the status of being a respected Pharisee, probable rabbi, and the stature it brought. In contrast, Paul considered that "to be a loss because of Christ." He further explained that it paled when compared to "the surpassing value of knowing Christ Jesus [his] Lord" (3:8). Furthermore, he considered those gains to be dung "so that [he] may gain Christ" (3:8).[198] In Phil 3 his Christian gain was knowing Christ and the life he brings to a believer. In 1:21 Paul engaged in a discussion that in death he might "be with Christ" which is "far better" (1:23). Paul's joy in life was his knowledge of Christ, his deep desire to know him, and his hope to honor him "by life or by death" (1:20). Death brings to a Christian more complete knowledge of Christ since the cataracts of fleshly life and earthly orientation are removed. Clear vision of Christ represents a new phase of Christian experience. Seeing Christ better also brings complete transformation from sin to righteousness. Fitting to this context, it also will enable completely honoring Christ in the body, which will be transformed at the resurrection into the newness it will have for eternity. Death, then, brings gain. The offer of salvation should not be reduced to going to heaven. At conversion one sees Jesus as the provision for a new life. Commitment to Jesus becomes the focal point of life. Christian growth brings a more encompassing commitment and an increasingly strong desire to know Christ fully. Since that can only be accomplished ultimately at death, death is gain.

3 BODY OF THE LETTER: PAUL'S CONCERNS FOR THE CHURCH (1:27–4:9)

With this set of exhortations, Paul turns to the body of the letter. From now through 4:9 he explains some deep concerns for the growth of the church (1:27–2:18), the ability to withstand false teachers (3:1–21), and the repairing of a breach in fellowship in the church (4:2–4). He is equally concerned that they understand the principles that bring peace.

SECTION OUTLINE

3 Body of the Letter: Paul's Concerns for the Church (1:27–4:9)
 3.1 Exhortation to Christlike Character (1:27–2:18)
  3.1.1 A Unified Stand (1:27–30)
   Theological and Practical Points
  3.1.2 A Unified Mind (2:1–4)
  3.1.3 A Unified Focus: The Example of Christ (2:5–11)
   Theological and Practical Points

[198] In Phil 3:7–8 Paul used both the noun form for "gain" and the verb form "I may gain."

3.1.4 The Command to Obedience (2:12–18)
Theological and Practical Points
3.2 Paul's Future Plans Related to Philippi (2:19–30)
3.2.1 Concerning Timothy (2:19–24)
3.2.2 Concerning Epaphroditus (2:25–30)
Theological and Practical Points
3.3 Exhortation to Avoid False Teachers (3:1–21)
3.3.1 Paul's Experience Explained (3:1–16)
3.3.2 The False Teachers' Character Exposed (3:17–21)
Theological and Practical Points
3.4 Exhortations to the Philippians (4:1–9)
3.4.1 Exhortation to Steadfastness (4:1)
3.4.2 Exhortation to Unity (4:2–3)
3.4.3 Exhortation to Joy and Peace (4:4–9)
Theological and Practical Points

3.1 Exhortation to Christlike Character (1:27–2:18)

Philippians 1:27 begins a new section of the letter. The change of tone signals a change of direction. Paul moved from information to exhortation, and three primary exhortations occur: 1:27–30; 2:1–4; 2:12–18. Both before (1:12–26) and after (2:19–30) the exhortations, Paul shared information about himself and his intent to send Timothy and Epaphroditus to the church. The change of tone is noted most dramatically in grammar and style. The text changes from indicative first person verbs to imperative second person commands. The switch in verbal moods between indicative and imperative indicates a major stylistic feature of the letter This is further emphasized by the interchange of subjects expressed primarily by personal pronouns. The indicative sections have Paul as the subject, and therefore the pronoun "I" predominates. The imperative sections have the church as the subject, and therefore the pronoun "you" does (see above at 1:12).

The phrase "[j]ust one thing" (in Greek literally "only") also marks a change such as seen in Gal 2:7–9.[199] Paul's concerns about Christian relationships surface during this discussion. The CSB translation makes Paul's concerns here central to his thoughts as his mind embraces their responsibility to implement the mind of Christ. Given

[199] See Silva, *Philippians*, 89–90, for a good discussion of this.

his recounting of the divided Roman church situation, Paul naturally begins with unity.

3.1.1 A Unified Stand (1:27–30)

[27] *Just one thing: As citizens of heaven, live your life worthy of the gospel of Christ. Then, whether I come and see you or am absent, I will hear about you that you are standing firm in one spirit, in one accord, contending together for the faith of the gospel,* [28] *not being frightened in any way by your opponents. This is a sign of destruction for them, but of your salvation—and this is from God.* [29] *For it has been granted to you on Christ's behalf not only to believe in him, but also to suffer for him,* [30] *since you are engaged in the same struggle that you saw I had and now hear that I have.*

Structure

Just one thing:

live your life worthy of the gospel of Christ
["as citizens of heaven," implied by the word "live"]
in order that . . . I will hear about you
whether I come and see you
or am absent,
that you are standing firm in one spirit, in one accord,
contending together for the faith
of the gospel
not being frightened in any way
by your opponents.
This is a sign of
destruction for them
but of your salvation—
and this is from God.
For it has been granted to you on Christ's behalf,
not only to believe in him
but also to suffer for him
since you are engaged in the same struggle
that you saw I had
and how hear that I have.

As pictured, the primary elements of the structure are these:

1) There is one main sentence in these verses ("[L]ive your life worthy of the gospel"). The other comments support it.
2) Dual reasons are given to support this statement, given their situation.
    a) purpose: in order that Paul may hear they stand in one spirit, and
    b) reason: for it has been granted to them on Christ's behalf . . . to suffer.

Interpretation

In this first section of commands, Paul urged the church to be true to the faith. "[T] o live . . . worthy of the gospel of Christ" is a command that may be understood broadly, but Paul's specific concern was a unified stand for the gospel. Both of these elements were important.

The churches at Rome stood for the gospel but there was no unity, and among other things, this disunity impeded its witness. The Philippians had the opportunity to witness to the world by their unified stand for the gospel. This would be particularly impressive if they stood strong through the sufferings they were called to endure. Two matters need to be discussed: the nature of their stand (1:27–28) and Christian suffering (1:29–30).

3.1.1.1 The Nature of their Stand (1:27–28)

The main verb "live your life" (*politeuesthe*) called the church to appropriate conduct. It is an unusual term, and the verb form occurs only here and in Acts 23:1. There, presenting his defense before the Sanhedrin, Paul stated, "I have lived my life before God in all good conscience to this day." Normally Paul used the verb "walk" (*peripateuo*) to describe a Christian's conduct. Sometimes he used the word "live" (*zao*). Here in Philippians he used the verb "conduct yourselves as citizens" (*politeuo*). Scholars differ as to the exact force of the word in this text. It is a term built upon the Greek *polis* (city) and had overtones of citizenship responsibilities. Paul made conscious use of the term. The noun form occurs in 3:20 in calling the Philippians to appropriate ethical conduct. There he stated that "our citizenship is in heaven." No doubt the earliest readers would have associated the word with the Roman citizenship which they prized so much. This was Paul's way of reminding them of the obligations of people who participate in a society. In this case, the society was of Christians whose strongest ties were in heaven.

It is possible, and in some senses correct, to read 3:20 into 1:27. While Paul's ultimate concern is the same, the particular expressions differ. The three occurrences of the word *politeuo,* including the one in Acts, have slightly different nuances. In Acts 23:1, Paul stated he has lived his life appropriately before God. This assumes there is some standard by which life is to be measured and that it is one's responsibility to live oriented to it.[200] In Phil 1:27, Paul's concern is "the gospel of Christ." More will be said later regarding this expression, but clearly the gospel brings its own lifestyle expectations, which Paul expected of the church. In 3:20, Paul pointed them to their citizenship in heaven. Only in that spot did the term have the specific definition of "citizen."

Paul urged the church to live according to the expectations brought by being part of the gospel of Christ. The Greek term *politeuo* derived from the Greek political organization of the city. The Greeks called the official Greek cities *polis*, the root of the word found here. In Greek usage, the *polis* was far more than a geographical description. It was more than a way to organize the populous. It was a way of inculcating Greek philosophy and culture through a total experience that was "Greek."[201] Rome built on the *polis* idea to reinforce their rule in the empire. Consequently, the term is usually associated with Greco-Roman citizenship. No doubt the Philippians would understand that connotation. Rome expected its citizens to live in light of and to perpetuate the greatness of Rome. Paul chose the word intentionally since he and they lived under the supervision of Rome. As will be noted later, however, Paul did not mean by this word that they were citizens of Rome. In fact, he never stated that churches or Christians had any citizenship on earth.[202] Even so, several texts suggest the responsibil-

[200] Paul's statement before the Sanhedrin seems to suggest he lived his life pre- and post-conversion in good conscience. If so, that would mean his former life as an active Pharisee was done innocently, led by his conscience and Jewish interpretation of the Torah.

[201] For example, central to the *polis* was the gymnasium. The gymnasium was a place of athletic activities, but only because the physical body was to reflect the philosophical ideals of Gk. culture. The gymnasium taught Gk. culture.

[202] In several places Paul urged Christians to live their lives in peace by acknowledging their responsibility to governing authorities and the people within them (Rom 13, for example).

ity of earthly citizenship should also guide (Rom 13). The use of the word in Acts 23:1 does not refer to Roman citizenship (or any other). It refers to an ordered life lived in good conscience before God. Similarly, the Philippian Christians were to order their lives by the gospel.

The standard for conduct here is "the gospel of Christ." The construction "gospel of Christ" could mean "the gospel *about* Christ" (either a descriptive or an objective genitive). It could also mean "the gospel *spoken* by Christ." Though Paul indicates he has traditions recalling the words of Christ (1 Thess 4:15; 1 Cor 7:10), he does not describe these words as gospel. It seems "the gospel [about] Christ" is the better understanding.

Paul expressed his concern for the church earlier (1:24–26). Now he hoped to hear good news about them, particularly that they are standing firm in unity. Before, he expressed his preference and the likelihood he would continue his ministry on earth (1:25). He so longed for the church's maturity he was convinced that God would leave him on earth to help it grow in faith. Here he expressed less certainty: "[W]hether I come and see you or am absent" suggests either concern that he would not be released, or a change in travel and ministry plans. Many assume it means Paul lost his optimism about his circumstances. It is strange, however, that in two adjoining verses Paul would express confidence in his release and pessimism about it (1:25, 27). The better understanding is that Paul said no matter what happened to him he hoped for their well-being. In reality the church could grow with or without him, and now he spoke of the possibility that he might not come to them. If he were absent, perhaps because of an unfavorable verdict in his trial or unexpected delays, he still longed to hear of its good spiritual condition. Paul had no inflated ideas about his importance. The church was capable of standing by itself for the gospel.

Regardless of his personal circumstances, Paul expected continued communication between him and the church. He looked to continued reports from them about their progress. "I will hear . . . that you are standing firm" does not necessarily reinforce concern about his absence.[203] He modified that statement by "whether I come . . . or am

---

Yet, he does not affirm Christians are citizens of any earthly kingdom. They have a new citizenship. For an excellent discussion of the word "citizenship" in Philippians with the backdrop of Roman citizenship, see Witherington, III, *Paul's Letters*, 99–102.

[203] It should be noted a textual variant influences translations here. The question is whether the text reads "I will hear" (future indicative) or "I may hear" (subjunctive). The CSB

absent." "Hearing," therefore, is a way of stating that he expected the best. He was sending Timothy to them shortly, and no doubt he would return with good news.

Paul wanted to hear that the church was "standing firm." He often used words of posture to describe Christian privilege and responsibility. We are "seated" (Eph 2:6) with Christ in the heaven lies, for example. As already noted, the Christian's life is often described as a "walk." Commonly, as here, Christians are to stand.[204] Obviously this is metaphor implying a ready state, not in repose as sitting, nor in aggression as walking or running. Nor is it the posture of weakness nor of the victim of violence. It does imply that the church is to stand firm regardless of the theological and cultural winds that oppose them. Paul knew and expected opposition to the church, against which the church must be firm.[205] This anticipates verses 1:28–30, where opposition is clearly expressed.

Christians' stand is "in one spirit." This is the first of the several words for unity that bind together 1:27–2:4. The word "spirit" is used in parallel with the word "soul" (1:27b; "in one accord," CSB), and refers to the attitude that should characterize the church. Many commentators make the case this refers to the Holy Spirit. Fee offers four points in favor of that interpretation. (1) The Greek expression "in one spirit" is not found elsewhere in Paul or Greek literature generally. (2) In Paul, when the verb stand is followed by "in," it invariably provides the sphere of the stand (locative case). (3) There is a parallel in 2:1–4 which he interprets as the Holy Spirit. (4) Paul uses the expression elsewhere to refer to the Holy Spirit (Eph 2:18; 1 Cor 12:13).[206] The interpretation is accepted by other commentators as well. Alternatively, many interpret this as referring to the human spirit. This fits well with the complementary following statement "with one soul"

---

opts for the future tense. It is the more difficult reading, a canon of acceptance. The grammar, however, calls for a subjunctive verb to follow the subordinate clause introduced by *hina* (ἵνα). Perhaps some scribes were concerned that the subjunctive read with too much uncertainty, and therefore read the future. The Greek inflected form is the same. Ultimately, the meaning is the same, but the better reading is the subjunctive in a purpose clause.

[204] See 1 Cor 16:13; Gal 5:1. Interestingly, Watchman Nee organizes the Letter to the Ephesians with posture predominate: *Sit, Walk, Stand* [Carol Stream, IL: Tyndale House Publishers, 1977].

[205] Allowing for the Roman context of Philippi, there may be a slight overtone of the Roman soldier whose primary task in battle was to stand. Defeat meant disgrace, often punishable by death.

[206] Fee, *Philippians*, 164–66.

(translated "one accord" by CSB). The two statements do not stand in apposition, but rather stress metaphorically the "soul" of the church collectively, which expresses itself in unity with "one spirit." Hawthorne describes the meaning well. He says the church can "resist the challenge and overcome the adversary by joint effort, by a community spirit . . . ."[207]

In Philippians, "spirit" occurs six times: 1:19, deliverance comes through the "Spirit of Jesus Christ"; 1:27, "in one spirit"; 2:1 ,"fellowship with the spirit"; 2:2, "united in spirit"; 3:3, "worship by the Spirit"; and 4:23 "grace of the Lord Jesus Christ be with your spirit." Three of the six have clarifying modifiers to explain the term "spirit" (1:19; 3:3; 4:23). Two of those explicitly refer to the Holy Spirit (1:19; 3:3), and one clearly refers to the group spirit (of the church, 4:23). Those without modifiers are left to context to determine their precise meaning (1:27; 2:2). Significantly, Paul closes the letter with the prayer that Christ be "with [their] spirit." Not only is the modifier clear that it refers to the church, but the form is singular so as to refer to the group.[208] The group is considered as one entity that reflects Christian characteristics together.[209]

This use of spirit does not refer to the Holy Spirit. The word is ambiguous and some indicator as to its meaning would be helpful. The combination of the Holy Spirit working to strengthen the human spirit, accepted by some commentators, does not satisfy the parallel constructions. The interpretation rests on context or theology. The NLT and the CSB translate it with a lower case: "spirit." Paul drew on the imagery of persons to describe the function of the body of Christ. It is unnecessary to distinguish between "spirit" and "soul" here. They both explain the immaterial part of persons, and the point Paul made was the church was to unite inside and out. Both "one spirit" and "one soul" (CSB says "one accord") mean there was no divisiveness. The differences between the words are minimal.

---

[207] Hawthorne, *Philippians*, 56.

[208] Though some epistolary plurals are distributive, pertaining to each of the readers individually, this refers to the whole.

[209] The same issue and construction occurs in Eph 5:18 where the grammatical evidence favors "be being filled in spirit" (encouraging the inner strength of the church). This is the only statement in Paul about the "filling of the spirit," often translated "be filled with." "Filled with (of) spirit" is a Lucan distinctive occurring only in Luke/Acts. CSB says, "[B]e filled by the Spirit."

The stand is explained in two complementary ways.[210] The positive statement is "contending" for the faith of the gospel. The imagery changes again. Previously, Paul used the idea of a Greek *polis* to explain the Philippians' relationship to the Lord. Then he used the metaphor "stand," which was taken from the military. Next Paul's mind moved to the athletic games where he had seen team sports in action, a striving together. The metaphor is rare, occurring only twice in the NT (cf. Phil 4:3). If the Roman military element appreciated the military associations with the word "stand," the Greek population would identify with the necessity of "contending" as one man as was demanded in some athletic games. It does little good for individuals on a team to contend individually rather than as part of the team. Similarly, the church was to contend as one soul. Complete harmony of purpose and coordination of various elements was necessary to achieve God's purposes.[211]

The struggle was described in positive terms. The Philippians were to contend "for the faith of the gospel." The expression "faith of the gospel" has many possible interpretations, and there is little clear precedent in the NT that favors any one of them.[212] The context assumes people opposed the church and its message, so this construction probably relates to the church's taking the gospel to the world. Paul must have meant "contending for the advance of the gospel." The CSB and NIV translators have captured that meaning by the statement "for the faith."[213] The team effort supplied by the church would present the gospel to the world. Together the members also would explore

---

[210] Two participles modify the verb "stand." They are "contending together" and "not being frightened."

[211] Many Greek and Roman sports were contested individually. For example, gladiator sport was always a crowd pleaser. There were, however, team sports. The chariot races increasingly developed into team sports with four main teams: Red, White, Blue, and Green. The riders contested for their cities (and colors) for victory. Chariot racing was very popular in Rome. Though disdained by the social elite for the most part, Emperor Nero drove his own chariot and owned horses. Since Paul was in Rome at the time of this writing, he may have been hearing the partisan crowd discussing the chariot races. See Thomas F. Scanion, *Sport in the Greek and Roman Worlds*, vol. 2 (Oxford: Oxford University Press, 2014).

[212] Bockmuehl, *A Commentary*, 99, states it does not occur elsewhere in the NT. The genitive construction "of the gospel" could be descriptive ("a gospel-faith"), objective ("a faith directed toward the gospel"), subjective ("faith produced by the gospel"), or appositional ("a faith which is the gospel"). Of these, the second is the least likely. The word "faith" (πίστις) is also capable of a semantically active ("faith") or passive ("faithfulness") translation, and can even be a synonym for "message."

[213] This takes the construction τῇ πίστει with a true dative force.

the implications of the gospel in each other's lives. Bockmuehl states, "Christians are to contend for gospel-based faith."[214]

1:28 The second explanation of standing firm is negatively stated: "not being frightened." The term occurs only here in the NT and suggests a reflex action resulting from being startled.[215] The church was to have unflinching steadfastness even in the midst of persecution. Whoever the opponents were at this point, they were not to intimidate the Philippians.[216] Paul later equates their opposition with what he received and receives (1:30).

Often the opponents are assumed to be one of two possibilities. The opponents could be the Roman authorities who opposed Christians and the practice of Christianity. In Philippi, they were the ones who troubled Paul and Silas when they founded the church (Acts 16). Although that was approximately ten years earlier, Christianity still had not been declared legal. Since Paul stated the opposition was what they saw previously and persists in Rome, this is likely. From what we know of Paul's situation, however, in Caesarea he voluntarily requested to be in Rome's protectorate. From that time forward (ca. AD 58) Rome took care to provide for their citizen while he awaited trial. We know of no specific opposition from Roman officials while Paul was in Rome. Others suggest the opponents are the same as found in 3:2, Judaizers. These people harassed Paul from the time of his first missionary journey with increasing intensity. They threatened to seduce the Philippian church with energy enough that Paul needed to warn them. The problem with this approach is twofold: we know of no Judaizer opposition to Paul at Philippi, and it is very unlikely Judaizers were at Rome. Those against him in Rome were definitely Christian. Paul accepts their Christian message as correct, but he vehemently opposes the message of the Judaizers in 3:1. There is inadequate information to define the opponents Paul mentions here. Whoever they were, they, or others like them, harassed Paul for years.

---

[214] Bockmuehl, 99.

[215] It was used of horses which "spook" because of something that scares them, particularly in competition or war.

[216] The opponents in mind may have been Gentiles from outside the church, or they may have been Judaizers about whom Paul spoke in 3:2. Apparently, these opponents were used to having their way with Christians, for Paul urged the believers not to give in to intimidation.

The fact that the church stood fast became a sign.[217] The question is, To whom was it a sign? Scholars have taken two positions regarding the rest of this verse. First, some see the steadfastness as a confrontation to unbelievers and a confirmation to believers. Therefore, the same situation produced a twofold result. Unbelievers would see the stand of the church and know destruction was coming. They would be warned to accept the truth. On the other hand, the church will be encouraged by its own stand, knowing God strengthened it and that her salvation was sure. This interpretation contrasts the words "to them" (*autois*) and "of you" (*humon*) in 1:28.[218]

Following what he considers the historical position of the church, Fowl interprets both aspects as relating to believers. Ostensibly, it is difficult to see how "destruction for them" fits either the Roman or Philippian church. His interpretation is that the church will be saved but through martyrdom, their destruction.[219]

Others interpret the destruction with reference to the non-Christian world entirely. They point out that the words "for them" precede the rest of the sentence and must mean that both aspects of the church's steadfastness were a sign to unbelievers. They would know of their destruction and the believers' salvation. This makes better sense of the passage. The fact that the Philippians could stand firm in the face of adversity proved their relationship to the Lord. Unbelievers could see a hidden and unexpected strength. Paul did not enumerate the ways he knew the church would be confronted by such a proof. Apparently, it was the inner strength to live and die for what the Philippians believed. Such strength had to come from God himself, not from mere human resources.

---

[217] The Gk. text again is ambiguous. The pronoun "which" is feminine, and scholars question its antecedent. It could be "sign" (ἔνδειξις within the clause it introduces, by attraction), "faith" (1:27), or the entire situation. Paul normally used the neuter pronoun to refer to a previous clause or list of commands (see Eph 2:8–9; 1 Thess 5:17–18). Here the flow of thought suggests the entire clause, with the verb "stand" and the two participles ("contending . . . not frightened"), form the antecedent. The gender probably results from an attraction to "sign" within the clause.

[218] Hawthorne, *Philippians*, 59–60, makes a good case for this interpretation. His syntactical reconstruction is entirely possible, but one must question whether it is the best. Silva, *Philippians*, 95, states, "The sense thus achieved is attractive but the syntax is barely defensible."

[219] Fowl, *Philippians*, 66–69.

3.1.1.2 Christian Suffering (1:29–30)

The reason unbelievers would arrive at that conclusion is because God granted suffering to Christians. The text makes a direct connection between the "sign" and suffering, using a Greek word which must be taken as providing a reason.[220] These verses speak to the nature of Christian suffering (1:29) and the Pauline model of suffering (1:30).

3.1.1.2.1 The Nature of Christian Suffering (1:29)

Paul spoke straightforwardly about Christian suffering. In this text he clearly said it was a privilege, that God had in fact graced them with suffering.[221] Translators often use something like "it was given." It should be noted Paul's word is not the normal word for "to give." This word is built on the root of "grace" (*charis*). As a passive form, it means "it was given as an act of grace." The obvious giver is God, who graced them suffering. That raises serious questions, and it is necessary to study Paul's thought carefully. The suffering was on behalf of Christ, as stated in 1:29. The words "on Christ's behalf" appear to be vicarious, that is, in his place. They recall Col 1:24, where Paul stated he suffered eschatologically, essentially for the sake of Christ's body. Here the expression is more general. It is a distinctively Christian suffering, without a doubt. It is because of their standing firm for the faith of the gospel. The phrase points out that Paul had in mind the specific suffering that comes to Christians as they serve Christ.

The fact that suffering was connected with believing reinforces Paul's claim that it is a grace gift. Paul lived with persecution and he realized its redemptive value, but here he did not address that. The key to this phrase, "on Christ's behalf," is Phil 3:10, where Paul revealed his deepest desire of knowing Christ. That knowledge involved knowing resurrection power and the fellowship of suffering. Suffering confirms Christians' faith, brings them into closer contact with the Lord who suffered, and provides a vehicle for making commitment real and tangible. It is one thing to accept suffering and resign oneself to it. It is another to realize the privileges it brings.

---

220 The word is ὅτι, but one might expect γάρ.

221 The word translated "granted" is *charizomai* (χαρίζομαι), "granted as an act of grace."

3.1.1.2.2 The Pauline Model of Suffering (1:30)

Paul's life provided the model of the suffering he identified here. In 1:30 he used athletic imagery again ("struggle," *agon*) to remind the believers they would go through what he did.[222] In a parallel, 1 Thess 2:14–16, Paul explained his suffering related to calling the Gentiles to Christ so they could be saved. The universal nature of the gospel presented a problem to Gentiles, who had their own religions, and to Jews, who wanted the Gentiles to accept Judaism. The result was that Paul suffered at the hands of both groups, and the church at Philippi would do so as well. Paul had to develop a theology of suffering. He did so without becoming calloused to human need and without accepting suffering as good. The danger for Christians at Philippi and elsewhere was as they endured suffering, they would have one of those reactions. Suffering is evil because it comes from sin in the world. Those who oppose Jesus and Christians often unknowingly side with evil against God and the gospel. Paul stopped far short of mixing good and evil, which would make evil (suffering) a good thing. He did, however, realize the benefits and privileges of being involved in a battle for the truth and that battle scars were inevitable. The supreme model of that is Christ. Similarly, Christians should remember that general suffering sometimes comes because they live in a world which suffers as a result of sin, that Christians are called to a unique Christian suffering because of their identification with righteousness in an evil world, that it is a divinely given privilege to be involved in this battle, and that the struggle becomes redemptive in attesting the grace gift in their own experiences. The Philippians were, therefore, to take heart if they were called to suffer. Their steadfastness would demonstrate the reality of their relationship to God.

Theological and Practical Points

1. *A life worthy of the gospel of Christ.* Paul introduced this section with the command for Christians to live in an appropriate manner as "citizens of "heaven" (1:27). As noted above, the Greco/Roman idea of the city, *polis*, metaphorically pictures what this means. Since Paul seldom used the word picture, the questions may be asked, Why use

[222] The word is sometimes understood as a military term, but see Steven C. Hallum, "The Agon Motif in Philippians: Rhetorical Intertexture and Analytic Function of the Topos," PhD diss, Golden Gate Baptist Theological Seminary, 2010.

it here, and why in this context? The city of Philippi was a Roman colony, a coveted status not bestowed on all cities in the empire. When the city was repopulated by defeated Roman soldiers approximately a century before Paul's letter, allegiance to Rome was even more pronounced than before. Philippians were governed like Rome, dressed like the people of Rome, and implemented the values found in Rome. Ethnic pride characterized them.

The metaphor Paul used was intentionally chosen. Belonging to Christ brought its own privileges and responsibilities. The Christians were more specifically identified as being citizens of heaven based on faith in the gospel of Christ. Only the relatively few Christ-followers in Philippi enjoyed that privilege, and it was incumbent they demonstrate their unique identity to those around them.

What does it mean to be a "citizen of heaven"? First, this citizenship has no geographical boundaries. Unlike the borders of a country, the reach of the gospel has no defined local borders. Those who belong do so ideologically. They find comfort in their being rooted in the gospel and in their shared identity as citizens of God's kingdom.

Paul defined the gospel in 1 Cor 15:3–5. Christians are a defined-by-the-gospel people. Paul preached it, the Corinthians received it, they have taken their stand on it, and in so doing are being saved, assuming they internalize the message. This defining text reflects parallels with Philippians. In 1:27 Paul explained his expectation that the people would be "standing firm" as citizens of heaven. The components of the gospel they embrace may be put in parallel form with the two pivotal points at the head of each, as presented in 1 Cor 15:3-5:

Christ died for our sins	he (Christ) was raised on the third day
according to the Scriptures	according to the Scriptures
he was buried	he appeared.

The two focal points of the gospel correspond to the two stanzas of the poem about Christ (Phil 2:6–11). The death of Christ is clearly stated in Phil 2:6–8, but the resurrection, though not explicit in the poem, contains the parallels that God exalted Jesus, gave him the supreme name, and placed him as the proper object of worship. The Philippians are called to live consistently with the death of Christ and his resurrection. Living the death of Christ is most pointedly evidenced by service to one another as Christ's death expressed his supreme act of servanthood. Living the resurrection of Christ is most pointedly evidenced by willingly positioning oneself in the realm of the lordship of Jesus, where "every knee will bow . . . and every tongue will confess."

With this understanding the Philippian believers were encouraged to stand firm, to contend for the faith of the gospel, and not to fear their opponents. After all, they were the recipients of the servant-death of Christ and the beneficiaries of the power of Christ's resurrection. They were to live in triumph though conscious of enemy opposition and suffering. The specific concern is the ability to live under pressure, the pressure from unbelievers. It is to keep perspective, to stand firm, and to advance the gospel.

2. *Contending together for the faith of the gospel, 1:27b–28.* Paul used an unusual phrase for him: "faith of the gospel." Whether this means the faith communicated by the gospel or the faith in the veracity of the gospel, the gospel is primary. Two basic activities are associated with this emphasis. First, believers must stand firm. Paul possibly pictured the military phalanx involving Roman soldiers standing side by side as a firm and almost impenetrable human wall. In many ways it was the reason for the success of both Greek and Roman soldiers. The phalanx only worked because the soldiers stood together, and each understood his role in the conflict. They believed in each other. In the same way, Paul's imagery teaches that in spiritual battles there is the need of a spiritual phalanx. Every believer must understand the nature of the battle and be united with other believers.

The phalanx worked both offensively and defensively. The wall of soldiers could move ahead in lock step, or the men could stand shoulder to shoulder. Since Paul urges standing, he had in mind an advancing foe coming against them with the possibility of inflicting harm or even destruction. Standing together without discord, in the unity of "one spirit," brings greater effectiveness. Paul firmly believed standing firm was more than a nice, parade ground formation. It protected life.

Paul turned his imagery away from defense to offense. Again, the Roman military may have prompted his mind and its vocabulary. The church was to "[contend] together for the faith of the gospel." Phalanx soldiers moved in step, one step at a time, to "sweep" enemies into defeat. Similarly, the church was to move together in one accord. The idea behind "in one accord" is "one mind," the phrase so common in Philippians. If they moved together, the battle could be won.

Their "contending . . . for the faith of the gospel" was to be accompanied by confidence. They were not to be "frightened." Nothing so inhibits success as fear. There may be apprehension, but the gospel dispels fear. The inability of the enemy to put the church to flight evidences that the gospel has had its effect—the faith of the gospel has brought them salvation. Supernatural comfort and spiritual camaraderie confirm the truth. The truth reveals the error of the enemy: those who reject the faith of the gospel are destined for destruction.

The goal was to see the faith presented in the gospel move forward. Paul had stated as much earlier of his own circumstances. He wrote, "[W]hat has happened to me has actually advanced the gospel" (1:12). They were to join in unison to help spread the gospel.

All this produces a question, Who is the enemy? Paul spoke of discord at Rome, but he belittled the preachers' wrong motives because they joined with him in preaching Christ. They accepted and promoted the faith of the gospel. The Judaizers of 3:2 opposed Paul and the gospel. They were "enemies of the cross of Christ" (3:18). Though they were only on the horizon of Philippi, their ominous approach could be in mind. In this same context (1:29–30), Paul indicated the church suffered the same things he did, in presumably the same way. That likely refers to political or official opposition to the church.

The point of these verses is in order to be effective in its task, the church must stand together. The stand is not only in partnering with Paul. The apostle urged this whether he was with them or not. The spread of the gospel could not be accomplished by one man—no matter how energetic. The church had its own spiritual battleground, calling for collective and unified resources.

3. *Suffering for Christ.* Paul recognized that in spiritual battles, there would be suffering. Suffering, in fact, accompanies belief. The church was engaged in the same struggle that Paul experienced and continued to endure. Suffering was caused from the scars of battle as the gospel went forth. And the suffering of the past was caused by both Jews and Gentiles. The word Paul used for suffering in this passage is different from the word often translated "tribulations." "Tribulations" means pressure from the outside, being "between a rock and a hard place." "To suffer" is what Christ did for his church and is all-encompassing. Paul said the suffering was "on Christ's behalf" and "for him" (1:29). At Paul's conversion on the Damascus Road, Jesus told him he would "suffer" for Christ's name (Acts 9:16). Those who align with and promote the same gospel message as Paul can be expected to suffer as did Jesus and Paul. Suffering for Christ may be inevitable. It

is only temporary, however, since one day all will be made right when the Sovereign Lord actively and visibly reigns on earth (Phil 2:10–11). Christian suffering is another evidence the church stands with and for the Lord. It is inevitable, but temporary.

3.1.2 A Unified Mind (2:1–4)

[1] If, then, there is any encouragement in Christ, if any consolation of love, if any fellowship with the Spirit, if any affection and mercy,
[2] make my joy complete by thinking the same way, having the same love, united in spirit, intent on one purpose. [3] Do nothing out of selfish ambition or conceit, but in humility consider others as more important than yourselves. [4] Everyone should look not to his own interests, but rather to the interests of others.

Paul's thoughts turned from the need to withstand pressure from the outside to the characterizing attitudes of Christians individually and toward one another. Like so much of this epistle, the exhortations related to the church and its internal functions also relate to the church's ability to accomplish its mission to the world. In 1:27 he exhorted them to a unified walk worthy of the gospel, and here he continued the thought of church unity. The passage unfolds in three parts: the basis of Paul's appeal to unity (2:1); the essence of unity (2:2a); and the expression of unity (2:3–4). These three sub-points comprise part of another long sentence in the Greek text, and there is one basic command: "Make my joy complete." This is the second of three commands that mark this major division of the epistle.

Structure

[M]ake my joy complete
        by thinking the same way,
        having the same love,
                (being)united in spirit,
                (being) intent on one purpose.
        do[ing] nothing out of selfish ambition or conceit,
        but in humility consider others as more important than yourselves.
                Everyone should look not to his own interests,
                but rather to the interests of others.
if there is any encouragement in Christ
if any consolation of love
   if any fellowship with the Spirit
   if any affection and mercy

Interpretation

2:1 Four statements form the basis of Paul's appeal to the Philippians. The statements are introduced by the protasis (introduction) "if" in both Greek and English, and all four modify "make my joy complete" (v. 2). Although the word "if" brings doubt to the minds of English readers, these clauses express little hesitancy. They should be translated "assuming [this] . . . then make my joy complete."[223] All four statements introduce the command to unity of 2:2, and they identify Paul's concerns in approaching the church. Paul gently reminded the believers of what he and they shared in common. These four are more than relational characteristics. They call the church to recognize the common bond among them is the working of God in their midst. It was the God who began a good work who would also continue it (1:6). The corporate side of this statement consists of recalling the privileges and responsibilities of being "in Christ." There were deep spiritual bonds that tied them together, made all the more binding because they are shared relationship characteristics that apply to all believers. Paul appealed to them based on the spiritual connections that transcend earthly possibilities.

The four statements recall the blessings of serving in a Christian community. The first statement is, "If, then, there is any encouragement in Christ." Commentators differ on the precise meaning of the word translated "encouragement" (*paraklesis*). The Greek word is capable of meaning "encouragement, exhortation," or even "comfort/consolation." Since Paul continues immediately with the Greek word that more specifically means "comfort or consolation," it seems best to rule that meaning out here. Otherwise, the redundancy of statements is difficult to explain. Furthermore, the tone of this section is warm and gentle as Paul appealed to their common experience of Christ. The best understanding of the word seems to be "encouragement" that comes from Christian commitment, with both Paul and them being "in Christ." Without doubt, Paul has been exhorting them previously,

[223] The clauses are the fourfold protasis of a first-class conditional sentence. The apodosis is the imperative in 2:2. First-class conditions are translated "since" by many, but it is clear that translation cannot be sustained (see Matt 12:27). This class of condition sets up a logical relationship where an assumption occurs in the protasis ("if") and a conclusion ("then") based upon it occurs in the apodosis.

but this section contains a change of tone.[224] Second is the blessing of "consolation of love." The NIV correctly translates this as affirming Christ's love for his people, but other translations follow the Greek text literally. Like the CSB, they translate "any consolation of love," without designating whether it is an objective or subjective genitive, making it uncertain whether it is Christ's love or the love characterizing consolation of God. It could also reflect Paul's love for the church, or the reverse, the church's love for Paul. Finally, it could be the shared love between or among the persons implied. Obviously, there can be overlap in how the syntactical function of the word is used here. Since the first statement of the group identifies "encouragement in Christ," it seems best to take this in the same way: as God's love.

The "fellowship with the spirit" is the third statement of blessing. Virtually all agree this refers to the Holy Spirit. Paul referred to the Holy Spirit previously (1:19) in noting his circumstances would lead to his salvation in part because of the "help from the Spirit of Jesus Christ." In both cases there is a mutuality between the church and the Spirit. First, the Spirit provides energy to affect the affairs of things of earth (Paul's salvation). Second, the partnership in the Spirit enables the unity of the church.[225] The question is whether this is fellowship brought by the Spirit or fellowship in the Spirit.[226]

Finally, there is "affection and mercy." These qualities are often used of God himself (Jas 5:11). Paul, therefore, subtly reminds them of the privilege and responsibility of being like God. These are social qualities, effectively urging the church to express compassion and forgiveness toward each other. The word "compassion," (CSB "affection") is the strong word most often used as a characteristic of God. It literally refers to the movement in the intestines caused by emotion (*splagxna*).[227] The term "mercy" also points to God himself. Grace is a characteristic of God, a quality of his immutable nature. Mercy identifies the action when God's grace is put into service toward a specific person. Paul urges the church to recognize the strong, sympathetic

---

[224] Many take the word to mean "exhortation." See Lightfoot, Philippians, 107. Caird, Philippians, 116, takes "in Christ" as going with all the four statements, but its position and the symmetry of the four argue against it.

[225] The syntax opens several possibilities of meaning. It seems best to take this as a subjective genitive: "fellowship produced by the Spirit." That brings a collective sense of direction and corporate unity.

[226] Second Cor 13:13 speaks in favor of "fellowship produced by the Spirit."

[227] Paul is the only NT writer to use this word.

connection between the believers and that it is accompanied by genuine action motivated by God's grace. These statements make a strong emotional appeal, although their impact cannot be limited to emotion. Their rhetorical value clearly surfaces, and while Paul approached the Philippians gently here, the combined effect of the statements was powerful. Holloway states, "Paul's aim is not to produce a list of finely nuanced reasons for action but to create pathos, which he does by painting in very broad strokes: 'consolation . . . comfort . . . love . . . fellowship . . . deep affection and compassion.'"[228] He continues: "The language is more evocative than referential, which means that its interpretation lies not in a close analysis of the sort New Testament scholars are wont to perform, but in the larger context."[229] The church had a common experience of grace, and Paul built upon that in his exhortation. These qualities seem to be spiritual in nature, and it is best to take this as a fellowship the Holy Spirit provides.

2:2a Paul wrote to produce like-mindedness. His approach shifted from the blessings they shared in Christ to the Philippians' responsibility to Paul, their spiritual father. Paul's joy would be complete when they stood together in unity. The grammar of the text indicates this is Paul's primary concern. It is the apodosis, the "then" clause, of the four-fold protasis, "if clauses," that occur immediately before it. The clauses that follow further describe this statement by refining it to "thinking the same way." The prominence of this sentence is further highlighted by the fact that "make my joy complete" is only the second imperative so far in Philippians. The first occurs in the same larger context: "live your life worthy of the gospel of Christ" (1:27). Following the unique description of his personal situation (1:12–26), two striking commands urge their consistency in Christian living: "live your life worthy of the gospel," and "make my joy complete" by the church's unity. It is a climax of concern to which all of chapter one points, and it is the watershed on which chapter 2 depends. Paul's references to joy here suggested the anticipation of presenting a mature group of Christians to the Lord. His joy was that his life's work would amount to something good in God's economy and in the lives of other people (1 Thess 2:19–20). This should not be misunderstood in some egocentric way. Chapter 1 demonstrates Paul's

---

[228] Holloway, *Philippians*, 112.

[229] Holloway, 112. He calls it "rhetorical amplification."

lack of primary concern for himself. It is as though he provided details of his situation as a necessity because of their concern. Building on their concern for his personal situation, Paul informed them of what meant the most to him: their corporate spiritual growth. This personal appeal was a way of encouraging them onward for the glory of God.

The verb "complete" is often translated "fill or fulfill." It implies the completion of an act logically begun in the past. Paul has expressed his joy in the advance of the gospel. His joy began with the conversion of individuals to Christ through the gospel. Paul recognized conversion was not the end goal. This differs radically from some today who focus only on winning the lost. Winning them is the beginning. Maturity in Christ follows, with complete holiness as the end. Paul's joy in their conversion should be completed with his joy in their spiritual transformation, which would only take place when they were "like Christ" because of seeing him as he is (2 Cor 3:18). Paul's thoughts, however, were not on the eschaton or the final day of transformation. He focused more on the process of becoming mature in both character and witness. The church was to be in complete unity, explained by what follows. The unity of the church had immediate sanctifying power to the individuals in it, but it also had revelatory impact to those outside. Their common "stand" in unity was a sign of their salvation and unbelievers' destruction (Phil 1:27–28). Previously their stand was related to living up to the gospel's demands. Here their unity is to encourage each other by exemplifying the character perfectly revealed in Christ. One supports the other.

The content of his exhortation is that they be "like-minded" (*phroneo*). The verb used here for "thinking the same way" occurs ten times in Philippians (of twenty-three times in the Pauline corpus). It speaks to the intellect, but it goes beyond that. It incorporates the will and emotions into a comprehensive outlook which affects the attitude. With this idea and the contexts in which it occurs, Paul spoke of the values and ambitions which surface through the mind as the individuals shared the same Christian values. This is unity. It is not found in an identical lifestyle or personality, but occurs when Christian people have the same values and loves. Paul sought that in this church.

2:2b–4 Three characteristics express the unity of the church. They are goals for which to strive, and they provide the measurement of success. Each modifies "make my joy complete" by showing the manner it can be accomplished. So "same love," "united in spirit," and "intent on one purpose" tell how to achieve Paul's concern. Furthermore, the three modifiers basically restate three of the former protases ("if" clauses) of the conditional construction (2:1). By doing that, Paul emphasizes that the qualities the church and Paul share (2:1) also mirror the completion of his joy. The church is on its way to maturity; Paul hopes these qualities will deepen in their lives.

The four qualities following "make my joy complete" form a lexical chiasm. In fact, the first and fourth are the same verb in different forms:

A "thinking the same way"
 B "having the same love
 B′ "united in spirit"
A′ "intent on one purpose."

Understood this way, the primary point is to have the same values, to think "the same way" or be "intent on one purpose." This is a lexical chiasm relating to the definition of words. Grammatically, the text unfolds differently. The "A" of the chiasm is actually a subjunctive verb and is the primary verb of the subordinate clause. This verb is followed by three verbal statements that modify it ("B, B′, A′"): "having the same love," "[being] united in spirit," and "intent on one purpose."[230] The final word "intent" reflects the introductory verb "thinking." The restatement of the verb suggests "thinking the same way" is achieved through "same love" and same "spirit." The "one purpose," then, accentuates "thinking the same way." If the church should ask, "What does it mean to 'think the same way'?," the three reveal that: "having the same love," being "united in spirit," and "intent on one purpose." Paul reinforces this immediately in 2:5, where the church is commanded to "Adopt the same attitude as . . . Christ" (same Greek verb).

The three are stated in different ways, and either grammatical or logical units express them. The first is the same outlook. Three ideas combine to emphasize its different aspects: having the same love as Christ did; having a harmonious affection;[231] and valuing the same

---

[230] These three are statements involving predicate participles which modify the verb adverbially. The second implies the insertion of "being" to match the other two surrounding it. The CSB translates the same verb in two different ways: "thinking the same way" and "intent on one purpose" to demonstrate some progression.

[231] The Gk. is literally "like-souled," a term that occurs only here in the NT. It recalls "one spirit" of 1:27 and suggests the sharing of a life principle.

thing. There is nothing superficial about it. This unity comes from the core of one's being.

2:3 Paul expressed this both negatively and positively. Negatively, the Philippians were to avoid "selfish ambition" and "conceit." The former motivated the preachers Paul described in 1:17. Perhaps that was fresh in his mind. It led him to think about conceit, seeking glory which is, in reality, empty because it focuses on the individual rather than on the Lord. The positive side corrects improper attitudes. They were to act "in humility."[232] Before the NT era, the word "humility" had a negative connotation. The adjective related to it "was frequently employed, and especially so, to describe the mentality of a slave. It conveyed the ideas of being 'base, unfit, shabby, mean,' or 'of no account,' so 'humility' could not have been regarded by the pagan as a virtue to be sought after."[233]

Nonetheless, "humility" introduces a key theme of the passage. Paul further described it in 2:3 and 2:5–11. He urged the Philippians literally to "count others as excelling over themselves." This also relates to the mind and values. The word "excelling" ("more important," CSB) occurs in 3:8, where the pursuit of Christ excels anything Paul had before he engaged in it. The word "consider" occurs in the poem about Christ (2:6), as does the word for "humbled" (2:8). Since the model of Christ loomed in Paul's mind, Christ's actions provided the necessary motivation. Christ's humility is the standard for evaluating the worth of others and actions toward them. This does not mean personal concerns should be overlooked. Elsewhere Paul clearly stated Christians must take care of their own affairs as an act of love for the congregation (1 Thess 4:9–12). The next verse implies the same truth. Humility begins with a realistic appraisal of oneself and others as being in the image of God.[234] This relates intimately to the next characteristic, where the topic is continued.

Christian humility is often assumed to be reflected in self-abasement, particularly while in the presence of others. This meaning is

---

[232] A significant grammatical distinction is to be made between the negative and positive attributes. The negative is expressed by κατά and the accusative; the positive, by the locative or dative. It could be that this is a locative of sphere (operate within the sphere of humility) or a dative of reference (with reference to humility, consider others as excelling).

[233] Hawthorne, *Philippians*, 70. See also W. Grundmann, "humility," TDNT, 8:1–27.

[234] Martin, *Philippians*, 89, says, "The practice of humility consists in giving to other people a dignity and respect which Christians expect of themselves, especially as both parties are seen in God's sight (cf. Rom 12:3, 10)."

too superficial, individually paralyzing, and detrimental to the church. True Christian humility includes four basic elements that Christians must realize. (1) They must acknowledge God has gifted them to serve in his economy in some way, and they must find that/those gift(s); (2) God enabled them to do what they do; (3) they do not have every gift, but need what others have as well; and (4) they must answer to God for how they use their gift(s) for his kingdom. When these characterize the church, the church is effectively standing together.

2:4 The third measurement is consideration. The Philippians were to "look" out for others' interests as well as their own. Some Greek texts insert the word "also" in this sentence so it reads "also the [interests] of others." This may reflect an early interpretation, and it surely is a correct inference. Some, then, interpret this exhortation to mean the church is to focus on the good qualities of others in the church.[235] A way to unity, then, is watching to see how God works in others the qualities he desires in everyone. The focus shifts to others rather than personal spiritual qualities. The interpretation is attractive. It answers the problem of self-centeredness and false glory. It also does not relieve Christians of an obligation to care for their own matters. It expresses the dynamics of church relationships and fits the example of Christ. In reading the text, however, it seems Paul had more in mind. A natural reading suggests a broader reference point than merely spiritual qualities. Any concerns of others were to become the concerns of all! The Philippians were to imitate Christ. Jesus did not focus on the good spiritual qualities of the people for whom he left heaven. He died in spite of the fact that they were not spiritually attractive. The Philippians were to appreciate and serve each other regardless of external appearances or personalities. They were to realize that since Christ died for all, unified service had no boundaries.

3.1.3 A Unified Focus: The Example of Christ (2:5–11)

5 *Adopt the same attitude as that of Christ Jesus,*

6 *who, existing in the form of God,*
did not consider equality with God
as something to be exploited.

---

235 The interpretation is aided by the meaning and use of the word "look" (σκοπέω). It generally means to make something an aim or object of concern. That would mean each person was to make the good qualities in others his aim, asking that God work them in him or her as well.

7 *Instead he emptied himself*
by assuming the form of a servant,
taking on the likeness of humanity.
And when he had come as a man,
8 *he humbled himself by becoming obedient*
to the point of death—
even to death on a cross.
9 *For this reason God highly exalted him*
and gave him the name
that is above every name,
10 *so that at the name of Jesus*
every knee will bow—
in heaven and on earth
and under the earth—
11 *and every tongue will confess*
that Jesus Christ is Lord,
to the glory of God the Father.

Paul exhorted the Philippians to proper attitudes in 2:1–4. In 2:5 he repeated that exhortation in summary. The repetition emphasizes its importance. Even more, however, it introduces the ultimate model of humility and servanthood: the Lord himself. Philippians 2:6–11 recalls the attitude and actions of Christ as he left the glories of his preincarnate, eternal state to assume humanity and die vicariously. This is included as a model for the church. The Philippian believers were to imitate Christ because, among other things, the problems of disunity would be solved.

The thrust of the passage is clear, but scholars have debated almost every aspect of these verses.[236] They debate the form of the text. Is it a pre-Pauline hymn known and appreciated by the early church? If it were a hymn, what is its arrangement and order? In addition to the form of the text, they debate the function of the passage in the context of the letter. Is it theological, presenting Christology and soteriology as a foundation for the Philippians' action? Is it ecclesiological, exhorting

[236] Hellerman, *Philippians*, 105, states, "The literature on Philippians 2:5–11 has become virtually unmanageable. Scholars have produced whole books on single terms in the passage." Bochmuehl, *A Commentary*, 115, states in the twentieth century this text "has been the subject of an uncontainable deluge of scholarly debate, quite possibly more so than any other New Testament text." He adds, "Contemporary biblical scholars tend to gather like vultures over a suspected carcass."

them to unity in the church? Is it psychological, explaining how persons are to view themselves and their positions in life? Is it ethical, reinforcing a habitual behavior expected of genuine Christians? Is it sociological, about how to implement genuine Christian principles in the group? Once questions of form and function are answered, there are questions about the details of exegesis. Almost every word of the text has been debated. The following analysis cannot indicate the breadth of the debate. Rather, significant conclusions are presented, along with suggestions as to how the poem functions in its context.

The form of the text. The basic question regarding form is whether these verses are an early Christian hymn.[237] In the last half of the twentieth century, most contemporary scholars interpreted these verses as a hymn because of the rhythmical quality, rare words and phrases, and motifs (themes). Furthermore, this portion of the text seems hardly Pauline. At the least, it does not parallel Paul's normal style of writing nor are some of the themes in it typical of Paul. In the minds of many, the second portion of the passage, 2:9–11, goes beyond the demands of the immediate context. The poem is included to illustrate the nature of genuine servanthood. The second verse is about exaltation, not servanthood. It seems to be the second stanza of an independent hymn about Christ. Although the exaltation theme presented there contributes to the context, here Paul advocated humility rather than exaltation.

Those who accept it as a hymn warn against superimposing contemporary expectations of hymnology on the ancient text. Hymns today are distinct because of both technical and literary features. Most listeners today would recognize hymns because of their musical form. They combine a harmonious melody with a formal, often stately presentation. Time has hidden these features of Greco-Roman music if they were present. Obviously, they do not enter discussion of ancient hymns. Literary features receive more scrutiny. Particularly, hymns may be characterized by strict poetic meter and/or rhyme. These characteristics are expected in modern hymnology and found in some

---

[237] The literature on this subject is extensive and bewildering. Perhaps the best presentation is in Martin's works on the passage: *Carmen Christi, Philippians 2:5–11 in Recent Interpretation and in the Setting of Early Christian Worship* (Cambridge: University Press, 1967) and *An Early Christian Confession: Philippians 2:5–11 in Recent Interpretation* (London: Tyndale, 1960). V. Taylor also has a helpful study of the issues involved in this passage: *The Person of Christ in New Testament Teaching* (London: MacMillan, 1966), 62–79. An extensive bibliography is provided in Hawthorne, *Philippians*, 71–75. Keown, *Philippians 1:1–2:18*, 444–48, has an excellent and more current selected bibliography on this passage.

Greek or Semitic texts. This section does not fit those patterns well. Even so, there is a poetic feel. Without question the early church sang hymns. Colossians 3:16 and Eph 5:19 are often presented as proof. Perhaps the practice began with Jesus who, after he instituted the Lord's Supper, led them in a hymn before they left the room.[238] One of the earliest secular references to Jesus contains the statement that Christians sing "to Christ as a god."[239]

Most commentators point out the many aspects of this text that are unusual for Paul. For example: form (*morphe*); exploit[ing] (*harpagmos*); equality with God (*isa theo*); highly exalted (*huperupsoo*); and under the earth (*kataxthonios*) are not typically Pauline terms or phrases. These are sometimes explained as consistent with Pauline theology and therefore quite possibly attributed to Paul. Theologically, typical for him, the death of Christ and the cross occur here. The poem, however, does not include Jesus's resurrection and ascension, so essential to Paul's gospel presentations.

Those who advocate Pauline authorship point out 1) the absence of the word "hymn" in the text; 2) the argumentative nature of vv. 9–11(rather than attributing praise to deity as is typical of ancient hymns); and 3) the fact that no one has found a similar "hymn" to this in Greek literature.[240] The form of vv. 9–11 argues against complete symmetry in the two stanzas. The purpose clause modifying "God highly exalted him" serves to provide an intended reason for Jesus's exaltation rather than describing his personal attributes.

There is much discussion of authorship. Those advocating the pre-Pauline and hymnic nature of the passage contend it presents insight into the early church's worship. "Known" hymns (mostly interpretations of rhythmic style in the NT) indicate that worship was directed to Christ as God, included Jesus's death, and were generally "God-focused" rather than "person" or "experience" focused. Some seem to suggest if this material is not Pauline, it may not represent his theology. This conclusion is unnecessary. The text has a confessional nature which could be assumed to be based on the understood and shared Christology of the various churches. Whether Paul originated these words or simply included previously existing materials, he

---

[238] Matthew records the incident: "After singing a hymn, they went out to the Mount of Olives" (26:30).

[239] This is in Pliny's letter to Trajan (ca. AD 112–113).

[240] See Fee, *Philippians*, 192–4, n. 1–6, for a more complete analysis.

certainly put his approval on them as expressing his own theological commitments. Otherwise, Paul would likely have appended some corrective statements here. The passage certainly could be Pauline.

Considering these factors, it is difficult to determine if Paul actually wrote this section or only incorporated it. Apart from the unusual words for Paul found here (see above), the most significant factor is that there is no reference to the resurrection of Jesus. Paul spoke about the resurrection and/or lordship of Jesus more in his recorded preaching than he did Jesus's death. In his letters however, he wrote about Jesus's death with clarity and theological precision. No author wrote more insightfully or powerfully about the reality of Jesus's death or comprehensively about its meaning for the believer and the universe (Col 1:19–20). Whether Paul originated it or chose it for its well-known content in the early church, the text is one of the most powerful presentations of Jesus's person and work in cryptic form.[241]

Whether or not the verses reflect an early Christian hymn, they reveal the theology and worship of the early church. At least two characteristics predominate: they express a depth of theology which reveals a highly developed Christology; they reveal that the early church had formulated—or was being led to formulate—its Christology in enigmatic but powerful language.[242]

Scholars agree on little about the precise form of the text. Commentators accept from two to six verses with various arrangements. They normally appeal to theological themes for structure rather than to grammatical indicators.[243] Some believe Paul added his own comments so that the structure is irregular.[244] It seems clear the verses move in two directions, which must be considered the focuses of the text. Verses 2:6–8 speaks of Jesus's servanthood and vv. 9–11 speak of his exaltation. Literary analysis confirms these two segments. Further,

---

[241] It should be noted, of course, that until recent times many people were illiterate. Theology was learned through rhetoric and song. This is still the case in some parts of the world.

[242] Hellerman, *Philippians*, 106, following Reumann, *Philippians*, 364, considers this a Gk. *encomium*. Such is a "hymn of praise" extolling the virtues or activities of a particular subject. Even so, "Identifying Philippians 2:6–11 as an encomium contributes little to the interpretation of the text, but it does show that the Philippians would have been in familiar territory when they heard this portion of the letter for the first time."

[243] Hawthorne, *Philippians*, 6–77, presents a good representation of these various positions.

[244] Thus, theological or other reasons compelled him to amplify what the Philippians already knew, assuming pre-Pauline authorship.

a change of subjects from Jesus as actor (vv. 6–8) to God as initiator (vv. 9–11) affirms these divisions.

From a strictly grammatical perspective, the passage contains an interchange between independent and subordinate ideas. To aid envisioning this, the layout below presents the primary statements (independent clauses) first with the secondary and explanative statements (subordinate clauses) underneath. In the first emphasis, Jesus's servanthood (vv. 6–8), there are three statements: (1) who . . . did not consider equality with God as something to be exploited; (2) he emptied himself; and (3) he humbled himself. In the text, Jesus's emptying and humbling are linked by the conjunction "and," forming one main idea. Subordinate statements modify each of these: (1) existing in the form of God; (2) by assuming the form of a servant, taking on the likeness of humanity; and (3) when he had come as a man . . . becoming obedient to the point of death.

who [Christ Jesus of 2:5],
  existing in the form of God,
did not consider equality with God as something to be exploited.
Instead he emptied himself
        by assuming the form of a servant
        taking on the likeness of humanity.
And . . . he humbled himself
        when he had come as a man
        by becoming obedient to the point of death—
        even to death on a cross.

The section of God's response (vv. 9–11) contains two primary statements in parallel. These are modified by three subordinate clauses, one with the first statement and two modifying the second statement. The primary statements are (1) God highly exalted him, and (2) [God] gave him the name that is above every name. These two statements are linked together by "and." The supporting statements are (1) for this reason, and (2) so that at the name of Jesus every knee will bow, and every tongue will confess.

God highly exalted him
    For this reason
and gave him the name that is above every name
    so that at the name of Jesus every knee will bow—
        in heaven
        and on earth
        and under the earth—
    and every tongue will confess
        that Jesus Christ is Lord to the glory of God the Father.

In these two primary segments, vv. 6–8 and vv. 9–11, the main verbs carry the movements. Each section highlights two movements. First, [he] did not consider . . . . he emptied/humbled himself. Second, God highly exalted him . . . gave him the name, reflecting the movement of Christ to earth ending in death, followed by God's exaltation of him to the highest level.

Grammatically and thematically this appraisal fits. Some commentators have chosen to approach the structure differently. Most often they attempt to make the section conform to Hebrew parallelism, often assuming Paul inserts his own interpretations into it.[245] All agree the section is poetic, though not perhaps a poem in the modern sense. It has a rhythmic structure, especially when spoken. The repetition of key words is intentional. It was constructed carefully and thoughtfully. The approach in this commentary is a two-stanza poem, 2:6–8 and 2:9–11.

The function of the text. The discussion of how the poem contributes to the letter occupies the thoughts of scholars. In general, three positions attempt to answer the question. First, some consider the function of the poem to be primarily theological. Especially among older commentators, attention was devoted to discussions of the meaning and theological emphases. For some, context mattered little. In other words, the text was approached for its own interests without considering the impact of the problem at Philippi or the surrounding contexts. For example, they minimize any application to the problems caused by Euodia and Syntyche, addressed in 4:2. They hoped instead to fit the text into an early Christology. Second, some were concerned with the ecclesiological aspects. Since the problem which prompted including the poem concerned the fellowship of the church, its application to the church naturally predominated. Another aspect of the ecclesiological interpretations was that some became preoccupied with what the poem revealed about the setting of the early church. Employing form and source techniques, the text was viewed as a window by which to view early church order and worship. Naturally many interesting and fruitful suggestions arose when it was viewed this way. The problem which frustrated much of this study, however, is the fact that the only context that has survived is within the letter to the Philippians. No

[245] Keown, *Philippians 1:1–2:13,* 168–69, identifies the following: Weiss (two strophes with four lines in each); Lohmeyer (six stanzas, each of three lines); Jeremias (three strophes of four lines each); Eckman, (five strophes of varying length); Hooker (a chiastic structure).

one can be sure the material even had another context. Some became so preoccupied with their interests that their application to Paul's concerns at Philippi seem minor. Third, some scholars focused on the psychological, sociological, or ethical aspects. They assumed that Paul wanted the individuals of the church to implement the model of self-sacrifice seen in Christ, which was true, but at the expense of its powerful integration into Philippians. This view sometimes overlooked the theological significance of the poem. As noted earlier, sometimes these verses are isolated from their immediate context. Presumably for those who do so, since the poem had a "freestanding" life of its own, it merited separate consideration. Studying these verses in this way informs us more of early Christianity in general than any specific concern at Philippi.

Each of these approaches to the text is valid. Two major questions arise from the options. Is it necessary to isolate one of these approaches at the expense of the other two? Most today want to do just that. They assume if a psychological/sociological or ethical motif predominates, for example, then the theological (or other) has little importance.[246] There is no reason multiple reasons could not have guided Paul in his application of this text to the church. Typically, in his letters, Paul expressed theological truths, then described their application to a specific context.[247] It would be natural to use a theologically loaded text to make a practical point. In fact, that procedure strengthens the argument by providing the application to the church with a solid foundation. No matter what the primary focus, the passage is a window into the early church. The church had theological interests. The church applied theology to practical problems. The church used rhetorically powerful techniques to communicate truth so the masses would remember it.

The second question pertains to the theology of the poem. Is it proper to exegete the poem theologically if its ethical function is primary? Rather than explore the meaning of the poem, some bypass the

[246] Basically, interpretations follow either strictly theological lines (systematic or biblical) or "behavioral" lines. Often the latter is described as "ethical," stressing proper activity. Sometimes interpreters prefer "sociological," assumedly because of the plural intention of the exhortations. I have used "psychological," hoping to stress the individual reader's responsibility of self-identification with Jesus which would, of course, influence the entire group and be sociological.

[247] This occurs in small portions of the text (e.g., Col 2:8–3:4), as well as the larger progress of the letters, where most of them begin with theology and move to ethics.

difficult questions it poses in favor of making an application. They assume that since Paul's concern was moral/ethical (the nature of self-sacrifice), the illustration is the point. Generally, these interpreters do not seek the explanation of important words and ideas. Rather, the impact of the hymn in its totality, as opposed to its content, becomes the total message.

Such a procedure fails at two important points. First, it does not take account of the point of illustration. Paul penned these words because they conveyed what he wanted, implying he accepted the content of the poem and saw in it the greatest example of proper attitudes. Second, the illustration loses its impact if the details have no significance. The distance Jesus traveled from the "form of God" to "death on a cross" dramatically reveals the servant mindset that each believer should adopt. Hermeneutically, this material first calls for a serious exegesis of the content of the poem as a freestanding theological expression. Further, the hermeneutical task involves applying that servant attitude to the church. In actuality the two intertwine. No one in the church could repeat what Christ did. They did not begin where he started, they could not suffer the way he suffered, and they could not be exalted to the position he occupied. That is not the point. The attitude of Christ is the point of application, and that loses its impact without its theological foundation. The interpreters who ask questions about the Christology of the passage, the meaning of the emptying, and the nature of the exaltation ask the proper questions since that dimension is essential to a clear understanding. Concomitantly, the application of the text to individuals and the church at large completes the text as it stands in its canonical form. One theological interest captivates the minds of many: What does "he emptied himself" mean? The proposed answers to that question occupy many thousands of pages and vary widely. Trying to answer the *kenosis* of Jesus led many beyond the scope of the text and its purposes. While interesting, nothing in the text itself leads to a definitive answer.

One final concern, mentioned earlier, must be explored. Many interpreters question the Pauline authorship of these verses. Specifically, they point out this hymn has a decidedly Semitic background which seems to translate an Aramaic original;[248] typical Pauline themes

[248] These are participles functioning as main verbs, non-Greek constructions like "having been found . . . as," repetition of "threes" (three stresses to a line, three lines to a strophe, three-fold division of the cosmos, three-fold theme of preexistence, humiliation, exaltation).

are missing;[249] and there is, according to some, an un-Pauline emphasis on the "servant of the Lord" from the OT.[250] The situation, however, could account for many differences in wording; linguistic data are not conclusive; Paul could write in poetic style (1 Cor 13; Rom 8:31); and many Pauline elements are present in the poem. It matters little in the interpretation of this text, although it contributes to an understanding of Pauline Christology. What matters is that Paul chose to use this material to make his point; it is consistent with his views about Jesus; and he put his approval on it by building his argument around it. The poem serves to illustrate and explain the exhortations of, particularly, 2:1–4.[251]

Consequently, it is impossible to miss the point. The Philippian believers were to eschew the self-seeking values of the surrounding culture and embrace the virtues demonstrated by Christ. In this, they were to think and live with a reversal of the world's ambitions. They were not only to reject braggadocios and egocentric displays of honors and accomplishments, but they were also to reject the attitudes that fostered them. Such a radical and genuine change of attitude parallels a deeper understanding of the attitudes and actions of Jesus himself.[252] They are the exact opposite, a complete reversal, of the ambitions of the power conscious Philippians in their culture.

Analysis of the text. These verses contain two parts: an introduction in the form of a command (2:5) and the example of Christ (2:6–11). The Christ example has two movements: the humility of Christ (2:6–8) and the resulting exaltation of Christ (2:9–11). The following

---

[249] Such as redemption (no ὑπέρ, περὶ ἡμῶν, or any substitutionary idea is explicit), resurrection (the hymn moves directly to exaltation), the church.

[250] These come from E. Lohmeyer, *Die Briefe an die Philipper, und die Kolosser und an Philemon* (Göttingen: Vandenhoeck, 1953).

[251] E.g., W. S. Kurz, "Kenotic Imitation of Paul and of Christ in Philippians 2 and 3," *Discipleship in the New Testament* (Philadelphia: Fortress, 1985), 103–26, argues the letter basically urges the church to imitation of Christ (primarily) and of Paul (secondarily). In this, these verses are central to the exhortation. The point is well made but may be overdone. He argues persuasively the letter is a unity because of the literary parallels.

[252] Hellerman, *Philippians*, 1067, provides a powerful and exacting illustration of the difference in Philippi. He quotes the (self?) description of a noted aristocrat of Philippi, and provides a detailed explanation of what these accolades meant in contrast to the humility expected of all Christians.

"Publius Marius Valens, son of Publius, from the tribe Voltinia, honored with the decorations of a decurion, aedile, also decurion of Philippi, priest of divine Antoninus Pius, duumvir, sponsor of games (395/L780)."

commentary will focus on conclusions and major questions. Space forbids the type of analysis that deals adequately with each portion.

2:5 Paul introduced this section by looking both backward and forward. In retrospect, he picked up the theme of the proper attitude which he commended in 2:2 ("thinking the same way") and 2:3 (with the word "consider," found in 2:3, 6). Looking ahead, Paul anticipated the epitome of those with the proper mind: Jesus.

Two primary questions arise from the Greek in 2:5. What is the meaning of "your attitude should be the same as," and what is the sense of "Christ Jesus"? The CSB handles these problems by presenting a more dynamic translation: "Adopt the same attitude." The KJV says, "Let this mind be in you." The differences come from the Greek text chosen as well as the translator's preference. The first question relates to the verb translated "adopt the same attitude" by CSB. Is the verb active (*phroneite*) or passive (*phroneistho*)? The KJV adopts the passive: "Let this mind be." The interpretation is based on later manuscripts of the Majority Text which made their way into the KJV.[253] Following these manuscripts, the readers are enjoined to allow the proper attitude to come to them, presumably from God as the actor and provider. Most translations have the active form, and that is the better reading.[254] Technically, it should be translated something like, "You think this in you." The CSB "adopt" captures the point well. The active command force of the text indicates that the readers should embrace the proper attitude as a matter of choice.

The second question concerns "of Christ Jesus," which occurs at the end of the verse. As the Greek text stands, another verb is needed to make a complete statement, and some translators add "was." The sense, then, is "have this mind in you which was in Christ Jesus." Others have repeated the main verb of the first part of the sentence for a translation like, "You think this in you which you think in Christ Jesus,"[255] meaning the Philippians were exhorted to think properly as Christians, as those "in Christ Jesus." The translation has much to

---

[253] Primarily C^3, Ψ, 075, 0278.

[254] Hawthorne, *Philippians*, 80, takes the passive form as best. Almost no one agrees with him.

[255] This comes from A. Deissmann, *Die Neutestamentliche Formal "in Christo Jesu"* (Marburg: N. G. Elwert'sche Verlagsbuchhandlung, 1892), 113–17; E. Käsemann, "A Critical Analysis of Philippians 2:5–11," in *God and Christ: Existence and Providence in Journal for Theology and Church* (New York: Harper & Row, 1968), 45–88, and a good case is made by Silva, Philippians, 107–111, who also quotes these sources.

commend it.[256] Immediately, however, Paul appealed to the attitude of Christ, and the most natural reading is to understand Paul to say, "Think this in you which Christ thought in him." This is supported by the words "which also," referring to that which Christ thought in his incarnation.[257]

Both of these verbal insertions assume Jesus's past attitude. It is more common with elliptical expressions to insert a present verb form. This opens the choice of whether the attitude "was" in Christ Jesus or "is" in him. The difference is more than semantic. Understanding the insertion of "is" rather than "was" identifies an ongoing attribute of Jesus. Advocates say his servanthood should not be limited to a specific point in time since the qualities necessary for deity to assume humanity have existed eternally. They are part of the immutable attributes of deity. Though difficult to imagine-God the Son is eternally a servant, coinciding with his attribute of grace and, as grace is put into action, mercy. In that sense, Jesus was and is a servant while still being sovereign. Jesus always had the capacity within to display his servanthood at any specific point in time. The issue depends on whether one assumes the poem to follow focuses on a specific time action—when Jesus came to earth—or whether the poem extols the eternal attribute as illustrated in the incarnation.

2:6–11 Paul commended Jesus's disposition by appealing to his attitude (2:6) and his actions (2:7–8). The order is both logical and chronological. One led to the other. The question of sequence (time) may be significant when speaking about deity. Perhaps there are no time progressions in eternity. That is a subject of significant debate. This text, however, presents Jesus's actions sequentially. Jesus, thus, is to be viewed in time and space. The text points to a movement when Jesus entered history and took on himself humanity. Humans can identify with that. Paul employed the same order in 2:1–4, where he addressed the attitude (v. 2) first, then actions toward others (vv. 3–4). Perhaps Paul's exhortation was based on the poem which he anticipated. In this text Christ's attitude (presented negatively to make a positive point) led to his redemptive actions.

---

[256] Most notably, it makes good, straightforward sense of the Gk. text which is difficult at best, and it takes the usual sense of Paul's phrase "in Christ"—the soteriological environment of the church.

[257] The construction is a Gk. neuter relative pronoun and the conjunction, ὃ καὶ.

2:6–8 The main verbs are the key to the structure, and Jesus's attitude is presented in the first. Jesus "did not consider equality with God something to be exploited." Precise knowledge of why that was so remarkable comes from the phrases which modify and explain the significance of his attitude. The Greek verb "consider" repeats from 2:3, where Paul encouraged the church to "consider others as more important than" self. It implies a value system of thought followed by action, which is usually identified in the context. It is a stronger verb than "think," and is a fitting compliment to the often-occurring verb "to be minded." Indeed, the verbs occur in the same contexts here: one for the proper attitude of the church and the other for the exemplary attitude of Jesus.

Two parallel statements show the exemplary nature of Jesus's thoughts. The first is "the form of God" which is compared to the second, "equality with God." Fee states that "together . . . they are among the strongest expressions of Christ's deity in the NT."[258] The former is normally translated by the English word "form," which is true to the literal meaning of the Greek *morphe,* though some, such as the NIV, translate it "being in very nature God." Commentators have debated hotly the meaning of the word "form."[259] Basically, the word means "form, outward appearance, shape";[260] but since the noun form occurs only in 2:6 and 2:7 in the NT, the context must determine its precise meaning. In the expressions the "form of God" (2:6) and the "form of a servant" (2:7), form must mean the same thing since the same word occurs of both. Some take outward appearance to mean that the visible appearance of God is not a factor because he is invisible, and therefore the text calls for a nuance of the word. This meaning should not be dismissed too quickly. The poem called the readers to consider the pre-human state of Jesus. Then he was in the form of God. Physical eyes cannot see spiritual realities, only spiritual eyes can. Given the context, it would not be uncommon to use the term to state that he actually "appeared as God" to those who could

---

[258] Fee, *Philippians*, 207-8. He continues: "This means further that "equality with God" is not that which he desired which was not his, but precisely that which was *always* his."

[259] Hawthorne, *Philippians*, 81–84, provides perhaps the most complete survey of possibilities. He includes: "form" is equal to "glory" (μορφή = δόξα), based upon parallel passages; "form" is equal to "image" (μορφή = εἰκών), based on Gen 1:26–27 and 3:1–5; "form" is "mode of being," based on the Gnostic parallels; and "form" is "condition" or "status." Each of these has extensive support and implications for Paul's (the hymn's) motif. Hawthorne does not accept any of them.

[260] BAGD, 528.

see him.[261] Nothing in the context requires that human eyes see the pre-human form.

In 2 Tim 3:5 Paul condemns false teachers because they have a "form of godliness but [deny] its power."[262] Paul's concern there was the outward appearance did not resemble the inside. The form, then, was something that could be assumed, that is, adapted for some specific purpose, in that text assumed for pragmatic reasons. The form is equated to a garment of clothing which, perhaps, reveals a person's attributes. This may illumine Paul's concerns in Philippi since proper clothing was appropriate to one's status. In Philippi it may have been true that the clothing revealed the person. O'Brien well states this view, assuming it presents "a picture of the preexistent Christ clothed in the garments of divine majesty and splendour [sic]."[263] The statement would certainly resonate with the class conscious Philippians, some of whom were likely in the church. It seems, however, Paul's use of the phrase goes deeper than the metaphor of clothing. The parallel phrase "equality with God" serves in part to define "form," surely indicating that "form" was more than utilitarian. Further, while the word "form" may have been chosen for its visual connotation—that is what could be seen, its use is consistent with the inner aspect of Christ's pre-human condition.

Other places where the idea of "form" occur help define it here. In Phil 2:7, Paul states Jesus took "the form of a servant." There is some contrast since his being in the form of God is introduced with "being" (*huparxo; CSB says "existing"*) and the form of a servant is connected to "taking" (*lambano*). Did Jesus change forms to the visible eyes who beheld him? Similarly, in the transfiguration accounts of the Gospels, Jesus's pre-human form eclipsed his human form so he visibly went from mere man to obviously God (Mark 9:2–4). This event assumes that his "form [as] God" always characterized him, even while on earth and living as a man. It was, however, hidden so that the servant form predominated.

---

[261] J Behm, *TDNT* 4:745–46, states the word means that "which may be perceived by the senses."

[262] Second Timothy 3:5 contains a word on the same lema, *morphosin* (μόρφωσιν). The word in 2:6, 7 is (μορφή).

[263] O'Brien, *The Epistle*, 209. This certainly resonates with the concern for social order that characterized Philippi. See Hellerman, *Philippians*, 110 and elsewhere.

Similarly, the "form of a servant" does not require that human eyes be able to see that servant as a servant, although with spiritually enlightened eyes one sees it. The question is whether Jesus had that form. Surely the actions described of him here are appropriate to the servant role, and they appear in his death on the cross. The word "form" means an outward appearance consistent with what is true. The form perfectly expresses the inner reality.[264] When asking "What does God look like," the partial answer is "look at the pre-human Jesus," though of course that is impossible for humans. When asking "What does a servant look like?," the answer is to look at the incarnate Jesus.

The description "form of God" parallels "equality with God." "Equality with God" is, therefore, another explanation of Jesus's nature. The form of the expression stresses the manner of his existence since the word "equal" is actually a term helping to show how he existed.[265] In the Greek text, the phrase is introduced with an article so that it should read "the equality with God," referring back to something already identified as equality.[266] Thus "form of God" and "equality with God" refer to the same state of existence,[267] and the CSB correctly translates "in the form of God" as implying the very nature of God. Fowl provides a good definition of "form of God" that also relates to "equality with God." "Thus, the claim that Christ was

---

[264] Lightfoot, *Saint Paul*, 127–33, drew a correct distinction between μορφή and σχῆμα by saying "that which is intrinsic and essential with that which is accidental and outward." The distinctions will not always hold, but they seem generally true. He preferred to equate the form with "attributes" and spoke of a transfer from "objects of sense to the conceptions of the mind."

[265] J. Müller, *The Epistles of Paul to the Philippians and to Philemon*, NICNT (Grand Rapids: Eerdmans, 1955), 80, says, "Christ could have existed and have appeared only as God, only in a manner equal to God: it was a right which was due to him; he need not have gone into another manner of existence." This captures the thought well.

[266] The Gk. text uses an infinitive to express this phrase. Infinitives may occur with or without the article and have generally the same force. Here the article appears to call to mind the previous reference since the same sense could be achieved without the article.

[267] Some scholars point out that literally the text states "in the form of God" and not that he was the form of God. The locative sense they affirm means "in the sphere of God"; apparently the sense would be that Jesus existed "within God's sphere," rather than "as God." The point of that distinction would be difficult to understand. All beings exist "within God's sphere" (presence) as Paul reasoned in Acts 17:28. Paul's point must have been that Jesus was uniquely "in the form of God." If anything, he meant Jesus "emerged within God's form." Given this difficulty, and Paul's general Christology, this phrase must mean he was in nature God.

in the 'form' of God can be taken as a reference to Christ's sharing in the eternal glory of God and making that glory visible."[268]

Two other matters relate to Jesus's pre-incarnate state. The first is the meaning and force of the Greek participle often translated "being" (CSB says "existing"). The basic meaning of the word is "to exist originally,"[269] but later the term was used as an intensive form which meant "really exist." The result is that Jesus "really existed" in that form. The force of the participle is debated as well. Most interpreters understand it with a concessive force ("although being"), stressing the dramatic nature of Christ's humility.[270] Alternatively, the verb may have the syntactical force of cause: "since" he was in the form of God. As will be argued below, God is always a servant as part of his divine attributes. His self emptying may be the ultimate expression of who he really is. While attractive, and certainly true, the point of this discussion highlights the amazing truth that God did not allow himself to get in the way of his purposes.

The second matter is the meaning of "something to be exploited." Some understand the words to mean "something to hold on to," while others take them to mean "something to rob."[271] Often Jesus is contrasted with Adam, who selfishly attempted to rob God of what he had no right to possess. He wanted to be "like God" (see Gen 3:5). This contrast may have been in Paul's mind, but any suggestion that requires the sense of aspiration to "equality with God," as though it were not already a characteristic of Jesus, cannot fit the passage.[272]

---

[268] Fowl, *Philippians*, 94.

[269] The etymology of the term means "under the beginning," stressing the original state of affairs. In actuality, it is somewhat synonymous with "to be," but stresses the reality of existence (BAGD, 838).

[270] Hawthorne, *Philippians*, 85, takes the participle causally: "Precisely because he was in the form of God." The idea is attractive, but the text speaks of giving up what one has, and the concessive emphasizes that more. See also Bockmuehl, *A Commentary*, 133. The choice depends on the nature of the context and its force, since it is not a matter of grammar or lexicography.

[271] The question is whether *ἁρπαγμόν* is active ("to rob") or passive ("to be held"). It is difficult to see how "equality with God" should be robbed since he already possessed it. If a grasping were to take place, it would have to be a grasping of something other than equality with God, but that is precisely what the text identifies.

[272] Many interpreters have pointed out the Adam/Christ contrast lay behind Paul's thinking when he spoke of the human Jesus. The contrast helpfully explains the "in Adam"/"in Christ" motif. The objection here is to any idea Adam and Christ were equal in what they wanted, to grasp equality with God. Jesus had it; Adam sought it. Though other texts assume the Adam/Christ motif, it is difficult to see it here. There is no supporting context or parallel to make this explicit. It is an unlikely comparison.

With this understanding, Christ would have refused to do what Adam did. He refused to grasp what was not his.

Two factors argue against the concept of "something to be grasped." First, the text more naturally reads "not to be clutched." Since he already possessed "equality with God," Jesus had nothing to grasp. He was able to release the appearance of deity. Second, when the word "grasped/clutched" is studied with words like "consider" (*heμgeomai* 2:3, 6) the "idiomatic expression refers to something already present and at one's disposal."[273] The passage may mean that Christ did not think of his equality as "something to use for his own advantage."[274]

Indeed, scholars have taken considerable interest in the word translated "exploited" (CSB). The word *harpgmon* may be understood in one of two different senses. As noted above, it may mean "snatched away for some good purpose" (a "positive" meaning of the word), or it may mean "steal or plunder" (a negative meaning). This is explained by some as active and passive. The active meaning is that Christ could have sought to seize (active) equality with God. The passive meaning is that Christ had (passive) equality with God but chose not to use it. The active meaning, "to seize," has some support from the structure of the poem as it moves to a crescendo of God rewarding Jesus with an exalted name. This meaning is not clear. God exalted Jesus to a new position, but that is not equated to "form of God" or "equality with God." On the other hand, the passive meaning finds support from the phrases "form of God" and "equality with God" as translated in their obvious sense to describe deity. The passive meaning is surely correct. The wording indicates Jesus did not use what he had, or better who he was, to his own advantage.[275] As Fowl states, "Although this term has generated a long scholarly debate, it now appears that there is a consensus emerging, which is that in contexts such as this one we should understand the word indicating something that is used for one's own advantage."[276] Thus, translations like the CSB, "exploited," well capture the meaning.

---

[273] R. W. Hoover, "The *Harpagmos* Enigma: A Philological Solution," *HTR* 64 (1971): 95–119. See also N. T. Wright, "*Harpagmos* and the Meaning of Philippians 2:5–11," *JTS* 37 (1986): 321–52.

[274] Hoover, "The *Harpagmos*," 118.

[275] A full, recent discussion of this can be found in Keown, *Philippians 1:1–2:13*, 393–401. He concludes that Jesus did not use what he had for his own advantage.

[276] Fowl, *Philippians*, 94.

Every aspect of vv. 1–11 stands in stark contrast to the attitudes and actions characteristic of the values of ancient Rome. The culture expected its citizens to seek to rise to the top. At Philippi this certainly was their pattern of thinking. It was, therefore, almost unthinkable that someone would not use "what he had" or "what she was" for personal benefit. The status-conscious society took advantage of everything possible to get ahead. Jesus displayed an opposite and higher value: you advance in God's kingdom by service!

This first description of Jesus as the ultimate model for Christians is packed with theological importance. Verse 6 should be read like this: though (concessive) he really existed in the form of God, he did not consider that (state of) equality with God to be something to exploit.[277] The concessive use of the participle in Greek presents an obstacle necessary to overcome. Christ's success in "succeeding" in that victory highlights the power of this statement. The obstacles to servanthood were significant: he existed in the form of God, which was equal to being God. For most, including the Romans and Philippians, God could not be pictured as a servant. Furthermore, successful humans could not serve in the role of servant. The remarkable aspect of Jesus's attitude and subsequent actions is that deity did not stand in the way of servanthood. Rather, as will be seen, servanthood is entirely consistent with deity. To grasp and live that understanding is revolutionary!

2:7 The poem moves from attitude to actions. Two verbs describe successive actions as Jesus gave himself for humanity: "he emptied himself" and "he humbled himself." Each has a phrase modifying it and combined they make the one point, though in two stages: the first to become human; the second to endure death. The first of Jesus's choices was to empty himself. The CSB translation "he emptied himself" captures the spirit of the passage. Historically, interpreters have wondered of what did Jesus empty himself? The question shows that, for them, a theological interest predominates in the passage. Most modern interpreters, however, point out the hymn does not speak to that point. The contrasts between "Lord" (v. 11) and "servant" (v. 7), and "form of God" (v. 6) and "likeness of humanity" (v. 7) express the emptying. As a result, the emptying is that God became human, Lord

[277] This follows the previous discussion and the flow of the Gk. text. 1) The participle "existing . . . " should be concessive. 2) The participle phrase modifies the verb "consider." 3) The verb "consider" has a double object: a) something to hold on to, and b) the equality with God.

became servant, and obedience took him to death. The verb "emptied" does not require knowledge of what was emptied (Rom 4:14; 1 Cor 1:17). Often it is translated simply "to render void, of no effect."[278] This passage affirms simply that Christ left his position, rank, and privilege. They were of no effect given the task that lay before him.

The theological question is important and should not be totally cast aside. This passage, however, does not provide enough information to make judgments about it. The text only states explicitly that he "emptied himself." The addition of the word "himself" provides the object of the verb and, therefore, the focus of emptying. The most that can be said here is Jesus left the appearance of deity to accept the form of a servant. Some argue for a low Christology on the basis that he really became human. Nothing in the text suggests being human required him to be less than God. Most of the theological discussion regarding the *kenosis* of Christ involves reading in other assumptions, either high or low, regarding Christ. It is best to leave unanswered questions the text does not raise and, therefore, does not answer.[279] [See further the section below under "Theological and Practical Points."]

One relevant theological question related directly to the text is the power of Jesus while in his state of humiliation, being human. Could the human Jesus accomplish what Paul and other NT writers state? Christians have always affirmed that in some way divine energy was operative in Jesus. The questions of when and for what purpose require more consideration than space allows. One of the most crucial points to discuss from this text, however, is the statement that Jesus was obedient to "the point of death—even to death on a cross" (2:8). Paul spoke of the death of Jesus strategically. He made the theological connection between the death of Christ and salvation/redemption. One specific place this occurs is Rom 5:6–11. Verse 6 of that passage says, "Christ died for the ungodly." In his death he demonstrated God's love (5:8) and brought reconciliation between humanity and God (5:10). Four times in these verses Paul mentioned the death of Christ. His point repeatedly emphasizes that Jesus's death is vicarious,

---

[278] BAGD, 428.

[279] It may be that some interpreters wish to make Christ's emptying paralleled in thought with the statement in 2:3: Paul warns against "vain or empty glory." Thus, there is a desire to add some type of genitive modifier to the verb "empty," suggesting "emptied of something." The text, however, presents a change of "rank" or "activity," the most extreme imaginable: from deity to servant!

reconciliatory, and salvific. The connection between Jesus's death in Rom 5 and Phil 2 is more than symbolic. In Phil 2:8 the point is the extent of Jesus's servanthood. Paul left unsaid what that servanthood means in providing forgiveness and new life for believers. Elsewhere he makes it clear. The physical death of Jesus reveals his complete obedience. Romans 5, however, provides the immediate reason for Jesus's death. It is to provide salvation. It is missiological. The connection is direct.

Paul also connects the cross to more than a human death. Philippians 2:8 completes the extent of Jesus's humility by his being subject to "death on a cross." Colossians 1:20 explicitly connects reconciliation to "through his blood, shed on the cross." The two passages link with the cross as the center. In Philippians God exalted Jesus because of the cross, making him the central person of the Godhead for adoration. In Col 1:20 the entire universe and all within it are reconciled to Jesus, providing peace. Connecting the theological thread of the cross in both passages indicates the divine purpose at work in and through Jesus. Barclay comments, "'Even the death on a cross' (2:8) evokes numerous associations in the letters of Paul, for whom 'the cross' is never a bare fact, but the site of God's saving power."[280]

Paul argued for the unique power of the cross, a power beyond human ability and comprehension. In 1 Cor 1:20–25 he defended his life and ministry by appealing to the cross. In the natural human conception, the most powerful or wise win the day. The Jews "ask for signs" (1:22). After all, who should follow someone who was not powerful enough to avoid his own death on a cross? On the other hand, the native people of Corinth, "the Greeks seek wisdom" (1:22). Who should follow one not wise enough to prohibit his own death? Yet Paul's message was "Christ crucified, a stumbling block to the Jews and foolishness to the Gentiles" (1:23). He preached "Christ is the power of God and the wisdom of God, because God's foolishness is wiser than human wisdom, and God's weakness is stronger than human strength" (1:24–25). Therefore he "decided to know nothing among [them] except Jesus Christ and him crucified" (1 Cor 2:2–3).

---

[280] John M.G. Barclay, "Kenosis and the Drama of Salvation I Philippians 2," in *Kenosis: The Self-Emptying of Christ in Scripture & Theology*, ed Paul T. Nimmo and Keith L. Johnson (Grand Rapids: Eerdmans, 2022), 32–39. The question of whether Paul authored or incorporated the words of these two poems is insignificant. By including them, Paul certainly put his approval on the theology they conveyed.

The point is relevant. God's supreme power occurs in Jesus's cross. It is not that God enhances human strength and wisdom, enabling them to be superior. Barclay explains,"The crucified Jesus can be 'the power of God' only if God's power is *qualitatively different* from human power—not greater on the same scale, but operating on a different plane."[281] Human weakness, therefore, is prerequisite to God's power. Death on the cross expresses the ultimate human weakness. Jesus's death on the cross enabled human power to be perfectly suppressed so that divine power, saving power, could fulfill God's plan.

Two ideas modify the verb "emptied himself" in Phil 2:7. They are "assuming the form of a servant" and "taking on the likeness of humanity." These statements explain both how this took place and what it means. Paradoxically, they mean adding humanity to deity rather than subtracting deity from his person. The language has vagueness to it which allows for theology which cannot be expressed easily, a theology of the relationships between the divine and human in Christ.

The connection between these ideas reveals further the movement to death. Some interpreters understand the two ideas to be simultaneous, so that being a servant and becoming human explain each other and refer to the same action. Others see a progression: first servanthood, then humanity. Certainly, the first, assuming the very nature of a servant, speaks to an attitude which produced the action of assuming humanity. It logically precedes.

Their content should be seen in parallel, rather than with fine distinctions of meaning because of the close relationship between these modifying ideas. The "form of a servant" means that Jesus's outer actions (appearances) conformed to the inner reality. Jesus's servanthood issued in humanity and, later, obedience to death. Some assume his servanthood was his humanity.

That brings questions of how humanity is servant and to what is its slavery?[282] These questions go beyond the text, and they cannot be answered from the passage. This text says simply that he was genuinely

---

[281] Barclay, "Kenosis," 18.

[282] F. Craddock, *Philippians, Interpretation: A Bible Commentary for Teaching and Preaching* (Atlanta: John Knox, 1985), 41, represents many commentators who suggest that Jesus became subject to the "elements" like all persons are. They point to Gal 4:3–5 and 1 Cor 2:8 as proof passages. The suggestion is interesting but leaves many questions unanswered. Further, as pointed out in the text, it is doubtful the nature of the slavery is important to the hymn.

a servant. Furthermore, the passage implies, at least, that Jesus's servanthood was eternal. Thus, Jesus could take "the form of a servant" because he was—and always was—a servant in his relationships in the divine Trinity, not in terms of essential equality or an eternal hierarchy, but in terms of an eternal mutual self-giving.[283] Doubtless servanthood expresses one of the highest and most beautiful of all characteristics. Though each person of the Trinity (Father, Son, and Spirit) displays the dominance and ruling character of God at times and for specific reasons, each member also displays service. The entire character of salvation indicates that God chose to serve. In that sense, grace itself implies service to the recipient. This is a defining characteristic of deity, and clearly this context indicates that Jesus's service focused on mission. A specific set of actions come together to provide evidence of Jesus's servitude, so his entire human life is seen in one primary attribute: he was servant. The passage involves movement. It moves from eternity to time, to a lifetime of service, to a culminating act of sacrificial death in the most horrible manner. The text does not explain what "emptying" and "servanthood" mean, other than Jesus's becoming human and the giving of his life in death.[284]

The description "likeness of humanity" stresses Jesus being not just God but man. While on the surface it may seem to say Jesus was not really man, that conclusion finds no support. In fact, Beare points out that likeness "does not suggest any degree of unreality in Christ's humanity; the word is almost a synonym for 'form' (*morpheo*) and 'image' (*eikoµn*), but it leaves room for the thought that the human likeness is not the whole story."[285] It must be seen in light of the next statement, that he "had come as a man." The change from the plural ("likeness of humanity," literally "the likeness of men") to the singular ("as a man") may reinforce that conclusion. It reveals that Jesus was certainly one of a class: a man of men. He existed originally in the

---

[283] Fowl, *Philippians*, 97, states intriguingly, "Self-emptying is not so much a single act as the fundamental disposition of the eternal relationship of the Father, Son, and Spirit. The incarnation, life, death, and resurrection of Jesus become the decisive revelation to us of that 'self-emptying' that eternally characterizes the triune life of God."

[284] It also has become common to link the "form of a servant" with the "Servant of the Lord" texts of Isaiah. See Martin, *Philippians*, 97. They are noteworthy because of their suffering motif, but the legitimate objection may be made that the Servant of the Lord was an honored position, and that is far from the obvious meaning and point of this poem, which is to serve rather than seek honor.

[285] Beare, *The Epistle*, 83. This well states the point.

form of God; but at a specific point, he became human.[286] With these words, the text praises the attitude of Jesus. Bockmuehl says,"He came into the same conditions of human life as the rest of us."[287]

Philippians 2:5-11 was to be used in worship, and as such, it was doxological. The total impact was to move the church to appreciate and imitate Jesus's action in an ethical application. Each word contributes to the meaning. Certainly, interpreters need not read more into the text than was intended, but overtones of Christology exist which cannot be dismissed. First, it affirms Jesus's pre-human state. Before he came to earth, he existed fully as God, in essence and appearance. Second, he became human. Like the movement from riches to poverty in 2 Cor 8:9, this text follows the movement from the exercise of lordship to the obedience of the servant. This teaches Jesus added the movement of servanthood to lordship as he added humanity to deity. In so doing, he elevated humanity beyond what it had known before, as Heb 2:6–8 affirms (quoting a fulfillment of Ps 8:5–6, LXX). Paul easily affirmed both the deity and humanity of Jesus. If this were a poem, he affirmed its content by using and not correcting it. The words convey significant theological meaning that adds reality to the impact of the worship experience. Recalling Jesus's servanthood also exhorted the believers to unity.

The two occurrences of "form" (*morphe*) here present a remarkable understanding of deity. It might be possible to assume when Jesus took the form of a slave he relinquished the form of God. If form identifies only outward appearance, that would be a necessity. The text, however, gives no indication of that. We are to understand God may remain God even while being a slave. Deity contains within himself both capacities at the same time. By using the words "assuming the form of a servant," however, Paul describes something as being added to Jesus's visible person. The newly adopted humanity (fashioned like *men*) tells how he became a slave. Jesus added humanity to deity. While God always has the capacity for servanthood, it was at this point in time Jesus added humanity. That was something new. It seems better to recognize that at the same time both the form of God and the form a slave were possible, rendering servanthood consistent with deity. Nevertheless, we see God's servanthood most clearly in

[286] In 2:6 the verb is a verb of state being used like εἰμι (ὑπάρχω; 2:7 uses γενόμαι).

[287] Bockmuehl, *A Commentary*, 137.

his gracious, sacrificial death on the cross with its power to transform individuals and the cosmos.

In applying this to the Philippian church, Paul seeks a similar understanding. This corrects those who consider the highest form of humanity to be dominating over others, having better positions or possessions. Servanthood in no way diminishes being human. It is a dimension of life most like Christ. Persons may be at their best and still serve. In fact, service defines the highest and best. The danger in the church resembled the flawed understanding of the culture. Having positions and possessions at all costs warps human existence and tarnishes the image of God in humanity. True self-fulfillment is found in the context of service, no matter what positions or possessions God allows one to enjoy.

2:8 Having entered the world of humanity, Jesus "humbled himself." This describes a second stage in Jesus's journey to death. Here is one of the most important connections between this poetic passage and Paul's commands to the church. In 2:3 Paul exhorted the church to genuine consideration of others (as being "more important than" themselves). Such consideration was to come as an expression of humility. It was "in humility," and therefore "from humility" that they were to so appraise others.[288] Here in 2:8, Paul speaks of Jesus humbling himself. In his description, he used the same root word for humility as in 2:3. Paul encouraged the church to choose to let their humility govern interpersonal relationships like Jesus's humility characterized his servant actions.

Like the first statement, he emptied himself; two ideas modify this one explaining the extent of Jesus's actions. First, when he was found in fashion like a specific (singular) man, he chose humility. This statement reinforces the previous section of the poem, but it also introduces a new phase of Jesus's action. When the poem moves from Jesus as in the "likeness of humanity" it becomes more specific. The form of a man is how people saw him. He was found to be that. The word used for "form" here differs from the previous, though the two are synonyms. Though closely related, there seems to be a slight emphasis on "a specific form" (*skema*, instead of *morphe*)—a man. His servanthood and ultimate death was not as "men," but as a man.

[288] The word "humility" (*ταπεινοφροσύνη*) comes from two words (*φρον*, understanding, and *ταπεινος*, humble), both of which in some form or another convey the message of Philippians.

The individuality implied in the statement stresses the reality and distastefulness of his death. At this point, people can identify with him. Second, he became obedient to death. The text does not suggest to whom Jesus was obedient, though most obviously God willed such an action.[289] It is best to understand Jesus was obedient to the divine plan and calling, embraced by each person of the Trinity, including himself. Through obedience he accomplished the divine purpose. As a true servant, Jesus chose to obey even when it cost his life, and that in a most ignoble way. Death came through crucifixion. The impact of crucifixion on the Philippians would be great. By Roman law, no Roman could be subjected to such a death, and the Jews took crucifixion as a sign that the victim was cursed (Deut 21:23; Gal 3:13). Perhaps it made a point to Paul's opponents as well, whom he described as "enemies of the cross of Christ" (Phil 3:18). The cross, so dear to Paul and other devout Christians, was an embarrassment to many, demonstrating the extent of Jesus's earthly journey.[290]

Although here is a literal presentation of Jesus's death, this phrase combines two of Paul's descriptions regarding Jesus's work. First, he spoke of Jesus's death. His was a death of substitution for believers' spiritual death. Second, Paul spoke of the cross. The cross was the means of death, and crucifixion on one was the most painful and horrible of punishments enforceable in that day. When Paul speaks of the cross, therefore, he intentionally calls to mind the extreme price Jesus paid to remove the curse of sin.

Paul seldom spoke about the cross. The word occurs ten times in his epistles. One other time he used it in Philippians (3:18), perhaps with intentional reference to this poetic text. He also used it in 1 Corinthians (1:17, 18), Galatians (5:11; 6:12; 6:14), Ephesians (2:16), and Colossians (1:20; 2:14). Philippians 3:18 represents succinctly how Paul used the word. The Judaistic heretics who threatened the church were "enemies of the cross." On the surface, no one would befriend the cross—the word stood for torture and Rome's power to inflict it. In God's strange economy, however, this horror becomes beauty. To deny the cross of Jesus for any reason is to fail to

---

[289] This is the only time Paul uses slave as a descriptor of Jesus, though it is not apparent in CSB.

[290] Silva, *Philippians*, 121–22, points out the one other time "obedience" occurs of Jesus in the Pauline corpus is Rom 5:19, where Paul contrasted Adam's disobedience with Jesus's obedience. The parallel has fruitful possibilities.

acknowledge God's plan and to oppose him. It belittles the pain and suffering required to pay for sin. To be an enemy of the cross is to be opposed to God and his plans in Christ, but it also diminishes the seriousness of personal sin. The cross is a necessity.

The terms "death" and "the cross" are, then, almost used interchangeably. In some ways they become synonyms. On the other hand, Paul has clear reasons why he chose one over the other. For him, the "death on a cross" had significant meaning. [See also previous discussion of death and the "power of the cross."]

2:9 The passage changes both tone and structure. The poetic character continues, but God becomes the subject, rather than Christ, and the purpose of God's actions becomes evident. The language of deity in this poem conforms to a common use in Paul: God is often descriptive of "God the Father." It does not imply that Jesus is less than God. The text to this point affirms Jesus's deity ("form of God"; "equality with God"). Using the term here indicates the first person of the Triunity (Trinity) of God. God the Father exalted Jesus, his eternal Son who took on flesh.

These verses are introduced by "For this reason" (CSB). Clearly there is a connection in Paul's thought. God was pleased with Jesus's actions: his servant attitude, his becoming human, his journey to death as a man, and the obedience that guided it. Introducing the second stanza of the poem in this way prompts the deeper question of how the two fit together. It is misguided to assume the two form a necessary combination in the same way. Is it a spiritual law that those who follow Christ's example will be rewarded with the highest esteem? Thinking that way can easily decay into thinking service is the way to the top: that self-giving always means God will reward with a position of privilege or power, rendering service as an alternate way to glory; it is climbing the ladder to success. Several points counter that notion. First, the poem is descriptive and not a promise. It is what God did and not a promise of what he will (must) always do in the same way. Of course, it is difficult to see what equivalent exaltation is for the Philippians to that of Jesus if status is the goal. Second, this is the story of Jesus, a unique story of a unique person, the God-Man. The text says because of Jesus's servanthood and self-sacrifice, God chose to exalt him. Third, this portion of the poem does not have a parallel in 2:1–4, Paul's primary point for introducing the illustration. God surely honors his people who choose to serve, but he does not always exalt them in the way the world sees exaltation. The connection between the two stanzas cannot be assumed to be simply an alternate way to exaltation. Such a stance mitigates against the attitude of a servant and the commands of 2:1–4. Genuine servants serve. They do not serve with one eye on the reward.[291]

For some, the opposite understanding to reward is that 2:9–11 do not actually fit the Philippian situation and Paul's commands to the church. They are an afterthought simply to complete the story of Jesus. If this were sung as a hymn of praise to Christ, therefore, it would be counter-productive to end the hymn on the down note of the cross. Nor did Jesus's earthly life end there. Praise for Jesus's actions is completed by acknowledging his high and lofty position. Is 2:9–11 therefore irrelevant to the actions of the Philippians other than lifting their eyes to Jesus, the Lord they serve? There are problems with this understanding as well. First, why would Paul include these verses if they were irrelevant? The complications of writing in that day demonstrate including unnecessary text was both expensive and cumbersome. If these verses had no immediate significance, why would Paul include them? Second, it may be assumed if this material is pre-Pauline it was well-known in the churches. That being so, there was no need for Paul to reiterate the remainder of a text known to them, yet he did. Surely there is an application to the first readers.

Theologically, the exaltation of Jesus is important. It is demanded by the nature of God. Bockmuehl says,"Theodicy requires that innocent suffering should be vindicated: only thus can it be meaningful, and only so can God be seen to be just."[292] This provides a better understanding for the inclusion of the verses. How could a moral God allow immorality to be the end? Although 2:9–11 describe what God did for Christ, they also have a deeper significance concerning what God did to vindicate Jesus's suffering. The Philippians can expect that

---

[291] This conclusion makes an important point but is not to be misunderstood. Many texts of the NT teach, or assume, God rewards the faithful. That is a strong motivation and comfort. The point here is the uniqueness of Christ and the Christ poem was not to encourage Philippian pride of accomplishment. Verses 1-11 affirm exactly the opposite. In support of a nuanced reward understanding, however, Keown, *Philippians 1:1–2:13*, 422, says "There is no need to resist the idea of reward here if one takes care to avoid pushing it toward a works theology."

[292] Bockmuehl, *A Commentary*, 140. Holloway, *Philippians*, 125, represents those who take the verses as indicating a reward for Christ rather than a vindication of God. "As reward . . . for the radical self-humbling and obedience of vv.6–8, God grants Christ a kind of celestial promotion."

God will vindicate them for their self-sacrifices done as Christians and in the name of Christ.

Two statements reveal the nature of God's actions. First, he "highly exalted him"; second, he "gave him the name that is above every name." The two relate to each other so that combined they express God's action.

Jesus's exaltation is stated graphically. The word translated "highly exalted" actually means super exalted.[293] Some scholars understand the word in a comparative sense, that God exalted him more than before, suggesting a new position for Jesus after his ascension.[294] Others, however, point out this is a superlative degree. He was exalted "to the highest," a contrast which compares the lowliness of the "death on a cross" (v. 8) with the exaltation of restored glory.[295] Finally, many interpret this in the context of the human Jesus. The hymn describes the exaltation of humanity in Christ.[296]

In determining a solution, several matters must be kept in mind. First, the action of "super exaltation" occurred as a consequence of Jesus's voluntary humility.[297] It came because of his servant-like attitude and actions. Second, these actions began in eternity past. The sequence of thought is his attitude was such that he was able to add humanity. A position that rewards Jesus as man, therefore, seems to enter the drama in the second act. Surely God's blessings took into account the attitude which prevailed in Jesus's pre-human state. Third, "super exaltation" should be taken seriously. It was not something that happened to the earthly Jesus only; it, too, began in eternity past. Fourth, it has overtones of a change in position, even though exaltation

---

[293] BAGD, 842, says "to raise someone to the loftiest height." Literally it means to exalt above.

[294] H. A. Kent, "Philippians," EBC (Grand Rapids: Zondervan, 1978), says, "Implicit in this exaltation is the coming consummation mentioned in the next verses, when his triumph over sin and his lordship will be acknowledged by every being" (11:124–25). The new status, therefore, is the acknowledgment of his rule.

[295] Beare, *The Epistle*, 85.

[296] Caird, *Paul's Letters*, 123, says, "It is the man Jesus of whom it is said that God has highly exalted him. The heavenly Christ returns to the high dignity he possessed before, but with this difference that he returns as man, and as a man who by his self-humbling has made common cause with his fellow men and become their representative."

[297] The introductory conjunctions to 2:9 make that clear. They are διὸκαί ("wherefore also"). They naturally suggest that God chose to bless Jesus for his actions.

lies at the heart of its usage.[298] Fifth, the exaltation involved granting to Jesus the title "Lord" (v. 11). This places the focus on function as well as being. The "super exaltation," therefore, is as much a functional matter as an ontological one. These argue for an interpretation that elevates Jesus in position more than before, while recognizing he could be no more than God before or after the incarnation.

Given these parameters, Paul affirms God granted Jesus a functional superiority over what he had before. He could hardly at this point have become deity, since Paul has affirmed he was in the form of God and equal to God. God could, however, by virtue of his humanity and death have put Christ in a place of prominence in the eyes and experiences of humans. Jesus was certainly understood better after the incarnation than before. After his death and resurrection (assumed by Paul though not stated here), Jesus provided access to the Godhead through himself. This begins with conversion but continues throughout a believer's Christian life. Thus, after Jesus's exaltation people are instructed to approach God "through Jesus." Prayers are offered and heard "in the name of Jesus." Faith that God will ultimately triumph rests on Jesus accomplishing God's will.

The second portion of the exaltation is that God "gave him the name that is above every name." Though the introduction to this portion of the poem suggests God's blessings were the outcome of Jesus's humility, this verb implies a gratuitous giving of honor. The verb has as its root the word for grace (*karizomai*). Jesus was not paid for his servanthood; nevertheless, as a consequence, God chose freely to grant him a high name to which every knee will bow.

The "name that is above every name" is the title "Lord." The title refers to Jesus's character as well as to his function.[299] Some have argued the name is Jesus, supported in part by the next phrase "so that at the name of Jesus every knee will bow." This runs into the difficulty that the name "Jesus" was given him at his human birth, and that by divine command. The insertion of the name Jesus (2:10) is to identify the new acclaim afforded the human Jesus. Others take the

---

[298] Martin, *Philippians*, 101, points out Paul's terms introduced with ὑπέρ are "generally elative in force."

[299] Caird, *Paul's Letters*, says concerning the view of those who take "Jesus" as the name given, "There is an obvious difficulty . . . in identifying a name given at Christ's exaltation with that by which he was known to his contemporaries during his earthly life. For this reason, the majority opinion is that the new name is 'Lord'" (123).

word name to mean “fame,” or “reputation.” In v. 9, Hellerman says, “The emphasis falls decidedly upon the public status associated with that name: God has granted Jesus ‘the reputation and is above every reputation.’ ”[300]

Isaiah provides more insight as to the identity of the granted name. In a text describing the unique and powerful rule of God (YHWH), Isaiah states, “Every knee will bow . . . every tongue will swear allegiance” (Isa 45:23). This parallel to Phil 2:10–11 is obviously borrowed from Isaiah. That prophet continues, “It will be said . . . , ‘Righteousness and strength are found only in the Lord’ ” (45:24). Consistently through this text the word translated Lord is YHWH. The Hebrew is translated into Greek as *kurios,* Lord. With Isaiah’s text in mind, Paul applies the truth to Jesus—he is Lord!

This corresponds to Peter’s preaching at Pentecost (Acts 2:36) and to the view of the early church generally. The new factor is that, by virtue of Jesus’s humility, he became the primary object of adoration in the Godhead (at least until all enter eternity[301]), as well as the administrator of God’s affairs. The worship accorded him in 2:10–11 supports this fact. Other passages speak to his function of Lord as well (1 Cor 15:24–28; Eph 1:20–23). Now, since Jesus’s ascension, all that God is comes to us through Jesus, and all who come to God do so through Jesus.

2:10–11 The hymn explains the goal or purpose of God’s exalting Jesus. Quoting the LXX of Isa 45:23, with its own additions, the two parallel ideas express Jesus as the object of worship. “Every knee will bow” and “every tongue will confess” employ typical imagery of *metonomy* or the part for the whole; the knee and the tongue stand for the person’s worship and confession that Jesus Christ is Lord. Ultimately, every creature in the universe will acknowledge who Jesus is.

Two concerns must be discussed: the meaning of “at the name of Jesus” and the description of which persons acknowledge him. The phrase “at the name of Jesus” may mean he is the object of worship,[302]

---

[300] Hellerman, *Philippians*, 120. One advantage of seeing it this way is the text puts Jesus central in human adoration and worship (10–11).

[301] This caveat is based on 1 Cor 15:28, after Jesus subdues everything: “[T]hen the Son himself will also be subject to the one who subjected everything to him, so that God may be all in all.” The best interpretation of this verse is not clearly understood yet.

[302] In which case the phrase ἐντῷὀνόματι is basically equivalent to πρός showing the object. Those who argue for this unique use of the preposition ἐν point out the necessity of it because of context.

that he is the medium of worship,[303] or that he provides the occasion and focus of worship.[304] The context reveals Jesus is to be the object of worship, as the name "Lord" and his exalted position indicate, eliminating the notion Jesus is a medium of worship, but more may be required by this expression. In fact, more is intended. Wherever Jesus's name (and character) has authority, he will be worshiped. Since his authority extends to every place, as the next phrase indicates, he will be worshiped everywhere. The emphasis of this text, however, is not directly on the worship of Jesus. The language is that of triumph. The bending of the knee was a posture of submission, as was confessing "Jesus Christ is Lord." The poem speaks of Jesus as the conqueror of all and should be seen as parallel to such texts as 1 Cor 15:24–28. Everyone will acknowledge the unique position of Jesus in the universe. The context is of rulership and sovereignty in contrast to humility and ignominious death.

The second concern of this first purpose clause is those who submit to Jesus's lordship. In Phil 2:10 the text states, "in heaven and on earth and under the earth." The meaning of the text is that it is the knees of beings located in these places that will bend to Christ.[305] Paul could and did use personification to speak of the relation of inanimate objects to Christ (Rom 8:19–22; Col 1:19–20), but this context is confined to personalities.[306] Jesus's lordship encompasses spiritual beings (those of "heaven"—good or evil),[307] living human beings (those of "earth"), and dead people as well (those "under the earth").[308] This includes every conceivable habitation of personal beings.

The second part of the purpose statement is that "every tongue will confess that Jesus Christ is Lord." In a parallelism typical of

---

[303] This takes the preposition ἐν in an instrumental sense and makes it equivalent to διά with a genitive. Some commentators who take this position remind the readers this is the language of prayer, and that in prayer the worshiper comes to God "through Jesus's name."

[304] This may take ἐν as a normal locative of sphere. It is in the sphere of his name that people worship. This is accepted here.

[305] The adjectives are masculine, not neuter, since they imply persons whose knees are the point of reference.

[306] Lightfoot, *Philippians*, 115, Martin, *Philippians*, 101, and a host of others broaden the reference to include "things." Paul's theology does include creation itself giving glory to God (Col 1:20), but that seems foreign to his thought here. There is no reason to extend it beyond persons.

[307] "The heavens" are often considered the place of all spiritual beings, both good and bad: Col 1:15–20 and Ephesians, especially 6:12. The term seems to be broad here, including all living spiritual beings.

[308] This phrase seems to be the equivalent of Hades or Sheol, the place of the dead.

poetry, both the universal nature of Jesus's lordship and the acknowledgment of it are reemphasized. "[E]very tongue" includes the same beings as "every knee" which bows. The confession "Jesus Christ is Lord" encapsulates this aspect of the Christian faith and may well have been the earliest Christian confession.[309]

Honoring Jesus in this way fulfills God's plan. He elevated Jesus to the position of lordship (2:9), and the confession is "to the glory of God the Father." There is perfect unity in the Godhead. The actions of Jesus in his exaltation bring glory to God the Father. The Father honors the Son and the Son honors the Father. In this dynamic, both display selflessness, and both receive honor.

This is an eschatological picture. The hymn brings the future into view by describing the culmination of history when all persons will acknowledge Jesus's lordship. No evidence states such acknowledgment will bring salvation, however. That must be cared for in the present before Jesus conquers his enemies. The church bears witness to Jesus's lordship by confessing to the world "Jesus Christ is Lord" and offering salvation to those who accept that confession and make it the central part of their lives (Rom 10:9–10). Paul recognized, therefore, that some people will voluntarily accept the reality that Jesus is Lord and participate in his reign of glory. Others will deny that lordship and, in the end, be conquered by the Lord himself. For them, it will be too late to participate voluntarily in the glory, and they will be destined to the punishment appropriate for those who resist the conquering Lord.

Paul reminded the Philippians of the greatest example of servanthood. The first section, on selflessness, applied directly to them. They were to be like Christ, the chief servant. Christ's attitude was to become theirs. They were to focus on giving rather than receiving. If God chose to exalt them, they would be truly exalted, but there were no guarantees of what that meant. True servanthood can never be perceived as simply an alternate route to the top, to exaltation.

Christ acted selflessly to accomplish the will of God. He even died to provide salvation as a part of the divine plan. God chose to honor

---

[309] The title "Lord" had relevance to Gentiles, who identified it with sovereignty, and to Jews, who associated it with the Jehovah of the OT. Sometimes a fuller confession included "Lord Jesus Christ," which included the messianic significance of this sovereign one. An older but still helpful work in this regard is Vernon Neufeld, *The Earliest Christian Confessions*, NTTS (Leiden: Brill, 1963).

him, determining that Christ would be the focus of the Godhead in its interactions with creation. Because of Jesus's actions, the way to honor God is to honor Christ. Even so, the glory Christ receives is a glory given to the Father. Again, shared servanthood works to the mutual benefit of all involved. The church had to learn this lesson. It would do so by focusing on Christ himself.

Theological and Practical Points

1. *"Adopt the same attitude" that was in Christ Jesus (2:5).* Paul begins the section with an action expected of every person in the church. The active nature of the choice highlights the possibilities: the church was to choose to follow Christ, and the alternative is to remain in discord and sectarianism. The poem to Christ clearly expresses the option before them: they are to choose servanthood. Paul assumed that attitude is available in Christ and there is no reason why his followers cannot be characterized by Christ-like service. The state of being "in Christ," to use Paul's very common designation of believers, makes available new vistas of imagination and experience. The "mind of Christ" mentioned in 1 Cor 2:16 is only available to those who have accepted the person and work of Christ as their own. In this context, true servanthood, like that of Christ, is only available to the church and it is in the church that this divine attribute can be seen.

Relating to the point above, the availability of "the mind of Christ" is itself the product of grace. Even as the work of Christ providing salvation is by grace (Eph 2:8–10), the attributes of Christian character can only be attained through the grace received at conversion. As Paul notes in Phil 2:1–4 the persuasive argument for developing Christ-servanthood, as well as the mandate for it, comes from God himself. Unbelievers should be confronted by Christ-servanthood as they observe the inner-workings and outward ministries of the church. The church alone stands as a trophy to God's grace.

Mistakenly, many Christians only extol the grace of God's ability to transform their lives into the righteousness God expects and which the human heart longs to have. Although that is an exciting and necessary application of God's grace, few praise God's grace for enabling them to be slaves of Christ and of others in and outside their congregations. Yet being "in Christ" shapes one's life into all of Christlikeness, including having the attitude of a servant. Paul's exhortation to "[a]dopt the same attitude as . . . Christ" means he expects it as normal for Christians and is available to all. As for the Philippian congregation(s), the known division in the church championed by Euodia and Syntyche (4:2) is the direct opposite of the Christ-example and the commands that introduce it. So it is with all followers of Christ.

2. *Jesus as servant and Lord.* The two stanzas of the Christ poem complement each other in presenting the picture of who Christ is. The first (2:6–8) describes an unfathomable descent from eternity and deity to earth and human death. The second (2:9–11) describes an equally unfathomable ascent into honor and sovereignty. Both movements are critical to understanding Jesus and since we are to be like him, bring challenges to both individuals and congregations. As Paul commands, attention should be given to both; hours of meditation on the matters bring Christian enrichment.

The narrative of Christ's experience also brings questions as both are understood together. How does a servant rule? Leaders in the business and political worlds struggle with this. Servant leadership is an ideal, but few really strive to combine the two together. If it is difficult in the earthly arena, it is more difficult for individuals to mentally blend these two qualities into the persons of the Godhead. The clearest picture comes from observations of Jesus's life, mixed with the theology that his life demands (virgin birth, sacrificial death, resurrection to life, and ascension to honor). Perhaps no texts require as much reflection of the hypostatic union as 2:5–11. The greatest thinkers of history have struggled, usually inadequately, to join the two natures successfully in the life of Christ.

The purpose of this writing is commentary, not systematic theology. Reading the text at face value, the conflict is between God as servant and God as sovereign. Some mistakenly assume Jesus adopted servanthood when he journeyed to earth as a man among men, and such an approach begins at the wrong place. Servanthood was always part of the divine constituency or Christ could not have conceived of making the journey he did in order to accomplish our salvation. Service is an essential attribute of God. It is only in Christ that we see it so clearly. Therefore, in many ways, the "attitude . . . of Christ" is the reflection of an eternally necessary and appreciated attribute. It can be assumed that God cannot exist and cannot function without it.

In contrast, God is expected to be sovereign. Sovereignty resides in the definition of deity—what god exists subject to human whims? The second part of the Christ-poem is no surprise at that point. Every tongue should confess and every knee should bow to the One who rules the universe. The difficult part of the poem is how Christ arrived at that point, and what does it mean? When the text says "[f]or [this] reason" (2:6), clearly there is a relationship between the servant attitude/action and the exaltation. It is suggested the exaltation, although ontologically certain, is described from the eyes of the beholders. Christ became the visible focus for humanity of the Godhead. All see God clearest through Christ. In another text Paul described the complete work of reconciling everything (personal and impersonal) because of the "blood . . . shed on the cross" (Col 1:19–20). Jesus is not only the place where we see God triumph; he is the one who brings that triumph.

Sovereign control is essential to service. One cannot do for others what is outside his or her ability to perform, no matter how much the wish to do so is present. Furthermore, the goal of service is to benefit those one serves. Selfless actions are directed to that point. Understanding the goal of service and the appropriate acts of service requires knowledge of the circumstances and the benefits the service-act will produce, as well as a familiarity with those in need. God alone knows what makes his creatures better. It is that created and fallen humans may have the capacity to glorify God by being what he intended them to be: holy and righteous in the image of his Son (Col 3:10). This brings glory to God, which is the purpose of Christ's death and our salvation (Phil 2:11). He alone knows what actions will bring them to the completeness for which he created them. He alone knows the timing and the extent of his enabling required to meet the need. In the sovereignty of God, Christ's service was necessary to accomplish the completed redemption of sinful humanity. It took the cross!

As for the Philippians, they were to serve each other as described in 2:1–4 and illustrated beautifully in 2:6–11. Enlightened by having "the mind of Christ," they were to exercise what they controlled to accomplish the exaltation of their fellow-believers. Each was to provide a visual example and helpful resources for others to become conformed to the image of Christ. In some sense personal control and enabling always work together in life, as they do in the Godhead.

3. *The death on the cross (2:8)*. Both death and the cross occupy a significant place in Paul's theology. The two cannot be separated, and each assumes the other since they inform one another. The cross is critical to the Christ-poem. It marks the end of the long and painful

journey from the bliss of eternity to the worst "earth" can do. Jesus's death, Barclay points out, "is as far removed from God as a human can be, the nadir in human alienation from the life of God, which seems to be the point. Jesus fully embraces human misery in full solidarity with a broken world."[310] The cross is central to Christian theology. It separates Christianity from the religions of the world. It was Paul's pride (1 Cor 2:2) and the ultimate explanation of his power.

Paul applied the cross of Christ to the confused Christians at Corinth. He carefully explained the importance of keeping the cross central. Enamored with the surrounding culture, many at Corinth tried to influence the church to use the rhetorical conventions of the Gentile culture. They tried, in part, to form an apologetic to communicate on the same level as the culture. They accused Paul of lack of familiarity with oratorical and rhetorical conventions. Concomitantly, there were Jewish elements who reasoned the better way was to communicate through the preferences of Jewish values. Neither was correct. In 1 Cor 1:20–25 Paul stated "the Greeks seek wisdom." They basically asked, "How can you follow someone who was not smart enough to reason himself out of death?" They accused Paul of a lack of wisdom too. He also spoke to the Jewish element: "Jews ask for signs." They basically asked, "How can you follow someone too weak to prevent his own death?" Many were curious one way or another. Paul's response to both was "we preach Christ crucified, a stumbling block to the Jews and foolishness to the Gentiles." Paul knew "Christ is the power of God and the wisdom of God."

The cross is central to the Christian message. The death of Christ is explained with theological significance. Although the cross adds little theological information to the meaning of Paul's theological explanations of the death of Jesus, it consistently points to the extent to which Jesus humbled himself. Death by crucifixion exemplified the weakest of human conditions. That weakness, however, opened the door to God's power in the place of human effort. The cross powerfully describes God's wisdom as superior to the world's. It also presents a pattern of living for the Christian: the life of complete service—to the greatest extent required—brings God's power to any situation.

The cross also symbolized the nature of Christian living in ways beyond service to others. Jesus died in our place, and his crucifixion

---

[310] Barclay, "Kenosis" 32.

serves as a significant and important part of conversion. In conversion one dies to sin and the patterns of life sin brings, and lives a new life empowered by Christ. It is critical for believers to understand they are identified with the death of Jesus (Rom 6). In our identification with Christ's death, sin no more dominates. In dying with Christ, believers move from the realm of death (now satisfied because of Jesus's actions) to the realm of life.

Believers worship Jesus in horror of the pain he endured with an appreciation of the benefits of life which could be secured only that way. The Christ poem does not end in death but moves to life.

In the pro-Roman city Philippi, appealing to the cross forms a striking contrast between choices: why would anyone choose crucifixion? To them, that was the height of folly. Nevertheless, for Christians it is the ultimate symbol of power and love.

4. *Focus on Christ.* The church was not only to reject braggadocios and egocentric displays of honors and accomplishments, but they were also to reject the attitudes that fostered them. Typical of Paul's exhortations to proper Christian living, the example of Jesus stands supreme. It provides a corrective to the frequent approaches of even well-meaning Christians today. Following the intuitive patterns of the surrounding cultures, it is easy to adopt one or more of the various theories of discipleship prevalent in contemporary Christianity. One can easily slip into a group mentality exclusive of others as evident in the church at Corinth. The way to spiritual success may easily become confused with the way of the program! Similarly, there is an almost universal movement to measure success by the successes of others. Other Christians may become the standards of success or failure. Perhaps either or both of these characterized at least some elements of the Philippian church. Certainly, they were vulnerable to success by human effort or Paul's warnings of the threat brought by the Judaizers were needless. Likely, some looked to either Euodia or Synteche as the model of proper Christianity.

Either way, the church would miss the point. True spirituality comes as a result of a clear focus on Jesus. The church is to adopt the mind of Christ with its concomitant attitude and actions and not even "the mind" of other Christians. While Paul urged his followers to use him, Timothy, and Epaphroditus as examples, he did so because they pointed to Christ.

5. The kenosis of Jesus. Thousands of pages have explored the concept of Jesus having "emptied himself," formally known as kenosis. The lexical meaning of the word is simple: "emptying" or "make void." The theological use of the word is amazingly complex. Most of the discussion involves the theology. It is far too broad a topic to describe even the movements associated with kenosis. Nimmo and Johnson observe, "Its substance . . . bears upon the doctrine of the Trinity, the doctrines of creation and providence, the doctrine of the church, and the discipline of theological ethics."[311] Here a few simple comments are in order. First, until the Reformation, orthodox thinking generally did not conceive of Jesus's emptying as setting something aside.[312] The focus on the deity of Jesus as the Son of God overruled any ability to diminish him. They spoke in terms of the divine attributes being hidden from view. Second, particularly in Lutheran theology, theologians began to think in terms of the divine attributes being imparted to the human so that Jesus was fully God and fully human. What, then, happened to the divine attributes while Jesus was on earth? Two answers were provided: (1) the incarnate Jesus refrained from using the divine attributes; or (2) they were used in secret.[313] In the eighteenth century German scholarship emphasized the humanity of Jesus (some questioning the divinity) and that the divine attributes were emptied at the incarnation. This effectively left Jesus with only one nature—human. This idea characterized many in mainline scholarship in the nineteenth and twentieth centuries.[314] Third, there is somewhat of a divide between biblical scholars and theologians. The latter have tended to read the text as "he emptied himself *of*" something, which involves inserting the word "of" into the text. While "*of what?*" is a logical question, nothing in Philippians gives a hint of how to handle that. People read into it their own assumptions as to

[311] Paul T. Nimmo and Keith L. Johnson, ed., *Kenosis: The Self-Emptying of Christ*, 1. This excellent volume provides stimulating essays that cover textual, historical, and theological approaches to kenosis.

[312] Nimmo and Johnson, 4, state " . . . in the patristic era, there was a general willingness to subscribe to the view that the being of God in Jesus Christ was not subject to change or suffering, and that the assumption of flesh at the incarnation represented kenosis by way of addition and concealment: the addition of human being to the Son of God and a consequent concealment of the divine glory during his life on earth."

[313] Nimmo and Johnson, 4.

[314] Nimmo and Johnson, 6, attribute a refueled kenosis to the stress of the historical Jesus, questions of theodicy after the two world wars, and the harmful effects of self-denial in liberationist theology which sought elevation rather than humiliation.

the nature of Jesus, particularly the hypostatic union and its possibility in the earthly Jesus. Even more conservative theologians wrestle with this. Biblical scholars are more prone to handle the text within its own limits. In the Greek text, "emptied" is followed by "himself" in the accusative case, the normal case of the object. Thus, "himself" is the direct object—that is what is emptied. It is not necessary, therefore, to ask "What did he give up?" in the incarnation. The text is satisfied by the early church position that Jesus emptied by "adding" humanity to the divine nature, with its necessary temporary limitations. This is the position taken in this commentary.

Nevertheless, some of the contours may help orient us to some of the recent discussion. The word "contours" is intended to highlight critical points of discussion. As noted, however, rather than attempt a thorough discussion of each, identifying the most significant reference points of debate may prove helpful. Additional comments guide to the conclusions of this commentary.

At the most foundational level since the seventeenth century, questions arose and guided scholarship regarding the issue of Jesus's divinity. A presupposition of many interpreters was Jesus could not be both human and divine, so one nature or the other had to be dismissed. Given the prevailing philosophical climate, most discarded theological statements about Jesus's divinity. It was, perhaps, easier to refute the orthodox claims about the historical Jesus than to reconceive the essential ontology of God. In fact, the arguments against the divine nature in Jesus often took the form of what it would mean to describe God with the human limitations that kenosis suggested. This argument required rethinking the propositions of Phil 2:6–11 to make them acceptable to the current assumptions. This exercise challenged orthodox Christian thinking as expressed in the Creed of Chalcedon that Jesus had two natures simultaneously.

For millennia orthodox Christians have held at least two major tensions in this regard. First, the essential nature of God requires at least two fundamental, ontological categories. God is both *immutable* (incapable of change) and *impassible* (incapable of emotion). In *kenosis* his immutability is challenged if at any time or for any reason there is a fundamental change in God's nature. If God were to divest himself of his attributes of deity to become human, he is no longer immutable. On the other hand, if God were to assume human characteristics, particularly those of emotion, he would be capable of suffering. The supreme expression of that would be the suffering brought by death on a cross.[315] Second, the tension must be maintained between the two natures of Jesus: the God-man. Furthermore, the two natures exist in the one person. Postulating two personalities in Jesus leads to multiple problems. Orthodox theologians have differed on the balance between the two—as to which one was dominant at any given time in Jesus's life—but Jesus's two natures have been consistently considered a necessary Christian tenet.

Some in the early church struggled with the human nature of Jesus. Could one who so displayed the power of God on earth and accomplished eternal salvation really be human? This is the central position of docetic theologians who argue Jesus only *seemed* to be human. The Gnostic inroads into some so-called Christian communities tended to err in the same way. It was declared heretical. This position is certainly uncommon today. A less-than-human Jesus makes him nothing more than a theophany.

One area of postulate involves the ontology of God. When and what did the kenosis mean? As for when, two possibilities exist in current thought. First, the kenosis took place before the incarnation, or simultaneous to it. This is often referred to as *asarkos*—literally, "without" flesh. Perhaps more commonly it is defined as the *Logos*, or *Logos asarkos,* based on John 1:1. Both refer to the eternal state pre-existing the incarnation. Thus, the self-emptying took place as an activity of God in eternity. This is explained as (1) he divested himself of deity while Jesus lived on earth. This would involve an ontological change in God, therefore challenging his immutable nature. Furthermore, it raises the question of how he was able to reassume his deity at Jesus's ascension. It also separates the Trinity for at least a temporary timeframe. This is to be rejected. (2) God should be understood as having both "essential" and "relative" (non-essential) attributes. The relative attributes are those that manifest God's glory to the world. They are omnipotence, omniscience, and omnipresence. Others may use different terminology, but the point is that God divested, or laid

---

[315] The position that God can and does suffer was usually linked to *Patripassianism*, a third-century heresy addressed by Tertullian. Praxeas, its promoter, denied the Trinity and claimed that "each person" designated an appearance of the one God in different modes. Therefore, all of God experienced what is described of each of the three persons of the Trinity. This was a trinitarian heresy. God's suffering has been a renewed concept in some modern liberationist theologies.

aside, these attributes in Jesus while keeping the essential-to-deity attributes. If that were the case, is it possible to state Jesus was fully God? Further, can God's attributes be so divided without the loss of his person in its perfection? This, too, should be rejected. (3) Emptying himself meant he did not rely on those attributes that would, by exercising them, overshadow the necessary human attributes. Jesus, as a man, could grow in knowledge and social relationships, obey to be perfected, and become the source of eternal salvation (Heb 5:8–10).

The second suggestion as to when kenosis occurred is "while he was a man." It is often referred to as *ensarkos*—literally "in flesh." The emptying related to the man Jesus as he moved toward the ultimate suffering and death on the cross. The difficulty with this is the order of Phil 2:7. The description of emptying is "by assuming the form of a servant" and "taking on the likeness of humanity." The words "assuming" and "taking" grammatically and logically modify "he emptied." All are aorist forms in parallel (two are aorist participial phrases showing contemporary time to the main verb). The best reading is that when or by taking the form of a servant and becoming in the likeness of men, he emptied. These point to the entry of *Logos* to earth (cf. John 1:14). The humbling of Jesus is presented as occurring in a state of humanity. The better understanding is that the kenosis was an action of the *Logos* and was *asarkos*.

In common parlance Jesus is often described as completely God and completely man. The intent is to reaffirm Christian orthodoxy and is well-meaning. The term "completely," however, brings some connotations that may not express the theology well. Does "completely" mean the totality of God? Does it mean everything about God? Orthodox theologians have generally followed the wording of the Chalcedonian Creed. Jesus was "fully" God and "fully" man. That relieves some misunderstanding in communicating the nature of Jesus's person.

Finally, for this presentation of some contours of kenosis, what was the ultimate nature of kenosis? Could it be the emptying was actually a revealing? Doubtless, in Jesus God's attributes of grace and love find new vistas of understanding. Grace and love resonate with humans and form a clear passage to knowing the God who is otherwise somewhat veiled. It is well argued Jesus is the ultimate "special revelation" of God, displaying in himself the invisible attributes of deity (Heb 1:1–4). The introduction to the Christ poem calls the reader to "see" and "be like" the humble Christ. While there is an ethical impact to the poem, its primary content informs as to who Jesus was, the amazing sacrifice of what he did, and the powerful place he now occupies in all of creation. The emptying should be understood primarily as a covering and only secondarily, perhaps, as a revealing of God's love. Without doubt, the poem is cast in a missional setting leading to the death on the cross, but its second stanza, describing the reigning Jesus, restores vision and understanding of sovereignty.[316]

The orthodox Christian statement adopted in AD 451 at the fourth ecumenical council held in Chalcedon, Asia Minor, remains the standard declaration of Christ's nature:

> We, then, following the holy Fathers, all with one consent, teach men to confess one and the same Son, our Lord Jesus Christ, the same perfect in Godhead and also perfect in manhood; truly God and truly man, of a reasonable [or rational] soul and body; consubstantial with the Father according to the Godhead, and consubstantial with us according to the Manhood; in all things like unto us, without sin; begotten before all ages of the Father according to the Godhead, and in these latter days, for us and for our salvation, born of the Virgin Mary, the Mother of God, according to the Manhood; one and the same Christ, Son, Lord, Only-begotten, to be acknowledged in two natures, without confusion, without change, without division, without separation; the distinction of natures being by no means taken away by the union, but rather the property of each nature being preserved, and concurring in one Person and one Subsistence, not parted or divided into two persons, but one and the same Son, and only begotten, God the Word, the Lord Jesus Christ, as the prophets from the beginning [have declared] concerning him, and the Lord Jesus Christ himself has taught us, and the Creed of the holy Fathers has handed down to us.[317]

---

[316] There are many good surveys of kenosis taking different approaches. All are helpful. In particular, see Bruce L. McCormack, "Kenoticism in Modern Christology," in *The Oxford Handbook of Christology*, ed. Francesca Aran Murphy, 444–458: https://doi.org/10.1093/oxfordhb/9780199641901.013.26. Also, the essays in *Kenosis: The Self-Emptying of Christ in Scripture and Theology*, ed. Paul T. Nimmo and Keith L. Johnson are very helpful.

[317] Philip Schaff, ed., *The Creeds of Christendom: Volume 2: The Greek and Latin Creeds* (Grand Rapids: Baker, 1990), 62–63.

The kenosis question encourages deep and careful thought, taking the mind into new territory and uncomfortable categories of theological reasoning . The issue should be handled like the remainder of the Christ poem. It is doxological and ethical: doxological, to promote worship, and ethical to model servanthood. Like much of Christian hymnody and poetry, often it is easier to sing and praise than to understand.

6. *A contemporary interpretation of the Christ-poem.* Translators always seek to balance ancient lexicography with contemporary idiom. This involves different languages, cross-cultural thought patterns and values, and socio-economic differences. An example of this is in a recent translation by David Alan Black. The translation attempts to remain true to the text and theology of the poem while seeking to remain true to the emotion that poem brings by its literary features. It is presented to stimulate thought:

In God's own form existed he,
And shared with God equality,
Deemed nothing needed grasping.
Instead, poured out in emptiness,
A servant's form did he possess,
A mortal man becoming.
In human form he chose to be,
And lived in all humility,
Death on a cross obeying.
Now lifted up by God to heaven,
A name above all others given,
This matchless name possessing.
And so, when Jesus's name is called,
The knees of everyone should fall
Where'er they are residing.
Then every tongue in one accord,
Will say that Jesus Christ is Lord,
While God the Father praising.[318]

[318] *Philippians 2:6–11, International Standard Version* (Davidson Press, 2011).

3.1.4 The Command to Obedience (2:12–18)

[12] Therefore, my dear friends, just as you have always obeyed, so now, not only in my presence but even more in my absence, work out your own salvation with fear and trembling. [13] For it is God who is working in you both to will and to work according to his good purpose. [14] Do everything without grumbling and arguing, [15] so that you may be blameless and pure, children of God who are faultless in a crooked and perverted generation, among whom you shine like stars in the world, [16] by holding firm to the word of life. Then I can boast in the day of Christ that I didn't run or labor for nothing. [17] But even if I am poured out as a drink offering on the sacrificial service of your faith, I am glad and rejoice with all of you. [18] In the same way you should also be glad and rejoice with me.

Paul resumed his thoughts with concern for the well-being of the Philippians. This section contains Paul's third and final command in this unit of the letter (1:27–2:18). As noted above, these verses are marked by second person commands rather than first person narrative. The second and third commands are separated by the poem of Christ's journey to earth and death, and God's super exaltation of him. Each of the commands urges the hearers to implement attitudes appropriate to their standing as Christians.

1:27–30 Live worthy of the gospel
2:1–4 Fulfill Paul's joy by being like-minded
  [2:5–11 Illustration of Christ's attitude and action]
2:12–18 Work out your own salvation

Structure

12 Therefore, my dear friends, . . . work out your own salvation
with fear and trembling.
just as you have always obeyed,
so now,
not only in my presence
but even more in my absence
13 For it is God
who is working in you both to will
and to work according to his good purpose.
14 Do everything without grumbling and arguing,
15 so that you may be blameless and pure = children of God who are faultless
in a crooked and perverted generation,
among whom you shine like stars in the world,
16 by holding firm to the word of life.
17 I am glad and rejoice with all of you
even if I am poured out as a drink offering on the sacrificial service of your faith.
18 You should also be glad and rejoice with me
in the same way.

Following the extended hymn regarding Christ, Paul returned to his primary concern. The passage resumes the thought of 1:27 with the matter of Paul's presence or absence. More importantly, however, Paul identified and applied what he considered the central thrust of Jesus's attitude: obedience (2:8). For Paul, obedience was also a primary responsibility of the church and expressed an essential ingredient in Christian living. These verses consist of three movements which extend the central idea of obedience. First, the Philippians were to devote themselves to practical Christianity (2:12–13) by working out their salvation in tangible ways. They were to be characterized by positive steadfastness (2:14–16), never succumbing to complaining or grumbling. Finally, they were to participate in Paul's personal joy in ministry (2:17–18), not only rejoicing with him but also sharing his perspective. These last two points (2:14–16 and 2:17–18) are parallel, joined with the conjunction but. They make separate assertions, but they should be considered together in thought.

The connections with the previous sections are obvious. First, the introductory word translated "[t]herefore" draws a strong conclusion from the previous. Second, verbal parallels tie these verses to the previous section. These include unity (2:1–4, 14); salvation even in difficult circumstances (1:28; 2:12, 16); Christian character in an opposing world (1:27–30; 2:15); and obedience (2:8, 12).

Moving from one of the loftiest Christological passages in Scripture, Paul applies one aspect of it warmly. His use of "my dear friends" locates his exhortation in a supportive and encouraging atmosphere rather than a confrontational one. Two indicators reveal this. First, Paul refers to them as "dear." Second, he attaches the personal pronoun "my." Doubtless this is a cryptic title more fully expressed in 4:1: "my dearly loved and longed for brothers and sisters." Paul is not distant from them emotionally. His personal involvement with them and his appreciation for them appears again in the letter.

Interpretation

3.1.4.1 Living Salvation (2:12–13)

Paul immediately applied the example of Christ to the problems in the Philippian church. In so doing, he urged the believers to work out their salvation (v. 12) and provided a reason for doing so (v. 13).

2:12 One central theme ties these verses together. The Philippians were to make salvation work in their lives. It will be helpful to determine the nature of the word "salvation" and whether this refers to the church at large or the individuals within it.

Salvation was central to Paul's theology. Normally the word embraces its full soteriological sense of spiritual deliverance from sin and the world.[319] Paul described salvation as a past event (Eph 2:8–9) and as a future consummation (Rom 13:11). Here he spoke of working out salvation, a present application to life. Many recent commentators have opted for the meaning "well-being" as a better translation for *soteria* ("salvation" in CSB), although this is highly unlikely.[320] Personal salvation brings with it responsibilities which Paul related to Christians' obedience. The responsibility is to live in accord with their

---

[319] Paul used the word "salvation" nineteen times in his writings. The majority carry the full soteriological sense. Philippians 1:19 is the most likely time when it may refer to a generic deliverance. BAGD, 801, gives "deliverance" as a meaning of the term but indicates no Pauline references in their listing. The volume states 1:19 means "to appropriate it for oneself."

[320] Representing this view, Martin, *Philippians*, says it is "the health of the church which was sorely distressed by rivalries and petty squabbles" (102). He provides five reasons for taking it that way: "salvation" can mean wholeness; after 2:5–11 it is inappropriate to stress individual salvation; "your own" cannot mean each church member concentrating on his own soul's salvation; the state of the Philippian church needed just this call; and "fear and trembling" are manward attitudes involving a healthy respect for each other. Silva, *Philippians*, 135ff., consistently refers to this as "the new view," pointing out that it is not the view of the older commentaries.

salvation, letting the implications of their relationship with Christ transform their personal and social relationships. Paul meant, in the first place, that they were to act like Christians.

To do so, the Philippians were to have an attitude of obedience. The obedience was not to Paul, although apparently his presence encouraged it in their lives.[321] The obedience was to God. The church participants were to solve their problems as an act of obedience to the Lord. Such obedience confirmed the fact they were genuinely saved. Perseverance was expected of Christians, whether in individual purity or harmonious group relations.

Obedience characterized the Philippian believers. Paul gently encouraged rather than rebuked them since they had always obeyed. This central Christian characteristic marked the church from the beginning. Paul had no reservations about this. Further, their obedience was genuine. They did not feign it simply as a show to their beloved church founder. Whether Paul was with them or away from them, obedience to God was an essential part of their identity. Their life in the Roman Empire demanded obedience to the political machine and its operatives, so their obedience to God subtly indicates the ultimate commitment of the Philippian church. Paul's was a reminder to be obedient to God regardless of political or social pressures.

Their obedience to God was manifested in their obedience to the expectations of the gospel. They were to live consistently with a gospel lifestyle as a process. It is unclear what specifically was Paul's concern about obedience. Perhaps he encouraged them to proudly display Christian expectations in their daily lives. Alternatively, Paul may have been admonishing them to correct errant behavior endangering the witness of the group. Either way, conformity to the gospel and the attitude/actions of Christ occupied Paul's thoughts. As in Christ's case, obedience exacts a cost. If the tides turned against them, they were to recall how Christ remained faithful. The salvation evidenced in conversion will be completed in deliverance from this evil world. In the meantime, the Philippians were to recognize the tensions of being in some sense "in between." Their obedience took them away from the values of the past (at conversion) and implanted the deep anticipation of completed character in the future. This dual recognition changed

[321] He wrote with some apprehension they would act differently if he were not there. This may well mean that he entertained the idea that he would die before seeing them again.

the present. It brought understanding of both individual and corporate relationships in Christ. Obedience meant a change from self-elevation to servanthood. The outlook changed from personal achievements to the success of the whole, the church. In that sense, their obedience was ultimately to God and his purposes (see below), secondarily to Paul who interpreted salvation for them, and to the fellowship of believers with whom they were to live in Christian responsibility.

In light of having obedience described in this way, one more aspect needs consideration. Paul urged them to be obedient "in [his] presence but even more in [his] absence." With this, Paul clearly assumed he had continuing value to them. Perhaps it was in providing an ongoing model of what Christian living is like. Perhaps it was in his being aware of the day-to-day aspects of church life on which he could, and likely would, make comment. At the least, he had an ongoing sense of responsibility for their continued growth. This may reflect, therefore, his consistent desire to be with those who were converted under his leadership. His task was to see them successfully living as Christians in light of the return of Christ.

In addition to obeying, the Philippians were to be sober minded. The precise words are "fear and trembling." These terms reminded them of their relationship to God and that they were to conduct their lives with the seriousness and reverence due him. After all, God worked in them.

Paul used the words "fear and trembling" only three times, two in addition to this instance. In 2 Cor 7:15 Paul commended the Corinthian believers for the way they handled his instructions regarding the man who had an affair.[322] Verbal parallels occur: salvation (7:10), pure (7:11), "devotion to us" possibly (7:12), the "obedience of all of you" (7:15), and "fear and trembling" (7:15). Both there and in Philippians, Paul commends believers for their obedience, for their proper behavior as saved, and for their proper action even without Paul's presence. Paul commended Corinth's Christians for their obedience which Titus remembered, and how they received Titus with "fear and trembling." Consequently, the church had appropriate responsiveness in light of their salvation. They also had proper respect for Titus, as Paul's representative. They worked out their salvation in obedience

[322] This well-known situation was a major issue in the Corinthian church. Most likely Paul wrote four letters that contained this as a major concern. In 2 Cor 7 he commends them for their responsiveness to him and ultimately to God's expectations of them as a church.

(to Paul and to God) accompanied by due respect. The other time Paul used the expression is Eph 6:5. There he encouraged slaves to obey their human masters. Again, the context contains parallels: obedience (6:5–8), "fear and trembling" (6:5), obedience without being watched (6:6), service (obedience) to the Lord (6:6), and doing God's will from the heart (6:8).

The two other contexts suggest how Paul used "fear and trembling." Obedience is often assumed to be the least desired characteristic since it may be perceived to be contrary to human freedom. It is often only a response done in a mandatory authoritarian relationship. In Paul's three cases of using "fear and trembling," however, obedience has a voluntary aspect.[323] Paul's encouragement, therefore, turned things around. Obedience was a part of God's will and an imperative to implementing the process of salvation-change in those who believe. Fear and trembling appropriately suggest a proper attitude of respect. Respect tempers the negative emotions that may accompany obedience. Respect comes from a proper understanding of the situation. In Philippi, the believers were to respect and enthusiastically accept what God was doing in their lives. Obedience is heartfelt and voluntary.

Did Paul's exhortation refer to individuals or to the church at large? Many contemporary interpreters understand the words to address the church collectively. This position recognizes Paul was concerned with a group problem, a problem in the church. In order to promote harmony and unity, he told the group to work out their salvation.[324] This view has some difficulties and some strengths. Those who advocate for that position correctly interpret the text in light of the context of Philippians. Paul wanted to correct the group, but in addressing a group he often provided more detailed instructions for dealing with a problem, as he did in 4:2–3, where he invoked the help of a third party, his "true partner." Further, the group would have had difficulty correcting the problem of disunity without the individuals devoting themselves to the task of personal change as well. Finally, this approach must make salvation refer to the wholeness of the group, and that would be very

---

[323] One may question the voluntary aspect of obedience to human masters. Yet the purpose of writing the domestic codes is to produce a willingness of heart to submit or obey.

[324] Fowl, *Philippians*, 121, represents this view. He states Paul "is not talking here about individual Philippian Christians so much as the salvation of the Christian community in Philippi. Obviously, Paul is often concerned about the spiritual health of individuals (see 4:1–3). Generally, however, this is not his primary focus. It certainly is not his focus here."

strange for Paul. Instead, Paul must have meant the individuals of the group were to live consistently with their salvation. If they did so, the group problems would be solved.

2:13 Paul often provided reasons for ethical commands. The reason the Philippians were to work out their salvation was the sober realization that God worked in them. The text emphasizes God.[325] Using a play on words, Paul said they were to "work out" because God "works in." God's work in them provided both the motivation and the ability to do his good pleasure. Two factors indicate Paul meant God initiated their interest in him. First, the context was one of salvation. Although the beginning events of personal salvation concerned Paul, they could not be separated from the total experience of salvation: past, present, and future. Second, the work of God culminated in "his good purpose." The phrase generally relates to the ultimate will of God (see Eph 1:5, 9), his own glory. The application to the Philippians should have been clear. First, without God taking the initiative, they would not have had the opportunity to work out salvation because they would neither want nor be able to do so. Second, the fact that God began the work in them gave them a stewardship responsibility. They were to be true to his purposes, handling the gift of salvation with utmost care. After all, they were God's "workmanship" (Eph 2:10), and the way they handled their salvation reflected on the God who gave it. This passage closely resembles Phil 1:6, where Paul expressed his confidence in them because God began a work in them and would complete it.

In that light, the church was to respond in obedience "with fear and trembling" (2:12). As noted above, Paul identifies those emotions with a voluntary, heartfelt recognition of the seriousness of the situation and the desire to promote the work of God within them.

The emphatic use of words for "work," built on the same root in Greek, presents an unusual contrast. Paul presented both the work of God ("working in," *energeo*) and the work of the individual Christian ("work out" *katergazomai*). Paul recognized the place of each. Divine initiative called for a human response. While he believed ultimately all of salvation, considered in its broadest scope, depended on God's initiative and power, he never tolerated passive Christianity.

[325] The actual subject of the sentence is "the one working in you"; "God" occurs in the normal predicate position, first in the sentence. Even though a normal construction and "God" is not the subject, the predicate position is typically emphatic in these constructions.

Human energy could never accomplish the work of God, yet God did not accomplish his purposes without it. The two functioned in perfect harmony, and people cooperated with and contributed to what God did in them and in the world.[326] It is both comforting and sobering to realize God initiated the relationship. It is equally sobering to realize nothing short of full cooperation with God's working confirms and matures personal salvation. The divine initiative and human response accomplish his purposes. Here, the Philippians were to apply their salvation to the problems of selfish ambition, strife, and egocentric actions which divided the church (2:3–4). Their salvation demanded it; their responsibility to God called for it.

3.1.4.2 Standing Tall in a Crooked World (2:14–16)

The second sentence of the paragraph changes directions slightly. Paul applied his point to specific concerns within the church. Appealing perhaps to an OT precedent, Paul warned of the dangers of grumbling (*gongusmos*) and arguing (*dialogismos*). Paul knew selfishness and vainglory (2:3) led to complaining and arguments.

Paul may have recalled Deut 32:5 in Phil 2:15. Deuteronomy records Moses's farewell address. He complained that Israel was a "devious and crooked generation," recollecting the people's grumblings against Moses in the wilderness.[327] Paul may have used the text because he thought in terms of his own farewell or absence (2:12). The combination of the two seemingly different ideas of "work out your . . . salvation" and "[d]o everything without grumbling" could have come from his realization of Moses's disappointment with Israel's failures in both these points. Whether Paul intentionally used the OT parallel is uncertain; even less certain is what such a parallel would signify in the Philippian church. Paul does not relate to the church as though they were in danger of departing the faith or failing in God's intended will for them. Perhaps Paul just wanted to be sure his fruit lasted. All

---

[326] Bockmuehl, *A Commentary*, 153–54, states this is "both thoroughly Pharisaic and thoroughly Pauline. On the one hand, the free will and accountability of individuals are fully compatible with the sovereign work of God." For the Pharisee perspective he quotes R. Akiba: "Everything is foreseen, yet freedom of choice is given; and the world is judged by grace, yet all is according to the amount of the work" (m. Abot 3.19).

[327] Significantly, Paul used the word "grumbling" (γογγυσμός) only here in the NT. He did use a cognate form (γογγύζω, "to grumble") in 1 Cor 10:10, describing the wilderness experience of Israel. Conceivably, the wilderness experience governed his thoughts at this point.

three of the major portions of this section fit that motif, including the idea of sacrifice with which Paul ended the section. The Philippians had the possibility of being blameless among a crooked generation. By contrast, Israel was blameworthy, and Moses called them the crooked generation.[328] In this section Paul issued a command (v. 14) and gave an extended purpose for the command (vv. 15–16).

2:14 The command has positive force although it is framed negatively. The use of the words no doubt comes from the OT text, but their application to the Philippians is a question. What would the positive command be? Would it be to trust God in everything since complaining is at the root a failure to accept God's plans and provisions? This aim seems unlikely because the problems within the group still govern the context. Perhaps the application sought to encourage the Philippians to accept the practices and efforts of others in the church since Paul warned about self-seeking (2:3–4). Whatever the problem, it was a concern which affected the moral life of the church and its witness to the world. Paul implied if dissension stopped the church would be on its way to purity of life and action.[329]

2:15–16 Employing terminology like his prayer in 1:9–11, Paul looked for the completion of the Philippians' character. They were to become pure and blameless. The terms speak to the moral nature of their lives. They were to have complete Christian character, and they were to have no offense in relation to others.[330] This hope was further expressed by Paul's statement, "children of God who are faultless in a crooked and perverted generation." This statement explains the first so that "faultless" incorporates "blameless and pure." They were children of God already; Paul hoped they would consistently aim to live in light of it.

---

[328] The clear reference to Deut 32:5 makes this suggestion a real possibility and provides a good rationale for what is otherwise a disconnected thought (Beare, *The Epistle*, 89, boldly associates these ideas). It also subtly but perhaps powerfully countered the Judaizers who prided themselves as the people of God, the heirs of Israel.

[329] The plural words and the fact that "arguing" may be a strong word might suggest a deep problem of continual arguments within the congregation. Martin, *Philippians*, 104, suggests they were actually going to court before unbelievers as at Corinth. He probably goes beyond the evidence since Paul did not handle it the same way as he did there.

[330] The words "blameless," "pure," and "faultless" are likely synonyms which should not be pressed into strong differences of interpretation. Two emphasize personal relationships ("blameless," and "without fault"), and one emphasizes personal character ("pure").

This consistent character is particularly striking when viewed against the backdrop of the world. Two metaphors describe the contrast between Christians and non-believers. First, using a word from Deut 32:5, Paul described the world as "crooked." The use of such language stressed the moral distinctiveness of Christians. Purity and blamelessness were the standard by which the distortions of the world were measured. Thus, Paul meant the world was morally crooked, distorted by its failure to understand and embrace the word of God. The ministry of the church was to provide a straight model for distorted lives.

The second metaphor comes from astronomy. The Philippians, with their unblemished moral character, shone "like stars" in the sin-darkened culture. Even with their imperfections, they were the light of the world to those in darkness.[331] This mission was accomplished by their holding out "the word of life."[332] All assume the "word of life" is the gospel, of which Paul had so much to say in this letter. The Greek word *epeko*, however, may mean "holding fast"[333] or "proffering."[334] The immediate context supports "holding fast" because Paul's discussion concerned moral conduct. By their lives, the Philippians were actually holding tightly to the gospel. By so doing, their lives also became both the measuring rod and the place of illumination for the world around them.

Paul ended this section with a personal appeal. His converts were his life. Equally, his life was Christ. Like other seeming biblical paradoxes, this one blended perfectly in Paul's mind. He urged them to progress in their lives so his efforts would be profitable, literally that he would have cause to boast on judgment day.[335] Looking to the day

---

[331] Some interpret the word "shine" as a command and translate it "you must shine" (the Gk. form is the same for indicative and imperative). It is highly unlikely an imperative would be found in a subordinate clause (relative) which is itself subordinate to a purpose clause. The indicative reading is the better. Paul described their function. There is also significant discussion regarding the voice of the verb: passive ("you appear") or active ("you shine"). The active sense is attested in Matt 24:27 and should be accepted here

[332] The NIV takes this as temporal and ministry oriented ("as you are holding out"), but the commentary, and CSB make this manner and related to steadfastness ("by holding fast").

[333] BAGD, 285.

[334] Caird, *Paul's Letters*, 126, believes this translation accords better with the star metaphor and with the theme of living for others.

[335] The word translated "boast" seems prideful to us. A better translation might be "have pride in." Therefore, what brought Paul joy and satisfaction was that those he led to faith ran their races well.

of Christ, the day of judgment, he wanted to have fruit from his labor. Using athletic imagery, he stated he wanted to be able to say "that [he] didn't run or labor for nothing." At other places, he expressed that desire in terms of his personal understanding of Christ (3:12–14).

Here he related it to his ministry ("I didn't run or labor for nothing"). Was he selfishly motivated in this? Two factors require a negative answer to the question. First, Paul's life was Christ (1:20–21). Paul knew in everything he did, Christ actually motivated and empowered (2:13), and all of the acclaim given him was for Jesus's glory. Paul's energies contributed to the glory of Christ whom he so loved. Second, it hardly seems consistent in a context devoted to selflessness and warning about personal ambition that Paul would so blatantly express his own selfish wish. Suggesting that the Philippians were to live a certain way for his benefit would be the height of egoism. In bearing his concerns, Paul openly spoke in terms of his ministry. He had previously just as openly revealed his deepest motivation to please Christ. There was no conflict!

3.1.4.3 Personal Joy in Ministry (2:17–18)

In 2:17–18, Paul's concern for the Philippians' steadfastness did not replace his joy for them and their service to the Lord. In this last portion of 2:12–18, Paul employed sacrificial terms to explain he was not dissatisfied. The introductory words are "[b]ut even if." They suggest a sharp contrast. The question is the nature of the contrast. Paul did not merely accept his lot as an apostle; he rejoiced in the faith of the church no matter what the cost to him. The words introduce a deliberate affirmation of Paul's trust in the Lord. Whatever happened—whether he was released from prison or died a martyr's death—he was confident the Lord had called him into apostolic ministry on behalf of the Philippians, and not even the prospect of death could diminish his joy.

2:17 The terminology of these verses supplies another metaphor. Three terms recall the OT sacrificial system: "poured out" (*spendomai*), "sacrificial" (*thysia*), and "service" (*leitourgia*). "Poured out" refers to a drink offering that accompanied the sacrifices. "Sacrificial" relates to the offering, and "service" enabled the offering. The first two terms speak of a sacrifice: the first, "poured out," referred to the practice of pouring a drink offering either before or after the offering itself. Paul figuratively describes himself as being "poured out." The present tense verb suggests an already occurring act with possible implications for the future. Some interpret this metaphor to refer to his impending martyrdom, of which Paul was certain. Others think of it in terms of his apostolic ministry which often included suffering. While Paul may have considered the idea of martyrdom, he was not unduly pessimistic at this point. His language is reflective. It seems to be a verbalization of thoughts about his life and its meaning. The conditional sentence in which this occurs ("even if") suggests an element of doubt about the matter.

Regardless of its interpretation, Paul's being "poured out" accompanied their service. While many think of Paul's life as the primary offering, that view blurs the metaphor. Further, there is no reason he would not use more direct terminology to express sacrifice, as he did in Rom 12:1. The sacrifice was that of the Philippians, their "sacrificial service" of faith. It is possible that Paul referred to their support of him, including the gift mentioned in Phil 4:10, as sacrifice and service to God. He used the same terminology in 2:30 and 4:18 when speaking of the gift. Understood this way, the "sacrificial service of [their] faith" would refer to tangible evidence of their faith in their lives. The Philippians' response to God in faith produced the sacrificial gift to Paul.[336] Perhaps it is better to propose the term "sacrificial" to describe the calling and proper actions of the Philippian church and their entire Christian experience. Since he has exhorted them to be "blameless and pure, children of God" in the world, their sacrificial service may consist of constant effort to walk in Christ. Their faith produced the quality of life that represented Christ well. The service was their effective living as Christians which Paul enabled by his own apostolic ministry. Paul perceived his work in bringing them the gospel as in some sense preparatory to the "greater" good of the Philippian church honoring God through Christ. This seems to fit the context.[337] Either way, the use of this terminology reveals Paul's humility about his own importance. In the ritual, the sacrifice was primary and the drink offering was secondary. Paul placed himself in the position of the drink offering, and he saw them (perhaps exemplified by their gift of support) as the primary matter and his own circumstances as secondary. If it refers

[336] This takes the construction to be a subjective genitive.

[337] Caird, *Paul's Letters*, 127. Many have equated the "pouring out" with the sacrifice itself so that they believe Paul was speaking of his own death as the sacrifice which was directed toward them. That does not seem to fit the context or the grammar.

to their support, that enabled him to be a drink offering not only to them but, by extension, to others as well. This balances the statement of 2:16 that Paul boasted in their continuing to the end as a source of pride. If that seemed arrogant, his being "poured out" countered it. They were the important ones and his role was complementary.

2:18 Rather than being discouraged about his circumstances, Paul experienced great joy. In 2:17b–18 four times "joy" is prominent. Twice the words "glad and rejoice with" occur. One time Paul used them to explain his feelings about being a part of their offering (2:17b). The other urged them to feel the same way (2:18). The power of this encouragement is reflected in the repetition of the two verbal forms used in 2:17b–18 ("I rejoice"—*kairo*; "I rejoice with"—*sunkairo*), which are translated "I am glad and rejoice with all of you." Paul expressed he was glad and rejoiced with them. He then hoped they would "be glad (rejoice) and rejoice with" him, using the exact verbal parallels. The power of the rhetoric reinforced their need to be like Paul as he and they sought to implement the servant attitude of Christ.

In this section, the attitude of Christ occurs in the thoughts of Paul. He urged the Philippians toward the goal of blamelessness. As for him, he was happy with his service to them and with them. Christ's act was one of sacrifice, and Paul's life was too. It was "poured out [like] a drink offering," along with those whom he loved so much.[338]

This ends the first section of exhortations. From 1:27–2:18 Paul's commands provide the tone and organization of the text. He urged the Philippians to stand true, to have the attitude of Christ, and to work out their salvation in obedience. Above all, they were called to be like Jesus.

Theological and Practical Points

1. *Living Salvation.* Paul's words are striking: "[W]ork out your own salvation" (2:12). The statement could easily be misunderstood. Most religions would approach this subject with the statement "work *for* your own salvation." They stress what one can do to attain deliverance

[338] Often commentators point out the use of sacrificial terminology in Paul. In Rom 15:16 he spoke of his priestly function of offering up the Gentiles. In Rom 15:27 Gentile "service" is commended. In 2 Tim 4:6 Paul used the term "poured out" of his martyrdom. In Rom 12:1–2 cultic language is compounded. Finally, in 2 Cor 9:12 sacrificial language describes the gift that meets the needs of the saints. The closest reference to Phil 2:17 is 2 Tim 4:6, and the idea of martyrdom in 2 Timothy may well have been in Paul's mind while writing in Philippians.

from this world, usually at death. All of Paul's writings oppose that idea, especially in contexts where salvation is central. For example, Eph 2:8–9 parallels this: "For you are saved by grace through faith." Salvation is consistently presented as by the grace of God rather than by human effort. It is not something one can work to attain.

This statement uniquely takes a different perspective. As noted in the commentary, salvation may be considered as a past event (conversion), a present reality (sanctification), and a future hope (glorification). Paul implies all three have a bearing on a Christian's life. Working out salvation means to allow the implications of your conversion to progressively transform your life in anticipation of your ultimate state of purity. Living in the middle, so to speak, brings responsibility. Understanding that counters those who view salvation as a compartmental decision affecting only one aspect of life. It secures heaven no matter what happens on earth. Genuine conversion secures heaven and future heavenly bliss (Rom 8:28–30). Entering heaven, however, is not the goal of salvation.

Salvation means deliverance *from* the control of sin and sin's spiritual consequences. The preposition "from" is often misunderstood or only partially understood. Paul seldom speaks of deliverance from hell, though that is often the way salvation is presented. Hell is the destination and punishment for those who are unrighteous since righteousness is the prerequisite for fellowship with God. The core issue is righteousness. Salvation is deliverance from unrighteousness and its harmful effects. Salvation is deliverance from sin that comes with righteousness from God, enabling fellowship with God. The beginning point is the desire to be free from sin and its penalty.

Salvation also involves putting one in conditions that enable real life. Freedom from both the penalty of sin (at conversion) and the power of sin (through sanctification) enable the spiritual life God desires. Realizing sin is the core problem brings a deep desire to live above the power of sin in one's daily life. That comes from God's power through the Holy Spirit applied to life. At conversion this power is made available to the believer.

Genuine believers intend to overcome sin now, in this present life, since sin is the core problem personally and in social relationships. This involves serious attention given to overcoming both personal and social sin. It is progressively overcoming the destructive habits of the past and embracing the new values and lifestyles that will completely characterize the heavenly future. Salvation represents a progressive and radically different change into righteous living. It is only possible because God provides new life and power and the believer chooses to accept and implement them. Paul's statement "work out your own salvation," therefore, is a call to cooperate with God's intent and available resources to become what he wishes. God's work within a believer provides the incentive and means to accomplish the goal.

2. *Standing tall in a crooked world . . . shining as lights: Paul used these two metaphors to describe the properly functioning Christian community*. Though the related commands are plural, it is difficult to see how he could be addressing a corporate group. The grammatically distributive plurals intend for each person to respond so as to build the reputation of the entire group. Following the first metaphor, those who are crooked look up to the straight (tall) as the normal posture all should have. The problem is sin has so distorted everyone that all fail in achieving the erect posture God intended. It is both a universal and reversible characteristic. The phrase "shine like stars" describes the illuminating aspect of the church. It assumes the world is dark and needs illumination. Proper Christian character penetrates the darkness as a constant reminder of what light looks like. Using both metaphors, Paul provides a picture of the functions of the church in and to the world. The church is a standard and a revelation of what God intends for humans—when it holds "firm to the word of life."

The standard and revelation starkly contrast with the world around. But Paul stated the problem is "grumbling and arguing" (2:14). Reflecting on Israel's experience in the wilderness, Paul identified a core problem. Grumbling reveals discontent in Israel, who failed to appreciate deliverance from slavery and the hope of a new and better life in the promised land. They were preoccupied with the present. Grumbling represents a failure to appreciate the goodness of God. It also fails to recognize and believe in the sovereignty of God. In the case of the Philippians, since God had worked in them both the willingness and the ability to do his good pleasure, they were different. Their salvation brought them new potential. They should appreciate God's goodness in their lives even though at times it may have been difficult to see. Paul stood as a primary model for trusting God and his purposes in spite of circumstances. Arguing describes the group side of discontent and failure. It reveals both dissatisfaction with God and with others, signaling failure to trust each other.

These destructive attitudes come from feeling neglected. In this case, some of the believers doubtless felt they were neither honored by God nor others as they should be. Arguing accompanies grumblings, which come from selfishness. The latter seeks to protect personal identity by ensuring needs and wants are met, often by expecting others to contribute to them. Vainglory accompanies them. Glory that comes from self-seeking is an empty glory (see 2:1–4). Once achieved, it pales in satisfaction since humanity, created in the image of God, exists to magnify God's glory, not its own. When selfishness comes from personal inadequacy, it leads to complaints. Similarly, gaining empty goals in life leads to disillusionment and often bitterness. Murmuring, complaining, and arguing evidence substandard Christianity. With these warnings, Paul may have sought to prevent the development of further problems in the community. They may reveal the discord was deeper than apparent.

The divided and dissatisfied church fails in its mission. Its mission is to present a standard for individual and group character. It is to call people to that as the way to spiritual fulfillment. When observing grumbling and contention among the church family, the world sees itself as better than the church and the church is disgraced.

That Paul spoke so pointedly immediately after giving his call to unity (2:1–4) and the model of Christ (2:5–11) illuminates this point. Living in humility as God's servant heals broken relationships. Christ stood taller and shined brighter than anyone. He is the model.

3. *Paul functions as the assistant in the sacrificial service.* Drawing on OT imagery of the sacrificial system, Paul reminded the church of their privilege to contribute to God's glory. Living out of his own servanthood and humility, he described himself as the "drink offering" being "poured out" as part of the sacrifice. Less humble servants may have referred to themselves as the sacrifice. Paul resists that in this context. He saw himself only as the enabler by example and encouragement. His goal was to compel the church to see their service as a sacrifice acceptable to God. The OT sacrificial system required the offering to be pure, blameless, and appropriate. Similarly, the church is to be pure, blameless, and faultless (2:15). Paul was a catalyst, and his efforts toward that end brought him joy as long as the church responded properly. Paul's imprisonment seemed a tragedy. Nevertheless, the church was to realize Paul's experiences were the assisting

activities necessary to prepare the service. They all should rejoice in that.

3.2 Paul's Future Plans Related to Philippi (2:19–30)

[19] *Now I hope in the Lord Jesus to send Timothy to you soon so that I too may be encouraged by news about you.* [20] *For I have no one else like-minded who will genuinely care about your interests;* [21] *all seek their own interests, not those of Jesus Christ.* [22] *But you know his proven character, because he has served with me in the gospel ministry like a son with a father.* [23] *Therefore, I hope to send him as soon as I see how things go with me.* [24] *I am confident in the Lord that I myself will also come soon.*

[25] *But I considered it necessary to send you Epaphroditus—my brother, coworker, and fellow soldier, as well as your messenger and minister to my need—*[26] *since he has been longing for all of you and was distressed because you heard that he was sick.* [27] *Indeed, he was so sick that he nearly died. However, God had mercy on him, and not only on him but also on me, so that I would not have sorrow upon sorrow.* [28] *For this reason, I am very eager to send him so that you may rejoice again when you see him and I may be less anxious.* [29] *Therefore, welcome him in the Lord with great joy and hold people like him in honor,* [30] *because he came close to death for the work of Christ, risking his life to make up what was lacking in your ministry to me.*

This section forms a break or a digression in the letter. Paul exhorted through commands in 1:27–2:18, and he returned to exhortation in 3:1–4:9. Here he provided information about his situation and his intent to visit the Philippian church when able. In these verses, Paul promised to send Timothy and Epaphroditus and praised them for their good character and service to him and to the Lord. These two men stand as further examples of those having the attitude of Christ. They both served unselfishly, considering others better than themselves. They were of value to the church at Philippi, but they were of equal importance to Paul at this time in his life.

The character of Timothy and Epaphroditus does not explain why Paul wrote about them. This section has often been called a travelogue because it reveals Paul's travel plans, and Timothy and Epaphroditus fit into those plans.[339] This raises the question of why Paul would reveal his plans to the Philippians. Perhaps they were concerned about when he would see them and anxiously awaited some news regarding his situation since they had both a financial and a fraternal interest in the apostle. No doubt that was a primary concern of Paul in disclosing this information. Even so, it is necessary to explain why these verses occur in this part of the text. The answer must be that while Paul thought of the attitude of Christ, he was reminded of two men who represented that character and had been especially selfless in their service to him. Since they each had a special relationship to the church at Philippi, Paul took the opportunity to discuss their character, their value to the ministry, and their proposed journey(s) to Philippi. If Paul were not enough of a model of Christlikeness, these two beloved friends were. They complemented Paul in illustrating the mindset of Christ.

Both Timothy and Epaphroditus received significant commendations. The commendation of Timothy contains 100 words in the CSB (seventy-two in the Greek text). The commendation of Epaphroditus contains 144 words in the CSB (100 in the Greek text).[340] In the case of Timothy, Paul identified his genuine care for them, his obvious proven character, and his loyal service to Paul. When speaking of Epaphroditus, Paul commended his relationship to Paul, his sickness and the joy they would have seeing him well, his sacrificial service on their behalf, and his heartfelt desire to represent the church well to Paul. The apostle necessarily stressed the relationship Epaphroditus had as a trusted envoy from the church. The differences commend Timothy for his good service and reputation standing with Paul and commend Epaphroditus for his determination to fulfill the church's commission even amidst trial.

Paul's plans for Timothy were still future. He *hoped* to send Timothy. Previous to this writing, Paul had been severely criticized for

---

[339] Generally, such travelogues come at the end of a letter, though not always. The fact one occurs here fuels the fire of those who see multiple letters incorporated into this canonical one. The matter is not definitive enough to be a substantive argument in favor of fragments since 1 Cor 4:17–19 has almost identical content, including Timothy as an envoy for Paul. Travelogues may be studied from R. W. Funk, "The Apostolic Parousia: Form and Significance," in *Christian History and Interpretation: Studies Presented to John Knox*, ed. W. R. Farmer, C. F. D. Moule, and R. R. Niebuhr (Cambridge: University Press, 1967), 249–68.

[340] The larger CSB numbers reflect the nature of translating the Gk. original into English. The percentage of words in both Gk. and English are the same in this section of the letter: Timothy 41 percent and Epaphroditus 59 percent.

outlining his travel plans and not being able to keep them. It was one of the major points the false apostles at Corinth used to discredit Paul. He told the church at Corinth he planned a visit to them yet had not made it there by the time of writing 2 Corinthians (1:15–2:4).[341] Perhaps these stinging charges caused Paul to be somewhat tentative in projecting what his own future would hold. He still had the uncertainty of the outcome of the trial before Nero as well.

3.2.1 Concerning Timothy (2:19–24)

Structure

Now I hope in the Lord Jesus to send Timothy to you soon
so that I too may be encouraged
by news about you.
For I have no one else like-minded
who will genuinely care about our interests
all seek their own interests
not those of Jesus Christ.
But you know his proven character,
because he has served with me in the gospel ministry
like a son with a father.
Therefore, I hope to send him
as soon as I see how things go with me.
I am confident in the Lord
that I myself will also come soon.

Interpretation

Timothy is mentioned first. He was Paul's companion, and Paul refers to Timothy as a servant of Jesus, too (1:1). Often Paul sent Timothy on missions for him, and he intended to do that again.[342] Timothy was well suited to be an envoy for Paul for reasons identified below. It is helpful, however, to recall that Timothy was well-known in Macedonia. He was with Paul ten years earlier when Paul and Silas founded the

[341] The false apostles' attacks against Paul involved twisting circumstances to make their point that Paul was unfit to be their model, much less their leader. In the Corinthian letters they accused Paul of no character (not fulfilling his promise to come to them, 2 Cor 1:15–23); no credentials (he did not match up to other apostles, 2 Cor 11:5–7); no charisma (his public speaking seemed somewhat dry, 2 Cor 10:1–2; 10–11); and no confidence (as he stated he was weak among them, 2 Cor 10:12–18) redundancy issue.

[342] Timothy's character is noted in how Paul used him on these trips as well. Paul sent him to troubled spots where he could be oil on the waters (1 Cor 4:17). Most notably Timothy had a significant ministry in Macedonia. Paul sent him to three churches in that province, Berea (Acts 17:14), Thessalonica (1 Thess 3:1–2), and Philippi.

church at Philippi, and in Thessalonica thereafter (1 Thess 3:2). Paul also sent Timothy to Corinth in his stead when events in Ephesus mitigated against Paul's going himself (1 Cor 4:17; 16:10). Timothy was a trusted son-like companion whom Paul regularly sent on his behalf. A church should be honored to receive Timothy as Paul's envoy. Even so, perhaps the Philippian church would be surprised to see Timothy and Epaphroditus, rather than Paul, and some explanation was needed. Paul first explained his plans to send Timothy (Phil 2:19), commended Timothy for his character (vv. 20–23), and explained that Timothy was only a temporary substitute for his own presence (v. 24). For several reasons Paul chose to send Timothy, but primary in his mind was that he, too, might "be encouraged by news about [the believers there]" (v. 19). Timothy was to report to Paul the situation of the Philippian church. Paul expected it would be encouraging news.[343]

2:19 Knowing he could not visit Philippi, Paul hoped to send Timothy. As always, his plans were subject to the will of God so he stated, "I hope in the Lord Jesus." The expression was not simply tacked on to Paul's statement, nor was it only an escape clause in case his plans did not materialize. Rather, Paul naturally thought in terms of commitment to God's will, and the expression disclosed the principle by which he lived. Even amid the criticisms leveled at him in Corinth, Paul steadfastly claimed he operated "in the Lord," following God's will. Perhaps part of that hope was Timothy would be sent soon. Paul could not release him yet (2:23), but he hoped things would change and Timothy could be on his way quickly.[344]

Paul also hoped to receive news concerning the church. Good news would lift his spirits, which may have been depressed by the reports of difficulty in the church. Paul used an unusual term for the expected lift of his spirits, "cheered" (*eupsycheo*), which showed how important this was to him (CSB simply says "encouraged"). Literally the word means "to have a good soul," which suggests being in good spirits. Of course, other means of gathering information were available to Paul. If there were no better courier of news (2:20), there was certainly the possibility of mail. These did not suffice. Paul wanted accurate,

---

[343] For information on Timothy's background, see the introduction under authorship.

[344] Some have suggested Paul was disposed to send him before he was really ready to do so since he obviously needed Timothy for some reason. Perhaps even some problem at Philippi caused Paul to change his plans. These ideas are purely speculative, and the text does not suggest them.

reliable information. No matter what way Paul chose to communicate, some time lapse was inevitable before Paul would receive the hoped-for news.[345] Timothy knew them well, having been with Paul in the founding of the church. He could read between the lines of their comments should they have questions. Further, Paul appreciated this church and, in his absence, his right-hand man should go. Thus, he planned to send Timothy on another important mission.

2:20–21 These verses contain one of the highest commendations possible and deserve comment. The commendation includes a statement and three reasons to support it. They convey the sincerity of Paul's words. Paul sent Timothy because he was "like-souled" ("I have no one else like-minded" CSB; *isopsukos*). Some have questioned whether Paul meant Timothy was like Paul, but all the evidence suggests Timothy was a partner in ministry, sharing Paul's commitments and burdens.[346] Significantly, Paul did not commend Timothy for like desires. His word choice suggests the basic life principles coincided. Apparently, for Timothy to live was Christ as well and he conducted his affairs in that way.

Paul provided three reasons what he said was true. First, Timothy had a genuine interest in the affairs of the church at Philippi. The translation weakens a strong statement in the Greek text. The word root has the idea of "legitimate" ("born in wedlock," *gnesios*),[347] and the adjective form is used of Timothy in 1 Tim 1:2, leading some to suggest Timothy was Paul's son and as a son he "naturally" inherited the interests of his father.[348] This proposal, however, goes beyond the normal sense.[349] Paul's commendation was that Timothy had acquired

---

[345] It would take approximately a month to travel the 800 miles from Rome to Philippi, though professional couriers could reduce that. Couriers were, however, both expensive and detached. Timothy would bring reciprocal news from Paul and to Paul as a dear brother. Perhaps the two-month minimum turn-around from Rome to Philippi suggests neither the situation with Paul in Rome nor the impending threat to the church at Philippi were imminent. Perhaps, but there was no faster way to communicate effectively. Paul's harsh and emotional address to the heretics (3:1) certainly suggests concern.

[346] "Like-souled" could mean 1) no one else like Timothy; 2) no one else who cared so deeply about the church at Philippi; or 3) no one so like Paul. Most likely the point is Timothy's unique likeness to Paul.

[347] BAGD, 163.

[348] Martin, *Philippians*, 117.

[349] Every use of the word in the NT is metaphorical. It is used of Timothy and Titus as true sons in the faith (1 Tim 1:2; Titus 1:4), but that probably does not mean they were brought to Christ by Paul. The events surrounding their salvation are unknown, but Paul gave credit to Timothy's mother and grandmother for their impact on his life (2 Tim 1:5). Further, in 2 Cor 8:8 it

a concern for others that had become second nature in its genuineness. This point is further reinforced by the term for "care" for your interests. The term occurring in 4:6 is translated "worry" and is the same word used in Jesus's Sermon on the Mount in a similar sense.[350] It does not convey an improper sense of worry—something that might be wrong. Here it points out the deep and obvious interest Timothy had in the believers at Philippi.

2:22 Timothy's concern for others manifested itself in other ways. The second reason for commendation was Timothy sought the things of Jesus Christ rather than his own interests. This contrasts with "all seek their own interests" (2:21). This is not likely a condemnation of all other Christians, some of whom supported Paul in Rome in spite of what might have been their best interests (1:15–16). Rather, it could be Paul's reflection on the self-seeking and ambitious citizens of Rome who may have been caught up in building their own fortunes. Most likely, it refers to the cadre of persons who surrounded Paul in his imprisonment. Yet it is difficult to think those who sacrificed to be with Paul would be so classified. Regardless, this commends Timothy, marking him as unique in compassion. Perhaps it was a personality trait, but it was certainly enhanced by his Christian character displayed through action. Natural qualities may be enhanced by supernatural (spiritual) enabling. The wording recalls 2:4: "Everyone should look not to his own interests, but rather to the interests of others." With it Paul provided Timothy as a model of what he meant. The church would do well to imitate Timothy as well as Paul in following the example of Jesus.

Finally, Timothy's worth was found in his commitment to Paul. Paul had no biological sons. Timothy, however, took care of Paul as though Timothy were a natural son. The dangers he endured in that service, such as at Philippi (Acts 16:19–40), proved his genuineness even in life-threatening situations.[351] Paul sometimes used the metaphor of parent to child(ren).[352] Paul added to Timothy's commenda-

---

refers to genuine love. Perhaps most telling is the one other use of the adjective in Phil 4:3, where the expression "true partner" occurs. Surely there the "true partner" was not born to it. The adverb is used only here (Phil 2:20).

[350] (μεριμνάω). See Matt 6:25–34 where the word occurs eight times. It is often translated with regard to anxiety.

[351] The Gk. word is "tried by the fire and refined" (δοκιμήν), therefore "tested."

[352] For example, fatherhood (1 Cor 4:15); motherhood (1 Thess 2:7); and parent (Phlm 10).

tion by pointing out that though Timothy served as a son, his primary commitment was to the gospel, not to Paul.

Why did Paul go to such lengths to commend someone the Philippians already knew well? It is unlikely they would be disappointed with seeing Timothy because they apparently had a positive relationship with him. It is unlikely they hoped instead for Paul to come. They were already aware of Paul's circumstances, so much so they anticipated his needs in Rome and sent Epaphroditus ahead of Paul's arrival at Rome. Surely they knew Paul could not come even if he wanted to as he still awaited trial. Any word from Paul would have been welcomed. Some have suggested Epaphroditus failed in the mission given him by the Philippian church, and perhaps they would be disappointed in seeing him since he was supposed to stay with Paul as their helper. Yet they knew of his serious illness, and they had responded to it in a way that increased Epaphroditus's desire to see them. If they were angry with him, he hardly would have sought to return home. Further, even if Timothy were sent to soften the impact of Epaphroditus's return, that was no reason to commend Timothy as Paul did.

Apparently, Paul commended him simply because he remembered Timothy's value to the ministry. Paul quickly praised his fellow-workers, and after thinking about Christ's servanthood, he remembered he lived with a servant, Timothy, who had the same disposition. Further, in Paul's sending such a valued helper, the church in Philippi would realize his esteem for them as well. They could not be disappointed with Paul's actions.

2:23–24 Timothy functioned in a significant role in Paul's work. Although he represented Paul in delicate situations, Paul reluctantly allowed him to do so. Two statements in the text reveal Timothy's importance to Paul and the work of the gospel. First, Paul needed Timothy a while longer (2:23). When he knew "how things [would] go," Timothy would be free to travel. No one knows why Paul felt that way. What is certain is that Timothy uniquely sustained Paul during the uncertainty of his trials, and Paul felt he could hardly get along without him.[353] Later, after Paul learned of his impending death, he called for Timothy to stand with him (2 Tim 4:9–11). Second, Timothy

[353] Perhaps physical difficulties combined with a natural anxiety regarding the long-awaited trial. Paul was sixty to seventy years old and had known physical problems. Additionally, the church at Rome was divided regarding his worth as an apostle and preacher (Phil 1:12–18), and few were there to comfort him.

replaced Paul, who desired to come when he could. In sending Timothy, Paul sent the best he had and a costly gift—an extension of himself. After all, they had sacrificed for him as well.

3.2.2 Concerning Epaphroditus (2:25–30)

With a similar style of commendation, Paul explained why he sent Epaphroditus back to the Philippians. This section has a commendation of Epaphroditus (v. 25), a reason Paul sent him (vv. 26–28), and a command to honor him (vv. 29–30).

Structure

25 But I considered it necessary to send you Epaphroditus—
my brother, coworker, and fellow soldier,
as well as your messenger
and minister to my need—
26 since he has been longing for all of you
and was distressed because you heard that he was sick.
27 Indeed, he was so sick that he nearly died.
However, God had mercy on him,
and not only on him but also on me,
so that I would not have sorrow upon sorrow.
28 For this reason, I am very eager to send him
so that you may rejoice again when you see him
and I may be less anxious.
29 Therefore, welcome him in the Lord with great joy
and hold people like him in honor,
30 because he came close to death for the work of Christ,
risking his life to make up what was lacking
in your ministry to me.

Interpretation

2:25 Paul found it necessary to send Epaphroditus, which raises many questions. Why would Paul have felt that way? Would Epaphroditus not be of service to Paul as the church originally intended? Did something happen to sour him or Paul? Was he physically impaired in a way that limited his usefulness? Further, Epaphroditus could make the trip without Timothy, so perhaps Timothy accompanied him for his sake as well as to find out about the church. The text provides no answers to these questions. For that reason, even though imaginative suggestions abound, it is best to understand what the text *says*, and leave the rest to conjecture.

The necessity of sending Epaphroditus came from Paul's own judgment. He stated, "I considered it necessary." His use of the word "considered" recalls other instances of this word in Philippians (*hegeomai*). In 2:3 he urged the church to "consider" others in humility as excelling themselves. Reinforcing the importance of the mind in Christian discipleship, he explained Jesus "did not consider" even equality with God something to exploit (2:6). Later, Paul stated he "considered" his former life to be loss and garbage (3:7–8) for the sake of gaining Christ. In Paul's circumstance, it suggests the resolution of a dilemma. Should he allow Epaphroditus to complete his intended mission, or should he send him back to the ones who loved him at Philippi? His considerations led him to the better alternative: sending him back.

Such a simple statement reveals volumes about Paul. At a deeper level Paul chose between his own needs or comfort above the joy of the church. Doubtless another helper in Rome could ease the strictures of his confinement and provide another source of personal encouragement. Yet Paul stated Epaphroditus could help meet Paul's "need" (2:25). Epaphroditus's presence would be a constant, tangible reminder that others cared for Paul, even from a distance. Sending Epaphroditus back to the church was a tangible expression of Paul's consideration of their need above his own. The contrast in his language regarding sending these two men reinforces that. Paul hoped to send Timothy; Paul needed to send Epaphroditus. In this, Paul acted like Christ would act.

Paul commended Epaphroditus as he identified him. He was valuable both to Paul and to the Philippian congregation. First, he mentioned Epaphroditus's relationship to Paul. Obviously Paul felt fondness and deep appreciation for him. Paul reminded them of Epaphroditus's relationship to him on their behalf. As for Paul, Epaphroditus was a brother, a fellow worker and a fellow soldier These descriptions emphasize partnership by employing familial, vocational, and military terms. Each provides insight as to how Paul saw the work of the gospel. The three terms go together as indicated by the grammar. The three are introduced by one Greek article, indicating they refer generally to the same idea.[354] Furthermore, the triad is concluded with the possessive pronoun "my," which naturally modifies all three. Epaphroditus was an equal; there was no hint of inferiority or failure.

[354] The last of the three descriptors, "fellow soldier is modified by "my" (συστριώτην μου).

"Brother" was a common term among Christians, indicating their close relationships in Christ regardless of whatever natural or ethnic circumstances could have distanced them. This is more than a general term, however. Used in parallel with three specific characteristics, this word expresses closer endearment. Epaphroditus's relationship to Paul resembles more of a "brother among brothers" in closeness and appreciation. Certainly his work in the promotion of the gospel brought deep affinity as indicated in the following two descriptions.

Epaphroditus was a "coworker," literally a "worker with" Paul (*sunergos*).[355] Paul seldom used this word to refer to his companions, but he applies it to Prisca and Aquila (Rom 16:3), Urbanus (Rom 16:9), Timothy (Rom 16:21), Titus (2 Cor 8:23), Clement and others at Philippi (Phil 4:3), Jesus (Justus, Col 4:11), Philemon (Phlm 1), and Mark, Aristarchus, Demas, and Luke (Phlm 24).[356] Some are described in detail elsewhere, like Epaphroditus here; others remain in relative obscurity. "Coworker" is not the title of an office or position, but a descriptor of respect and honor. It does not suggest a lower position in Paul's thinking. Using it, Paul appreciates these people, doubtless among unnamed others, as equals. Further, the nomenclature is reserved for those who share Paul's mission to advance the gospel. Identifying Epaphroditus this way indicates the place of Epaphroditus in mission. He was more than a helper to Paul's need; he was a participant in Paul's vision and calling.

The third description references the military: "fellow soldier" (*suspatiotes*). Paul's language is rich with athletic and military metaphors. These words contained clear picture references gained from the prevalence of Roman military and athletic games inherited from the Greeks. He seldom used the word of his colleagues, however. Timothy is reminded of the proper life-focus of Christian leaders, like soldiers (2 Tim 2:4). Archippus's ministry is not described, but he is a soldier (Phlm 2).[357] Soldiers both defend and advance their causes. The term used here implies activity. Epaphroditus expended energy in promoting the gospel. It is unclear what specific ministry he served in or where

---

[355] The two words that complete this triad of commendation are parallel in that they have the prefix "with" (Gk. συν) prefixed to them. This makes a tight expression, literally "with worker" and "with soldier."

[356] Keown, *Philippians 2:19–4:23*, 36.

[357] In a different context, Paul reminds the Corinthian church of the obligation to pay for its ministers who are like soldiers (1 Cor 9:7).

he employed his gifts. It is clear he was active and on mission with Paul to defend and advance the gospel. Paul found an affinity with him in this. Extending the military analogy, Keown says Epaphroditus was "a wounded military hero . . . returning home, to be welcomed with great honor and joy."[358]

Paul continues his description of Epaphroditus by indicating his relationship to the Philippian church. Epaphroditus's service was a gift from the church to Paul. The CSB translation describes Epaphroditus as "your messenger (*apostolon*) and minister (*leitourgon*) to my needs." The words "messenger" and "minister," a word suggesting religious service, or related to temple service, state his mission. Epaphroditus came with news of the church's love and a gift from them. He also determined to stay and care for Paul. This action demonstrated the love of the church in sending and supporting Paul, and it showed the selfless character of Epaphroditus, who left home to serve in difficult circumstances.

Paul described Epaphroditus as an apostle, more specifically "your apostle." The CSB, however, translates it as "your messenger." The term is used in two ways in the NT. The designation "apostle" describes the Twelve who were appointed by Christ to serve uniquely in providing oversight and direction for the theology and mission of the early church. In this sense, when Luke describes the qualification to replace Judas, he said it must be one of those "who have accompanied us during the whole time the Lord Jesus went in and out among us—beginning from the baptism of John until the day he was taken up from us—from among these, it is necessary that one become a witness with us of his resurrection" (Acts 1:21–23). This reflected Jesus's choosing of twelve to be his apostles (Matt 10:2; Mark 3:14; Luke 6:13). Paul identified himself with this group because "[Christ] also appeared to [him]." Even so, Paul described himself as "the least of the apostles" (1 Cor 15:8–9).

On the other hand, there is evidence of a broader use of the term "apostle." At times the word referred to some who wished to be recognized as an apostle but who were not commissioned to the task by Jesus. For example, there were numerous false apostles who claimed the title but lacked the characteristics of true apostles. Paul argued

---

[358] Keown, *Philippians 2:19–4:23*, 27.

against them at Corinth. They were "super apostles" by their own self-designation, and false apostles by Paul's (2 Cor 11–12).

Further, the term is used of those sent by an authorizing group to accomplish a specific mission. For example, when Paul collected a major offering for the poor in Jerusalem, the churches appointed men of renown to accompany their gifts. Paul identified these as *apostoloi*. Highly respected, they were men selected by each church for the specific mission of bearing the financial gifts to Jerusalem (2 Cor 8:23). These men, like Epaphroditus, should be understood as those charged with a specific (temporary?) mission. CSB's "messengers" is the better translation. This is a functional use ("sent with a mission") rather than official.[359]

2:26–28 Before discussing the reason he sent Epaphroditus back to the church, Paul described the circumstances that had befallen his visitor. Perhaps he had some concern they would not understand. After all, Epaphroditus was well enough to travel, and they may not know of all his past difficulties. The verses tell of his sickness. On the way to Rome Epaphroditus fell ill. He traveled on to Rome after some delay for healing and met Paul. When he arrived, however, the situation was not like it was when he started. The church at Philippi heard of Epaphroditus's sickness and made known its concern about Epaphroditus's well-being. Paul wanted to assure the believers their messenger was well.

The travel assumed in Paul's account has been much discussed. Some scholars have even suggested the letter was written from a closer-to-Philippi location because of it (see Introduction). Among others, Fee suggests how the necessary factors fit together.[360] Since Epaphroditus was carrying money, probably a large sum to care for the trip and to minister to Paul's needs, it is likely he had others with him. Such arrangements are made clear with respect to Paul's collection for the poor in Jerusalem that occupied much of his energy on his third missionary journey. Paul specifically commanded the various churches to select men to accompany the gift and Paul as they traveled with increasing amounts of cash (2 Cor 8:16–24). So, when Epaphroditus fell ill it is likely at least one fellow traveler would have returned to

[359] Keown, *Philippians 2:19–4:23*, 38–45. For a more extensive presentation, see M. J. Keown, "Congregational Evangelism in Paul: The Paul of Acts," *Colloquium* 44, no 2 (2010): 231–51.

[360] Fee, *Philippians*, 278.

Philippi to alert them to the situation, which may also explain how Epaphroditus knew the Philippians were aware of his illness. The sickness took him near death (Phil 2:27, 30). Upon healing, Epaphroditus and his other fellow traveler(s) would have made their way on to Rome. He would be joined later by the traveler who bore the news to Philippi or another of their designees who informed him of their concern and prayers.

The discussion of his sickness has the theme of selflessness about it. Epaphroditus was concerned only for the impact his illness would have on them (v. 26). He had been "longing for" them and was "distressed" over their concern for him. Paul felt Epaphroditus's return to Philippi would be more profitable than any service he might render to the apostle (v. 28).

Epaphroditus's infirmity was severe. Twice Paul informed them of that fact (2:27, 30). It almost cost Epaphroditus his life, and Paul understood that kind of service. Though it had heard Epaphroditus had been sick, the church had no way of knowing the extent of what he went through; therefore, Paul reinforced Epaphroditus's situation by this disclosure.

The scene is filled with emotion as well. Epaphroditus was filled with deep emotion over the Philippians' reaction to his circumstances.[361] Some have suggested he was homesick. That is not as likely as the fact that he felt his sense of responsibility toward them and wondered how they would respond to his inability to carry out their wishes. If that theory is correct, this feeling grew from his sense of responsibility. Perhaps he was anxious about how they would treat him, but the text seems to indicate he participated fully in the decision to return, and that would be unlikely if he had dreaded seeing them.

The return to health is described simply but powerfully: "God had mercy on him" (v. 27). The expression contributed to understanding the seriousness of Epaphroditus's illness. The expected outcome of it was death. The text does not identify his illness but only its life-threatening nature. The recovery was due to God's mercy. Although some have suggested natural means of treatment, such as medicine, or special applications of spiritual resources, such as the laying on of hands or direct response to a Christian healer, nothing reveals how it took

[361] The words "ἐπιποθῶνῆν" (periphrastic construction) and "ἀδημονῶν" are strong terms individually, and together they make a powerful statement.

place. Paul was not opposed to medicine and, at least once, recommended it (1 Tim 5:23). Understanding the healing process was not necessary. Ultimately, through whatever means, God healed.

Paul also expressed his emotion. He took Epaphroditus's sickness to heart, undoubtedly realizing he was sick because of his concern for Paul. A special relationship develops when someone willingly risks his life for another. Paul expressed his own feelings by the word "sorrow" (*lupe*), which occurs three times in the Greek text of vv. 27–28 (the third usage in v. 28 is a form of *lupe* and is translated "less anxious" in the CSB).[362] The term conveys a matter of serous pain physically or, as here, emotionally. Why did Paul have sorrow? After all, he expressed his own conviction that death was better than life because it meant to be with Christ (1:21–26). Paul's theology governed his feelings; nevertheless, Paul recognized the natural sorrow and distress that occurs with the loss of a loved one (1 Thess 4:13). Epaphroditus was a brother. His death would mean "sorrow upon sorrow." As with so much of Paul's writing, more information would be helpful for us to grasp the full meaning of his words. There is no evidence for what the first sorrow could be, and the text is equally unclear about the second. The construction "sorrow upon sorrow" simply states the depth of suffering something could cause, and that one negative event can be compounded by after events to make the whole extreme. Paul expected the church would be eager to see the convalescent.

All of this culminates in understanding Paul's actions demonstrate concern for others first before himself. He wanted the church to see Epaphroditus. Nothing so comforts the heart when going through the severe sickness of a loved one than to see him or her well again. When they saw Epaphroditus's health for themselves, their reaction would be one of returning joy (v. 28). This does not suggest the sum total of their joy concerned Epaphroditus. It does reveal Paul's awareness of the bonds in Christ and that each member of the fellowship mattered. Epaphroditus may have been a leader in the Philippian congregation, but that is conjecture. Their joy is that one of their own was restored to health. He had overcome the difficulty encountered in doing the will of the church on their behalf. They would rejoice. Paul would rejoice over thoughts of their joy. Once again he demonstrated his concern

---

[362] Twice the noun occurs in 2:27 (λύπην ἐπὶ λύπην), and once the negative adjective occurs in 2:28 (ἀλυπότερος). The word may be used of intense sorrow *or pain*, even that caused by childbirth. BAGD, 482.

for others rather than himself. Philippi's representative was valuable to Paul, but Paul understood the church's needs. It was also good for Epaphroditus.

2:29 Was there any doubt the church would honor Epaphroditus? Paul wanted to make sure it would. Therefore, he urged the members to welcome Epaphroditus appropriately,[363] with the respect due to men like him. If they had concerns about whether Epaphroditus had failed, Paul relieved those fears. Men like him deserved honor, and the Philippians were to provide it. He had risked his life for Paul, but he also had done it in demonstration of his love for them. The man endured sickness near to death for Paul and for them. Paul's words "welcome him in the Lord" once again reveal Paul's philosophy of life. To him, every aspect of life was to be lived "in, and for, the Lord." To welcome "in the Lord" is to share the deeper meaning of living "in Christ." Their welcome included appreciation for the shared relationships that occur thanks to shared faith in Jesus.

2:30 Paul ended this section by reminding the Philippians Epaphroditus really served them, but because of his illness, he had no chance to serve Paul. They were to realize this man attempted to do what others could not or would not do. He had acted on their behalf, "to make up what was lacking in [their] ministry to [Paul]." The terminology suggests something was missing. In fact, it was. Although the word "lacking" (*hysterema*) does not necessarily mean they had failed or that Paul judged them because of it,[364] here "lacking" seems to have its normal meaning. The church intended to do more than it could do without Epaphroditus or someone like him. The gift had to be carried to Paul, and it came with a promise that someone would be with Paul to care for him. It was a special way the church chose to honor the beloved apostle. Their gift, as they intended it, had three stages. First, they collected financial resources. Second, they selected a courier to go to Paul. Third, that courier was to remain with Paul for an extended time, presumably at the church's expense. They intended to offer Paul all three things, but the church at large could only do one. The rest was the responsibility of Epaphroditus. What they could not do, the lack in their ministry, he attempted to do. The word for "lacking" may reflect the remainder of what was intended but which

---

[363] Gk. is προσδέχομαι (*prosdexomai*).

[364] Silva, *Philippians*, 163, points to Col 1:24 and 1 Cor 16:17–18 as parallel statements to this one.

had not been accomplished. In confirmation of this interpretation, the word for "ministry" seems to be the equivalent of "gift."[365]

Paul ended this section of the letter by commending the service of these two Christlike men: Timothy and Epaphroditus. Both thought of others before their own concerns, and both served the Lord and the church. Epaphroditus, and Timothy in time, would journey to the church in Paul's stead in the hopes that he would soon follow.

Theological and Practical Points

1. *Early church travel.* Even today travel always has a purpose and such was the case when early Christians journeyed. Theirs was not travel for entertainment or exploration's sake. The early church was characterized in part by the mobility of its leaders and envoys doing the church's service and Christ's work.

Travel conditions will be surveyed below. Here it is appropriate to note the kind of distance traversed in church planting. Doubtless difficult, certainly by modern standards, the distances traveled by foot were limited. In the days of the divided kingdom, even fairly small distances could take people to multiple countries. Traveling from Dan in northern Israel to Beersheba in southern Judah covered approximately 173 miles, which would be about three hours of modern driving time. In the NT, Jerusalem and Rome were 1,500 miles apart in a straight-line measurement. The leaders of the early church invested much time and many resources in accomplishing their mission to spread the gospel worldwide.

The reason for travel is more important than the distances. Jesus traveled within the same length dimensions of the Holy Land as had the OT prophets. After his death and resurrection, however, he commanded his people to take their message to "Jerusalem, [to] all Judea and Samaria, and to the ends of the earth" (Acts 1:8). The differences in distance are remarkable. The directions they were to travel reveal more. The OT expectation, by in large, was that Gentiles would come to Jerusalem when the Messiah was on earth in a centripetal movement with Jerusalem at the center. Most of the concerns of the OT saints involved how to make Jerusalem and the Jewish people, and the believers of the world, receptive to the Messiah. Jesus, by contrast, envisioned world-wide evangelism. The distinctive message given to

[365] See notes on 2:17.

Paul at his conversion was to preach to "Gentiles" and "kings," and by that time in history Israel no longer had a human king (see Acts 9:15). This and the Great Commission started a centrifugal movement from Jerusalem. Paul took this commission seriously, as did the early church.

Most are familiar with Paul's three missionary trips and his journey to Rome. Additionally, Peter traveled in Syria, Cappadocia, and Rome. Other Christians, possibly Mark, went to North Africa, and Eusebius records the apostle Thomas took the gospel to India. Still more first-century Christ-followers went to places unknown to us.

Ancient Rome prided itself on its miles of paved road. Indeed, the road system made traveling better than at any previous time in the history of the world. The Pax Romana opened up world commerce, empire-wide peace, and safety in the Mediterranean and navigable rivers. There was little fear of personal harm or piracy as a result. The Roman roads made travel possible year-round, regardless of weather. The Roman army protected travelers to facilitate movement from place to place.

Even so, ancient travel was difficult. Modern conceptions of it often assume the conveniences of modern times, easily glossing over the trials and dangers involved then.[366] If voyagers were hearty, they could average up to twenty miles per day on foot. Other options were to ride by carriage or horseback.[367] Travel by road was expensive. Travel by sea was much less expensive and, generally, faster. Ships were military or cargo based, and passengers had to persuade captains to allow them aboard. Passengers usually remained on deck, regardless of weather. Much more could be said about travel conditions.

The early church paid a price to advance the gospel. Their routes often took them into strange cities, where they encountered unfamiliar

---

[366] Interested readers should consult the recent resource ORBIS: The Stanford Geospacial Network of the Roman World, done by Stanford University. Accessible at orbis.stanford.edu: "For the first time, ORBIS allow us to express Roman communication costs in terms of both time and expense. By simulating movement along the principal routes in the Mediterranean, Black Sea and coastal Atlantic, this interactive model reconstructs the duration and financial cost of travel in antiquity."

[367] Public carriages, available for a fee, could hold six passengers. They had metal wheels and only the upper class had access to any suspension for comfort. Horses were likewise expensive. A system of way stations, called *mutaiones*, were spaced every twelve miles and provided overnight accommodations, stables, and refreshments. See "Hadrian's Travels," World History Encyclopedia, www.worldhistory.org, accessed Dec 26, 2023.

faces and uncertain schedules. Many suffered illness, as did Epaphroditus, and dying on a journey was common. When people left home, there was no assurance they would return in good health. Only the most hearty or driven could venture into such unknown circumstances. People usually traveled with more than one in the party for medical and safety reasons, given the need to carry cash. Paul traveled with a group of men who had immediately employable vocations and who could generate sufficient funds to care for their needs as they went.[368]

Fulfilling the Great Commission in the first century took great effort, resiliency, and resolve. In addition to the travel difficulties, early Christians often faced serious opposition. Luke attributes the zeal, the vision, and the success of the gospel bearers to the leadership of the Holy Spirit and the lordship of Jesus.

Epaphroditus was a hero. Timothy and the aging apostle Paul spent their lives on divine, though difficult, mission. All such people were driven for one purpose. They took the message of Christ to places where it was unknown and to people for whom Christ died.

3.3 Exhortation to Avoid False Teachers (3:1–21)

At this point in the letter, Paul turned his thoughts more directly to the false teachers and to Christian living.[369] The epistle contains an interchange of instruction and exhortation. Here commands predominate again. Instruction, in the form of information to the church, occurs in 1:12–26, and again in 2:19–29. Exhortation, in the form of commands, occurs in 1:27–2:18. Commands continue until 4:9, and then Paul thanked the Philippians for their gifts to him.

Two concerns occupied Paul's mind. First, certain persons attempted to undermine his ministry, and Paul had to counter them. They were outside the bounds of Christian orthodoxy. Second, the problem of church disunity demanded one final appeal, and Paul

---

[368] For example, Paul was a leather worker, Luke a physician, and normally there was at least someone who was a scribe (Silvanus or Timothy are suggested). With these vocations there could be immediate employment and remuneration.

[369] The passage does not end decisively. Fee, *Philippians*, 285–86, takes the section to be 3:1–4:3, with the dual mentions of "[r]ejoice" starting a new section. Marshall, *Philippians, 76*, ends it at 4:1 with "stand firm" ending in the discussion of the Judaizers. However, chapter 4 seems to continue the issue of discord in the church (4:2) and continued Christian growth (4:4–9).

provided it with more direct and confrontational language. These two concerns form the logical divisions of the text.

A further concern arises regarding the somewhat abrupt rift between 3:1 and 3:2. For more on the topic, consult the commentary introduction, but a review with additional material may be helpful here. The tone in 3:2 is harsher and direct. Further, "rejoice" in 3:1 is seemingly strengthened by repetition in 4:4. There Paul twice commands them to rejoice. Is Paul resuming thoughts that had been interrupted by 3:1–4:3? Perhaps the stronger command to rejoice, apparent by the word repetition, served to put Paul and the readers back on track after a digression, giving rise to the suggestion that (1) Paul was sidetracked in his thought and writing at 3:2. Perhaps his mind recalled the severity of the attack against the church, and he took advantage of the opportunity to address it directly. Or (2), a later editor combined two Pauline writings, fusing them into one document.

Regarding the suggestion that two letters are now merged, one would have to question a later editor inserting another writing at this point. The break seems severe enough that if Paul did not intend it, a later editor inserting it without a smoother transition from one letter to another makes little sense. The content of 3:2–21 differs from what precedes and what follows. If this is an insertion, the question must be asked, Why here? Why not at the end of the letter, allowing him to build his argument of the common bond of friendship before his warning? Or, it may be better to insert it in chapter 1 while he is speaking of those who oppose him. It may make more sense to have an introduction to the letter which addresses the problems both Paul and the church were facing: unsympathetic preachers in Paul's situation and unorthodox teachers in theirs. Having cleared the air about both, Paul could return to the warm, friendly correspondence he intended to write in the first place.

Regarding the first suggestion that Paul was distracted, it should be noted the same questions arise. Does it make better sense to think something prompted Paul so that he approached this with an afterthought? The assumption would be that Paul's content in 4:1 and 4:10 are what he originally intended to write before distraction. Indeed, Paul "resumes" his letter with "[s]o then" in 4:1. Must it be the same as intended in 3:1? It should be noted Paul's exact repetition, if there is one, occurs in 4:8 rather than 4:1. In 3:1 the word is literally "so then, my brothers," tying it more directly to 3:2–21.[370] Additionally, Paul "returns" to "[r]ejoice in the Lord" in 4:4 (followed by the emphatic repetition of "rejoice"). Is he resuming his thought of 3:1 with rejoice? It should be noted his command to rejoice occurs well before his statement "finally" (4:4 and 4:8). He cannot mean that rejoicing is to be the content of his final section since it precedes it.

Despite the abruptness of 3:2, Paul anticipates it. He is writing "again" as a "safeguard." It is logical but unnecessary to assume Paul is *writing* a second time (or more). As noted above, he may mean he is addressing it in writing "this time." Of more importance is not the when and how he previously communicated, but it is that he has connected it to "[s]o then" and "rejoice." Paul's thought flows smoothly from "[r]ejoice in the Lord" to "write to [them] again." The question is, What did Paul communicate previously?

Either there was another letter or something earlier in this letter. We know of no previous correspondence between Paul and the Philippian church. This letter from prison was written approximately ten years after the founding of the church. Surely there was some communication. We know Paul traveled through Macedonia in the mid-50s. His custom was to visit Christians, encouraging them in the faith. Surely, therefore, he had communication between the church's founding and this letter. As far as we know, however, there was no written communication.

It is possible Paul refers to something previous in this missive. Most likely, that would come from 1:27–30. There is parallel thought and language to 4:1: "stand firm in the Lord." The same root verb "stand" occurs in both. Further, the parallels include harmony ("in one spirit" with the commands to unity between Euodia and Synteche in 4:2). This assumes 3:1–27 is an unplanned insertion. Even so, these connections seem too vague and minor to satisfy Paul's statement. It is best to view the passage as one intentional and connected text.

3.3.1 The Identity of Paul's Opponents (3:1–16)

Before addressing the concerns of the text, a brief discussion of the identity of Paul's opponents will be helpful. Two questions must be answered regarding them, and scholars have been significantly divided

[370] The difference is between the expression τὸ λοιπόν ("finally") and ὥστε ("thus, or so then").

regarding both questions. First, were these the same persons who were addressed in chapter 1? Second, were the same persons addressed throughout chapter 3? The following information is supplementary to the discussion in the introduction. It is prudent to explore the issue here as well.

Some discussions of these matters assume there are multiple letters contained in this one and, therefore, the suggestions have no contextual boundaries. The primary evidence for the opponents' identity comes from the pieces of information contained in these fragments. Thus, for example, 3:1–16 may be totally unrelated to 3:17–21. The fragment hypothesis, however, leaves many unanswered questions.[371] It is best to discuss the opponents within the context of Philippians itself.

Were the persons identified in 3:2 the same as those of chapter 1? Major differences surface in ecclesiology and Christology. Primarily, in chapter 1 Paul accepted the opponents' message even though he objected to their motivations. They preached Christ. Here he warned about the message, exposing it as non-Christian. In chapter 1 the opponents were within the church, but those of chapter 3 were outside, though their approach to Christians takes the posture that they are within the early Christian movement or environment. Otherwise, they probably would not have received a hearing from the congregations they infiltrated. Further, Paul's criticisms were different. In chapter 1 he said nothing negative about their theology. In chapter 3 his criticisms focused on theology though he implied their positions indirectly by warning his readers about the persons themselves rather than what they taught. The opponents of these two chapters could not have been the same people.

Did Paul address the same persons throughout chapter 3? That question is not as easily answered. Scholars debate whether Paul addressed one, two, or three different groups. Advocates of the one-group interpretation assume either Jewish or Jewish-Gnostic opposition. Many, if not most, assume they are Christian Jews who remain devoted to their Jewish heritage, seeking to preserve it along with their new faith. The Jewish nature of the attackers appears, for example, in their boast of circumcision (3:2); their methods of operation which

371 See the Introduction to this commentary for some of these questions.

reminded Paul of "dogs" (3:2); their claim to perfection (3:12–14);[372] their obsession with food ("their god is their stomach," 3:19), which may refer to rituals and Jewish food laws; and their boast in their shame (3:19), which refers to circumcision. Some contend, however, that Paul did not denounce Jews by claiming they opposed the church.[373] Others see a Jewish-Gnostic opponent. They point out Paul's argument included the typical Gnostic themes of knowledge, perfection, resurrection from the dead (presumably avoiding suffering), and that the nature of 3:17 fits a Gnostic audience better. Nevertheless Paul's argument against them assumed they were preoccupied with the flesh and fleshly attainments (3:2) which hardly fits the typical Gnostic message.

A strong case has been made for one group of opponents from the rhetorical perspective. Verses 2–16 and vv. 17–21 are often perceived as difficult to reconcile if they are the same group. They are usually understood as representing a legalistic group and a perfectionist one. Holloway, however, presents a different picture. His key to understanding this section is Paul's use of two commonly understood conventions of speech: comparison (*suncrisis*) and self-correction (*epidiorthosis*). The term translated "comparison" occurs in 3:2–3, 4–11, and 17–21. The notion of self-correction occurs in 3:17–21. Paul has not changed opponents; he has changed "figures of speech."[374] Holloway notes, "It is precisely on the basis of misunderstanding these shifts in rhetorical figure that a number of scholars assume Paul to be arguing on two or more fronts."[375] For him, the passage discloses Paul's approach rather than his opponents' theology.[376] His point should be heard. Their message lies in the background as Paul speaks to the messengers. It is difficult to accept that fully, however, given the strong and emotional introduction in 3:2, with terse sentences and imperative verbs, and sharp criticisms describing them (3:2, 18–19). These could not have originated without any connection to his opponents' message.

---

[372] These verses do not represent their claims, but Paul revealed his attitudes because of their claim to perfection. Paul countered it by his confession of not having arrived.

[373] This seems difficult to see in light of 1 Thess 2:13–16, where he described the Jews as those who "are hostile to everyone."

[374] Holloway, *Philippians*, 148.

[375] Holloway, 133, n. 13. Witherington, III, *Paul's Letter*, 183, also argues for σύνκρισις and the unity of this passage. He does not, however, speak of ἐπιδιόρθωσις by name.

[376] Witherington, III, *Paul's Letter*, 148–49, writes, "It has been crafted to serve his own argument and tells us little, if anything, about his opponents: not how they might have appeared to a more neutral third party and certainly not how they would have described themselves."

Other interpreters contend Paul addressed two or three groups. Evidence for two groups occurs in the differences between 3:1–16 and 3:17–21.[377] Advocates point out the tone changes between these two sections and there are, in reality, two kinds of arguments. The greatest obstacle for them is the lack of transition between the two passages, which would seem appropriate if Paul changed his focus. Keown, for example, advocates two different kinds of opponents. In his thinking, Paul first addressed the threat "based on a Jewish worldview (3:1–9 in particular) and then a Graeco-Roman worldview (3:18–19)."[378] These incorporate the major challenges to the Christian faith in the first century. Paul, Keown adds, "reframes Judaism around relationship with the Christ and simultaneously rejects Graeco-Roman libertine life and any syncretistic corruption of the gospel in either direction."[379]

Recently some have advocated three groups. Generally, the three are Jewish legalists who advocated strict adherence to the law (3:1–6); libertines who had the opposite view of law (3:17–21); and perfectionists who believed they had attained already (3:12–14). These verses, however, are not mutually exclusive in the characteristics they describe. It is entirely possible one or two groups held a theology that united these seemingly diverse positions.

The resolution of these approaches may await more evidence. Those who point to the Jewish nature of the opposition may well explain everything in the chapter. Strict legalism could easily produce a sense of perfectionism,[380] and Paul certainly could have described them as preoccupied with their appetites and genitals and totally oriented to this life. That is easy enough to see, but the question remains: Does that answer a natural reading of the text? Strong evidence exists for one group of opponents. Since the chapter may be naturally read with these being Jewish or non-Christian opponents, that approach will be assumed. This makes the problem of Phil 3 similar to that of Galatians and Colossians. The Jewish reaction to the gospel made

---

[377] Proponents include J. B. Lightfoot, Philippians; Vincent, *Critical and Exegetical Commentary*; and Beare, Philippians.

[378] Keown, *Philippians 2:19–4:23*, 75. He documents others who accept some form of this.

[379] Keown, 75.

[380] Paul himself claimed to be previously "alive." This refers to his self-awareness before his conversion and his confidence that he kept the law. Perhaps that is close to a perfectionistic outlook in Jewish life. "Once I was alive apart from the law, but when the commandment came, sin sprang to life again" (Rom 7:9). His point in that context, however, is the law is good and his argument is that sin is the culprit in our spiritual failures.

inroads into the church and threatened syncretism between them.[381] While Paul initially addressed Jews outside the church, he purposed to warn Christians within the church who might have been influenced by them, resulting in a mixed argumentation and exhortation.

The Judaizers were one of the strongest and most effective groups to undermine pure faith in Christ. They appear early in the Christian movement. Their impact is significant enough that a major, "universal" church council was called to discuss the purity of salvation by grace through faith. Acts 15, which mentions the council, described events that took place in approximately AD 50. Luke records the issue as "[s]ome men came down from Judea and began to teach the brothers, 'Unless you are circumcised according to the custom prescribed by Moses, you cannot be saved'" (Acts 15:1). Two important aspects of this account predominate: (1) the men came from Judea, and (2) they clearly taught the necessity of keeping the law for salvation. Thus, they were Jewish legalists. Usually this is considered the observable origins of the Judaizers.

Judaizers are often described as Torah-oriented Christians. Questions arise as to whether that fits the profile here. It is unlikely they are believers in Christ, given Paul's harsh description of them. His metaphor of "dogs" indicates they seek to recapture ("devour?") believers. They live as "enemies of the cross" (Phil 3:18) and their "end is destruction" (3:19). They are "focused on earthly things" (3:19), in sharp contrast to Paul and genuine believers who have a heavenly perspective. Assuming these texts address the same group of people, they cannot be Christian.

Why would non-Christians have an interest in correcting or seducing Christians? The energy required to travel surely indicates a considerable animosity toward the faith. There was a strong Jewish reaction to Christianity. Both Judaism and Christianity based their theology on the OT, though Christians interpreted it through the life, death, and resurrection of Jesus. Both looked to a coming Messiah to bring in the age of peace promised by the prophets. The church claimed that age began in Jesus; establishment Jews strongly opposed that. The fast-growing Christian movement began in the synagogues. Jerusalem was filled with the teaching about Christ (Acts 5:28). Furthermore,

---

[381] This may also have affected Ephesians since it contains a major discussion of the relationships between Jews and Gentiles in Christ. If so, that means some form of the problem prevailed in all of Asia.

Paul's pattern of seeking to worship with synagogue Jews in the cities where he traveled bore significant fruit. Many devout Jews turned to Christ from these efforts. Christianity represented a serious threat to Judaism.

Most of the opposition to Christianity in the early years came from those within Judaism. That is discussed below. It should be noted, however, that initially the Roman government seemed to view Christianity as a variety of Judaism, legally protected by the sanctioned religion of the Jews. There is scant concrete evidence supporting that point, but the following should be noted. (1) The earliest record of Roman opposition refers to Emperor Claudius expelling the Jews from Rome. The occasion was discussions of "Chrestus," most likely a Latin version of Christos, recorded by the Roman historian Suetonius in approximately AD 120: "Since the Jews constantly made disturbances at the instigation of Chrestus, [Claudius] expelled them from Rome."[382] Luke mentions that in Acts 18:2. The significant point here is Claudius blamed the disturbance on Chrestus, but his disciplinary action was against Jews, not specifically followers of Chrestus. The Roman historian Tacitus, writing about AD 115–117, stated Christians were persecuted by Nero as culprits. Even though Christus was killed by Pontius Pilate, Christianity was "to break out once more, not merely in Judea, the home of the disease, but in the capital itself. . ."[383] These two secular references indicate that early on Christians were not distinguished from Jews by Rome, that the Christian movement came from Judea (and was therefore Jewish), and that Emperor Nero used Christians as culprits ten years after Claudius allowed Jews to return to Rome. (2) In AD 52, Paul appeared before Gallio in Corinth, accused of inciting unlawful worship. Gallio refused to hear the case, stating he assumed this was a matter of Jewish law and not worthy of Roman judicial time (Acts 18:14–16). (3) In AD 58, Paul appeared before King Agrippa in Caesarea, accused by Jews of the crime of Christianity. After hearing Paul's case—which included explicit testimony of Paul's conversion—King Agrippa replied, "This

382 Suetonius, *The Deified Claudius* 25.4, Book V of *Lives of the Caesars*, in *Suetonius*, with an English Translation by J. C. Rolfe, Loeb Classical Library 38 (Cambridge, MA: Harvard University Press, 1914), 2:52–53. There is discussion of the connection between Chrestus and Christ, but the identity is assumed by many, if not most, scholars.

383 Tacitus, *Annals* 15.44, in *Tacitus V: Annals Books 13-16,* translated by John Jackson, Loeb Classical Library 322 (Cambridge, MA: Harvard University Press, 1937), 283.

man could have been released if he had not appealed to Caesar" (Acts 26:32). Thus, in the decade of AD 49–59 the known evidence suggests Roman officials considered Paul's message Jewish and not distinctively Christian.

The stronger early opposition to Christianity came from Jewish sources. History records at least one example of strong Jewish, non-Christian reactions to Christ. After the stoning of Stephen in Jerusalem, Luke wrote, "Saul agreed with putting him to death" (Acts 8:1). His opposition took active form: "Saul . . . was ravaging the church. He would enter house after house, drag off men and women, and put them in prison" (Acts 8:3). He took legal action: "still breathing threats and murder against the disciples of the Lord. He went to the high priest and requested letters from him to the synagogues in Damascus, so that if he found any men or women who belonged to the Way, he might bring them as prisoners to Jerusalem" (Acts 9:1–3). His personal testimony confirmed this zeal (Acts 22:3–5 before the crowds in Jerusalem; 26:9–11 before Agrippa). Relevant to this issue, Paul stated, "I pursued [Christians] even to foreign cities" (Acts 26:11). For Paul it was a matter of zeal (to be discussed below) as a devout Jew. Eradicating Christianity was a primary motivator of Paul's former life. When Paul used rhetorical and pointed language to describe his opponents, he knew them well because he had been there. Had he been a dog, an evil-worker, and a mutilator of the flesh? Most likely so.

A survey of texts in Acts and the Pauline letters reveals approximately thirty-five references to Jewish opposition to Paul and/or Christians. There was a "circumcision party," apparently within the church, which is mentioned a few times (Acts 11:2; Gal 2:12). Perhaps from the same group are the Jewish believers who are "zealous for the law" (Acts 21:20; 15:1). The Letter to the Galatians reflects opposition at Galatia. The opponents are Jews with the same concern (Gal 1:6; 2:3) since they are identified with those of the circumcision party (Gal 2:12). Paul also had personal opposition to him as an apostle. Since these opponents claim apostleship, they are Jewish (2 Cor 11:5; 11:13; 12:11). There were at least thousands of Jewish believers within the church who remained committed to the law. The activities of the circumcision party do not seem aggressive toward the church, however, given the way they are described. That, of course, may be an argument from silence. These are the only references where it is explicitly stated that opposition comes from believers sympathetic to the law.

On the other hand, there are explicit and more numerous references to Jewish opposition from outside the church. Descriptions of their activities reveal a much more vindictive attitude toward the church and Paul in particular. Their attitudes often turned to physical persecution. The references include the Jewish leadership in Jerusalem (Acts 4:1, 18); Saul (9:1); King Herod(12:1); the Jews (23:12, 27); chief priests and leaders (25:1); the Jews from Jerusalem(25:6; 26:2); and Jews in Judea (1 Thess 2:14).

Finally, there are descriptions of Jews who actively pursue Paul and seek to recapture Jewish Christians. These have a greater bearing on the nature of the opponents Paul addressed in this letter. On the first missionary journey, Jews in Antioch (Pisidia) were "filled with jealousy" (Acts 13:45) and "incited the prominent God-fearing women and the leading men of the city" who "stirred up persecution against Paul and Barnabas and expelled them from their district" (Acts 13:50). In Iconium, the next city Paul visited, "an attempt was made by both the Gentiles and Jews, with their rulers, to mistreat and stone them" (Acts 14:5). Paul and Barnabas escaped Iconium, traveling to Lystra. There, "[s]ome Jews came from Antioch and Iconium" who "stoned Paul and dragged him out of the city, thinking he was dead" (Acts 14:19).

During Paul's the second missionary journey, opposition continued. After Paul founded the church in Philippi (Acts 16), he, Silas, and the group traveled to Thessalonica some ninety-nine miles away. Although they ministered in the synagogue only three weeks at Thessalonica, "the Jews became jealous . . . and started a riot in the city," looking for Paul (17:5). Paul and Silas went to Berea, about forty-five miles distant. "[W]hen the Jews from Thessalonica found out that the word of God had been proclaimed by Paul at Berea, they [went] there too, agitating and upsetting the crowds" (17:13). Paul then went to Corinth where, again, the Jews "resisted and blasphemed" (18:6). Then, "[w]hile Gallio was proconsul of Achaia, the Jews made a united attack against Paul and brought him to the tribunal" (18:12). Later, while in Macedonia, "[t]he Jews plotted against him when he was about to set sail for Syria" (20:3). Finally, back in Jerusalem "some Jews from the province of Asia saw him in the temple, stirred up the whole crowd, and seized him" (21:27), and later, "the Jews formed a conspiracy and bound themselves under a curse not to eat or drink until they had killed Paul" (23:12).

The evidence provided in the NT indicates wide-spread opposition. It came from Gentiles on occasion. Additionally, there were Jewish believers in the church, but Scripture does not record they had a significant and violent reaction to Paul and his message. The case is different, however, with the Jewish establishment and leaders of synagogues. They opposed Paul when he preached in the synagogues and planted new churches. The Jews stirred opposition from Gentiles. Most significantly, it was these Jews who are recorded as pursuing Paul from city to city to discredit him and silence his movement. Since Corinth, Berea, and Thessalonica are relatively close to Philippi, and with evidence that Macedonian Jews plotted against him, it seems best to think of the potential threat as coming from Jews who cared enough to travel to neighboring cities to counter Paul and his message. This survey reinforces the understanding that the Jewish opponents of whom Paul writes in Philippians were non-Christian Jews. They were, most likely, some of "the Jews" who followed Paul to discredit him and his message. They also stood against the church.

Another question is why people of Philippi would be vulnerable to the Jewish attacks. There were relatively few Jews in Philippi, judging from the account of the founding of the church (Acts 16). Paul and his team could not find a synagogue there and so worshiped with sympathetic women at the river. They were probably proselytes. Jews were expected to have a synagogue where there were ten Jewish male heads of households (otherwise known as a *minyan*). The pro-Roman city officials seemed surprised that Paul, Silas, and probably Timothy as Jewish males came into the city since the prevailing attitude at Rome was that Jews were troublemakers and the emperor, Claudius, expelled them in AD 49. Likely Philippi followed suit so that in AD 52, the approximate date of the founding of the church, no Jews lived within the city limits. At the writing of Philippians, AD 62–64, it is likely that few Jews moved back into the hostile environment even though Claudius allowed their return in Rome in AD 54. Who, then, were the targets of the approaching Torah advocates? Some have suggested at least some Christians in Philippi were concerned that Rome had not declared Christianity legal. For their own protection they may have moved "back" toward Judaism, which was legal. While interesting, there is little but conjecture to support that position.[384]

It should be noted Paul's opponents were not yet in Philippi. His warning assumes they may appear, and the church should be on the lookout for them. Thessalonica was a neighboring city. Paul taught in the synagogue there with some success amidst serious Jewish opposition (Acts 17:1–9). Perhaps Paul received word of impending theological danger from that sister city.

The apostle chose to infuse his warning with his own experience. He did not produce a narrative explaining their theological inadequacies. His most articulate theological defense against such occurs in Galatians and Colossians. Rather than propositions, he chose comparison. He compared his experience with the opponents' to persuade them his was now better. He chose this approach in part because of his personal relationship with the church, knowing their esteem for him. They would listen to their founder and friend. He had traveled the road his opponents were on but found something far better. The better came when he renounced that path and followed Christ. By comparison between Paul and the Jewish opponents, the church should be adequately put on guard and warned.

Paul did not state what his opponents believed. Apparently, they were well-known to early church believers. There are few glimpses into the content of their message. Four verses out of twenty-one contain them (Phil 3:2–3, 18–19). Even these theological portholes reveal little of what they said. Paul continues his pattern of comparison rather than refuting their message straightforwardly. What we know about them comes from his appraisal and, assuming these same persons surface elsewhere in the letters, from other texts. They are clearly Jewish since Paul calls them "those who mutilate the flesh" and contrasts that with the true circumcision, that of Paul and genuine believers. True circumcision contains three descriptors: worship by the Spirit of God, take pride in Christ Jesus, and put no confidence in the flesh. For him, the circumcision God acknowledged was spiritual, whether or not his advocates were also physically circumcised (see

[384] It may be that one of Luke's purposes in writing Luke/Acts was to commend Christianity to the government officials in hopes they would be favorable toward it. In both Luke and Acts, no Roman people or government officials are presented in a negative light. Approximately thirty years had passed since Jesus's resurrection, however, and it was becoming clear that Christianity was not Judaism.

Rom 2:25–29, especially 28). His opponents were preoccupied with earthly things. They were committed to a literal understanding of the Torah and opposed to any suggestion that Jesus fulfilled it.

3.3.2 Warning and Paul's Experience (3:1–16)

[1] In addition, my brothers and sisters, rejoice in the Lord. To write to you again about this is no trouble for me and is a safeguard for you.

[2] Watch out for the dogs, watch out for the evil workers, watch out for those who mutilate the flesh. [3] For we are the circumcision, the ones who worship by the Spirit of God, boast in Christ Jesus, and do not put confidence in the flesh—[4] although I have reasons for confidence in the flesh. If anyone else thinks he has grounds for confidence in the flesh, I have more: [5] circumcised the eighth day; of the nation of Israel, of the tribe of Benjamin, a Hebrew born of Hebrews; regarding the law, a Pharisee; [6] regarding zeal, persecuting the church; regarding the righteousness that is in the law, blameless.

[7] But everything that was a gain to me, I have considered to be a loss because of Christ. [8] More than that, I also consider everything to be a loss in view of the surpassing value of knowing Christ Jesus my Lord. Because of him I have suffered the loss of all things and consider them as dung, so that I may gain Christ [9] and be found in him, not having a righteousness of my own from the law, but one that is through faith in Christ—the righteousness from God based on faith. [10] My goal is to know him and the power of his resurrection and the fellowship of his sufferings, being conformed to his death, [11] assuming that I will somehow reach the resurrection from among the dead.

Paul had traveled the road the false teachers traveled. In this passage, Paul drew on his theological pilgrimage. He knew the weaknesses of a legalistic approach to salvation, and he knew the joys of coming to God through Christ. In his career he had experienced both, and he knew that one excluded the other. A subtle danger, however, was the threat that some in Philippi might become legalistic Christians. In their enthusiasm they would hold together two polar theologies, their untrained theological minds allowing them to practice what threatened the very existence of the church they loved. The best means of countering both was for Paul to explain his experience.

Structure (3:1)

In addition, my brothers and sisters,
rejoice in the Lord.
To write to you again about this is no trouble for me
and is a safeguard for you.

Interpretation: (3:1)

3:1 Paul began this section with a verse of transition. Three matters in it call for brief discussion: the use of the phrase "[i]n addition"; the command to rejoice; and the statement that he was repeating his warning. First, the opening of this chapter has been misunderstood by many. Often translated "finally," it literally means to (toward) the rest, and that meaning fits here.[385] There are numerous examples in Greek literature where "finally" points toward the next point. English readers may mistake its meaning. The word occurs again in 4:8, where CSB does translate it that way. He may well be picking up the thought introduced in 3:1.

Second, Paul commanded them to rejoice. The word "rejoice" occurs nine times in the letter including two which are compound words with the prefixed preposition "with."[386] As many note, rejoice/joy could be considered a major theme of the book, if not the primary theme.[387] Focusing on joy as the theme coordinates well with the idea that Philippians is a personal letter to friends who have interest in Paul's well-being. Their concerns would have been alleviated somewhat by Paul's insistence on his joy regardless of circumstances.

The nine occurrences of the word "rejoice" follow a pattern. They contribute to the contexts Paul discusses. First, Paul uses the word four times in the first person, "I" being the subject of the verb. In 1:18, Paul discloses his attitude toward the well-known division of allegiance of preachers at Rome. Some opposed and some supported Paul. Even so, Paul responds emphatically: "I rejoice . . . and I will continue to rejoice" (1:18). After urging the Philippians to work out

---

[385] C. F. D. Moule, *Idiom Book of New Testament Greek* (Cambridge: University Press, 1953), 16ff., says it may imply the end in a final sense ("finally"), or it may point to the rest ("and so" or "it follows then, that"). Some theories of multiple letters have supported their cases by the use of "finally," but there is common enough usage of it in the second sense in Paul so that no case can be made based on this adverb alone (1 Thess 4:1, 2; 2 Thess 3:1).

[386] See Phil 2:17-18.

[387] For example, A. T. Robertson, *Paul's Joy*.

their salvation with faithfulness, which was Paul's pride, he described himself as potentially used up ("poured out") for their benefit as a sacrifice to God. His servant attitude, like that of the Lord he previously described (2:5–11), enabled him to rejoice. He hoped they would adopt his perspective and he could rejoice with them (2:17). Adopting Paul's perspective should also cause them to rejoice and rejoice with him (2:18). After 2:19, however, Paul continues to encourage them to rejoice. The first cause of their joy independent of Paul's circumstances was to rejoice when they welcomed their own Epaphroditus home healthy (2:28).

Beginning in 3:1 both the subject matter of the letter and the nuanced use of the word rejoice change. In 3:1–4:8 Paul encouraged the church to stability, guarding against division from the outside (3:1–21) and from destructive tensions within (4:1–8). He introduced these sections with the command to rejoice (3:1), and he concluded it by calling them again to rejoice (4:4 twice). His last use of that word expressed his own joy upon receiving the financial support from the church (4:10–21).

Perhaps more significant than the previous pattern is the last three occurrences. Each of them introduce a new situation of Paul's concerns: the threat from outside (3:1–21), the concerns about internal stability (4:1–8), and Paul's thankfulness (4:10–20). As such, rejoicing gains literary significance. More significantly, perhaps, is these last three occurrences are accompanied by the prepositional phrase "in the Lord." This is a new expression for Paul in Philippians. Both of Paul's previous disclosures of his personal joy in spite of difficult circumstances and his urging the Philippians to share in that perspective were possible because of Paul's relationship to Christ, but that remains unstated there. Here Paul explicitly states the point.

The phrase "in the Lord" provides the atmosphere (location) for their joy. It is distinctively Christian and enabled by their relationship to Christ. It could mean their rejoicing is to be "*for* the Lord" in the sense that their circumstances are known and allowed by him. Thus, their joy is to be directed toward him. If so, however, the normal Greek expression would be literally "rejoice toward the Lord" (the verb followed by the accusative case). Alternatively, it could be their rejoicing is to be because of their situation "*within* the Lord." A Christian commitment brings both a relationship of joy and the ability to apply that relationship with the Lord to any circumstance. Used in this way, it reflects Paul's very common expression elsewhere, "in Christ."[388] Because they are "in Christ" they are to "rejoice in the Lord." Their spiritual location, "in the Lord," though somewhat mystical, provided both a higher perspective about life and emotional equilibrium. As so often seen in Paul's writings, joy occurs because of one's relationship to Jesus instead of one's perspective of surrounding events. The Christian's joy, then, is qualitatively different from happiness. Joy is a settled disposition of the soul based on the fact that God controls. Happiness is based on positive experiences and circumstances. Paul demonstrated his confidence in God and his understanding of joy in his experience. He rejoiced in spite of the divided churches at Rome (1:12–20). With these final three uses of the phrase ("rejoice in the Lord"), he cautions readers to embrace the principle of joy apart from specific circumstances in which joy would be unexpected.

Third, Paul claimed to repeat what he stated earlier, "[t]o write to you again about this." Some relate that repetition only to the command to rejoice, which precedes it,[389] but that construction seems awkward as do the defenses for it. The largest objection to this is how joy could be a "safeguard." Supporting that notion requires default to the fact that the joy of the Lord is always our protection. Would joy protect from theological heretics? Others understand the expression to refer to the warnings about the Jewish opponents. Previously, when present with them, Paul had spoken against these same people; now he wrote against them. It was, then, at least a second warning. The Greek text does not say Paul wrote before; that idea comes from the statement "[t]o write to you again about this."[390] When did he express these concerns? Some say it was in a previous letter. Others say it occurred in some oral communication, possibly even through Timothy and Epaphroditus, who carried the letter. Any of these explanations would suffice and do not violate the meaning of the text. In any case, from this warning come two observations: Paul believed this matter was significant enough to address repeatedly, and the problem most likely persisted long enough for continued communication about it. The Philippians needed to realize Paul lived for the spiritual well-being

[388] The phrase "in Christ" occurs repeatedly in Ephesians and Colossians. These are the classical locations for deriving interpretation.

[389] G. Hawthorne, *Philippians*, 124. More recently, Bockmuehl, *A Commentary*, 180–82, advocates this with extended support. He claims it is "the most likely reading."

[390] Literally the text says, "to write the same to you," τὰ αὐτὰ γράφειν ὑμῖν.

of his converts and that his instruction was intended to prepare them for the attacks against their faith.

From Paul's perspective, writing again is not "trouble for [him]." The word translated "trouble" is often translated "lazy, lack" (*oknaros*). It suggests Paul has no hesitation in writing—it does not unnecessarily take his time. Writing to them is important, even a necessity. Taking the church's perspective, it is for their good. Paul uses the term "safe" ("a safeguard" CSB, *asphales*). It is the wise thing to warn the church, and it is for their own good. Such a rationale strengthens Paul's motive for writing. In Paul's mind this demands greater attention than has been given previously. It is doubtful that 4:1 (occurring later) fits that concern.

Paul had communicated to them before this letter. Assuming that, he is burdened to warn the church of the impending theological danger. The false teachers had influence earlier, and their energies increased as time passed. There is no evidence the Jews had made inroads into the church, but their threat was real and, perhaps, imminent. Paul's pastoral desire for the church's protection is seen in both the facts that this was at least a second warning and Paul's reasons he felt he must include it in this letter for both his and their sakes.[391] He found it no problem to write; they would find the instruction helpful.

[391] Bockmuehl, *A Commentary*, 183, contributes an interesting comparison: "But if, say, a government minister sat down one evening to begin writing a letter to her constituents, it is not difficult to imagine how abruptly different her tone might be the next evening if in the meantime her government had suffered a serious political setback, or if slanderous allegations had been raised against her in the press."

Structure (3:2–6)

Watch out for the dogs,
watch out for the evil workers,
watch out for those who mutilate the flesh.
For we are the circumcision = the ones who worship by the Spirit of God,
boast in Christ Jesus,
and do not put confidence in the flesh
although I have reasons for confidence in the flesh.

If anyone else thinks he has grounds for confidence in the flesh
[I have more confidence]: circumcised the eighth day;
of the nation of Israel,
of the tribe of Benjamin,
a Hebrew born of Hebrews;
regarding the law, a Pharisee;
regarding zeal, persecuting the church;
regarding the righteousness that is in the law, blameless.

Interpretation (3:2–6)

3.3.1.1 True Circumcision (3:2–6)

Paul addressed the problem immediately. Although he focused on the veiled message of the false teachers—circumcision and law—Paul also discussed their methods. There can be no doubt as to his conviction regarding them and their religious activities. Paul's writing revealed his concern that the church recognize the nature of its opponents. His style became graphic and picturesque, a sign of his interest in the subject.[392] Both the terms which describe the opponents and the contrasting definition of true Christians would interest a Jewish audience.

3.3.1.1.1 Decrying the False (3:2)

3:2 Holloway notes, "Nowhere is Paul's skill at invective more in evidence than in Phil 3:2."[393] With three rapid, terse statements

---

[392] This is known in the quick, pithy sentences which open the passage and in the frequency of figures of speech here. Hawthorne, Philippians, 123, lists six figures of speech found here: anaphora (repetition of the same word), paronomasia (sound-alike words), polysyndeton (repetition of *καί* in close succession), alliteration, short disjointed sentences, and chiasm.

[393] Holloway, *Philippians*, 152.

Paul warned the church about the false teachers. The warnings also described the false teachers. The rhetorical devices employed are intended to alert the readers—and the likely many illiterate listeners—to his concern. Each of the three descriptions begin with the Greek letter "k." Three times the verb "watch out for" (*blepete*) occurs.[394] The objects of the verb also reveal the false teachers for what they really were. First, they were "dogs." Eastern people generally hated dogs,[395] with the exception of guard dogs.[396] Jews often described Gentiles as dogs, but here Paul applied the term to Jews. Perhaps he envisioned the packs of ravenous canines which roamed the countryside as scavengers. With this definition, Paul implied they were simply following him, anxious to pick up those who were not theologically grounded after his missionary activity. Paul uses irony to address these false teachers.

The term "dogs" occurs more frequently in the OT than in the NT, and figuratively describes distasteful and/or immoral activity. They eat garbage (Exod 22:31) and corpses, even unburied people (1 Kgs 14:11). It is descriptive of people: 'dead dog' refers to someone of no value (2 Sam 16:9); metaphorically of male prostitutes (Deut 23:15); and evildoers (Ps 22:16).[397]

The appearance of "dogs" in Philippians is the only Pauline use. Jesus is recorded as using the word twice with a literal meaning.[398] Peter used the imagery to describe lapsed believers.[399] In Revelation, John records some are outside the heavenly city, unable to eat from the tree of life: "Outside are the dogs, the sorcerers, the sexually immoral, the murderers, the idolaters, and everyone who loves and practices falsehood" (Rev 22:15). This use comes closest to Paul's and is the only other time the word is use figuratively in the NT. In both cases it

---

394 Three factors reveal the urgency of his address: the imperative mood verbs; the repetition of the same verb, "watch out for" (βλέπετε), even when it is unnecessary; and the fact that the clauses are in asyndeton (no connective conjunctions). Some do not believe the verb deserves such attention and have concluded there were no opponents outside the church. See Garland, "The Composition," 165–66.

395 Michel, *TDNT*, 3:1101–02.

396 See Witherington, III, *Paul's Letter*, 188, for a description of the frequency of guard dogs in Roman houses.

397 Bockmuehl, *A Commentary*, 185–86. He notes the possible exception in the Near East of Phoenicians in the Persian period.

398 In Matt 7:6 he says, "Don't give what is holy to dogs or toss your pearls before pigs." In Luke 16:21, the dogs licked the poor man Lazarus's sores.

399 In 2 Pet 2:2 he writes, "A dog returns to its own vomit."

is used of unbelievers. Revelation is more descriptive than Philippians, but both writers clearly use the word to refer to those who are outside of the faith. In Revelation, "dogs" is a personification of individuals known by their sins. Paul used a strong term applied metaphorically, describing heretics. His powerful language clearly separates these Jews from genuine Jewish or Gentile believers. Observing the use of the word in the NT confirms the false teachers were outside of the church and outside of Christian orthodoxy.

The two other descriptions of the opponents were direct plays on words with Jewish ideas. The second was "evil workers." These Jews, oriented to salvation by the good works of the law, took pride in their exemplary lives. Like the Paul of the past, they considered themselves blameless. But in reality what they assumed were good works were not. They hindered the gospel, providing a stumbling block to genuine faith. Describing their character as evil, Paul warned against them.[400] Third, they were mutilators. In a figure of speech employing *homonyms* or words that sound alike, Paul turned his thoughts to circumcision.[401] Circumcision represented the first requirement of the law and symbolized their approach to God. They took great pride in the ritual as 3:19 reveals. Paul recognized their circumcision was simply a cutting; it had no value apart from genuine faith in Christ.[402] Paul used a similar expression when speaking of those who advocated such circumcision. He urged them to have themselves emasculated. Speaking again in irony, if cutting brought God's blessings why not cut off everything, presumably for more blessing (Gal 5:12)?

Paul was not opposed to the ritual of circumcision. He described his own circumcision later in this passage in a positive way (Phil 3:5). On his second missionary journey he added young Timothy to his team in Derbe/Lystra (Acts 16:1–3). Before traveling, he circumcised him. He did so "because of the Jews who were in those places, since

[400] Significantly, Paul did not say, "They do evil works." That would focus on their activities. He said they were evil workers, placing the emphasis on their character and motivation.

[401] The sound-alike is with the ending of the words "circumcision" (*peritome*, περιτομή) and "mutilation" (*katatome*, κατατομή). The KJV attempts to capture this pattern by translating the contrasts as "circumcision . . . concision." The NIV misses Paul's rhetorical device entirely. The CSB correctly translates "mutilate the flesh," but fails to capture the strong rhetoric of the Gk. text.

[402] Witherington, III, *Paul's Letter*, 190, relates this to the pagan priests like the prophets of Baal who mutilate themselves. Or, "if Greco-Roman models are in view the worshipers of Cybele, who even cut off their testicles and placed them in a box in the temple."

they all knew that his father was a Greek." While Jewish heritage was a derivative of the father and his lineage, Jewish ethnic identity came through the mother. Timothy was a Jew even though his father was a Greek. Circumcision was important to Paul. Jewish members of his team needed to be without reproach to the Jewish community.[403] The Jewish opponents made circumcision a requirement to enter the kingdom of God. For them it had a strong spiritual meaning qualifying one for God's blessings. Paul realized the futility of this for several reasons. Ritual Jewish circumcision would limit God's blessings to one ethnic group rather than making salvation available to everyone. Further, it directly countered the simplicity of faith in Jesus's life, death, and resurrection. Paul knew if Jesus's death was sufficient for forgiveness of sins and entrance into God's kingdom, nothing else was significant. Adding anything to the work of Jesus through requiring circumcision meant denying the work of Jesus. He used the strongest of terms, "mutilate," to describe the meritless activity.

3.3.1.1.2 Describing the True (3:3–6)

Paul described the genuine response to God in two ways. In 3:3–4a he characterized Christians generally, consciously contrasting them to his Jewish opponents. In 3:4b–6, he appealed to his own religious background as proof of the validity of his theology. Significantly, in contrasting reasons for confidence Paul rightly faults the opponents for having "confidence in the flesh." Yet Paul states twice he has grounds for confidence in the flesh. Given his backward glance to his former life in this text, it surprises to find he used present tense language here. He does not say "I *had* confidence" in the flesh, but rather "I *have* more confidence" (3:3b, 4). This subtly reveals Paul did not reject his background, as will be noted below. He just counted it useless in terms of gaining Christ. In his argument against those who claimed a better Jewish pedigree, Paul still had a stronger reason for confidence in the flesh than they. He had been—and remained—at least an equal Jew to them, and better than most of them!

3:3–4a It is easy to miss Paul's opening and contrasting first words: "For *we* are the circumcision" (emphasis added). Later he argued from his own experience ("I have reasons for confidence in the

---

[403] For similar reasons, Paul refused to allow Titus to be circumcised when he joined Paul's team. Titus was a Gk. with no Jewish background (Gal 2:3).

flesh . . . ."), but here he joined with true believers as the true circumcision. Most immediately he contrasted "those who mutilate" (plural) with the believers (plural). He made such contrasts three times in this chapter: here, in 3:18, "For . . . many live as enemies of the cross," and 3:20, for "Our citizenship is in heaven" as opposed to their minding earthly things. In so doing, he began and ended his argument against them by referring to theology affirmed by genuine Christians. This enabled him to move to his personal experience as the embodiment of theology and as the prime example of the true believers. In these cases, Paul's use of the plural contrasts in relation to those he described as his opponents. The first is mutilators versus circumcision (3:2–3); second is modelers (a "type") of the proper attitudes compared to those opposed (3:17–19); third is the earthly-minded and heaven's citizens (3:19–20). It is as though the baseline theology is primary, including ecclesiology. Combining these sections, the confessional theology goes something like this: We believers are the actual, or true circumcision, in contrast to the mutilators (3:2) . . . We seek perfection which is the proper goal (3:15–18a) . . . We belong to a higher order than earth (heaven) in contrast to those who mind earthly things (3:20)! He supplements these foundational points with his own experience, which is theologically grounded and packed as well.[404]

In 3:3–6, Paul's response to his opponents stressed circumcision. He mentioned it first in describing true believers (3:3), and it is the first characteristic he identified when describing his own pre-Christian qualifications as a Jew. In this, he moved to the heart of the issue for him and the catchword for his opponents' position. In his three previous descriptions of his opponents, he did not mention circumcision directly, although it was obviously in mind when he said they "mutilate the flesh" (3:2). He may also have an indirect reference to it when he later says "their glory is in their shame" (3:19), perhaps a reference to their pride in their circumcised genitals. The allusions are unmistakable. Paul, however, introduced circumcision specifically by referring to it metaphorically. His three descriptions of the truly circumcised are spiritual rather than physical.

---

[404] It will be noted Paul includes two exhortations that are plural directed to himself and all believers (3:16, 17). They are grammatically different, joined to the previous by "therefore" (οὖν) rather than "for" (γάρ). For provides a reason or rationale; therefore provides an application. The theological points are reasons supporting Paul's theology; the applications urge proper behavior.

In the OT, God commanded Abraham to be circumcised as a symbol of his previous commitment to God. He further commanded all Abraham's male children were to be circumcised to remind them of their special identity as Abraham's offspring and part of the covenant God made with Abraham. The ritual of circumcision had symbolic importance as an ethnic identifier and reminder of the covenant. The spiritual aspect of the covenant and circumcision had an early Jewish connection. Apart from the command to circumcise all Jewish males and proselytes even in Israel's wilderness era, circumcision was necessary to participate in the Passover celebration (Exod 12:43–49). At the same time in Israel's history, Moses commanded the people to "circumcise [their] hearts and [not] be stiff-necked any longer" (Deut 10:16). This is explained as "[y]ou are . . . to love the resident alien," (10:19), and to "fear the LORD your God and worship him. Remain faithful to him" (10:20). Jeremiah warned about rebelling against God. His remedy was to "Circumcise [self] to the Lord; remove the foreskin of your [heart]" (Jer 4:4) because his people were "uncircumcised in heart" (9:26). In God's economy, spiritual circumcision was always more important; the OT affirms it (see also Jer 31:31–34; Ezek 36:26) and Paul confirmed it elsewhere (Rom 2:25–29). Circumcision of the heart became a primary emphasis of the early church. Physical circumcision served to identify a man with the Jewish nation and had value for purposes of ministry, but it had no value in commending someone to God.[405] Spiritual circumcision was a matter of the heart (Col 2:11).

The spiritually circumcised are described three ways. Each part of the description is linked together in the Greek text because the three are preceded by one article. The three together characterize genuine Christians, the truly circumcised. Paul identified himself with that group, even though he also had physical circumcision. By so doing, he anticipated the discussion of the choices which became apparent when he chose Christ (3:7). By stating that "we" are the true circumcision, Paul associated himself with Gentiles and Jews who relied on Christ rather than trusting in religious ritual, representing a significant theological point. Jewish circumcision was ethnic and limited to

[405] This is clear in Paul's dealings with Timothy and Titus. Timothy was circumcised before his journeys with Paul (Acts 16:3) in order not to be offensive to his Jewish countrymen. Paul forbade Titus to be circumcised, however, because he was Gk.; circumcision would only hinder his ministry to his countrymen (Gal 2:3).

one people. Paul clearly enlarges spiritual circumcision to include both Jews and Gentiles, to anyone who believes. Perhaps the best statement of this is Gal 3:27–29.

The three characteristics of the spiritually circumcised involve worship, glory, and confidence. First, true believers "worship by the Spirit of God." Using a term that often referred to temple service (*latreuo*), Paul contrasted inward, spiritual worship with the legalism of outward conformity to the law. Furthermore, he employed the word consistently used for activity as worship—what the singers and assistants at the temple did. He could have stated they "glorify God" using the word for "glory" (*doxa*, δόξα), but that word is absent from this context. Perhaps he is focused on his previous comment that his opponents are "evil workers." Christians actively worship by the Spirit. Their work serves as a contrast to that of the "evil workers." The Spirit energizes and focuses Christian worship. In a similar context, Paul wrote to his Gentile Christian readers at Galatia, "if you get yourselves circumcised, Christ will not benefit you at all" (5:2). Further, "For we eagerly await through the Spirit, by faith, the hope of righteousness. For in Christ Jesus neither circumcision nor uncircumcision accomplishes anything" (5:5–6). In Philippians Paul implies "the dogs" attempt worship, but it is on their own terms and by their own power. Effective worship is prompted by and enabled by the Spirit, a resource his opponents do not possess.

Second, true believers as the true circumcision "boast in Christ Jesus." The term "glory" means to "boast" (*kauchaomai*), and Paul consciously contrasted the boasting of good works (by unbelievers) with the boasting that is in the work of Christ (by believers). Later he will accuse his opponents because "their glory is in their shame" (3:19). Two different words give instruction. Paul's boasting is in "that of which he is most proud" (*kauchomai*). Thus, Paul is most proud of Christ Jesus and the work he has done on behalf of believers. Later, he would reveal his opponents have a point of pride which they honor ("glory," *doxa*)—their shame. It is likely a veiled reference to their circumcised genitals. Paul's life and conversation—his boast—was Christ, but the Judaizers could not get beyond physical circumcision.

Third, true believers have no "confidence in the flesh." He refers again to righteousness that trusts in human initiative and energy to gain spiritual blessing. Paul came to the place where he realized his own efforts were useless and that attitude paved the way for his trust in Christ. His opponents' confidence began with circumcision, a humanly performed ritual, and continued with actively trying to keep the law. Paul often used the word "flesh" in contrasting true believers, those in the Spirit, from others (Gal 5:16–26). The flesh figuratively denotes the values, outlook, and activities of people unaided by the Holy Spirit. They live their lives like everyone else. The flesh describes an environment and what that environment does to its participants. It motivates them to self-appeasement. Alternatively, the realm of the Spirit produces values, an outlook, and activities motivated by the Spirit of God.

Unlike physical circumcision, spiritual circumcision produces a change of character and activity. The threefold description of the truly circumcised—those who have experienced the deeper point and meaning of (spiritual) circumcision even without the physical act—reveals genuine faith. The spiritually circumcised worship differently, talk about someone (Jesus) beyond themselves and their achievements, and trust in Christ rather than their own efforts.

In these first few verses addressing the threat to the Philippian church, Paul easily moves between literal and metaphorical language. For the most part he follows his Jewish training as a rabbi and rabbinic interpretation of the OT. Early in Jewish history devout prophets sought to encourage the people to realize the true meaning which lay behind circumcision since these prophets recognized the importance of the ritual and what it symbolized. They recognized the physical ritual that promised God's blessings did so only if there was a deeper, inner commitment to the God who promised. Similarly, Paul moves beyond the physical flesh to what human energy (flesh) achieves. Those who "mutilate the flesh" through circumcision without belief put their confidence in themselves and their achievement. Flesh, then, symbolized the efforts of humanity rather than simply the physical body. Without commitment to Christ, circumcision is done only to the body, not the soul (Gal 5:3–6).

This is Paul's most pithy but pointed description of his opponents. It is a mistake to assume he levels his attacks against all Jews and Jewish practices. It is a vindictive against certain Jews who militantly seek to recapture the church and bring Christians under the Torah. Paul would certainly argue against Judaism because of his theology of the uniqueness of Christ and the "better" way he found in him. He believed the Jewish nation failed because they did not recognize Jesus as the Christ (Rom 10:1–6). Paul would not call all of them dogs, however. His opponents were aggressive Jewish zealots whose activity was characteristic of a few individuals.

Following his general description of Christians, Paul appealed to his background as proof of his point. The immediate concern was "confidence in the flesh." Since that attitude is basic to all human life—all naturally trust in their own abilities—Paul picked up that point. Further, it seemed to be the pride of the Jewish opponents and, therefore, their downfall. They trusted in their flesh to gain salvation.

Paul's background naturally divides into two logical categories: heredity and achievement. Neither were sufficient. Gordon Fee aptly entitles this section "There Is No Future to the Past."[406] Paul listed seven components which spoke of his background. The first four form the first group, and each identifies some part of Paul's heredity. The last three are introduced by the preceding preposition *kata*. They belong together since *kata* provides a standard of measurement and refers to achievements. Although he had the best of advantages by birth and made the most of his religious opportunities, they fostered a spirit of pride which kept him away from his goal of gaining salvation.

3:4b–5a Natural attributes are identified in a list that includes four components, but their exact relationship to each other is difficult to understand. The pattern of these relationships is one of inclusion.[407] Two statements occur: Paul was "an eighth-day person" ("circumcised the eighth day,") and he was a "Hebrew born of Hebrews." Each of these has a modifier, and the effect is to divide them into two distinct points. First, Paul was a true Israelite. Starting at the point of their interest, he disclosed with reference to circumcision, he was an "eighth-day one."[408] If his opponents were circumcised, he was too, and his procedure had been completely in accord with the law. Further explaining the value of his circumcision, he was "of the nation

[406] Fee, *Philippians*, 305.

[407] The inclusion is a grammatical pattern that helps explain the semantic relationships between the components. The first and last components are in the nominative case, and the second and third are in the genitive/ablative case. This suggests the second and third are secondary. Two possibilities exist: The genitives/ablatives modify the first nominative, or the genitives/ablatives modify one nominative each so that a chiasm results. This latter explanation is more likely. This enabled Paul to build his argument to a climax with a "Hebrew born of Hebrews," the high point of his pedigree.

[408] "Circumcision" is a dative of reference which serves to introduce a statement. Literally this reads "in circumcision, eighth-day."

of Israel." This set him apart from Gentile proselytes. Circumcision was a boundary marker, clearly identifying Paul with the nation. Jews who were circumcised fulfilled the physical aspect of God's command to Abraham, who was to circumcise his offspring (Gen 17:11), a sign of the Abrahamic covenant. Centuries later Moses reiterated the same (Lev 12:3).[409] Paul was an authorized Jew, properly circumcised when a Jewish baby. His circumcision indicated he belonged to the people of Israel.

Second, Paul was a Hebrew. The chiastic arrangement (an inverted relationship between the elements of parallel phrases) places the tribe of Benjamin first. The tribe of Benjamin was significant to the nation and to Paul. Benjamin was the last of Jacob's sons from whom the tribes were named. Also, he was the only son born in Canaan, the Promised Land. Although Paul was a Diaspora Jew, he was proud of his strong national background. That pride existed in his parents first when Paul's parents named him Saul,[410] after Israel's first monarch, King Saul, who also was of the tribe of Benjamin. His parents aspired for their son to live with the conscious awareness of his ancestor. Indeed, he had an enviable ancestry and remained true to that heritage. He was a Hebrew of Hebrews. On one hand, this may have meant he was not a Hellenist or Hellenist sympathizer. Since he was born in Tarsus, his opponents could have assumed he was. Furthermore, Paul's understanding of Jewish history paralleled that of Stephen, the first martyr. Saul/Paul witnessed Stephen's message and martyrdom. His early Christian understanding, in fact, may have derived from Stephen as well. His opponents could well have understood Saul/Paul to be sympathetic to the Hellenistic branch of Jewish/Christian theology (Acts 7). On the other hand, it may have referred to Paul's ability to read the Scriptures in Hebrew. In any case, the stress on the correct

---

[409] Abraham was the father of the Jewish people; Moses was the founder of the Jewish nation. The reiterated command reinforces the idea that circumcision set the people apart as a national and ethnic boundary-marker.

[410] Acts 13:9 says, "But Saul—also called Paul—filled with the Holy Spirit, stared straight at Elymas . . . " This was on the first missionary journey. It is not clear why Luke changed at this point from Saul to Paul. Throughout the remainder of Acts and through the Pauline Letters, Paul is called Paul. Peter accepts this name, seemingly with ease (2 Pet 3:15). Some suggest the change is from the Hb. "Saul" to the Gk. "Paul" because it was easier to say in the Gentile world. There is no rationale given, however.

pedigree removed a potential question about Paul's credentials when he confronted the Jewish teachers.[411]

Although the primary thrust of presenting his pedigree was to counter his opponents' pride, could Paul have subtly taken this approach to parallel the kenosis of Jesus? Both his heredity and his achievements placed him in an enviable category in Jewish life. Paul's previous status exceeded that of his opponents. He was at the top in Judaism. When he met Christ, however, his attitude changed. Who he was previously paled in insignificance compared to the greater joy of service. The apostle served Christ and people out of his newfound situation—a "[servant] of Christ" (Phil 1:1)—rather than expecting the adulation that could have come because of who he was in his previous life. There is no evidence Paul completely disavowed the past; perhaps he used his Pharisee/rabbi status to gain access to the podium in the synagogues. Toward the end of his active ministry as recounted by Luke, Paul claimed, "I am a Pharisee" (Acts 23:6; see also 26:5). Paul's primary point is clear: nothing of what he received or earned commended him to God as he had previously thought and hoped. His Jewish opponents, therefore, should follow the same path that he did.

3:5b–6a Paul had made the correct choices as a Jewish boy and adult. Three items provide the standard to measure these achievements: the law, zeal for the nation, and righteousness.[412] Paul obviously had excelled in all three (see Acts 22:3; 26:5). First, Paul chose to be a Pharisee. Each devout Jewish male would sympathize with some organized approach to the law since it was the heart of Jewish life.[413] The Pharisees were noted for their love for the law, strict interpretation of it, and ethical consistency. According to Josephus, there were "above" 6,000 Pharisees in first-century Judea.[414] This was a select group which was popular and generally appreciated by the people. Even though they could be legitimately criticized for their methods of

---

[411] Lightfoot, *Saint Paul's*, 146–47, provided a good description of the importance of these statements. He also pointed out the four are in an ascending order, reaching a climax with the fourth statement. This is the third way of reading the statements. As above, however, since two are ablative modifiers, it seems best to see a chiasm.

[412] Each of these is introduced by κατά.

[413] The well-known choices included the Pharisees, Sadducees, Zealots, and Herodians. The situation was far more complex than this, however. For example, there were Essenes. It is likely not every boy chose to identify with one of these groups. The groups served similarly to a combination between political and religious affiliations.

[414] Jos. Antiq. XVII. ii. 4

protecting and applying the law,[415] they brought Jewish faith to the people through the synagogue and their teaching in it. In a sense, they kept the people "Jewish." Paul's credentials are cryptically presented. One wonders how common it was for a Diaspora Jew to align with one of the groups. Paul's family was conservative Pharisees since they sent their son to study in Jerusalem under Gamaliel the Elder. Gamaliel was one of the two leading rabbis of the day (Acts 22:3); Hillel was the other. That alone would have given Paul influence in Jerusalem, which he had before his conversion. He was quite ambitious in school, excelling in both rabbinic methodologies and political opportunities. Paul would have chosen to be a Pharisee as a young teenager,[416] the time he would have begun his studies under Gamaliel. Many assume that as a young man he was appointed to the Sanhedrin, the highest Jewish court of law.[417] Although Paul could have boasted of his attainments as a Pharisee, he simply introduced them as "regarding the law, a Pharisee." The law was his point of contention with the opponents. The title "Pharisee" spoke for itself in terms of attitudes about the law and approaches to it. Pharisees knew the law and interpreted it conservatively.[418] In that light, it is important to note Paul still saw himself as a Pharisee (Acts 23:6) and sometimes debated with the Jews with that identity.

Second, concerning "zeal," Paul persecuted the church. Identifying himself with regard to zeal had more significance than many assume. It is incorrect to think of it simply that "Paul was a fervent religionist."

---

[415] Pharisees put a hedge around the law to protect it by making applications and implications requirements. In their minds, their oral interpretations were necessary and sanctioned by God. In Exod 20 Moses gave an oral interpretation of the Ten Commandments. They followed in that train.

[416] Much has been written about Paul's life, pieced together from Scripture and the likely experiences he would have had given his biographical statements. Not everyone could gain appointment to study under Gamaliel, and certainly it was not likely for one whose family had lived outside Judea for generations. Paul's devout, wealthy parents surely had influence both abroad (Judea) and at home (Tarsus). They not only passed to him a love of the law, they passed the coveted prize of Roman citizenship, which he found helpful in Philippi.

[417] His age is unknown but given the length of his life and ministry, he must have been accomplished in Judaism at an early age. The assumption he was on the supreme court (Sanhedrin) comes from his statement that he "cast [his] vote against [saints]" (Acts 22:10, ESV).

[418] The word *Pharisee* comes from "to separate." They separated themselves to the law, developing strict principles of how to interpret it. Paul reveals his Pharisaic background in his exegesis of the OT. Interestingly, Gamaliel had a more lenient attitude toward those who interpreted differently (Acts 5:33–39). Though Paul studied under him, his attitude toward Jewish nationalism was like that of Hillel, who had a much stricter political perspective.

Zeal was different from enthusiasm. N. T. Wright traces Israelite zeal to Phinehas, who took bloody action when the nation was drawn to the Moabites in the wilderness before they conquered the Promised Land. Some Israelites took Moabite women and some worshipped Moabite deities, particularly Baal. Phineas turned the nation around in a single act. He killed a man and his prostitute who were having sex in the man's tent. Through this act, Phineas became a hero known for his zeal. Of him, the Lord said, "he was zealous among them with my zeal, so that I did not destroy the Israelites in my zeal." He was granted "[God's] covenant of peace." Scripture says his zeal "made atonement for the Israelites" (Num 25:6–14). Psalm 106:30–31 records that Phinehas's act "was credited to him as righteousness throughout all generations." A similar phrase was used earlier of Abraham.[419] Zeal was the desired, even necessary quality for preserving Jewish life, especially in a Gentile culture. Phinehas had God's zeal empowering his own. In the first century, Jewish men often measured their commitment to God and the nation by how they opposed foreign religion and rule. Young Paul obviously saw the emerging church as a threat to Israel. For him, it was dangerous because it was a messianic movement that arose within Israel. Paul saw the rise of early Christianity[420] as another threat calling for a man with zeal like Phinehas. He should rise to the occasion to preserve Israel. Like those of Phinehas, perhaps Paul's actions could be counted as righteousness for him.[421] Since Paul persecuted the church, he had put into action his love for the nation and the law. He had taken his beliefs to an extreme that even his opponents did not, using physical force to eradicate Christianity (see Acts

[419] N. T. Wright, *Paul*, 30–31. Wright entitles his first chapter "Zeal," describing the formative influences on Paul as a young man. Of course, Paul was called Saul then and he kept that name for a while as a Christian leader. Unceremoniously, in Acts Luke simply changed describing Saul to Paul. The reason is unclear.

[420] At that time the church was not called Christian and believers were not called Christians. The name Christians was given to them by the unsaved community in Antioch, Syria. Since it later described true believers, the word is used here, though anachronistically, to provide continuity with later generations of believers who are called universally "Christians."

[421] It is worth noting by the first mid-century AD, the party known as Zealots (from zeal) armed themselves and became a militant group. There is no evidence Paul supported them, since he was a committed Pharisee. In another note, Jesus cleansed the temple because of his own zeal (John 2:17). Paul understood the zeal of the nation of Israel was not directed toward the true Messiah (Rom 10:2).

9:1–2).[422] His zeal went beyond that of his opponents. He secured legal documents and military assistance to incarcerate Christians. He stated his zeal more positively in his testimony before the crowds in Jerusalem. He was "educated at the feet of Gamaliel according to the strictness of . . . ancestral law. [He] was zealous for God . . . " (Acts 22:3). He explained his zeal for "persecuting the church" as evidence of his zeal for God. Every Jewish person understood the importance of zeal in protecting Jewish heritage and mission. Paul did not acknowledge the zeal of his opponents other than that they were "evil workers." He mentioned zeal because of its significance to loyalist Jewish patriots and their love for their nation. He recognized his opponents expended significant energy against Christians. Their activity was motivated by zeal. The fact that he does not call their efforts zeal may be a subtle way of showing his previous superiority to them, however. What they wanted, he had wanted more than they!

3:6b Paul had attained the righteousness of the law. Obviously, Paul did not mean he had lived perfectly in accordance with the law. In this context, he boasted of externally verifiable qualities that demonstrated the religious standing he had before he became a Christian. If the other two points regarding achievement could be verified, becoming a Pharisee and possessing zeal, which was the case, this one must have the same capability. Paul's point was he had an outwardly perfect record. He had never been accused of breaking any law[423] and, therefore, "showed himself to be blameless."[424] This does not cancel out the testimony of Rom 7:7–12. At one time, he perceived himself as "alive, apart from the law" (Rom 7:9), but that time passed quickly. He knew his inner spiritual condition, but publicly he was above reproach.[425]

The three descriptions of his attainments relate individually and together to the law. Judging from Paul's condemnation of his

---

[422] Lightfoot, *Saint Paul's*, 148, stated graphically the sense of Paul's statement: "I persecuted, imprisoned, slew these infatuated Christians; this was my great claim to God's favour [sic]."

[423] So Silva, *Philippians*, 175. His discussion of this verse is quite to the point. It is difficult to determine whether or not the NIV translation "legalistic righteousness" means this or not. It is a good attempt to translate in light of the contextual considerations.

[424] Lightfoot, *Saint Paul's*, 148.

[425] K. Stendahl, "The Apostle Paul and the Introspective Conscience of the West," *HTR* 56 (1963): 199–215, takes a different view which has had significant impact on interpretation. He argues Paul simply chose a better way, and that he had no sense of guilt about his sin. The context, however, seems to support the view taken in this commentary.

opponents, that was the primary issue. Would one gain righteousness and favor with God by law? Paul had traveled the road of his opponents, doubtless better than they. That road, however, was a dead end. These seven characteristics of heredity and achievement reveal Paul's acceptance of Christ did not occur because he was marginally Jewish. He had not failed in his own religion. Fleming states, "Paul's problem was not that he couldn't make the grade; it was that he did make it, only to find out that it was the wrong standard of measurement."[426] He had seen a better way and had chosen to follow it.

Based on this cryptic description of those who threatened the church at Philippi, it is necessary to repeat who they were. The people addressed in chapter three do not appear to be the same ones Paul describes in chapter one. Both groups opposed the apostle, but Paul writes differently about the two. The critical division is that in chapter one Paul affirms that they preach Christ. While they may have been guilty of wrong motives, their method and message were acceptable. In chapter three, nothing about them is correct theologically or practically. The telling point is they apparently boasted of what they could achieve in the flesh rather than boast in Christ Jesus. That alone revealed their unorthodox theology. As chapter three develops, this basic and foundational difference becomes more pronounced. Paul's personal testimony of the centrality of Jesus instructs and warns the readers (see the further discussion in the Introduction and below).

3.3.1.2 True Values (3:7–11)

The second section of this warning explains Paul's real values. The false teachers were "evil workers" (see 3:2). While Paul's evaluation was penetrating, he realized their outlook was the same as his had been. In fact, the burden of this entire section is carried by a theme of Paul's life before and after placing faith in Jesus as Lord. The real value Paul found was in knowing Christ personally. That brought true zeal for perfect character not found through the law.

This section is intensely theological, yet practical. After describing dissatisfaction with his natural attainments, Paul described succinctly and successively what has come to be known in the topical arrangements of classical systematic theology as "justification" (3:9), "sanctification" (3:10), and "glorification" (3:11). Since they occur

[426] Fleming, *Philippians*, 165.

together under one subject in Paul's testimony, he considered them to be linked, each growing out of the other. Further, the passage calls to mind 2:5–11, which combined theology and ethics. There are even verbal parallels between the two: "consider" (2:6; 3:7, 8), "form" (2:7, "taking . . . the likeness of humanity"; 3:10 "being conformed to"), and "Lord" (2:11; 3:8).[427] These links reinforce the descriptions Paul used of his own experience are chosen because they resemble the description of Jesus in 2:6–11. That would connect him further with genuine Christians who appreciate the movement of the Christ poem. Example and parallel characterize Paul's methodology. Paul probably linked these in his own mind, though they address two very different situations. This passage makes clear, however, that theology and life go together and that the antidote to poor living is proper theology. If the Philippians understood the richness of Paul's Christian life, they would not follow the false teachers.

Structure

I have considered . . . everything that was a gain to me . . . to be a loss
because of Christ.
More than that, I also consider everything to be a loss
in view of the surpassing value of knowing Christ Jesus my Lord.
I have suffered the loss of all things
and consider them as dung
[because of him]
so that I may gain Christ
and be found in him,
not having a righteousness of my own
from the law,
but one that is through faith in Christ—righteousness
from God
based on faith.
My goal is to know him
and the power of his resurrection
and the fellowship of his sufferings,
being conformed to his death,
assuming that I will somehow reach the resurrection from among the dead.

[427] This idea comes from Silva, *Philippians*, 178. His analysis of this section is particularly insightful.

Interpretation

3.3.1.2.1 Evaluation of Paul's Former Life (3:7–8)

These two verses are characterized by two consistently employed literary patterns. The first is comparison. Paul compared his pre-Christian life with his life with Christ. The second is progression. Paul described the former and the present life progressively, sometimes with the same words or cognates. This is a powerful passage. It combines personal experience with deep theology. Some have suggested this is Paul's theology in brief statement.[428]

Attitude	Reason
I have considered personal gain, loss	because of Christ
I do consider everything to be a loss	in view of the surpassing value of knowing Christ Jesus my Lord.
I consider all (previous) things as dung	so that I may gain Christ and be found in him.

3:7–8 The first side of the comparison is Paul's terminology for his former life. Three times he described it, and each is progressively more vivid. First, when he came to Christ at his conversion, he considered his previous gains as "loss." Remarkably, the word Paul used frequently in this section, "consider," is the same word of Jesus's attitude in 2:6, *hgeomai*. It has been used often in the letter. The first use here is in the perfect tense. The perfect tense form of "considered" suggests a completed evaluation with present effects.[429] He came to realize that gains were loss. The loss is everything that was a gain. In the NT, "gain" is a Pauline distinctive (*kerdos*). It occurs three times: Phil 1:21; 3:7; Titus 1:11. The word is likely a business term expressing "profit" instead of loss. Paul expressed "to live is Christ and to die is *gain*" (1:21, emphasis added). In that text, death adds value to his existence because he will have received what he longed to have, a more intimate, personal relationship with Christ. He also stated to Titus that rebellious people needed to be silenced because "they are

[428] Silva, *Philippians*, 177–78, calls this section "The Essence of Pauline Theology." He correctly captures the significance of these verses. They are theology expressed through personal testimony.

[429] This is not a matter of tense only because the perfect can stress the completion of the action or the abiding results. The idea comes from the tense in contrast with the present tense in 3:8 and from the impact of the context.

ruining entire households by teaching what they shouldn't in order to get *money* [that is, gain] dishonestly" (Titus 1:11, emphasis added). The word suggests something to be earned for personal benefit. The use of the term in Phil 3:7 fits into this pattern "[e]verything that was gain to me" reveals two important aspects of his new value system. First, it refers to his immediately preceding list of benefits: his heredity and his achievements. What he received from birth (see above) he certainly used to his advantage. What he achieved (see above) built on that foundation which brought him status in the Jewish community. Second, with a particular focus on his achievements, they were gained through self-effort: hard work and political opportunism. He thought in terms of these as proper payment for his effort. They were gain, which also brought him a sense of pride of accomplishment. It would be wrong to view Paul's previous life as entirely self-oriented, however. His discussions of his previous life always come in the context of being devout. He viewed himself as having accomplished what every Jewish boy should hope as a child of the covenant.

Nevertheless, Paul's Christian evaluation of his pre-Christian experience is described as "loss" (*zemia*). The well-chosen word is intentional, evidenced by its repetition in his second appraisal of his past (3:8). "Loss" occurs four times in the NT. Luke used it twice in his record of the shipwreck at Malta, during which the ship suffered "damage and loss" (Acts 27:10, 21). Damage described the ship; loss described the cargo and the destroyed vessel. The word has a financial sense. Losing the cargo was more than a loss of things. It deprived the owners of expected gain. The two uses here (3:7, 8) retain that meaning. Paul's achievements were misdirected. None can doubt the energy and focus required to attain what Paul did. What he expected to bring profit, however, was misdirected and the hoped-for gain became loss for the sake of Christ. The profit/loss metaphor spoke powerfully in Rome, the financial center of the world, and in Philippi where the values of Rome had a home.

Second, Paul continued to affirm that decision. Lest some of the readers interpret him as regretting past decisions, he continued with an adversative conjunction followed by another strong adversative: "More than that."[430] Though he continued the same thought even

[430] The Gk. verbal combination is strong, combining three particles: (μεν) "on the one hand," and *oun* (οὐν) "so then," *ge* (γέ) "indeed." μενοῦνγε is a strong contrast with the previous, "more than that" (CSB).

using some of the same key words, his point was now stronger. Considering gains loss was indeed a past decision, but it was not left in the past. There was more than that. The past decision remained a present evaluation. In 3:8 the present tense of "consider" joins with the object "loss." Paul meant this was a proper appraisal and a good choice.[431] He thus lived daily with the realization of his misdirected gain become loss.

Third, in 3:8 Paul expressed his conviction more firmly with the verb "consider" and the object "dung" (*skubala*).[432] Here is repetition of the word "loss" in a verbal form: "I lost all things." This side of the progression reaches its climax by using the verb "to be . . . loss," rather than the noun as before, and repeating "I consider." Though each statement progresses in meaning and emphasis, Paul used the same words in the core statement: "gain" and "loss." Using "loss" as the verb allowed another object of "I consider." He used the word "dung." Perhaps he used dung in anticipation of the Jewish opponents' insistence on proper diet. Paul said they worship their bellies. He paints the most dramatic picture of what is useless, dung, but is there also a veiled reference to the uselessness of the focus on foods? All foods pass through the body, after all. The imagery could well have come from Jesus himself. Discussing dietary laws, as Paul does here, Jesus explained the truth to his disciples who struggled with the concept of kosher foods: "Don't you realize that nothing going into a person from the outside can defile him? For it doesn't go into his heart but into the stomach *and is eliminated*; (thus he declared all foods clean)" (Mark 7:18–19, emphasis added). Since the ultimate "destination" of foods is the waste pit, perhaps Paul extended the metaphor based on Jesus's words. In so doing, he also anticipated his opponents' focus on foods/stomach which he discussed later (Phil 3:19). There is increasing intensity, as though the mere thought of the decision that what he previously considered gain was loss brought a renewed appraisal that his former life was useless compared to what really mattered.

---

[431] Here the tenses gain significance. Paul used the perfect tense for the past. As noted above, the perfect may stress the resulting state of the action of the verb. Because he followed the perfect with the present of the same verb, it seems likely he was referring to a past action. If not, the resulting state of the decision (present force of the perfect, which is normal) is presented as a background factor in contrast to the foreground emphasis on the continuing action (present).

[432] Some scholars are prone to translate this as "garbage." It is used for "dung," however, and the strongest possible contrast makes best sense of this passage.

Paul reflected on the Damascus road experience (Acts 9:1–31). At that time he saw the foolishness of his past life and embraced a new way. His conversion accounts in Acts do not include any direct idea of repentance. It is difficult to know, therefore, how much of Paul's prior life he discounted at that time. How did he understand and express repentance? A close look at the Acts narrative indicates he left the accompanying men, joined the believing community, preached Jesus as the Christ so effectively that the leaders of the city sought his life, and he sought to join himself to the Jewish Christian apostles (Gal 1). The impact of that event, when he was essentially captured by Jesus, caused immediate changes in values, biblical understanding, self-identity, and new directions far different from his former ambitions. His negative appraisal expressed an important component of salvation. No one can choose Christ who does not reach a similarly negative conclusion about personal efforts.

It has been popular to read into this passage significant remorse on Paul's part. Since Martin Luther's rant against the legalism of the Roman Catholic church, many have assumed Paul's situation was like Luther's. They equate Jews with the distorted Roman church of the Middle Ages. Luther was plagued by his awareness of his own sinfulness and the inability to relieve guilt through the activities prescribed by the priests. Was Luther's experience with Rome akin to Paul's with Judaism? Nothing in this passage suggests that. Paul's emotions are hidden, if there at all. This was a theological change of mind and heart without the agony of guilt and fear brought on by a dissatisfied prior life. Paul was surprisingly conquered by Jesus.

The other side of the contrast presented above explains why Paul considered his heredity and achievements so useless. They did not bring him to Christ. The strong language thrice repeated has made some think Paul completely discarded his former life, that his mind so changed he wished he had not lived the way he did. Nothing, however, in this text suggests that, exaggerating the negative side of his statements. Paul's Christian and mission experiences reveal just the opposite. Paul often presented and defended his Christian faith with rabbinic methodologies. There are multiple evidences of his rabbinic hermeneutics illuminating OT texts. In his mission, he stated the gospel was relevant "first to the Jew, and also to the Greek" (Rom 1:16). He demonstrated this first in his insistence that Christ fulfilled the OT and that the OT is the proper foundation for Christian truth. He also showed his commitment to this in his preference of going to the synagogues first in the towns he visited. Such a pattern could provide multiple benefits. It would get him into the Jewish population of a city, opening the possibility of a good reception. In every such account, Jewish persons were among the first believers. It is possible, though this is conjecture, that Paul took advantage of his status as a Pharisee to gain the platform to deliver his message in the synagogues.[433] The early church had Christian Pharisees in it (Acts 15:5). Finally, in this regard a striking statement occurs before Paul's last trip to Jerusalem and the lengthy imprisonments it brought. Fearing conflict, Paul's friends urged him to join with men who made a Jewish vow so that people would know Paul was "also careful about observing the law" (Acts 21:24). This suggests that at times Paul used his Jewish background to advance the gospel.

Perhaps the most obvious of evidences that he appreciated his background would be well-known in Philippi. Luke's record of the founding of the church includes Paul's disclosure to the Philippian jailor that he was a Roman citizen. It was only after he and Silas endured the suffering possibly inflicted by the jailer (Acts 16:37). Again, in Jerusalem the Roman officials ordered Paul to be scourged after Paul's message caused a riot. Paul said to the centurion, "Is it legal for you to scourge a man who is a Roman citizen and is uncondemned?" (Acts 22:25). His Roman citizenship is not at issue in confronting the opponents in Philippians. Nevertheless, it reveals Paul did not devalue everything in his past.[434] Fowl says, "Rather than having forgotten or erased the past, Paul has been offered a truthful vision of [it]."[435] The point is his heredity and achievements did not bring him to Christ. He could no longer rely on them to gain what he most wanted in life: a relationship with the God then known primarily through Judaism.

[433] There must have been some way synagogue Jews recognized Paul's stature and allowed him to speak to them in their formal services. It certainly was not his Christian status, though that may have earned him the right to return and speak. Could he have worn his Pharisee/rabbi robe to the synagogues? Possibly so!

[434] To these Jewish and Roman illustrations, a host of others could be added. For example, his proficiency in speaking and writing Gk. and Hb., and even his understanding of travel, come from his background benefits and experiences.

[435] Fowl, *Philippians*, 162. He further states, "It is only from the perspective of this truthful vision that he has any hope of directing his present and future in ways that will bring him to the goal for which Christ laid hold of him."

Three times Paul expressed the goal was Christ, each corresponding to the explanation of his Christian value system. First, he said it was "because of Christ" (3:7). This is the idea of exchange in seed form. This could mean he understood "Christ told him to," and he wanted to be obedient. More likely, Paul realized a choice had to be made between what he had worked so hard to gain and what he could be given by Christ. Doubtless Paul's deepest desire was to be properly related to God. His upbringing pointed him in one direction; now he saw a completely different way. He experienced a loss in exchange for Christ.[436] Second, he said it was for the sake of "the surpassing value of knowing Christ Jesus [his] Lord" (3:8). The advance in this statement is that knowledge of Jesus excelled what Paul had previously. The word "surpassing" suggests something of more excellence than that to which it is compared. The word translated "surpassing" here (*huperexon*) occurs only five times in the NT, three of which are in Philippians. In 2:3, Christians are to consider others "more important." In 4:7, the peace of God "surpasses" knowledge. Here, knowledge of Christ is better than the former ways. Therefore, knowing Christ was better than the combined value of his former life. Some interpret this knowledge in a Gnostic context and claim Paul spoke of a general religious knowledge. This is a supremely Jewish context, however, and the knowledge of which he spoke is to be understood in light of the OT knowledge of God, now applied to Christ. Seen this way, knowledge means "a personal response of faith and obedience to God's self-revelation."[437]

As though he relived his experience chronologically, Paul added twice to the understanding of "Christ." The messianic title used thus far now took more personal form. It is the first reference to Jesus in this particular context. One's relationship to the law was the point of argumentation between Paul and his opponents. However there is now a new dimension. It is that "Christ Jesus" brought the gain which he previously thought the law would. This will be explained further later with the statements "I make every effort to take hold of

---

[436] The Gk. construction is the preposition *dia*, δία, with the accusative case.

[437] Caird, *Paul's Letters*, 137. He states further, "Here he takes up the Old Testament phrase and fills it with a specifically Christian content and with a peculiarly personal intensity." Since the Jewish teachers would be particularly offended by Gnostic concepts, it seems best to understand this in terms of its Jewish origins. To this point, at least, there is no hint of Gnostic influence in the letter.

[perfection] because I also have been taken hold of by Christ Jesus" (3:12) and "I pursue as my goal the prize promised by God's heavenly call in Christ Jesus" (3:14). These are the only three occasions in chapter 3 where Christ is joined with Jesus, giving a specific identity to "the Christ." Again, this was the topic of debate between Christians and non-Christian Jews. Who was the Christ? Paul may have intentionally combined Jesus with Christ throughout much of this chapter to reinforce his point. The combination of his personal name, Jesus, with the title, Christ, was selectively chosen. Together they complement Paul's cryptic theology. He hoped for the knowledge of Christ Jesus because Christ Jesus initiated his conversion, and in the messiah (Christ) Jesus he would be granted the rewards God promises to his followers.

Another addition occurs here of significance. Paul said, "Christ Jesus" is "my Lord" (3:8). The title Lord occurs frequently (fifteen times) in Philippians. The majority are in the prepositional phrase "in the Lord" (ten times). "In the Lord" occurs in a variety of statements, but all commonly express the believer's spiritual location. It is in some ways the equivalent to "in Christ," found prominently in Ephesians and Colossians. Christians can "rejoice in the Lord" (Phil 3:1; 4:4, 10), "stand firm in the Lord" (4:1), "agree in the Lord" (4:2), and welcome each other "in the Lord" (2:29). Personal decisions were framed as "in the Lord" (2:19, 24), suggesting it was an alternate way of expressing the will of God and that decisions for travel were subject to the Lord's approval. Paul also acknowledged other believers as "brothers . . . in the Lord" (1:14). At a deeper level, the expression acknowledges the purpose and joy of being Christian. Life has deeper significance for believers: it is to be lived in harmony with God's plans, which are expressed as "in the Lord." The remaining occurrences include "Jesus Christ Lord" in different order. Apart from 3:8, grace and peace come from "the Lord Jesus Christ" (1:2), every tongue will confess "Jesus Christ is Lord" (2:11), on earth believers "eagerly wait for . . . the Lord Jesus Christ" (3:20), and in conclusion of the letter the "grace of the Lord Jesus Christ" is mentioned (4:23). Each of these identify the Lord Jesus Christ by his position or his gifts. In 3:8, however, two nuances occur. Most obviously, Paul personalized Jesus Christ by referring to him as "Christ Jesus my Lord." The statement resembles the opening salutation where Paul declared himself a servant "of Christ Jesus" (1:1, with the term *doulos*). Additionally, this unique statement in Philippians comes in the context of Paul's change from a follower of the law as primary to a follower of Jesus. He alluded to his conversion in Acts 9. In response to the light and the voice, Paul asked, "Who are you, Lord?" (Acts 9:5). He immediately understood that he was conquered by one greater than he. To the question, Jesus replied, "I am Jesus." From that time, "the Lord" became Paul's Lord in a uniquely personal way.

The apostle further expressed his personal relationship to Jesus with his new value of knowing Christ. This is the first of two occurrences of the words built on the root "know" (noun *gnosis* and verb *ginosko*) in this chapter (3:8, 10). Both enhance the personal aspects of Paul's faith. Paul knew about Jesus well, learning of him both before his conversion and after. Here, however, he chose words more conducive to personal knowledge (built on the *gno* root in Greek), knowing him.[438] The statement is cast in the present rather than the past. In this triad of explanations about his experience with Christ, he first used the Greek perfect tense, "[E]verything . . . I have considered to be a loss" (3:7), stressing the continuing state of the past decision. Here he used the present tense: "I . . . consider everything to be a loss" (3:8), which he continues with the third statement, "I . . . consider them as dung" (3:8). At his conversion he recognized the importance of gaining Christ. Over the years, he grew in his understanding of the privilege of knowing Christ. The statement in 3:8 anticipates his developed statement of knowledge of Christ in 3:10.

Third, Paul said he counted all things as loss "that [he] may gain Christ" (3:8). Here Paul clearly developed the idea of exchange. It was impossible to hold on to the former values and still have Christ. It was one or the other, and Christ exceeded anything and everything else. The growing intensity of his statements on his former life end with the evaluation that the assumed gain was mere dung. In the Roman world, dung had little value. Similarly, Paul recognized his former direction which he thought then would pay off (be gain) was basically useless.[439]

The three statements of 3:7–8 express repentance regarding Paul's former attitudes about salvation. He turned away from the past to

---

[438] He used the verb *ginosko* (γινώσκω) rather than *oida* (οἶδα), a verb implying experience rather than actual knowledge.

[439] The meaning of "all things" as loss is clear. It may be, however, that he is thinking of his parents, his standing in Judaism, or property. It is best not to try to delineate what specifics are involved.

gain Christ.[440] In recent decades some have questioned whether Paul was repentant and, if so, of what. The so-called New Perspective on Paul, now fifty years old, questioned the traditional, "western" understanding of Paul's conversion.[441] More recent scholars have reinforced the traditional view of Paul. The latter is accepted here.

3.3.1.2.2 Aspiration of the New Life (3:9–11)

Paul explained what was better. The structure of the text is somewhat confusing. First, two verbs are parallel, but one explains the other. The parallels are "that I may gain Christ" (v. 8) and "be found in him" (v. 9). Second, a parenthesis explains what that means—it is having a Christ-righteousness, not a legal one. Third, the idea is restated: "[t]hat I may know him" (3:10, KJV). The CSB makes this a new sentence, picking up the purpose clause of the Greek text: "My goal is to know him." Fourth, three clauses are joined with "and," which calls for explanation: "to know him and the power of his resurrection and the fellowship of his sufferings." Sixth, Paul concludes with the death to life motif, which serves as what he actually wants to know about Christ. Finally, the ultimate concern is expressed in v. 11: "resurrection from among the dead." The section has three movements, one for each verse division.

3:9 The first statement expresses Paul's existence in relation to Christ. Being in Christ was at the heart of Paul's theology. He saw all persons as either in Adam or in Christ (Rom 5:12–21). His desire to be in Christ meant to be in union with the Lord and to have the covering of Christ's righteousness surrounding him and the resources of Christ available to him. Paul equated the words "gain Christ" (3:8) and "found in him" (3:9). Together they present two different points of view. From one perspective, Paul gained Christ. That is, using business terms again as he so often has in this context, Paul's encounter with Christ on the Damascus road enabled him to embrace another point of

---

440 Repentance is primarily a change of attitude about God, salvation, and sin. The attitude toward sin does not predominate here. There is, however, a definite change of attitude about the way of salvation; thus, the passage stresses one aspect of repentance.

441 Stendahl, "The Apostle Paul." Stendahl's article prompted a "New Perspective" on Paul. The idea was furthered by E. P. Sanders, *Paul and Palestinian Judaism* (Minneapolis: Fortress Press, 1977) and a host of other writers. For more balanced presentations, see James G. D. Dunn, *The New Perspective on Paul* (Grand Rapids: Eerdmans Publishing Co, 2007), Scott McKnight and B. J. Oropeza, *Perspectives on Paul: Five Views* (Ada, MI: Baker Academic, 2020).

view. He was now associated with Christ. From another perspective, he was found in him. The passive verb, "found in him," often has the meaning of "prove to be" or "be present."[442] It takes the perspective of a divine investigation of one's relationships. At the great day of judgment, Paul wanted to be found in Christ. By using the passive voice "Paul subtly shifts from being the subject of his own story to being part of a story in which Christ is now the subject," Fowl observes.[443]

Paul used the phrase "in Christ" ten times in Philippians. Here he used the pronoun construction "in him" to avoid redundancy, making an eleventh occurrence . Similarly, ten times the synonymous construction "in the Lord" occurs with the same meaning.[444] In each use, it refers to the ideological location of Christians: they are identified by commitment with Christ alone. As such, they live with a sensitivity to their position in Christ, seeking to be true to him and to represent him correctly. When Paul hoped to "be found in him" he referred to the most basic idea from which all other uses flow. To be found "in him" is to be manifest as Christian, as siding with Christ, and with a stewardship responsibility of life to Jesus. The context of the passage is eschatological: "found in him" refers to judgment day, when Paul wanted to be seen in Christ as his hope.

Significantly, Paul defined being in Christ in terms of righteousness. Being found in Christ means being clothed with God's righteousness rather than one's own. It is righteousness "based on faith" (3:9). This is the heart of the matter. Fellowship with God is always predicated on righteousness. The OT makes that clear, as in the case of Abraham (Gen 15:6; see also Ps 143:12), and Paul continually affirmed it (Rom 4). The basic question for all persons is that of righteousness. Only the righteous will be saved. The issue is what righteousness suffices for salvation. Paul previously had his own righteousness, which he discovered was inadequate. It was "righteousness that is in the law," and he was "blameless" (Phil 3:6). But it did not bring him into living contact with Christ.

In Scripture, righteousness is often a legal term, not a moral one. It means a judge would pronounce someone righteous. Naturally, the ideal was that the person would actually be righteous, but the focal

---

[442] Caird, *Paul's Letters*, 137.

[443] Fowl, *Philippians*, 154.

[444] "in Christ": 1:2, 13, 26; 2:1, 5; 3: 3, 14; 4:7, 19, 21. "in the Lord": 1:14; 2:19, 24, 29; 3:1; 4:1, 2, 4, 10.

point is on what the judge said (pronounced). The verdict did not necessarily depend on the moral realities of the defendant. In accord with that, the primary question of both Judaism and Christianity was, Caird notes, "What must a man do if God is to declare that he is in the right and so give judgment in his favor? The Jewish answer was that he must obey the Law of Moses."[445] But for Paul, righteousness attained by the law was only a relative self-righteousness. The best that could be hoped for was the blamelessness of which he spoke in 3:6b, but which he nonetheless found inadequate for gaining salvation. Thus, the law provides one approach to righteousness, but it is a flawed approach. The problem is not the law. Paul taught the law is good (Rom 7). The problem is sin, which indwells each person (Rom 7:13–25). When God examines one's life on judgment day, no one has the kind of righteousness that will secure a verdict of innocence by personal effort.

The alternative to law righteousness is God's righteousness. Twice in the context of God's righteousness "righteousness" and "faith" occur (one time "righteousness" is assumed as the subject of the clause). Although they parallel each other, one explains the other by adding to the concept to complete it. First, Paul simply stated righteousness is through the "faith of Christ" ("faith in Christ," CSB). Further, he clarified that it is a righteousness from God and based upon faith.

The construction "faith of Christ" is ambiguous in Greek. Two questions emerge regarding it, one semantic and the other syntactical. The first is the meaning of the word "faith." The second is the precise meaning of the genitive Greek construction "of Christ."[446] Regarding

---

[445] Caird, *Paul's Letters*, 138.

[446] The literature is growing on this subject. The most comprehensive recent monograph on the subject is R. Hays, *The Faith of Jesus Christ: An Investigation of the Narrative Substructure of Galatians 3:1–4:11*, SBLDS 56 (Chico, CA: Scholars, 1983), esp. 158ff. An earlier historical, syntactical, and theological survey may be found by this author in Richard R. Melick, Jr. "A Study in the Concept of Belief: A Comparison of the Gospel of John and the Epistle to the Romans" (PhD diss, Southwestern Baptist Theological Seminary, 1976), 173–89. For more recent discussions see Nijay K. Gupta, *Paul and the Language of Faith* (Grand Rapids: Wm B. Eerdman's Publishing Co, 2020) and Archie W. England, "The Righteous, By 'His' Faithfulness Will Live: Habakkuk 2:4 Re-examined," in *Anchored to the Text: Essays in Honor of Dr. Richard R. Melick, Jr.*, ed. Shawn Buice and Roger Duke (Ontario, CA: Gateway Seminary, 2023). Other significant contributions include J. Barr, *The Semantics of Biblical Language* (London: Oxford University Press, 1961), 161–205; and criticisms of Hays by M. Silva in *Conflict and Context: Hermeneutics in the Americas*, ed. M. L. Branson and C. R. Padilla (Grand Rapids: Eerdmans, 1986), 274–80.

the meaning of the word "faith" (*pistis*), the tension is between the semantically objective meaning (trust) and the semantically subjective meaning (faithfulness). Both are attested in Scripture (objective, Rom 4:9; subjective, Rom 3:3). Normally Paul meant "faithfulness" when the word was a quality of "God" or "Christ," as it is here.[447] Furthermore, of the twenty-four times Paul uses faith with the genitive case it refers to faith, or faithfulness, as the characteristic of the individual identified in the genitive case. It never makes that person the object of faith. Faith is always a quality of the one identified in the genitive case. In Jesus's case, Paul never says Jesus must trust. When faith occurs with Jesus (in the genitive case) it is an attribute of Jesus. The normal use of "faith" (*pistis*) in these contexts, which is "faithfulness," should govern interpretation.[448]

The syntactical question is the nature of the statement "of Christ," which CSB translates as another instance of "in Christ." It could mean belonging to Christ, produced by Christ, directed to Christ, or simply of Christ.[449] Most likely, it is the faithfulness which is in Christ and should be read "of Christ." This first statement, therefore, means that righteousness is made available to people through the faithfulness of Christ. This fits the construction well and also conforms to Phil 2:5–11. Jesus was faithful (obedient) even to death. Paul continues his discussion of his new life to include conformity to Jesus's death. The parallel is powerful.

This construction has been much debated in recent years. More traditionally, the genitive "Christ" is considered an objective genitive construction meaning "faith *in* Christ." If understood this way, Paul expressed his faith directed toward Christ. The second understanding, that taken above, considers the genitive "Christ" as a subjective genitive meaning "faith (faithfulness) *of* Christ." This moves the faith, or

---

[447] The adjective πιστός occurs frequently with "God" and "Christ" as a quality meaning "faithful," so the idea is not foreign to NT thought (of God: 1 Cor 1:9; 10:13; 2 Cor 1:18; 1 Thess 5:24; 2 Tim 2:13; Heb 10:23; 1 Pet 4:19; 1 John 1:9; of Christ: 2 Thess 3:3; Heb 2:17; 3:2; Rev 1:5; 3:14). When πίστις is followed by a genitive of person, faith is a quality of that person, i.e., God (Rom 3:3), Abraham (Rom 4:12), and Christ (Rom 3:22). When it occurs with God or Christ, however, the objective meaning of "trust" does not apply since "trust" is not a quality of God. A rule develops: when applied to deity, it means faithfulness; when applied to man, it may mean either.

[448] It is worth noting the Hb. word for faith (*aman*, *emunah* in normal form), translated by the LXX as *pistis*, probably never means "trust" in the OT. It always means trustworthy.

[449] These would be possessive, subjective, objective, or descriptive genitives respectively.

faithfulness, to Jesus rather than Paul. No place in Scripture speaks of the *faith* Jesus had, much less that believers are to trust the *faith* of Jesus. The Lord is never spoken of as having faith. The construction here must be considered in its more usual sense of *faithfulness of Jesus*. He was faithful to God's plan for his life both in living perfectly and dying as substitution for believers. The result is that Jesus's faithfulness is the hope of the believer.[450]

The arguments in favor of the subjective ("faithfulness of Christ") position include the following. (1) Every time Paul uses faith (*pistis*) in the genitive with a possessive pronoun it is subjective (Rom 4:5, for example). (2) When the construction is used of a person of the Trinity it is subjective (Rom 3:3, for example). (3) Clearly in other passages, such as Hebrews, the faithfulness of Jesus forms the foundation for God's accepting believers.[451]

Arguments in favor of the objective ("faith in Christ") approach are worth consideration. These include the following: (1) Paul never directly equates the obedience of Christ to his faith or faithfulness. (2) The two texts used by Paul that are analogous to "faith of Christ" refer to people's faith in God (Gal 3:6–12; Rom 1:17; 4:3). (3) Elsewhere in Philippians, Paul uses "faith" (*pistis*) three times (1:25, 27; 2:17) and the verb "believe" once (1:29). Each of these refer to faith in Christ. (4) Paul uses faith language nearly two hundred times, none of which speak of Jesus having faith. Rather, God and Christ are often the objects of faith.[452] Paul continues the discussion with the statement "the righteousness from God based *on faith* (*epi te pistei*). This construction means that righteousness is *based* on faith. It is best to take this passage as stating the previously mentioned "faithfulness of Christ."

Righteousness comes to people from God and based on that faithfulness (*epi te pistei*).[453] Paul rejected his own faithfulness to the law, realizing it was insufficient. His hope was the faithfulness of Christ.

---

450 A good, recent survey of this occurs in Keown, *Philippians 2:19–4:23*, 154–63.

451 Paul's foundational statement in Rom 1:17 also contributes to this understanding. There are multiple interpretations of "faith to faith." This writer accepts the translation "out of faithfulness (of Christ) unto faith (of believers)." The only parallel to this construction is 2 Cor 2:16: "death . . . to death" and "life . . . to life."

452 Keown, *Philippians 2:19–4:23*, 160.

453 The same argument occurs in Rom 3:21ff. and Gal 2:20. A related idea occurs in Gal 3:26 which states "faith in Jesus Christ," and one wonders why the difference in the construction (ἐν rather than the simple genitive).

This verse, then, brings knowledge of how God makes his righteousness available: It is through Jesus's faithfulness and a person's total reliance on him.[454]

The passage further contrasts Christ and the law. Paul never spoke against the law. Rather, he spoke about the individual's inability to keep it. In this text he contrasted two approaches to coming to God: by works (through adherence to law) and by grace (through faith). If one chooses works, the law sets the standards and determines the success of that endeavor. Paul tried that and found it unacceptable. If one chooses grace, Christ's life and death become the hope. Paul found grace and faith to be the only way to have fellowship with God. The grace approach means that persons cast themselves on God's mercy, trusting that what Jesus did will be applied to them. Grace freed Paul from self-effort to gain salvation and enabled him to devote himself to the things that accompany salvation. One big problem with the false teachers Paul countered was they had not learned what Paul had learned.

It should be noted Paul does not use the word "grace" in this context. It is not his primary concern or argument The lack of mentioning it does not negate the presence of the concept, however. Paul counted on someone else's faithfulness (Jesus'). In so doing, he was eligible to receive the benefits of Jesus's faithfulness by Jesus's benevolence. So it is with trusting God. To rely on Jesus's work instead of personal effort implies a benefactor who provides to you what someone else has. Indeed, God is the benefactor who applies Jesus's faithfulness to the one who counts on it.

There is also a contrast between two types of "righteousness." Keeping the law produced an *achieved righteousness*; trusting Christ brought an *imputed righteousness*. This passage does not explicitly speak of imputed righteousness. It points us to trusting the righteousness of another: Christ. His righteousness covers the believer. Since righteousness is imperative in order to have a right relationship with God, the Father sees the covering of Christ's righteousness when he looks at the believer. The one who trusts in Christ is seen to be righteous. God declares the believer righteous because he is "found in Christ." Outside that covering, human imperfections mar the attempts

---

[454] As Bockmuehl, *A Commentary*, 211, notes, "Human faith is not itself the means of bringing about the righteousness 'derived from God', but merely the mode of its reception. It is certainly only the work of Christ which is in any theologically significant sense instrumental to the righteousness of God."

at righteousness and, of necessity, bring God's judgment. Paul states this explicitly in 2 Cor 5:21: "He made the one who did not know sin to be sin for us, so that in him we might become the righteousness of God." Paul's hope was the righteousness God gave.

Trusting in the benefits provided by someone else was not a totally foreign thought in Jewish theology. Both John the Baptist and Jesus warned the Pharisees not to begin to say "we are Abraham's children" as though that guaranteed inclusion in the kingdom of God (John, Luke 3:8; Jesus, John 8:39–41). This common apologetic against the Jews reveals many/most of the Jews expected to benefit from Abraham, specifically from his meritorious life. Though their individual works contributed, their foundation was that they trusted in Abraham, being his offspring. This is seen in a boast from Rabbi Simeon ben Yohai (AD 140–165):

> If Abraham likes to justify (by his merits) all people from his time up to my time, my merits will justify them from now up to the time of the Messiah. If not I join with Achiah, ha-shilone (sic), and we will justify by our merits all creatures from Abraham up to the time of the Messiah.[455]

The point is there was a doctrine of trusting others for what they provided. It supports the fact that the issue is trusting *Christ's* righteousness. The question is not can I trust another, but who is the appropriate object of trust? Paul discussed this in a more theological discourse in Gal 3:16–18. He explicitly stated Abraham's seed, being singular not plural, refers to Jesus, the promised heir. Therefore, to be "in Abraham," a Jew had to be in Jesus! The only righteousness that commends one to God is that of his Son, Jesus.

3:10 Paul turned his thoughts to knowing Christ. Some understand the words "know him" (which is an infinitive in Greek) to express the purpose of gaining Christ and being found in him. In this sense, the purpose of being found in him would be to come to know him. That seems somewhat awkward for Paul but is a possibility.[456] A better approach is to understand the infinitive as consecutive,

[455] Quoted in W. E. Davies, *Paul and Rabbinic Judaism* (London: Society for the Promotion of Christian Knowledge, 1948), 270–71. This quote concerns the Doctrine of Merits, which Davies finds fully developed in Judaism.

[456] The CSB takes this position: "My goal is to know him and the power of his resurrection . . ."

further defining to "be found in him" (3:9). This, then, gives the content of Paul's deep desire, that is, to know Christ in a life-shaping way. The particular verb chosen for knowledge (*ginosko*) supports this. It implies relationship. When used of individuals, it is the knowledge of personal relationships. It also is the preferred word for learning by experience. It implies that the knowledge it defines comes from experience in contrast to a completely intellectual, factual knowledge. Awareness and enjoyment of persons comes from the interrelationships and interactions of the two. Paul's choice of words suggests his desire to understand Christ through an ongoing experience with him. It further suggests such knowledge is not one dimensional. It includes good times (power) and challenging, difficult times (suffering). Both are required to gain complete knowledge of Christ. Paul had in mind the pattern of Christ's life found in 2:6–11. If God rewarded Jesus for his extreme obedience even to the point of death on a cross, surely God's blessings granted to Jesus's followers come from that same pattern in believers' lives. The believer's life includes both obedience and exaltation. In this verse two ideas complement each other: the power of Christ's resurrection and the fellowship of sharing in his sufferings. They provide a theological foundation for Paul's thought, as well as a model for Christian growth.

Christians must be like their Lord.[457] Here another chiasm occurs. The primary elements are "the power of his resurrection" (v. 10) and attaining "the resurrection from among the dead" (v. 11). The secondary elements are sharing "the fellowship of his sufferings" (v. 10) and "being conformed to his death" (v. 10). The literary arrangement indicates Paul's deepest ambition was resurrection power. While the chiasm expresses these four statements in two ideas, the logical order preserved Paul's theology. In literary chiasms, the outside members receive the primary emphasis. Thus, Paul's stress is on resurrection life rather than suffering and death. Subtly, this confirms Paul's focus was completely on living with Christ. In order to experience Christ's life fully, he realized that his own suffering and death were inevitable.

A the power of his resurrection
    B and the fellowship of his sufferings,
    B′ being conformed to his death,
A′ assuming that I will somehow reach the resurrection from among the dead.

[457] The frequent references to Christ in this passage unmistakably speak to this point.

3:11 The acquisition of resurrection power has a prerequisite of Christ's experience since the only available model is Christ. The power displayed through Jesus's resurrection is also available through Christ to those found in him. It is divine power. Resurrection power has two phases. First, at conversion believers experience the power of a spiritual resurrection (3:10). They are given new life. A new spiritual energy characterizes the new life in Christ. Yet this powerful life only begins at conversion. Successively and progressively the moral life must be changed, the physical body ultimately transformed, and believers brought to the eternal resting place of resurrection, heaven itself. The transformation does not happen all at once. It culminates in the attaining of the resurrection from the dead. Paul called this "the resurrection from among the dead" (v. 11). It refers to reinvigorating the remains of believers which after death are located in cemeteries and the like ("among the dead") so that they are made new. The resurrection of the believer's physical body occurs at the time of the Lord's return "in the clouds" (1 Thess 4:13–18). That will finalize the application of resurrection power to the Christian. Paul's ultimate goal, therefore, was to be with Christ in his complete identity: soul/spirit perfected by seeing Christ as he is, and body transformed in resurrection by God's power.

Paul used this word for power (*dunamis*) only once in Philippians. Selecting "power" here, he placed the emphasis on the present resurrection power in his life. In Col 2:20–3:4 Paul made explicit the point implied here. The believer died with Christ and has already been raised with Christ in one sense. A spiritual resurrection has taken place. The power accomplishing resurrection has been applied to a Christian already. It is power enabling life within and above the difficulties suffering brings. Resurrection power was applied to Paul's life in the present and it continued into the future. In the chiasm, the word resurrection ties the two components together. The present power of the resurrection enables present endurance and guarantees the believer's future resurrection from the dead.

Paul longed for the complete resurrection in his own life. Any contemplation of existence without the completed process of bodily resurrection made him uncomfortable. No one can conceive of a person without a body.[458] Resurrection power, however, achieves an entire process. Paul's longing to know Christ, therefore, was ultimately a longing to be like Christ in his glorified state.

Knowing Christ also meant identifying with his death. This involved participating in suffering and being conformed to his death. Paul spoke of sharing in Christ's sufferings in various ways,[459] but here he paralleled Rom 6:1–11. In Romans the suffering was the death of Christ into which Paul had been baptized. He thus participated in what Christ did for him when he died.[460] Paul did not expect to contribute to Christ's sufferings, that is, by taking on himself some redemptive suffering as Jesus did, neither did he mean he would suffer and die as Jesus did. The theological substructure of this passage is the Christian's identification with Christ.[461]

Paul understood that knowing Jesus would mean identification with Christ's sufferings. Suffering is a major theme in Scripture as well as in life on a fallen planet. People question suffering. Why do we experience it? How long does it last? Is it necessary in a believer's life? In this text, Paul does not deal directly with the theological or moral aspects of suffering. It should be noted, however, that the sufferings of Christ were not intended to improve Christ's moral life. Jesus was perfect. Paul hoped participation in Christ's sufferings would bring deeper knowledge of Jesus, who chose to undergo even death to redeem fallen humanity.

Paul used the noun "suffering(s)" (*pathema*) nine times. The closest parallel to his thought here is most likely 2 Cor 1:5–7. There he also described one of the benefits of participation in Christ's sufferings:

---

[458] This is the burden of 2 Cor 5:1–10. There Paul spoke of how he longed to be clothed with his new body, at which time the work of salvation will be complete. In that text, he also implied he expected a time when he would be in heaven without his body, i.e., in a "naked" state. Since the body is both the vehicle through which we communicate and receive communication and the housing which shapes our self-identity, we cannot conceive of comfortable existence without it. Nevertheless, the dead in Christ will have an intermediate state of existence. Paul, however, looked forward to the completion of salvation when the material aspects of a person (body) will join with the immaterial (soul/spirit) for completion of the person in resurrection.

[459] See, for example, Acts 9:16; Rom 8:17; 2 Cor 1:5; Col 1:24.

[460] This preserves the basic meaning of "participation," which the Gk. κοινωνία implies. It has little to do with "completing . . . afflictions," as Col 1:24 states. Rather, it is expressive of "benefitting from" by participation.

[461] W. Grundmann, TDNT, 7:786–87, provides a full range of compound words used to express the theology of identification with Christ.

> [J]ust as the sufferings of Christ overflow to us, so also through Christ our comfort overflows. If we are afflicted, it is for your comfort and salvation. If we are comforted, it is for your comfort, which produces in you patient endurance of the same sufferings that we suffer. And our hope for you is firm, because we know that as you share in the sufferings, so you will also share in the comfort.

Paul's ability to apply the benefits of suffering to his converts comes from his awareness that Christ's sufferings also brought comfort. Knowing Christ through his sufferings brought a deeper sense of the kind of encouragement Christ brings through them. Paul experienced that in his own life and assured the Corinthian believers they should expect the same. This can only be learned by participating in Christ's sufferings. Going through suffering enables the purifying focus of Christian obedience (following Christ) and provides the most comprehensive scenario for obedience to be expressed (in difficulty). Suffering provides the opportunity to experience resurrection power, to be like Jesus, "becoming obedient to the point of death—even to death on a cross" (Phil 2:8).

Paul also spoke of his identification with Christ's death. He expressed it with a term unique in the NT and one not found in Hellenistic Jewish literature: "conformed.[462] It means "to cause to be similar in form or style to something else, grant or invest with the same form as."[463] What is unique about the word is joining the preposition "with" to "form." It recalls the Christ poem of 2:5–11, where twice "form" (*morphe*) is used of Jesus. He was in the "form" of God but emptied himself by taking the "form" of a servant. The latter is exemplified in the servant's obedience, an obedience by Christ even to death. For Paul, conformity to the death of Christ included the obedience of following Christ throughout life: particularly in suffering. Just as Christ's obedience was complete, so Paul hoped his obedience would be complete. It would bring him conformity to Jesus if he were to share the same kinds of experiences. Unification with Christ in his death was a spiritual reality from conversion on, but being conformed to his death was the daily process of living in obedience. Romans 6:11 provides the theological parallel. The task of the Christian is partially to realize that one major aspect of salvation is death to self. The choice

[462] Keown, *Philippians 2:19–4:23*, 173. The Gk. word is συμμορφιζόμενος (*summorphizomenos*).
[463] BAGD, 958.

to die to self occurs at conversion. By consistently choosing to live with the awareness of that initial decision of death to sin and self, conformity to Jesus's death occurs. Jesus completely died to self and became a sacrifice for others. It was the greatest demonstration of commitment to the will of God, and it was that death which brought his resurrection life. Paul realized conformity to Jesus's death made him a candidate for resurrection power. It should be noted the Greek word translated is passive in form. It implies conformity is something done to Paul. His choices of obedience enabled God to work in him the kind of death to self that would enable resurrection, also an act done to him by God, just as it was God who raised Jesus from the dead. This helps explain the spiritual discipline mentioned in Phil 3:12–16.

The chiastic pattern ends with "assuming that I will somehow reach the resurrection from among the dead" (3:11). The CSB translation well translates a rare Greek construction: literally "if how" (*ei pos*). It is more a stress on the manner of arriving at resurrection than a lack of confidence. It is conformity to Christ's death that brings the same resurrection that Christ had. "Assuming" stresses the hope Paul here expressed.

The chiasm begins with the knowledge of the "power of [Christ's] resurrection" and ends with "the resurrection from among the dead." It is important to catch the nuance of Paul's thought here. The first use of "resurrection" is the simple noun form, while the second use of "resurrection" is a combined noun with a preposition form. When a preposition is attached to a word it is either directional, anticipating what comes next, or intensive, emphasizing what comes next. Since the phrase "from among the dead" uses the same preposition as that attached to "resurrection," this could be directional, simply anticipating "from the dead." Since, however, it picks up—reflects—the previous use of resurrection, Paul seems to intend a contrast. The first, the simple word "resurrection," speaks to the realization of resurrection power in general. It refers to knowing God's supernatural power in this life, which is most dramatically displayed in times of suffering. The second, the compound word "resurrection from among," clearly points to the final resurrection of the body. "From among the dead" consistently means from the realm of dead persons. Paul's hope involved the ultimate resurrection of the physical body. His hope was to know resurrection power now—in life—and resurrection from the dead ultimately.

Paul's hope of resurrection from the dead was thoroughly Christian. Paul acknowledged a general resurrection of all humans to life—dwelling with God through Christ—or to death—dwelling without Christ or God and in punishment. His primary focus, however, was on the resurrection of believers (1 Thess 4:13–18). That was his hope here. It makes little sense to think of Paul striving to attain what is guaranteed for all people. His expectation was to be counted among those who are raised from the dead to live in a completed state with Christ forever.

In longing to know Christ, the apostle sought a complete relationship with him. Situations may differ, but each Christian has the hope that resurrection power results from death and that conformity to Jesus's death brings life. In fact, the more obedient one is to Christ, thus conformed to his death, the more resurrection power becomes available in this life. Further, Paul longed for the completion of his Christian hope. Someday he would enjoy complete transformation of character, newness of body, and a perfect environment. He would live forever with his Lord (see Rev 21:1-5). Fee notes, "This is one of the truly 'surpassing' moments in the Pauline corpus: it would be a tragedy if its splendor were lost in analysis. Finally, therefore, one should go back and read it again and again, until what one learns in the analysis is absorbed in praise and worship over the surpassing worth of knowing Christ Jesus our Lord."[464]

3.3.1.3 True Zeal (3:12–16)

Paul's attention turned to true zeal in living the Christian life. He continued his argument against his Jewish opponents through his personal experience. What should occupy the thoughts and focus the energy of genuine Christians?

The passage falls into two distinct parts. First, in 3:12–14, Paul expressed his desire to achieve what God had in store for him. Then, in 3:15–16, he issued a call to follow his pattern of living. The Greek of this section is particularly difficult, but the thrust is abundantly clear. Paul was in the process of achieving. In case he was misunderstood in 3:4–11, he clarified that he had not yet arrived.

One of the key words of the passage is "pursue" ("press on," CSB-*dioko,* 3:14). It stresses active commitment to the call of Christ.

---

[464] Fee, *Philippians*, 315.

Previously Paul had been a zealous Pharisee. Exhibit one demonstrating this was "persecuting the church" (3:6). Here Paul used the same Greek word three times, which serves to tie this passage to the previous. It occurs in "*make every effort* to take hold of it" (3:12) and in "*I pursue* as my goal the prize promised by God's heavenly call" (3:14; emphasis added). Before, he pursued eradication of the church (3:6); now it was completing God's call on his life. It seems best to link 3:12–16 with 3:6 by showing the contrasts between the former zeal and righteousness of his past and zeal and righteousness that accompany conversion.

Some commentators suggest in this section Paul addressed his opponents. They say he consciously countered a perfectionistic group, sometimes called "divine men," who claimed their own completeness. Others suggest Paul produced this section because the Jewish opponents of 3:2 taught perfection could be achieved by keeping the law. Still others see Paul continuing the logic of 3:4–11, issuing a warning because of a tendency to misunderstand his teaching. His introduction of 3:15 with the words "all of us who are mature," (lit., "perfect") suggests those with the proper spiritual attitude. Since he is countering some who claim perfection, he certainly does not mean there are a group of people like himself who are perfect (see below, 3:15). He has refuted that. The context does not require an opponent, and it is unlikely that he envisioned one. It is possible that a group within the church may have misunderstood his teaching on righteousness and taken it to their own logical conclusions, which were theologically unacceptable.

3.3.1.3.1 Paul's Desire to Fulfill His Call (3:12–14)

Structure

[it is] Not that I have already reached the goal
        or am already perfect,
but I make every effort to take hold of it
        because I also have been taken hold of by Christ Jesus.
Brothers and sisters, I do not consider myself to have taken hold of it.
But one thing I do . . . I pursue as my goal the prize promised by God's
        heavenly call
                in Christ Jesus
        forgetting what is behind
        and reaching forward to what is ahead

Interpretation

3:12–13a Twice, in similar terms, Paul expressed his imperfection. The first expression presents this in three ways (v. 12), and the second expression summarizes the three ways into one (v. 13). The three are "Not that I have already reached the goal," "or am already perfect," and "I pursue." The basic question is, What did Paul lack and, therefore, seek? Three times the word root for "received" occurs (3:12; *lambano*; *katalambano* twice). The word is ambiguous, and no object occurs with it.

The precise definition may refer to mental or experiential attainment. Used of the mind, it means to "understand" (or "understand fully" with *katalambano*).[465] This would mean that Paul did not yet understand the significance of Christ or that he did not know him completely. If the use were experiential, "to grasp something," Paul stated he did not yet have in hand what he desired. The understood object of the verbs would determine which definition applies.

What did Paul hope to attain? In these verses two phrases suggest an answer: "am already perfect" and "taken hold of by Christ Jesus." "Have already been made perfect" (*teteleioμmai*) occurs only here in the Pauline corpus. It contrasts with the verb "obtained." Through his past experiences ("obtained," aorist tense), Paul had not yet achieved completion (*katalambano*, perfect tense).[466] The question is whether Paul referred to perfect knowledge or experience. Was his call to complete knowledge of Christ or to complete identification with him in character?

The context has a bearing on the problem (3:9–11).[467] Those who understand Paul's desire in the mental sense, to know Christ completely, point out the primary verb in these verses is "to know him" (see 3:10). That knowledge involved knowing Christ's power and suffering. Paul wanted to know in his experience the full implications of his union with Christ because that knowledge was related

---

[465] See, e.g., John 1:5; Acts 4:13; Eph 3:18. BAGD, 464–65, lists several meanings for the term. It states that Phil 3:12 means "to make one's own, apprehend or comprehend mentally or spiritually." Here is another word with a prefixed preposition.

[466] See A. T. Robertson, *A Grammar of the Greek New Testament in the Light of Historical Research* (Nashville: Broadman, 1934), 901.

[467] This is known by the flow of thought and the fact that the objects of these verbs are omitted. The rule of thumb is that no object needs to be supplied if the existing subject naturally supplies it. That rule applies here. Thus, the Gk. text looks back to these previous verses to find its object.

closely to experience. The text, however, seems to argue against that understanding.[468]

Those who understand Paul's desire in the experiential sense point out the object of the verb in "reached the goal" is "the resurrection from among the dead" of 3:11. It seems best to understand Paul as saying he had not completed the experiential process begun in his salvation. He looked forward to the resurrection from the dead and, secondarily, to the process of conformity to death which would bring it forth.

"The resurrection" fits this context and answers the problems raised in the text. First, it easily explains why Paul had not attained. He looked to the end of time when the resurrection would occur. Second, it is helpful to remember a first-century heresy stated that the resurrection was already past. Paul countered it in 2 Tim 2:18 (cf. 1 Cor 15:12–20; 2 Thess 2:2). Something similar may have concerned Paul here when he pointedly affirmed the necessity of continued growth.[469] Third, this fits well with Paul's prayer in 1:9–11. He hoped to be pure and blameless at the day of Christ. Fourth, the idea of "the power of [the] resurrection" (3:10) must be taken with the death that precedes it. As a result, he thought of conformity to the will of God ("being conformed to [Christ's] death," 3:10) continued to be a goal because resurrection power is available in death. The best explanation of this desire is that Paul looked ahead to the completion of his salvation in resurrection.

3:13b–14 The content of Paul's goal is given. Repeating the word "press on" of 3:12 ("make every effort," CSB), Paul employed athletic imagery to make his point.[470] Since the Greek athletic games captured the imaginations of all persons on the Greek peninsula, Macedonia included, it spoke vividly to the first readers.[471] The manner of attain-

---

[468] This objection is that, in typical Jewish fashion, Paul thought of knowledge as applied to action: it was experiential. Therefore, even if the stress of these verses is on knowledge, it is on knowing by experience, a concept quite in keeping with the meaning of the verb chosen, γινώσκω. For a complete defense of the "knowledge" position, see Hawthorne, *Philippians*, 151ff.

[469] The theological misunderstanding involved the denial of a physical resurrection, which Paul countered by implication here as well.

[470] The word CSB translates in v. 12 as "make every effort," διώκω, means "to run swiftly in order to catch some person or thing." It was used in both hunting and athletics. As to the former, it described the pursuit of game, stalking it with relentlessness. In athletics it meant to run so as to gain the victory.

[471] The imagery is well developed by Hawthorne, *Philippians*, 154.

ment, pressing on ("I pursue as my goal" in CSB), is explained by two participles of manner. First, "[f]orgetting what is behind" comprehensively expresses Paul's future orientation. Obviously, one cannot erase the experiences of the past. Indeed, Paul was recalling them as a warning to the Philippians. But "[f]orgetting the past" implied he would not build on the past, letting the misdirected motivations and ambitions of the past shackle him so that the race could not be won. What was done was done! Both focusing on the nostalgia of the former life and the good old days of his Christian life would paralyze him in terms of what God wanted in the future. Every day was a new adventure. Second, he was "reaching forward to what is ahead." This continues the athletic metaphor. It is particularly graphic, bringing to mind the straining muscles, clear focus, and complete dedication of the runner in his race for the prize. Both mental and physical discipline were necessary.

The goal is "God's heavenly call in Christ Jesus." The text is ambiguous here. The term *skopos* is technically "goal marker" in English.[472] Such was the focus of the eye when a runner ran a race. For Paul, it was the model provided in Christ who demonstrated both obedience unto death and the resurrection. The prize is explained as the "heavenly call" (*ano kleseos*). The CSB translates it "the prize promised by God's heavenly call in Christ Jesus," correctly seeing the word *ano* refers to heaven as opposed to earth. Is the call at the beginning of the race, however, or the end? The statement "I also have been taken hold of by Christ Jesus"(3:12) may refer to the Damascus road experience when Paul was conquered by Christ. In history, that was the time of Paul's conversion and the beginning of his participation in the race. The CSB translates "because I have been taken hold by Christ." Literally the expression in v. 12 is "I may take hold *upon which* I was laid hold by Christ." "Because" is a good translation, but the primary emphasis of the word is what Christ intended in capturing Paul, which corresponds to Paul's life if the call is understood as at the time of conversion, but there is no hint of that here. Paul's language is more general. He understood God's call to begin in time in the womb (Gal 1:15), but he also understood God's election as being eternal. God's call on the believer is for him or her to be like Christ, completely glorified by God's power (Rom 8:29–30). "Perfected" and

[472] Hawthorne, *Philippians*, 154.

"taking hold" are synonymous, referring to the completion of salvation and the complete union of the perfected person (body and soul) at the resurrection. It seems best to understand the call as associated with the resurrection. At that day there will be a call to heaven. Further, in 3:21, Paul mentioned the resurrection and the transformation that will occur then. He lived for the day when the heavenward call would come, like a victory in a race. In the ancient competitions, at the end of the race the winner would be called up on the platform to receive his laurel-wreath crown of success. Paul viewed his present life as in a race begun ultimately in eternity past but in time at conversion. The race is completed already in God's mind (Rom 8:29–30), but historically it occurs at the resurrection. In the meantime, Paul is actively seeking to obey his Lord even to conformity to death. There is no hint of doubt in Paul's mind. He was certain of his direction. The energy exerted in the past was now devoted to the future. Rather than slack off, as some were prone to do, he allowed the thought to motivate him to further purity and service.[473] He would get to know every dimension of Christ (reign and suffering), through every means. The joy of the process kept him going, but he realized the ultimate joy was the completion of God's work in his life.[474]

Speaking of the resurrection points to the actual completion of the process of maturation, of sanctification. Resurrection from the dead (glorification) takes place at the return of Christ. Resurrection means the restoring of life to the body, the physical body, which will be transformed at the resurrection much as Christ's was on the third day (1 Cor 15:12–28; 2 Cor 5:1–10). By focusing on the resurrection, Paul looked to the completed end of God's working in the believer. The expected perfection unites body and soul.

[473] Witherington, III, *Paul's Letter*, 208, quotes the outstanding preacher Fred Craddock: "Trust in God's grace did not make Paul less active than the Judaizers but rather set him free now to run without watching his feet, without counting his steps, without competing with other servants of Christ." Craddock, *Philippians*, 339.

[474] The syntax of the interpretation is as follows: "toward the goal" (κατὰ σκοπόν) provides a standard of measurement, strictly, and is not the goal in sight (therefore Christ is the model and standard); "unto the prize" expresses the direction of the striving; "of the heavenly call" (τῆς ἄνω κλήσεως) is appositional, expressing what the call is. It is a call to "come up" to heaven, just as victors ascended the victory platforms.

3.3.1.3.2 Paul's Encouragement to Believers (3:15–16)

Paul came to his point at the end of this section. His experience correctly set a pattern for all believers. If they would understand it and join with him, they would avoid the influence of the false teachers. Three movements occur in this command to the church: a call to unity, a warning of misconduct, and an exhortation to continue.

Structure

Therefore [vv. 12–14]
let all of us who are mature think this way.
And . . . God will reveal this also to you
if you think differently about anything.
In any case, we should live up to whatever truth we have attained.

Interpretation

3:15a First, Paul called the Philippians to unity. The words "think this way" translate the verb "be minded," which characterized 2:1–11 (e.g., 2:5 "[a]dopt the same attitude," CSB). The word occurs again later in this verse, and includes both thoughts and values. The church was to value these truths as Paul did.

Several problems occur in this verse. First, who did Paul mean by the word "mature"? He called both himself and the believers "mature" ("perfect," *teleios*), but in light of the relative infrequency of the word as a description of people, questions arise.[475] Two primary possibilities exist. Conceivably, Paul addressed a group of people who shared his outlook and clearly understood their imperfection in their desires to be perfected. This meaning requires different uses of two words built on the same root, which is awkward.[476] On the other hand, Paul could have been speaking in irony, addressing a group of people who assumed they were perfect. If so, he was calling them to admit their imperfect knowledge about such matters and accept his evaluation.[477] The choice between the meanings is difficult. One of the critical issues,

---

[475] Paul employed the term eight times, but only descriptively of persons who had attained perfection twice (1 Cor 2:6; Phil 3:15). He did speak of it as a goal several times (1 Cor 14:20; Eph 4:13; Col 1:28; 4:12).

[476] The verb τελειόω (3:12) expressed his imperfection; the adjective τέλειος (3:15) would be awkward in a different meaning.

[477] This was suggested by Lightfoot, Philippians, 153, and developed more fully by Hawthorne, Philippians, 156.

however, is that Paul includes himself among the mature ("let all of us who are mature"). Christian maturity does not mean perfection, but rather having found and adopted the proper attitude about life. Paul took the unfounded claim of the perfectionists and applied it to the proper attitude rather than their claim of perfect performance. It is the proper understanding of the process that makes one "mature."

3:15b Second, Paul warned about misconduct. The interpretation depends in part on knowing who Paul addressed. It could have been a correction to the false teachers or instructions to mature Christians. Some scholars take the position Paul meant those who differed with him had a right to their own positions because ultimately the way they thought did not matter. That hardly seems consistent with Paul's attitude.[478] Others argue Paul really meant it would do little good to try to convince the false teachers of their error. God would reveal it to them.[479] Another possibility is Paul turned his thoughts to the general problem of disunity in the congregation, which he addressed in chapter 4.[480] Paul addressed the mature and realized that God would work in them.

Further, his words were corrective in the sense that God would adjust their wrong attitudes in the course of time. Their misunderstanding involved their perfectionistic ideas, which had reached a deep level of personal commitment, evidenced by Paul's use of the term "think differently" (*phroneo*).[481] There is no indication of when or how God will reveal it to those in error. It is unlikely to be the eschaton, at the Second Coming or in judgment, since that seems foreign to this context. It is best to understand this as Paul's confidence in God's leading and informing his people through the Spirit as part of the Spirit's work. Life correction naturally occurs as individuals mature in their walks with Christ. In light of the fact that Paul includes himself in "let all of us . . . " and "we should live up to," this statement indicates he places himself among those who have experienced God's corrective revelation. Even so, his specific concern in this statement is

---

[478] Caird, *Paul's Letters*, 144–45, provides eight convincing reasons why that approach cannot be correct.

[479] Hawthorne, *Philippians*, 156.

[480] Silva, *Philippians*, 206. This seems quite unlikely since it makes an abrupt shift in the text.

[481] The Gk. adverb "differently" occurs only here in the NT. Outside the NT, it has the idea of having "the wrong frame of mind." Silva, *Philippians*, 207.

for "you," not "us." He is confident he has both the correct goal and is in the proper race.

3:16 Third, Paul gave an exhortation. The believers were to remain steadfast. What they had achieved to this point was to guide them into the future as the standard by which they would walk collectively. Here Paul used another relatively rare term, which the CSB translates "we should live up to" (*stoicheo*). Generally, the term means an orderly or a disciplined walk. It has overtones of collective discipline in the sense of all walking in the same row or by the same measure.[482] Two emphases appear in this sentence. First, they were to remain true to what they had. Second, they were to remain true with collective discipline that was to characterize the entire church. This meant that they would not follow the infatuating teachings of Paul's opponents, and it also meant that they would seek to implement in their own lives what they already knew to do,[483] which included honoring Christ and looking forward to the resurrection.

The last sentence summarizes this section by presenting a challenge to continue in the faith. Obviously, some believers had tendencies toward deviating from what they had learned from Paul. In rebuking the false teachers, Paul presented his own testimony and urged the group at large to have the same attitude. While the exhortation related primarily to 3:12–16, it ended Paul's first line of apology against his opponents. It also placed faith in the church members' attitudes and ability to continue in the things they had learned.

3.3.2 The False Teachers' Character Exposed (3:17–21)

[17] Join in imitating me, brothers and sisters, and pay careful attention to those who live according to the example you have in us. [18] For I have often told you, and now say again with tears, that many live as enemies of the cross of Christ. [19] Their end is destruction; their god is their stomach; their glory is in their shame; and they are focused on earthly things. [20] Our citizenship is in heaven, and we eagerly wait for a Savior from there, the Lord Jesus Christ. [21] He will transform the

---

[482] BAGD, 769, says "be in line with, stand beside, hold to, agree with, follow." It occurs in the NT in Acts 21:24; Rom 4:12; Gal 5:25; 6:16.

[483] W. Schenk, *Die Philipperbrief des Paulus Kommentar* (Stuttgart: W. Kohlhammer, 1984). Cited in Silva, *Philippians*, 207. Schenk states ἐφθάσαμεν is equivalent to κατελήμφθην, so that "what we have already attained" equals "what we received." That would tie the passage together and form a fitting end to the section.

body of our humble condition into the likeness of his glorious body, by the power that enables him to subject everything to himself.

Structure

Join in imitating me, brothers and sisters,
and pay careful attention to those
who live according to the example you have in us.
For I have often told you . . . that many live as enemies of the cross of Christ.
and now say again with tears
Their end is destruction;
their god is their stomach;
their glory is in their shame;
and they are focused on earthly things.
Our citizenship is in heaven,
and we eagerly wait for a Savior from there, the Lord Jesus Christ.
He will transform the body of our humble condition into the likeness of his glorious body,
by the power that enables him to subject everything to himself.

Interpretation

Paul continued to warn the church about the false teachers. The format remains the same as 3:1–16: the literary pattern is comparison and contrast. Now, however, the text moves to plural rather than singular subjects so that the entire church is included (3:20–21). Some interpreters see a change of opponents to the libertines; others see a consistent reference to enthusiastic Jewish teachers as in vv. 1–16. They were probably the same opponents. If they were a new group, Paul handled them in a veiled manner, with no introduction and no conclusion to their teaching. Paul also implicitly described them as non-Christian. They were "enemies of the cross" (3:18), their citizenship was on earth rather than heaven (3:20), and they did not have the same destiny as Paul and the church (3:21).[484] Structurally, after an introductory statement setting the direction for these verses (v. 17), Paul described the opponents (vv. 18–19) and then contrasted them with true believers (vv. 20–21).

3.3.2.1 Encouragement to Imitate Paul (3:17)

3:17 Earlier Paul urged the church to imitate Christ (2:5–11); here he urged the Philippians to imitate him. The theme occurs in other

[484] This is an implication from the way the contrast proceeds.

places in Paul's writing (1 Cor 4:16; 11:1; 2 Thess 3:7–9), but it seems awkward to the present-day Christian. There is no egotism here, however, as two factors in the text make apparent. First, he realized they would follow other Christian models as well. The words "imitating me" naturally meant they would follow Paul, but later in the verse he urged them to follow others with the same goal.[485] They were to "pay careful attention to those who live according to the example you have in us." Second, 3:1–16 reveals that imitation is the literary style Paul used. He recalled his own experience to persuade them to follow him. To state they should follow him was no more prideful than the pattern he employed in this entire chapter. Rather, it grew out of it.[486] Again the extended passage about Christ (2:6–11) provides the backdrop for Paul's thought. As he instructed them to have the attitude of Christ (2:5), he now implored them to have his own proper attitude. It is worth repeating. Paul's primary systematic presentation of the inadequacy of the law occurs in Galatians and Colossians. Personal testimony, however, also has its unique power. Paul counted on it here. It was impossible to separate his doctrinal foundation from his life. Paul presented some of the deepest theological concepts by personal illustration: by the newfound goal of his life. Among these theological insights are faith in Christ's faithfulness rather than one's own; the danger of adding the law (Moses) to Christ; and the completed, perfected person coming into being only at the resurrection.

In addition, Paul urged them to imitate others who were likeminded. The words "pay careful attention to" translates one Greek verb (*skopeo*) and occurs elsewhere in this passage. Previously the noun form was used in 3:14: "my goal," in running the race. It meant the Philippians were to have the lives of others like Paul in their sights and to make living like these people their aim. In Paul's absence they were to find other models who were true to his commitments. Given the persons commended in this letter, certainly Timothy and Epaphroditus are among those whose walk was admirable. Once again Paul expressed the importance of the individuals comprising the church.

[485] The word has the common Gk. prefix "with" (σύν), which typically describes the theme of being "in Christ." The reference does not explicitly mean others were following Paul—it could be he meant others along with him were following Christ. The former would not be too harsh, however, because Paul did in fact set the pace for many people.

[486] Robertson, *Paul's Joy*, 118, insightfully says, "Keep your eye on the goal if you can see it. If not, keep your eye on one who knows the way to the goal and who is going there."

3.3.2.2 *Characteristics of Paul's Opponents (3:18–19)*

The Greek text grammar presents an ordered description of the opponents (3:19). The subject of the section is "many" who "live as enemies of the cross." Paul warns about them with three descriptive clauses, beginning with his own attitude when thinking about them ("with tears"). These are followed by a nominative participle phrase that should modify a nominative subject grammatically. That is, the phrase "they are focused on earthly things" should be placed with the subject/verb of the sentence, "many live as enemies of the cross of Christ."[487] The best understanding, based on the Greek grammar, is this:

Structure

For . . . many live as enemies of the cross of Christ (object of the verb live)
[of whom-literal Greek] I often told you
and now say again with tears
[of whom—literal Greek] their end is destruction
[of whom—literal Greek] the God is their stomach
and their glory is in their shame
[the many] are focused on earthly things (nominative participle phrase)

Interpretation

This makes the primary statement of the paragraph "many live as enemies of the cross of Christ . . . focused on earthly things." Paul had two primary concerns, with modifying sub-points. The opponents were (1) enemies of the cross, and (2) they minded earthly things.

3:18 Paul delivered his final blow against the false teachers. Previously he contrasted the false teachers with true believers (3:2–6). He ends this section of warning with the same pattern: they stood in opposition to true believers in theology and life. Even so, there is no need for repetition. Paul sharpened his criticisms of them. Emotion characterizes the text, and Paul confessed his tears as he wrote. It is the only recorded instance of the apostle Paul weeping. The

[487] It is possible to understand the nominative participle to modify the subjects (in pronoun form) of the three descriptive clauses, thereby incorporating the three into one category. It is also possible to see the nominative participle as a general reference without a specific subject to modify. This is very unlikely since at least two references are possible in the text. The most natural reading is the one taken here—nominative modifier with primary nominative subject ("many"). See Fee, *Philippians*, 368, n. 26.

word for "tears" (*klaiw*) means a "loud crying from grief."[488] Why was there such emotional involvement with these deceptive teachers? Paul described them and then explained their characteristics. He was sad, first of all, because he had to make repeated warnings about them. They followed him about, seeking to entice people away from the truth. Doubtless, repeated efforts to counter that brought in some sense emotional fatigue. Second, he called them "enemies of the cross." The sobering statement must mean more than they refused to accept the cross as God's way of reconciliation. Rather, they actively opposed the message of the cross and hindered those who would take advantage of its work. Paul, by contrast, rightly cherished the cross. For him the biggest concern was the false teachers did not reveal who they were. A subtle nuance enters the text here: they "*live* as enemies of the cross" (emphasis added). The word live (*peripateo*) is the common word for lifestyle, to "walk around." It contrasts with the use of "live" which occurs above (*stoicheo*, 3:16), the focused and purposeful gait toward a specific goal. Such was to be the characteristic of true believers. While Paul consistently teaches living comes from thinking and commitments work their way into life, here he bypasses the thinking to stress the living. They have put into action what they believe, but both their belief and their actions are wrong and *detrimental to them and their hearers*. The strong emotion parallels the emotion of Rom 9:1–3 where Paul expressed his desire to be cut off from the Lord himself if that meant his kinsmen would place faith in Jesus. These teachers were his own people who should have accepted the Messiah, but they chose instead to hinder the truth wherever they could.[489] This was organized, active opposition to the gospel. More is said below about them and Paul's description.

3:19 Paul exposed these teachers by revealing their true situation. He accomplished this by explaining what "enemies of the cross" meant as applied to them. Three statements explain their theology and

---

[488] An interesting contrast occurs between Paul's crying and that of Jesus. In John 11:35, the one recorded instance of Jesus crying, his emotion is expressed as quietly weeping (*dakruo*-δακρύω). In John 11:33 it stands in contrast to Mary and the professional "criers" at Lazarus's death, the latter being described with the same word as Paul here (*klaio*-κλαίω). Since there are two different authors, the distinction may be insignificant. It does, however, highlight Paul's feelings.

[489] In a similar vein, Paul explained the Jewish opposition as "hostile to everyone" in 1 Thess 2:13–16. The similarities between the passages and Rom 9:1–3 suggest he had the same persons in mind.

practice, although little is developed about them. The three occur in quick, pointed statements involving or implying contrasts. Thus "end" contrasts with "destruction"; "god" with "stomach"; "glory" with "shame"; and (as a later statement) "earthly" with the heavenly "citizenship."[490] As will be noted below, the fourth characteristic, minding earthly things, parallels and actually describes enemies of the cross. Paul described both their values and their destiny, providing more detail about who they were and the seriousness of their opposition.

The first description of enemies of the cross looks to their eternal condition: their end was destruction. That term does not mean loss of existence since it contrasts with salvation (1:28).[491] Paul typically used the word of the eternal punishment coming to those who reject Christ. Their end—*telos*—was the opposite of that of the life shared by believers. Though they devoted significant energy to their religious activities, their living was pointless when considering eternity. Everything was oriented to and only had meaning in this life, since their destination was destruction. This describes their hopelessness compared to Paul, who looked forward with anticipation to the resurrection from the dead.

The second and third descriptions of enemies of the cross point to their religious values and activities while on earth. These two belong together because they are linked in the Greek text by one relative pronoun.[492] The early church knew who these described, but there is scant evidence to identify them now. The critical interpretive issues here involve "stomach" (*koilia*) and "shame" (*aisxune*). Both may function as metaphors or as metonymy, parts for the whole. One major divide is whether or not these are Christians. Those who suggest they are believers are persuaded by the introductory pronoun "many" who walk in v. 18. They say that Paul used the term "many" only of Christians. Furthermore, they say it is unlikely Paul would be tearful over the fate of non-Christians. Perhaps they are lapsed Christians whose lifestyle betrays the faith in ethics, not theology.[493] Others note there is a consistent argument from 3:2 onward so that these persons are the

[490] Keown, *Philippians 2:19–4:23*, 254.

[491] It is also used of the lost who are physically alive in Luke 19:10.

[492] Two relative pronouns introduce the first three characteristics. The first, ὧν, literally reads "whose end is destruction." The second relative ὧν joins the two into one clause and reads literally "whose God is their stomach and their glory is in their shame." The next characteristic does not have the relative pronoun introducing it.

[493] Bockmuehl, *A Commentary*, 232.

same as the "dogs" there. A few others see here a new group of opponents who are libertarians and, possibly, perfectionists, and perhaps they are gluttonous and boastful about it. This last group, however, has little concrete evidence to support it in this context.[494] Some are willing to remain silent about who they are and simply describe their characteristics.[495] The consistent position of the early church seems to be these are Judaizers, like those addressed earlier, who harass both Paul and the churches.[496] Since what is known from the context is Paul is concerned about Jewish opponents, and no others are explicitly mentioned, it seems the weight of evidence is in favor of the same Jewish opponents. Consequently, both of these second and third characteristics reflect strongly Jewish practices, which is why they are joined.

The second description refers to Jewish dietary laws. They had become so preoccupied with kosher food laws they spent more time contemplating them than thinking about God.[497] This statement, like the next, reveals the emotion Paul has when thinking of them. He speaks in irony, but with reality as its base. Their time is spent in preoccupation with their stomachs, and the food that goes in them, rather than time spent focusing on God, contemplating making Christ's righteousness characteristic of them and living for the resurrection. The description resembles his earlier warning "to watch out for those who create divisions and obstacles contrary to the teaching that you learned. Avoid them, because such people do not serve our Lord Christ but their own appetites" (lit. "belly," Rom 16:17–18). Both here and in Romans they are identified as non-Christian. The preoccupation with their stomachs (proper foods) replaces proper concern about God, so the stomach becomes their god. Paul may have anticipated this in a veiled way when he stated earlier that he considered his past "gain" as "dung" (Phil 3:8). He summarized later by stating they focus on

---

[494] Witherington, III, *Paul's Letter*, 213, says, "Nowhere else in this discourse are such folk critiqued or mentioned, nor is moral laxness or antinomianism in evidence as a problem in Philippi."

[495] Fee, *Philippians*, 372.

[496] Fee, 372, n. 9. Fowl, *Philippians*, 171, states, "A common interpretive move going back as far as the patristic period is to take these terms as euphemistic references to Jewish food laws and circumcision."

[497] Food was a major concern to the religions of the first century. Overemphasis came into the Christian churches as well (e.g., Rom 14–15; 1 Cor 8–10; Col 2:8–10). The issues were complex, but this one seems to be rooted in the OT regulations. Paul may have reflected on Jesus's comments about food in Mark 7:1–16.

what is earthly. Rather than the prize of the upward call, in effect they worship their stomachs. In Paul's vivid metaphorical language, their stomachs are their gods!

Dietary laws place the focus on self-effort, living out what, to them, nationalistic circumcision brings. They represent discipline as a virtue with the confidence that in so living they will be noticed and approved by God. For them, the cross is unnecessary and ineffective since those who claim the cross and resurrection as the resting place of their own faith are often lax in living by the discipline required. Paul, in fact, was sometimes wrongly accused of promoting sinful living by his emphasis on grace. The argument was if God accepts those who earn their way, those who do not are outside God's blessings. The choice is either their focus on self-discipline or forgiveness through Christ's blood, the cross. This activity is symptomatic of rejecting, denying, and opposing God's way through the cross of Christ.

The third characteristic of these enemies of the cross was they glory "in their shame." As stated above, this seems to be a veiled reference to their genitals. Paul never spoke negatively about circumcision. It is as though even a misunderstood meaning was to be treated with some reverence. Paul, however, does not call this issue circumcision. He simply referred to it as "shame." As some note, this could refer to the entire situation in which they find themselves as enemies of the cross. Opposing God is shameful. They not only sit in that position, but they boast of it everywhere. As noted earlier, this characteristic is joined with the previous idea that they are governed by physical wants rather than occupied with spiritual needs. Joining them grammatically reveals that for Paul they are in a similar category. Since many interpreters identify this as the proper meaning of "shame," it is worth serious consideration. Alternatively, Paul leaves the word circumcision out of his conversation here. The entire context is filled with hidden meanings and some vitriol. Their shame is their preoccupation with their genitals, unacceptable in both Jewish and Gentile society. Whether circumcised or not, talking about genitals was improper. They were circumcised, being Jewish, but Paul refrains from writing "circumcision" to avoid denigrating a sign God gave to identify his special people. Rather, he spoke of their preoccupation with genitals. Paul introduced this subject in 3:2 by calling the opponents "dogs." Speaking of their pride in their immodesty would fit his tone. In the context of chapter 3 Paul does contrast circumcision between the opponents and true believers. After calling the opponents "those who mutilate," he contrasts them with "the true circumcision." The mutilation idea refers to the activity of those who circumcise themselves while disregarding its true meaning. Mutilators, then, is a way of speaking against the circumcision of those who would require it instead of faith in Christ. The description is strong and pointed. The Mosaic law focused on the Sabbath and foods. Circumcision was the entry ritual qualifying one for the supposed benefits of keeping the law. Circumcision became the distinguishing mark of Jewish males and, in many cases, their source of pride in being Jewish. Although Paul did not speak against circumcision by name, using "those who mutilate" instead, here "shame" may apply to it because of the focus on the genitals, which should have been a private matter.

Either way, Paul's issue with them goes beyond simply speaking about their shame. He states their shame is their "glory," literally "the glory is in their shame." The word "glory" is not Paul's common word for boasting (*kaukametha*), which speaks to pride in something and often the communication of that pride. This word, *doxa*, is used of the manifest characteristic(s) of someone. It is used of God's glory—the summation of his divine characteristics which are manifest to others. A person's glory is that which most clearly and obviously manifests who he is. Here, their shame most clearly defines who they are—it is their basic manifested characteristic. This enhances the irony; who they are was represented by their shame. Paul's point is they organize their lives—their walk—around shame. It is their glory. In contrast, Paul's glory was his commitment to Christ, his gratitude for being considered as within the scope of Christ's righteousness, his desire to run a faithful race, and his expectation of participating in the resurrection. Paul's picturesque descriptions of his opponents reveal these matters engendered pride in the false teachers, and Paul criticized them severely.[498]

Finally, they were preoccupied with "earthly things." This obsession with material things was not an afterthought to Paul, as the grammar and the verbiage suggest. First, this is an odd place for this Greek construction in several ways. It is a nominative participle construction,

---

[498] O'Brien, *The Epistle*, 457, states, "There is no evidence that αἰσχύνη means 'shameful member.' The best alternative, therefore, is that once again Paul is speaking of destruction: their shame is their eternal destiny. The difficulty with that, however, is it does not seem parallel to join destruction with food laws. The two characteristics are joined as noted above.

and the previous descriptions in 3:19 are introduced by the genitive case pronoun. This statement includes a stated verbal idea, "they are focused on earthly things" (a Greek participle rather than a finite verb). The other three descriptions have no stated verb, which calls for inserting one. The CSB correctly inserts "is" as the verb. In this fourth contrast, the verbal idea changes from the verb of state, "is," to a more powerful accusation, the active verb "focused" (see more below).

The two primary descriptions, then, carry the weight of Paul's concern. First, they are enemies of the cross of Christ and second, they focus on earthly things. Regarding the first, the manifestation of their opposition to the cross is two-fold. On the one hand, their end is destruction. Since nothing and no one can stand against the power of the cross, their activities of active opposition will lead them to perdition. Putting this first emphasizes the futility of their living. On the other hand, their living is given over to two sets of legalistic and useless principles. They worship their stomachs through attention to food laws. They glory in their shame. The self-efforts of Paul's opponents are not only directed in opposition to Paul, but they also are in active opposition to the cross. Jesus's death on the cross applies beyond any national boundaries, providing availability of salvation for all.

This is only the second time in Philippians Paul mentions the cross. The first was in the account of Jesus humbling himself to "death on a cross" (2:8). Paul typically speaks more often of the lordship of Jesus than his crucifixion, though he clearly articulated passages about the death of Christ and what it means to the believer (Rom 3:23; 5:1–11, for example). Paul's use of the cross in this context suggests two important accusations about his opponents. First, their self-effort directly counters God's provision of salvation through the cross. Second, they equally reject the ethical dimensions of the cross that would lead to their own spiritual well-being. Jesus's example in 2:5–11 demonstrates both the power of his life and death as being acceptable to God, but also the example of Jesus as to how to live as followers of him. As Paul stated, "Adopt the same attitude as that of Christ Jesus." Their dependence on personal activities and, through them, achievements revealed their lack of understanding of Jesus, who emptied and humbled himself. They misunderstood and misapplied Jesus's cross: its power and its example.

The second concern is "they are focused on earthly things." This is a different condemnation, though it certainly included opposition to the cross and technically the statement further describes the "many." Paul chose his familiar and oft-used term in Philippians: "They are focused" (*phroneo*). It is used in a positive sense in 2:5: "[a]dopt the same attitude as that of Christ Jesus." Being focused on earthly things presents the exact opposite of the mind of Christ and the focus expected of Christians. Jesus emptied and humbled himself! These opponents exalt themselves, filled with self-pride. "Earthly" occurs seven times in the NT, five of which are in Paul's writings. Of the five, three occur in the Corinthian correspondence and two in Philippians. Those in Corinthians are in contexts of resurrection, the same as here. In 1 Cor 15:40 Paul says, "There are heavenly bodies and *earthly* bodies, but the splendor of the heavenly bodies is different from that of the *earthly* ones" (emphasis added). In 2 Cor 5:1 he states, "For we know that if our *earthly* tent we live in is destroyed, we have a building from God, an eternal dwelling in the heavens, not made with hands." Earlier in Philippians it is used of the reigning Christ who will receive homage even from the bowed knees and confessions of people "on earth" (2:10). Elsewhere, it is used of "earthly things" (Jesus to Nicodemus, John 3:12) and of "earthly" wisdom (Jas 3:15).

Perhaps the theme of attaining the resurrection prompted Paul's use of the term "earthly." As noted previously, Paul normally used it in connection with the earthly body. His choice of terms may, however, have more significance. In discussing false teachers elsewhere, two times he used the word "elementary." The Greek word *stoicheion* means the "elementary" or "basic things." In Gal 4:3 of CSB Paul explains that before Christ, "when we were children, [we] were in slavery under the *elements* of the world" (emphasis added). He contrasts that with the coming of Christ enabling "adoption as sons" rather than merely acceptance as children.[499] The law, then, had its place as a guardian to regulate life until Christ came. In Col 2:8 Paul warned the church of those who may call them to spiritual slavery through a specific deceitful philosophy "based on human tradition, based on the *elements* of the world, rather than Christ" (emphasis added). In both

[499] In Galatians, Paul's use of adoption actually has the force of "adoption as sons" rather than "children." The argument in Gal 4:1–7, in particular, distinguishes between children and sons.

cases *stoicheion* described Jewish practices and rituals.[500] While their intended purpose was completed when Christ came, Paul acknowledged limited value. He never spoke against the law. He did consider it elementary, merely preparing the way for the Messiah.

In this passage, however, Paul did not use the term stoicheion. He is not concerned with the value of the law or of its divine origins which he considered worthwhile for its intended purpose (Rom 7). His concern was the preoccupation of the false teachers with the rituals associated with protecting the law (Gal 3). The focus on the efficacy of the rituals, particularly those associated with the body, was misdirected. Inasmuch as the body is earthly, rituals associated with it for spiritual gain become earthly as well. His use of earthly does not give them even the value of being "elementary" as above. They are simply devoid of spiritual value when practiced and advocated in the manner of these false teachers.

A caution is in order. It should be noted Paul was not opposed to discipline in a Christian's life. His common use of athletic metaphors assumed the discipline and training demanded of athletes (1 Cor 9:24–27). His employment of athletic terms in this context supports an orderly and focused lifestyle: "pressing on," "mark," "heavenly call," and "attained the prize." The discipline he advocated, however, was not related to the law, from which believers have been set free. He did not run the race with markers to measure his achievement; he did not run looking over his shoulder to see how far he had gone. Both require objective standards which the law provided. Instead, he ran looking ahead to the prize, the upward call of attaining the perfection awarded at the resurrection. The experience of grace alone, embracing the cross of Christ (of which his opponents were enemies), provided the freedom to run and to attain. The race cannot be won with the impairments of guilt, introspection, and failure which characterized the activity of the legalists. Being covered by the righteousness of Christ brought freedom.

One more grammatical/literary nuance contributes to understanding. It was explained above the participial phrase "they are focused on

---

[500] The heresy threatening the Colossians used to be considered by many as Gnostic and στοιχεῖον was taken as supportive. It was used of "spirits" who emanated from the creator God. I agree with the prevailing scholarship, however, that this was a Jewish heresy with practices similar to what occurred in Qumran. There is no evidence of Gnosticism in the area in the early 60s when Colossians was written. See Melick, *Philippians*, 171–83.

earthly things" (which in Greek is literally "who mind earthly things") should directly modify the primary subject/verb of the sentence. It is dislocated from its primary relationships to provide an emphasis. It serves as a bridge in thought to the contrast between true believers and these opponents. They "focus on earthly things" but "our citizenship is in heaven." Since they were earthly in orientation, their religious shortsightedness came because they could not see beyond time into eternity. Nothing in theology provides a more remarkable contrast between believers in Christ and the advocates of non-Christian religions.

3.3.2.3 Characteristics of True Believers (3:20–21)

3:20–21 Paul ended this comparison by presenting a Christian perspective. He specifically contrasted the earthly with the heavenly. Paul stated that "[o]ur citizenship is in heaven."

In some ways beginning a new idea with 3:20 is artificial and interrupts the flow of the text. The contrasts below argue for an integrated understanding of Paul's argument. The text should not be radically divided. On the other hand, Paul shifts from a focus on opponents to the characteristic of genuine believers. For the first time, he completes the picture of what he argued throughout. Although correct, it is insufficient to stop at renouncing the law and legal approaches to a relationship with God. It is inadequate but necessary to argue the necessity of trusting in the faithfulness of Christ and thereby having his righteousness as a cover. It is imperative to have in life the passion of getting to know everything about Christ. That occurs through gaining knowledge, obedience, and sacrifice. Even so, there is more. As though the passage moves logically through what it means to be a Christian, it naturally has a *telos*, an end point. This is treated as a separate section because of the singular importance of understanding the whole and the emphasis Paul put on proper focus. It should not be considered separate from what precedes, however.

Paul began with a blatant and shocking reality. "Our citizenship is in heaven!" The metaphor had rich meaning to the Philippians.[501] The untranslated Greek "for" that introduces these verses is explanatory in a strongly contrasting way. Citizenship contrasts with the life walk of the enemies of the cross. Employing "citizenship" as the location

---

501 See the Introduction for the significance of the city as a colony with Roman citizenship.

of genuine believers recalls a more comprehensive idea than mere living. The descriptions of the enemies are present—how they live now but with their future in mind (destruction). The benefits of believers comprehensively involve the present and the future. They incorporate both their hope and their ultimate location. Paul recognized Christians belong to the resurrection ultimately. Witherington observes in essence Paul said "the Christian's commonwealth, ruling principles, and constitutive government come from Christ who is reigning from heaven, not from the Emperor who is ruling from Rome."[502] Immediately their thoughts would have turned to an analogy with their earthly citizenship. They were proud of their Roman citizenship, but the analogy would have conveyed more. Philippi was an outpost colony, and Paul was at the home base in Rome. Regularly they awaited news from the capital to know how to conduct their business. When Paul said they belonged to a citizenship, he spoke directly to them. Similarly, the church was an outpost of an entity which had its own capitol, heaven.

The certainty of this is emphasized by the verb Paul chose to use, which is not apparent in CSB. Rather than saying our citizenship "is," Paul actually wrote that our citizenship "exists" (*huparchei*) in heaven. It is an active verb ("is" has no action, it is a verb of state) combining a preposition and the verb into the meaning "exist, be present, possess." The verb occurred earlier (2:6) of Christ's "existing in the form of God." It was his primary state. Used here, it indicates the believer's primary, or ultimate, reality. Where we belong, in heaven, is really there!

Although "citizenship" may call to mind a place, Paul used it of a people. They awaited the Savior from that citizenship. He would come with power sufficient to subdue everything and with ability to transform their bodies to be like his resurrected one. They would naturally associate subduing power with a Roman emperor, but transforming power was unique to Christ. Once again, Paul spoke of the resurrection as the climax of his Christian experience. By implication, the false teachers would not share in the resurrection of the just because their orientation was earthly rather than heavenly.

One final point occurs in v. 21. Paul focused on the physical body which would be transformed so that it becomes like Christ's. Two factors are significant. First, the body is destined for eternity. It should be

---

502 Witherington, III, *Paul's Letter*, 217.

treated accordingly, and people should not make earthly existence in the body their ultimate concern. The tragedy of the false teachers was, in part, that they did just that. They focused on aspects of the body that would not last beyond this life. This makes the commitments of the opponents discussed in this chapter elementary and earthly, if not foolish. It should be remembered that Paul disciplined his body. In Acts 21:23–24, Paul's friends told him to take a vow so everyone would know he was "careful about observing the law." Presumably they recognized Paul's life patterns reflected Jewish concerns about the Torah (see also 1 Cor 9:1–9, 24–27). Discipline enables focus. It does not necessarily reveal trust in self-effort.[503] Second, Paul's hope involved physical transformation. His theology included the fact that redemption culminated in a change of the body itself. The spirit was already joined in resurrection with Christ; the body awaited the change to a spiritually maintained version of itself.[504] This statement reiterates the hope expressed in Phil 3:10. The power of the resurrection would be complete when Jesus exerted his resurrection power toward the bodies of believers. Paul characterized the body now as one of humiliation, of "humble condition" (*tapeinoseos*). The root of this word is the same as used in the description of Jesus in 2:8. Jesus "humbled" himself. The attitude of humility exists as an attribute of Christ eternally, coexisting with his eternal authority. In 2:8, however, Jesus's humility expressed itself in its move toward the death of the cross. Death was a temporary experience for Jesus, though his humility is eternal. With Paul using the root "humility" in connection with the body it suggests that the body is in a temporary lowly state. In so doing, Paul addressed the limitations Christians have on this fallen earth. The body is not suited to heaven unless a transformation takes place. In that sense, it symbolizes a Christian's state of humiliation. Someday, however, it will be a body of glory, fully suited to the environment of heaven and displaying the glory of Christ himself. After that transformation, the body will have reached its fullest development, able to display the glory God intended for it in creation. The primary limitations imposed on this body of "humble condition" come because of its contamination with sin. It currently has limitations of age, health, and perception. When the impact of sin is fully removed, at the resurrection,

503 Paul's discipline was so as not to hurt his work, his walk, or the weak (1 Cor 8–10).

504 E.g., Rom 8:19–25; 1 Cor 15:42–44, 50–54.

these limitations will be removed as well. The body will have reached a state of glory. This is a significant hope, fully pastoral in motivation. It should cause believers to press on until that great day.

Theological and Practical Points

1. *Theology through biography.* Chapter three contains the most pointed rebuke of the opponents of Christianity threatening the church at Philippi. The chapter is both theological and biographical. These verses contain the most theology of any text in Philippians apart from, perhaps, the poem about Christ. The poem about Christ brings Christ' experience from pre-humanity to humanity and back to his exalted state. It provides theological concepts that defy complete understanding as they describe the unfathomable: God became human! It is supremely Christological.

In a similar manner, in Gal 3 Paul describes the application of the death of Christ by appealing to his own experience. Thus, the experience of Christ illustrates theology; likewise, the experience of Paul illustrates theology. Paul was uniquely suited to teach by biography. Born a Diaspora Jew, he understood both Jewish history and thought and Gentile patterns of thinking. His background suited him to didactic sections of text explaining Christ to both Gentile (1–2 Thess; Romans and Jewish thinkers (Galatians; Romans). Much of his apologetic required verbal and logical conventions. He excelled at both. In Philippians, however, the challenge called for a more personal rebuttal. First, he was writing to friends who knew him well. Second, he wrote against those who followed his pre-Christian values which he could address better by example. This fits the primary genre of the entire "letter" since it models patterns of truth. It also conforms to common Greco-Roman patterns of imitation as a way of instruction.

God values human experience. In the canonical Scriptures, major sections are historical and embedded in history, biography. Old Testament narratives not only tell the story, they inform the reader as to how to be a part of the story. Rather than giving abstract principles to follow, the OT illustrates theology through the lives of people who lived it. Some persons were bad examples, others good. Most were both good and bad. Either way, theology matched life in ways that compelled the reader to side with one or the other. Sometimes both good and bad actions tell the ongoing story of redemption.

In the NT a similar pattern emerges. The four Gospels narrate Jesus's experiences and sermons. The authors present a biographical picture of Jesus with nuances that enable the four documents to impact different ethnic and cultural groups. The book of Acts describes the growth of the early church. Theology is in the forefront in the sermons that are available, but for the most part the theology of Acts is encased in history. The NT does have a mixture greater than the OT. The many letters and Revelation are written in a more focused, didactic pattern so that the points are made propositionally. In both cases, the narrative and biological genres differ from most religious literature, containing their own beauty. They are also the style God used to describe his most precious gift, Jesus's life and work.

For the most part, Paul follows the narrative/biography pattern in Philippians. There are comparatively few commands. Theology and lifestyle issues must be discerned from the individuals described in the book: Timothy, Epaphroditus, Clement (with the negative examples Euodia and Syntyche), and ultimately Christ whose life pattern in the Christ poem permeates the entire letter. Paul chose a biblical pattern in confronting his opponents. The lives of Israel's heroes like Noah, Abraham, Joseph, Moses, and David taught divine truths to generation after generation. Reading their lives and exploits instructed in many ways; reading of Paul's experience followed in their train.

All of this points to some simple but powerful truths. First, God's truth is largely incarnational. Like God become flesh, truth became flesh as well, often incarnated in those who accepted and followed it. Second, those who live as God intends become models for others who sometimes need a picture to grasp how the relationships work. Third, there is power in personal testimony. Yet testimony to experience must always be grounded in objective truth. That truth is found in the composite teaching of Scripture. As Paul observed from his years of study, however, truth is often personal and powerful through personal testimony to it.

2. *The components of genuine holiness*. Even in telling his story, Paul worked almost systematically through the process of salvation. He first provides an overview beginning with circumcision. Although he does not call his Jewish opponents' activity circumcision, preferring to call it mutilation of the flesh, he immediately contrasts their situation with that of true believers. Genuine God-followers "worship by the Spirit of God, boast in Christ Jesus, and do not put confidence in

the flesh" (3:3). The differences are stark. The opponents' great failure is they "glory" in their "shame" (3:19), their circumcision, rather than in Christ Jesus. That is the critical dividing line. For Paul to get there, he had to have a radical reappraisal of his former life. Though repentance does not occur explicitly in this text, disavowing his past involved a change of attitude toward God and Christ. It also brought a reexamination of his own personal values, which he found errant. Loving his past stood in the way of his entrance into future joy.

The negative appraisal of the past gave way to the replacement values of the present. Paul's goal in life changed to "knowing Christ Jesus [his] Lord" (3:8). He spoke of knowing Christ with synonyms "gain[ing] Christ" and "be[ing] found in him." Prerequisite to knowing Christ is to have another righteousness, different from the one before. The requirement is more than one naturally possesses. It is not a law righteousness, one acquired by diligently and energetically striving to keep the commandments. The energy involved in such an endeavor may be commendable, but it is errant. No matter how devout, one's efforts at law righteousness do not "gain Christ." Such disregards Christ in preference for standing on one's own. God provides the necessary righteousness in making Jesus's righteousness available to the believer. In Paul's mind the contrasts between righteousness lie at the heart of successfully relating to God or not.

Personal effort is countered by trust. Through faith in Christ the appropriate righteousness is granted to the believer. It is the faithfulness of Jesus who was faithful to keep the law and to complete the divine plan. Faith in the faithfulness of Jesus, rather than oneself, brings God's righteousness, the basis of salvation. The new goal is to know Christ completely and to be like him in complete holiness.

Every event in life enables more intimate knowledge of Christ. Using the model from the Christ poem, Paul expected his life to imitate Jesus'. Rising above negative events in a supernatural enabling evidenced that Christ is operative in believers' lives. The power is that of Christ's resurrection. On the other hand, passing through difficulties and painful experiences brings a comfort found only in connection with Christ, the one who suffered on his way to exaltation. All events are interpreted through the lens of the life of Jesus—what it means to be like him and experience his presence. Christian living is going through life with the mixture of Jesus's power and his comfort.

All of this has a goal. It is the goal of creation: that humanity would be like Christ and enjoy its Creator forever. At conversion, the Christian becomes aware of new values, new ambitions, and new pleasures. Christ followers find an all-encompassing desire to be holy. The latent desire becomes a passion. It is to be completely like Jesus, including the immaterial parts of being human and the material. The transformed, resurrected body joined with the perfected soul is the ultimate stage of holiness, of being what God intended in creation. Meanwhile, the passion for holiness enables a proper perspective on difficulties, including suffering. It strips away the superfluous and brings to the forefront the core commitments of those who suffer. Suffering enhances the longing to be pure, away from the world of evil, and more like Jesus. The comfort of the one who suffered most brings peace and guidance.

The journey toward holiness is both a personal and a group activity. "Citizens of heaven" model how to get there. Citizens of heaven who live on earth temporarily join in unity and live focused on the goal together. All the while, citizens of heaven anticipate and eagerly await their deliverer, who will bring transformation into reality and transport each to their permanent heavenly home. There the longings of the heart will be satisfied. We will be holy.

3. *Righteousness*. Righteousness is central to the argument of Phil 3. Paul stated in a somewhat summary fashion in 3:9 he wanted to "be found in [Christ], not having a *righteousness of [his] own* from the law, but one that is through faith in Christ—*the righteousness from God* based on faith" (emphasis added). Several aspects of this verse are striking and take us to the heart of Paul's theology. First, the core issue is righteousness. This is consistently Pauline, that without righteousness there is no relationship with God. Personal salvation is intimately related to and based on righteousness. Second, there are two approaches to righteousness. On the one hand, there was Paul's previous life pattern, representative of all non-Christian persons, which he described as "my own from the law." On the other hand, there is God's righteousness "based on faith" available to believers. In the context of chapter 3, Paul's opponents advocated their own righteousness attained by keeping the law. Paul found this lacking in his own thinking and experience. The questions raised center on 1) what righteousness is and 2) how it is attained. The discussion of righteousness has been analyzed and debated for millennia. In the context

of a biblical commentary, both purpose and space forbid adequate discussion. Nevertheless, the following is an attempt to provide some contours for understanding and to apply them to Paul and Phil 3.

Several general reference points should be noted at the outset. First, regarding righteousness, is it an activity, or a defining personal quality? In thinking of God's righteousness, a third option appears: is it God's relation-restoring love? Second, regarding the Christian's righteousness, 1) is it imputed, or 2) is it imparted? Imputed righteousness is God's *declaring* one to be righteous. Imparted is God's *changing the nature* of the believer so there is actual righteousness. Third, what does righteousness mean in the believer's life before God and others?

The most common word for righteousness in Hebrew is *sedeq* (in various grammatical forms); it has the basic meaning of "straightness, justness, rightness."[505] Sometimes the word is used in relation to God and his covenant with Israel. It informs readers God has remained faithful to his promises even if his people stray. Like most OT descriptions of God, it focuses more on activity than abstract qualities. For example, the OT writers may say "God loves" rather than "God is love." In the NT, the Greek words most translated "right . . . " are built on the *dik* root ("just," "right") in both secular and biblical Greek. The Greeks tended to describe their gods in abstract terms rather than with action qualities. Some NT interpreters follow that pattern.

The foundational platform for Paul's thought here is "righteousness of God," which CSB translates as being "from God" (3:9). Two of the most informative texts involving the former phrase occur in Romans, which also contains almost one half of all Paul's uses. Paul used the phrase in almost half of the occurrences in the NT. Both Rom 1:17 and 3:21 occur in pivotal places in Paul's systematic presentation of the need for and provision of salvation. Both refer to God's saving activity in the gospel and in Jesus's death. Romans 3:21–25 in some ways reiterates and further describes the gospel of 1:17. In 1:16–17 Paul's pride in the gospel is 1) because it is God's power to effect salvation, and 2) it reveals God's righteousness, the necessary component

[505] K. L. Onesti and M. T. Brauch, "Righteousness, Righteousness of God," in *Dictionary of Paul and His Letters: A Compendium of Contemporary Biblical Scholarship,* ed. Gerald F. Hawthorne, Ralph P. Martin, Daniel G. Reid (Downers Grove, IL: InterVarsity Press, 1993), 828. Though somewhat dated, the articles in this volume remain very helpful.

of salvation because "the righteous will live by faith."[506] "God's righteousness" is literally "righteousness of God." The lack of the Greek article "the" (anarthrous noun) in both occurrences indicates Paul is speaking of the gospel as being at least one way of God revealing his righteousness, rather than the gospel as *the* (totality of) righteousness of God.[507] These texts are grammatically identical. Both are followed by concerns related to God's righteousness.

Romans 1:18–20 presents a serious difficulty requiring the judgment side of God's righteousness: humans are sinful (1:18 for Gentiles; 3:3 for Jews). Does that affect God's promises made throughout history? Rather than human failure redirecting God's purposes, God is righteousness in spite of it (Rom 3:5). In 3:9–11, God's righteousness is seen in his providing Jesus, in part, to demonstrate he remained righteous. Consequently, the gospel —Jesus's death and resurrection benefits available to believers—accomplished two important aspects of God's righteousness. First, it provided salvation to believers; second, it vindicated God's actions in blessing OT sinners. God's promise of redemption, his spoken righteousness, began in one of the earliest events in history when God made promises of redemption to Adam and Eve who sinned (Gen 3:15). His promises of blessing continued throughout OT history, both in word and action in spite of the failures of his people. Now, in Jesus's life and death, the world could see that God was faithful—righteous—all along.

There are alternate interpretations. The phrase "righteousness of God" as defined above takes righteousness to be descriptive of God (it is a genitive of description). Others see God as the source of Christian righteousness ("God" is a subjective genitive or, more accurately, an ablative case). That interpretation makes righteousness an attribute given to humans by God. It is equivalent to God making believers

---

[506] There are multiple well-known difficulties with this text both in Hab 2:4 and Rom 1:17, though neither affect the meaning of "the righteous." First, as for Habakkuk, the Hb. text (MT) reads literally "the just will live by his faith" (or faithfulness, as generally *aman* is translated in the OT). The LXX translation interpreted it as "the just will live by *my* faith" (or faithfulness) since it is a direct quote from God. Romans leaves out the pronoun "his" and "my" completely, thereby making it a principle of faith. Second, the two prepositional phrases require analysis: "out of faith unto faith" (ἐκ πίστεως εἰς πίστιν). Third, is πίστις subjective (faithfulness) or objective (faith)? However interpreted, the combination emphasizes faith, typical of Paul.

[507] In Gk., nouns with articles specify *identity* and nouns without the article indicate *quality*. It is similar to the difference between "Paul is the man" (articular) and "Paul is man" (anarthrous). God's working in Christ is indeed a revelation of his righteousness but not every revelation of it.

righteousness. While it is true God grants righteousness to those who believe in Christ, that reads broader Pauline theology into these two texts. Both Rom 1:17 and 3:21 are followed by activities, one relating to sinful behavior and the other relating to God's remedy for sin. Paul usually employed the word "righteousness" in contexts of right and wrong, most often contrasting it with keeping or violating the law. The Letter to the Romans is primarily about God—it defends God and his working in the world. It is best to interpret "righteousness of God" in Rom 1:17 and 3:21 as God's own consistency.

"Righteousness" is seen in activity. It defines a way of doing. God's righteousness is known by his consistent actions in light of his word. As an activity, righteousness implies consistency to a standard, a norm of conduct, which raises the question of by what standard God can be considered righteous. God's righteousness is measured by his holiness. Holiness describes God's perfect being. His holy nature determines the standard by which his activity is measured. Righteousness means doing right in light of that standard. As a result, righteousness is the activity of God enforcing his holiness. Right working is more than consistency with the spoken word; it is consistency with the objective standard of conduct. When one does right it reveals that he or she is right. Therefore, God may be understood to be righteous because he does right in light of what his holiness demands. As this relates to humans, God also expects activity consistent with the ultimate standard: God's holiness. Punishment occurs when people fail to act rightly in light of that standard (Rom 1:18; 2:8; 3:5–6, 23). His holiness demands punishment for sin. To be consistent with his character, God will either grant blessings (theoretically) or punishment according to human ability to achieve holiness. Such judgment is always based on what one does: God "will repay each one according to his works" (Rom 2:6; Ps 62:12). Either way, righteousness characterizes God whose actions always correlate to his holiness. Repeated acts of righteousness may lead to calling God righteous, since he habitually acts in that way. On the other hand, righteous character is always measured by how it coincides with holiness.

The majority of Paul's discussions about righteousness occur in contexts of law and faith. The ultimate goal for humans is to have righteousness sufficient to be in fellowship with God. This includes doing right, which then can be categorized as being righteous. One place God revealed his standard for human behavior was at Sinai at the origin of Israel as a nation, after the exodus: he gave the Ten Commandments (Exod 20:3–17).[508] Moses explained the people's obligations in light of them (Exod 20–23), to which the people responded, "We will do everything that the has commanded" (Exod 24:3). If they could accomplish that, their righteousness would be measured by the Commandments; so began the religious codification of law as necessary for fellowship with God. Jewish scholars projected this same obedience to Abraham who lived centuries earlier and before the Ten Commandments. Abraham obeyed God by instituting family circumcision. Circumcision was an act of obedience, but it also marked the Jewish nation as Abraham's own. By Paul's day, these legal structures regulated the people's religious activity and, in many ways, provided the national identity. For Paul's opponents, God's command, the weight of history and tradition, and Israel's national identity were identified by circumcision and the law. Righteousness was measured by conformity to it.

After his conversion, Paul understood Israel's history and responsibility differently. Consider what is revealed in Gen 15:6:"Abraham believed the Lord, and he credited it to him as righteousness." At least two foundational principles come from the exegesis of Abraham's life. 1) Abraham was "credited" righteousness when he believed. Clearly a righteousness was available that was given rather than earned. From the time of the father of the Jews, Abraham, then, faith brought the desired relationship with God (Rom 4:3–5). Possessing credited righteousness overcame human failures, even as David experienced and recorded (Rom 4:7 quoting Ps 32:1–2). The same statement was made of Phineas as noted earlier (see commentary on Phil 3:6). The righteousness given to Abraham came from God himself, who qualified Abraham for a relationship with him. Even Abraham's failures, some attempting to accomplish God's purposes, did not affect the fact he was righteous in God's sight. 2) Abraham demonstrated God's righteousness is available for everyone (Jew and Gentile), since he believed and received righteousness before he was circumcised. Paul argued, "It was not while he was circumcised, but uncircumcised" (Rom 4:10). It was, therefore, "to make him the father of all who believe but are not circumcised, so that righteousness may be credited to them also"

---

[508] Abraham was the father of the Jewish people. Moses was the father of the nation.

(Rom 4:11). It is possible to "follow in the footsteps of the faith our father Abraham had while he was still uncircumcised" (Rom 4:12), having righteousness credited to those who believe in him "who raised Jesus from the dead" (Rom 8:11).

Paul's argument in Phil 3 is at the core of the gospel, Israel's history, and God's righteousness. Advocates of circumcision and law aspire to righteousness by achievement. Those with faith in Christ trust what God gives. The contrasts are these: principle—law versus grace, activity—works of law versus faith in Jesus, goal—righteousness by law versus righteousness credited. The options are not equal. No one can achieve the righteousness they hope through law. Both Jews and Greeks are under sin (Rom 3:10–18) and "no one will be justified in [God's] sight by works of the law" (Rom 3:20; Gal 2:21). The problem is not with the law, it is with people, none of whom can measure up to the demands of the law (Rom 7:7, 12–13). In God's righteousness, however, he provided another way (Rom 8:3–4). He had determined to redeem, but the law had no redemptive mechanism for those who fail, and all do. God's faithfulness in sending Jesus, the effective approach to righteousness, is the only way to fellowship with God. It is through Jesus that God can "be just (righteous) and justify (give righteousness to) the one who has faith in Jesus" (Rom 3:26, clarity added).

Through faith in Christ, the believer receives "righteousness from God" (Phil 3:9). He considers the believer righteous by his own standard of holiness and makes available all the blessings suited to the righteous. In declaring the believer righteous of character, God also declares his activities righteous. One cannot be true without the other. Actions are considered covered in God's righteousness as the believer aligns with God's righteous character and activity. Since holiness and righteousness is the true identity of the believer by faith in Christ, Paul urges the believer to act righteously. The goal is personal holiness, actual righteousness in human experience somehow measuring up to God's declaration. In Phil 1:9–11 righteous character and activity enable the believer to be "pure and blameless." Christian growth involves presenting the parts of the body "as slaves to righteousness, which results in sanctification (holiness)" (Rom 6:19; clarity added). Believers are to pursue righteousness (1 Tim 6:11; 2 Tim 2:2) and be trained in righteousness (2 Tim 3:16), all the while realizing salvation is not "by works of righteousness that we had done, but according to [God's] mercy" (Titus 3:5).

The issues of Phil 3 have eternal significance. Paul's opponents saw circumcision and law as their way to righteousness. They refused the true righteousness of God, lived as enemies of the cross, and sealed their own damnation (3:19). Their threat to the church was not only an errant message, but it was also devastating to those desiring to be holy. It simply could not produce fellowship with the holy God. Paul had traveled that road. He now saw its deception, that it misunderstood God's righteous character and activity. "Righteousness that is in the law" was empty (3:6). God's righteousness combined with his love provided salvation through Jesus. It brought the ability to be and do right by God's power. No wonder Paul's strongest aspiration was "the righteousness from God based on faith" (3:9).

3.4 Exhortations to the Philippians (4:1–9)

Paul's mind turned to various matters in the church. Throughout the letter there are hints of disunity among the congregation, and Paul countered that disunity with strong doctrinal (2:1–11) and practical (2:12–18) instruction. This chapter presents the only tangible evidence as to what the problem might have been, and the evidence is scarce. Several exhortations occur in these verses: to steadfastness (4:1), to unity (4:2–3), to joy and peace (4:4–7), and to the proper outlook (4:8–9).

There is a question as to where this section begins. Since 4:1 is obviously transitional, a case may be made for including it in the previous section. Grammatically it is natural for a "so then" (*hoste*) clause to look forward.[509] There is a parallel in 2:12, which, looking forward in the text, applies the truths of Jesus's self-emptying to the church. Here, Paul applied the truths of chapter 3 to practical church life. For that reason, 4:1 is included in the exhortations of the final chapter. It is further noteworthy that Paul used his phrase "in the Lord" four times in 4:1–20. These four reinforce and emphasize the statements associated with them, and three are commands. The church is to "stand firm in the Lord" (4:1); Euodia and Syntyche are to "agree in the Lord" (4:2); and the church is to "[r]ejoice in the Lord" (4:4) as

[509] Moule, *The Epistle*, 144, says it is an inferential particle, meaning "and so, accordingly." These suggest the possibility of a forward-looking idea as well.

they remember that Paul "rejoiced in the Lord greatly" for their gift to him (4:10).[510] Paul introduces 3:1 with the same phrase "rejoice in the Lord." He follows it with a warning about encroaching heresy which takes a drastic turn of warning unlike 4:1 and following, which are all positive commands about Christian living. Finally, there is no connection between the matters discussed in chapter 4 and those of chapter 3. The latter warns of matters external to the church; the former concerns those internal.

Paul's challenge is directed to the entire church. It naturally follows from the conclusion of chapter 3, when he spoke of "[o]ur citizenship" in contrast to those whose is earthly (3:20). As noted, "[s]o then" applies that text to the church by indicating the blessings true believers have collectively. It is impossible to achieve the collective goal without the individuals within the church adopting them as well. Further, though immediately Paul's thought reflects his eschatological perspective ending chapter three, the specific command to stand firm recalls 1:27, the only other time Paul used the verb meaning stand firm in Philippians. There he urged the church to stand firm in one spirit and one soul while striving for the faith of the gospel. The exhortations that follow here echo that concern, though the focus is internal rather than external. Before, they were to guard the gospel by their actions. Here, they are to live out the implications of the gospel in church life. The connection to stand firm in 1:27 (which continues through 2:18) is reinforced by another use of the term "to adopt the same attitude" (*phroneo*) that occurs in 2:5. It occurs in 4:2, translated here "agree." Philippians 4:1–9 should be read recalling 1:27–2:18, applying the mind of Christ to the church. These verses should also be read with sensitivity to the true gospel explained by example in 3:1–21.

---

[510] These may well be literary markers indicating Paul's movement from theme to theme as he closes the letter. This is another evidence that v. 1 belongs with chapter 4 rather than 3.

3.4.1 Exhortation to Steadfastness (4:1)

[1] So then, my dearly loved and longed for brothers and sisters, my joy and crown, in this manner stand firm in the Lord, dear friends.

Structure

So then . . . stand firm in the Lord, dear friends
in this manner
my dearly loved and longed for brothers and sisters,
my joy and my crown

Interpretation

4:1 Immediately Paul changed his tone in this verse. The previous passage contains the emotion of argumentation; now he spoke with the warmth of a dear friend. Two sections occur in this verse: the address to the readers and the exhortation.

3.4.1.1 The Address to the Readers (4:1)

In the address Paul made three statements about the church. Central is the idea the believers there were his spiritual "brothers and sisters." The term occurs frequently in Philippians and helps express the unity they enjoyed with each other and with Paul.[511] As previously, the use of the masculine plural is not gender restrictive, but rather incorporates the group—the church—as a whole. The immediate appeal to two Christian women, who must be included in the exhortation of 4:1, evidences the breadth of the appellation. Furthermore, Paul called this group those who were "dearly loved and longed for." The first term, built on a form of *agape* (*agapetos*) stresses the strong tie that bound them together in love. The second word, "longed for" (*epipothetos*), occurs only here in the NT. It speaks of Paul's desire to fellowship with them.[512] Just because they were Christian brothers and sisters did not guarantee Paul would feel this way about them. Their relationship had grown out of the fellowship in the gospel. Their history with Paul brought this unusual commendation. He longed to be with them, and the statement echoes 1:8. Perhaps the tensions he

[511] 1:12; 3:1, 13, 17; 4:1, 8, 21.

[512] BAGD translates ἐπιπόθητοι "longed for, desired," 298. Hawthorne, Philippians, 178, says it is the emotion of "homesick tenderness."

observed and felt in Rome with its divided congregations caused him to wish for the fellowship of those who understood and agreed with his mission. Further, the general support financially in sending one of their own to assist Paul, and their obvious concern for his well-being, brought a deep desire to be with them either in Rome or Philippi. Finally, Paul called them his "joy and crown." These terms turned the readers' thoughts to the end of time. Joy is a common theme in the letter. This use is unique, however, because the church was Paul's joy. He did not mean they replaced the joy of the Lord, but rather that life was better because he knew them. They brought him joy even while he was awaiting trial! Further, their response to the gospel would bring him joy on judgment day. In a sense, when that day arrived Paul's life and ministry would be validated and rewarded by the consistency of his converts. The imagery of the crown speaks of the reward God gives. The Philippian believers were Paul's crown.[513] The fact they believed guaranteed Paul's rewards. A strong tie existed between Paul and the church.[514]

Out of this friendship grew exhortation. Paul urged them to steadfastness. Perhaps the language came from the military and, therefore, had significant meaning for the city populated by military families. The Roman armies were known for standing unmoved against the enemy. The church was to stand in the same way. The words "in this manner" translate the Greek *houtos*, a word that shows the customary way. The church was not to be weakened by disunity, turmoil, or wrong values. It was to stand together to accomplish God's will. The "how" likely reflects 3:15–16. The exhortation recalls 1:27, and it was an important aspect of church life.

With this second use of the verb "stand firm," it is worth noting that the idea is a defensive one. While there are other metaphors illuminating how the church should advance the gospel, this one urges the church to be unmoved. Referring to the two Pauline appearances of the word, the general warnings look back to division (1:15–17) and forward to disharmony (4:2). In both, believers may become disheartened or defeated. In 4:1, "stand firm" emphasizes the defensive bulwark of the church against false theologies that will likely appear.

---

[513] Perhaps athletic imagery continues from 3:14 since in a race the winner won a crown. See Keown, *Philippians 2:19–4:23, 302*, for the number of ways crowns were used. It seems here the athletic metaphor continues.

[514] The passage parallels 1 Thess 2:19–20 and Phil 2:16.

They are on the horizon (3:1–21). Earlier, in 1:27, "standing firm" was modified in part by "contending together for the faith of the gospel." The verbal picture there is mixed: they are to stand firm *as* they advance the gospel (defense and offense). Here it is primarily defensive. Roman soldiers never ran! Similarly, the church must stand strong in theology and relationships. The gospel demands it.

Paul closed this exhortation with a reminder of his love for them. Essentially, the text ends as it begins. "My dearly loved . . ." as an introduction is matched with "dear friends" in the conclusion. Both translate the same word "loved" (*agapetoi*). It may be best to translate them alike to capture the rhetorical power of this sentence: "my *dearly loved* and longed for brothers and sisters . . . *dearly loved.*"

3.4.2 Exhortation to Unity (4:2–3)

[2] I urge Euodia and I urge Syntyche to agree in the Lord. [3] Yes, I also ask you, true partner, to help these women who have contended for the gospel at my side, along with Clement and the rest of my coworkers whose names are in the book of life.

Structure

I urge Euodia
and I urge Syntyche to agree in the Lord.
Yes, I also ask you—true partner—to help these women
who have contended for the gospel at my side,
along with Clement
and the rest of my coworkers
whose names are in the Book of Life.

Interpretation

4:2–3 At this point Paul directly addressed the problem of unity. It is the first specific problem known about the church, but Paul may have been concerned with it from the beginning of the epistle. The location of this discussion in the epistle suggests two different characteristics of the problem. On one hand, its occurrence in a prominent place in this section of the epistle suggests the problem had some significance. It was more than a passing disagreement. It had the potential of splitting the church into at least two groups. On the other hand, it occurs near the end of the letter and is handled in a relatively soft manner. Apparently it was not enough of a problem to cause Paul undue alarm.

Paul had faith in the women themselves and in the church's ability to address the problem.

Nothing is known about these women or the dispute between them. Many scholars have attempted to identify them, but the conclusions are all conjecture. Were they deaconesses, house church leaders, patronesses, administrators (perhaps of common funds), missionaries? The best course of action is to stay within the bounds of Scripture.[515] Some suggestions may be drawn from the knowledge of the founding of the church (see Acts 16) and Philippi itself. Women occupied a prominent place in the church. They were among the first converts. Though the founding of the church had happened approximately ten years earlier, it is quite possible Euodia and Syntyche were among the early converts. Nothing is stated, however, about their longevity in serving the church. Apparently they were well known so that it was needless to say more about them or their dispute. The way Paul addressed them and his concern for a mediator suggests they had significant influence and either they and/or their issue could divide the church. Since Paul addressed the letter in part to "overseers and deacons" (1:1), soon after men joined the congregation, the church may have gained size and maturity quickly. Paul never includes women in the his instructions relating to the offices of overseer and deacon.[516] Any suggestions they had specific offices in the church is speculation, though, of course, some responsibility—official or not—cannot be ruled out.

The controversy occurred between two notable women who played a major part in church life. Whatever the cause, several factors emerge about the problem. It was significant enough that the women could not, or would not, solve it themselves; it probably was not a doctrinal problem since Paul spoke to such matters when they arose; it was divisive enough to cause the church to write to Paul about it; the entire church was asked to intercede on behalf of these women;[517]

---

[515] Lightfoot, *Saint Paul's*, 158, provided the evidence for the names in the inscriptions. Hawthorne, Philippians, 179, surveys the kinds of suggestions that have been made regarding their identity.

[516] The one notable exception, much discussed, is Phoebe (Rom 16:1) who is a servant (διάκονος, *deaconos*). The Pauline Pastoral Epistles, written a few years later, lists the qualifications of bishops and deacons with masculine descriptors (1 Tim 3:1–13, esp. 2, 12)

[517] Certainly that was the point of making the problem public in an epistolary form. Some go further and suggest the "true partner" is the church at large, an unlikely conclusion. (Hawthorne, Philippians, 180, reaches this conclusion perhaps because Clement was also named in the text.)

and the fellowship and ministry of the church faced a major crisis because of it. Keown contributes some relevant information about the situation: "That Paul wrote at all shows that this is no small matter. Further, Paul is so concerned about the situation in Philippi that he is giving up two of his very best coworkers, Epaphroditus and Timothy, and changing his own travel plans in order to [go] to Philippi."[518] Keown assumes this dispute was a major reason for Paul's writing the church. Church unity is a primary theme that permeates the letter. Judging by space and content, however, the problem with these two ladies does not occupy a major concern.[519] Most likely the issue involved personality or pride, causing some rallying of persons to stand with them against the other. The church was on the way to division.

In writing about how to solve the problem, Paul identified a process and a reason for it. The process began with the women themselves. In addressing them, Paul used the term translated "I urge" twice, once before each woman's name. The terse repetition stressed the personal interest Paul felt for each. He could have stated "I urge Euodia and Syntyche," but repeating the verb, giving each woman equal weight in the verbiage, puts them on level ground with each other and in Paul's mind. It is extremely rare to mention dissenters by name, as Paul does here. Again, only conjecture posits a reason for this unique approach to them. The address also called them to reconciliation. Naturally, the best solution was for them to solve their own problem. The word translated "agree" (*phroneo*) is encountered frequently in this letter (ten times). These women were to have the same attitudes and values that Christ had (2:5–11), that Epaphroditus and Timothy had, and that characterized Paul.

If the women could not resolve the problem themselves, they were to secure a mediator. Apparently the dispute was not moral, and neither woman was guilty of theological heresy. If so, Paul would have urged the erring one to submit to the Lord and the church.[520] This was a true disagreement, and a third party could help resolve it. Paul

---

[518] Keown, *Philippians 2:19–4:23*, 310.

[519] It is certainly not the same as the divisions in Corinth, the misunderstood theology of Thessalonica, or the immorality addressed in both. Other lesser issues warranted Paul's care, such as meat offered to idols (1 Cor 8–10); vegetarianism (Rom 14); cultural and religious celebrations (Rom 14); or the use and abuse of spiritual gifts (1 Cor 12).

[520] This is clear in 1 Cor 5:1–5 in morality and in Gal 2:11–14 and 2 Tim 4:10 in theology (assuming Demas's departure was theological). Paul did not hesitate to address persons when he felt they were in error.

simply identified the third party as "true partner." "True" was seldom used by Paul. The adverbial form of the word occurs as a description of Timothy who would "genuinely" care for them (2:20). Paul's request that the "true partner" assist differs from his urging the two women to agree. The CSB well translates the difference between the two: "I urge Euodia and I urge Syntyche . . . I also ask you, true partner."[521] This, too, indicates the relatively minor dispute that should be resolved easily. Throughout history, many scholars have attempted to identify this person, but too little evidence exists.[522] Some conclude this is a name, Syzygus, and therefore Paul appealed to a prominent person in the church. That, however, has not been widely accepted.

Next, Paul presented reasons for helping the women. First, they fought alongside Paul for the gospel. Employing a word picture again, he spoke of their value in the spread of it. They not only helped Paul in his work but also fought alongside Clement and other unnamed coworkers.[523] The description recalls 1:27, where Paul urged the church to "[contend] together for the faith of the gospel." What he encouraged of the church already characterized these two, they "contended" ("strove"). They were not passive Christians. They exerted energy in what they believed.[524] The three named persons, along with the unknown number of unnamed, were the kinds of people necessary for the spread of the gospel and the well-being of the church.

Strangely, nothing is known about Clement. He obviously was well-known in Philippi though the text does not give any indication of his origin or his current residence. He need not be in Philippi at the time of the letter. He was, however, occasionally associated with the Pauline group. Others, too, were known associates of Paul, but they are unnamed. Others may have been known by the church, but Clement is named! That makes him significant to them. It may be noted he has a Latin name. Some would, therefore, locate him as a Roman. Given the pervasive presence of the Roman Empire and the far-reaching effects of the Pax Roma, it would not surprise to have

---

[521] The first Gk. word is "beseech" or "urge" (παρακαλέω, *parakaleo*), a stronger verb than "ask" (ἐρωτάω).

[522] Hawthorne, *Philippians*, 179–80, provides an excellent list of these attempts. Some are totally speculative, including Paul's wife (possibly Lydia). A more recent, good survey is Keown, *Philippians 2:19–4:23*, 317–20. The best course is silence.

[523] Paul frequently acknowledged women for their contribution to the gospel. Romans 16 contains a list of ten women who significantly helped in his ministry.

[524] The Gk. word in both texts is συναθλέω (*sunathleo*).

a Roman in Macedonian Philippi. The name adds little to knowing who he was. Apparently, knowing more about Euodia, Syntyche, the true partner, and Clement was unimportant. Barth comments, "God knows them, and that too as righteous, as his own."[525]

Second, the women were Christian sisters. The Greek pronoun that introduces this last statement is masculine plural (*hon*), while the former introduction is feminine plural (*haitines*). Both by gender and proximity, this pronoun refers back to the women who "contended for the gospel." The latter pronoun is not so clear. Its proximity to "coworkers" demonstrates it is modifying Clement and the rest (all masculine). On the other hand, it is likely the masculine plural incorporates all of the persons mentioned in 4:2–3.[526] Further, the subject of the paragraph is Euodia and Syntyche. It would be natural for Paul to include the women as being recorded in the Book of Life.

The statement that their names were there is rare for Paul and seldom found in all of Scripture.[527] Further, Paul seldom stated such confidence about people.[528] When he commended them, he did so because of their association with him, their status in the church, or their relationship to Jesus. Claiming they were in the Book of Life reflects confidence about these people and their faith in Christ. "The Book of Life" is the listing of those who inherit eternal life. The imagery is used as the criteria for unbelievers and believers alike. The phrase echoes Moses, who interceded for Israel after they formed the golden calf. In praying for them, Moses identified with erring Israel to the degree that if God could not forgive them, he should "erase [him] from the book" (Exod 32:32). Later, David, in an imprecatory psalm against his enemies, asked God to "[l]et them be erased from the book of life and not be recorded with the righteous" (Ps 69:28). Revelation confirms this: "[T]he one who conquers will be dressed in white clothes, and [the

---

[525] Barth, *The Epistle*, 120.

[526] Masculine gender is appropriately used in Gk. for a group unless all are feminine gender.

[527] The statement regarding the Book of Life may refer to the fellow workers of Clement and Paul or to the women. The Gk. is unclear. Commentators have taken it both ways. Beare concludes Paul's certainty regarding it seems to convey the idea "of comrades who have died in the faith" (145). The text more naturally includes these living women in the word "whose." The gender is ambiguous (ὧν), and the phrase "Clement and the rest of my fellow workers" seems parenthetical. The Gk. text NA27 puts an interpretive comma after "my fellow workers," possibly suggesting the "Book of Life" phrase refers to the women. The CSB does not follow that suggestion. As noted, the masculine plural could refer to the entire group.

[528] For the Book of Life, see Exod 32:32–33; Ps 69:28; 139:16; Dan 12:1; Qumran (1QM 12:3); Luke 10:20; Rev 3:5; 20:15; 21:27.

Lord] will never erase his name from the book of life" (3:5). "And anyone whose name was not found written in the book of life was thrown into the lake of fire" (Rev 20:15). Conversely, Jesus stated to his disciples,"[R]ejoice that your names are written in heaven" (Luke 10:20). The metaphor is used sparingly and sometimes with mystery. Is everyone's name written in the Book of Life and those who fail to confess Christ stricken from it? Every occurrence of the metaphor suggests erasing rather than entering names. Those whose names are in it receive the life with God promised in the gospel. Euodia and Syntyche, with the others, are commended for their unquestioned inclusion in the Book of Life. They are true Christians.

Church government is another interest sparked by this passage. Some suggest the women had leadership roles in the congregation. Paul, however, said nothing about the offices of these women, nor did he say they preached as they labored for the Lord. Nevertheless, two indications of church order emerge here. First, Paul's appeal to an individual to mediate the problem may indicate that this individual was in a place of authority. Everyone knew both his identity and his right to intervene. Perhaps he was the pastor of the church.[529] Second, the matter became public, and the church was to handle such matters in a way that few do today. The congregation was a partnership. As the body of Christ, the members were to address such matters objectively, frankly, lovingly, and spiritually.[530]

3.4.3 Exhortation to Joy and Peace (4:4–9)

[4] Rejoice in the Lord always. I will say it again: Rejoice! [5] Let your graciousness be known to everyone. The Lord is near. [6] Don't worry about anything, but in everything, through prayer and petition with thanksgiving, present your requests to God. [7] And the peace of God, which surpasses all understanding, will guard your hearts and minds in Christ Jesus.

---

[529] Some apply the passage as though Paul was the pastor of this church. They derive pastoral principles from the text. While some of the principles may apply, Paul was not the pastor of the congregation, nor was he a former pastor intruding into the affairs of a current pastorate. Care must be exercised in these analogies.

[530] F. Craddock, *Philippians*, 70, speaks well at this point: "Notice that Paul does not, as some pastors do, regard matters such as this as private, to be settled outside the church lest anyone be disturbed. No, in Paul's view, this is precisely the nature and function of the congregation as a partnership."

[8] Finally brothers and sisters, whatever is true, whatever is honorable, whatever is just, whatever is pure, whatever is lovely, whatever is commendable—if there is any moral excellence and if there is anything praiseworthy—dwell on these things. [9] Do what you have learned and received and heard from me, and seen in me, and the God of peace will be with you.

Structure

Rejoice in the Lord always.
I will say it again: Rejoice!
Let your graciousness be known to everyone.
The Lord is near.
Don't worry about anything,
but . . . present your requests to God
        in everything
        through prayer
        and petition with thanksgiving
And the peace of God . . . will guard your hearts and minds
        which surpasses all understanding in Christ Jesus.
Finally brothers and sisters . . . dwell on these things = whatever is true,
                whatever is honorable,
                whatever is just
                whatever is pure
                whatever is lovely
                whatever is commendable
            if there is any moral excellence
            and if there is anything praiseworthy
Do what you have learned and received and heard . . . and seen.
            from me   in me
and the God of peace will be with you

This section contains the third time the phrase "in the Lord" occurs (4:1, 2, 4). These are also followed by the fourth occurrence in 4:10, though there Paul says he rejoiced in the Lord rather than commanding them to do so. The repetition of "in the Lord" seems to identify the logical text groupings. This is the last of Paul's sections of exhortation. In 4:10 he changes to his appreciation for them. There is no connecting link between vv. 3 and 4, and v. 4 introduces a series of three commands without grammatical connection which raises questions of how these verses relate to each other and the previous verses. Some assume 4:4 is a continuation of 4:2–3. If so, that specifically suggests Euodia and Syntyche are not only to agree, but they are to rejoice. If that is the case, vv. 5 and 6 should also relate primarily to them. Both the flow of the text and intuitive reading mitigate against that and suggest a new section of thought. For instance, it is strange

Paul would move from confrontation to the command to rejoice. Did he consider reconciliation to counter joy? Furthermore, certainly the command to stop worry in 4:6 cannot be delimited only to these women and/or their mediator, even if the command to graciousness (4:5) could apply. It is better to begin a new thought in 4:4 that relates primarily to action all but accomplished only if individuals comply as well.[531] Understanding these verses as a new command also fits the section dividers of the repetition of "in the Lord," as mentioned earlier.

Interpretation

Combined, these verses naturally divide into four concerns: joy (4:4), graciousness (4:5), peace (4:6–7), and focus (4:8–9). The discussion of peace breaks the pattern of simple commands found in vv. 4–5. Verses 6–7 and 8–9 have extended explanations of how peace becomes operative in life. Understanding these commands as part of a unit makes it difficult to discern a connecting thread. It seems possible "peace" is the binding thought since Paul describes genuine peace in two major and complementary sections. Joy and graciousness certainly enhance that discussion, but they are unconnected grammatically. The four commands of 4:4–9 refer together to a general sense of calmness, of spiritual characteristics that enable equilibrium regardless of circumstances. If that is the case, what are the immediate circumstances? Paul has described discord in the church at Rome (1:15–17), possible self-seeking within the church at Philippi (2:1–11), possible challenges to the doctrinal purity of the faith (3:1–20), and pressure on individuals in Philippi to side with either Euodia or Syntyche. To these may be added the external pressures from practicing a religion not yet declared legal by the government in a decidedly pro-government city, and the normal tensions brought by the uniqueness of the gospel. There were many situations that could interfere with joy, tempting one to react less than Christian and to worry.[532]

4:4 Paul commanded the Philippians to rejoice. He repeated the command immediately so the first and last words of the sentence call them to joy, thereby emphasizing its importance. The theme of joy

---

[531] The CSB joins many scholars in making 4:2–9 a unit of thought rather than 4:4–9.

[532] Fee, *Philippians*, 402, takes the theme to be piety.

permeates the letter.[533] In many ways this is remarkable given the difficulties described. Their joy was to be in the Lord, and it was to be unchanging. The circumstances of Paul's life reminded him of the joy available in the Lord, and he wished that joy for them as well. The command to rejoice introduces the first plural command of the chapter; such joy is given to the church rather than to some specific individual. Even so, it is difficult to see how a group could choose joy without the individuals within affirming it. The emphasis of the text falls upon the individuals to be what they should in order for the church to be what it should. Here the distributive force of plural commands predominates. "All" means "each one" in order to become "all." The plural aspect suggests the corporate meeting of the church must provide the theology and atmosphere of real joy, along with opportunities to express it. Praise and thankfulness point the group to their position "in the Lord." Additionally, Paul urges joy in spite of the pressures and difficulties of being in Christ in an alien environment. Reading the entire letter reveals suffering and various difficulties are a part of life even for the Christian. Joy is not the absence of difficulties, but rather the choice of recognizing and implementing the realities of being in Christ. Paul knew no situation is beyond the Lord's help. Christians can always rejoice in that, if nothing else. Indeed, "the joy of the Lord is [our] strength" (Neh 8:10).

The oft-repeated phrase "in the Lord" calls the Philippian church to a higher standard of conduct. As believers, they are "in the Lord." The phrase encapsulates Paul's previous words of spiritual location in this letter. They have a new citizenship; they are challenged by the Christ poem to be like Christ and concomitantly promised resources to enable that life transformation. They are to have clear focus on Christian things rather than earthly. They are to appreciate their salvation past and anticipate with enthusiasm their salvation future—deliverance from this world and the completion of the transformation God has in store for them. They are to participate with each other in the Christian community, serving out of genuine humility, considering others as excelling over them. The list of responsibilities and resources could continue. As Paul stated introducing the Christ poem in 2:5, "Adopt the same attitude as . . . Christ." Choices made bring

[533] The verb occurs, usually twice in proximity, in 1:18; 2:17–19; 3:1; 4:4, 10. The noun form is in 1:25; 2:2, 29; 4:1.

new stature, outlook, and energy as Christians embrace their new lives in Christ. "In the Lord" is more than a simple statement. It is a reminder of who they are. They are expected to live commensurate to that identity.

4:5 Second, Paul exhorted them to graciousness. No single word translates "graciousness" (*epieikes*) well, although commentators consistently insist that the term contains an element of selflessness. At times it may be translated "gentleness." The gentle person does not insist on personal rights. Rather, he has "that considerate courtesy and respect for the integrity of others which prompts [him] not to be forever standing on his rights; and it is preeminently the character of Jesus (2 Cor 10:1)."[534] The word occurs in Paul's writing as a required characteristic of Christian leaders (1 Tim 3:3, of bishops; Titus 3:2), and a characteristic of Christ (2 Cor 10:1). Perhaps most immediately Paul implied Euodia and Syntyche were to demonstrate gentleness toward each other, although he does not use the word itself. Gentleness softens attitudes so that one can enter into deliberations with a sense of humility and openness to instruction. The command is to the entire church since the form is plural. Rather than the militancy that sometimes characterizes Christians, gentleness requires humility motivated by love. It does not imply weakness or the acceptance of all variant ideas. Believers must stand firm in the gospel. Fairness and magnanimity are to be developed so they are visible to all. The Greek command is "let [graciousness] be known" (*ginosko*). Gentleness is not something to broadcast. It is something to be seen and felt. It will be observable in the actions and earned reputation of the church. That it is to be known by all ("everyone") indicates that within and without the church, gentleness is a primary feature of Christlikeness.

Paul made this emphatic by reminding them the Lord was at hand. The nearness of the Lord raises questions. Does Paul mean he expects the second coming of Christ soon? Or does Paul mean that Christ's presence and all he brings is readily available to assist the believer? Paul used the phrase both ways, eschatologically (Rom 13:11, see also 1 Cor 16:22) or with his presence (Rom 10:8; Eph 2:13, 17). He could have been purposefully ambiguous. Any of these are possible. The temporal use does not necessarily imply an immediate return of Christ. Like other NT writers, Paul understood that the events of Jesus's life

---

[534] This excellent definition comes from Caird, *Paul's Letter*, 150.

bring in the new age expected in the OT. Appropriately, Christians are to live with the realization the last days began with Christ's incarnation. Christianity itself is eschatological. The statement sobers Christians: the Lord will come as Judge, expecting to see gentleness in his people. Having personified the quality himself, he knows what it is like.

4:6–9 In these verses, Paul wrote of "the peace of God" that sustains Christians during times of hardship. In 4:8–9, he wrote of the result of proper thought life (4:8): "the God of peace" will be present.

These two commands differ in significant ways. Philippians 4:6–7 speaks primarily to those occasions in life when peace is lacking. They are the times when troublesome circumstances interrupt the normal flow of events. Paul gave three commands to help the readers navigate such problems. In 4:8–9, Paul organized his thoughts to address the need for a peaceful environment. The cultivation of the proper environment brings with it the God who is peace. Some commentators see these commands as applying to the church collectively rather than to individual Christians. It is impossible to determine whether that is true because of the distributive nature of the Greek plurals. Commands made collectively must be implemented individually, so they relate to the believer and the congregation. The commands also occur in passages describing the application of truth. In these Paul moved from the problems of the church to individual concerns. He probably had both individual Christians and the church family in mind.

4:6 The command is negative, but it has a positive thrust: "Don't worry about anything." Reading this literally, the form means "stop being anxious" as a negative present imperative which implies ceasing an activity already in progress. The same word is used positively of Timothy who (literally) "naturally will be anxious for things concerning you" (2:20). Generally, the word has the negative connotation of worry. Jesus spoke about anxiety in the Sermon on the Mount (Matt 6:25–34), where he stated the most common causes of worry. They are physical attributes (v. 27), clothing (v. 28) or food and drink needs (v. 31), and the future (v. 34). Even in contemporary life with its complexities, the same simple matters cause worry. Prayer, however, cures anxiety.

Here three words describe prayer. Each contributes to a proper understanding of the comprehensive nature of the prayer life. Kent observes, "In this context, the three have the following meanings:

'Prayer' (προσευχῄ) denotes the petitioner's attitude of mind as worshipful. 'Petition' (δεήσει) denotes prayers as expressions of need . . . 'Requests' (αἰτήματα) refers to the things asked for."[535] While these distinctions usually hold true, the primary point in combining the words is to emphasize the necessity and reality of prayer. The basic sentence is "in everything . . . present your requests to God." The third word for prayer, "requests," is the object of the verb: "let the *asks* (requests) be known to God." The structure of the Greek sentence translates this way: "Let your requests be known to God in prayer and petitions and with thanksgiving."

"Thanksgiving" adds another term to the list of words for prayer, the fourth in the sentence. The way requests reach God is through prayer and petitions. The proper attitude in presenting them is with thanksgiving. Generally, thanksgiving is a response to a benevolent act. The word is composed of the term for grace, *xaris*, heightened with the prefix "well." Strictly, thanksgiving appreciates God's gifts (in contrast, praise appreciates who God is, although that word is not used here). Through prayer with thanksgiving the church is to "present" their requests to God. It is somewhat unusual to use the verb "make known." Through prayer one reveals personal concerns to him. God, of course, knows well—even better—the concerns of each heart. Making known has the benefit of conversation with God about the points of worry. The focus is on the one presenting rather than on the one receiving revelation. With such a union of various words for prayer, four in all, Paul emphasizes the antidote to worry: prayer. Worry often dominates the human mind and heart. Paul suggests if believers really pray with proper attitude and specificity, worry ceases. The point of the statement is prayer relieves the problem of anxiety. The center of the verse is the significant part: Prayer is to be offered "with thanksgiving." The attitude of gratitude should accompany approaches to the Father. It is impossible to worry when appreciating God's goodness.

4:7 The counter to anxiety is "the peace of God." Paul made three statements about this peace. First, it is divine peace, a characteristic of God which invades the Christian. This is not peace *from* God, as though God is just the giver of peace. It is true, of course, that

---

[535] Kent, "Philippians," 11:152. These distinctions are based on the context and should not be pressed here or in other texts.

God provides peace. This must be understood in light of what it is: it "surpasses all understanding." The emphasis is on the kind of peace as qualitatively different (God's) and quantitatively different. This peace should be understood as "God's peace" that will provide a guard in the life.[536] It is the same as Jesus promised: "Peace I leave with you. My peace I give to you. I do not give to you as the world gives. Don't let your heart be troubled or fearful" (John 14:27). Second, God's peace "surpasses all understanding." "Surpasses" translates the Greek word *hyperechousa,* "excellent," which is found in 2:3; 3:8; and here in a compound form. Paul contrasted understanding and peace at one point: peace excels over understanding. No doubt he had in mind situations in which both knowledge and understanding are insufficient. Sometimes they cannot explain, and sometimes explanations do not help. Peace, however, is always appropriate and meets the need for the heart. The word often interpreted knowledge is "mind" (*nous*). Capable of a wide range of meanings, it is basically a Pauline distinctive in the NT.[537] Paul often used the word to express some function of the mind. Here it means the ability to understand. This is contrasted with anxiety which, in this context, is another function of the mind. Some understand this peace as providing calm in the face of anxiety, providing it when one's thoughts cannot arrive at a good conclusion. At a deeper level, however, it seems Paul described God's peace as beyond the capacity of human understanding. The construction literally reads "the peace of God, the surpassing all understanding one." "All understanding," therefore, further describes God's peace, which is qualitatively different from anything known in humanity without God's intervention.

Finally, this peace will "guard . . . hearts and . . . minds in Christ Jesus." "Guard" is a military term, implying peace stands on duty to resolve anything that brings anxiety. A guard may be hired to keep something in as well as to keep something out. Sometimes guards function in both ways. In this case, the guard prohibits the "hearts and minds" from escaping and getting out of control. Specifically, the

---

[536] Some have suggested this is peace God bestows at conversion, "peace with God" as mentioned in Rom 5:1 (O'Brien, 496). Others wish to relate it to the Euodia-Syntyche conflict in this context. Neither seems to satisfy the demands of the text.

[537] Paul used it twenty times. It is only found three times in the NT outside the Pauline writings. The variety of meanings in Paul include: "the faculty of intellectual perception . . . a way of thinking, mind, attitude . . . or the result of thinking, mind, thought, opinion, decree." Keown, *Philippians 2:19–4:23*, 351.

heart and thoughts may entertain ideas that damage a Christian's relationship to Christ. The heart speaks to the inner person, though often it is the "place" of values that inform and feed the will (choices). The thoughts are the out-workings of the mind, which can be consistent with Christian belief or a regression to former non-Christian ways of thinking. Either or both are dangerous since they can lead a person to act improperly and embrace the anxieties that arise. The peace of God allows its recipient to live above the circumstances, confident in the God who provides it. For these reasons, prayerful people are peaceful people.

4:8–9 Paul turned his thoughts to providing an environment of peace by unified and focused thought. The church was to make these matters its collective goal. If they did, God would rule in them. Individual Christians also were to conduct their lives in this way. This speaks to the need of rearranging life and thought through discipline so that the God of peace can freely work.[538]

It was noted these verses speak to proper focus. Following these instructions provides a spiritual environment that calms the mind and provides an environment in which the God of peace can produce his work. Within this focus, there are two different emphases, noted by the grammar as well as vocabulary. First, there is a contrast between parts of speech. In the first part, the qualities are described with adjectives ("true," "honorable," "just," "pure," "lovely," "commendable"). It is unclear what the adjectives modify here other than the abstract "whatever." In the second part, 4:9, Paul describes what to value by use of verbs found in separate clauses. There are two clauses ("if . . . any moral excellence; if anything . . . praiseworthy") which serve as *protasis* ("if") in a first class conditional sentence with "dwell" as the apodosis ("then"). The sentence has the sense of "assuming there is any moral excellence and assuming (if) there is anything praiseworthy, then dwell on these things." The grammatical difference between the sentences of vv. 8–9 lies in the adjectives and verbal clauses. Second, there is a contrast in the two primary commands that complement each other. Verse 8 urges the believers "to count on" or, as CSB says, to "dwell." The verb speaks to the mind. The mind is to be disciplined to explore the qualities identified. Verse 9 urges the believers to "do"

---

[538] The former, 4:6–7, seems to speak to occasions of outbreaks of anxiety. This speaks to ordering a personal environment to prohibit such outbreaks.

(that is, practice) the life patterns they have observed in their mentors. This difference is between exploring the depths of positive things and doing, that is, forming habits of life. Both proper thinking and living provide the atmosphere of peace.

These verses have a definite structure. They contain two lists, each with its own verb. The first list (4:8) provides objects with the main verb "think about such things" (*logizesthe*). The word indicate far more than a simple thought, to "think on these things." The church was to count on these things and to chart its course according to them. The CSB translates it "dwell on these things." The second list (4:9) has multiple objects described in verbs ("learned, received, heard, seen") and completes the verb "put into practice" (*prassete*). The CSB translates it with the simple "do" (these things). By using these two verbs, dwell and do, Paul combined the mental and ethical concerns of his Jewish background with Christian thought. For him, knowledge always led to responsible Christian living. Some scholars point out many secular moral philosophers could have produced the lists in 4:8 since there is little distinctive to Christianity. These scholars suggest Paul probably borrowed them because he seldom used many of these terms. True, Paul may have discovered a list of virtues which was acceptable to him, but the motivations and resources to develop these qualities in a Christian manner come only from the Holy Spirit who produces such fruit within.

The question of borrowing or even sharing contemporary vocabulary, or lists in this case, has been much discussed. Beare states the case strongly and representatively:

> It is almost as if he had taken a current list from a textbook of ethical instruction, and made it his own; these are nothing else than the virtues of the copybook maxims. It follows that Paul had come to recognize that there was a genuine capacity for moral discernment in the pagan society around him, and that the things which were counted as honourable [sic] by good men everywhere were in fact worthy of honour [sic], worthy to be cultivated by a Christian believer.[539]

---

[539] Beare, *The Epistle*, 148. Many accept this type of conclusion. If Paul did borrow a philosophical list and approve it, that does not mean Christians should cultivate the qualities of the pagan society around them. Surely Paul Christianized the list.

It would not be necessarily un-Christian to borrow in such a way. It is customary for Paul to recognize good behavior. He noted everyone is capable of it to some degree since all are created in the image of God. Christ followers, of course, have the indwelling power of the Holy Spirit to develop these traits and to exercise them for the glory of God. Yet there are weaknesses with the argument that suggest they come from secular sources. Witherington, III, states, "There are no Hellenistic or Roman virtue lists that are closely parallel in content to this one."[540] Bockmuehl notes "that missing in action here are the four cardinal Greek virtues of prudence, justice, courage, and self-control."[541] Others have looked to the LXX for evidence of Paul's quotation of existing material. Most of the words in this list are found in the LXX and have become part of Jewish aspirations. Even so, there are no lists with these words included. It is possible Paul appeals to either Stoic philosophy's ideals or to Jewish qualities, but there can be no certainty. Regardless of the origin of the lists, these have become Christianized in Paul's encouragement to the church.

The literary style of 4:8–9 is unusual. The structure of v. 8 reveals quick, staccato like utterances that surely means Paul's thoughts flowed quickly. The first six characteristics are introduced with the pronoun "whatever" (*osa*) and all end with the "a" sound (either *η* or *α* in Greek). They have strong rhetorical impact. They are in apposition to and explain the words "these things" which occurs at the end of the sentence. The list of "these things" is reduced to six attributes. As noted above, the six statements are followed by two parallel clauses beginning with "if there . . .." Greek grammar indicates they are both indefinite and together provide the first part (protasis, "if") of a first-class conditional sentence. The condition is completed (apodosis, "then") with the indicative command "count ("dwell") on these things (*logizesthe*). The basic sentence is: "Assuming there is moral excellence (and there is) and assuming there is anything praiseworthy (and there is), dwell on these things, (that is, specifically) whatever is true, whatever is honorable, whatever is just, whatever is pure,

540 Witherington, III, *Paul's Letter*, 250. He continues, however, "Paul appears to believe that virtue should be recognized and affirmed wherever one finds it."

541 Bockmuehl, *A Commentary*, 251.

whatever is lovely, whatever is commendable." The first class conditional sentence strengthens Paul's statement.[542]

Verse 9 has a similar literary power. The primary verb is "do," which translates a word generally meaning "practice" (*prasso*) and provides a connotation of discipline or focus. What they are to do is explained by a clause introduced by one pronoun, "what," but includes four verbal ideas within it: "what you have learned and received and heard from me, and seen in me" (CSB). "From me" goes with "learned and received and heard" and "in me" goes with "seen," occurring at the end. "From me" is inserted by the CSB to better explain the logic of Paul's statement. Its placement separates what Paul taught from how Paul lived ("they saw"). His appeal throughout the letter is for them to follow him in following Christ. He was their spiritual father in every way.

Paul addressed the thought life first in 4:8. He identified eight qualities that should characterize Christians. "True," (*alethe*) in the ethical sense as used here, indicates "truthfulness, dependability."[543] "Honorable" (*semna*) translates a rare word which has a broad meaning. Used primarily by Paul in the Pastoral Epistles, it reflects the notion of "worthy of respect, honor, noble."[544] It is primarily used of church leaders where various persons are urged to be respectable. "Just" (*dikaia*) implies giving to God and people the integrity that is due them. It is the characteristic of doing right. This definition differs from Paul's normal use, but it well describes the ideal Christian virtue. "Pure" translates a word meaning "pure" or "holy" in relation to God (*hagna*). "Lovely," found only here in the NT, has a fundamental meaning of "that which calls forth love" (*prosphile*).[545] It covers a host of qualities but basically indicates "attractive, lovable." "Commendable" (*euphema*) also occurs only here in the NT, and it means whatever is "praiseworthy, attractive,"[546] therefore not likely to offend. "Moral excellence" (*arete*) was seldom used by Paul, but in 1 Pet 2:9 and 2 Pet 1:3, 5 the same Greek term describes Christian

---

[542] The first class condition is often thought to indicate certainty and is translated "since . . . . " Not all first class conditions are, however (cf. Matt 12:27). The better translation is "assuming . . . then." The assumption is considered true for logical purposes. Of the four conditional sentences in Koine Greek, this is the condition that most expresses reality.

[543] BAGD, 36.

[544] BAGD, 746–47.

[545] Hawthorne, *Philippians*, 188.

[546] BAGD, 327.

virtue. Finally, "praiseworthy" (*epainos*) means "worthy of praising God" or capable of being appreciated by others. In a Christian perspective, the two blend. These characteristics would unite the church and present a good testimony to the world.

After presenting the standard for the spiritual life, Paul turned to Christian practice in 4:9. The church was to cultivate the things it heard from and saw exemplified by Paul. Four words emphasize this as Paul continues with lists. They should give attention to what they learned, received, heard, and saw in Paul. Three of these terms describe what they would have observed in him in person: "learned," "received," and "seen." One describes what could or may not have required physical presence: "heard." Since the four are listed in parallel, it is best to take all four together emphasizing the completeness of how they nurtured the church. Both words and actions teach. Paul was obviously at Philippi when he founded the church. The tumultuous times surely taught them significantly about being like Christ as they both interacted with and saw Paul. As far as we know, later he would have traveled through Philippi as he made his way through Macedonia. Again, the theme of imitation predominates. In Paul's brief visits they observed his lifestyle. Perhaps including his comments in 3:1–17, Paul urged them to use him as a model of effective Christian living. This kind of living results in the God of peace being with them.

Paul disclosed one of his principles of discipleship. The church would grow by observing Paul in various circumstances in person, by letter, or by reports from other Christians. Implicitly, Paul was confident in his relationship with the Lord. His radical conversion further impacted by Jesus's presence in difficulties affirmed his belief in the risen Lord as God's Son. His life so devoted to Christ was an adequate model for Christian living.

Much of Philippians is filled with the words and concepts of Jesus's kenosis (2:6–11). The words encourage the readers to be like Jesus in their own lives. This list of eight characteristics, however, does not resemble 2:5–11. These are qualities that could have been discussed by the general populous of the day. Philosophers could have taught them; learners could have emulated them. They were commendable. Subtly, Paul teaches that God desires this focus of his followers since he dwells with those who can truly value them. Since Paul links them with his own experience, and his thoughts throughout the letter are

Christocentric, doubtless Paul believed these characteristics were actualized as a result of the power of Christ in the life.

Often Paul greeted his friends with a prayer for peace, such as in the salutation of this letter (1:2). In this passage the means to the answer of that prayer appear. God's peace especially resides in those who have ordered their lives in accordance with God's will. This includes proper and disciplined thinking and good Christian living. Thus, the two sets of instructions on peace complement each other. When anxiety arises, the cure is prayer. When the life is disorderly, the cure is mental, practical, and focused discipline.

This section ends the body of the letter. Paul has comforted them regarding his situation in Rome, has urged them to unity unlike the divided Roman church(es), has refuted false teaching by using the example of his own life, has spoken to the problem of Euodia and Syntyche, and has urged them to live in peace through prayer and proper focus. One more subject remains. He must thank them for their financial gift. He does so in more length than seems necessary. Paul, however, is the constant theologian, thinking of motivations behind actions and the theological impact actions reveal. Furthermore, the church at Philippi was the only one who supported him as they did.

Theological and Practical Points

Peace. Nothing so satisfies as peace! Everyone has times of stress. Sometimes circumstances produce unsettledness. Political, economic, and cataclysmic events often bring restlessness about life and the future. Inward turmoil also produces lack of peace. Life is sometimes beset by broken relationships, wayward children, disease, and mental/emotional frustrations. Everyone lives in a fallen world shaped too often by the hardships of life rather than the joys the Creator intended to receive focus.

Paul faced the same kinds of issues. At first he was successful in politics, but his Jewish world turned upside down with his conversion to Christ. Throughout his life after that, Jews oppressed him. Rome was no friend. He had a long and strong Roman heritage. He was a citizen! Yet Rome disdained controversy, particularly in its cities. And outside of Judea, Jews had no recourse to bring their charges against Paul except to appeal to Rome. Judicial hearings absolved Paul of criminal activity at first, but he lived his life under the scrutiny of a powerful, skeptical government. It would eventually bring his life to an end. Constant travel was expensive and temporary relocation in new places difficult. Paul learned to be without (4:11–13), having to earn his way with the team God provided. His exposures caused physical sickness (2 Cor 1:8–11). His ministry sometimes brought physical persecution (Acts 14:19; 2 Cor 12:7; 2 Cor 11:24–29) and calamity (Acts 27:13–44). At times he was alone when he wanted friends nearby (2 Tim 4:11–18). Those from whom he expected encouragement sometimes opposed him unnecessarily (Phil 1:12–14). He had every reason to be without peace! Even so, writing out of the background of his varied experiences, he exhorted the church to welcome the unique peace of God in their lives and the congregation.

Paul used the word peace (*eirene*) forty-two times.[547] Its importance is often overlooked largely because readers assume the English and the Greek emphases are primarily the same. While the breadth of the connotations of peace may be similar, the contexts in which peace occur have deeper significance in Paul's writings. The secular Greek concept of peace, Foerster explains, did "not primarily denote a relationship between several people, or an attitude, but a state, i.e., 'time of peace' or 'state of peace,' originally conceived of purely as an interlude in the everlasting state of war."[548] While it may at times signify an attitude of peace, tranquility, it was primarily used of relationships among warring nations or the emperor and his people. Paul employs the word in a similar way but broadens it by the implications that peace brings to the believer.

At the most foundational level, it should be noted peace is a quality of God. That seems patently obvious, but it is worth exploring. For God to be peace implies several truths.

(1) Where God rules things will have proper order, therefore peace. Fallen earth does not see universal peace and therefore does not see the visible reign of God. According to Col 1:20, however, God was pleased "through [Christ] to reconcile everything to himself, whether things on earth or things in heaven, by making peace through his blood, shed on the cross." The words "reconcile" and "making peace" indicate God's intent ultimately is a cosmic reign of order. This means every aspect of

---

[547] Examples appear in the Gk. behind Rom 9; 1–2 Cor 6; Gal 3; Phlm 3; 1–2 Tim 3; Col 2; and Titus 1.

[548] Werner Foerster, TDNT accessed through Logos Bible Software. Paul sometimes used the word "silence" (*sigao*, *σιγάω*) when speaking of the need for harmony in group relationships. See, for example, 1 Cor 14:28, 30, 34.

creation (human, supernatural—angels/demons, and material) will be put into a proper relationship to Christ and therefore to God.[549] When that reconciliation takes place, there will be peace. Through Christ's sacrifice, there is a restoration of peace, bringing creation into alignment with what it was before sin entered the world with the exception that rebellion will be silenced and punished. The movement in Colossians resembles and echoes that of the movement in the Christ poem of Phil 2:6–11. Particularly, both move from harmony to disharmony and back to harmony with the cross as central.

(2) Christ and God (the Father) have and share peace. One central characteristic of deity is peace—proper order. The trinitarian relationships among Father, Son, and Spirit are bonded by peace and love. Peace is more passive, while love is the more dynamic. Their perfect unity manifests itself in perfect order and peace.

(3) The peace found in the Trinity is shared with believers. Paul's common prayer "Grace to you and peace from God our Father and the Lord Jesus Christ" (1:2) contains a deeper request than that the saints will feel good. That will be discussed below.

(4) The peace offered by God is not of this world. Jesus promised his disciples, "My peace I give to you. I do not give to you as the world gives" (John 14:27). This means more than a promise of tranquility that may be somewhat—and at some times—mixed with trouble. It is peace of a quality unknown by human minds and hearts. Paul echoes this in Phil 4:7 with the "peace of God, which surpasses all understanding." Such otherworldliness is also described in Eph 3:19 in extolling the amazing love of Christ.

Gaining such peace puts the believer into harmony—the proper order—with God and his intent in creation: that all creation would glorify him. Salvation is about that peace. Paul stated in Rom 3:23 that all persons are sinners. Quoting Isa 59:7–8 he said in Rom 3:17, "the path of peace they have not known." Their disorder is because there is no fear of God among them. With more positive news, Rom 5:1 states of Christ followers, "Since we have been justified by faith, we have peace with God through our Lord Jesus Christ." Described as the first and overarching benefit to believers, this is "peace *with* God," not the "peace *of* God." Through Christ's sacrifice God declares the

---

[549] This does not mean everyone and everything will be "saved." It does mean through Christ's blood those who accept him will be saved and those who reject will be punished. Both imply a proper relationship to Christ given the choices made.

believer innocent (justified) and therefore restored to the harmony God originally intended. Paul prays, "May peace come to all those who follow this standard," living as the new creation (Gal 6:16).

Peace with God brings peace with others, particularly believers. Christ "is our peace" (Eph 2:14–17) and creates "in himself one new man from the two, resulting in peace." Since believers have been made partakers of God's peace, they should relate to each other the way God relates to himself: there is order among the three persons of the Trinity. It is no wonder, then, that the "fruit of the Spirit is . . . peace" (Gal 5:22); that God has called believers to live in peace (1 Cor 7:15); that believers should exert effort to "keep the unity of the Spirit through the bond of peace" (Eph 4:3); and that all believers are to pursue it (2 Tim 2:22). In Christ the believer is opened to the same qualities that characterize the Godhead. As the visible body of Christ, the church is to look like God.

Sin temporarily disrupts peace in the universe. Similarly, disorder interferes with the believer's intentions of being what God desires. Group dynamics may fail to reflect true unity (Rom 14:17; 1 Cor 7:15). The church must constantly be reminded that "God is not of disorder but of peace" (1 Cor 14:33), that "the peace of Christ" should rule in the heart (Col 3:15), and that it is necessary to "pursue what promotes peace" (Rom 14:19). Individual fears and concerns may also disrupt the peace that should characterize believers. That concerned Paul as he admonished the Philippians: "Don't worry about anything," then noting the "peace of God" will guard the heart and mind through prayer and thanksgiving (4:6–7, see the previous discussion). Similarly, Jesus warned about anxiety (Matt 6:25–34). He also stated the challenge to his peace in his disciples is "trouble" (John 14:27). The answer to both personal and group difficulties is to allow the peace of God to reign individually and corporately. Finally, one of Paul's most common expressions is to associate God with peace, such as "the God of peace." The "God of peace will soon crush Satan" (Rom 16:20) whose energies are directed explicitly toward God's order of peace in the universe. The God of peace will "sanctify you completely" (1 Thess 5:23) and "[m]ay the Lord of peace himself give you peace always in every way" (2 Thess 3:16). These representative texts call to mind the sovereignty of God and one of his most prized attributes: peace. These last two are also found in the common salutation of praying for God and Christ to give peace.

There is a rich context for the two verses in Philippians that speak directly about peace. Philippians 4:7 uniquely associates peace with human anxiety. This is unusual for Paul and is his only reference to individual anxiety. The word, however, is sometimes correctly translated as "care" as found in 2:20. In anxiety, the cares of this world so occupy the mind that even the believer fails to experience God's proper order (peace). Though called to peace, and placed there by the work of Christ, ambivalence often comes from existence in this unreconciled world. Christians may lose confidence that in Christ believers belong to and live in the orderly environment secured for them by Christ's death and resurrection. But through prayer, with thanksgiving, perspective may be restored and confidence in God's control reaffirmed. The recognition of "peace with God" brings with it the "peace of God" that triumphs over everything else. It is peace not fully understood by the human heart and mind, but which dominates them both, bringing awareness of God's control through Christ. The negative emotions caused by disorder are overcome by the positive emotions of rightness that emerges from within. That is the peace of God.

The second text is 4:9: "the God of peace will be with you." Typical of most references to God in Scripture, "God" is modified by a designation of one of his attributes. Here, God is the God of perfect and proper order whose presence applies that order to those seeking it. Believers will recognize themselves to be within the environment of God's peace again. Philippians 4:8–9 lead to the promise of God's presence. As noted above, in the commentary on those verses, the verses contain lists of qualities to seek in life and encouragement as to how to attain them (following those who seek the same). Focusing on these things brings excellence in living. Inasmuch as Paul locates them in a Christian context, they result in the God of peace being "with" his people. Thus, the degree to which one lives in that way is the degree to which one experiences divine order. God progressively reorders the life to bring peace—the ability to live characterized by the same peace that is found resident in the Father and the Son.

4 CONCLUDING MATTERS: EXPRESSION OF THANKS FOR THE PHILIPPIANS' SUPPORT (4:10–20)

SECTION OUTLINE

- 4.1 Paul's Situation (4:10–14)
  - 4.1.1 Appreciation (4:10)
  - 4.1.2 Contentment (4:11)
  - 4.1.3 Adaptability (4:12)
  - 4.1.4 Dependency (4:13)
  - 4.1.5 Blessing (4:14)
- 4.2 Paul's Attitude Toward Those Who Gave (4:15–20)
  - 4.2.1 Commendation (4:15–17)
  - 4.2.2 Blessings (4:18–19)
  - 4.2.3 Doxology (4:20)

Theological and Practical Points

The final section of the letter addresses finances. Paul thanked the Philippians for remembering him and his needs, as they had before. Because of their pattern of giving, they were a double blessing. Typical of Paul, he used this occasion to teach the church spiritual truths. An introductory statement of thanks led to an explanation of Paul's outlook on things. This was followed by identifying some of the benefits (*blessings*) for those who gave.

Several factors point to this as a change in thought, different from 4:1–9. First, as is obvious, the subject of the section is Paul. The grammar changes from second person subject to first (from "you" to "I"). Second, he uses the transitional conjunction "but" (*de*) which both continues the thought and often, for Paul, introduces a new direction.[550] Third, the repetition of "in the Lord" is a transition marker (4:1, 2, 10) in this chapter. This time the phrase differs from the other two, however. It changes from the environment of his exhortations to his own personal joy because he is "in the Lord." Fourth, Paul moves from discussing their situation to revealing his. Fifth, he picks up the subject introduced in 1:5: joy resulting from their partnership in ministry from the beginning.

Having noticed these factors, however, it is worth noting the context in which most of 4:10–22 occurs. The section under discussion clearly reveals Paul's thankfulness, the church's concern for Paul, and at a deeper level a partial theology of money. Following the movement

---

[550] The conjunction is not always translated.

of the letter, Paul's immediately previous commands to the church involved securing God's peace in the midst of anxiety. Perhaps nothing causes worry more than concern for finances. Jesus, of course, addressed anxiety as including other aspects of life, but a significant portion of his teachings involve the proper understanding and use of money. The Philippians may have shared some anxiety. Paul notes the rock bottom poverty of the churches of Macedonia (2 Cor 8:1–2). In general, Philippi was economically stable, though not to the degree of the time of its founding, the days of gold mines and abundant physical resources. For some reason(s), Paul stressed having peace through prayer and proper focus, reinforced by his own experience. It could be Paul's disclosure of his sufficiency in Christ came directly from the possible lack of peace among some in the church family.

Without diminishing Paul's deep appreciation for the church's financial support, more is involved than simply finances here. Social patterns predominate in how Paul relates to the Philippians. The church is more than a financial supporter. The letter reveals that friendship among the parties permeates Paul's communication and theirs to him. They communicated by sending emissaries with a financial gift, including most recently Epaphroditus. Perhaps they also communicated by letter as was often the case. Either form of communication was done by courier, professional or personal, and Paul would have responded in the same way. Communication could take up to two months round trip. Despite the relative difficulty of such communication, the fact that it occurred revealed strong commitment between the apostle and the believers at Philippi.

Both the style and content of this communication reveals friendship based on social norms of the day. This would, of course, be expected in ancient times, but is not always understood with more modern forms of communication.

4.1 Paul's Situation (4:10–14)

[10] I rejoiced in the Lord greatly because once again you renewed your care for me. You were, in fact, concerned about me but lacked the opportunity to show it. [11] I don't say this out of need, for I have learned to be content in whatever circumstances I find myself. [12] I know how to make do with little, and I know how to make do with a lot. In any and all circumstances I have learned the secret of being content—whether well fed or hungry, whether in abundance or in need.

[13] I am able to do all things through him who strengthens me.[14] Still, you did well by partnering with me in my hardship.

Structure

[10] I rejoiced in the Lord greatly
because once again you renewed your care for me.

You were, in fact, concerned about me
but lacked the opportunity to show it.

[11] I don't say this out of need,
for I have learned to be content in whatever circumstances I find myself.
[12] I know how to make do with little,
and I know how to make do with a lot.

I have learned the secret of being content
in any and all circumstances
—whether well fed or hungry,
whether in abundance or in need.

[13] I am able to do all things
through him who strengthens me.

[14] Still, you did well by partnering with me in my hardship.

Interpretation

4.1.1 Appreciation (4:10)

Apparently, some time elapsed between gifts from the Philippian church since Paul said "once again you renewed your care for me." The expression implies the culmination of a time interval now concluded. [551] It may have been years between the gifts mentioned in 2 Cor 8 and the one delivered by Epaphroditus. Perhaps Paul had despaired of their love for him since so much time elapsed and since they were the ones who remembered him financially. A financial gift uniquely expressed love. Their gift was a cause of joy in the Lord. In that light, it should be noted Paul does not mention a gift specifically until Phil 4:15, which he refers to as "giving and receiving," and more specifically with the word "gifts" in 4:16. He couched his appreciation in the deeper significance of their gift: their care for him (4:10 twice)

[551] BAGD, 344.

and their partnership in Paul's hardship (4:14). Even so, in this text several synonyms for gift occur: care and concern (4:10), partnering (4:14), giving and receiving (4:15), gifts (4:16), and what you provided (4:18). Paul's thoughts are stirred by their financial support. Nevertheless, spiritual relationships brought the most satisfaction: their love for him because of Christ's love and his love for the Lord and for them. It was natural for a material gift to become an occasion for Christian joy. The Christian nature of this relationship is supported by the word Paul used for concern. It is the key verb of the epistle, *phroneo*. Twice it occurs in 4:10: "your care (*phonein*) for me," and "concerned (*phroneo*) about me." Paul used it consistently to point out proper Christian attitudes in following the mind of Christ. He consciously alluded to that in his choice of the word.

Although some time elapsed between the gifts, Paul remained in the Philippians' thoughts. He explained they were mindful of him all along (the same verb occurs, *phroneo*), but they lacked opportunity. The lack was that Paul did not have need, but some interpret it as the church's inability to provide what they desired because of their poverty (2 Cor 8). According to 2 Cor 8:2, "extreme poverty" was not an obstacle to their sending financial support since they gave in spite of their economic distresses. They created the opportunity to give by sending Epaphroditus as their minister to Paul. This was no small undertaking. Presumably they provided Epaphroditus with enough money (or some equivalent way to get money) to cover his travel, lodging, and food as he journeyed, and funds to sustain him while he visited Paul in Rome. Since Epaphroditus was sent to minister to Paul while he was under house arrest, it would obviously be counter to his purpose to live from funds they directed to Paul. The Pauline team lived primarily by paying their own way. The persons identified as his companions were spiritually gifted in ministry, but most had some means of immediate profitable work. Each would most likely have expertise in some profession or craft that could be recognized and valuable wherever they traveled in the empire. Paul modeled this by using his father taught trade of being a canvas worker, so it is likely Epaphroditus had some skill that could be quickly negotiated to bring immediate financial support. That does not diminish the amount or value of the Philippians' gift to Paul. No matter what, sending Epaphroditus on the 800-mile journey one way would require sacrifice, but that did not derail their giving. Their lack of opportunity likely came from Paul's situation, which best explains the reference. This is affirmed by his later explanation of his own attitudes amid the fluctuations of life.

Paul was sympathetic of them. On one hand, lest some misunderstand him as being too critical, he explained they had no occasion to give.[552] On the other hand, the phrase translated "You were, in fact, concerned" is introduced by a causal construction (*eph ho kai*), meaning "you have renewed your concern for me *because* you have been concerned."[553] Rather than a rebuke, this makes Paul's situation the reason they could not respond and implies they wanted to give all along.

Paul's statement did not reflect his own need. He had learned to be at home with whatever God supplied to him. He stated three reasons why and how he fared well even without their gifts.

4.1.2 Contentment (4:11)

The first reason Paul did not need the gift was his own contentment. Twice in these verses he stated he had learned contentment. He used two different words as synonyms. The first Greek word "learned" (*emathon*) conveys the general sense of education. It speaks to having arrived at a place of understanding, and implies arriving after a process of growth. In this case, the learning would have come from his experiences traveling to promote the gospel. From what we know of Paul, the lesson learned came after his conversion to Christ. It was a Christian principle. As Jews with inherited citizenship, Paul's family would have been financially secure. They were apparently able to support their son in his studies, including sending him to Jerusalem to study under Gamaliel. His pre-conversion life was likely one of some privilege on which he built his own reputation. If Paul had to learn contentment, the assumption is his source of family support was curtailed. His commitment to Christ took him away from the historical family faith. Often one who deserted Judaism was considered reprobate and the privileges of family were withdrawn. Paul did not

---

[552] Caird, *Paul's Letters*, expresses the idea of many by interpreting this as, "You lacked the means" (153). Silva, *Philippians*, 231–32, suggests the awkwardness of the passage is partly cultural, in that we do not understand their ways, and partly circumstantial. The awkwardness also comes in the natural difficulty of expressing thanks without asking for more.

[553] The construction occurs four times in Paul's writing, and each time it appears to make a correction of thought (Rom 5:12; 2 Cor 5:4; Phil 3:12; 4:10). See BAGD, 235.2, 123.

consider himself to have renounced Judaism, however. He saw Jesus as the continuation of Israel's history and messianic hopes. Rather than departing the faith, Paul understood that he lived in the fulfillment of it. Of course, most Jews did not see Christianity that way.[554] In short, confessing Christ likely meant, for Paul, the loss of family support. As a Christian, he learned what he did not as a Jewish Pharisee and possibly Sanhedrin member—but as a Christian. There would be hard times. Getting through them required more than personal will power and resolve. His source of strength was the Christ whom he loved and served.

The other word translated "learned" (*memyeμmai)* occurs in 4:12. The term is explained by its context in v. 12, but its contrast with "learned" in 4:11 makes it important to define here. The two words together continue to paint a picture of Paul's Christian situation rather than his pre-salvation one. The Greek word *memyeμmai* means to "learn the secret" and conveys the idea of a secret knowledge; for example, that to which adherents of the mystery religions, in particular, aspired.[555] It need not come through experiences, and in general lifted the recipient above experiences good or bad. Employing it here conveyed the nuance Paul desired. Contentment is learned only in part through experience. Paul used another rare word for "to be content." The etymology means "self-reliant" (*autarkes*),[556] and the context supports that meaning. It is self-sufficiency because of Christ, however, as Paul clearly stated in 4:13. He meant he came to grips with his circumstances and fared well in and through them because of his own relationship to Jesus. He did not need help from human sources since his understanding and application of spiritual resources provided what he needed.[557]

In this verse Paul used terms well known outside of Christianity. The "secret" life lesson word used earlier employed a term most

---

[554] Paul's understanding is manifest in his preaching and writing (e.g., Rom 9–11; Eph 2:11–13). Historically it is significant and instructive that the earliest church was composed of primarily Jews. There was an overwhelmingly positive response to the apostles' preaching in Jerusalem, Judea, and in Gentile territory. By the time of Paul's Roman imprisonment, however, the balance between Jews and Gentiles in the church probably shifted to more Gentile.

[555] Paul may have deliberately chosen the word to explain in irony that Christians have their secrets too.

[556] BAGD, 122. It only occurs here in the NT.

[557] J. B. Lightfoot, *Saint Paul's*, 163, stated well that the meaning of the word ἀυτάρκης is "independence of external circumstances."

associated with the mystery religions. The word "self-reliant" was a favorite of the Stoic philosophers. Their ideal was to live unmoved by the circumstances of life. Achieving self-sufficiency was a highly praised and prized virtue. It referred to the will power to become detached from events and the fluctuations that occur in various situations. This meant to be removed from personal need as well as the needs of other people. Happiness involved emotional isolation from the joys and pains that accompany all relationships. Self-reliant meant to triumph by personal strength and resolve. Many Romans aspired to this Stoic ideal. As Fee notes, "Some Stoics may have reveled in 'want'; none of them would tolerate 'humiliation,' which often headed their lists of attitudes to be avoided."[558]

As Paul used the word "self-reliant," however, he removed self reliance from common associations. In this passage his self-reliant triumph was not in passively removing himself from the circumstances of life. He triumphed through and in them. At times he had need and at times he had plenty. His goal was not to remove himself from the impact of these external pressures and joys but to live in victory within and through them. In fact, it was the very issues of life that enabled him to be self-reliant. He "learned" through them, arrived at a disposition related to them and in many ways indebted to them.

4.1.3 Adaptability (4:12)

Circumstances were one arena of spiritual growth, and through them Paul developed adaptability. Adaptability was the second reason he gave for his lack of need. In this verse, Paul presented three contrasts that provided the occasion for learning and explained the nature of contentment. The first and last speak to physical needs in general, while the middle refers to food. In these varied experiences, Paul displayed spiritual equilibrium. He was equally unaffected by poverty and riches.

The text provides an interesting structure with, perhaps, veiled theological underpinnings. Paul's first contrast contains structural emphases that should be observed. (1) The contrasts occur in couplets:

[558] Fee, *Philippians*, 433. He continues, "Whether deliberately chosen over against them or not, and that is moot, for Paul this verb not only indicates 'poverty,' but embraces a way of life similar to that of his Lord (2:8; cf Matt 11:28), a way of life that finds expression elsewhere in his various "hardship lists."

"whether in abundance or in need"; "whether well fed or hungry"; "to make do with a little . . . to make do with a lot." (2) In each of the first two parts of the couplet, the situations are introduced by "I know" (*oida*), which does not occur with the other two couplets. (3) The first couplet has the lower situation mentioned first (make do with little); the next two couplets change the order so that the higher condition is mentioned first (well fed . . . in abundance). (4) The word abound occurs twice, once contrasted with humility and once contrasted with lack. (5) After the first couplet, the negative to positive order, the prepositional phrases "in any and all circumstances" (first singular then plural) occur followed by the two sets of couplets. These last two sets are presented positive to negative, the reverse of the first. They are "whether well fed or hungry, whether in abundance or in need."

How should this section be understood? The sense of it is obvious even to the casual reader, but the nuanced structure may call for more precise understanding. Paul provided first an overview statement followed by more specific detail. Thus, "I know how to make do with little, and I know how to make do with a lot" give the basics of his concern. This is shown by both the negative to positive couplet and the repetition of the verb "I know" with each member. The prominence of the negative may reflect the primary subject in his mind, that he is not speaking out "of need" (4:11). Rather, he knew how to live in this "humble" state of need, and Paul knew how to abound! Second, Paul stressed his knowledge throughout this section. Already he has used the verb "I learned" (4:11, "to be self-reliant"). He also referred to his knowledge as "the secret" (4:12). The repetition of "I know" indicates Paul learned his lesson well. His process of learning resulted in intellectual certainty (*oida*). He turned his experience of learning into a principle that he knew. He actually knew humility and abundance.[559]

The CSB translates this phrase as "I know how to make do with little." The actual Greek word behind the phrase means "to be humble." It is used as a description of Jesus after his incarnation and in his movement to death. After emptying himself by becoming human, he humbled himself becoming obedient to death on the cross (2:8). For

559 This is not based on the tense of οἶδα, which is perfect and may imply the changed state after some action. The verb is always used in the perfect tense with a present tense sense (at least in the NT). In this case, "I know" means Paul went through the process of learning (4:11) so that he actually learned.

Paul, adopting humility meant he was given the privilege of following the trajectory of Jesus in his movement to death. Paul does not speak of not having need. Rather, he speaks of their not having opportunity to address Paul's need. In fact, his need became the environment for learning Christ's sufficiency. Choosing the word "to humble" was hardly accidental. This is the first line of the couplet beginning "I know how to make do with little . . . ." The couplet continues, "I know how to make do with a lot." It replicates further the movements in Jesus's experience. As God "highly exalted [Jesus]," so Paul knew what it means to abound. "To make do with little" is more than a physical condition. While it certainly was prompted by the environment in which Paul found himself, it cannot be confined to that. As noted, this couplet introduced and covered the following two couplets which restate or in part explain it. So the pattern of Paul's thinking moves from need and humility to provision and abundance. The same sequence, though not in the same kind of experiences necessarily, occurred with Jesus.

Paul now moved to "the secret" he learned (see the previous discussion on the verb "learned"). It continues explaining how the general principle of humbling to abundance manifests itself. The environment is comprehensive, noted by the two prepositional phrases that introduce it: "[i]n any and all circumstances." Together they purposely focus on each individual aspect of life ("in any"), but also take the individual experiences together into a whole ("and all circumstances"). The statement is reminiscent of Paul's theological statement in Rom 8:28: "[A]ll things work together for good . . .." Approaching all of life with a conscious commitment to Christ as Lord brings "the secret." Unknown and unexperienced by non-believers, it is a Christian privilege and kingdom perspective. The secret is identified by both backward glances in the text and looking forward. In retrospect, Paul explained it as contentment. Looking ahead, it is defined by the two following couplets which reverse the previous pattern by stating the positive before the negative.

The rather subtle change from describing negative situations first to positive situations first may give a hint as to Paul's deeper understanding. Perhaps Paul continued to have in mind the account of Jesus's story on earth. He humbled himself, only to be exalted. For Paul, the ultimate humbling was in bowing to the Lord who conquered him on the Damascus Road. After that experience it was difficult to see himself as in real need. He followed his Lord who cared for him. Consequently, in the second and third couplets Paul's thoughts begin with victory, what his Lord provided. Beginning with food, he moves to a general statement of life situations. The three couplets together move from "make do with little" to "make do with a lot"; then from "well fed" to "hungry," followed by "abundance" to "need."

Life's lessons come from experience. Paul did not affirm here, nor does he teach elsewhere, that life will be free from need and hunger. He accepted both need and abounding as equal partners in his Christian experience. Both contributed to learning "the secret." The Philippians had no need to contribute to Paul and his well-being because of Paul's understanding of life. Both good times and hard times taught him how to rely on Christ. At a deeper, more foundational level, Paul expected his Christian pilgrimage would replicate that of Christ. Paul would progressively know Christ as he experienced power and suffering (Phil 3:10) as Jesus did.

This knowledge is learned by walking with the sufficient one and by developing a solid theology of material things. Things ultimately do not matter. Relationships do. Paul's attitude contrasted with the false teachers'. They were preoccupied with food and other earthly matters; Paul could rise above any set of circumstances.

4.1.4 Dependency (4:13)

Like most translations, the CSB says, "I am able to do all things through him who strengthens me." This is perhaps the most misunderstood and therefore misused verse in Philippians, if not the entire NT. The text involves two synonyms and a simple statement of relationships. The synonyms are the words for "power." First, Paul explains "[he is] strong to everything (*panta isxuo*)." Though it may be implied, there is no "to do" in this statement. It may be better to read this verse to say this:"I am strong related to all things."[560] The idea is better understood as enduring successfully. The verb "strengthens" connotes actual power in motion toward a given situation. Thus, "I am strong to all things" may be the more literal understanding. The actualized strength is toward "all things." The pronoun "all things" (note that

[560] The construction is the verb followed by the accusative case. The accusative focuses the action of the verb toward its object. The "all things" completes the verbal idea. It is not a locative idea ("in all things"), though that comes close to the contextual meaning.

"things" is supplied in English because the Greek nominative neuter plural is things rather than persons) demands some previous reference if it is available. Here it repeats the pronouns "any" and "all" of 4:12. These pronouns are explained in the text as "well fed or hungry . . . abundance or . . . need." Perhaps the better paraphrase of Paul's thought is this: "I am strong when feasting or in famine; when in abundance or in poverty." It is "the secret" (4:12) that makes this possible. It is strange to hear such an outstanding Christian describe his life as sometimes in need. Paul was no stranger to difficulty, nor was he a stranger to the power available to strengthen him in it.

Technically, the first word for power used in the verse means "I am strong." The second, a synonym, is the word "empowering" (*endunamounti*). Literally the phrase reads "in the one empowering me," from the second word for power, *dunamis*. This implies a latent power ready to be expressed but not necessarily already in action. It is available power to be applied according to need. Thus Paul is strong because of available power. The empowering comes from outside Paul, which is clear by the pronoun "me" that completes "strengthens." The source of Paul's power is not of his own making or ability. It comes from one empowering him. This construction involves location (locative case) and indicates "source."[561] Paul literally states "in the one who empowers me." This equals one of his favorite expressions "in Christ," so commonly used in Ephesians and Colossians in particular. The word "Christ" does not appear in the text. One could just as easily insert the word Jesus: "in Jesus who empowers me." In Philippians, however, Paul frequently refers to Jesus with his regnant title Christ. Paul also approached this subject previously, in 3:10, where he stated knowing Christ brings resurrection power and fellowship suffering. Perhaps even more relevant to the Philippian church was Paul's own experience of being beaten and incarcerated for the gospel. Hard times do come. This assurance is hardly the triumph many hope to have in Christ, that their problems will be erased. Rather, it promises the power to go through various experiences without failure.

Paul depended on Christ for strength. The expression "through him who strengthens me" refers to the indwelling Christ, and Paul

[561] Some may well interpret the Gk. preposition "in" as "by." The preposition is often used in an instrumental sense. That would not violate this text. Paul typically uses "in" with Christ in a locative sense rather than instrumental. In this text, the one empowering is Christ, therefore, this is the equivalent of "in Christ." It is often supplied by the translators.

could accomplish all that God wanted through the strength he provided. Some people abuse this verse by taking it out of context. They assume Paul was making a comprehensive statement about the spiritual abilities of a Christian. Some even act as if there were nothing they could not do. But Paul did not mean to suggest that. Two factors in the text reveal why. First, the passage discussed material and physical needs. In the day-to-day economic fluctuations, Paul knew stability that enabled him to rise above them. The rule of context means this must be applied to economic matters.[562] Second, Paul expressed his dependence on the power of the Lord. In this, he knew that where the Lord led him, he had power. The will of God limited the application of the strength he knew. Many who misapply this verse step out of God's will for their lives. They hope to cover their actions by a blanket promise of power, but power comes in the will of God. Thus, Paul expressed a crucial paradox. He was strong when he was weak! He was independent (self-sufficient) only when he was dependent! Although Paul realized the necessity of living in a Christian community, he also knew what it meant to face life's problems alone and still triumph through them.

It may be more difficult to triumph in the good times than in the bad. A Christian's victory comes from conscious dependence on the Lord and his power, after all, and that is sometimes easier understood when times get tough. One mark of maturity in Christ is knowing how to depend on the Lord in every situation of life, not only in those for which one assumes he or she needs help. Paul modeled this lesson for them; thus, even in his thankfulness he taught the truths of Christian living.

4.1.5 Blessing (4:14)

As a summary of this section, Paul reminded the readers their share in his work was good. The CSB translates this accurately: "[Y]ou did well by partnering with me in my hardship." Two important terms indicate the significance of their financial contribution to Paul. First, they participated with him. The Greek *sugkoinoneo* emphasizes that

[562] This does not directly refer to Paul's ministry, even though it was in the course of ministry he encountered these circumstances. It certainly does not apply to spiritual powers, although in some ways the principle remains. The apostle meant he could get along well in this life because of Christ.

participation. "Partnering" means a deep partnership of two going the same direction. This is heightened by the preposition "with" (*syn*), which has a perfective force here.[563] Second, Paul identified their partnership specifically as with his *thlipsis*. The term implies hardships of any kind, but it had a deeper significance for Paul.[564] In Col 1:24 he spoke of suffering "Christ's afflictions" (the same Greek word) so that his difficulties in spreading the gospel actually related to the Messiah.[565] In reflecting on his tribulations, Paul realized the eschatological significance of his ministry and that those who supported him participated in that. Their gifts evidenced their willingness to identify with the new era inaugurated by Jesus.

This expression contains the first hint of the significance of Christian giving. It also explains something of Paul's hesitancy in expressing his own needs to them. The Philippians recognized Paul's strategic place in the spread of the gospel, the mystery revealed to him (Eph 3:1–13). Others, particularly some of the Jewish Christians, had difficulty accepting Paul's ministry. The gifts from Philippi meant the church there eagerly participated in the work of God and their gifts were, in reality, contributions to the spread of the gospel to other Gentiles. Paul knew he would suffer because of his distinctive apostolic calling. He accepted this suffering joyfully and learned the secret of triumph over and in any circumstance. Paul's ministry simply provided an occasion for sharing in the gospel. He knew he handled sacred resources when gifts came from God's people (see Phil 4:18). Their gift was good because it demonstrated they understood God's working in the world and they willingly supported it.

4.2 Paul's Attitude toward Those Who Gave (4:15–20)

Paul's thankfulness turned to commendation and promise of reward. Both the nature of their giving and its motivation pleased the Lord.

---

[563] Such compounds may be directive, pointing to an object, or perfective, stressing the meaning of the verb. Here the perfective force comes through. It stresses a complete, deep partnership with Paul.

[564] BAGD, 362, says this is primarily about "the distress that is brought about by outward circumstances."

[565] See Col 1:24–29. There Paul expressed his call to fill up the tribulations of Jesus. In other words, he viewed his hardships as in themselves contributing to the spread of the messianic era brought in by Christ. The same word for hardship (afflictions- θλιψις) suggests his understanding here. See Melick, *Philippians*, 239–40.

[15] And you Philippians know that in the early days of the gospel, when I left Macedonia, no church shared with me in the matter of giving and receiving except you alone. [16] For even in Thessalonica you sent gifts for my need several times. [17] Not that I seek the gift, but I seek the profit that is increasing to your account. [18] But I have received everything in full, and I have an abundance. I am fully supplied, having received from Epaphroditus what you provided—a fragrant offering, an acceptable sacrifice, pleasing to God. [19] And my God will supply all your needs according to his riches in glory in Christ Jesus. [20] Now to our God and Father be glory forever and ever. Amen.

Structure

[15] And you Philippians know that . . . no church shared with me . . . except you alone
in the matter of giving and receiving
in the early days of the gospel,
when I left Macedonia
[16] For you sent gifts for my need several times
even in Thessalonica
[17] Not that I seek the gift,
but I seek the profit
that is increasing to your account.
[18] But I have received everything in full,
and I have an abundance.
I am fully supplied,
having received from Epaphroditus what you provided—a fragrant offering,
an acceptable sacrifice,
pleasing to God.
[19] And my God will supply all your needs
according to his riches in glory in Christ Jesus.
[20] Now to our God and Father be glory forever and ever. Amen.

Interpretation

4.2.1 Commendation (4:15–17)

4:15 Paul commended the church for the way it supported him. Its support was unique. It was the only Macedonian church to support him, at least in the early days. Paul referred to these as "early days of the gospel." The date was about AD 51, approximately eighteen years after Jesus's death and resurrection . The gospel had spread like wildfire in Jerusalem. Then it reached Judea and Samaria, and now toward the uttermost parts of the earth (following Acts 1:8). It is best to see the beginning of the gospel similarly to their "partnership in the gospel from the first day until now" (1:5). The beginning of the gospel in this context thus refers to the European mission, from Macedonia south. Philippi was the first place a church was planted in Macedonia. From there Paul moved down the Via Ignatia to Thessalonica, which was also in Macedonia. Athens and Corinth were further south. Paul disclosed one of the reasons he remembered the Philippians fondly "from the first day" (1:5).[566] When they first heard the gospel, they saw its implications for others and shared in its propagation. Since Paul committed his life to the progress of the gospel (1:12) and measured his success by the proclamation of it (1:18), their giving promoted a natural friendship. The early days in Macedonia had been difficult. Paul suffered physically in Philippi. In Thessalonica his work caused an uproar (1 Thess 2:9), which resulted in his departing the city (Acts 17:5–9). These difficulties were only external. Perhaps the greatest difficulty was that the other churches failed to help him. In describing this sad situation, Paul used the very strong negative "but not one" church (*oudemia* rather than "no church" as in CSB) partnered with him. In this, Philippi was different! From the very first it supported his work, evidencing the genuineness of salvation and love for Paul.

The other churches failed in their obligations to the gospel. Paul called the Philippian support a matter "of giving and receiving" (4:15). When he stated other churches did not support him, he used the common word for "fellowship" (*koinonia*) which so characterizes this book. Subtly and without complaining, Paul pointed out others had received but not given. They had a one-way relationship with the gospel. Paul expected rejection and loneliness in his work; it came as no surprise. He was, however, troubled for two reasons. First, when people received Christ, they had a responsibility to share. Second, those who did not missed the spiritual blessings that came from giving. The Philippians understood both principles and acted on them. That brought joy to Paul's heart.

[566] It is interesting Paul addressed the church personally, but he used a noun based on the Latin rather than the Gk.. His word is based on the Latin "*Philippenses*." Perhaps it was normal to use the Latin in addressing those of a Roman colony. There seems to be no reason other than that for its form here. In the opening salutation Paul used the Gk. Φιλίπποις rather than the Latin (cf. 1:1).

The apostle used two words to express the relationship between himself and the churches, particularly the church at Philippi. First, in 4:14 he recalls their partnership in his hardship. The word "partnering" is the common word in Philippians usually translated "fellowship" (*sugkoinoneo*). Their gift evidenced a reciprocal partnership with Paul's hardship. In a sense, what he felt they felt, and they wanted to demonstrate that to him. Paul commonly used the word translated "hardship" (*thlipsis*) of the difficult circumstances he encountered. The word is singular. Paul viewed the individual events as though they were in one group. His hardship was the entire trip to and time in Rome.[567]

Second, he described the subject he addressed as "giving and receiving." Using both words, rather than simply "giving" (that is, supporting) implied mutuality. As John Barclay has well explained, gifts in the ancient world were seldom pure gifts. Givers expected a return in some form, though perhaps not of the same kind as the gift.[568] "Against modern notions of 'altruism' . . . benefits were generally intended to foster mutuality, by creating or maintaining social bonds."[569] Consequently, "giving and receiving" was a technical way of introducing the expected response of the church to Paul. Even perhaps unknowingly, the church had entered that sociological relationship with its founder, quite apart from the spiritual bond that existed. Paul used the technical term *logos*, best translated as this "matter," to identify the subject with them. *Logos* often has business or financial overtones.

In light of the context of Paul's letter and the history of the Macedonian churches, one would expect Paul to say the matter of "receiving and giving" rather than "giving and receiving." Paul did not stress his activity as the gift but in this context was centered on their gift response to him. He preached the gospel, which they received. The gospel may be considered a gift Paul offered the churches, and so his work was to their benefit. At a deeper level, Paul brought the gift of

[567] It is quite possible Paul viewed his hardship as an ongoing part of his ministry from his conversion. He was told he would suffer (see Acts 9). It seems best to limit hardship here to the time of his first relationship to those in Philippi. He is expressing gratitude for the friendship evidenced by the gift.

[568] John M. G. Barclay, *Paul and the Gift* (Grand Rapids: William B. Eerdmans Publishing Company, 2015), 11–65, explains responding to a gift was a universal expectation in the ancient Greco-Roman world.

[569] Barclay, 562.

the gospel from God himself, emphasizing that they received God's gift. Their primary responsibility was to acknowledge God as the giver and respond properly to him with a gift of some type. Paul explained the Philippians' gift to him related to that responsibility.

Earlier, Paul's third missionary journey had a major emphasis on collecting gifts to send to the Jerusalem church. Judea had suffered a famine in the mid-40s AD, and many Jews still struggled economically even though ten years had passed. Paul's clearest presentation of his motivation and expectations of Christians is found in 2 Cor 8–9. He commends the churches of Macedonia for their generosity in deep poverty. They, primarily the church at Philippi, became a model of giving, which is consistent with Paul's commendation here. The 2 Corinthians text reveals some of Paul's understanding of the responsibility Gentiles had to Jews. The latter brought the Christ into the world. All Christians benefited from that, and one part of the Gentile Christian response was to give to the Jews in their need.

Several of Paul's expressions and instructions relate to this idea of "giving and receiving." Again, 2 Cor 8–9 illustrates. Consistently, Paul calls giving an "act of grace" (e.g., 8:6–7). He thus locates their benevolence as part of the grace gift category. Additionally, the gift was evidence of their love (cp. 8:9). It was a tangible completion of their love for distant Christians. Thus, Paul thanked them for their love by putting it in the form of a gift.

Paul's circumstances in Rome differed from the hardship of the Jews in Judea. Yet, the appreciation for the Philippians' gifts to him may be best explained by his words to Corinth. The gift was an act of grace, evidence of God's grace operative in their lives. Further, it was the tangible expression and fulfillment of their love for Paul. Finally, it was the natural response from those who had received. Other churches fell short of both social and spiritual obligations and opportunities. Paul did not seem to press blame here. He simply recounted the facts. His purpose was to commend the church family in Philippi and to thank them for all their gift meant.

4:16 Paul also commended them because their support was immediate and consistent. He remembered they supported him "in Thessalonica," the city he had entered after being asked to leave Philippi. Paul was in Thessalonica for three Sabbaths only (Acts 17:2). Because of the public nature of the Jewish reaction to Paul's message, some consider the "three Sabbath days" to be longer than three consecutive weeks. In Thessalonica there was a public trial which suggests significant time for the accusers to gain popular support for their accusations.[570] The normal way to read this text, however, is three consecutive Sabbaths, three chronological weeks, suggesting there was a sudden, strong, and serious objection to Paul's message. Even in the short time Paul was in Thessalonica, the Philippian church sent at least two support offerings to assist Paul and his mission, indicating the reality of the Philippian church's conversion to Christ, their immediate love for Paul, and their understanding of the Pauline mission. Paul's statement in Phil 4:10 reveals that, at some time, their support ceased. Perhaps they stopped when Paul left Thessalonica or Berea and went to Athens alone. Their resumed giving enhanced Paul's joy ten years later when Paul was in Rome, serving as proof the intervening years had not diminished their love for him.

4:17 Paul commended them because their gifts were an investment. Financial terms dominate this passage.[571] The gifts were an investment in the work of God and in their future. Some believers may have mistakenly assumed Paul sought gifts, but he clearly stated he sought the blessings such brought to the givers.[572] Paul saw beyond the physical act to the spiritual transactions taking place. The phrase "I seek the profit that is increasing to your account" reveals Paul was sure of God's awareness of their actions. He used a more descriptive word, "the fruit to your account," which may be translated as profit. Both fruit and profit suggest a return on labor or investment. Though the church focused on giving as pure gift, Paul recognized their activity was to mature into greater blessing, perhaps in the day of Christ. He was confident their actions were what God expected. They acted in accord with his will. Three aspects of this are noteworthy: 1) the church responded as they should in supporting Paul; 2) supporting

---

[570] It is noteworthy the Jewish accusation was that Paul acted "contrary to Caesar's decrees, saying there is another king—Jesus" (Acts 17:7). At that time Christianity had not been declared legal, and thus was against the laws of the Roman Empire Their bigger problem, however, seems to be the lordship of Jesus. Here is another indication the early church, particularly the Pauline churches, preached the resurrection of Jesus evidencing that Jesus is Lord over all things.

[571] This was pointed out long ago by H. A. A. Kennedy, "The Financial Colouring of Phil. 4:15–18," *ExpTim* 12 (1900–1901): 43ff. Some of these terms in CSB are "increasing," "account," and "in full."

[572] The Gk. is graphic. "Gifts" is really *τὸ δόμα*, "the gift." It stressed the giving/receiving aspect. It is contrasted with another articular expression *τὸν καρπόν*, "the fruit."

Paul was actually involvement in God's interests in the world (Paul was confident he represented God as called by him); and 3) God knew their activity and would reward them for their contribution to his work. Even in acknowledging their support, Paul's servant attitude surfaced. He thought of their growth and blessings.

4.2.2 Blessings (4:18–19)

Paul's commendation led him to speak of how the Philippians benefited from supporting him. He understood well that genuine giving seeks no personal benefits. He lived that way, and so did they.[573] Nevertheless, giving brings blessings to both giver and receiver. First, Paul stated what he received from their gifts. Further, using financial language, Paul stated his need was met. He had sufficient resources to carry on God's work. Any obligation they had to him had been paid in full. Their responsibility was satisfied. The gift brought by Epaphroditus exceeded what Paul might have expected, and they were to feel no obligation to give more. Including this first in acknowledging the benefit to the church indicates Paul's desire to let them know he was pleased with the gift. They need do nothing more. In fact, this has the form of being a receipt of "paid in full" given to the church. The CSB translates "I have received everything in full" (4:18). Paul wrote this way to assure the church he wanted nothing from them. He put that first to reinforce his point.

4:18 Paul also listed two benefits to the giver. For one thing, God was pleased. In terms reminiscent of Rom 12:1–2, Paul pointed out that their gift was "a fragrant offering, an acceptable sacrifice, pleasing to God." Like Rom 12, this passage teaches physical activity can become spiritual in motivation and importance. Romans states that dedicating the body to God is a spiritual act. Here, Paul revealed giving material items can be a spiritual exercise. Since Paul used the language of the OT sacrificial system, perhaps even his terms subtly countered the Jewish false teachers.

Paul had developed a comprehensive theology of stewardship. As noted, its most thorough statement occurs in 2 Cor 8–9, where he

---

[573] In our day, it helps to be reminded of this truth. Giving should not be perceived as an alternate way of receiving. That is a contradiction of terms. In God's economy, however, giving is blessed, and the blessings outweigh the sacrifice. That is the main point of Paul's commendation, even with the previous discussion of "giving and receiving."

solicited support for a famine relief offering.[574] Their giving was exemplary because they gave out of "rock-bottom poverty."[575] Their contribution was a "fragrant offering" to God because of its sacrifice, its Christian motivation, and its significance to the spread of the gospel.

4:19 Another benefit to the believers was they would experience God's provision. Just as God had met Paul's needs in the work of the gospel, so God would meet their needs. The context of this promise deserves careful attention. Paul spoke to those who actively supported the work of the Lord. His statement of 4:19 indicates what he meant: God meets the needs of those who honor him through stewardship of finances, giving freely to his purposes.[576]

God's supply is "according to his riches in glory in Christ Jesus." The text says "according to" and not "out of."[577] "According to" means the supply is suited to the resource and like it in kind and extent. God, therefore, bountifully blesses those who give with glorious provision in accord with his glory and for his purposes.[578] Since the glory is associated with Christ—it is "in Christ Jesus"—Paul spoke of one of the benefits brought to those who are in Christ. God's "riches" are available to those who give as the Philippians did. This expectation of God's provision came from Paul's own experience. It should be kept in balance with his earlier assertion that he was in humility and poverty as well as abundance. Contrary to those who expect God to treat every Christian lavishly simply because they are Christians, Paul believed God would take care of those who honor him so that their needs are met. This is not a statement that Christians will be wealthy.

---

574 The theological aspects of giving as presented in 2 Cor 8–9 are developed in R. Melick, "Collection for the Saints: 2 Corinthians 8–9," *CTR* 4 (Fall, 1989): 97–117. There are soteriological aspects: It is a Christian grace demonstrating the completion of grace in the heart; it is true to the example of Jesus Christ; and it expresses the concept of Christian community. In that text there are also eschatological aspects which overlap with Philippians.

575 The Gk. of 2 Cor 8:2 describes their poverty as "according to the depth" or bottom. The expression "rock-bottom" comes from P. Hughes, *Commentary on the Second Epistle to the Corinthians* (Grand Rapids: Eerdmans, 1962), 228.

576 This is much the same as the Lord's prayer: "forgive us . . . as we . . . have forgiven" (Matt 6:12).

577 The Gk. is *κατά* rather than *ἐκ*.

578 The construction "in glory" (*ἐν δόξῃ*) has been taken as in a glorious manner he will provide, in the kingdom of glory after this life, and equal to his glorious riches. This latter seems best suited to the context.

4.2.3 *Doxology (4:20)*

[20] *Now to our God and Father be glory forever and ever. Amen.*

4:20 The section closes with a doxology to God the Father. The thought of the glorious nature of what the Lord supplies no doubt prompted Paul to think of the ultimate purpose of life: to bring glory to God forever.[579] The doxology expresses a prayer concerning all the affairs discussed in the letter. Through whatever means, in every age, and through all creatures, may God be glorified. Once again, Paul's thoughts moved beyond the present to the future, or, as in other places in the letter he consciously remembered the ultimate purpose of life. It is to bring glory to God now and forever. In so doing, the believer will join a great host glorifying God for eternity.

Theological and Practical Points

Money ("gift"). Paul's discussions about money occur with specific concerns related to stewardship. He does not use the word "money," which often causes strong emotional reactions; rather, he uses synonyms in its place. Nevertheless, money is at the heart of many of Paul's concerns. As has been often noted, the letter to Philippi may be occasioned by a gift from the church to Paul. If it is not the occasion for writing, it certainly occupies a prominent place in the letter as it should. The church(es) at Philippi were known for their generosity even in the midst of poverty (2 Cor 8:2). Paul preferred synonyms in his writing, but he developed and revealed a clear theology of material things and money.

One reference point for Paul's theology is he spoke against financial irresponsibility. He explained to Timothy that "if anyone does not provide for his own family, especially for his own household, he has denied the faith and is worse than an unbeliever" (1 Tim 5:8). He encouraged the Thessalonian believers to continue in brotherly love, which manifested itself in leading "a quiet life, [in minding one's] own business, and [working] with [one's] own hands" (1 Thess 4:11) for reputation's sake and so as not to be dependent on anyone. He continued in the second letter to them: "If anyone isn't willing to work, he should not eat" and that they were "to work quietly and provide for

[579] The idiom translated "forever and ever" really captures the idea of the ages to come. It is based on the Hb. idea of heaven as a future age.

themselves" (2 Thess 3:10, 12). If someone refused this instruction, the church was informed "don't associate with him, so that he may be ashamed. . . . [W]arn him as a brother" (2 Thess 3:14–15). Paul's own example provided a powerful witness to that point: "For you remember our labor and hardship, brothers and sisters. Working night and day so that we would not burden any of you, we preached God's gospel to you" (1 Thess 2:9). This pattern persisted as he wrote ten years later: "You were . . . concerned about me but lacked the opportunity to show it" (Phil 4:10). Other passages could support these. Clearly Paul took care of himself and urged believers to take similar personal responsibility. Providing for personal and family needs was a priority.

Paul also wrote that workers should be paid. Arguing against opponents at Corinth, he stated, "Do not muzzle an ox while it treads out grain" (1 Cor 9:9), an idea originating from God through Moses (Deut 25:4). He applied that to the right of Christian apostles to be paid for their service to the church: "Let the one who is taught the word share all his good things with the teacher" (Gal 6:6). Doubtless drawing on his Jewish background where rabbis were paid for teaching and administrative work, he knew the church had its counterparts who propagated the faith. Yet he and Barnabas did not expect the churches to support them in their daily lives: "[D]o only Barnabas and I have no right to refrain from working" (1 Cor 9:6)? These texts teach the expectation that churches care for their spiritual leaders.

Beyond these types of text, Paul wrote about the practice of Christians sharing their resources with those in need. The early church incorporated benevolence as an important part of their community. Acts repeatedly reports the believers took care of their own (Acts 2:44–45; 4:32–35; 6:1).[580] Early on Paul incorporated this into his Christian experience when the Antioch church sent a relief offering to the Jerusalem Christians who had suffered a devastating famine (Acts 11:27–30). The church selected Barnabas and Saul to carry the offering to Jerusalem. Later, much of the energy of his third missionary journey related to collecting a relief offering to help the suffering Christians in Jerusalem (Rom 15:25–28). He considered the offering a proper gift since the Jews brought spiritual benefits to Gentiles. The Gentiles should repay as they could with material blessings. There

---

[580] This was not a form of socialism or communism since they willingly brought what they could rather than being coerced or shamed into it.

were no dues or fixed percentages required (2 Cor 8:5). Each was to give "according to what [he had], not according to what he [did not] (2 Cor 8:12), and it was because of God's blessing enabling them (2 Cor 8:14). Significantly, in this text Paul mentioned the example of the Macedonians (8:1) who "begged . . . earnestly for the privilege of sharing in the ministry to the saints" (8:4).

This generosity had a powerful theological foundation: "For you know the grace of our Lord Jesus Christ: Though he was rich, for your sake he became poor, so that by his poverty you might become rich" (2 Cor 8:9). The parallel to Phil 2:6–11 is remarkable. Christ was rich ("existing in the form of God") but became poor ("he emptied himself by assuming the form of a servant") for the benefit of those who believed in him. Attitudes change when pondering "his indescribable gift" (2 Cor 9:15). The grace of God in sending Christ becomes the grace of God in reciprocal generosity. It is one evidence of the reality of the believer being in Christ (2 Cor 8:8).

Such Christian generosity is an investment in eternity. Ultimately it comes from a clear understanding of God's grace. It is evidence the giver has experienced God's grace and has allowed personal values and activities to be shaped by that. It is a spiritual experience, "a fragrant offering, an acceptable sacrifice, pleasing to God" (Phil 4:18). Though it is a gift, Christian stewardship will bring "the profit that is increasing to [one's] account" (4:17).

Money may be used for good. It is the product of work that enables care for the family. It can bring blessings to many in times of distress and need. It can enable the gospel to go forth promoted by those gifted and called, freeing them from the obligation of time intensive earning. Its proper use evidences genuine Christian commitment, understanding the grace of God in Christ. Christian stewardship of money and things pleases God and is an investment in future blessing for those whose hearts are touched by grace.

Along with Paul's instructions about the wise use of material things, he also warned about the unique dangers associated with money and possessions. Writing to Timothy in his last known communication, Paul warned Timothy that "[h]ard times will come in the last days" (2 Tim 3:1). Among the evidences of these hard times, Paul mentioned that people will be "lovers of money" (2 Tim 3:2). That phrase translates one Greek word, *philarguroi,* literally "lovers of silver." The word comes in the context of eighteen vices that will characterize people in the last days, when Christ comes again. Since it is coupled with another word meaning "lover of selves" (*philautoi*) that is built in the same way, most see the two as an introduction to the entire list, in part because they come first. Thus "lovers of self" and "lovers of money" go together and introduce an environment of egocentricity. The particular word translated "lovers of money" occurs only one other place in Scripture. In Luke 16:14 Jesus describes the Pharisees as "lovers of money." The description of religious professionals misdirected for personal gain serves as a warning to all Christians. Jesus spoke of the tantalizing tendency to put self and money first. It is an especially difficult temptation to avoid. Using similar words, Paul often warned Timothy and Titus of its danger (1 Tim 6:3–10; 2 Tim 3:3–8; Titus 1:7). The warning occurs three times with the command that those who succumb to the temptation are disqualified from church leadership (overseers, 1 Tim 3:1–4; deacons, 1 Tim 3:8; overseers in Titus 1:7). The passion for money is at the core of all evil ("love of money is *a* root of all kinds of evil," 1 Tim 6:10).

In these various contexts, Paul echoed a common theme found throughout Scripture: the importance of using material things for the correct purposes. Jesus warned about building an empire in a self-congratulatory way without considering God, who allowed such success (Luke 12:16–21). More positively, he taught that wise people "store up . . . treasures in heaven," which cannot be lost due to the impermanent characteristics of the earthly environment (Matt 6:19–21). In one of his most puzzling and powerful parables, Jesus commended an unjust steward for his cunning approach to preparing for the afterlife (Luke 16:1–9). Conversely, Jesus's followers are to remember the poor (Matt 6:1–4). He accepted, for instance, the support from women who believed in him and his mission (Luke 8:3), obviously affirming their investments in their eternal future. Jesus taught about the close connection between the heart and the pocketbook.

More than one Christian, including many Christian leaders, have been derailed because of their love of money and, particularly, the lifestyle it can bring. Paul is not naïve about the temptation of wealth, nor is he blind to its spiritual power for good or evil. The fact that the Philippians gave to him and others repeatedly (as in the relief offering, for instance) demonstrated they understood the positive power of money.

One's attitude toward money and material things, therefore, often reveals more than most other spiritual markers. Money earned represents time, and time equates to life. Life values reveal themselves in the use of time and the allocation of money. When Paul commended the Philippians for their financial support, he was cognizant of its deeper meaning. It revealed the life-change brought by conversion and developed by following Christ. Promoting the kingdom of God through its messengers like Paul demonstrated the church's embrace of God's value system. Material possessions can be a uniquely sweet offering to God. Such is, in fact, the NT equivalent of the sacrifices commanded of Israel who also offered to God the sweet aroma of sacrifice. Paul affirmed, as Jesus taught, that "where your treasure is, there your heart will be also" (Luke 12:34).

5 CONCLUSION: GREETINGS FROM ROME (4:21–23)

SECTION OUTLINE

5.1 From Paul (4:21)
5.2 From the Brothers with Paul (4:21)
5.3 From All the Saints at Rome (4:22)
5.4 From Believers in Caesar's Household (4:22)

[21] *Greet every saint in Christ Jesus. The brothers who are with*
me send you greetings. [22]*All the saints send you greetings, especially*
those who belong to Caesar's household. [23] *The grace of the Lord Jesus*
Christ be with your spirit.

Structure

Greet every saint in Christ Jesus.
The brothers who are with me send you greetings.
All the saints send you greetings,
especially those who belong to Caesar's household.
The grace of our Lord Jesus Christ be with your spirit.

Interpretation

The conclusion of Philippians is typical of other letters, including exhortations to greet the brothers and sisters and including greetings from Christians in the place of writing. These concluding remarks are abbreviated, but significant. Paul sent greetings from three groups of persons with him. Each Greek sentence begins with the command "greet" (*aspasasoµai*). He specifically identified some "saints . . . who belong to Caesar's household." Though they are grammatically a part of the third group, their specific designation indicates they are a fourth group to send greetings.

5.1 From Paul (4:21a)

Initially, the letter concludes with a greeting from Paul himself. The second person command indicates the writer is speaking to others to implement the contents of the letter. Interestingly, his command is to a plural readership. It is "you," plural, who were to greet. The text could be read in a redundant sense at face value: "you all greet everyone" (the insertion of "all" is to make the plural obvious). Are all saints to greet every saint? The object of the commanded greetings is "every saint" (singular). The change from the plural command to the singular recipient of the greetings emphasizes Paul's intent to include all Christians in Philippi. Each Christian is to know Paul's love.[581] There is, therefore, a personalizing of the letter so that each receives the message. The statement stands in grammatical contrast with 1:1. In the initial salutation, Paul writes to the leadership of the church and "all the saints." That is a true distributive force. All means everyone. Paul's obvious intent to include everyone at the end comes from his awareness of how his letter must impact each of the congregants in order to make his concerns characteristic of the whole. More directly, Paul has just commended the church for its support. He was aware such support involved a group activity. Thus, his plural greeting for them to greet every saint may come from his sensitivity to include each one who participated in the group offering. This counters the human tendency to place greater value on those who offer greater gifts. Rather than overlooking some who may have given out of "deeper poverty" than others, Paul seems eager to appreciate every gift by acknowledging the giver.[582]

Of equal interest, the phrase "in Christ Jesus" seems quite unnecessary. Like the greeting to every saint, this mirrors 1:1, "To all the saints in Christ Jesus." The redundancy is that "saints" are by

---

[581] Fee, *Philippians*, 456, suggests the intent is a "kind of 'distributive' way." Paul's language is clear enough. The singular included each one.

[582] There is a tendency among all humans to measure their value by how much they can give and conversely to depreciate those whose gifts are smaller. Paul spoke against this clearly in his previous instructions about the relief offering: "Each person should do as he has decided in his heart—not reluctantly or out of compulsion, since God loves a cheerful giver" (2 Cor 9:7).

definition "in Christ Jesus." In strict grammatical form, the phrase "in Christ Jesus" modifies the verb, not the noun. It is thus connected with "greet" rather than "every saint." Therefore, the command to greet every saint is to be done consistently with, and in the energy and acceptance of, being in Christ Jesus. Philippi had enough party spirit, already addressed throughout the letter.[583] The model of Christ's emptying and humbling teaches everyone matters both to Christ and to the church. Greeting "in Christ Jesus" means acknowledging the uniquely spiritual relationships in the church that include each one.

5.2 From Brothers (and Sisters) with Paul (4:21b)

Second, Paul sends greetings from the brethren who surrounded him, his team of people who supported him and served with him. In some instances Paul took time to mention by name at least a few of those with him. This probably reflected his desire to include those known and appreciated by the church that was receiving the letter.[584] Though Timothy and Epaphroditus have been named in the letter Paul's final greetings exclude their names. "The brothers . . . with me" incorporates more than these two men. No doubt the brothers knew the church well, and because of the multiple communications between Philippi and Paul at Rome the church knew well who they were.

5.3 From All the Saints at Rome (4:22a)

Third, greetings were sent from other saints with whom Paul had contact. The term "[a]ll the saints" must mean all those in the church at Rome, even those who were not specifically a part of Paul's band of supporting people. Given the divided nature of Christianity in Rome, evidenced by the differing opinions of Paul's ministry and message, many who were included in "all" were likely unaware of Paul's writing. Even so, just as Paul made sure to include "every saint" in Philippi, all saints in Rome were included (the word saints is, again,

---

583 See, for example, 1:9–11 (abounding love); 1:27 (stand in one spirit); 2:1–4 (think the same way with the same love and purpose, united in spirit, looking to the interests of others); 2:14 (no grumbling and arguing).

584 There are multiple persons named in Rom 16:21–23; 1 Cor 16:19; Col 4:10–14; 2 Tim 4:21; Titus 3:12–13; and Phlm 23–24. Some of Paul's letters do not include individual greetings: 2 Corinthians, Galatians, Ephesians, 1 Thessalonians, 1 Timothy.

plural). Such greetings were commonly exchanged as a mark of Christian friendship and brotherhood.

5.4 From Believers in Caesar's Household (4:22b)

The last group to send greetings included specifically Christians in Caesar's household. "[T]hose who belong to Caesar's household" may mean, of course, that there were Christians in Nero's family. It is a vague description, however. The unusual manner of identifying them as belonging to a "household" suggests they were not family members. Bockmuehl notes some interesting connections of names with Rom 16. The "household of Narcissus" (Rom 16:11), the "household of Aristobulus" (Rom 16:10), and Herodion (Paul's relative, Rom 16:11).[585] He believes there may have been some connection between the church at Philippi and Rome. He notes Herodion may have been a relative of Paul so Paul could have had a kinship connection with Rome (see the n. in CSB). That, of course, is conjecture. Most assume the greeting came from persons in Caesar's civil service, rather than his personal family. Perhaps because of Philippi's importance as a colony and financial center, some of Caesar's assistants had regular business contacts with the Christians at Philippi.[586] The interchange of greetings was an important way of maintaining contacts with the Christians around the empire.

4:23 Paul's final words implored the grace of God. He ended like he began—with a prayer for grace. In 1:2 Paul greeted the church with "[g]race to you and peace from God our Father and the Lord Jesus Christ." As noted there, God the Father and Jesus act jointly in providing these two qualities. Here Paul simply stated, "The grace of our Lord Jesus." Perhaps he omitted peace because earlier he mentioned both the "peace of God" (4:7) and "the God of peace" (4:9). With peace already in mind, the closing simply refers to grace and associates it with Jesus Christ's provision to believers.

Here Paul provides a source of grace as well. Grace is a characteristic of Jesus Christ, therefore coming from him. Paul specifically states grace should be "with your spirit." The word spirit is singular.

---

[585] Bockmuehl, *A Commentary*, 270.

[586] Beare, *The Epistle*, 158, points out that one Poppaea, a proselyte to Judaism, was Nero's mistress. It is not likely that she became a Christian, but it shows that the household included people of other faiths than the preferred religions of Rome.

Possibly he had the collective church spirit in mind, but most likely he referred to the spirits of individuals. Paul sometimes used the singular with the plural pronoun to mean each person is included. Here, each of the listeners'/readers' spirits were to receive grace from Jesus Christ. Rather than thinking of an environment in which believers are located (Rom 5:1–4, "this grace in which we stand"), this "grace" brings calm despite difficulties. It comes from the unchanging attributes of God himself in Christ. Grace is God's way of looking at a world in need. Thus grace, like peace, brings God's presence into the life. God communicates with the spirits of his people and through them, he brings the riches of his grace wherever it is needed. Grace in action is mercy. In a letter which clearly presents the polarities between law and grace, works and faith, and self-righteousness and divinely imputed righteousness, it is significant that the final line should focus on grace. Fittingly, Paul reminded them everything good they had resulted from God's grace.

BIBLIOGRAPHY

Abbott, K. *Short Notes on St. Paul's Epistles to the Romans, Corinthians, Galatians, Ephesians, and Philippians.* Dublin University Press Series. Leopold Classic Library, 2015.

Armistead, J. G. "The Social Setting of the Early Christian Community at Philippi." M.A. thesis. University of Mississippi, 1987.

Bahr, C. J. "The Subscriptions in the Pauline Letters," *JBL 87:1* (1968): 27–41.

Barclay, W. *The Letters to the Philippians, Colossians, and Thessalonians.* Philadelphia: Westminster, 1975.

Barclay, John M. G. *Paul and the Gift.* Grand Rapids: Eerdmans, 2015.

________. "Kenosis and the Drama of Salvation in Philippians 2." In *Kenosis: The Self-Emptying of Christ in Scripture and Theology,* ed. Paul T. Nimmo and Keith L. Johnson. Grand Rapids: William B. Eerdmans Publishing Company, 2022.

Barth, Karl. *Epistle to the Philippians: 40th Anniversary Edition.* Louisville: Westminster John Knox Press, 2002.

________. *The Epistle to the Philippians.* Hymns Ancient and Modern LLC. [reprint] Norwich, UK, 2012.

Baur, F. C. *Paul: The Apostle of Jesus Christ*, 2 vols. London: Williams & Norgate, 1875

Beare, F. W. *The Epistle to the Philippians.* Harper New Testament Commentaries. New York, NY: Harper and Row, 1987.

Bingham, Sandra. *The Praetorian Guard: A History of Rome's Elite Special Forces.* Waco, TX: Baylor University Press, 2013.

Bird, Michael F., and Preston M. Sprinkle. *The Faith of Jesus Christ: Exegetical, Biblical, and Theological Studies.* Milton Keynes: Peabody, MA: Hendrickson, 2010.

Bockmuehl, Markus. *A Commentary on The Epistle to the Philippians.* Black's New Testament Commentaries, ed. Henry Chadwick. London: A & C Black, 1997.

Boice, J. M. *Philippians: An Expositional Commentary.* Grand Rapids: Zondervan, 1971.

Braune, Karl. *The Epistle of Paul to the Philippians and Colossians: An Exegetical and Doctrinal Commentary.* Lange's Commentary on the Holy Scripture. Wipf & Stock, 2007.

Bruce, F. F. *Philippians*. NIBCNT. Peabody, MA: Hendrickson, 1989.
Buchanan, C. O. "Epaphroditus' Sickness and the Letter to the Philippians" *EQ* 36:3, 1964.
Caird, G. B. *Paul's Letters from Prison*. Oxford: University Press, 1976.
Calvin, John. *Calvin's New Testament Commentaries on the New Testament (Volume 11): Galatians, Ephesians, Philippians, Colossians*. Calvin's New Testament Commentaries Series. Grand Rapids: Wm. B. Eerdmans Publishing, 1996.
Casson, S. *Macedonia, Thrace, and Illyria*. Oxford: University Press, 1926.
Cohick, Lynn H. *Philippians*. SGBC. Grand Rapids: Zondervan, 2013.
Collange, Jean-Francois. *The Epistle of Saint Paul to the Philippians*. Trans. by A. W. Heathcote. Eugene, OR: Wipf & Stock, 2009.
Collart, P. *Philippes, ville de Macedoine depuis ses origines jusqu'a la fin de l'époque romaine*. Paris: E. deBoccard, 1937.
Cousar, Charles B. *Philippians and Philemon: A Commentary*. Louisville: Westminster John Knox, 2009.
Craddock, F. B. *Philippians. Interpretation*. Atlanta: John Knox, 1985.
Dana, H. E., and Julius R. Mantey. *A Manual Grammar of the Greek New Testament*. New York: Macmillan, 1969.
Danker, Frederick W., Walter Bauer, and William Arndt, eds. *A Greek-English Lexicon of the New Testament and Other Early Christian Literature*. 3rd ed. Chicago: University of Chicago Press, 2000.
Davies, Paul. "The Macedonian Scene of Paul's Journeys," *BA* 26 (1963): 91–106.
Davis, Valentine D. *Biblical Manuals. The Epistles of St Paul to the Philippians and to Philemon: Explained and Illustrated*. Classical Reprint. London: Forgotten Books, 2019.
Deissmann, A. *Die Neutestamentliche Formal "in Christo Jesu."* Marburg: N. G. Elwert'sche Verlagsbuchhandlung, 1892.
Denniston, J. D., and K. J. Dover. *The Greek Particles*. London: Duckworth [Bristol Classical Press]; Indianapolis: Hackett, 1996.
Dodd, C. H. *New Testament Studies*. Manchester: University Press, 1953.
Ducrey, Pierre. "The Rock Reliefs of Philippi," *Arch* 30 (1977): 102–107.
Duncan, G. S. *St. Paul's Ephesian Ministry*. London: Hodder & Stoughton, 1929.
Dunn, James D. G. "Once More, Πιστις Χριστου." Pages 61–81 in *Pauline Theology, Volume IV: Looking Back, Pressing On*. ed. E. Elizabeth Johnson and David M. Hay. Atlanta: Scholars Press, 1997.
________. *The New Perspective on Paul*. Grand Rapids: Wm B. Eerdmans Publishing Co, 2007.
Edwards, Mark J., ed. *Galatians, Ephesians, Philippians*. ACCS 8. Downers Grove, IL: IVP Academic, 1999.
Ellicott, Charles John. *A Critical and Grammatical Commentary on St. Paul's Epistles to the Philippians, Colossians, and to Philemon, with a Revised Translation*. London: John W. Parker and Son, 1861.
England, Archie, W. "The Righteous, By 'His' Faithfulness Will Live: Habakkuk 2:4 Re-examined.'" In *Anchored to the Text: Essays in Honor of Dr. Richard R. Melick, Jr*., ed. Shawn Buice and Roger Duke. Ontario, CA: Gateway Seminary, 2023.
Fabricatore, Daniel J. *Form of God, Form of a Servant: An Examination of the Greek Noun μορφη in Philippians 2:6–7*. Lanham, MD: University Press of America, 2010.
Fee, Gordon D. *Paul's Letter to the Philippians*. NICNT. Grand Rapids: William B. Eerdmans, 1995.

________. Philippians. NTC 1. Downers Grove, IL: InterVarsity Press, 1999.

Fitzmyer, J. A. "Philippians." In *Jerome Biblical Commentary*, ed. R. E. Brown. J. A. Fitzmyer, and R. E. Murphy, 2:247–53. Englewood Cliffs, NJ: Prentice-Hall, 1968.

Flemming, D. *Philippians: A Commentary in the Wesleyan Tradition.* NBBC. Kansas City, MO: Beacon Hill, 2009.

Flexsenhar, III, Michael. "The Provenance of Philippians and Why it Matters: Old Questions, New Approaches" *JSNT* 42:1 (2019): 18–45.

Fowl, Stephen E. *Philippians.* The Two Horizons New Testament Commentary, ed. Joel B. Green and Max Turner. Grand Rapids: William B. Eerdmans Publishing Company, 2005.

Funk, Robert W. "The Apostolic Parousia: Form and Significance." In *Christian History and Interpretation: Studies Presented to John Knox*, ed. W. R. Farmer, C. F. D. Moule, and R. R. Niebuhr. Cambridge: University Press, 1967.

Garland, David E. "The Composition and Unity of Philippians: Some Neglected Literary Factors." *NovT* 27 (1985): 141–73.

Geoffrion, Timothy C. *The Rhetorical Purpose and the Political and Military Character of Philippians: A Call to Stand Firm.* Lewiston, NY: Mellen Press, 1993.

Greenlee, Harold J. *An Exegetical Summary of Philippians.* Dallas: SIL International, 2008.

Guthrie, George H. *Philippians.* Zondervan Exegetical Commentary on the New Testament, ed. Clinton E. Arnold. Grand Rapids, Zondervan Academic, 2023.

______. "Cohesion Shifts and Stitches in Philippians." In *Discourse Analysis and Other Topics in Biblical Greek*, ed. S. E. Porter and D. A. Carson, 36–59. JSNTSup 13. Sheffield: Sheffield Academic, 1995.

Gundry, Robert H. SOMA in *Biblical Theology: With Emphasis on Pauline Anthropology*, SNTSMS 29. Cambridge: University Press, 1976.

Gupta, Nijay K. *Paul and the Language of Faith.* Grand Rapids: Wm B. Eerdman's Publishing Co, 2020.

Hafemann, Scott, J. *Biblical Theology: Retrospect and Prospect.* Downer's Grove, IL: IVP Academic, 2022.

Hallum, Stephen C. "The Agon Motif in Rhetorical Intertexture and Analytic Function of the Topos." PhD diss Golden Gate Baptist Theological Seminary, 2010.

Hammond, N. G. L., and G. T. Griffith. *A History of Macedonia.* Oxford: Clarendon, 1972.

Hansen, G. W. *The Letter to the Philippians.* PNTC. Grand Rapids: Eerdmans, 2009.

Harris, Murray J. *Prepositions and Theology in the Greek New Testament: An Essential Reference Resource for Exegesis.* Grand Rapids: Zondervan, 2012.

Harrison, James R., and L. L. Welborn, eds. *The First Urban Churches 4: Roman Philippi.* WGRWSup 13. Atlanta: SBL Press, 2018.

Hawthorne, Gerald F., and Ralph P. Martin. *Philippians. WBC* 43. Dallas: Word, 2004.

Hays, Richard B. *The Faith of Jesus Christ: An Investigation of the Narrative Substructure of Galatians 3:1–4:11.* Atlanta: Scholars Press, 1983.

Hellerman, Joseph H. *Philippians.* Exegetical Guide to the Greek New Testament. Ed Andreas J. Kostenberger, Robert W. Yarbrough. Nashville: B&H Academic, 2015.

Hendriksen, William. *Exposition of Ephesians.* NTC. Grand Rapids: Baker, 1967.

Holloway, Paul A. *Philippians, A Commentary.* Hermeneia—A Critical and Historical Commentary on the Bible, ed. Adela Yarbro Collins. Minneapolis: Fortress Press. 2017.

________. *Consolation in Philippians: Philosophical Sources and Rhetorical Strategy. SNTSMS* 12. Cambridge: Cambridge University Press, 2001.

Hoover, R. W. "The *Harpagmos* Enigma: A Philological Solution." *HTR* 64 (1971): 95–119.

Hunsinger, George. *Philippians*. Brazos Theological Commentary on the Bible, ed. R. R. Reno. Grand Rapids: Brazos Press, 2020.

Jeremias, Joachim. *Jerusalem in the Time of Jesus*. Philadelphia: Fortress, 1969.

Jewett, Robert. "Conflicting Movements in the Early Church as Reflected in Philippians." *NovT* 12 (1970): 362–390.

Käsemann, E., "A Critical Analysis of Philippians 2:5–11." In *God and Christ: Existence and Providence in Journal for Theology and Church*. New York: Harper & Row, 1968.

Keown, Mark, J. *Philippians 1:1–2:18*. Evangelical Exegetical Commentary, ed. H. Wayne House. Bellingham, WA: Lexham Press, 2017.

______. *Philippians 2:19–4:23*. Evangelical Exegetical Commentary. ed. H. Wayne House. Bellingham, WA: Lexham Press, 2017.

Kennedy, H. A. A. "The Epistle to the Philippians." *The Expositor's Greek Testament*, ed. W. R. Nicol, 3:397–474. 1903; reprint, Grand Rapids: Eerdmans, 1976.

Kent, H. A. "Philippians." EBC. Grand Rapids: Zondervan, 1978.

Klauck, Hans-Josef, and Daniel P. Bailey. *Ancient Letters and the New Testament: A Guide to Context and Exegesis*. Waco, TX: Baylor University Press, 2006.

Kostenberger, Andreas J., L. Scott Kellum, and Charles L. Quarles. *The Cradle, The Cross, and the Crown*. Nashville: B&H Academic, 2009.

Knight, III, George W. *The Pastoral Epistles: A Commentary on the Greek Text*. The New International Greek Testament Commentary. Grand Rapids: William B. Eerdmans Publishing Company, 1992.

Kurz, W. S. "Kenotic Imitation of Paul and of Christ in Philippians 2 and 3." In *Discipleship in the New Testament*. Philadelphia: Fortress, 1985.

Lenski, Richard C. H. "The Interpretation of St Paul's Epistles to the Ephesians and Philippians." *Lenski's Commentary on the New Testament*. Augsburg Fortress Publishers, 2008.

Levick, B. *Roman Colonies in Southern Asia Minor*. Oxford: Clarendon, 1967.

Liddell, Henry George, Robert Scott, and Henry Stuart Jones. *A Greek-English Lexicon*. 9th ed. Oxford: Clarendon, 1996.

Lightfoot, J. B. *Saint Paul's Epistle to the Philippians: A Revised Text with Introduction, Notes, and Dissertations*. London: Macmillan, 1898.

Lohmeyer, Ernst. *Die Briefe an die Philipper, und die Kolosser und an Philemon*. Göttingen: Vandenhoeck, 1953.

Louw, J. P., and A. Nida. *A Handbook on Paul's Letter to the Philippians*. UBS Handbook Series 19. New York: United Bible Societies, 1995.

________, and Eugene A. Nida. *Greek-English Lexicon of the New Testament: Based on Semantic Domains*. New York: United Bible Societies, 1988.

Marshall, I. Howard. *A Hymn of Christ: Philippians 2:5–11 in Recent Interpretation and in the Setting of Early Christian Worship*. Downers Grove, IL: IVP Academic, 1997.

_______. *The Epistle to the Philippians*. Epworth Commentary Series. London: Epworth Press,1992.

_______. "The Theology of Philippians." In *The Theology of the Shorter Pauline Letters*, ed. K. P. Donfried and I. H. Marshall, 115–74. Cambridge: Cambridge University Press, 1993.

Martin, Ralph P. *Carmen Christi, Philippians 2:5–11* in *Recent Interpretation and in the Setting of Early Christian Worship*. Cambridge: University Press, 1967.

______. *An Early Christian Confession: Philippians 2:5–11 in Recent Interpretation.* London: Tyndale, 1960.

______.*The Epistle of Paul to the Philippians: An Introduction and Commentary.* Tyndale New Testament Commentaries. Grand Rapids, MI: Eerdmans, 1988.

______. *Philippians*, NCB. London: Oliphants, 1976.

McKnight, Scott, and B. J. Oropeza. *Perspectives on Paul: Five Views.* Ada, MI: Baker Academic, 2020.

Melick, Richard R. *Philippians, Colossians, Philemon.* NAC 32. Nashville: Broadman &Holman, 1991.

______. "Collection for the Saints: 2 Corinthians 8–9." *CTR* 4 (Fall 1989): 97–117.

Metzger, Bruce M. *A Textual Commentary on the Greek New Testament.* 2nd ed. Stuttgart: United Bible Societies, 1994.

Meyer, Heinrich August Wilhelm. *The Epistles to the Philippians and Colossians.* Translated by John C. Moore and William P. Dickson. CECNT. Edinburgh: T&T Clark, 1875.

Motyer, J. Alec. *The Message of Philippians.* Bible Speaks Today. London: Inter-Varsity Press, 1984.

Moore, Thomas. *Philippians: An Exegetical Guide for Preaching and Teaching. The Big Idea Series,* ed. Herbert W. Bateman, IV. Grand Rapids: Kregel Academic. 2019.

Moule, H. C. G. *The Epistle to the Philippians, with Introduction and Notes.* The Cambridge Bible for Schools and Colleges. Cambridge: The University Press, 1899.

______. *Idiom Book of New Testament Greek.* Cambridge: University Press, 1953.

Muller, Jacobus J. *Epistles of Paul to the Philippians.* New International Commentary on the New Testament. William B. Eerdmans Publishing Co, 1985.

Nee, Watchman. *Sit, Walk, Stand.* Carol Stream, IL: Tyndale House Publishers, 1977.

Neufeld, Vernon. *The Earliest Christian Confessions*, NTTS. Leiden: Brill, 1963.

Nimmo, Paul T., and Keith L. Johnson ed. *Kenosis: The Self-Emptying of Christ in Scripture and Theology.* Grand Rapids: William B. Eerdmans Publishing Company, 2022.

Novakovic, Lidija. ed. *Philippians: A Handbook on the Greek Text.* Baylor Handbook on the Greek New Testament. Waco: Baylor University Press, 2020.

Oakes, Peter. *Philippians: From People to Letter.* SNTSMS. Cambridge: Cambridge University Press, 2001.

______. *Rome in the Bible and the Early Church.* Carlisle: Paternoster, 2002.

O'Brien, Peter. *The Epistle to the Philippians.* New International Greek Testament Commentary. Grand Rapids: Wm. B. Eerdmans Publishing, 1991.

ORBIS: The Stanford Geospacial Network of the Roman World, done by Stanford University. Accessible at orbis.stanford.edu.

Park, M. Sydney. *Submission within the Godhead and the Church in the Epistle to the Philippians: An Exegetical and Theological Examination of the Concept of Submission in Philippians 2 and 3.* Library of New Testament Studies, ed. Mark Goodacre. London: T & T Clark, 2007.

Pelekanidis, St. "Excavations in Philippi," *BalSt* 8:1 (1967): 123–26.

Pentecost, J. D. *The Joy of Living: A Study of Philippians.* Grand Rapids: Kregel, 1996.

Peterman, Gerald W. *Paul's Gift from Philippi: Conventions of Gift Exchange and Christian Giving.* SNTSMS 92. Cambridge: Cambridge University Press, 1997.

Polhill, J. B. *Acts.* The New American Commentary Vol. 26. Nashville: Broadman & Holman Publishers, 1992.

Porter, Stanley E., and Carson, D. A., eds. *Discourse Analysis and Other Topics in Biblical Greek*. Sheffield: Sheffield Academic Press, 1995.

Porter, Stanley E., and Sean A. Adams, eds. *Paul and the Ancient Letter Form*. Pauline Studies 6. Leiden: Brill, 2010.

Plummer, Alfred. *A Commentary on St. Paul's Epistle to the Philippians*. Wipf & Stock, 1997.

Ramsay, William. "Roads and Travel (NT)." Harper Dictionary of the Bible 5 (New York, NY: Harper Collins, 375–402.

Reed, Jeffrey T. *A Discourse Analysis of Philippians: Method and Rhetoric in the Debate over Literary Integrity*. JSNTSup 136. Sheffield: Sheffield Academic Press, 1997.

Reumann, John. *Philippians: A New Translation with Introduction and Commentary* AYB. New Haven: Yale University Press, 2008.

Robertson, A. T. *A Grammar of the Greek New Testament in the Light of Historical Research*. Nashville: Broadman, 1934.

_________ . *Paul's Joy in Christ: Studies in Philippians*. Nashville: Broadman, n.d.

Runge, S. E. *High Definition Commentary: Philippians*. Bellingham, WA: Lexham Press, 2011.

Sanders, E. P. *Paul and Palestinian Judaism*. Minneapolis: Fortress Press, 1977.

Scanion, Thomas F. *Sport in the Greek and Roman Worlds*, Vol. 2. Oxford University Press, 2014.

Schaff, Philip ed., *The Creeds of Christendom: Volume 2: The Greek and Latin Creeds*. Grand Rapids: Baker, 1990.

Schenk, Wolfgang., *Die Philipperbrief des Paulus Kommentar*. Stuttgart: W. Kohlhammer, 1984.

Scott, E. F. *"The Epistle to the Philippians."* In The Interpreter's Bible, ed. G. Buttrick et al., 11:3–129. New York: Abingdon, 1950.

Silva, Moisés. *Philippians*. BECNT. Grand Rapids: Baker Academic, 2005.

_________. *Philippians, WEC*. Chicago: Moody, 1988.

Stendahl, Krister. "The Apostle Paul and the Introspective Conscience of the West," *HTR* 56 (1963): 199–215.

Stevenson, G. H. *Roman Provincial Administration*. New York: Strechert, 1939.

Still, Todd. *Philippians and Philemon*. SHBC. Macon, GA: Smyth & Helwys, 2011.

Synge, F. C. *Philippians and Colossians*. London: Torch Bible Commentaries, 1951.

Taylor, Vincent. *The Person of Christ in New Testament Teaching*. London: MacMillan, 1966.

Thielman, Frank S. *Philippians*. NIVAC. Grand Rapids: Zondervan, 1995.

______. "Philippians." *Zondervan Illustrated Bible Backgrounds Commentary*, vol. 3, Romans to Philemon, ed. C. E. Arnold, 342–67. Grand Rapids: Zondervan Publishing, 2002.

______. *Theology of the New Testament*. Grand Rapids: Zondervan, 2005.

Thrall, Margaret E. *Greek Particles in the New Testament: Linguistic and Exegetical Studies*. New Testament Tools, Studies and Documents 3. Leiden: Brill, 1962.

Varner, William C. *Philippians: A Handbook on the Greek Text*. BHGNT. Waco, TX: Baylor University Press, 2016.

______. *Philippians: An Exegetical Commentary*. Dallas: Fontes Press, 2021.

Verhoef, Eduard. *How Christianity Began in Europe: The Epistle to Philippians and the Excavations at Philippi*. London: Bloomsbury, 2013.

Vincent, Marvin R. *A Critical and Exegetical Commentary on the Epistles to the Philippians and to Philemon*. ICC. Edinburgh: T&T Clark, 1897.

Wallace, Daniel B. *Greek Grammar beyond the Basics: An Exegetical Syntax of the New Testament*. Grand Rapids: Zondervan, 1996.

Walvoord, John F. *To Live is Christ: An Exposition of the Epistle of Paul to the Philippians*. Dunham Publishing, 1961.

Wiefel, W. "The Jewish Community in Ancient Rome and the Origins of Roman Christianity," reprinted in *The Romans Debate*, ed. Karl Donfried. Minneapolis: Augsburg, 1977.

Witherington, III, Ben. *Paul's Letter to the Philippians: A Socio-Rhetorical Commentary*. Grand Rapids: William B. Eerdmans Publishing, 2011.

Wright, N. T. *Paul for Everyone: The Prison Letters: Ephesians, Philippians, Colossians, and Philemon*. The New Testament for Everyone. Westminster: John Knox Press, 2004.

_______*Paul: A Biography* San Francisco: Harper One, 2018

_______. "*Harpagmos and the Meaning of Philippians 2:5–11*," *JTS* 37 (1986): 321–352.

NAME INDEX

A

Armistead, J. G. *6, 7, 8, 11, 12*

B

Bahr, C. J. *36*
Barclay, J. *213, 214, 229, 397*
Barr, J. *313*
Barth, K. *56, 132, 363*
Baur, F. C. *24, 25*
Beare, F. W. *14, 15, 42, 43, 44, 45, 46, 50, 56, 76, 110, 118, 119, 143, 215, 221, 245, 275, 363, 373, 409*
Behm, J. *207*
Bockmuehl, M. *34, 38, 40, 41, 162, 179, 180, 209, 216, 220, 244, 285, 286, 288, 316, 336, 374, 409*
Brauch, M. T. *350*
Buchanan, C. O. *44*

C

Caird, G. B. *21, 25, 36, 132, 133, 143, 161, 162, 189, 221, 222, 246, 248, 308, 312, 313, 330, 368, 386*
Carson, D. A. *36, 38*
Casson, S. *6, 7*
Collart, P. *6, 9, 10*
Craddock, F. *214, 328, 364*

D

Dalton, W. J. *36*
Davies, P. *6, 12*
Davies, W. E. *317*
Deissmann, A. *43, 204*
Dibelius, M. *56*
Dodd, C. H. *46*
Ducrey, P. *6*
Duncan, G. S. *46*
Dunn, J. G. D. *311*

E

England, A. W. *313*

F

Fee, G. D. *xvii, 48, 49, 52, 61, 68, 89, 90, 92, 101, 109, 118, 125, 133, 138, 141, 149, 153, 160, 177, 197, 206, 264, 270, 295, 323, 334, 337, 366, 388, 407*
Fleming *301*
Flexsenhar III, M. *47, 48, 52, 133*
Foerster, W. *378*
Fowl, S. F. *xvii, 38, 40, 41, 52, 141, 157, 181, 208, 209, 210, 215, 242, 307, 312, 337*
Funk, R. W. *254*

G

Garland, D. *38, 39, 288*
Gnilka, J. *56*
Greenlee, J. H. *37*
Griffith, G. T. *7*
Gupta, N. K. *313*
Guthrie, G. H. *xvii, 11, 36, 39, 61, 69, 76*

H

Hallum, S. C. *183*

Hammond, N. G. L. *7*
Harrison, P. N. *46*
Hawthorne, G. *37, 38, 42, 43, 46, 49, 50, 51, 56, 68, 70, 97, 98, 99, 101, 110, 111, 115, 116, 119, 142, 149, 150, 154, 178, 181, 193, 196, 198, 204, 206, 209, 285, 287, 326, 327, 329, 330, 357, 360, 362, 375*
Hays, R. *313*
Hellerman, J. H. *106, 149, 195, 198, 203, 207, 223*
Hendriksen *53*
Holloway, P. A. *xvii, 32, 34, 36, 37, 38, 61, 113, 160, 162, 190, 220, 274, 287*
Hoover, R. W. *210*
Hughes, P. *401*
Hunsinger, G. *114*

J

Jeremias, J. *76, 200*
Jewett, R. *143*
Johnson, K. L. *213, 231, 235*

K

Käsemann, E. *204*
Kellum, L. S. *49*
Kennedy, H. *399*
Kent, H. A. *221, 370*
Keown, M. J. *11, 35, 38, 42, 52, 68, 69, 72, 92, 118, 134, 141, 149, 154, 196, 200, 210, 220, 262, 263, 264, 275, 315, 321, 336, 358, 361, 362, 371*
Knight III, G. W. *75*
Kostenberger, A. J. *37, 49, 106*
Kurz, W. S. *203*

L

Levick, B. *9*
Lightfoot, J. B. *33, 47, 78, 112, 117, 118, 132, 189, 208, 224, 275, 297, 300, 329, 360, 387*
Lohmeyer, E. *200, 203*

M

Martin, R. *15, 32, 33, 37, 43, 44, 50, 51, 56, 99, 100, 111, 193, 196, 215, 222, 224, 239, 245, 257*
McCormack, B. L. *235*
McKnight, S. *311*
Melick, R. R, Jr. *57, 313, 342, 394, 401*
Michaelis, O. *56*
Michel *288*
Mitton, C. L. *25, 45*
Moore, T. *149*
Moule, C. F. D. *283, 355*
Müller, J. *208*

N

Neufeld, V. *225*
Nimmo, P. T. *213, 231, 235*

O

Oakes, P. *11, 76*
O'Brien *207, 339*
Onesti, K. L. *350*
Oropeza, B. J. *311*

P

Peterman, G. *39*
Polhill, J. B. *15*
Porter, S. *36, 38*

Q

Quarles, C. L. *49*

R

Ramsay, W. *43*
Reed, J. T. *xvii, 36, 38*
Reumann, J. *xvii, 107, 198*
Robertson, A. T. *130, 131, 283, 325, 333*

S

Sanders, E. P. *311*
Schaff, P. *235*
Schenk, W. *331, 416*
Silva, M. *23, 43, 46, 56, 70, 99, 102, 108, 112, 151, 172, 181, 204, 218, 239, 267, 300, 302, 303, 313, 330, 331, 386*
Stendahl, K. *300, 311*
Stevenson, G. H. *9*
Synge, F. C. *143*

T

Taylor, V. *196*
Thielman, F. *22*
Thrall, M. E. *149*

V

Vincent, M .R. *150, 164, 275*

W

Witherington III, B. *39, 40, 68, 69, 128, 176, 274, 288, 289, 328, 337, 344, 374*

Wright, N. T. *17, 210, 299*

Y

Yarbrough, R. W. *37, 106*

SCRIPTURE INDEX

GENESIS

1 *99*
1:1 *85*
1:26 *85*
1:26–27 *206*
1:27 *168*
3:15 *351*
15:6 *312*
17:11 *296*

EXODUS

12:43–49 *292*
20 *298*
20:3–17 *353*
20–23 *353*
22:31 *288*
24:3 *353*
32:32 *363*
32:32–33 *363*

LEVITICUS

12:3 *296*

NUMBERS

12:7 *72*
25:6–14 *299*

DEUTERONOMY

6:5 *109*
10:16 *292*
10:19 *292*
10:20 *292*
21:23 *218*
23:15 *288*
25:4 *403*
30:6 *56*
32:5 *244, 245, 246*

JOSHUA

14:7 *72*

2 SAMUEL

7:5–8 *72*
16:9 *288*

1 KINGS

14:11 *288*

2 KINGS

10:10 *72*

NEHEMIAH

8:10 *367*

JOB

13:13–18 *151, 152*

PSALMS

8:5–6 *216*
16:11 *162*
22:16 *288*

32:1–2 *353*
62:12 *352*
69:28 *363*
89:3 *72*
106:30–31 *299*
110 *82*
110:1 *82*
139:16 *363*
143:12 *312*

ISAIAH

2:9–11 *220*
28:16 *155*
43:10 *72*
45:23 *223*
45:24 *223*
59:7–8 *379*

JEREMIAH

1:5 *139*
4:4 *292*
9:26 *292*
31:31–34 *292*

EZEKIEL

36:26 *292*

DANIEL

12:1 *363*

HOSEA

10:12 *118*

JOEL

2:1 *99*

AMOS

5:20 *99*

HABAKKUK

2:4 *351*

MATTHEW

1:21 *82*
1:23 *82*
5:29–30 *167*
6:1–4 *405*
6:12 *401*
6:19–21 *405*
6:25–34 *258, 369, 380*
10:2 *263*
11:28 *388*
12:27 *188, 375*
22:43–45 *82*
24:27 *246*
26:30 *197*

MARK

1:24 *16*
3:14 *263*
7:1–16 *337*
7:18–19 *305*
9:2–4 *207*

LUKE

3:8 *317*
6:13 *263*
8:3 *405*
10:20 *363, 364*
10:25–37 *110*
10:27 *109*
10:29 *110*
10:36 *110*
12:16–21 *405*
12:34 *406*
16:1–9 *405*
16:14 *405*
16:21 *288*
19:10 *336*
23:39–43 *161*

JOHN

1:1 *xiv, 233*
1:1–2 *85*
1:5 *325*
1:14 *234*
2:17 *299*
3:12 *341*
3:16 *109*
8:39–41 *317*
11:11 *162*
11:35 *335*
13:35 *109*
14:16 *154*

14:27 *81, 371, 379, 380*
15:26 *154*
16:7 *154*
16:33 *81*
20:25 *82*

ACTS

1:8 *268*
1:21–23 *263*
2 *96*
2:10 *10*
2:36 *86, 223*
2:44–45 *403*
4:1 *279*
4.13 *325*
4:18 *279*
4:32–35 *403*
5:28 *276*
5:33–39 *298*
6 *79, 84*
6:1 *403*
6:1–6 *78*
6:2 *78*
7 *296*
8:1 *27, 278*
8:3 *278*
9 *310*
9:1 *279*
9:1–2 *300*
9:1–3 *278*
9:1–9 *28*
9:1–31 *306*
9:5 *86, 310*
9:5–6 *86*
9:15 *145*
9:16 *139, 186, 320*
9:19–25 *29*
9:26–30 *29*
11:2 *278*
11:27–30 *403*
12:1 *279*
13:1–14:28 *29*
13:2–3 *29*
13:9 *296*
13:13–52 *30*
13:36 *122*
13:39 *30*
13:45 *279*
13:50 *279*
14:5 *279*
14:19 *19, 279, 378*
15 *55, 276*
15:1 *276, 278*
15:5 *307*
15:36–18:22 *29*
16 *13, 17, 96, 180, 279, 280, 360*
16:1–3 *26, 289*
16:3 *292*
16:6–7 *14*
16:11–21 *15*
16:11–40 *14*
16:13 *10*
16:15 *18*
16:16 *12*
16:17 *19*
16–18 *70*
16:19 *12*
16:19–40 *258*
16:21 *12, 16*
16:23–31 *42*
16:25 *169*
16:31 *17*
16:32 *18*
16:37 *18, 28, 307*
16:38–40 *31*
17:1–4 *20*
17:1–9 *281*
17:2 *398*
17:3 *30*
17:4 *15*
17:5 *279*
17:5–9 *396*
17:6–9 *140*
17:12 *15*
17:14 *255*
17:28 *208*
17:32 *30*
17:34 *15*
18:2 *15, 277*
18:5 *30*
18:6 *279*
18:12 *51, 279*
18:12–14 *140*
18:13 *31*
18:14–16 *277*
18:16 *31*
18:18–26 *50*
18:23–21:3 *29*
19:1–9 *27*
19:8 *30*
19:22 *26*

19:24–41 *140*
19:40 *31*
20:1 *19*
20:3 *279*
20:4 *45*
20:17 *77, 78*
20:17–38 *77*
20:28 *75, 76, 77, 78*
21:15–26:23 *29*
21:20 *278*
21:23–24 *345*
21:24 *307, 331*
21:27 *279*
21:28–29 *31*
21:37 *28*
21:39 *28*
22:1–21 *28*
22:1–22 *102*
22:3 *27, 297, 298, 300*
22:3–5 *278*
22:10 *298*
22:24–23:22 *42*
22:25 *307*
22:28 *18*
23:1 *174, 175, 176*
23:1–10 *102*
23:6 *297, 298*
23:12 *279, 280*
23:27 *279*
23:33–26:32 *42*
23:35 *47, 50*
24:1–21 *102*
24:15 *30*
24:16 *117*
24:20–21 *51*
24:23 *51*
24:24–27 *102*
25:6 *279*
25:10–11 *28*
25:11–12 *31*
25:25 *28*
25:412 *102*
26:1–32 *102*
26:2 *279*
26:5 *27, 297*
26:8 *30*
26:9–11 *278*
26:10 *27*
26:11 *278*
26:12–23 *28*
26:19–20 *140*
26:23 *30*
26:31–32 *31*
26:32 *28, 151, 278*
27:10 *304*
27:13–44 *378*
27:21 *304*
28 *29*
28:15 *29*
28:16 *47*
28:17–31 *42*
28:23 *29, 30*
28:30 *133*
28:30–31 *29*

ROMANS

1:8 *87, 127*
1:10–12 *166*
1:16 *29, 306*
1:16–17 *350*
1:17 *315, 350, 351, 352*
1:18 *351, 352*
1:18–20 *351*
1:29 *137*
2:6 *352*
2:8 *352*
2:25–29 *282, 292*
2:29 *56*
3:3 *314, 315, 351*
3:5 *351*
3:5–6 *352*
3:9–11 *351*
3:10–18 *354*
3:20 *354*
3:21 *315, 350, 352*
3:21–25 *350*
3:22 *314*
3:23 *340, 352, 379*
3:26 *354*
4:1 *312*
4:3 *315*
4:3–5 *353*
4:5 *315*
4:7 *353*
4:9 *314*
4:10 *353*
4:11 *354*
4:12 *314, 331*
4:14 *212*
5 *213*
5:1 *80, 123, 371, 379*

5:1–4 *410*
5:1–11 *340*
5:2 *80*
5:6–8 *109*
5:6–11 *212*
5:8 *212*
5:10 *212*
5:12 *386*
5:12–21 *311*
5:19 *218*
6 *230*
6:1–11 *320*
6:6 *156*
6:11 *321*
6:12–14 *156*
6:19 *354*
7 *313, 342*
7:7 *354*
7:7–12 *300*
7:9 *275, 300*
7:12–13 *354*
7:13–25 *313*
8:3–4 *354*
8:17 *320*
8:18–25 *161*
8:19–22 *224*
8:19–25 *345*
8:28 *390*
8:28–30 *250*
8:29–30 *327, 328*
8:31 *203*
8:33–34 *117*
9 *378*
9:1–3 *335*
9–11 *387*
9:33 *155*
10:1–6 *295*
10:2 *299*
10:2–3 *123*
10:8 *368*
10:9–10 *225*
10:10–11 *155*
10:11 *155*
12 *400*
12:1 *169, 248*
12:1–2 *114, 156, 249, 400*
12:3–8 *84*
12–15 *101*
13 *175, 176*
13:11 *239, 368*
14 *361*
14:1–15:6 *55, 127, 144*
14:4 *146*
14:8 *146*
14:14 *135*
14–15 *138, 337*
14:17 *380*
14:19 *380*
15:16 *249*
15:23–24 *166*
15:23–29 *44*
15:25–28 *403*
15:26 *95*
15:27 *249*
15:28 *126*
16 *362, 409*
16:1 *70, 360*
16:3 *262*
16:9 *262*
16:10 *409*
16:11 *409*
16:16–19 *37*
16:17–18 *337*
16:20 *380*
16:21 *262*
16:21–23 *408*
16:26 *160*

1 CORINTHIANS

1–4 *145*
1:4 *87*
1:5 *87*
1:9 *95, 314*
1:17 *212, 218*
1:20–25 *213*
1:23 *213*
1:24–25 *213*
2:2 *229*
2:2–3 *213*
2:6 *329*
2:8 *214*
3:6 *79*
4:15 *258*
4:16 *333*
4:17 *26, 255, 256*
4:17–19 *254*
5:1–5 *361*
5:8 *116*
6:13 *168*
7:10 *176, 241*
7:11 *241*

7:12 *241*
7:15 *241, 380*
8:1–3 *151*
8–10 *337, 345, 361*
9:1–9 *345*
9:6 *403*
9:7 *262*
9:9 *403*
9:24–27 *342, 345*
9:27 *169*
10:10 *244*
10:13 *314*
10:16 *95*
10:32 *117*
11:1 *333*
12 *361*
12:4–11 *84*
12:13 *177*
13 *203*
13:8 *114*
14:20 *329*
14:28 *378*
14:30 *378*
14:33 *380*
14:34 *378*
15 *xiv, 96*
15:3–5 *184*
15:8–9 *263*
15:12–20 *326*
15:12–28 *328*
15:24–28 *223, 224*
15:27–28 *85*
15:28 *223*
15:35–55 *161*
15:40 *341*
15:42–44 *345*
15:50 *168*
15:50–54 *345*
16:10 *256*
16:13 *177*
16:17–18 *267*
16:19 *408*
16:22 *368*

2 CORINTHIANS

1:3 *87*
1:5 *320*
1:5–7 *320*
1:8–10 *46*
1:8–11 *125, 378*
1:15–2:4 *255*
1:15–23 *255*
1:18 *314*
2:16 *315*
3:12 *156*
3:18 *191*
5:1 *341*
5:1–10 *161, 320, 328*
5:4 *386*
5:8 *162*
5:14–15 *91*
5:16 *28*
5:21 *123, 317*
6 *378*
7 *241*
7:1 *99*
7:4 *156*
7:15 *241*
8 *384, 385*
8:1 *21, 160, 398*
8:1–2 *383*
8:1–5 *19*
8:1–6 *109*
8:1–7 *99*
8:2 *385, 401, 402*
8:2–4 *21*
8:4 *95*
8:5 *404*
8:6–7 *398*
8:7 *98*
8:8 *257, 404*
8–9 *398, 400, 401*
8:9 *216, 398, 404*
8:12 *404*
8:14 *404*
8:16–24 *264*
8:23 *262, 264*
9:7 *407*
9:12 *249*
9:13 *95*
9:15 *404*
10:1 *368*
10:1–2 *255*
10:10–11 *255*
10:12–18 *255*
11:5 *278*
11:5–7 *255*
11:9 *19*
11–12 *264*
11:13 *278*
11:21 *278*

11:23 *42, 46*
11:24–29 *378*
12:7 *378*
12:11 *278*
13:13 *95, 189*

GALATIANS

1 *306*
1:6 *278*
1:6–9 *56, 147*
1:11 *160*
1:15 *139, 327*
1:15–16 *139*
1:18–20 *29*
2:3 *278, 290, 292*
2:7–9 *172*
2:11–14 *361*
2:12 *278*
2:20 *158, 315*
2:21 *354*
3 *342, 378*
3:3 *99*
3:5 *153*
3:6–12 *315*
3:13 *218*
3:16–18 *317*
3:26 *315*
3:27–29 *293*
4:1–7 *341*
4:3 *341*
4:3–5 *214*
5:1 *177*
5:2 *293*
5:3–6 *294*
5:5–6 *293*
5:11 *218*
5:12 *289*
5:16–26 *294*
5:21 *137*
5:22 *119, 380*
5:25 *331*
6 *36*
6:6 *403*
6:11 *36*
6:12 *218*
6:14 *218*
6:16 *331, 380*

EPHESIANS

1:3 *87*
1:3–14 *81, 119*
1:4–6 *85*
1:5 *243*
1:7–12 *85*
1:9 *243*
1:13–14 *85*
1:20–23 *223*
2:6 *177*
2:8 *80*
2:8–9 *181, 239, 250*
2:8–10 *226*
2:10 *243*
2:11–13 *387*
2:13 *368*
2:14–17 *380*
2:16 *218*
2:17 *368*
2:18 *177*
3:1 *132*
3:1–7 *145*
3:1–13 *394*
3:3–7 *166*
3:6 *166*
3:7 *79*
3:17–19 *114*
3:18 *325*
3:19 *379*
4:3 *380*
4:11–13 *76*
4:11–14 *84*
4:13 *329*
5:18 *178*
5:19 *197*
5:22–6:9 *18*
6:5 *242*
6:5–8 *242*
6:5–9 *72, 73*
6:6 *242*
6:8 *242*
6:12 *224*
6:19 *156*
6:21 *30*
6:21–22 *53*

PHILIPPIANS

1 *34, 47, 50, 52, 144*
1:1 *45, 70, 71, 74, 75, 83, 132, 255, 297, 309, 312, 360, 396, 407*
1:1–2 *40*
1:1–3:1 *35, 36*

1:2 *79, 80, 82, 83, 309, 377, 379, 409*
1:3 *22, 87, 91, 93, 120*
1:3–8 *87, 88*
1:3–11 *39, 40*
1:4 *90, 92, 93, 104, 120*
1:4–5 *90, 93*
1:4–6 *150*
1:5 *33, 36, 87, 91, 92, 93, 95, 96, 382, 396*
1:5–7 *146*
1:6 *xv, 82, 83, 90, 97, 118, 150, 243*
1:7 *22, 33, 90, 95, 96, 100, 101, 121*
1:7–8 *90*
1:8 *82, 103, 357*
1:9 *87, 104, 109, 111, 120, 150, 154*
1:9–10 *108, 109*
1:9–11 *62, 63, 87, 88, 108, 245, 354, 408*
1:10 *82, 83, 99, 104, 105, 115, 116, 117*
1:10–11 *99, 108*
1:11 *82, 83, 99, 118, 119, 123*
1:12 *10, 61, 96, 124, 125, 128, 130, 131, 149, 163, 164, 166, 172, 186, 357, 396*
1:12–4:9 *39*
1:12–14 *378*
1:12–15 *30, 31*
1:12–17 *142*
1:12–18 *50, 128*
1:12–20 *285*
1:12–26 *40, 58, 124, 125, 126, 127, 128, 172, 190, 270*
1:13 *46, 47, 82, 83, 102, 128, 130, 131, 158*
1:13–14 *130*
1:14 *134, 136, 141, 309, 312*
1:14–15 *137*
1:14–17 *24, 130*
1:14–18 *144*
1:14–28 *97*
1:15 *55, 57, 82, 83, 129, 137, 138, 141*
1:15–16 *258*
1:15–17 *23, 37, 54, 96, 129, 136, 358, 366*
1:15–18 *128, 141*
1:16 *82, 96, 110, 129, 141*
1:17 *32, 34, 129, 141, 193*
1:18 *82, 83, 130, 141, 142, 145, 148, 149, 150, 169, 283, 367, 396*
1:18–19 *149*
1:18–20 *149, 150, 163*
1:18–25 *142*
1:18–26 *128, 148*
1:19 *81, 82, 83, 128, 152, 153, 178, 189, 239*
1:20 *xv, 82, 128, 149, 154, 163, 169*
1:20–21 *247*
1:21 *xv, 82, 83, 128, 131, 152, 158, 171, 303*
1:21–24 *148, 149, 150, 152, 157, 158*
1:21–26 *266*
1:22 *159, 160*
1:22–24 *158*
1:23 *128, 162, 171*
1:24 *148, 157, 159, 160*
1:24–26 *176*
1:25 *128, 149, 150, 151, 163, 166, 176, 315*
1:25–26 *148, 149, 150*
1:26 *75, 82, 83, 128, 149, 160, 164*
1:27 *19, 61, 82, 83, 96, 128, 175, 176, 177, 178, 184, 187, 190, 192, 238, 315, 356, 358, 359, 362, 408*
1:27–2:4 *39, 177*
1:27–2:18 *58, 124, 125, 127, 171, 237, 249, 253, 270, 356*
1:27–28 *22, 54, 174, 191*
1:27–30 *40, 127, 128, 172, 237, 238, 272*
1:28 *34, 37, 180, 181, 238, 336*
1:29 *37, 82, 83, 145, 182, 186, 315*
1:29–30 *174, 186*
1:30 *180, 182, 183*
2 *203, 213*
2:1 *81, 82, 83, 95, 110, 178, 187, 188, 192, 312*
2:1–4 *22, 172, 177, 195, 205, 219, 220, 226, 228, 237, 238, 252, 408*
2:1–4:3 *40*
2:1–11 *127, 220, 329, 355, 366*
2:2 *101, 110, 178, 187, 188, 190, 191, 204, 205, 367*
2:3 *193, 204, 206, 212, 217, 244, 261, 308, 371*
2:3–4 *187, 205, 244, 245*
2:4 *194, 258*
2:5 *82, 83, 101, 150, 195, 199, 203, 204, 226, 329, 333, 341, 356*
2:5–11 *23, 58, 69, 73, 101, 124, 125, 193, 195, 204, 210, 227, 237, 239, 252, 284, 302, 314, 321, 332, 340, 361, 376*
2:6 *193, 204, 205, 206, 228, 261, 302*
2:6–8 *59, 184, 198, 200, 203, 206, 227*
2:6–11 *22, 23, 25, 61, 73, 84, 184, 195, 198, 203, 205, 228, 232, 302, 318, 333, 376, 379, 404*
2:7 *206, 207, 211, 234, 302*
2:7–8 *205*
2:8 *193, 212, 213, 217, 228, 238, 340, 345, 389*
2:9 *219, 225*
2:9–11 *82, 196, 200, 203, 220, 227*

2:10 *222, 341*
2:10–11 *187, 223*
2:11 *82, 83, 302, 309*
2:12 *37, 61, 98, 128, 238, 239, 244, 355*
2:12–13 *238*
2:12–18 *127, 172, 237, 247, 355*
2:13 *243, 247*
2:14 *245, 251, 408*
2:14–16 *22, 37, 238*
2:15 *238, 244, 252*
2:15–16 *245*
2:16 *22, 82, 238, 358*
2:17 *247, 249, 284, 315*
2:17–18 *238, 247, 249*
2:17–19 *367*
2:18 *83, 249, 284, 356*
2:19 *22, 61, 70, 83, 256, 284, 309, 312*
2:19–3:1 *34, 35*
2:19–3:14 *124*
2:19–21 *49, 51*
2:19–29 *270*
2:19–30 *23, 172*
2:20 *70, 256, 258, 362, 381*
2:20–21 *257*
2:20–22 *23*
2:20–24 *70*
2:21 *82, 258*
2:22 *96, 258*
2:23 *61, 150, 256, 259*
2:23–24 *43, 259*
2:24 *22, 53, 135*
2:25 *43, 260, 261*
2:25–30 *33, 34*
2:26 *43*
2:26–28 *264*
2:27 *265, 266*
2:28 *23, 33, 266, 284*
2:29 *83, 267, 309, 367*
2:29–30 *23*
2:30 *36, 82, 248, 265, 267*
3 *31, 57, 96, 123, 142, 144, 275, 349, 350, 354, 355, 356*
3:1 *37, 65, 128, 180, 271, 272, 283, 284, 309, 312, 356, 357, 367*
3:1–2 *63*
3:1–4:1 *20*
3:1–4:3 *270, 271*
3:1–4:8 *284*
3:1–4:9 *253*
3:1–6 *275*
3:1–9 *275*
3:1–14 *126*
3:1–16 *273, 275, 332, 333*
3:1–17 *376*
3:1–20 *366*
3:1–21 *24, 171, 284, 356, 359*
3:1–27 *272*
3:2 *22, 23, 34, 35, 37, 51, 54, 55, 57, 119, 124, 180, 186, 271, 272, 273, 274, 287, 291, 301, 324, 338*
3:2–3 *274, 281, 291*
3:2–6 *334*
3:2–21 *37, 58, 271, 272*
3:3 *75, 178, 290, 291, 312, 348*
3:3–4 *135, 290*
3:3–6 *291*
3:4 *82, 290, 295*
3:4–6 *119, 290*
3:4–11 *274, 323, 324*
3:5 *27, 289, 297*
3:6 *123, 300, 312, 313, 324, 353*
3:7 *37, 82, 83, 170, 292, 302, 303, 304, 308, 310*
3:7–8 *171, 261, 303*
3:8 *82, 83, 170, 171, 302, 304, 305, 308, 309, 310, 311, 337, 348, 371*
3:9 *xvi, 82, 83, 123, 301, 311, 312, 318, 354*
3:9–11 *325*
3:10 *xv, 95, 139, 182, 301, 302, 310, 317, 318, 319, 325, 326, 345, 391, 392*
3:10–11 *xv*
3:11 *301, 318, 319, 326*
3:11–21 *61*
3:12 *82, 309, 324, 325, 326, 327, 329, 386*
3:12–13 *325*
3:12–14 *247, 274, 275, 323*
3:12–16 *56, 322, 324, 331*
3:13 *326, 357*
3:14 *75, 82, 83, 309, 323, 324, 333*
3:15 *83, 101, 324, 329, 330*
3:15–4:4 *39*
3:15–4:9 *124, 125*
3:15–16 *323, 358*
3:15–18 *291*
3:16 *331, 335*
3:17 *274, 332, 357*
3:17–19 *291*
3:17–21 *273, 274, 275*
3:18 *82, 83, 186, 218, 276, 291, 332, 334*
3:18–19 *54, 56, 274, 275, 281*
3:19 *56, 57, 101, 274, 276, 291, 293, 305, 334, 335, 340, 348, 355*

3:19–20 *291*
3:20 *xv, 82, 83, 174, 175, 291, 309, 332, 343, 356*
3:20–21 *146, 332, 343*
3:21 *328, 332*
4 *270, 356*
4:1 *34, 63, 128, 239, 270, 271, 272, 309, 312, 355, 356, 357, 358, 365, 367, 382*
4:1–3 *242*
4:1–8 *284*
4:1–9 *382*
4:1–10 *61*
4:1–20 *355*
4:2 *15, 21, 23, 58, 101, 113, 200, 227, 270, 309, 330, 355, 356, 358, 365, 382*
4:2–3 *59, 242, 355, 359, 363, 365*
4:2–4 *22, 171*
4:2–7 *20*
4:2–9 *366*
4:3 *34, 77, 96, 179, 258, 262*
4:4 *83, 145, 271, 272, 284, 309, 355, 365, 366, 367*
4:4–7 *355*
4:4–9 *40, 270, 366*
4:5 *83, 366, 368*
4:6 *258, 366, 369*
4:6–7 *366, 369*
4:6–9 *369*
4:7 *xv, 75, 80, 82, 83, 308, 312, 370, 381, 409*
4:7–9 *80*
4:8 *37, 100, 128, 271, 272, 283, 369, 372, 373*
4:8–9 *355, 366, 369, 372, 374, 381*
4:9 *23, 171, 270, 372, 373, 376, 381, 409*
4:10 *34, 101, 164, 248, 271, 356, 365, 367, 382, 384, 385, 399, 403*
4:10–19 *124, 125*
4:10–20 *22, 33, 34, 35, 36, 39, 40, 126, 284*
4:10–21 *284*
4:10–22 *382*
4:10–23 *39*
4:11 *387, 389*
4:11–13 *77, 378*
4:12 *169, 387, 389, 392*
4:13 *75, 387*
4:14 *61, 95, 385, 397*
4:15 *19, 23, 92, 95, 96, 384, 385, 396*
4:16 *83, 384, 385, 398*
4:17 *399, 404*
4:18 *248, 385, 394, 400, 404*
4:19 *xv, 82, 83, 124, 401*
4:20 *402*
4:21 *75, 82, 83, 357*
4:21–23 *40, 80*
4:22 *46, 47, 72*
4:23 *79, 82, 83, 178, 309, 409*

COLOSSIANS

1:1 *45, 71*
1:3 *87*
1:3–8 *90*
1:6 *90*
1:7 *70, 79*
1:9–11 *107, 108*
1:15–20 *xiv, 224*
1:16 *85*
1:18 *75*
1:19–20 *198, 224, 228*
1:20 *213, 218, 224, 378*
1:24 *139, 169, 182, 267, 320, 394*
1:24–29 *394*
1:27 *75*
1:28 *329*
2:8 *341*
2:8–3:4 *57, 201*
2:8–10 *337*
2:11 *292*
2:14 *218*
2:20–3:4 *319*
3:4 *158*
3:10 *228*
3:15 *380*
3:16 *197*
3:18–4:1 *18*
3:22–4:1 *72, 73*
4:7 *70*
4:7–8 *53*
4:9 *53*
4:10–14 *26, 30, 408*
4:11 *262*
4:12 *70, 329*
4:17 *53*

1 THESSALONIANS

1:1–5 *90*
1–2 *145*
1:2 *87*
1:3 *87*
2 *258*
2:4 *96, 121*
2:9 *396, 403*
2:13 *121*

2:13–16 *37, 274, 335*
2:14 *279*
2:14–16 *183*
2:19 *91*
2:19–20 *190, 358*
3:1–2 *255*
3:2 *256*
3:12 *114*
4:1 *283*
4:9 *68*
4:9–12 *193*
4:11 *402*
4:13 *266*
4:13–5:11 *161*
4:13–18 *118, 161, 162, 319, 323*
4:15 *176*
5:1 *68*
5:17–18 *181*
5:23 *380*
5:24 *314*

2 THESSALONIANS

1:8 *151*
2:1–12 *99*
2:2 *326*
3:1 *283*
3:3 *314*
3:4 *135*
3:7–9 *333*
3:10 *403*
3:12 *403*
3:14–15 *403*
3:16 *380*

1 TIMOTHY

1 *75*
1:2 *257*
3:1 *75, 77*
3:1–4 *405*
3:1–7 *78*
3:1–13 *360*
3:2 *75*
3:3 *368*
3:8 *78, 405*
3:8–13 *71*
4:6 *79*
4:12 *26*
4:15 *131*
5:8 *402*
5:17–19 *78*
5:23 *266*
6:3–4 *137*
6:3–10 *147, 405*
6:10 *405*
6:11 *354*

2 TIMOTHY

1:5 *25, 257*
2:2 *354*
2:4 *262*
2:13 *314*
2:18 *326*
2:22 *380*
3 *378*
3:1 *404*
3:1–9 *145*
3:2 *404*
3:3–8 *405*
3:5 *207*
3:15–17 *xiv*
3:16 *354*
3:16–17 *xiii*
4:6 *249*
4:9–11 *259*
4:10 *361*
4:11–18 *378*
4:21 *408*

TITUS

1 *378*
1:4 *257*
1:5–7 *78*
1:5–9 *78*
1:7 *75, 405*
1:10–11 *145*
1:11 *303, 304*
2:11–14 *81*
3:2 *368*
3:5 *355*
3:12–13 *408*

PHILEMON

1 *262*
2 *262*
3 *378*
4 *87*
6 *95*
10 *258*
12 *53*

15–16 *72*
22 *53*
23–24 *30, 408*
24 *262*

HEBREWS

1:1 *xiii, xiv*
1:1–3 *85*
1:1–4 *234*
2:6–8 *216*
2:17 *314*
4:12 *xiv*
5:8–10 *234*
5:14 *112*
10:23 *314*
12:2 *145*

JAMES

3:15 *341*

1 PETER

2:9 *375*
2:12 *75*
2:25 *75*
4:19 *314*
5:1–2 *78*

2 PETER

1:3 *375*
1:5 *375*
3:1 *116*
3:15 *296*

1 JOHN

1:9 *314*
2:7–11 *109*

REVELATION

1:5 *314*
3:5 *363, 364*
20:15 *363, 364*
21:5 *xiv*
21:27 *363*
22:15 *288*